Praise for *The Taste of War*

"Collingham's book masterfully corrects our understanding of the great conflict that made America what it is, and thus prepares us for the conflicts that are all too likely to come. Its usefulness is hard to overstate."
—Tim Snyder, *The New York Times Book Review*

"Superb . . . Examining in detail the role played by food in the greatest of all political conflicts, the Second World War, was a brilliant idea on Collingham's part. *The Taste of War* is breathtaking in its breadth and scope, global in coverage, and yet anchored in detailed research."
—Richard J. Evans, *The Nation*

"An enlivening entry into unexplored areas."
—*The New Yorker*

"This fascinating calorie-centric history of the greatest conflict in world history is scholarly and well-written but, above all, wholly convincing. After this book, no historian will be able to write a comprehensive history of the Second World War without putting the multifarious issues of food production and consumption center stage."
—Andrew Roberts, *Financial Times*

"Ambitious, compelling, fascinating."
—*The Guardian* (London)

"Amazing . . . [Collingham] makes it impossible to think of the war in the old terms."
—*Daily Mail* (London)

"The great merits of [this] book . . . lie in its extraordinary range . . . and in the entirely new perspective it throws on the Second World War."
—Bernard Potter, *London Review of Books*

"Lizzie Collingham's book possesses the notable virtue of originality. . . . [She] has gathered many strands to pursue an important theme across a global canvas. She reminds us of the timeless truth that all human and political behavior is relative."
—Max Hastings, *The Sunday Times* (London)

"Powerful and important . . . Like all the best ideas, Collingham's means that a lot of events fall satisfyingly into place. . . . One of the beauties of this book is its savage unpicking of cherished myths."
—Diane Purkiss, *The Independent* (London)

"An important, original contribution."
—*Booklist*

"A definitive work of World War II scholarship."
—*Kirkus Reviews*

W9-CZY-627

ABOUT THE AUTHOR

Lizzie Collingham is the author of *Imperial Bodies: The Physical Experience of the Raj* and *Curry: A Tale of Cooks and Conquerors*. Having taught history at Warwick University she became a Research Fellow at Jesus College, Cambridge. She is now an independent scholar and writer. She has lived in Australia, France, and Germany and now lives near Cambridge with her husband and small daughter.

The Taste of War

World War II and the Battle for Food

LIZZIE COLLINGHAM

PENGUIN BOOKS

PENGUIN BOOKS

Published by the Penguin Group
Penguin Group (USA) Inc., 375 Hudson Street,
New York, New York 10014, USA

USA | Canada | UK | Ireland | Australia | New Zealand | India | South Africa | China
Penguin Books Ltd, Registered Offices: 80 Strand, London WC2R 0RL, England
For more information about the Penguin Group visit penguin.com

First published in Great Britain by Allen Lane, 2011
First published in the United States of America by The Penguin Press,
a member of Penguin Group (USA) Inc., 2012
Published in Penguin Books 2013

Illustration credits appear on pages xi–xii.

THE LIBRARY OF CONGRESS HAS CATALOGED THE HARDCOVER EDITION AS FOLLOWS:
Collingham, E. M. (Elizabeth M.)
The taste of war : World War Two and the battle for food / Lizzie Collingham.
p. cm.
Includes bibliographical references and index.
ISBN 978-1-59420-329-9 (hc.)
ISBN 978-0-14-312301-9 (pbk.)
1. World War, 1939–1945—Food supply. 2. Food supply—History—20th century.
3. Food security—History—20th century. 4. Nutrition policy—History—20th century.
5. Starvation—History—20th century. 6. Food habits—History—20th century. 7. War and
society—History—20th century. I. Title. II. Title: World War Two and the battle for food.
HD9000.5.C624 2012
940.53'1—dc23
2011043783

Printed in the United States of America
1 3 5 7 9 10 8 6 4 2

For Sarah

Contents

CONTENTS

PART II
The Battle for Food

PART III

The Politics of Food

CONTENTS

PART IV

The Aftermath

List of Illustrations

1. 'State Secretary Herbert Backe. Reich Minister for Food and Agriculture, NSDAP.' 2 June 1942. Bundesarchiv: Bild 183–J02034.

2. 'A re-settled Polish family (Matschak) from Skaradsch.' Photographer Wilhelm Holtfreter, c. 1939–41. Bundesarchiv: R-49 Bild-0129.

3. *Ours to fight for. Freedom from want.* Poster of an original painting by Norman Perceval Rockwell published by the Division of Public Inquiries, Office of War Information, US Government Printing Office, offset lithograph on paper, 71 x 50.9 cm. Australian War Memorial: ARTV00185.

4. *Potatoes set our shipping free.* British poster issued by the Ministry of Agriculture, c. 1939–45. HMSO, James Haworth & Brother, offset lithograph on paper, 74.6 x 49.6 cm. Australian War Memorial: ARTV01561.

5. *Hamster – shame on you!* Poster by Max Eschle. Published by the Reich Propaganda Department, NSDAP. December 1939. Bundesarchiv: Plak 003–023–077.

6. 'France, Paris. German soldiers buying cakes from a street seller with Notre Dame in the background.' Photographer Heinz Boesig. Summer 1940. Bundesarchiv: 101I-129–0480–05A.

7. 'The arrival of confiscated foodstuffs.' Archive Heinrich Hoffmann, September 1942. bpk, Berlin: Bild 50073634.

8. 'Registration of Jews. Violence against a Jewish man – mistreatment by a civilian next to a German sentry.' Photographer Franke. June 1941. Bundesarchiv: Bild 101I-186-0160-12.

9. 'Inhabitant of Stalingrad cooking on a makeshift oven.' September 1942. Bundesarchiv: Bild 169-0369.

10. 'Balikpapan, Borneo. Two Malayan natives, suffering from malnutrition after being ill-treated and starved by the Japanese, now receiving treatment at the Netherlands civil administration compound in 7 Division area.' 10 July 1945. Australian War Memorial: 111003.

11. 'Muchu Island, New Guinea. Japanese soldiers cooking their rations over a fire.' 11 September 1945. Australian War Memorial: 096143.

12. 'Papua, Sanananda area. After having been in action during which time their only food was bully beef and biscuits, these Americans prepare a hot meal – jungle stew.' Photographer Clifford Bottomley. 27 January 1943. Australian War Memorial: 014241.

13. 'Sandakan, North Borneo. A badly emaciated Japanese POW waiting to embark on a landing ship, Tank (LST) for the POW camp at Jesselton.' Photographer Frank Albert Charles Burke. 26 October 1945. Australian War Memorial: 121785.

14. 'Tokyo, Japan. A scene from one of Tokyo's tall buildings shows evidence of the shortage of food among the people.' 1945. Australian War Memorial: 019221.

15. 'Tokyo Bay, Japan. Australian Navy personnel who boarded USS *Sims* (an American assault destroyer) to take part in the naval landing of Tokyo Bay enjoy the food piled up on their American mess trays. They are Leading Writer Jack Norris of Sydney, NSW, and Leading Stores Assistant Jim Cumming of Essendon, Vic.' *c.* August 1945. Australian War Memorial: 019248.

Acknowledgements

For talking or writing to me about their experiences during the war and for putting me in contact with or interviewing their friends and relatives on my behalf I would like to thank: Alison Backhouse, Dorothy Bacon, Elfreda Bayly, Jill Beattie, Teruko Blair, Richard and Margot Eickelmann, Herbert Fröböse, Prof. Fujita, Reinhold Fellies, Elfriede Günter, Helmut Geidel, Doris Hallpike, Tom Kimura, Alois and Elizabeth Kleinemas, Professor Kusakabe, Mary, Doreen and Peter Laven, Jean Legas, Evdokiya Andreevna Levina, Robert Mair, Prof. Matsumoto Nakako, Elizabeth and Tony Minchin, Eva Norman, Oki, Chiyo, Catherine Oki, Clara and Emilia Olivier, Irmgard and Peter Seidel and Tosa, Mitsuhiro, Akiko and Hiroko. I would also like to thank the copyright holders of the papers held in the Imperial War Museum for permission to quote from their relatives' memoirs. I am grateful to the staff at the Imperial War Museum, Cambridge University Library, the National Library of Australia, the Australian National Archives and the Australian War Memorial for their assistance.

Generous friends have at various times lent me their homes and spare bedrooms during the writing of this book and I am very grateful to Stephen Barton and Maureen Langham, Sarah Burwood and John Hay, Pam and Vic Gatrell, Mike and Tricia O'Brien, Clare and Simon Redfern, Tim, Jan and Anna Rowse, Peter and Becky Ryan and Lionel and Deirdre Ward. I am especially grateful to Fiona, Andrew, Ali and Sarah Blake for providing me with a quiet room of my own and sustaining meals and conversation during a stressful period in the writing process.

Interesting conversations as well as helpful suggestions and assistance in finding information were provided by friends and colleagues. I would like to thank Clare Alexander, Olaf Blaschke, Steven Bullard, Adrian Caesar, John Cornwell, Joanna Cwiertka, Peter Garnsey, Sophie Gilmartin, Guðmundur Jonsson, Tsuchihashi Kenichiro, Barack Kushner, David Lowe, Veronique Mottier, Rachel Murphy, Mogens Rostgaard Nissen, Keith Richmond, Richard Overy, Tim Rowse, Wendy Way and Hans-Ulrich Wehler. In particular I would like to thank those who read and commented on the manuscript: Chris Bayly, Paul Brassley, Helen Conford, Adam Tooze, Rebecca Earle, Mike O'Brien and Rana Mitter. I am very grateful to Geoff Dunn for devising the maps. Thanks are also due to Rikin Trivedi and his team.

Finally, I am indebted to my sister, Sarah, for endlessly re-reading the manuscript and for generous help and cheerful support. Thomas Seidel knows how much I owe him and I especially thank him for his assistance with the research as well as his willingness to engage in discussion and for always asking challenging questions.

Note on Sources

Throughout the book I refer to Mass Observation and the Harvard Project on the Soviet Social System. Mass Observation was set up in Britain in 1937 by the anthropologist Tom Harrisson, the sociologist Charles Madge and film-maker Humphrey Jennings, to record the views of ordinary people. During the war around 3,000 people responded to questionnaires sent out to them by Mass Observation and others kept diaries which they would send in to Mass Observation in instalments. These are now held by the Mass Observation archive at the University of Sussex and many have since been published in various collections. The names given to Mass Observation observers are pseudonyms. The Harvard Project on the Soviet Social System consists of transcripts of interviews conducted in West Germany in 1950–51 with refugees and defectors from the Soviet Union, most of whom were living in camps for displaced persons at the time. The interviews were conducted on behalf of the United States government in order to gain an understanding of communism.

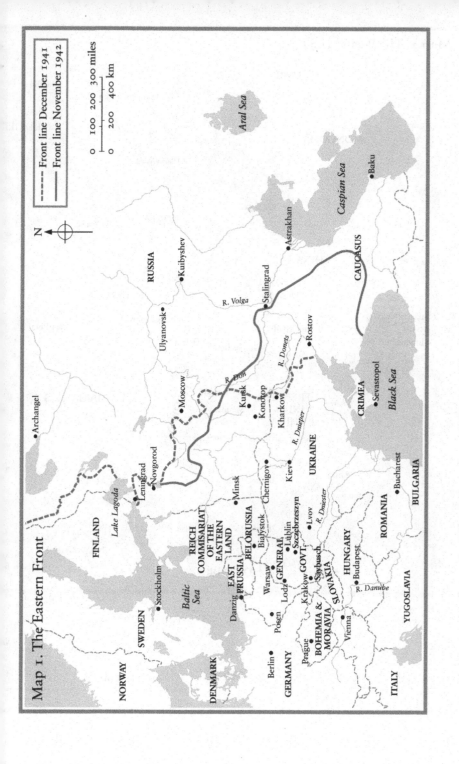

Map 1. The Eastern Front

- - - - - Front line December 1941
————— Front line November 1942

0   100   200   300 miles
0   200   400 km

N

NORWAY

SWEDEN

DENMARK

GERMANY

Berlin

Prague

BOHEMIA &
MORAVIA

Vienna

ITALY

YUGOSLAVIA

HUNGARY

Budapest

SLOVAKIA

R. Danube

ROMANIA

Bucharest

BULGARIA

Stockholm

Baltic
Sea

Danzig

EAST
PRUSSIA

Posen

Lodz

Warsaw

GENERAL
GOVT.

Kraków

Szybusch

Lublin

Szczebrzeszyn

Lvov

R. Dniester

FINLAND

Lake Lagoda

Leningrad

Novgorod

REICH
COMMISARIAT
OF THE
EASTERN
LAND

BELORUSSIA

Minsk

Białystok

Chernigov

Kiev

UKRAINE

R. Dnieper

Kharkov

Konotop

Kursk

R. Don

Moscow

Ulyanovsk

RUSSIA

Kuibyshev

R. Volga

Stalingrad

Rostov

R. Donets

CRIMEA

Sevastopol

Black Sea

CAUCASUS

Astrakhan

Caspian
Sea

Baku

Aral Sea

Archangel

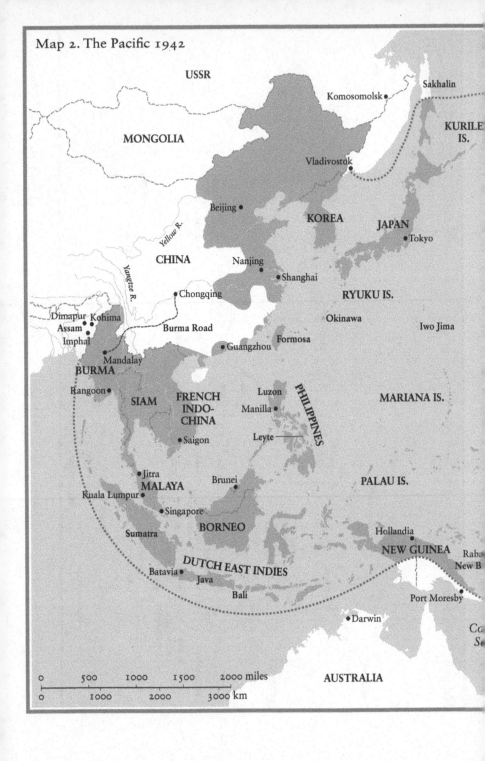

Map 2. The Pacific 1942

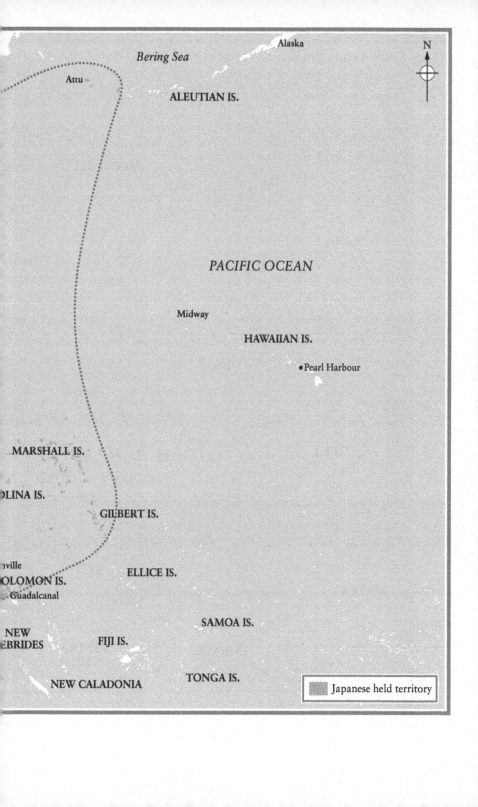

N

Bering Sea

Alaska

Attu

ALEUTIAN IS.

PACIFIC OCEAN

Midway

HAWAIIAN IS.

• Pearl Harbour

MARSHALL IS.

OLINA IS.

GILBERT IS.

nville

OLOMON IS.

ELLICE IS.

Guadalcanal

SAMOA IS.

NEW
EBRIDES

FIJI IS.

NEW CALADONIA

TONGA IS.

Japanese held territory

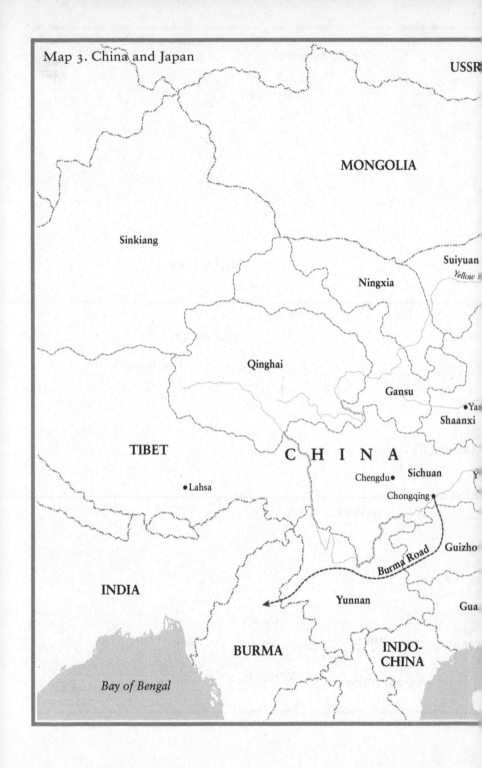

Map 3. China and Japan

USSR

MONGOLIA

Sinkiang

Suiyuan

Yellow

Ningxia

Qinghai

Gansu

•Ya

Shaanxi

TIBET

C H I N A

•Lahsa

Chengdu• Sichuan   Y

Chongqing•

Burma Road   Guizho

INDIA

Yunnan   Gua

BURMA

INDO-
CHINA

Bay of Bengal

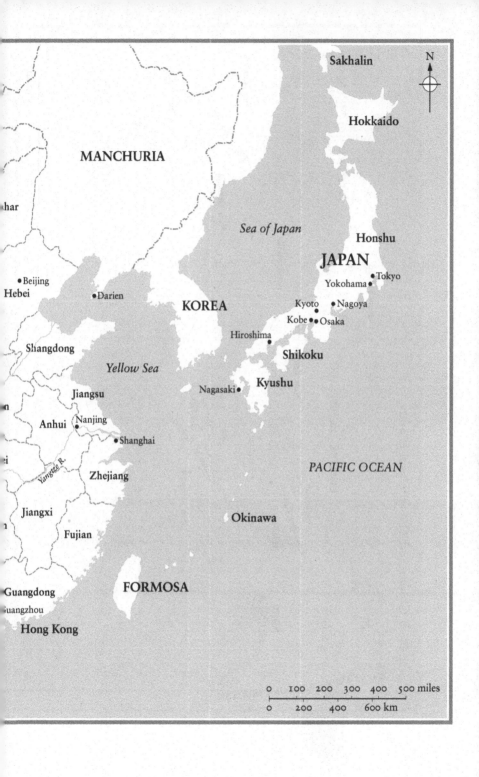

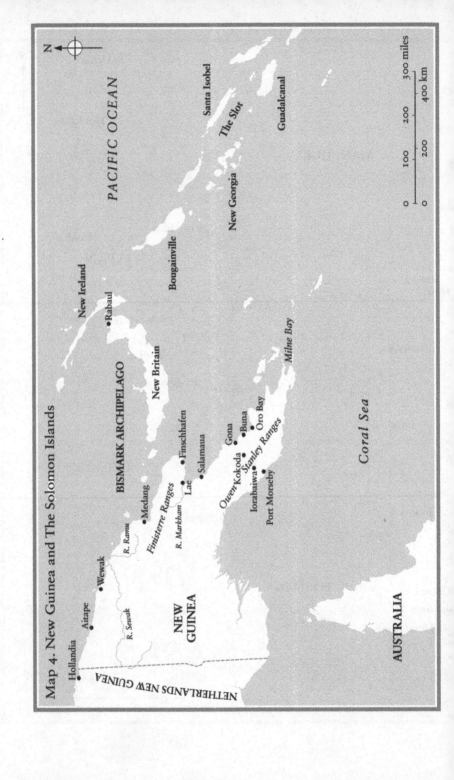

Map 4. New Guinea and The Solomon Islands

I

Introduction – War and Food

'Death by famine lacks drama. Bloody death, the deaths of many by slaughter as in riots or bombings is in itself blood-bestirring; it excites you, prints indelible images on the mind. But death by famine, a vast slow dispirited noiseless apathy, offers none of that. Horrid though it may be to say, multitudinous death from this cause . . . regarded without emotion as a spectacle, is until the crows get at it, the rats and kites and dogs and vultures very dull.'[1] This was the view of newspaper editor Ian Stephens commenting on the Bengal famine of 1943, which killed 3 million Indians. It is perhaps the quiet and unobtrusive nature of death by starvation which explains why many of those who died of hunger during the Second World War are largely forgotten today. While the Vietnam war is firmly embedded in the western collective memory, most westerners have never heard of the famine in the Vietnamese region of Tonkin in 1943–44 which probably killed more peasants than all the years of war which followed.[2] And yet 'one dies a very terrible death from starvation'.[3] As one of the survivors of the Leningrad siege was disturbed to discover, 'It's not so horrifying when a person . . . has been hit by a shell or a bomb. But what happened as a result of hunger, that was particularly awful, the way a person's face changed . . . a man became an animated corpse and . . . a corpse is a grim spectacle.'[4]

During the Second World War at least 20 million people died just such a terrible death from starvation, malnutrition and its associated diseases: a number to equal the 19.5 military deaths.[5] The impact of the war on food supplies was thus as deadly in its effect on the world population as military action. This book seeks to understand the role of food at the heart of the conflict. The focus on food is not intended to exclude other interpretations but rather to add an often overlooked dimension to our understanding of the Second World War.

The book begins by uncovering the important role food played in driving both Germany and Japan into conflict. During the nineteenth century Europe's urban industrial workforce substantially increased their consumption of meat, while the demand for rice rose significantly among Japan's urban population. Both countries feared that their agricultural sectors could not produce enough food to feed the cities. Britain had responded to the problem of feeding its urban population by embracing free trade and it imported large quantities of food and animal fodder. But Germany and Japan felt disadvantaged by the international economy dominated by Britain and America. Right-wing elements within both countries pushed for an alternative, more radical solution to the problem of food and trade. Rather than accepting subordination to the United States, Hitler preferred to engage in a struggle for world supremacy and looked to an eastern empire as a source of food and other resources which would make Germany self-sufficient and independent of world trade. This made war in eastern Europe inevitable. The Japanese army sought to reduce its country's dependence on the United States by consolidating its hold over mainland China which many officers saw as an area of settlement and resources, not the least of which was food. But Japanese belligerence in China set the country on a collision course with the United States in the Pacific.

This perspective on the causes of the Second World War is relevant to the contemporary global food situation. The problem which confronted Germany and Japan in the 1930s, of how to feed a growing urban population with the more nutritious but also more costly food which it demands, has returned to confront the developing world with even greater force and with the potential for an equally global impact at the beginning of the twenty-first century.

Rising living standards among the growing urban middle classes in developing countries such as China, India, Indonesia and Brazil have led to marked changes in eating habits. Zhang Xiuwen grew up a member of a poor farming family in the rural province of Yunnan. He often went hungry and he only ever ate meat on special holidays once or twice a year. He never drank milk. Now he is a tennis coach in Beijing and he and his family can afford to eat meat and drink milk every day. This shift from a grain-based vegetarian diet to one rich in meat and milk has been replicated across China and the rest of the developing world, where hundreds of millions of consumers' food preferences have changed as their nutritional status has improved. Chinese per capita consumption of meat has risen in the last twenty-eight years from 20 kilograms in 1980 to 54 kilograms in 2008. The wider impact of such changing tastes has been to divert ever more of the world's grain harvest into the stomachs of animals rather than humans. In 2007 China imported 45 per cent of the soya beans traded on the world market to feed pigs, poultry and farmed fish. Approximately 30 per cent of the world's grain crop is now fed to livestock.[6]

Diverting grain from humans to animals is an extremely inefficient use of food. The 3–4.5 kilograms of grain that have to be fed to a steer to obtain half a kilogram of beef contain as many as ten times more calories and four times as much protein as half a kilogram of beef.[7] At the same time increased demand for grain for feed has pushed up prices and made food more expensive for the poorer sections of the world's population who rely on grains for their staple diet. Even poorer countries have become increasingly dependent on food imports. In West Africa urbanization has produced a large body of townspeople who have switched from eating traditional staples such as millet and cassava to eating rice, which has to be imported. In Indonesia and India small improvements in income have led to a growing demand for imported vegetable oils.[8] Thus, development through industrialization and its inevitable corollary, urbanization, pushes countries into the difficult position of decreasing food self-sufficiency and increasing dependence on a volatile world food market in which the politically less influential countries, with less access to foreign exchange, are at a disadvantage. Sub-Saharan Africa's food import bill increased fourfold in the last decade even though the amount of food imported declined.[9] As the world population and the world's middle class continues to grow and food prices rise, this is likely to become an ever more pressing problem.

It is unlikely that food price rises will eventually be held in check by increased production, as many agricultural experts argue that the technological innovations of the green revolution have run their course, and there is little prospect of increasing yields as a result of new farming techniques. Meanwhile, the rising cost of fuel, fertilizer and increasingly scarce supplies of water is setting a limit on the improvement of agricultural methods in developing countries.[10] Climate change is only likely to make matters worse. While it is estimated that the world's population will increase by a further 3.3 billion in the next fifty years, scientists have warned that half of the world's arable land may become unproductive.[11] The dismal prospect is that as the world-wide demand for meat and livestock products, vegetable oil and grain grows, the share of food available for the world's poor will decline.

In 2007–2008 a food crisis was sparked by a variety of factors working together. An increase in the production of biofuels pushed up the price of sugar, maize, cassava, oilseeds and palm oil.[12] Drought pushed up the price of wheat. The surge in petrol prices increased the cost of fertilizers and doubled the cost of food transport. India responded to the threat that it would not be able to afford to import wheat by imposing an export ban on rice, and was followed by Thailand. The Philippines, anxious it would not be able to import enough food to feed its towns, panic-bought rice and pushed the price up to over $1,000 a ton. This, combined with speculation and the hoarding of foodstuffs, contributed to further food price spirals. In Egypt, where the government spends more on subsidized food for the poor than it does on health or education, more and more of the population resorted to buying cheap government-subsidized bread, with the result that the government was unable to meet the rise in demand. Bread queues lengthened and the poor found it increasingly difficult to sustain themselves. As grain prices continue to rise, the number of hungry people in the world grows exponentially and food is once more becoming a catalyst for political conflict. A ripple effect was felt around the world in 2007–2008 when food riots erupted not only in Egypt but in Senegal, Cameroon, Niger, Haiti and Mexico.[13]

One of the most powerful aspects of making food the central focus of an investigation into the Second World War is that the agrarian policy of the Nazi regime is revealed as one of the driving forces behind some of the worst atrocities committed during the conflict. The experience of the First World War had taught the National Socialist leadership that an adequate food supply was crucial to the maintenance of military and civilian morale. Food shortages among the soldiers on

4

the front and the civilians at home had pushed a deeply demoralized Germany towards capitulation in 1918. It was both fear of a repeat of the disastrous decline in civilian morale and a powerful sense of the German people's superior entitlement to food which made the National Socialists determined that the German population would not go hungry during this war. Instead, others would have to go without food.

The deliberate extermination by starvation of targeted groups became a defining feature of the National Socialist food system. It was the agronomist Herbert Backe who hatched the most radical plan to secure Germany's food supply. He argued that the Wehrmacht (the German armed services) could be fed by diverting Ukrainian grain from Soviet cities. This would solve the problem of feeding a vast army while conveniently eliminating the Soviet urban population, who would starve to death. Once the east was conquered and its former inhabitants had been forcibly eradicated, German agronomists intended to create an agricultural empire on the land. Altogether the regime's agrarian vision for the east generated plans to murder up to 100 million people. The siege of Leningrad, where 1 million died of starvation, the blockades of the Ukrainian cities of Kiev and Kharkov, which accounted for at least another 200,000 deaths from famine, were just the first steps towards the implementation of this murderous scheme.[14]

The National Socialists used the weapon of starvation against an array of other groups of people, who were allocated so little food that their eventual death was guaranteed. The daily ration for Polish Jews amounted to a derisory 184 calories. The majority of the 100,000 Jews who died in the Warsaw ghetto succumbed to starvation.[15] Even the 845 calories allocated to the Polish urban population condemned the recipients to death if they were unable to find alternative sources of food.[16] A proportion of the 200,000 mentally ill victims of Germany's euthanasia programme and 2.35 million Soviet prisoners of war were all given so little food that they were slowly but systematically starved to death.[17] In German concentration camps the number of calories in the food frequently fell below the minimum 1,200 which the World Health Organization recommends that everyone should eat daily, even clinically obese people trying to lose weight. A diet with fewer calories than this forces the body to begin to consume itself simply to perform normal bodily functions such as breathing, let alone hard physical labour. Primo Levi at a sub-camp of Auschwitz described how 'the Lager [camp] *is* hunger: we ourselves are hunger, living hunger'. At night the prisoners were tortured by dreams of food: 'many lick their lips and move their jaws. They are dreaming of eating.'[18]

Victims of starvation die of nutritional dystrophy, a process whereby, once the body has used up all its fat reserves, the muscles are broken down in order to obtain energy. The small intestine atrophies and it becomes increasingly difficult for the victim to absorb nutrients from what little food he or she is able to obtain. As a defence mechanism the body reduces the activity of the vital organs such as the heart and liver and the victim suffers not only from muscular debility but from a more general and overpowering fatigue. The Leningrader Anna Ivanovna Likhacheva, who 'survived all the stages of emaciation', recalled that 'it began simply with wasting, shortness of breath, slowed thought . . . And then everything went downhill. The darkness, the deadly cold, the hunger, the lack of strength.'[19] Others were afflicted by a painfully acute over-excitement. The water content of the body reduces at a slower rate than the wasting of the muscles and tissues and the flaccidity of the body increases. Some victims of starvation develop hunger oedema and swell up with excess water. The swelling begins in the abdomen and legs and spreads throughout the body. The skin becomes stretched, shiny and hypersensitive. Blood pressure drops and the victim is plagued by keratitis (redness and soreness of the cornea), sore gums, headaches, pains in the legs, neuralgic pains, tremors and ataxia (a loss of control over the limbs). These symptoms are accompanied by an intense craving for carbohydrates and salt, and uncontrollable diarrhoea. Just before death the victim veers wildly from depression to intense irritation and then a profound torpor.[20]

Eventually, the body has no alternative but to sustain itself by taking protein from the vital organs. Those who died in Leningrad were found to have livers that had reduced from a normal 1,800 grams to 860 grams (without blood) and spleens reduced from 180 grams to between 80 and 55 grams. Most importantly, the heart atrophies. Some victims in Leningrad had hearts that weighed as little as 90 grams, compared to an average adult heart which weighs 330 grams.[21] Organ failure is the final cause of death.

Starvation is a slow and excruciating process and the National

Socialists discovered that starving unwanted groups to death was far slower and less efficient than they had expected. When the east failed to deliver the hoped-for quantities of food, panic over the need for ration cuts for German civilians provoked a further radicalization of the regime. The decision was taken to eliminate as many 'useless eaters' as possible from the eastern area, with the result that the murder of Soviet and Polish Jews was given new impetus. Thus, food is implicated in the decision to speed up the Holocaust.

Even in cases where no deliberate plan existed to actively starve people to death, starvation and hunger were an inevitable by-product of National Socialist food policies. Although the National Socialists were at their most ruthless in exporting hunger to the Soviet Union and Poland, the plunder of foodstuffs from other occupied countries resulted in a famine which killed 500,000 in Greece, increased death and infant mortality rates and spread malnutrition, particularly among children, in Czechoslovakia, Poland, France, Belgium and Holland. During the Hunger Winter of 1944–45, 22,000 Dutch succumbed to starvation when the Germans cut off supplies to those parts of Holland which the Allies had failed to liberate.[22]

While Nazi Germany was unique in formulating plans for the systematic eradication of entire peoples, it was not the only combatant to inflict famine, hunger and malnutrition on its own inhabitants and those of occupied territories. In the gulags of the Soviet Union the death rate increased dramatically during the war as the prisoners struggled to perform hard physical labour on a starvation diet.[23] Among the 1 million German prisoners who died in Soviet hands, the 23,284 Allied prisoners and civilian internees who died in Japanese camps, and the 290,000 Asians who died while working as forced labourers for the Japanese, a substantial number will have lost their lives to hunger, malnutrition and diseases against which their starved bodies no longer had any resistance.[24] The Japanese made no overt plans systematically to eliminate the Chinese but in the 1930s thousands of farmers were evicted from their homes and left to starve in order to make way for Japanese settlers in Manchuria. The relentless extraction of food from China in order to feed the Japanese homeland caused chronic hunger and malnutrition among the Chinese population, while callous food requisitioning policies were directly responsible for a famine which killed at least 2 million Vietnamese in the district of Tonkin. Chinese military captives were annihilated by their captors. In 1945 only fifty-six Chinese prisoners of war were released by the Japanese.[25]

While the Axis powers ruthlessly exploited the food resources of the occupied territories, both the Axis and the Allies invested resources in denying their enemies access to food. The Japanese imposed a blockade on Nationalist China, while the United States in turn gradually tightened a net of submarines and mines around Japan; the British blockade of occupied Europe was matched by the German U-boat war on Allied shipping. The pre-war global food economy was thrown into disarray as the demand for imports of bulky foods such as fruits dried up, to be replaced by a growing clamour from Britain for concentrated foods such as meat and cheese. Canada, the United States, Australia, New Zealand and Argentina reorganized their agricultural economies to meet these new demands, while food-processing techniques were driven forward by the search for methods for condensing foodstuffs. Meanwhile, the colonies, whose agricultural economies were structured to supply cash crops in return for food imports, were suddenly forced to make themselves as self-sufficient in food as possible.

Indeed, securing a food supply became a central preoccupation for the governments of all the countries drawn into the conflict. Growing, transporting and distributing food took up resources such as manpower, raw materials and fuel which, particularly in the context of total war, were potentially valuable in other areas of the war effort. However, the human need for a relatively fixed minimum number of calories and nutrients in order to function meant that every sector of the war economy relied on the food sector. If the food supply failed this would impact not only on the army but also on the war industries and more diffusely on civilian morale.[26] Food was the fundamental basis for every wartime economy.

Levels of physical activity increased significantly. Men were drafted into the armed forces; women were recruited from the home to make up the deficit in the workforce. A larger section of the total workforce moved into heavy industry. The working day was lengthened, overtime hours increased, shift and night-work (which is more physically demanding) became increasingly common. Not only was the wartime working day more arduous, but so also was everyday life. After a long

8

shift at the Sheffield steel works where he was employed, my grandfather, Harry Collingham, put in a stint digging his vegetable garden
and then stayed up several nights a week doing his duties as an air raid
warden. In the Soviet Union just keeping warm in unheated apartments
used up many calories. Victor Kravchenko recalled that he and his wife
would sit in their Moscow flat in 'heavy coats, woollen shawls and
even gloves'.[27] His wife lost weight. Firewood for cooking had to be
carried home by hand or pulled on a sledge. Water had to be collected
from a communal tap in the yard and lugged up several flights of stairs,
clothes had to be washed by hand, and the walk to work was often
long, as the tram systems in many towns and cities broke down and
became unreliable. This dramatic increase in overall physical activity
in turn increased the number of calories required by each person. A
moderately active young man needs somewhere in the region of 2,800
to 3,000 calories a day, but a soldier in training needs about 3,429
calories a day; on active service in cold conditions, he needs 4,238
calories; and fighting in tropical conditions, 4,738 calories.[28] A comparable increase in calorie requirements is observable in workers in heavy
industry. The impact of too little food on the physical capacity of
workers was demonstrated by under-nourished foreign workers in a
factory in Essen who were 15–43 per cent less productive than their
German counterparts.[29]

Each country therefore needed to supply its population with substantially more food, and this required the agricultural sector to increase,
rather than simply maintain, production levels. As agricultural labour
was recruited into the army, factories stopped producing agricultural
machinery, and fertilizers competed with the explosives industry for
raw materials, food production in itself became a battle. America
possessed sufficient resources to rise to the challenge and devised and
implemented new agricultural techniques, the impact of which are still
felt long after the war. But for most combatant countries total war
placed an immense strain on the food system. Luxury foods fell by the
wayside, and farmers switched to cultivating bread grains and potatoes
rather than raising livestock for meat and milk. In the Soviet Union
the inability of the agricultural sector to produce enough food created
a serious and continual crisis which posed a real threat to the war
effort.

The Soviet government, however, in common with other non-democratic governments, exhibited a strong tendency to treat soldiers and civilians as expendable units in the service of the government. Thus, they were expected to fight valiantly and labour tirelessly despite inadequate food supplies. Conversely, the ability of a population to bear high levels of deprivation was often a reflection of low expectations of the government. The most extreme example of this is to be found among Japan's military commanders who believed that *bushido* (fighting spirit) was all that a Japanese soldier needed in order to fight. This resulted in a cavalier attitude towards food supplies for troops in the field and many Japanese soldiers found themselves fighting on the front line on a diet of wild grasses. This attitude, as well as the failure to protect supply lines properly, contributed greatly to the fact that 60 per cent of the 1.74 million Japanese military losses were due to starvation, not combat.[30]

All combatant nations were eager to harness the new science of nutrition in order to maximize the efficiency of food distribution and in order to squeeze as much physical labour as possible from soldiers and civilians. Obscure nutritionists suddenly found themselves in positions of power within government and the military and were able to exert varying levels of influence on food policies. Within the Japanese, British, Commonwealth and United States militaries a minor revolution occurred in the understanding of food as a tool for maintaining the health and fighting capacity of soldiers, which triggered significant changes in the way soldiers were fed. This, in turn, impacted on various food technologies and significant progress was made, particularly in the United States, in the processing, fortification, packaging and transportation of food. Most significantly, the democratic governments acknowledged that in return for the sacrifices soldiers and civilians made in order to win the war it was the responsibility of the government to safeguard the food supply and provide an adequate diet for the whole population. This resulted in food policies in Britain and America which were designed to benefit the welfare of the entire nation, not simply those directly contributing to the war effort.

Rationing systems were one of the most prominent faultlines exposing the weaknesses of the different ideologies – communism, capitalism, paternalism, National Socialism, ultranationalism – that operated within the combatant nations. Thus, the paradox developed within Germany of feeding starvation rations to Jews, forced labourers and concentration camp inmates, despite the fact that they were potentially valuable workers within a war economy desperately short of labour. In contrast, the communists in the Soviet Union showed a surprising willingness to jettison the ideological principle of centralized food collection and distribution and even re-introduced a free market in food. Meanwhile, Great Britain went in the opposite direction, centralizing the economy and adopting a form of war socialism which went against the grain for the Conservatives in the cabinet. The United States was the only country that possessed sufficient resources to preserve its ideology of laissez-faire in virtually all areas of the economy, and it was therefore able to keep food controls to a minimum. It was also the only country to emerge from the war with an agricultural sector strengthened by rationalization and innovation, and thus be in a position of power with regard to food.

In theory, rationing systems were designed to prevent hoarding and to ensure the fair and equal distribution of food, in other words, to protect the entitlement to food of all sections of the population. In practice, even where active policies of extermination were absent, a more passive process of exclusion and denial can be observed at work. The US rationing system was much less vigorous in its application of price controls in stores where black Americans bought their food. In the Soviet Union the absolute food shortage meant that routine decisions made by food officials about who would receive food marked out others at the same time who would not be supplied with food and who would most probably die of hunger. There are no accurate figures for the number of Soviet civilians who died of starvation but it seems safe to estimate that somewhere between 2 and 3 million died of hunger and malnutrition. In Nationalist China the food shortage was a result of the Japanese occupation and blockade but it was the Nationalist government's decision to prioritize the food needs of the army and the bureaucracy over those of the peasantry which made rural famine inevitable, with 2–3 million deaths in the province of Henan alone.[31] The British rationing system is often celebrated for having done a remarkably good job, with limited resources, of feeding the British people. But the British government was also responsible for the food security of its colonial subjects, and it was here that it often failed, most spectacularly in Bengal, where 3 million Indians died of a preventable man-made famine.[32] Thus, the Allied powers made their own substantial contribution to wartime hunger, malnutrition and starvation.

Food became a central and often all-consuming preoccupation for most of the world's population. A Ukrainian engineer who studied at a Siberian military institute during the war recalled the food served in the canteen. The students were given two sorts of soup: one was made by pouring flour into boiling water, the other the students referred to as 'green borscht' (green soup) because it was made with nettles. They also received 50 grams of fish and 50 grams of meat a week. Some idea of how tiny these quantities were is conveyed by the fact that a boneless pork chop weighs about 100 grams. 'You could live on this food for about a month,' he told his interviewer, 'but if you had to eat it for more than a month, you got so hungry that you didn't care anything more about your studies, you just tried to figure out how to get something to eat . . . Sometimes we would go down to the market and buy snails and boil them in our rooms with a few potatoes. It takes a long time for them to cook . . . as the water began to boil, the snails began to rattle in the pot and it made quite a noise. Even the table on which we had the hotplate began to shake. The commander of our company lived in the room below ours, and one day he came up to see what was making all the noise. He threw open the door and shouted, "What have you got in here – an airplane?" So from then on we called this dish "airplane". It was not too good, but it was quick and cheap.'[33]

The Ukrainian and his classmates also ran a scam forging blood donor certificates, which entitled them to more food: 200 grams of blood earned half a kilogram of rice, a kilogram of sausage and two kilograms of black bread. 'Many students sold their blood in order to eat. But . . . you cannot give 200 grams of blood every day.' Instead he and his friends forged the certificates. 'Practically our whole class ate this way . . . Once a professor noticed that our class seemed to be eating far better than the others and asked us about it, but we said, quite proudly, "We are giving blood to the Soviet regime." And he could not say anything more. Some men "gave" thirty litres of blood in a year this way!'[34]

Even in comparatively well-supplied countries, such as Britain and Germany, lack of fat meant that the diet became unpalatable. The British were used to a pre-war nutritional balance where fat made up 38 per cent of calorie intake.[35] Although this only dropped by a small percentage during the war, combined with a shift from meat to wholemeal bread and potatoes as the basis of the diet, the less fatty meals became so monotonous, and tasted so insipid, that Jean Legas recalled, 'we ate the same menu every week for nearly five years . . . we just ate without thinking about it'.[36] The Germans suffered from a similar fat problem. During the first half of the twentieth century animal fat became a central element in the food of the working classes, giving the food flavour and helping to induce a feeling of fullness. But the 48 grams of fat per week provided by the basic German ration meant that the fat content of many non-industrial workers' meals fell below the 20 per cent fat-content mark which most western Europeans regarded as essential for taste.[37]

There are no deficiency diseases associated with a lack of fat (as long as the diet has alternative sources of vitamins A and D) but a low-fat diet means that it is necessary to consume a greater quantity of food in order to obtain sufficient calories. In fact, it is quite difficult for a person to force himself to eat enough potato to maintain necessary calorie intake if this is the main source of energy. Contemporary workers engaged in hard physical labour, who need around 4,000 calories a day, would have to spend almost their entire day eating if they were to obtain sufficient energy from bulky carbohydrate foods alone. It is for this reason that such workers eat a high proportion of their food as fat.[38] But for the Soviet, German and Japanese workers, fat simply was not available in sufficient quantities. Fat and meat also stave off hunger pangs for longer. The lack of fat, combined with the very limited quantity of animal protein in the form of meat, eggs or cheese in virtually all wartime diets resulted in a nagging sensation of hunger, even if the food contained sufficient calories.[39] A lack of sugar and sweetness in the diet also provoked sometimes unbearable cravings. Mathilde Wolff-Mönckeberg longed for good things to eat. In a letter she wrote in 1944 she described how 'I often get myself a spoonful of sugar even though we are very short of it and we don't have any left over.'[40]

In all the countries drawn into the Second World War, civilians spent their days queuing for rations, wondering how they were going to scrape together enough food to make the next meal. Digging for Victory became a global activity. In every spare scrap of land people planted potatoes, which became the food of war. Comparatively easy to grow, potatoes were also nutritious, providing protein and vitamins as well as carbohydrate.[41] Levels of deprivation varied greatly but virtually everywhere the quality of food declined. Roy Lee Grover, an American B-25 pilot on New Guinea, was appalled by the Australian army rations he was given. 'Bully beef . . . gummey gooey rice, dried onions and not much else. The bully beef was boiled, baked and fried for the three meals each day.' In desperation while on a trip to Townsville he bought 'a case of twenty-four quart cans of sliced peaches in a sweet syrup'. But he was soon equally sick of peaches and 'on my return to the States, it was many months before I could include rice or peaches in any meal'.[42] Bully beef, 'mutton stew thick . . . like cold glue', rubbery powdered egg, Spam, gritty black bread, and potatoes – 'boiled potatoes, fried potatoes, roasted potatoes . . . potato cakes, potato soup, potato fritters' – endless potatoes, these were the tastes of war.[43]

PART I

Food – An Engine of War

Food was at the heart of many of the policies which set Germany, Italy and Japan on the path to war in the 1930s. The rise of fascism, the humiliation and resentment felt by the Germans as a result of the Treaty of Versailles and the economic and social instability which developed in the wake of the Great Depression more commonly spring to mind as factors which contributed towards conflict. However, changes in eating habits were equally powerful in their effect and the need to secure the food to satisfy new appetites played into the aggressive, expansionist policies of the dictatorial regimes of the Axis powers.

The story of food's role as one of the causes of international conflict in the twentieth century begins in the last quarter of the previous century when the urban population in Europe shifted from a grain- to a meat-based diet. This development went hand in hand with the emergence of a new global food economy. Germany felt disadvantaged by the terms of the international food trade, dominated as it was by the United States and Great Britain and its empire. Indeed, Germany went to war in 1914 hoping to establish for itself a stronger position in the balance of international powers. After 1918 nationalists within Germany, Italy and Japan continued to see international trade and politics as the stumbling block which prevented their respective nations from realizing their potential as great powers. In Japan concerns about the poverty and inefficiency of the agrarian sector and the security of the urban food supply allowed right-wing militarist groups to gain power and influence within the government. In ultranationalist Japan, fascist Italy and National Socialist Germany these anxieties fuelled the desire for empire which would not only provide the resources to wage war but transform these nations into great players on the world stage.

If dreams of agrarian empires drove Germany, Italy and Japan into waging war, the plans Germany and Japan hatched for transforming these empires resulted in some of the most murderous criminal actions of the war. The implementation of the German General Plan for the East in Poland and the Japanese Settlement of One Million Households in Manchuria demonstrate that food was an engine not only of war but also of German and Japanese atrocities.

2

Germany's Quest for Empire

*What India was for England, the territories of Russia will be
for us. If only I could make the German people understand
what this space means for our future!*

(Adolf Hitler, August 1941)[1]

FROM WHEAT TO MEAT

The standard meal of an eighteenth-century German rural labourer
was 'gruel and mush', a soupy combination of grains and lentils. This
was typical fare for the rural population throughout Europe. In 1796
Richard Walker, a farm labourer, bell ringer, grave digger and barber,
living in the Northamptonshire parish of Roade with his wife, a lace
maker, and their five children, spent half the family's annual income
of £26 8s. on bread. The bread was sometimes supplemented by a little
bacon, the occasional potato, a small amount of cheese, and washed
down with beer, sugared tea and tiny quantities of milk. In the eighteenth century three-quarters of all European foods were derived from
plants, and even the fat in the diet was drawn predominantly from
plant oils.[2]

Throughout the nineteenth century, but with a marked increase in
the 1870s, the amount of meat in the European diet steadily rose from
16 kilograms per person per year to 50 kilograms by 1914.[3] The diet
of Ben Turner, his father and brother, all mill workers in Huddersfield
in 1876, illustrates the change: 'On Monday a bit of cold meat, on
Tuesday a hash, on Wednesday a potato pie, on Thursday some fry
[liver] and onions, on Friday a bit of potted meat, on Saturday a bit of

sausage, and on Sunday the usual joint, always providing the funds ran to it.' For breakfast and tea they ate bread and dripping, 'sometimes a Spanish onion or some "craps" (pork fat made crisp), and on Sunday teatime, a bit of special home-made cake to make the distinction from the other days. At the worst times our cut of beef was brisket, because it went the farthest, and made the most "drip", besides being the cheapest cut.'[4] Bread still featured largely in working-class meals but they now revolved around meat dishes and were much richer in animal proteins and fats. The Germans ate more pork, the British more mutton and beef.

These changes in the European diet were made possible by the development of a new, global food economy. The globalization of food systems began in the last quarter of the nineteenth century when the growth of railways and the introduction of ocean-going steamships dramatically reduced the cost of transporting food. Whereas in the 1860s it had cost 4s. 7½ d. to ship a quarter* of wheat from New York to Liverpool, by 1902 it cost a mere 11½ d. Subsequently there was a corresponding fall in the price. Wheat production in America doubled, in Russia it trebled, and a global economy of specialized agriculture began to emerge.[5] North America, Argentina, Australia, New Zealand and Russia grew the wheat that made the European working man's loaf and fattened the cattle, sheep and pigs that were shipped as frozen meat for his table. European meat production also benefited, as cheap maize, barley, oilseeds and soya beans, grown in Australia and the Americas, were shipped in for animal feed. The slaughter weight of European livestock increased, the time it took to fatten animals was reduced, and milk yields rose. This made food cheaper and more plentiful for the expanding urban working classes.[6]

Britain was the first European country to follow the path of transferring the job of growing food to its colonies. From the mid-nineteenth century Britain's agricultural economy began to shrink as labourers left the countryside for the cities, and others travelled abroad, swapping a life of deference for one of greater dignity, if not wealth, farming in the colonies. The British food-import economy turned on its head as the spices, sugar, cocoa and tea which had been unloaded at the docks

---

* A quarter of a ton or eight bushels.

in the early eighteenth century as luxuries for the dining tables of the wealthy, were, during the nineteenth century, redirected into the kitchens of the masses. Sugar from the Caribbean, tea from India and China, wheat and meat from the Commonwealth countries, all connected the British working man to every part of Britain's empire, from the tropics to the temperate zones.[7] By 1914 Britain was reliant on imports for over half of its food (measured by value) and was Europe's major importer of grain. Indeed, the British developed a preference for the roller-ground hard wheat produced in Minneapolis and Buffalo over the soft European stone-ground wheat. The hard, glutinous American wheat produced a soft, moist loaf which stayed fresh for longer.[8]

The apparent improvement in the British working man's diet hid a decline in the nutritional quality of his food. Roller-grinding wheat to make flour is a process which discards much of the wheat germ, the source of wheat's protein, vitamins, minerals and fats. The softer loaf may have been more easily digestible than the old style stone-ground bread but it was far less nutritious. Even though the British working classes could afford more meat, the loss of vitamins and minerals in the bread was not compensated for by an increase in the consumption of vitamin-rich foods such as fruit, vegetables, cheese and eggs. In the towns fresh milk was hard to store and the urban population tended to rely on less nutritious imported cans of condensed and evaporated milk. Much of the energy in the working-class diet came from the sugar in their tea, and in the jam they spread on their bread. Sugar consumption per person increased dramatically over the nineteenth century until by the early twentieth century the British were eating about 36 kilograms a year. Thus, an unhealthy quantity of sugar had replaced the energy derived from plant carbohydrates that had been the main source of calories in the eighteenth century. This diet combined with urban poverty meant that hunger and malnutrition haunted the poorer sections of the working class, especially families with many children.[9]

However, the British celebrated their cheap white loaf; a direct product of free trade, it was regarded as a symbol of Britain's powerful international status and the benefits this brought Britain.[10] The country's dependence on imports was a positive force as 'the large food deficit acted as a pump for the world's commerce'.[11] The vast colonial agricultural hinterland provided a market (made wealthy by exporting food) for the manufactured goods that Britain needed to export in order to pay for its food. The ships that sailed for Canada, Jamaica and Australia were laden with Sheffield knives and Lancashire cloth, and returned with holds full of wheat, sugar and wool. British service industries invested in these same countries, further enriching British companies.[12]

Germany, in contrast, found itself in an uncomfortable position. Bismarck's protectionist tariffs had sheltered farmers from the growth in the global trade of cheap grain and had enabled the large farms owned by Junkers,* east of the River Elbe, to prosper. Germany's industrial revolution began almost half a century later than Britain's but, as the process began to gather speed, more liberal voices within the country advocated a less protectionist economic course. Germany, they argued, should follow a path similar to that of Britain and expand manufacturing in order to produce exports which would then pay for the import of primary products, including cheap food to feed the growing urban population.[13] In fact, protectionism ensured the German working classes ate a slightly healthier diet than the British. German-grown rye produced a far more nutritious loaf of bread and fewer imports meant that the Germans drank more fresh milk than the British and ate a more modest 21 kilograms of sugar per head.[14] But German workers also wanted to indulge in luxurious, light crusty white bread and they wanted more meat in their diet. In the 1890s Bismarck's successors began to dismantle the wall of tariffs in order to enable German export industries to develop. The economic writer and social reformer Karl Oldenberg warned that this would lead to ruin. Germany would become dependent on the United States and China for its food. The farming communities, which were the source of the nation's social health, would be destroyed. Meanwhile, the expanding urban areas would spread decay and undermine the nation's social fabric.[15] A fin-de-siècle fear of the anonymous and corrupting city was widespread throughout Europe, but in Germany conservative forces prevailed and in 1902 protectionist tariffs were reintroduced.[16]

Nevertheless, the German economy continued to expand and more and more imports of raw materials and food were required. The

---

* Prussian landed aristocracy.

German chancellor, Count Leo von Caprivi (1890–94), tried to solve the problem of dependence on food imports by increasing Germany's self-sufficiency in food and this was fairly successful. In 1916 German farmers were feeding about seventy people per 100 acres of cultivated land, in contrast to the British farmer who fed about forty-five people from an equivalent area. Only 19 per cent of the German population's calories came from imports. But these meat, livestock feed and fat imports were important sources of energy and taste, providing 27 per cent of the protein and 42 per cent of the fat consumed in Germany. By 1914 Germany (together with the Low Countries) formed the largest wheat-deficit area in the world.[17] But by delaying migration from the countryside to the cities, agricultural protectionism had burdened the nation with a large agricultural sector which held back the process of industrialization. It also kept food prices artificially high, with the result that urban working-class protests about the price of milk, butter, and especially meat, erupted between 1906 and 1912.[18] Those who advocated free trade within Germany argued that it was only by becoming a manufacturing and trading nation that Germany could hope to raise the standard of living of its growing urban population.[19]

For the British, the German loaf of rye bread symbolized the barbarism of autocratic German society, hemmed in by protectionism. German politicians were frustrated by their inability to challenge American and British dominance both over the world's wheat-growing areas and the sea lanes, and by Germany's lack of a dependent agricultural hinterland which could supply raw materials, or colonial markets to boost the German economy, in the same way that the empire created British wealth.[20] Behind the late nineteenth- and early twentieth-century jostle for a balance of power between Britain, Germany, Russia, Austria-Hungary and France, lurked the problem of how to feed a working population within the constraints of the economics of global trade. Within Germany, nationalist social commentators, and an increasing number of German Conservative Party politicians, thought that successful pursuit of profit, power and influence was contingent on the country finding a more equitable position in the global economy of food production, import and export, and the only way to achieve this was through war. If it fought a short war the German government felt confident that it could feed its people for the duration of the conflict.

Then, if Germany were victorious, it could defeat France and expand eastwards into a belt stretching from Finland to the Black Sea coast, thus establishing German dominance over western and eastern Europe. When they went to war in 1914 German politicians were hoping that the conflict would be decisive in disentangling the German nation from the world markets which put it at such a disadvantage.[21]

DEFEAT, HUNGER AND THE LEGACY OF THE FIRST WORLD WAR

If the problem of food supply was one of the factors which placed the great powers in hostile relations with each other, it was also one of the causes of Germany's downfall in 1918. The First World War is associated with stagnant trench warfare but the battle was also fought in the Atlantic. For the first time naval battles became subordinate to commercial warfare, and in this way the First World War prefigured the Second. The international specialization of food production made both Britain and Germany vulnerable to blockade. Both countries relied on imports of raw materials, food and fodder to keep the war economy afloat and to feed their people. Even a reduction in imports could cause food prices to skyrocket and cripple industry. Hungry, unemployed workers might then pressurize the government to negotiate a peace before a military victory was clear.

The British Admiralty planned to impose an economic blockade on Germany long before the war began, and a new dimension was added to the concept of blockade when the British revised the naval code in 1907 and 1908, extending the definition of an instrument of war to food, and changing the rules of engagement to allow for attacks on neutral shipping, if the ship was carrying supplies to the enemy.[22] When the war began Britain not only blockaded the German ports but extended the action to neutral continental countries by severely limiting the amount of imports they could receive, in an effort to prevent them from re-exporting surplus goods to Germany.[23] During the Second World War these principles were applied even more harshly when occupied countries came under a complete blockade and the amount of food and petrol allowed in to neutral countries such as Spain was strictly limited.[24]

The German Admiralty introduced their own crucial change in blockade techniques by using the submarine as a weapon against merchant shipping. They wanted to use the submarines to attack Britain's supply of wheat, but in the early years of the war the German military command hesitated to employ this strategy for fear of hitting an American ship and thus drawing the United States into the conflict.[25] The Germans did not adopt all-out submarine warfare until mid-1917, by which time America had entered the war. However, by then the Allies had begun to co-ordinate their use of shipping space and had introduced the system of grouping ships into convoys travelling together with escort vessels, which was very effective in reducing the number of sinkings.[26] German submarines did, however, inflict painful damage on Allied shipping and in 1917 Britain came close to using up its food reserves.[27] High food prices even caused a certain amount of industrial unrest but Britain was able to keep open its supply lines and feed its population adequately. Ultimately, the international system of maritime trade was not only a weakness but also a strength as it enabled Britain to draw on the economies of the Commonwealth and the colonies, which provided raw materials, men, clothing and food.[28] It was to prove equally crucial as a site of vulnerability and a source of strength during the Second World War.

The German submarine campaign was less successful than Britain's traditional blockade, which succeeded in cutting Germany off from 'direct imports from five enemy nations that together in 1913 had accounted for 46 per cent of Germany's total imports'.[29] When America entered the war in 1917 Germany's fate was sealed, as the United States placed an embargo on exports not only to Germany but also to neutral continental countries. This put an end to Germany's indirect trade with America while at the same time Britain gained better access to the boundless resources of the United States.[30] Eventually, a shortage of agricultural labour combined with the blockade to reduce the Germans to a miserable state of hunger.

Inspecting the food ration lines in Berlin in the autumn of 1916, the American newspaper correspondent George Schreiner wrote: 'among the 300 applicants for food there was not one who had had enough to eat for weeks. In the case of the younger women and children the skin was drawn hard to the bones and bloodless.'[31] Shortages began with bread, and then spread to potatoes, butter, fats and meat, until the Germans were forced to resort to eating turnips and swedes, which were normally fed to animals. The winter of 1916–17 became known as the turnip winter. Ethel Cooper, an Australian then living in Leipzig, wrote to her family: 'I think that if I were to bray . . . it is all that could be expected . . . after a month of living on parsnips and turnips.'[32] It was bitterly cold, coal ran out, electricity was cut off, the trams stopped running, even turnips were running short. 'Germany', Ethel wrote, 'has at last ceased to trumpet the fact that it can't be starved out.'[33] Life was thoroughly exhausting and uncomfortable, interspersed with periods of absolute deprivation when the urban population teetered on the verge of starvation. The Germans lost weight, the birth-rate fell and the mortality rate rose. Deaths from pneumonia and tuberculosis increased significantly, a strong indicator of malnutrition and poor sanitary conditions. Three-quarters of a million Germans died of malnutrition. George Schreiner noticed that the underfed bodies on the trams gave off an odour reminiscent of 'a cadaver'.[34]

Despondency and fatigue overwhelmed the nation. If the lack of food contributed to the German defeat it was not because the Germans were dying in vast numbers but because the grinding misery of never having quite enough to eat wore down the morale of the people. New recruits and soldiers returning from leave brought news of the misery to the front line, where the troops themselves were hungry and ill. They stole the barley feed meant for the horses and ground it in their coffee mills to make flour for pancakes.[35] The horses died; the soldiers' will to fight dissipated. The German request for an armistice in October was the result of failure on the battlefield. But to many of those who witnessed these events, it appeared as though hunger was the victor, and that it was starvation among the army and civilians which had brought about a humiliating defeat.[36]

Even after Germany had signed the armistice the British continued to impose an economic blockade. This was supposed to help suppress a communist revolution and pressurize the Germans into accepting the unfavourable terms of the Treaty of Versailles.[37] The winter of 1918–19 was the hungriest and most miserable for the German population. From the regimental barracks in Munich the twenty-nine-year old Adolf Hitler, who had served in the German army as a dispatch runner at the rank of corporal, watched how the city came under the rule of, first, a Jewish radical Social Democrat, and then of a number of Soviet-style councils, until it was eventually brought under control by the troops of the newly formed Weimar Republic.[38] These events, which demonstrated the vulnerability of a hungry and defeated Germany to the threat of communist revolution, ensured that Hitler (and many others who would later take up positions of power under the National Socialists) developed an acute awareness of the dangers of civilian hunger. Indeed, Hitler developed an obsession with the need to secure the German food supply, especially at a time of war. This would later provide him with one of the reasons for the attack on the Soviet Union, and add fuel to the fire of progressive radicalization which character-ized the National Socialist regime during the Second World War. On 8 March 1919, Lloyd George warned the Supreme War Council and the Allies that 'the memories of starvation might one day turn against them ... [T]he Allies were sowing hatred for the future: they were piling up agony, not for the Germans, but for themselves.'[39] Lloyd George's comments were alarmingly prescient. The hatred the Allies had sowed came back to haunt the British in 1940–42 during the height of the U-boat blockade. But it was the inhabitants of eastern Europe who experienced the worst of the agony that Lloyd George had foreseen. During the Second World War the National Socialists would argue that the need to secure a minimum food ration of 2,300 calories per day for ordinary Germans justified the extermination of 30 million urban Soviets, over 1 million Soviet prisoners of war, and at least as many Polish Jews.

AUTARKY AND *LEBENSRAUM*

The First World War intensified Germany's problems with regard to its position in the world food economy. The most critical problem was the country's lack of foreign exchange. Germany's manufacturing indus-try did not produce enough exports to earn sufficient foreign exchange to pay for all its import requirements. Food and fodder for livestock made up half of all Germany's imports, but it also needed raw materials to generate industrial growth and the war reparations imposed by the Treaty of Versailles swallowed up yet more foreign exchange. In 1927 the prominent agronomist Friedrich Aereboe published a study of the influence of the First World War on agricultural production and concluded that Germany would have been better off if it had followed the liberal course of integrating into the world economy in the nineteenth century. Agriculture should have been scaled down, freeing up workers for industry to produce manufactured goods for export which would then, in turn, have paid for increasing imports of food and consumer goods.[40] By not following this course Germany had burdened itself with an agricultural sector which was too large for a modern economy and farms which were too small, inefficient, and wallowing in debt.[41]

In the inter-war years it was not too late for Germany to choose to follow the liberal course mapped out by Aereboe, and fully (and peacefully) integrate itself into the global market economy. However, even Britain and America were moving towards protectionism in the 1930s. When the First World War came to an end a sudden drop in the demand for food left Europe and the United States with a surplus of foodstuffs. The interests of the farmer and the working man now converged. Both favoured a secure food supply and stable, if higher, prices. The economic impact of the Great Depression intensified the problem and in response the United States increased tariffs on both imports and exports. The days of British free trade came to an end with the Ottawa agreements of 1932, which gave favoured access to foodstuffs entering Britain from the Dominions in return for special privileges for British manufactured goods in the Dominions' home markets. France and Italy defended their low-productivity farms as the site of national identity and set up walls of protective tariffs, while injecting money into farming in an attempt to increase agricultural productivity.[42]

August Skalweit, another prominent agriculturalist, who published his analysis of the German food economy during the First World War in the same year as Aereboe, drew the opposite conclusion to his colleague. He argued that it was imperative that Germany should become less dependent on this hostile world market.[43] In conservative circles, which favoured this alternative course of action, food preferences were transformed into a political statement. German housewives' associations, with strong links to centre-right political parties, campaigned for patriotic consumption choices.[44] Germans preferred to eat crusty white rolls but two-thirds of the wheat to make them had to be imported. 'Good' German women were encouraged to support the German farmer and preserve the traditional social hierarchy and lifestyle, by purchasing rye bread made from home-grown grain. Housewives' associations also promoted German-produced potatoes, butter and fish. Even bananas and oranges were rejected as decadent fruits and shunned in favour of the German apple.[45] However, Skalweit warned that if Germany was really to become self-sufficient, and free of the need to spend precious foreign exchange on food, then its farmers would have to increase fodder production in order to feed the animals which would produce the protein and fat which Germany presently relied on imports to provide. He argued that this could only be achieved if a new, central organizational body was set up to co-ordinate the drive for self-sufficiency or autarky.[46]

The agronomists in the NSDAP (the National Socialist German Workers' Party) would probably have known Skalweit's work and they implemented many changes which resembled his recommendations. But their agenda was not simply to create a self-sufficient food economy which would secure the food supply for the German people but also to create a food economy which would provide the basis for military action.[47] As soon as the National Socialists came to power Walther Darré, Hitler's Minister for Food and Agriculture from June 1933, set up a new organizational body to co-ordinate the battle for self-sufficiency. Germany's woefully backward agricultural sector was completely removed from the market system and put under the control of the Reich Food Corporation (*Reichsnährstand*). Every farmer, agricultural labourer, trader or food processor was expected to join. This vast power complex administered all aspects of the food system from production to distribution, from the plants which farmers were instructed to cultivate to the price of essential foodstuffs in the shops.[48] German agriculture was cut off from international markets by protectionist tariffs. The prices farmers were paid for their products were often double what they were worth on the global market. Consequently, farm incomes rose and farm debt was reduced.[49] But the ideology of protection had shifted. It was no longer for the benefit of a small and powerful aristocratic Junker elite. National Socialist ideology maintained that farmers were working for the good of the German race.

Their primary motivation in cultivating the land was supposed to be not profit but feeding the nation.[50]

Darré idealized farmers as the backbone of the Aryan race and advocated a return to the soil as a way of reversing the dangerous racial deterioration brought about by urban life. A regenerated countryside would, he argued, benefit the entire *Volk* (people) by strengthening the 'life-source' of society. During the 1933 election campaign he was extremely successful at winning the farming vote for the NSDAP.[51] However, once the National Socialists had come to power he gradually fell from favour with Hitler and the rest of the National Socialist leadership. Darré's problem was that once power had been achieved Hitler quickly lost interest in the problems of farmers. Indeed, Hitler demonstrated just how much Darré's plans for internal agricultural restructuring bored him at a meeting in July 1934: while Darré was talking he picked up and began reading a newspaper.[52]

After 1933 agricultural reform was a low priority for the majority of the National Socialist leadership as they focused on preparing for war. But it is a mistake, which many historians have made, to conclude that issues of agriculture, farming and food supply were of little importance in determining wider National Socialist policy.[53] Food was a constant worry for Hitler. Darré's campaign for food self-sufficiency was modestly successful. The yield of key crops such as potatoes, sugar beet, cabbage and rye increased and in 1939 Germany was 83 per cent self-sufficient in the most important foodstuffs such as bread grains, potatoes, sugar and meat. However, this only represented a 3 per cent increase in self-sufficiency since the National Socialists had come to power.[54] The best efforts of the Reich Food Corporation could not solve the problem of the need for imported fodder. This brought Darré into conflict with Hjalmar Schacht, Reich Minister for Economics. While Darré wanted foreign currency for the purchase of oilseeds and food, Schacht wanted to prioritize raw materials for the armaments industry.[55] In 1936 food shortages and rising food prices combined with fears of inflation and a rise in unemployment to revive the spectre of November 1918. Hitler demanded that a brake should be put on food prices.[56] Two years later he warned that unless sufficient foreign exchange was made available to overcome food shortages the regime would face a crisis. It was by now clear to Hitler and his leadership that, as the German standard of living rose, the country would face a food disaster unless large quantities of food could be imported.[57] This would, of course, slow down rearmament. In February 1939 he told a meeting of troop commanders that the food question was the most urgent problem facing Germany.[58]

The solution lay, in Hitler's mind, in the conquest of *Lebensraum* (living space). In his never published 'Second Book', written in 1928, Hitler had already formulated the argument that in order to achieve the same level of wealth and prosperity as the United States, Germany needed its own version of the American west.[59] The Reich Food Corporation confirmed this belief in the need for expansion. It calculated that Germany needed another 7–8 million hectares of farmland.[60] If farms in the Reich were consolidated and rationalized many farmers would have to be evicted from their tiny farms. The plan was to send them east where they could settle new farms and supply the foodstuffs which Germany currently needed to import. *Lebensraum* would make Germany truly self-sufficient and immune to blockade and this would eventually enable Germany to challenge British and American hegemony.[61]

This vision of *Lebensraum* in the east was shared by many National Socialists, not least by Heinrich Himmler, head of the Gestapo (Secret State Police) and SS (*Schutzstaffel* or Protection Squad). His Race and Resettlement office was intended as the vehicle by which greater Germany would be settled by a racially healthy German People.[62] Darré, who in the early years was a friend of Himmler and director of the Race and Resettlement office, shared this vision, and as early as the summer of 1932 he can be found at a secret NSDAP leadership conference detailing plans for large eastern agricultural estates run by an aristocracy of SS members and worked by enslaved former inhabitants.[63] This perceived need to expand eastwards made conflict inevitable. In a secret speech to young military officers in May 1942, Hitler explained why Germany had gone to war. While it was the duty of the German people to multiply, they lacked the space to do so. If they failed to multiply they faced racial decline and therefore needed to capture living space. 'It is a *battle for food*, a battle for the basis for life, for *the raw materials* the earth offers, *the natural resources* that lie under the soil and *the fruits* that it offers to the one who cultivates it.'[64] The entire future of the *Volksgemeinschaft* (the classless People's Community which the National Socialists claimed they were striving to create) depended upon the creation of a new agrarian system throughout the Greater Reich.[65]

The desire for an agrarian empire can make National Socialism seem archaic and backward looking. Britain had long since outgrown the strategy of solving the problem of agricultural decline at home by promoting emigration overseas. But if it was impossible to emulate the United States, which was large and resource-rich enough to achieve autarky within the confines of its own borders, the only other contemporary model for achieving great power status was Great Britain's empire. And there were modern precedents for 'demographic colonization' within an empire. In the 1880s Czarist Russia had begun settling Russian peasantry in their newly acquired territories of Kazakh and Turkestan as a means of ensuring these territories were Russified and thus tied in to the empire.[66]

Likewise, Mussolini's war in Ethiopia in 1935 was born out of his desire to create a new Roman empire with Italy once more dominating the Mediterranean region. Agricultural experts were sent to Somalia, Eritrea and Ethiopia to assess whether the colonies could be transformed into a breadbasket for Italy. The cultivation of bananas, peanuts and sesame seeds were all considered. Bizarrely, given the fact that coffee plants were indigenous to the area, planners even looked into the viability of growing hibiscus flowers for a herbal tea which was an autarkic substitute for coffee. The Ethiopian campaign was ill-judged. It proved overly expensive, resulted in economic sanctions and caused food shortages throughout Italy. The Italian settlers were unsuccessful in establishing Italian-style agriculture and had to be sent food supplies from the home country.[67] In 1938 Italy again sought to invigorate food production in its empire and sent 20,000 peasants to Libya (which had been an Italian colony since 1912). They were settled on specially created farms and their role was to rebuild Libya as the erstwhile 'granary of Imperial Rome', and strengthen the Italian campaign for food autarky. They were also regarded as a reserve garrison of farmer-soldiers.[68]

At the same time the Japanese were implementing the Plan for the Settlement of One Million Households in Manchuria. Poor tenant farmers were encouraged to settle in northern China as a way of establishing Japanese culture on the Chinese mainland and to act as a reserve for the army should the Soviets invade. Thus, the German plan to acquire *Lebensraum* was not so much an attempt to set the clock back as a contemporary solution to the problems caused by industrialization. The Italians, Germans and Japanese all sought to remove from society those potentially destabilizing groups which had lost out in the process of modernization and, by using them to create utopian settler communities, to transform them into a positive by-product of modernity.[69]

HERBERT BACKE AND THE HUNGER PLAN

One of the most chilling aspects of Nazi Germany is the way in which various men, all with their own iniquitous plans, were able to exploit Hitler's seizure of power and his conveniently hazy vision of the future to realize their own designs. Herbert Backe was one of these men. For most National Socialists an eastern agrarian empire was a vision to be realized once the war was won, but Backe saw the agricultural riches of the east not as the eventual spoils of war but as the means to win the conflict.

In his position as representative for agriculture for the Four Year Plan, Backe managed, in the winter of 1940, to persuade first Hermann Göring, and then Hitler, that in order to win the war Germany would have to be self-sufficient, but in order to be self-sufficient it *must* first conquer the Soviet Union. While Darré found himself increasingly shut off from the Führer, Backe became increasingly influential and his solution to the problem of the wartime food supply contributed directly to Hitler's decision to go to war with the Soviet Union in the summer of 1941.

Until recently Backe's role in the National Socialist path to war and the regime's progressive radicalization has been overlooked. Many historians have regarded him as an innocuous agronomist whose involvement in National Socialism was confined to the apparently harmless sphere of food.[70] Neither Backe nor the National Socialist attitude towards food was harmless. In order to secure the German food supply for the duration of the war Backe devised the Hunger Plan, which proposed the mass murder of the Slavic inhabitants of the eastern

Soviet Union. Later his increasing worries over food shortages in the Reich fuelled the discussions which surrounded the decision to speed up the Holocaust and remove 'useless' Jewish eaters from Poland.

Backe's hatred of the Russian people stemmed from his traumatic experiences during the First World War. Born in 1896 to German parents in Georgia, then part of the Russian empire, he was interned as an enemy alien in the Urals in 1914. When he was eventually repatriated to Germany after the war he was appalled by the bitterness of the defeated Germans and shaken by his social decline into poverty. He supported his sick mother and three younger sisters by taking menial labouring jobs, eventually working as a farm agent. He later wrote to his wife, 'I realise that my tension and nervousness are a result of my development being distorted – hindered and destroyed: my hatred of the authors of this destruction [Russians] came about as a result of that.'[71]

Backe joined the Storm Troopers (*Sturmabteilung* or SA) in the early 1920s while working on an agrarian diploma at the University of Göttingen. He abandoned political agitation when he went to Hanover to work on a doctorate under Professor Erich Obst, an advocate of agrarian autarky. In his thesis Backe expounded the racial theories that he had developed in discussion with fellow SA members in Göttingen. He set out the argument that when Bolshevik rule disintegrated in Russia (as it surely must) 'The People without Space' (i.e. the Germans) would step into the vacuum to farm the east. His examiners failed the thesis on the grounds that it was a work of sociology, in other words of politics, and Backe set off into deserved obscurity to take up the tenancy of a dilapidated farm near the Harz mountains.[72] However, Darré's attention had been caught by some articles that Backe had published, and he repeatedly invited Backe to join him in the agrarian wing of the NSDAP in Munich. It was only after Backe had seen Hitler speak in 1931 that he finally acceded to the invitation and, having joined the NSDAP, was integrated into the National Socialist agricultural administration. In the autumn of 1936 Backe was recommended to Göring, who was looking for an agricultural representative on the Council of the Four Year Plan.[73]

Göring's office of the Four Year Plan was intended to rejuvenate German agriculture and industry and undertake a massive rearmament programme. Backe's position in charge of agriculture in the Four Year Plan made him effectively a second Minister of Food and Agriculture in competition with Darré. He enthusiastically undertook the task of liberating Germany from what he termed the 'Jewish' (i.e. American) liberal world economy by striving towards the achievement of 'nutritional freedom'.[74] If Hitler was bored by Darré's plans for fodder silos, Göring could barely disguise his impatience when asked to listen to Backe's plans to increase food self-sufficiency through land reclamation, fish farms, mechanization and artificial fertilizer. But while Darré fell from favour, Backe became increasingly influential. Alongside the internal agricultural reforms he developed a proposal which promised to resolve the impasse which the war and the German food situation had reached by the winter of 1940.[75]

The National Socialists began the Second World War well aware that a short war was essential for success and that only during a short war could adequate civilian rations be guaranteed.[76] Initially, things went according to plan and Germany achieved a string of rapid successes. First, Hitler made sure that the Soviet Union would not enter the war if he attacked Poland. The 1939 Treaty of Non-Aggression gave the Soviet Union eastern Poland, the Baltic states, Finland and parts of Romania. In return Stalin agreed to provide Germany with raw materials, oil and food, reasoning that if the Soviet Union generously provided Germany with all that it needed there would be no reason for it to attack.[77] On 1 September 1939 Hitler took Europe to war by invading Poland, which was defeated within a matter of weeks. Riding high on this rapid success, by June 1940 Germany had conquered Denmark, Norway, Holland, Belgium and France. But then the war stalled over Britain. The British government had not been willing (as Hitler had hoped) to negotiate for peace, and neither the Battle of Britain nor the Blitz had brought the British to their knees. Without air supremacy plans to invade had to be shelved and Germany now faced a protracted war of attrition with Britain, supported by the immense resources of the United States.[78]

Hitler turned his attention to the Soviet Union. Victory in the east was always his ultimate goal and he argued that Germany should make speed to defeat the Russians before the United States was officially drawn into the conflict. He also hoped that the rapid collapse of the Soviet Union would leave the British feeling even more isolated and perhaps persuade them to capitulate.[79]

Backe was aware that the limits of the German food supply system might hamper the execution of this plan. By the end of 1940 Germany was in possession of a number of occupied economies which had not prepared their agricultural sectors for war. All were dependent on food imports to a greater or lesser extent, ranging from Norway's reliance on imports for 57 per cent of its food, to France, where imports made up 17 per cent of the total food consumption.[80] In addition, the agricultural sectors of all of these countries were extremely dependent on fodder and fertilizer imports which would now be cut by the British blockade.[81] On 20 August 1940, Churchill announced a total blockade against Germany, its allies and all occupied countries. Every ship wishing to take cargo through the blockade had to apply for a 'navicert' which showed that its load was not contraband. Crucially, the British extended the definition of contraband to cover food if it could be used by the enemy's armed forces or government. In practice this cut continental Europe off from the rest of the world's food supplies. Only twelve ships broke the blockade in the year 1941–42.[82]

Even if the occupied territories comprehensively restructured their agricultural sectors it was clear that they, like Germany, would suffer from fodder, meat and fat shortages and a consequent decline in food production. Germany had no intention of exporting food to these countries, and even the food they were receiving from the Soviet Union under the terms of the 1939 Treaty of Non-Aggression was insufficient to cover the deficit. In a series of reports written in May 1940 Backe warned that in the light of the Allied blockade, 'if the war lasts more than two years it is lost'.[83] By December 1940 anxiety about Germany's food situation was widespread among the National Socialist leadership. Backe did nothing to assuage these concerns. Now was his opportunity to press for the solution to Germany's problems which he had been incubating since he first wrote his thesis in 1926. During the Christmas holidays of 1940 he spent his time redrafting, for the third time, the annual report of the Reich Ministry for Food and Agriculture on the food situation in Germany, the seriousness of which it was his purpose to emphasize to the leadership. In January he had the opportunity to put forward his concerns, and his ideas for a solution, not only to his direct boss, Göring, but also to Hitler, whom he met some time that month.[84]

One of the problems with piecing together the history of the National Socialist regime is that the leadership was wary of leaving behind incriminating evidence. Backe warned, 'clearly in case the enemy should hear of it, it is better not to cite the [Hunger] plan.'[85] Therefore records of what was said during meetings with Hitler were not always kept, or were later destroyed. How decisions were reached, and who influenced policy, has to be painstakingly pieced together from information about who attended specific meetings and knowledge of their political agenda at the time. Diary entries and other scattered references to such meetings often offer clues. A second complicating factor was that Hitler himself preferred to give orders orally and was frequently vague, leaving his subordinates to guess his intentions and to strive to fulfil his wishes according to their own interpretation of what exactly it was that he wanted them to do.

We do know that by February 1941 what would become known as the Hunger Plan had been formulated by Backe and had received both Göring's and Hitler's approval. Alfred Rosenberg, future Minister for the Occupied Eastern Territories, was informed about it in a meeting with Hitler on 2 April 1941. He noted in his diary that although he would never forget what the Führer had told him he would not write it down.[86] The plan does not seem to have been formulated on paper until 2 May, when it was summarized in a blandly entitled 'memorandum on the result of today's discussion with the state secretaries regarding Barbarossa',* which was later found among the papers of General Georg Thomas, head of the War Economy and Armaments Office. Only three copies of the plan now exist, one of which, known as the 'Yellow Folder', is a much shortened version which was circulated to agricultural functionaries. The original document came out of Backe's office and is covered in his handwriting.[87]

Backe's plan provided Hitler with a solution to the problem of a war of attrition with Britain and America by arguing that the Soviet Union could be transformed into a huge resource base *if* the needs of its inhabitants were ignored. In a vague way Hitler had for years been expounding the idea that 'the occupation of the Ukraine would liberate us from every economic worry'.[88] Already in 1939 he had told League of Nations High Commissioner for the city of Danzig, Carl

---

* The codename given to the invasion of the Soviet Union.

J. Burckhardt, 'I need the Ukraine, so that no one is able to starve us again, like in the last war.'[89] But most of Hitler's advisers were under no illusions about the difficulties involved in exploiting Soviet resources. Virtually all of the Ukraine's grain went to feed the vastly expanded cities of the Soviet Union. The process of collectivizing the farms had changed the social structure of Soviet society, creating an industrial proletariat out of peasants driven off the land. Whereas four-fifths of Soviets lived in the countryside in 1926, only one-half were still peasants in 1939. Officials in the German Food and Agriculture Ministry calculated that during the twentieth century more than 30 million people had moved into the Soviet Union's cities. While in the early years of the twentieth century Russia had produced a surplus of 11 million tons of grain, most of this was now disappearing into the stomachs of Russia's rapidly expanding urban population. This left only a small surplus which could be siphoned off to feed Germany.[90]

The memorandum outlining the Hunger Plan acknowledged this problem and the additional difficulties that the Soviet scorched earth policy, normal war damage and the emergence of a black market would cause. But the solution, it suggested, was simple. The memo spoke euphemistically of suppressing Russian consumption but what was actually intended was to shut down the flow of food from the Ukraine to the towns and cities of northern and central Russia. The food would be diverted on to the plates of German troops and civilians in the Reich. As a consequence, the document acknowledged, 'unbelievable hunger' would rule in northern Russia and the industrial areas, which would 'die out, so to speak'.[91] The meeting casually concluded that 'umpteen millions of people will be starved to death'.[92] The actual figure that Backe had in mind was 30 million, precisely the number by which his administrators calculated the Soviet Union's urban centres had grown in the past few decades. Those charged with implementing the plan were warned that any sympathy they might feel for the starving Soviets would be misplaced as 'the war can only be continued if the *entire* Wehrmacht is fed from Russia in the third year of the war'.[93]

Given the nature of the events that followed the invasion of the Soviet Union, much historical work understandably focuses on the racial and ideological motivation for the attack. It is only with the recent work of historians such as Christian Gerlach, Adam Tooze and Alex Kay that the centrality of food as an engine of the Second World War has become apparent. 'As hard as it may be for us to credit, agrarian ideology is crucial if we are to understand, not the archaism of Hitler's regime, but its extraordinary militancy.'[94] Hitler had always intended to wipe out Bolshevism and colonize the east. Backe's sinister plan now gave him a sound economic reason to set alongside the ideological reasons to launch an attack.[95]

Securing the nation's food supply was a primary war aim in Hitler's mind and the central importance of food was clear to the men charged with planning and executing Barbarossa. Germany was later to suffer from crippling fuel shortages and one might expect planners to have focused on capturing sources of mineral oil. But even General Thomas, who was assigned the task of assessing 'the military-economic consequences of invasion in the East', began his memorandum of that title with several pages on agricultural production. When he argued that the capture of the oil region of the Caucasus would be essential, he referred to the needs of agriculture, not to Germany's petrol shortage. Ukrainian farming was, he argued, highly mechanized, using 60 per cent of the Soviet Union's oil supplies, and it would be essential to secure the supply in order to ensure a plentiful grain harvest.[96] When Göring met with Rosenberg, Lammers, Keitel, Bormann and Hitler at military headquarters on 16 July 1941, he reiterated 'we must first of all think about the securing of our sustenance, everything else can be dealt with only much later'.[97] Once the attack began, the commander of Security Division 403, General-Major Wolfgang von Ditfurth, complained that the wild plunder of the eastern peasants' farms indicated that it did not seem to be universally understood among the troops and their officers 'that the war against Russia is not exclusively caused by a world view, but rather is supposed to simultaneously secure our supply zones, for greater Germany . . . that we must possess during the final conflict with England (USA)'.[98]

The Hunger Plan was never fully implemented but this was not because it was the pet project of an unimportant agrarian official. The scheme involved all levels of the regime from Hitler, to Göring and the officials of the Four Year Plan, to Rosenberg and the administrators in the Reich Ministry for the Occupied Eastern Territories. Even the

Wehrmacht, which preferred to be seen to distance itself from the more gruesome of the regime's plans, accepted it with alacrity because it solved seemingly insuperable logistical problems. If food could be taken directly from the occupied territories this would relieve pressure on overburdened supply lines. Erich von dem Bach-Zelewski, commander for the army in central Russia, coldly calculated that at least 20 million people would starve in his area.[99] The plan foundered and, as will be seen in a later chapter, was only implemented in a piecemeal, chaotic fashion. This was because co-ordination between the different organizations charged with administering the eastern territories was lacking and, despite the involvement of an array of political and economic bureaucrats in its conceptualization, the practical details of exactly how it was to be realized on the ground were never properly worked out.[100]

The attack on the Soviet Union has rightly been characterized as a war of annihilation. The exceptional brutality of the fighting on the eastern front, as well as the introduction of *Einsatzgruppen* (mobile task forces), which followed behind the army murdering Bolsheviks, the intelligentsia and Jews, have gained it this reputation. But if the Hunger Plan had been successfully executed then these acts of annihilation would have been overshadowed by the implementation of mass murder on an even larger scale. When he heard of the plan Franz Six, leader of one of the *Einsatzgruppen*, excitedly told a friend in the military that as the front pushed forwards along a line stretching from Baku to Stalingrad to Moscow to Leningrad, 'all life would be extinguished. In this strip of land about thirty million Russians would be decimated by hunger ... all those who took part in this action would be forbidden on pain of death to give a Russian even a piece of bread. The large cities of Leningrad and Moscow would be flattened.'[101] It was with these plans for utter devastation in mind that the German army invaded the Soviet Union on 22 June 1941.

GENOCIDE IN THE EAST

By the end of 1941 the Wehrmacht had taken the Baltic states and had reached Leningrad in the north, in the centre Belorussia had fallen and they were just a few kilometres from Moscow. In the south they occupied the Ukraine and then pushed into the Crimea, reaching the Caucasus by 1942. As soon as the attack started Himmler began making his own plans for the future of Germany's new empire in the east. He commissioned what has become known as the General Plan for the East from the office of the Reich Commissioner for the Strengthening of the German Race. The plans which these academics and bureaucrats produced, and the initial implementation of the scheme in Poland, demonstrate the way in which food and agrarian issues generated militancy within the National Socialist regime and resulted in murderous acts of aggression on the ground.

The architect of the General Plan for the East was the plant geneticist Konrad Meyer. Typically for the National Socialist power structure, he held a multitude of positions, as head of an office for environmental planning, as director of an academic agricultural institute, a position at the Ministry of Food and Agriculture, and he was also head of an SS planning department for settlement in the east. He was responsible for co-ordinating teams of German academics and agrarian experts, who worked on the details of the plan. A mass migration of Germans into the east was expected, one-third being designated to work in agriculture, made efficient by the application of modern technological advances, especially in plant and gene technology.[102] The rest would provide a support network of craftsmen and commercial and public servants. They would live in agricultural towns in German-style houses, surrounded by German plants and trees. Even the herbs and flowers growing in the cottage gardens were to be German, and the rubbish dumps were to be beautified.[103] This attention to seemingly innocent detail distracts from the fact that the General Plan for the East was one of the most atrocious plans hatched by the National Socialists. The idyllic new towns and ideal agricultural communities were to be built in a country which would have been subjected to a programme of terror and violence.

The academics who worked under Meyer were enthused by the task they had been given. On the clean slate of the east they could try out ideas without any of the limitations and intractable problems that faced them within the old Reich. Echoing Hitler's thoughts in his 'Second Book', an SS brochure outlining the planned agricultural reform described the east as a potential paradise, a 'European California' that had been left as a desert by the ruling system of the Slav sub-humans (*Untermenschen*).[104] The use of this term betrays the sinister attitudes underlying the misleadingly idyllic vision. The plans spoke euphemistically of 'resettlement', 'evacuation' and 'Germanization' of the indigenous population. Despite post-war denials, it was common knowledge among the hundreds of bureaucrats, officials, scientists and academics who worked on the plans that this would mean the death by extermination of millions. Indeed, the planners themselves urged the complete destruction of existing towns and villages as this would provide them with a truly blank canvas.[105] The justification for such brutal actions was provided by Heinrich Wiepking-Jürgensmann, a professor at the Institute for Landscape Design at the University of Berlin, and Himmler's special representative for questions concerning landscape formation. In his *Landscape Primer* of 1942 he described the Slavs as a quasi-ecological obstacle to the proper cultivation of the eastern landscape. If the environment was an expression of a people, their abilities and spirit, then, he argued, the murderous cruelty of the Slavs was written in their countryside. His book was filled with photographs of scruffy, poverty-stricken peasant huts to demonstrate his point. The Slavs had to be removed for the good of the land. The SS brochure took up the theme, arguing that the Germans would finally bring order and harmony to the 'impenetrable thickets of the steppes'.[106]

The General Plan for the East makes plain the fact that the Jews, together with the Soviet population in the cities who were the targets of the Hunger Plan, were to be only the first in a long line of peoples whom the Nazis intended to annihilate. It was decided that a few of the indigenous inhabitants in the eastern areas could be integrated into German society and another 14 million would be used as slaves; the rest would be deported.[107] In a secret speech in Prague about the plan Reinhard Heydrich, head of the powerful Reich Security Head Office, and later one of the architects of the Holocaust, outlined how, as soon as the war was won, un-Germanizable elements throughout eastern Europe and Russia would be sent to the Soviet Arctic zone to join the 11 million European Jews who it was anticipated would already be there. Indeed, the idea was that as the Jews died from overwork they would be replaced by waves of deported Slavs.[108] At the end of December 1942 the plan calculated that this would mean deporting 70 million people. It was expected that, like the Jews, the Slavs would also eventually die as a result of their labours. Once the regime acquired a taste for mass annihilation there was some discussion about whether it would be simpler just to execute them. Hitler extended the comparison of Germany's bid for the eastern territories to the western expansion of America by likening the fate of the Slavs to that of America's 'Red Indians'.[109] It is the genocidal intent that sets the German plans for colonial settlement apart from the Italian and Japanese plans for Libya and Manchuria.

Some of the most violent and brutal men in the east made the General Plan for the East their own. Hans Ehlich, a surgeon and racial eugenicist, was head of special security service groups in Poland charged with co-ordinating deportation, immigration and settlement. He trained a band of officials, all of whom believed in the project, who were then posted across German-occupied western and eastern Europe from France to the Crimea. Ehlich was impatient for the plan to be put into action even before the war was over and suggested that deportations should immediately begin of racially undesirable elements in the occupied territories to an unspecified area in the east. In October 1941, the equally impatient Heydrich argued that they should begin the work of categorizing the Czech population into those who could be Germanized and those who would be deported.[110]

The first eastern territory to be cleared of its inhabitants was the annexed part of Poland, known as the Warthegau. The plan was to Germanize the region by replacing the Poles with ethnic Germans (*Volksdeutsche*). In the eighteenth century thousands of Germans had emigrated east, repopulating lands that had formerly been occupied by the Ottoman Empire. German minority communities were dotted throughout the Baltic states, Poland, Czechoslovakia, Romania, Hungary, Croatia and Serbia, and there were a few German communities in Russia itself. No matter how long they had been settled in the east the National Socialists regarded these people as racially German. Under the 1939 Treaty of Non-Aggression they were encouraged to return to Germany and, fearful of oppression under the Soviet regime and hopeful that they would find a better life in the new greater German Reich, many did so.[111] The intention was that these settlers would establish a thriving agricultural community in the Warthegau, which Hitler and Göring planned would produce 'grain, grain and again grain', in fact become 'a grain factory'.[112] Ehlich's ambitious plans to deport 600,000 Jews and 3.4 million Poles from the Warthegau to the eastern half of Poland, known as the General Government, had to be scaled down once it became clear that it would be undesirable to create a sink state of the dispossessed between Germany and the Soviet Union. Nevertheless, throughout 1939–40, 365,000 Poles (one-third Jews) were rounded up, put on trains and deposited in the General Government.[113]

Zygmunt Klukowski, a doctor in charge of the hospital in the town of Szczebrzeszyn in the General Government treated some of these evacuees. A member of the Polish resistance, he kept a diary in which he recorded the criminal actions of the German occupiers. The story the evacuees told him was always the same. The Germans arrived in the village at night and gave the population less than an hour, often only fifteen minutes, to pack up a few necessities before they were rounded up, and loaded on to unheated railway cars for the journey east.[114] As time went by the conditions became increasingly harsh. The first evacuees to arrive in Szczebrzeszyn in December 1939 were allowed to bring 200 zloty with them, by July 1940 all money was confiscated. The group that Klukowski met in July 1940 were small farmers from Gostyn. 'They had been forced to leave their homes where their families had lived for hundreds of years. They were herded like cattle, pushed and beaten on the road from their villages to the railroad station. People who were too slow were shot.'[115] They were kept for one week in Lodz where the young teenagers and able-bodied men and women were selected out and sent to labour camps in Germany. The rest, a motley crowd of women, old men and small children, arrived in Szczebrzeszyn after another week on a train. They lay on the straw in their temporary accommodation, some too weak to sit up, virtually all the children suffering from diarrhoea, all of them 'pale, tired, and dirty, and . . . full of hatred toward Germany and the Germans'.[116] Klukowski wondered what was to become of them. The Germans had ordered that they should be relocated to the surrounding villages but here their welcome was uncertain. 'Our own farmers do not have enough even to feed themselves and many times have refused help.'[117] He was horrified by the way in which people who had been relatively prosperous farmers had become 'beggars in one hour'.[118]

In the autumn of 1940 there were 530,000 ethnic Germans living in miserable conditions in SS-run transit camps.[119] Something had to be done with them. Each of the planners in the four districts of the Warthegau was asked to choose a typical area where the ideas for the General Plan for the East could be tested. Saybusch (Zywiec), on the southern border with Slovakia, was eventually chosen. Between September and December 1940 17,000 Poles were deported from the area. Most ended up in concentration camps in the General Government. Fit young men were sent to the Reich as forced labourers. By the end of the year the Germans had seized 9.2 million hectares of land from Polish farmers in the Warthegau and 180,000 ethnic Germans from Galicia had taken over their farms.[120] However, the violence and dispossession did nothing to improve food production in annexed Poland. The farms lacked machines, fertilizer and labour, and the following year's harvest was jeopardized as those Poles who had not been evicted from their farms often did not plant crops as they feared they would be deported before the harvest.[121] Hitler's and Göring's vision of mountains of grain never became a reality.

In the autumn of 1942 German policy towards the General Government changed. It was no longer seen as an area in which to deposit the dispossessed and was redesignated for Germanization. The district of Zamosc in the eastern corner of the General Government was chosen as the first area where the General Plan for the East would be realized. Centred on Lublin, this was an important area for the SS. Here they had factories and concentration camps, and a magazine for SS troops. The area was fertile and it was hoped that the new German farms would be bountiful.[122] On 27 November the SS began rounding up Poles. They were given only minutes to collect together a few belongings. The town of Szczebrzeszyn, where Zygmunt Klukowski ran his hospital, was not far from Zamosc and on 2 December 1942 he noted in his diary that he could hear horse-drawn wagons rumbling through the town, carrying villagers who were fleeing their homes before the Germans arrived.[123] By the summer of 1943, over 100,000 Poles had been driven out of about 300 villages. Klukowski visited some of the evicted villagers in a nearby camp. They were 'barely moving, looking terrible'. In the camp hospital sick children lay 'like skeletons'.[124] Tens of thousands were sent to Germany as forced labourers, more than 4,000 children were chosen for Germanization in the Reich, where they would have been placed with childless families, 18,000 faced the horrors of the extermination camps at Majdanek and Auschwitz.[125] The operation backfired because the area became one of the most active for partisans. In December 1942 Klukowski reported that fighting units were forming in the forests around Zamosc. 'They are very well armed. Some try to burn down and completely destroy evacuated villages before the new owners, mostly German settlers from eastern Europe, take possession of them.'[126]

The empty farms were taken over by about 9,000 ethnic Germans and 4,000 Germans from the Reich. But Germanization was not the success the agronomists expected. The new farmers had little experience with the climate and soil conditions they found in Poland, and productivity on the seized land declined.[127] Klukowski observed that many of the new *Volksdeutschen* settlers from Bessarabia fled the villages for the safety of the towns, fearful of the vengeful return of escaped evacuees who sometimes returned to burn down their old houses and kill the new occupants.[128] Frieda Hagen, a twenty-nine-year-old agricultural teacher from Thuringia arrived in Zamosc in May 1943 to set up a school to train German women as village advisers. Their job was to refashion the ethnic German women into fine, upstanding examples of the Aryan race. They would go out to the settlers' villages and teach them the German arts of housekeeping, childcare and hygiene. They also ran German-language classes, schools and kindergartens. But Frieda found disappointment and disillusion among the settlers. They were depressed by the primitive conditions. Frieda was shocked to find that some of the clothes they had been given were 'dreadful, often still dirty, bloodstained from the ghetto and originating from Jews'.[129] Most of all they were resentful of their treatment as second-class citizens by the Reich Germans and angry that they were not given better protection from the vengeful partisans.[130]

Within Germany the majority of farmers rejected the idea of resettlement in the east. They did not want to move to a place which had been presented to them as cold and primitive. When anti-German farmers from Luxembourg were forcibly resettled in the General Government, resettlement became strongly associated with punishment. The 4,500 farmers who did apply to move in the first two and a half years of the war fell far short of the 40,000 who were expected according to the documents of the General Plan for the East.[131] Once it became clear there would not be enough German settlers the planners turned to Holland and Denmark for recruits. Hermann Roloff, a former eastern planner, now in charge of space in Holland and Belgium, began preparing figures for how many Dutch could be resettled. Again the figures were ambitious. He came up with a figure of 3 million but only 600 Dutch farmers went east between November 1941 and June 1942. Those who did not fall victim to partisans returned bitterly disappointed.[132] Those willing to move were certainly too few to create the 'blood wall', a swathe of territory settled by the racially pure, which Konrad Meyer envisioned.

Despite these difficulties on the ground, the experts in their offices lost none of their enthusiasm. In 1943 one of the scientists working on the plan wrote excitedly, 'the conquest of the east has brought into our possession those territories which will be of decisive importance for the future nutrition of the German people'.[133] Nor did lack of enthusiasm among German farmers have any impact on the planned number of deportations. However, the chaos which followed in the wake of the operation in Zamosc led the SS to speak of improving their methods, and the genocidal aspect of the plan began to be discussed more openly. In fact, the partisan activity in the area of Zamosc made the SS reconsider their intention of extending the operation into the district of Galicia. In January 1943, 5,000 Polish and Ukrainian families were expelled from the Rawa Ruska area and replaced by 1,500 Volhynian ethnic Germans and 200 Bosnians. But the massive operation which had been planned was never undertaken.[134] While lack of planning and the chaotic German administration of the eastern occupied territories prevented the full implementation of the Hunger Plan, the full realization of the General Plan for the East was thwarted by the turning tide of the war. By 1943 those ethnic Germans who were arriving in Poland were coming from the Volga, Caucasus and Donetz regions. They were no longer arriving in order to re-settle Polish farms but to escape the advancing Red Army.[135]

*

The extent of the agrarian radicalism of the Nazis is rarely fully appreciated because much of what they were planning remained on paper. There should be no doubt, however, that if the Germans had succeeded in defeating the Soviet Union they would have conducted a far more extensive and terrible genocide than that which they were able to carry out under the limitations of occupation while they were still fighting the war.[136] The full significance of the Nazi plans was certainly not realized by the lawyers at the Nuremberg trials. This is unsurprising given that it has taken many decades in the archives for historians to unravel the Nazi agrarian plans and their horrific implications.

Walther Darré was tried and found guilty of 'plunder, spoliation, enserfment and the expropriation' of land from Polish and Jewish farmers, as well as of depriving Jews of basic foods through ration cuts. He was imprisoned for five years but released three years before his death in September 1953.[137] Herbert Backe hung himself in his cell in April 1947, afraid that he might be sent to the Soviet Union for trial.[138] But many of the bureaucrats and officials involved in the projected programme of agrarian violence were overlooked. Given what we now know of the extent of Hans Ehlich's involvement in the genocidal aspect of the plan, his sentence of one year and nine months was uncomfortably lenient. He then moved to Brunswick, where he worked as a physician. He died in 1991.[139] Konrad Meyer's position in the SS Race and Settlement Office meant that he was captured and tried. However, by referring to one of the least incendiary early versions of the General Plan, and arguing that this was simply an academic study, not a plan which he expected to be implemented, Meyer successfully diverted the attention of the American prosecutors. He was set free in 1948, having already served his sentence of two years and ten months while awaiting trial.[140] Heinrich Wiepking-Jürgensmann, Himmler's special representative for questions concerning landscape formation, having served as a defence witness for Meyer, suffered no ill effects from his association with the murderous plan and became professor for horticulture and land culture at Backe's old university, the Technische Hochschule in Hanover. He was joined by Meyer in 1956, who took up a chair in land cultivation and land planning. Chillingly, Meyer turned his attention to the problem of Third World food supply and global over-population. In a 1953 publication he revealed that his thinking had changed little since his days in the Race and Settlement Office by suggesting that the strain on the world food balance could be relieved by redistributing people into what he sinisterly termed catchment areas. Wiepking-Jürgensmann was acclaimed as a conservationist and in 1952 the culture minister for Lower Saxony asked him to design a memorial for Bergen-Belsen.[141]

3

Japan's Quest for Empire

Our national state of affairs has reached an impasse. The critical problems of population and foodstuffs seem all without solution. The only avenue ... is boldly to open up Manchuria and Mongolia.

(Kwantung army officer in 1931)[1]

The issue of the food supply was to prove every bit as incendiary in 1930s Japan as it was in National Socialist Germany. Military and right-wing groups used the need to secure the urban food supply and crisis in the Japanese countryside to justify ever more radical actions, beginning with the seizure of Manchuria in 1931 and culminating in the war against Nationalist China in 1937. Finally, the Japanese determination to hold China in the face of American disapproval set them upon a collision course with the United States.

Japan first developed imperial ambitions during the period of the Meiji Restoration (1868–1912) when a group of aristocratic modernizers removed the warrior aristocracy from power and 'restored' the rule of the Emperor. The Japanese set their sights on the resources of mainland China. Since defeat in the Opium Wars of 1839–42 China had been forced to allow foreigners (including Americans, French, Germans, British and the Japanese) special political and trading concessions in various inland cities and what were known as the treaty ports. After war with China in 1894–95 and Russia in 1904–05 Japan acquired first the island of Formosa (now Taiwan), then Korea and, under the conditions of extraterritoriality, whereby the trading concession areas were outside the jurisdiction of the Chinese government,

Japan stationed a substantial number of troops in China, and established various commercial interests, the most important of which was the leasehold of a stretch of railway in southern Manchuria.[2] In 1911 the Qing dynasty collapsed and central government in China disintegrated to be replaced by regional warlords. During the First World War, Japan used the fact that the west was distracted to take advantage of the political instability and obtained 'exclusive political and trading rights in large parts of China'.[3]

The German defeat in 1918 came as a shock to a number of Japanese army officers who realized that Germany had lost because it was dependent on outside sources for the resources required to wage total war. This set them thinking about the vulnerability of Japan, which lacked primary resources and needed to import virtually all industrial raw materials. Crucially, Japan was dependent on the United States for one-third of its imports, particularly scrap metal and oil. But Britain, which, like Japan, was an island nation with limited natural resources, had drawn on the resources of its empire in order to win the First World War. It seemed clear to this group of 'total war officers' that Japan needed a similar maritime empire which would allow it to establish itself as a powerful world player, independent of the west and the US in particular.[4]

However, after 1919 the United States tried to rein in Japanese expansionism. In 1921–22 the American government convened the Washington Conference in an effort to restrain Japanese naval expansion. At the Conference they also persuaded the Japanese government to continue to uphold the open-door policy in China, which allowed the western powers equal access to the Chinese treaty ports. In return, America recognized Japan's special interest in Manchuria. But there was growing dissatisfaction among the Japanese military and political elite with the international status quo. The military were particularly bitter about the limitations the Conference placed on Japan's ability to arm.[5] The American refusal to integrate a racial equality clause into the charter of the League of Nations caused further disquiet, which was intensified by hostile American measures against Japanese immigration in 1924.[6] Meanwhile in 1928 the Chinese Nationalists under Chiang Kaishek had established a government at Nanjing which claimed to rule all of China. While the Nationalists were friendly towards the Americans, who provided them with funding, they became increasingly hostile towards the Japanese.[7] In addition, a growing awareness of the problem of rural poverty and anxieties about the country's ability to produce sufficient food to supply the growing industrial workforce in the towns contributed to a growing sense of national crisis.

A RADICAL ANSWER TO RURAL CRISIS

Until 1918 agriculture supported Japan's industrial and economic growth. Agricultural exports generated the foreign exchange needed to finance the import of raw materials. Farmers also supported economic development by paying a heavy cash tax on their goods.[8] But the Japanese countryside was plagued by a number of persistent problems which began seriously to hamper agricultural productivity in the 1920s. The concentration of property rights in the hands of a few rich landlords resulted in vast inequalities in wealth. Tenant farmers lacked the resources and motivation to modernize and for some their rent was so unreasonably high that it amounted to more than half their crop. For a sizeable minority, life in the countryside was marked by crippling poverty. Even the standard of living of middling farmers was well below that of the urban population and began to fall ever further behind.[9]

Modernization meant that Japanese eating habits were changing. Since the Meiji Restoration the government had been encouraging the consumption of milk and meat as a way of transforming Japanese bodies so that they could compete with the, supposedly superior, western physique. As part of the campaign, the public were told that the Emperor enjoyed eating beef.[10] But it was not until the inter-war years that meat consumption began to rise, virtually doubling between 1919 and 1937. The annual consumption of 2 kilograms of beef or pork per person was still tiny in comparison with the 50 kilograms eaten by Europeans. But, along with a rise in the consumption of fish, it represented a marked increase in the amount of animal protein in the Japanese diet.[11] Most importantly, urban Japanese began to eat more rice. By 1914 all Japanese were eating about a quarter more rice than they had in the 1890s. Then, from 1920, a marked gap began to open up between rural and urban diets. By 1929 city dwellers were eating at least 25 per cent more rice than those living in the countryside.[12]

The rising demand for rice was augmented by a 30 per cent increase in the population during the inter-war period and Japan looked to its colonies to make up the food deficit.[13] When Formosa became a Japanese colony in 1895 Japanese companies moved in and set up sugar planta-tions, farming organizations disseminated better farming techniques, improved irrigation and introduced Japanese rice varieties. Exports from Formosa to Japan of rice, sugar, tea, tobacco, pigs and poultry increased sixfold between 1897 and 1905.[14] Korea also exported rice to Japan. In 1918 wartime inflation meant that the price of rice virtually doubled. When rice riots broke out across the country these were interpreted as a sign that Japan's run-down agricultural sector simply could not provide enough food for the growing urban population.[15] A 'Rice Production Development Plan' was implemented to turn the colonies into 'reserve rice baskets'.[16] Rice imports from the colonies which had equalled 5 per cent of the Japanese domestic rice crop in 1915, equalled 20 per cent by 1935.[17] The problem of urban hunger had now been successfully exported to the peasants of Korea. Indeed, Japanese food officials and agricultural economists referred to the rice that Korea sent to Japan as 'starvation exports'. In Korea rice was transformed into a cash crop and the farmers were forced to sell such a large share of their crop that each year 'spring hunger' held them in its grip as the food from the previous harvest ran out before the next harvest came in. They survived by gathering wild grasses for food.[18] Fifty years later Ahn Juretsu, who grew up in Korea in the 1920s and 1930s, was still indignant. 'Because we were farmers under Japanese government control, the conditions of our lives were so poor, you can't imagine it. Just like beggars today.'[19]

If, to the satisfaction of its industrialists, Japan now had plenty of food with which to pacify its urban population, these measures only served to deepen the crisis in the countryside. Cheap colonial rice undercut the price of Japanese rice and further depressed domestic agricultural wages. In 1926, landlords, hit by a fall in the price of rice, began to demand that the imports be stopped.[20] The flood of Formosan and Korean rice was followed by the Depression, which pushed down world food prices. By 1931 the value of a bushel of rice, which cost between 20 and 23 yen to produce, had fallen from its 1925 price of 41 yen to 18 yen.[21] In addition, the American demand for silk fell dramatically, which impacted adversely on a large number of Japanese farmers for whom sericulture was a vital secondary source of income. Most farmers struggled through the Depression by mixing more barley with their rice, giving up small luxuries such as shop-bought soap and sugar, and cutting back on farm repairs.[22] But farm debt increased significantly. Even before the Depression, peasants were spending a worryingly high percentage of their income on food, ranging from 40 to 57 per cent.[23] Once the Depression hit, an increasing number of farming families had to buy in food. In the village of Sekishiba, in the north-eastern prefecture of Fukushima, over half the households ran out of food supplies from their own crop in 1932–33. The price they paid for food on the open market was far higher than the price they had received when they sold their crop immediately after the harvest. The only way they could find the money was to borrow, usually from private moneylenders and at devastating rates of interest from 12 to 20 per cent. In 1932 the government came up with the worrying conclusion that the farming debt now amounted to 4.7 billion yen, more than double the value of farm production, or a third of the GNP.[24]

That farming communities were living on the edge was indicated by the increasing number of villagers who could no longer pay their taxes. Numerous villages fell into arrears with payment of their schoolteachers' salaries. Farmers avoided attending funerals, or shamefacedly stuffed IOU notes into the hands of the bereaved, promising to make the customary payment 'when I sell some cocoons, or when the economy gets better'.[25] A government survey in July 1932 found that 200,000 children were turning up to school with nothing to eat for lunch.[26] One disgruntled farmer commented on his dinner of rice mixed with wheat, chopped yam leaves, and *daikon* (white radish), 'wealthy villagers and city people throw these things away, or else feed them to oxen or pigs'.[27]

In the northern provinces famine took hold. Cold, wet weather in 1934 in the north-eastern area of Tohoku resulted in crop failure. The farmers in the fields threw down their tools in despair as they realized that only a few bundles of grain could be collected from each paddy.[28] A Hokkaido farm girl lamented, 'It is really tragic that we farmers who grow rice are unable to eat it.' Even the supplies of inferior grains such as millet dried up. Her family survived by 'eating dried potatoes and herring dregs, which are used for fertiliser'. She and her sister dug up bracken roots, others scraped the soft edible parts from tree bark.[29] Infant mortality rates soared, around half a million died, and in order to relieve their families of the burden of feeding them, more than 11,000 girls were sold into prostitution, known as *musume jigoku*, 'hell for young women'.[30]

By the early 1930s a sense of crisis pervaded Japan. The Depression and industrial unemployment, combined with the growing magnitude of the rural problem, fed a general sense of 'stalemate, confusion and instability'.[31] Among right-wing groups the Depression confirmed the need for greater independence from western capitalism. Having learned the lesson of Germany's weakness during the First World War, the Army Minister Major-General Ugaki Kazunari, leader of the 'total war officers' within the armed forces, set up the Cabinet Resources Bureau. In 1931 it concluded that Japan's economy was woefully inadequate in terms of producing the materials for modern warfare.[32] At the same time Nationalist China began to protest at the level of Japanese influence in mainland China by boycotting Japanese goods. Two young officers in the Kwantung army (the Japanese army in China) took matters into their own hands in Manchuria. On the night of 18 September 1931 they planted a bomb on the Japanese-owned stretch of railway, which they then claimed was the work of bandits sponsored by the Chinese regional government. That night Japanese troops began their occupation of Manchuria, which resulted in the creation in 1932 of the puppet state of Manchukuo.[33] International disapproval led to Japan's withdrawal from the League of Nations in 1933. The army represented Manchuria as a treasure house of resources – gold, coal, livestock, soya beans, cotton. With Manchuria as part of Japan, they could withstand political isolation and the economic threat and military might of other powerful nations.[34] A rather romantic 1920s notion of a Japanese empire made up of one national people, all faithful to the Japanese way of life, gave way to a more aggressive vision of an economic bloc, self-sufficient and independent from the increasingly hostile western powers, which was later summed up by the rather mystical idea of a pan-Asian brotherhood or a 'New Order' in the 'Greater East Asian Co-Prosperity Sphere'.[35]

Those in Japan who favoured the development of democracy, the growth of independent political parties, and the liberal course which would place Japan on the world stage through peaceful trade and economic exchange, were silenced. A series of right-wing terrorist attacks ensured that those who were outspokenly in favour of internationalism lived in a certain degree of fear. Prime Minister Hamaguchi Osachi was assassinated in November 1930 after he signed a naval disarmament treaty in London. Between then and 1936 a series of advocates of a more liberal approach to Japan's problems were murdered.[36]

On 15 May 1932 Prime Minister Inukai Tsuyoshi was assassinated by a group of young army and navy officers in an attempted coup. At their trial the assassins invoked the agrarian crisis to justify their actions. One of the soldiers stated that, while farmers made model soldiers, 'it is extremely dangerous that . . . [they] should be worried about their starving families when they are at the front exposing themselves to death'. He went on to accuse big businessmen of making fat profits while 'the young children of the impoverished farmers . . . attend school without breakfast, and their families subsist on rotten potatoes'.[37] The men were treated with conspicuous leniency, and were allowed to use their trial to issue lengthy political statements, which the newspapers reported in full. The trials brought to public attention a number of issues which made up the pattern of crisis but which were not normally presented as part of a whole: 'the rural crisis, political and ideological corruption, fears of military weakness, Japan's international standing, and Manchuria'.[38] Discussion of them as interlinked problems strengthened the right-wing position advocated by the military. Militaristic nationalism attacked absentee landlords, nouveaux riches businessmen, power-seeking politicians and individualistic youth as representatives of the corrupting westernization of Japanese society. The people were urged to return to a more Japanese austerity, greater obedience to the state and to revive the Japanese military and moral spirit.[39]

While the extremists did not take over the government, more moderate exponents of their views did gain power. In 1932 parliamentary government was replaced by a cabinet of 'national unity' made up of military leaders and bureaucrats. The militaristic nature of Japanese government was reinforced by the fact that both the army and navy ministers in the cabinet were serving officers, and thus their allegiance was to the military rather than the government. In addition, they exercised rights of veto over the membership of the cabinet and could bring down any government which threatened to challenge the power of the military. Moreover, foreign policy was formed not within the cabinet but during Liaison Conferences where the prime minister, foreign, war, army and navy ministers met with the military chiefs of staff, whose power derived from the fact that they were directly answerable to the Emperor. The decision-making process at these conferences followed a distinctively Japanese pattern of lengthy discussion and debate, all carried on using an oblique language which meant that decisions appeared to arise out of the group rather than to emanate from a particular person. The decision was then ratified by a conference with the Emperor when it took on the appearance not only of consensus but of being sacrosanct.[40]

Each terrorist attack further intimidated the traditional ruling class, and after each of the five attempted coups the government which re-formed was progressively more isolationist. In June 1936 Prince Konoe Fumimaro became prime minister and appointed Hirota Koki as his foreign minister. Profoundly opposed to free trade and industrialization, and aggressive advocates of imperialism, they took Japan down an isolationist path which made war with the west ever more likely.[41] An ideological consensus began to emerge among the ruling elite which acknowledged that the only way to fulfil Japan's destiny would be to slip free of western domination and gain power and influence over east Asia. While the Emperor provided spiritual focus, military expansion was presented as the only way forward.[42]

Throughout the 1930s the military concentrated on building up a support base within rural society, conducting surveys of village health and addressing rural unemployment with public works schemes. Their concerns were less humanitarian than practical. Large numbers of applicants to the army were failing their physical examinations in the 1930s, and 500 of the soldiers dispatched to China to deal with the 'Manchurian Incident' had been pronounced unfit to fight within weeks of their arrival.[43] The army wanted to ensure a good supply of healthy recruits and to increase rural productivity in preparation for a possible war. But, when it came to the crunch, the military were adamantly opposed to sacrificing their lion's share of the budget to rural revitalization programmes. In fact, it was the villages which paid for most of the enormous military budget which the army secured in 1933.[44] Militarist and nationalist groups exploited the agrarian crisis to press for policies which pushed Japan towards war.[45] But it is unclear how much actual rural support for these groups and their policies there was. Real support was, however, relatively unimportant in securing their political position, given that Japanese politics consisted mainly of manoeuvres between small elite groups.

The countryside fed the growing isolationism and aggressive nationalism of 1930s Japan in a more diffuse way. In the 1930s a repressive 'collectivist ethic' dominated social relations and political thinking. Those who advocated democracy laid themselves open to charges of individualistic selfishness. Internationalism and the pursuit of open economic relations with the rest of the world could be dismissed as 'traitorous self-seeking, disloyalty to the national polity'.[46] Western liberalism was un-Japanese and therefore unworthy. This pattern of thought was particularly well entrenched in the villages where 'families ... bred into the personalities of their children a deference to all authoritarian demands to conform to the needs of the community as a whole'.[47] Three-quarters of all politically active adults came from this conformist rural background.

Conformism was strengthened by the Rural Revitalization campaign, the government's remedy for agriculture. There was no question of the campaign embarking on the painful process of restructuring landownership and challenge the position of landlords. Instead, farmers were urged to work harder and achieve more with less. Peasants were provided with training and shown more efficient planning and farming techniques. Women were urged to use their time more effectively and to engage in book-keeping, cottage industries and economizing kitchen improvements. Every aspect of daily life was implicated not only in the recovery of the village, but according to the rhetoric, in the economic health of the nation as a whole. These messages were transmitted through a variety of agricultural associations, co-operatives, youth leagues and women's organizations. Japan in the 1930s was supremely successful at making voluntary membership of an organization virtually compulsory. 'No one was left out. Not only could everyone be involved in reconstructing the village, but bureaucrats, activists, and, increasingly, rural Japanese themselves, believed that they should be.'[48] In this way the countryside was incorporated into a general process of spreading ultranationalism from above. Political parties, unions and religious organizations were either coerced into stating their support for the state or silenced by the police. Conformity was encouraged through education and 'voluntary' associations of which virtually everyone was a member. The citizen was redefined as a member of a family which owed its allegiance to the Emperor. Although there were certainly plenty of Japanese who did not share this view of themselves and the nation, to express dissent from this view became increasingly difficult and dangerous.[49]

By 1937 the resurgence of the industrial economy and a corresponding rise in the price of rice and silk had brought the countryside out of the depths of depression. Now the understanding of the causes of the crisis facing the nation shifted. Withdrawal from the League of Nations over Japan's annexation of Manchuria, the naval limitations conference of 1936 and the imposition of British and American protectionist trading tariffs in south-east Asia focused attention on Japan's need to find new markets and develop new territory.[50] The Japanese army were made wary by an alliance between Chinese Nationalists and communists against the Japanese in Manchuria. When a skirmish between Japanese and Chinese troops broke out in the small town of Wanping in July 1937 the Kwantung army took Japan into war with China. Thus, by the time Japan entered the wider international conflict in 1941 it had already been at war with China for four years.

In the Japanese countryside the focus shifted from revitalization to mobilization. The message did not change. The farmers were still urged to work harder and produce more with less. But the peasants were now striving for a stable home front rather than future prosperity. The agricultural associations and co-operatives of the Rural Revitalization campaign facilitated, and even made almost imperceptible, the deeper intrusion of the state into the lives of farmers. These organizations no longer made suggestions – they now determined which crops were grown, allocated fertilizer and collected the harvest for state distribution. The option to ignore or evade social control became less and less possible.[51]

ONE MILLION HOUSEHOLDS IN MANCHURIA

In the same year that Japan went to war in China, the Ministry of Agriculture adopted an agrarian emigration scheme under the characteristically long-winded title, 'Plan for the Settlement of One Million Households over Twenty Years'. An increase in landlord–tenant disputes over unfair eviction had given contemporary observers the impression that the agrarian problem was not so much that the countryside could not produce enough food, but that there were too many farmers competing for too little land. Finally the government acknowledged that it was not that the farmers needed to work harder but that a viable farm was the key to agricultural success. A survey by the Ministry of Agriculture worked out that the ideal farm size was a relatively small 1.6 *cho* (4 acres). According to this calculation, in order to ensure that every farm in Japan was the optimum size, 31 per cent of the farming population would have to leave the land.[52] Just as in Germany, the idea developed that the Japanese needed their own *Lebensraum*. This was to be in the puppet state of Manchukuo, which, like eastern Europe for Germany, was styled as Japan's equivalent to the American west. Agrarian advocates of the plan argued that, 'like the colonial days in American history, a new State is in the making, the vast virgin plains, unhampered by tradition, ready to welcome armies of fresh immigrants'.[53] While German agronomists claimed that the indigenous Slavs had no right to eastern land as they did not farm it properly, the Japanese simply ignored the presence of Chinese and Korean farmers and projected an image of Manchuria as an empty land. One woman who went to Manchuria in 1931 imagined that it was 'a limitless snowy plain containing only huts'.[54]

The suggestion that the social problem of poor tenant farmers could be solved by exporting them to the colonies had been on the political agenda since 1900. In 1904 the Japanese cabinet pronounced that 'If large numbers of emigrants from our country . . . can penetrate the [Korean] interior . . . we will acquire at a single stroke an emigration colony for our excess population and sufficient supplies of foodstuffs.'[55] In 1908 the Oriental Development Company was created with the purpose of subsidizing 10,000 Japanese annually to settle in Korea. The plan was not a success. Few farmers signed up for the project and those that did move to Korea often suffered from malnutrition to the point that they were too physically debilitated to work.[56] The only settlers who succeeded did so because they acted as landlords and moneylenders, renting out their land to Korean tenants. Korea was a profitable place for entrepreneurs, clerks, shopkeepers and others providing a service to the urban Japanese population but the peninsula was never going to be covered in prosperous Japanese smallholdings.[57] Ideas for Japanese settlement in Formosa were equally unrealistic. Japanese sugar companies had little interest in diverting land to settlers when they were making such a good profit using Formosan labourers. Both Korea and Formosa were far more successful as suppliers of food and as markets for Japanese goods.[58]

These failed attempts to create Japanese farming communities in the colonies did nothing to dampen the fervour for the plan to settle Manchuria in certain sections of Japanese political, military and academic circles. When campaigners managed to persuade the ministry to accept the scheme it was planned to move 1 million farmers, or one-fifth of the 1936 farming population, to China. Those who were targeted to leave were the very poor tenant farmers. If the poor left the villages and their land was redistributed, all Japanese farmers could be transformed into middle-class farmers and social inequalities in the rural areas could be ironed out without affecting the wealthy landlords. Thus, Japanese agriculture would be rehabilitated without disturbing the social order.[59]

Just as the German General Plan for the East envisaged the creation of a modern but idyllic version of German society, Japan's plan for Manchuria imagined an idealized agrarian version of Japanese society. The pioneers would live in a network of communities where each peasant would be allocated an equal holding with the same number of livestock. The entire village would work together as a co-operative using the most up-to-date farming techniques. By the end of the twenty years it would take to implement the scheme, 10 per cent of the population of Manchuria would be Japanese. Thus, the colony would have been assimilated into the Japanese polity. At the same time the farmers would double as 'mainland warriors of the plough', providing 'a shield for the nation' in the face of a possible attack by the Soviets.[60]

The Japanese plan did not go so far as the German one, in that it did not envisage wholesale extermination of the indigenous population. But the reality that lay behind the idyll was equally brutal and the impact on the Chinese farmers was comparable. The usual Japanese method of obtaining land for the settlers was simply to misclassify it as uncultivated, ignoring the Chinese and Korean peasants' farms. The farmers were evicted or coerced into 'selling' their land for artificially low prices. In 1941 many of them were still waiting for their payments.[61] Tsukui

Shin'ya, an official who organized forcible land purchases in 1938, later recognized that he had participated in a crime: 'We trampled underfoot the wishes of farmers who held fast to the land and, choking off their entreaties full of lamentations and kneeling, forced them to sell it. When we thrust on them a dirt-cheap selling price, even if the colonization group resettled the terrain, I was saddened that we would be leaving them to a future of calamity, and I felt that we had committed a crime by our actions.'[62] The Chinese twisted the name of the colonial office (*kaituoju*) and renamed it the 'office of murders' (*kaidaoju*).[63]

Reality did not, of course, live up to the ideal. Those Japanese settlers who were persuaded by their fellow villagers in Japan to make the journey to China were not pursuing some planner's dream of an ideal collective society. The idea that the Japanese settlements should function in self-sufficient isolation from Chinese society would have condemned the settlers to wearing home-made woollen clothes, and eating a basic diet of rice mixed with millet, local game and vegetables.[64] Instead, they chose to hire Chinese labour to farm the large plots and they grew rice and soya beans as cash crops so that they could pay farmhands and buy in household goods. For the majority of settlers life in Manchuria was unhappy and alienated. The army's plan that the Japanese settlements should be located in the strategically vulnerable north and east meant that farming was hard and life was brutal. The Japanese villages were surrounded by hostile Chinese and frequently subject to attack by 'bandits'.[65]

If the scheme was not an unqualified success in Manchuria, it did little to solve rural problems on the mainland. Settlers tended to come, not from the areas where overpopulation was a problem, but rather from those silk-producing areas which had been worst hit by the Depression.[66] By the time the emigration movement was in full swing, industrial expansion was absorbing labour from the farms and, in conjunction with increased conscription due to the war in China, villages were suffering from the new problem of a lack of labour. Urban youths, members of the Patriotic Farm Labour Brigades, had to be brought in to help with planting and harvesting. Increasingly, the pioneer settlers were recruited not from the farms but from youth brigades such as the Volunteer Army of Young Colonists.[67] Brides were found for them from among a variety of training institutes which taught young women how to be good wives. Those who hoped to escape from the exigencies of wartime Japan were fed the rhetoric that they would be a comfort and help to their pioneer husbands, while nurturing the future generation of Japanese Manchurians. The reality of life in an isolated village, detested by the indigenous inhabitants, was harsh.[68]

The eventual fate of the Japanese settlers was tragic. The army made no plans to evacuate them as the Soviet army advanced across Manchuria in August 1945. Many of the men formed a scarecrow contingent of soldiers while the women and children fled, 'hiding in the mountains during the day, running for their lives at night, carrying small children on their backs, feeding on whatever they could pick in the field, or aided by those Manchurians who remained humane.'[69] Kuramoto Kazuko, whose family fled from Manchuria to the house of an aunt in Dairen, recalled that winter of 1945 as 'a winter of death. It claimed hundreds of lives among the homeless Japanese refugees. They died of cold, hunger, and lack of sanitation ... Many hung themselves in the parks ... The hills behind the evergreen forest in the Central Park ... were now covered by piles of abandoned bodies. Wild dogs fed on them and multiplied fast.'[70] Of the 220,000 farmer settlers, around 80,000 died. About 11,000 of them met a violent end at the hands of the avenging Chinese, some committed suicide, and about 67,000 starved to death. The remaining 140,000 traumatized survivors were eventually repatriated to Japan.[71]

FROM NANJING TO PEARL HARBOR

While the settlement of Japanese farmers in Manchuria was under way, the conflict, which the Japanese called the 'China Incident' and the Chinese the 'War of Resistance against Japan', degenerated into a war of attrition. Japan's dogged determination to win the war in China placed it in opposition to the western powers of America, Britain and the Netherlands, whose interests were bound up with the fate of the Nationalists, whom they supported.[72] In response to Japan's war on China the Americans had given financial aid to the Nationalist government, hoping that it would be able to at least weaken, if not defeat, the Japanese. The Japanese army's orgy of rape and massacre in Nanjing in the winter of 1937–38 had severely damaged Japanese relations with the United States. However, the war in China also perversely made Japan even more dependent upon trade with the United States. By 1938 the Japanese were running out of weapons and, more importantly, their stocks of fuel were virtually exhausted. If the United States were not placated by a peace deal in China they might well place an embargo on the scrap metal and oil imports that Japan so badly needed to maintain the war effort.[73] However, 62,000 Japanese soldiers had already lost their lives in China and the Japanese military command felt that to withdraw would betray their sacrifice.[74]

Then, as Germany stormed across western Europe in the spring and summer of 1940, the weakness of the European colonial powers encouraged the Japanese chiefs of staff to think that they could take over the entire south-east Asian treasure house of resources.[75] Occupation of the French, British and Dutch colonies in south-east Asia would enable Japan to achieve decisive victory in the Chinese war by cutting off supplies of Indo-Chinese rice to Nationalist China.[76] They also set their sights on the oil supplies in the Dutch East Indies. Expansion into south-east Asia was a gamble but the potential rewards made it seem worth the risk. The Japanese military command felt that this was their only chance to end western dominance and establish their own claim as a great power in east Asia. In September 1940 Japan signed the Tripartite Pact, and became an official ally of Germany and Italy. Nevertheless, the military still hoped to secure Indo-China and the Dutch East Indies without drawing the United States into the conflict. However, the army began to follow a circular course of reasoning, which argued that they must prepare for war with America. This meant that they must take over the oil resources in the Dutch East Indies. But if they invaded the Dutch East Indies, this would inevitably lead to war with America. The navy was under no illusions that it could win a protracted war of attrition with the United States. Victory would have to be achieved quickly and in a decisive battle. But having justified their funding with arguments that they were preparing for war with the US they were not in a position to admit this to the army.[77]

Provoked by Japan's continued aggression in China in June 1940 the Americans had placed an embargo on exports of scrap metal. A year later, prompted by the German attack on the Soviet Union, the Japanese occupied French Indo-China and the United States cut off their oil supplies. The Japanese political and military leadership overestimated the abilities of their German ally and placed their faith in Germany managing to neutralize both Britain and the Soviet Union. The only way to avoid war with the United States was to capitulate in China, but the military were inexorable in their refusal to back down. The Japanese government had manoeuvred itself into a position where it felt that war with the United States was the only possible course of action. Japan's military commanders judged correctly that the United States possessed immense resources and could defeat Japan in a long war of attrition. However, unlike the National Socialists who hoped to defeat their enemies, Japan hoped to bring America to the negotiating table. They calculated that the Americans would be unwilling to sacrifice the lives of thousands of young men in the Pacific. When they authorized the attack on Pearl Harbor on 7 December 1941 Japan's leaders knew they were entering a war they could not really hope to win. Unfortunately, they woefully overestimated the willingness of the United States to enter peace negotiations once a war had begun.[78] And it was this utterly unrealistic determination to force America into a negotiated peace which provided the rationale for the refusal of the military leadership to surrender, even in the summer of 1945 when Japan's war effort lay in ruins.

The National Socialist solution to the problems associated with the global market in food, combined with a backward farming community in need of reform, pushed Germany into war in Europe. Rather than engaging with capitalist world markets, the National Socialists chose the alternative path of autarky and an aggressive search for land. Across the globe, Japan was placed in a similarly difficult position with regard to the international economic system. A weak and failing agricultural sector which was tipped into crisis by the Depression added to Japanese woes. In a parallel process, the agrarian problem propelled Japan's politicians into ever more conservative solutions, resulting in the decision to seek the same solution: autarky and expansion. Both Germany and Japan looked to their military to appropriate enough land not only to reverse the decline of agriculture but to recreate a 'flourishing farm economy [which] could hold its own against the pressures of industry and commerce'. Empire was seen by both regimes as a means of making 'peace with modernity'.[79] Unfortunately, it also guaranteed that they would be unable to make peace with their neighbours.

PART II

The Battle for Food

When Hitler took the world to war by invading Poland on 1 September 1939, many governments were caught off guard by the insatiable wartime appetite for food. The expansion of military forces created armies of voraciously hungry men. The corresponding growth of war industries created a second pool of men and women whose arduous physical labour meant that they too needed to eat an extra 500–1,000 calories a day. Employment and rising wages meant that even ordinary civilian demand for food (especially for meat and milk products) rose far more than most governments had expected. With the virtual disappearance of consumer goods, there was, after all, virtually nothing else on which people could spend their money.

The Allied governments had to switch quickly from the Depression mentality of trying to persuade farmers to grow less in order to reduce food surpluses, to encouraging farmers to cultivate every available inch of their land and to grow crops with the highest ratio of nutritional return for the effort expended. The need to increase agricultural yields was all the more urgent given that for many countries food imports disappeared, or were drastically reduced, because the war had thrown the global food trade into disarray. In August 1940 continental Europe was cut off from the world food market by the British blockade of Germany and all of occupied Europe. In June 1941 the German invasion effectively removed the Soviet Union from the market. By the end of 1942 Japan had imposed a blockade on Nationalist China and taken control of south-east Asia and large parts of the western Pacific. German U-boats patrolled the oceans, posing a threat to Allied shipping and this, combined with a shortage of ships, meant that every cubic inch of shipping space was hotly contested. Civilian food supplies had to compete for space on ships with coal and fuel, steel, phosphates for explosives, military supplies and troops.

In peacetime the British Isles sat at the centre of a complex web spun by its 3,000-strong merchant shipping fleet. Britain itself relied on ten to fifteen ships arriving in its ports each day, bringing in 68 million tons of imports a year, 22 million tons of which were food.[1] An intensive network of 'cross-trade' carried tea from India to Australia, beef cattle from Madagascar to sugar-producing Mauritius, cocoa beans from West Africa to America. Britain was now denied valuable imports of Danish and Dutch bacon, cheese and butter. Onions, which before the war were imported from Spain, France and the Channel Islands, disappeared from British greengrocers. Japanese successes in China, south-east Asia and the Pacific meant that the Allies lost access to a variety of essential raw materials such as Malayan rubber and tin and Dutch East Indian oil. One sign of the shortages was the disappearance of tinfoil wrappings on candy bars in America.[2] The Americans were denied Sumatran palm oil to manufacture margarine, Filipino coconut flesh and Chinese soya bean and peanut meal, which they used as fodder for livestock. The loss of Burma to the Japanese in May 1942 opened a gaping hole in the British empire's food network. Burmese rice was a staple food in India and Ceylon, the Gambia, Kenya, South Africa and Zanzibar, and in far-flung islands such as Mauritius and Fiji.

While the Allies were cut off from supplies of some foods, they faced the additional problem that vast quantities of other types of food were stranded in the wrong place. In Britain oranges and lemons became treasured objects. Doreen Laven recalled that her neighbour kept a lemon on her dresser. 'I was allowed to hold it. It was very hard and almost black.' Oranges were available 'once or perhaps twice a year', and the anxiety was acute when one Saturday Doreen's family came across a queue for oranges in the High Street, Bishops Stortford, and their father had to dash home for their ration books while the rest of the family waited anxiously in the queue, worried that the grocers would have sold out before he returned.[3] Cyprus, meanwhile, was afflicted with a glut of oranges. Britain could not afford to waste shipping space importing bulky fruits, and every effort was made to persuade the Cypriots to eat more oranges until they were undoubtedly sick of the sight of them. In Palestine the citrus fruit industry channelled its oranges into marmalade production. The marmalade was then fed to Allied troops in North Africa, who would have much preferred strawberry jam.[4] Western Australia and Tasmania suffered from a glut of apples and pears and much of the crop had to be left to rot on the trees. While the United States tried to boost the production of maize, the Argentinians burnt their excess maize crop as fuel.[5]

Latin American coffee farmers, cut off from continental Europe, lost 40 per cent of their market. While Europeans had to make do with an 'unholy concoction' made from ground chicory mixed with roasted acorns or barley, the coffee growers tried to off-load their surplus stock in the United States.[6] Anxious to keep Latin America out of the sphere of Axis influence, America eventually agreed to buy Latin American coffee at guaranteed prices. The arrangement turned out to be overly generous, and American civilians were forced to subsidize Latin American coffee farmers by paying artificially high prices for coffee throughout the war.[7] The cocoa farmers of the West African Gold Coast were just harvesting their beans when war was declared. Given the luxury nature of chocolate, it was clear that shipping space for their beans would not be a priority. Caribbean banana farmers and West Indian and Mauritian sugar planters faced the same problem.

The Allies responded to the disruption of the international food trade by fighting the U-boats in the Atlantic and trying to protect their merchant shipping. But, most vitally, the free market was abandoned in order to achieve maximum efficiency in reorganizing trade. The Arcadia conference between Churchill and Roosevelt in Washington in December 1941 gave rise to a number of boards charged with co-ordinating Allied efforts and pooling their resources as effectively as possible. The Combined Food Board co-ordinated the production and distribution of food throughout the Allied world. Responsible for food for more than half of the world's population, and covering agricultural production over two-thirds of the earth's land mass, it negotiated and co-ordinated agricultural output and trade within and between the United States, Great Britain, its empire and the Commonwealth, the Belgian and French colonies, the Soviet Union, Latin America, the Caribbean and the Middle East.[8] Its decisions were, however, always contingent on the availability of shipping. The Combined Shipping Adjustments Board presided over the Ministry of

War Transport in Britain, and the War Shipping Administration in the United States. It was in the committee rooms of the Shipping Board that the war, waged at sea between U-boats and convoy escorts, was mirrored by British and American officials who battled for access to shipping space. In this struggle, the competing claims of American and British civilians for food jostled with those of Allied troops and Britain's colonial subjects. 'International shipping control thus became international food control.'[9] This was to prove particularly disadvantageous for Britain's colonial subjects, the survival of many of whom was threatened by the disruption of the international food trade. Those in charge of shipping allocations often made decisions as to who would go hungry and, in some cases, who would starve.

Germany had been preparing for exclusion from the world food market since the National Socialists came to power in 1933. The campaign to increase agricultural self-sufficiency was combined with a gradual shift in food dependency towards the east. The percentage of all food imports from Hungary, Romania, Bulgaria and Yugoslavia rose from 10 to 30 per cent between 1932 and 1939.[10] In August 1939, under the terms of the non-aggression treaty, the Soviet Union agreed to supply Germany with grain and a variety of oilseeds, soya beans, and vegetable, fish and whale oils, all of which went some way towards compensating for Germany's failure to achieve self-sufficiency in fodder and fat production.[11] Fresh citrus and other fruits and vegetables were obtained from Italy. Nothing could be done to replace shipments of more exotic goods such as cocoa beans, cane sugar, coffee and tea. For the duration of the war Germany would have to find substitutes for these foods, eke out its stores or do without.

Germany and Japan intended to export wartime hunger. The Third Reich viewed the whole of occupied Europe, not just the Soviet Union, as a source of food for the Germans. While they did not plan to starve the inhabitants of occupied western Europe to death, the National Socialists had every intention of allowing them to suffer before they imposed food shortages on their own civilians. Japan dressed its expansion into south-east Asia in the language of pan-Asian nationalism. The Japanese would be liberating their east Asian brothers from the oppression of western colonial powers and bringing a 'New Order' to the outer area of the east Asian sphere.[12] This was empty rhetoric. The

Japanese planned to mercilessly exploit south-east Asian raw materials and cheap labour. The hope was that while they would suffer from initial shortages, by 1943 the production of oil, rubber, tungsten and rice would be fully recovered. If south-east Asians went hungry while this was achieved, this caused the Japanese few qualms.

Faced with a decline in food imports it made sense for every wartime government to follow Germany's agricultural example and strive for self-sufficiency in food. Even where this was impossible to achieve, the most sensible solution to the difficulties of farming in wartime was to reduce the loss of energy inherent in converting edible crops into meat and cut down livestock numbers. Grassland could then be ploughed up in order to expand the area under crops which went straight into human food, such as wheat, rice or potatoes. Potatoes became the food of the Second World War, not only grown by governments but in private gardens throughout the world. A reduction in animals brought with it a lack of animal fats in the form of butter and lard, so it was essential to grow more oilseed crops. The loss of sugar cane imports also meant that the area under sugar beet needed to be extended. These seemingly simple measures were a lot more complicated and difficult to implement in practice, and in 1939 worldwide agriculture did not appear to be in good enough shape to withstand the impact of total war.[13]

The Depression had left many agricultural communities across the world in a state of acute poverty. In the 1930s Japanese children in the northern prefecture of Fukushima were too ashamed of the boiled barley mixed with a little rice inside their lunch boxes to open them and show the food to their teachers.[14] A district nurse in Suffolk 'knew of quite a few children who came to school without any breakfast and who walked home to a dinner of just potatoes'.[15] In the American south, migrant agricultural labourers lived in dwellings constructed out of 'old tents, gunny sacks, dry-goods boxes and scrap tin' with absolutely no sanitary arrangements.[16] Under-nourishment left them listless and vulnerable to pellagra, malaria and hookworm. There were few rural doctors, virtually no rural hospitals and infant mortality, a good indicator of levels of health and nutrition, was, even in 1942, running at the shockingly high rate of 43 per 1,000.[17]

The conveniences of the modern world had yet to reach even the more prosperous farming households. Approximately 60 per cent of

American farmhouses were without electricity. The vast majority were in a dilapidated state and needed repairs or complete rebuilding. Most had no central heating or running water, and outside privies were the norm.[18] Two-thirds of German farms had neither sewage nor water connections, and their isolation from the modern world was reinforced by the fact that clocks and radios were rare luxuries in farming households.[19] During the war, when lower-middle-class British land girls from urban backgrounds and German evacuees from the bombed-out towns found themselves living with farmers, they were shocked to discover that the farmhouses had 'no gas, electricity or water, no bathroom, no indoor sanitation . . . neither wash basin nor kitchen sink'.[20] Land girl Anne Hall described the living conditions of the family she lodged with in a row of farm workers' cottages near Bournemouth. 'Water was drawn up out of the well . . . and it was hard work turning the handle to haul up the pail. The washing up was done in a basin on the kitchen table, the used water thrown into the garden. There was a garden hut down the side path in the back garden which housed an Elsan bucket loo.' Its contents had to be emptied daily into a hole dug in the garden.[21]

If the living standard on farms was low, the state of farmland itself was often equally poor. In the Great Plains of America, drought had reduced the farms to a dust bowl of wind-eroded soil. In Britain, demoralized farmers had reduced their costs by spreading less fertilizing lime on their land, and leaving ditches and hedges in a state of disrepair. Rather than improving their grassland they fed their animals with cheap imported fodder.[22] Similarly, Japanese farmers had cut back on repairs and improvements.[23] Mechanization of farming was only just beginning and draught animals and humans were the main sources of strength on most farms. Pesticides, weedkillers and artificial fertilizers were in their infancy. John Cherrington, on his farm in Hampshire, fought a losing battle against docks, ragwort, thistles, couch grass and charlock, wireworms, leatherjackets, slugs, rooks and rabbits, with ploughs, hoes and guns the only weapons at his disposal.[24] In many countries the productivity and efficiency of agriculture lagged far behind industry. In parts of Germany farmers wasted hours of each day walking between their widely dispersed fields.[25]

In the under-developed countries agricultural impoverishment was the norm. Surveys by the League of Nations revealed that across Africa and Asia the peasant populations scraped together only the most meagre of livings from the land. Debt, malnutrition, periodic hunger and famine characterized most of the colonial world.[26] Theodore White and Annalee Jacoby, American journalists who lived in China in the 1930s and 1940s, described the situation of the Chinese peasant: 'The Chinese farmer does not farm; he gardens. He, his wife, and his children pluck out the weeds one by one ... His techniques are primitive ... his sickles, crude ploughs, flails, and stone rollers are like those his forefathers used. Frugality governs all his actions ... the yield of his back-breaking labour is pitifully small ... [T]he Chinese farmer is constantly at war with starvation; he and his family live in the shadow of hunger.'[27] It is estimated that in the 1930s about 3 million Chinese died each year as a result of starvation.[28] These farmers, living at the margins of subsistence, would be extremely vulnerable to the disruptions of war.

There were some signs of hope. Most developed countries had addressed the problems of the Depression with various schemes, such as President Roosevelt's New Deal (1933–36) in America. In the United States the government put its faith in science, and agricultural research had begun to yield results, which the agricultural extension officers of the New Deal spread among farmers.[29] In Britain new techniques such as bail milking had created pockets of regeneration.[30] And a rise in farm prices in 1937 alongside the Rural Revitalization campaign had stimulated some recovery in Japan. But wartime conditions created a new set of problems which the weakened agricultural sectors of most countries struggled to overcome.

The conditions of total war created an internal competition for resources within all the combatant nations, a competition which agriculture often struggled to win. New employment opportunities, offering higher wages and a better standard of living, combined with military conscription to drain workers from the farms in Allied and Axis countries alike. The best way to compensate for a loss in farm workers is to mechanize. But the production of agricultural machinery declined precipitously as industrial plants switched to making tanks and arms. Fuel shortages and a lack of spare parts often prevented the proper use of those machines that were available.[31] It was safer to rely on draught animals, but the military demand for oxen and horses meant that they too were in short supply. Artificial fertilizers were made predominantly from nitrogen and phosphorus. These were also the basic ingredients in the manufacture of explosives and so the fertilizer industry competed with the munitions industry for scarce supplies. Lack of fertilizer meant that farmers struggled to increase the yield of their land.

One factor which took a surprising toll on farmland was the military use of land. The army took over coastal areas and borders for defence, anti-aircraft batteries and observer posts, and they needed vast areas for practising manoeuvres. The most land-hungry arm of the military was the air force. Runways and airports were best sited on high, well-drained arable land. In Japan there was competition from the military for the limited amount of flat land. In Britain the best efforts of the ploughing-up campaign, which sought to increase the amount of cultivated land, were counteracted by the military requisitioning of 750,000 acres in England and Wales. In Germany compulsory land purchases swallowed up tens of thousands of hectares for motorways, airfields, barracks, camps, army training areas and the 'West Wall' defences.[32] Loss of land to one's own military was one thing, but loss of land to enemy occupation was another. The Soviet Union lost vast swathes of vitally important agricultural land to the German invaders.

If the international free market in food had to be abandoned, it was even more important that governments took control of all food imports entering the country. In addition, all governments sought to control the allocation of every scrap of food produced by its farmers. In theory rationing enabled governments to ensure that every level of society received a fair share of the whole. In most countries the rural population was the easiest to feed as they could simply be permitted to keep a share of the food which they produced. But, if they were the section of the population with the best access to food, they were not the group the government most wanted to feed. The military received first priority for food, followed by industrial workers. A common problem that government collection agencies faced was that small-scale farmers were well placed to illegally hold back more than their fair share of food, much of which they would then channel on to the black market.

The chapters that follow ask how effectively the different combatant countries, beginning with the United States and ending with China, approached and solved these problems. How they overcame the disruption to trade, and reorganized their agriculture in response, how efficient they were at collecting food from the farmers and to what extent they were able to use the resources of their allies and occupied territories. To a large extent this part of the book looks at who was well fed during the war, who went hungry, who starved to death, and why. This part begins with those countries which were able to draw strength from their ability to command food, and ends with those which were weakened and disabled by their inability to overcome the challenges war posed to agricultural production and the food supply.

4

American Boom

We will emerge from this struggle as the dominant power, dominant in naval power, dominant in air power, dominant in industrial capacity, dominant in mineral production, dominant in agricultural production. These are the basic resources of power.

(Ralph Watkins of the US National Resource Planning Board, November 1942)[1]

The position of American farmers during the Second World War was exceptional. The wartime problems which they faced were minimal in comparison to those faced by farmers in other combatant nations. There was no danger of enemy invasion or the capture of vital agricultural land. Farmers had to compete with the arms and explosives industry for labour, fertilizers and machinery, but the United States was virtually the only country in the world which had sufficient resources to spare to divert raw materials into the production of large quantities of farm machinery, fertilizers and other chemical products. The Depression had left farmers with huge surpluses of food which the unemployed urban workers could not afford to buy. By providing American farmers with a market for their food, and with a healthy income, the war pulled agriculture out of the Depression. A process of modernization, which had begun tentatively in the 1930s, was accelerated and a new agricultural revolution occurred which began to transform farming into the industry which it is today. Crucially, modernization allowed fewer farmers to feed significantly more people. The wartime boom in American agriculture meant that the United States was not only able to provide its enormous army and civilian population with plentiful quantities of food, it was also able to feed the soldiers and civilians of the Soviet Union, China and Great Britain.

The outbreak of war in Europe was, however, viewed with gloom by American agriculturalists, their outlook shaped by years of over-production, unwanted agricultural surpluses and low farm prices. They feared that, as had been the case with the First World War, a period of increased demand and production would be followed by a post-war bust and a return to the problem of surpluses. The need for textiles for uniforms did empty US warehouses of depressing piles of cotton, built up during the 1930s, but war meant that Europeans needed to husband their dollar resources and as a result they cut back on food purchases. In 1939 France reduced the amount of wheat it bought and cancelled all purchases of apples and pears. The British cut their expenditure on American food from £62 million in 1939 to £38 million in 1941. The United States Department of Agriculture warned that unless some way of selling food to Britain was found, America would be burdened by warehouses bursting at the seams with yet more unwanted food.[2] America's problem was not that the war cut off its access to imports but that it had lost a large chunk of its export market.

In March 1941 President Franklin D. Roosevelt introduced lend-lease as a means by which the supposedly neutral United States could aid Britain's war effort. Lend-lease solved the problem of the British balance of payments by 'loaning' Britain war materiel and food. The Agriculture Minister, Claude Wickard, urged farmers to grow as much as they could, telling them 'this is our war and not anyone else's war'.[3] Farmers were provided with the incentive of guaranteed farm prices, fixed at 110 per cent parity with industrial goods for the duration of the war.[4] Wickard was proved right. By 1942 it was clear that food production was going to be a vital and highly profitable aspect of America's contribution to the conflict. American farmers now had plenty of customers. Even before the United States' official entry into the war large numbers of civilians had moved into work in the war industries where they earned good money and they had little other than food to spend it on. The civilian demand for dairy products rose by 22 per cent. In April 1941 the lend-lease system was extended to the Chinese Nationalists and in November 1941 to the Soviet Union.

Once America entered the war in December 1941 the expansion of the military pushed up the demand for food even further. The American military, together with Britain, China and the Soviet Red Army, swallowed up 15 per cent of American dairy products and 25 per cent of American eggs, although the British and the Russians would undoubtedly have preferred more canned meat to the dreaded powdered egg, which America over-produced.[5]

The United States' agricultural administration rivalled the German Reich Food Corporation in its complexity, but it exercised far less control. This was partly due to Roosevelt's failure to appoint a food administrator with overall authority. The obvious man for the job would have been Herbert Hoover. Hoover had played an important role in the United States Food Administration during the First World War and had organized famine relief for Europe and the Soviet Union in the 1920s. But Roosevelt loathed him.[6] Instead, food issues were divided between the Ministry of Agriculture (which itself broke down into the War Food Administration, the Forest Service and the Bureau of Agricultural Economics) and the Office of Foreign Agricultural Relations. In addition, the Nutrition Division of the Office of Defense Health and Welfare Services and the Office of Price Administration both had a role to play in the control of food. The antipathy between different administrators, each defending their own patch, resulted in an ineffective administration. And few bureaucratic directives were ever applied in the field. The Production Goals Committee, for example, set down guidelines as to what farmers should grow, but these had little impact on the actual planting of crops.[7]

Thus, American farmers continued to grow too much cotton when they could more usefully have cultivated peanuts and vegetable feed. In 1944 valuable resources were wasted when fruit farmers planted a bumper crop of water melons. The Office of Price Administration considered water melons so low in nutritional value that it was not worth setting a maximum price for them. In 1943 water melons had been so scarce and the demand for them so great that they became some fruit farmers' most profitable crop. By planting double the quantity in 1944 the relatively control-free farmers were simply responding to market forces.[8] Most importantly, the American agricultural administration failed to boost milk production as much as was needed. In order to keep the price down for the consumer, the decision was taken not to raise the price paid for milk to the farmer but to subsidize the cost of feed for the cows. The result was that farmers' incomes increased but milk production barely rose. The United States Food Administration would have been better off adopting the British solution whereby farmers were paid well, creating an incentive for the farmer to produce more milk, while a subsidy kept down the cost to the consumer.[9]

The government's relatively lax grip on farming was wasteful in a wartime context. Fortunately, American agriculture experienced a revolution in productivity which meant that the United States could afford some wastage. To many American farmers the Second World War certainly felt like a 'good' war. Farm incomes rose by 156 per cent.[10] 'As farm prices got better and better . . . farm times became good times,' recalled Laura Briggs, raised on a small farm in Idaho in the 1930s and 1940s. 'Dad started having his land improved, and of course we improved our home and the outbuildings. We and most other farmers went from a tarpaper shack to a new frame house with indoor plumbing. Now we had an electric stove instead of a wood burning one, and running water at the sink where we could do the dishes; and a hot water heater; and nice linoleum . . . It was just so modern we couldn't stand it.'[11]

The war also provided a painless solution to the problem of agricultural unemployment, caused by the Depression. Rural workers were attracted to the factories by a wage double that of a farm worker and which could be earned in a mere eight hours a day.[12] In the United States ex-farmers and farm labourers made up 35 per cent of wartime industry's mechanical engineers and 30 per cent of those working in production.[13] Including those called up into the military, 6 million people left the farms.[14] Mordecai Ezekiel, economic adviser to the Department of Agriculture, commented dryly that 'we will have conquered unemployment by the same means that the Fascist countries conquered it, by organizing our people and our resources into a military economy'.[15]

Indeed, by 1942 farming was doing so well that farmers began to regret the loss of labour to industry. Farmer's organizations began to campaign for farm workers to be exempted from the draft. So powerful was the farm lobby in Washington that they succeeded in pushing through the Tydings Amendment to the Selective Service Law, by which means about 3.5 million farmers managed to escape the draft in 1943. In 1944 for every industrial worker who received deferment, three farm workers were exempted.[16]

The United States overcame the shortage of agricultural labour with relative ease by using a variety of alternative sources of farm labour. A Women's Land Army was formed in 1943 but farmers on the Great Plains and in the Rocky Mountains resisted hiring in land girls. They preferred to rely on their wives and daughters, who extended their activities from the farmyard and vegetable-growing to working in the fields. Verda Peterson left college to work on her father's farm in Missouri, milking cows, driving the binder to harvest the oats, and using the tractor to make hay. She replaced her older brother, who had enrolled in the naval reserve. In an article on her life in the *Country Gentleman* she explained: 'I am needed there. I know how to farm and can do more for my country there than in industry.'[17] Officials in Iowa estimated that farmers' use of their wives and children to work on the farm increased from 13 to 36 per cent. One farmer summed up the general feeling: 'If I have to have a woman helping me in the field, I want my wife, not some green city girl.'[18] But those who overcame their prejudices against the Women's Land Army were often pleased. A dairy farmer in Massachusetts enthused that 'his [land] girls were the best of the lot'.[19]

In California schoolchildren were given the afternoons off to help bring in the 1942 fruit and vegetable harvest. By 1944 the state was employing 3 million schoolchildren part-time to pick fruit, milkweed and floss, which was used to make life jackets.[20] Farmers discovered that German prisoners of war made good farm labourers. 'They saved us!' commented one rancher. Edward Pierce from Hillboro County recounted, 'They do what they are told. They don't work quite as fast as Americans . . . but they damage less fruit in orchards . . . We couldn't have harvested our apple crop up here without help and the prisoners were the best solution.'[21] The Germans were as delighted with their food as the farmers were with their hard work. One prisoner reported that he ate more in America in one day than he had in a whole week at home. Another commented that 'at first we thought the Americans were making fun of us. Such a menu: Soup, vegetables, meat, fish, fruit, coffee and ice cream! Never in the army did we get such a meal.'[22]

When the US War Ministry, eager to get the prisoners off its hands, began to make plans for their repatriation in 1945 there was an outcry among farmers. Farmer George S. Sweet wrote to Senator Raymond E. Willis in desperation in August 1945, explaining that he would need his prisoners of war until at least '15 November, as the city folks will not come out and get these crops in'.[23]

In the summer of 1944, as the German atrocities in eastern Europe began to come to light, the German prisoners were sad to find that they were no longer fed as though they were American soldiers. Their rations were reduced but their food was still well above the standard received by any labourer on a German farm in 1945, let alone a prisoner of war or forced worker.[24] Despite condemning the 'Jewish' liberal conspiracy of American capitalism, Hitler had held up the United States as a country which had achieved a level of wealth and mass consumerism to which Germany should aspire. When they were repatriated these German prisoners of war will have taken home to their battered and defeated country a fuller understanding of the superiority of American resources and the meaning of American abundance.

If the Americans treated their prisoners of war well, one of the least triumphant aspects of American wartime agriculture was the *bracero* programme. About 50,000 Mexican workers, brought in specifically to work in the vegetable and cotton fields of California and the southwest, were corralled into work gangs, housed in the most basic of barracks, and paid derisory wages. The *braceros* provided large-scale agribusinesses with a supply of cheap, non-unionized, fully exploitable labour.[25] An even darker side of America's war in the countryside was its treatment of Japanese-American farmers. Japanese-Americans owned only 1 per cent of Californian land but produced 10 per cent of the state's agricultural produce. During the wave of hysterical hatred which followed the Japanese attack on Pearl Harbor Californian fruit and vegetable farmers saw their opportunity to rid themselves of the unwanted competition. C. L. Preisker, Chairman of the Board of Supervisors in the Santa Barbara district, said: 'if we begin now to shut out the Japanese, after the war we have the chance of accomplishing something'.[26] Japanese-Americans were interned in camps in 1942. Many sold their farms at bargain prices and left their fruit and vegetables to rot in the fields.[27]

The most effective way of compensating for the loss of farm labour was to mechanize. Mechanization had been progressing slowly in the 1930s but the lack of profits and farm capital held the process back. War guaranteed the farmers high prices for their produce but it also pushed up the wages for labour. This created an even greater incentive to replace men with machines, and increased profits enabled farmers to buy in new machinery. Steel shortages meant that agricultural machinery was rationed; nevertheless, of all the countries in the world the United States had sufficient raw materials and labour to spare in order to produce enough tractors, combine harvesters and milking machines for the number of these machines in use on American farms to double between 1941 and 1945. Maize- and cotton-pickers and threshers became commonplace.[28] The rural electrification programme, which had begun in the 1930s, was extended to the point where electricity had become a standard utility for nearly half of America's farms by 1945, allowing the introduction of electric milk-coolers, feed-grinders and heating systems for chicken coops.[29]

The spread of machinery was matched by increased use of fertilizers, herbicides and pesticides. The United States, Canada and Britain combined their resources and this meant that they were the only countries in the world with sufficient raw materials to allow them collectively to increase their use of artificial fertilizers while still producing explosives. The United States government set up ten synthetic-nitrogen-processing plants and greatly increased its mining of potash and phosphoric rock. Most of the production was channelled into the explosives industry but there was enough available for American farmers to triple the amount of fertilizer they used, thus ensuring that the United States, Canada and Britain were the only countries that possessed agricultural soil which had not been severely depleted of its nutrients by over-farming by the end of the war. There were extreme shortages of pyrethrins, most of which were made in Japanese-occupied south-east Asia. They were used to manufacture insecticides for use in agriculture and for troops fighting in the tropics. But imports of pyrethrum from daisies grown in Kenya meant that American farmers were able to increase the use of arsenate and calcium arsenate insecticides.[30] In addition, the widespread introduction of hybrid seeds and selective breeding for livestock allowed great strides to be made in increasing yields. Thus, while virtually every other nation struggled to maintain, let alone increase, its agricultural productivity, US agriculture ended the war with productivity having risen by somewhere between 11 and 30 per cent.[31]

In 1909 President Theodore Roosevelt extolled the virtues of America's farming population. He told Congress that 'our civilization rests at bottom on the wholesomeness, prosperity, of life in the country. The men and women on the farms stand for what is fundamentally best and most needed in our American life . . . [W]e need the development of men in the open country, who will be in the future, as in the past, the stay and strength of the nation in time of war, and its guiding and controlling spirit in time of peace.'[32] But this romanticized notion of farming as a way of life gave way as market forces reshaped farming into a business which faced the same sorts of competition and price pressures as industry, where the constant demand was that more should be produced for less.[33] By rejuvenating the market for food the war enabled farmers to take advantage of new scientific improvements. But fertilizers, insecticides, machines, hybrid seeds which needed to be bought in each year (formerly farmers had saved a part of the previous crop for seed), and selective breeding for livestock, all demanded more and more capital (rather than labour) investment. Small farms had begun to disappear in the 1930s as the New Deal's farming subsidies favoured the larger farms which agrarian reformers concluded were better able to meet efficiently the needs of the vast nation.[34] This process accelerated during the war. Just as the government awarded industrial war contracts to large businesses (more than half of the $175 billion spent went to 'just thirty-three firms'), agribusinesses were favoured by agricultural wartime spending.[35] Farm and commodity lobbies, which became increasingly influential, also tended to promote the interests of large-scale farmers at the expense of the small and marginal.[36] The size of America's farms increased, while their number declined.[37] In the south, large, fully mechanized agribusinesses moved in and the dispossession of the mainly black share-croppers, which had begun in the 1930s, was virtually completed.[38]

Seabrook Farms in New Jersey is an excellent example of the way in which, during the first half of the twentieth century, American agriculture transformed into an industry and of how this development was consolidated during the Second World War. Charles F. Seabrook, always known as C. F., took over a fruit and vegetable farm from his father in 1913. He hated the dirtiness of farming and his real ambition was to become a construction engineer. He did eventually qualify in engineering and set up a construction company. Meanwhile, he applied his engineering interests to farming. Having noticed an ingenious method whereby a neighbouring Danish farmer irrigated his vegetables by means of iron pipes, he experimented, and in 1920 Seabrook Farms possessed the largest overhead irrigation system in America. C. F. indulged his passion for construction by building a highway that linked his farm to the large customer bases in Philadelphia and New York. On the farm he built power- and food-processing plants, a cold-storage warehouse, a sawmill, water storage and pumping stations to feed the irrigation pipelines, as well as houses and a school for the workers and their families. By the First World War it was a small self-contained industrial village and the farm prospered, supplying the United States army with fresh and canned fruits and vegetables.[39]

C. F. failed to withstand the decline in demand once the war was over and in 1924 he went bankrupt and was bought out of the farm, only to buy it back in 1929 with the proceeds of his construction company. By then his sons Belford and Jack had joined him in the business and it was their ingenious ideas that kept the farm afloat through the difficult years of the Depression. Their strategy was to add value to low-priced and unwanted crops, which otherwise would have been left to rot in the fields. Cabbages were turned into cans of sauerkraut, and the farm bought up skinny mid-western cattle at low prices and added the meat to their potatoes and carrots to make canned beef stew. The cans were sold to the state for its programme of food distribution to the poor.[40]

But it was the freezing industry that really rejuvenated the farm. In the 1910s Clarence Birdseye had learnt about freezing food while living with the Innu in Labrador. General Foods patented Birdseye's freezing technique and in the late 1930s C. F. signed a contract with them. As a result Seabrook Farms became the largest frozen foods company in America, controlling the process from seed to packages of frozen food. The farm developed new varieties of vegetables which were more suitable for freezing. The latest technology was used in the 20,000 acres of fields, from power tractors, many-disc ploughs, four-row cultivators, and the latest fertilizers, which, alongside pesticides and fungicides, were sprayed on the crops by aircraft.[41] Large vegetable-processing assembly lines were built on the farm, and refrigeration and cold storage facilities expanded. The workers' village grew into a small town.[42]

When America entered the Second World War Seabrook Farms was poised to take advantage of the boom in demand for food, especially easily transportable food. Stimulated by domestic demand, as a result of the shortage of canned items, the frozen food industry doubled its output during the war. Indeed the amount of vegetables grown for processing in the United States increased by a staggering 91 per cent. Many of the potatoes, carrots, onions, sweet potatoes, cabbage, beets and tomatoes were dehydrated for the military. But realizing that dehydrated vegetables were unlikely to be a roaring success after the war, the food-processing industry was much more interested in expanding its freezing capacity.[43] Meanwhile, Belford Seabrook was sent to Australia to teach farmers there the art of industrialized vegetable production to feed the US troops fighting in the Pacific.

In 1943 Seabrook Farms produced 60 million pounds of vegetables and employed 7,500 workers around the clock at harvest time. The farms' demand for labour was insatiable and the Seabrooks solved the problem of wartime labour shortages with their customary ingenuity. Every summer a group of black female college students from Atlanta were flown in, along with a contingent of chaperones. The women slept in a large barrack with bunk beds, and sorted peas, beans, spinach, strawberries, corn and beets by day. The field work was done by hundreds of men hired in from the West Indies, who earned fifty cents an hour and sent most of what they earned back home to their families.[44] Once the Japanese-American internees were released from the camps in the west, Seabrook Farms took 2,500, who were joined in the summer of 1944 by German prisoners of war. In 1945 the farm found room for 600 Estonians from displaced-persons camps in Germany.[45] C. F. liked to present the farm as a paternal enterprise which humanely gave work to unwanted 'enemy aliens'. But his sons recalled a cold and rather heartless man and the memories of the workers confirm that while agribusiness was good for the farmer it was a rather less joyful development for agricultural labourers.[46] As it was a long way to the nearest towns, the workers were forced to buy their food and other necessities from over-priced company stores. Their dominant memories were of long hours, poor pay – unions had been withdrawn from the workers on the farm when strikes in the early 1930s had disrupted production – and segregated, purpose-built villages of concrete block houses.[47]

In the post-war years, American agricultural productivity increases continued until by the late 1980s one farmer, who would have been able to feed about ten people in the 1940s, could produce enough to feed ninety.[48] The face of American agriculture changed dramatically. In the south cotton was no longer the king of crops, and black farmers had virtually disappeared. In California rice became an important crop, while speciality crops (mainly fruits and vegetables) were now grown on large-scale holdings. Across the north dairy cattle remained important but in the mid-west corn, hogs, poultry and soya beans became the dominant crops.[49] Before the war the Americans had used soya beans to provide protein in animal feed but it was indigestible for chickens and pigs. It was not until the 1940s that research developed a technique for deactivating the enzyme inhibitor in the meal, which allowed these animals to tolerate the feed. Their high protein content made the beans a useful meat substitute and American soya bean flour became the main ingredient in British sausages. Vere Hodgson in London commented that 'Thursday I have an order with the Dairy for a pound of sausage. These make-do for Thursday, Friday and part Saturday. No taste much of sausage, but are of soya bean flour. We just pretend they are the real thing.'[50] The United States also sent out self-heating tins of soya chunks to help feed the Indian army, which by reason of religious taboos was not very keen on corned beef or canned pork. But they went down like 'a lead balloon'.[51]

Soya was given an immense boost by the loss of the vegetable-oil-producing countries in the Far East. The growing Allied reliance on margarine to compensate for the decline in butter production, and the use of glycerine (which could be extracted from the beans) to make explosives, led to the doubling of the area under soya from 5 to 11 million hectares.[52] Already in 1939 Illinois was known as the 'Manchuria' of the United States, producing more than one-half of America's soya beans. The farmers complained that the crop robbed the soil of nutrients but the profit motive for growing soya was too powerful. A new, fattier bean known as the Lincoln was developed by the Illinois Agricultural Experiment Station, and the Secretary of State for Agriculture guaranteed a generous wartime price per bushel which amounted to twice that paid for corn.[53]

Until the Second World War Americans were resistant to the charms of margarine. It had been invented by a French food chemist, Hippolyte Mège-Mouriès, in 1869 for the French navy as a cheap and calorific butter substitute which would not go rancid on long voyages. In 1902 the German discovery of hydrogenation (by which unsaturated fat in reaction to hydrogen turns into saturated fat) meant that margarine could be made from plant oils rather than the original ingredients, which included cow's udder, milk and sodium bicarbonate. Its name came from the Greek *magarítes* for pearl because of its pearly white sheen. Yellow dyes were mixed in to make it look more palatable and buttery.[54] By the 1930s Germany, in particular, had become dependent on margarine as a butter substitute for the poorer sections of society.[55] But in America dairy farmers did not want it to undermine butter production and they lobbied for heavy taxes on the substitute, especially the more appetizing yellow-coloured margarine, which was forbidden in some states.[56] The agricultural administration's failure to boost wartime milk production sufficiently meant that nutritionists recommended vitamin-A-fortified margarine as a replacement for butter. Housewives took to the product with enthusiasm. One reported that although 'all had been against it at the start', women were now 'unanimous in their praise of oleo [as in its original French name oleo-margarine] . . . Our butcher can't keep up with the demand.'[57] An Illinois state booklet, *Home Budgets for Victory*, recommended margarine in sixty-eight of its recipes. Surveys showed that even the households of the anti-margarine dairy farmers were using the butter substitute. In 1950 the extra taxes on margarine were abolished.[58] The war had firmly established margarine as an everyday American food. In turn, this helped to establish soya as an American crop.

At the end of the war American scientists learned from their defeated German colleagues how to counter soya oil's unpleasant smell. From then on soya's share of the United States' edible oil exports rose dramatically, reaching 20 per cent in 1950.[59] Soya flour was also seen as a way of meeting the need for high-protein flours to feed undernourished newly liberated European civilians. Facilities for milling the beans into flour were expanded. Under the Marshall Plan soya flour, oil and feed exports to Europe were heavily subsidized as a cheap way of feeding hungry Europeans.[60]

This has led to largely invisible but none the less significant changes in the western diet since 1945. Soya has now become a dominant element in European animal feed and is ubiquitous in processed foods, such as bread, biscuits, cakes, chocolate bars, breakfast cereals, soups, margarine and processed meat, to which it is added in a variety of forms as soya flour, oil, lecithin, protein or as a flavour enhancer.[61] From its pre-war position as a smelly and indigestible bean, soya has become one of the three staple crops eaten by Americans. Today soya provides 257 of the average contemporary American's daily intake of calories, while wheat provides a further 768 and corn another 554 calories.[62]

The enormous success of the lucrative American soya business also had its more dubious side-effects. The impact of soya products on human health is a matter for some concern. While the Japanese ferment soya beans to make tofu, miso and soya sauce, western processing of soya to produce vegetable oils and soya flour does not involve fermentation. Unfermented soya products contain phytoestrogens which mimic human oestrogen and some medics fear that if unfermented soya is consumed in large quantities it can affect the development of the reproductive system and fertility.[63] Soya beans also loosen the soil far more than other crops, and in the American west, which had already lost much of its soil in the 1930s, the expansion of the crop undermined a very real need to concentrate on soil conservation, especially when the problem of drought and soil erosion returned in the 1950s.[64] Nowadays, soya farming is expanding in environmentally sensitive areas in Latin America, undermining the ecosystem of the Brazilian Cerrados plateau and threatening to encroach on the Amazonian forest.[65]

America ended the war virtually the only country in the world with a booming agriculture sector. Its civilians barely suffered any hardship with regard to food supplies and its army was the best fed throughout the war. Yet the US was still able to supply its allies with large quantities of much-needed food. In price terms the amount of agricultural exports tripled.[66] In 1945 the United States War Food Administration summed up the importance of food as a 'weapon of war. As such, it ranks with ships, airplanes, tanks and guns. Food, particularly American food, has been especially crucial in the present war, because it has been essential to the fighting efficiency of our allies as well as our own military forces, and has been required to maintain colossal industrial productivity here and in other allied countries. Modern war demands enormous food production, not only for consumption by huge forces on land and sea, but for consumption by the personnel employed in war industries, in transport, and in related occupations.'[67] The United States' ability to fill this need for food gave it a hold over its allies and an advantage over its enemies. When America ended the war with a bumper harvest in 1945 the administration was to discover that the ability to command plentiful quantities of food continued to equate with power in the post-war world.

5

Feeding Britain

Wartime farming was not . . . as productive as it is today. Feeding stuffs for cattle were rationed and the techniques for making good quality hay and silage were still in their most rudimentary stages. There were shortages of fertilisers and none of the sprays which now keep weeds out of most of our crops. A yield of one ton an acre of all grain was quite good.

(John Cherrington, a farmer in Hampshire during the war)[1]

Britain entered the war as the combatant nation most dependent on wheat imports. But the Ministry of Agriculture's campaign to restructure farming and switch to growing wheat and potatoes was so successful that the government never had to ration bread. Many historians have celebrated the government-initiated ploughing-up campaign as a resounding success. It is portrayed as having taken British farming out of a depressed phase of low input, low productivity pastoral farming and, with the introduction of technological innovations, to have reoriented British farms towards much more productive arable farming. In *The People's War* Angus Calder argued that the campaign returned British agriculture to its mid-Victorian hey-day before the new global economy in food developed and Britain began to import cheap grains from abroad.[2] Certainly, farmers were the social group that benefited the most from the war. The generous pricing scheme which the government introduced meant that between 1939 and 1945 farm incomes quadrupled. Even farm labourers benefited as their wages doubled.[3] Consumers were protected from these rising costs by subsidies which kept the price of food in the shops at a reasonable level.[4] However,

89

recent research suggests that the agricultural achievements of wartime were less impressive than is usually suggested. Those gains in yields which were achieved were more the straightforward result of an increase in the cultivated area and old-fashioned hard work rather than the by-product of technological innovations.[5]

By expanding the area under crops British farmers were able to increase their contribution to the British diet from 33 per cent of calories to 44 per cent and Britain was able to extend the number of days a year when it could feed itself from 120 to 160.[6] These figures demonstrate that the reorganization of British agriculture by no means freed the island from its dependence on imports. Rather, the ploughing-up campaign enabled Britain to compensate for the fact that food imports fell by half from 22 million tons to somewhere between 15 and 11 million tons a year.[7] Britain stopped importing non-essential foodstuffs. The most important saving was in the area of animal feed, which virtually disappeared from supply ships. Another 2.5 million tons a year were saved by severely cutting imports of sugar, fresh fruit and nuts. By growing more wheat to make bread, British farmers enabled the government to prioritize the import of condensed high-energy foods such as meat and dairy products, which filled the protein and calcium gap in the workers' diets, and added variety and interest to a monotonous menu based on bread.[8]

FROM MEAT TO BREAD AND POTATOES

In the 1930s the only food in which Britain was entirely self-sufficient was liquid milk.[9] Most of British agricultural land was under pasture and livestock products made up 70 per cent of the value of farming output.[10] At the time it was calculated that while ten acres of grassland for stock-raising could feed twelve people, the same area under wheat could feed 200, while ten acres planted with potatoes could feed as many as 400.[11] With the reduction of food coming into the country it made more sense to extend the number of people Britain's farmland could feed and plans were made to reduce livestock and plough up pastures to plant with wheat, sugar beet and potatoes.[12] However, the Ministry of Agriculture still hoped to maintain a meat reserve on the hoof, rather than in cans which would be stored in warehouses vulnerable to the German aerial bombing campaign.[13] In the summer of 1941 the government realized that the shipping crisis was going to be much worse than they had expected and Cabinet Office economists protested that animals were being allowed 'to eat shipping space . . . at a rate comparable with the rate at which submarines are destroying it. No more costly reserve could be devised . . . A reserve ought to be held against an emergency. But a livestock reserve creates an emergency.'[14] In response the Food Policy Committee cut the annual import of animal feed to a mere 150,000 tons for the next three years. Dairy cattle were given first priority for imported feed as the government concentrated on maintaining milk production. Livestock farmers were required to become self-sufficient and grow their own feed grains.

In order to achieve the feat of ploughing up the pastures the government encouraged farmers to use tractors. Before the war, horses pulling the plough were a common sight in British fields. In 1939 only one in six British farmers owned a tractor. By 1946 the number of tractors on British farms had quadrupled.[15] It was also possible, via the county agricultural committees, to hire in a contractor who used government-owned machines.[16] The tractors, made by the Ford Motor Company at Dagenham, or shipped in from America as part of the lend-lease agreement, were by no means cutting edge. The Ministry of Agriculture preferred to stick to the well-known and temperamental Fordson rather than any of the new and innovative tractors on the market at the time.[17] But even the exasperatingly unreliable Fordsons made the task of ploughing up 2.5 million acres of pasture land a great deal easier. Although the tractors look antiquated to us now, the sight of a land girl using a tractor to plough pasture land was a powerful contemporary image of the modernity that the war was bringing in its wake.[18] There were limits, however, to the mechanical revolution. During the war most planting was done using cup feed drill machines which had been in production since the nineteenth century.[19]

In order to ensure the success of the ploughing-up campaign it was essential to increase the use of fertilizers, as much of the new land that was brought under cultivation was poor in phosphoric acid. One of Canada's most vital contributions to maintaining Britain's food supply was the expansion of its phosphate and nitrogen industry.[20] Nitrogen was essential for both explosives and artificial fertilizers and four large synthetic nitrogen plants were set up in Canada with British financial assistance. In this way Britain protected its vital source of nitrogen from German bombs and Canada acted as a safe warehouse for Britain's ammonium phosphate.[21] Through the auspices of the Combined Food Board, Canada also compensated for the disruption caused to the global fertilizer trade by becoming the main supplier of ammonium phosphate fertilizers to the rest of the Commonwealth and Britain's empire, which in turn also provided Britain with food.

Soviet supplies of potash were also channelled through Canada and the United States. Rather than burdening with yet more cargo the already overloaded rail lines leading to the eastern front, the Soviets mined the potash in the Urals and then sent it on a journey almost all the way round the globe, through Siberia and across North America, before it finally arrived in Britain.[22] Britain's fertilizer supply was also periodically boosted with shipments of potash and phosphate rock from the United States, Chile, Palestine and, with the Allied capture of North Africa, Morocco.[23] This enabled British farmers to more than double their use of nitrogen and phosphate fertilizers and significantly increase the amount of potash and lime they spread on the fields.[24]

The introduction of many more tractors and the increased use of fertilizers made the ploughing-up campaign possible *but* they did not amount to a revolution in agricultural methods. Tony Harman, a farmer in Buckinghamshire, recalled that a herbicide called Agroxone was tried out during the war and it wiped out the yellow mass of charlock flowers that had always accompanied the spring barley.[25] However, it was not until *after* 1945 that British farms really began to benefit from the extensive use of hybrid seeds, pesticides, herbicides and selective livestock breeding which came into use in the United States during the war. The cereal varieties British farmers used between 1939 and 1945 had been introduced before the First World War and most milk cows were not high-yielding cross-breeds but more often than not old-fashioned Shorthorns and were milked by hand. That dairy herds were not fully modernized was, in fact, fortunate. The normal cows did well on the bulky home-grown feed that was available and produced a steady 300–400 gallons a year on their austerity diet, unlike the fine breeds of high-yielding cows who failed to produce much milk without a concentrated, protein-rich diet.[26] It was not until after the war that the introduction of technological advances produced an immense leap in crop and livestock yields.

Nevertheless, in 1943 British farmers produced a bumper crop of wheat. At the beginning of the war virtually all of the country's wheat for bread was imported, but in 1943 Britain was able to cover one-half of its bread grain needs with home-grown wheat. Barley, oats, fodder crops and vegetables all showed significant gains and there was a modest increase in sugar beet yields, which were limited not by farming but by the processing abilities of the sugar factories.[27] Potato production increased by a staggering 87 per cent. But the Agriculture Ministry's policy on potatoes was probably one of the least efficient of its wartime food measures. It made sense to increase potato consumption as they are a simple and nutritious way of stretching meals when meat is in short supply. But the Ministry of Food treated potatoes as a substitute for bread and encouraged the cultivation of the maximum amount of potatoes rather than aiming for an optimum yield. The problem with potatoes is that they are a very unpredictable crop: 'the paradox of potato policy [was that] . . . there must be at once a greater stimulus to consumption, in order to avoid waste, and at the same time more and yet more careful planning against a shortage that, should it occur, would be made worse by the consumption increase.'[28] The end result was that Britain produced too many potatoes. While it is common for people to replace potatoes with bread, they rarely use potatoes instead of bread. Those who benefited were the privileged members of society who had the means to keep a pig, as they were provided with a plentiful and cheap feed.[29]

The impressive harvest of 1943 was the result of the doubling of the amount of arable land in Britain, and farmers also benefited from a good growing season.[30] Even though the harvest was a success in terms of providing Britain with the food it needed to survive the war, it was not necessarily a success in the terms in which many historians have described it, as an indication that the productivity of British agriculture had increased. 'There were no yield improvements, and output increases were the result of the change from pasture to arable and the increased inputs of labour, capital to pay for the mechanisation, and management.'[31] More than anything else the good harvest was due to the long hours the farmers and their labourers had invested working on the fields, a regressive tendency, which indicates that productivity may even have declined.[32]

Much of the back-breaking labour on British wartime farms was provided by the 80,000 land girls of the Women's Land Army.[33] The conditions were often miserable. Life was lonely and isolated, and cold bedrooms and a lack of bathing facilities made life particularly uncomfortable given the dirty nature of the work. Vera Campbell described washing on her farm in Scotland. After pumping water into pails it was heated in hens' pots, normally used for boiling scraps for poultry and the pig. Having poured the water into the old zinc bath she would first 'wash top half of body – dry – put on warm jersey and try to sit in the bath for the bottom half of body. Pretty grim in cold weather.'[34] The farmers were often hostile and obstinate, at best taciturn, and the girls were sometimes sexually harassed by male farm workers. They were always hungry. Bread and butter and potatoes were the mainstays of the diet and it was common for the farmers and the girls' landladies to keep the best foods, such as bacon or the land girls' extra ration of cheese, for themselves, which meant that more often than not they ended up with beetroot sandwiches for lunch.[35] The one-third of the Land Army who were organized into work gangs and lived in hostels were usually better off. The hostels were overcrowded, 'the Old Girl [in charge of the hostel] was a tartar. The house was damp' and cold but at least they had company and if 'the food was rotten' there was usually sufficient.[36]

The Women's Land Army was for most women an interesting, sometimes liberating, always exhausting, but ultimately rewarding way of contributing to the war effort. Anne Hall recalled that 'work, eat, sleep was the daily routine [but] I loved the cows'.[37] And Linda Shrigley, who joined as a shy seventeen-year-old who had 'never even been on a train', grew in confidence as she learned to handle an excavator and helped to clear the banks of the silted up River Skerne in Durham. The men she worked with were 'amazed when I got out of the machine. I was only four feet nine and a half.'[38] Once the women had proved their mettle, many farmers acknowledged that their help was invaluable. A farmer from Northamptonshire wrote to the *Land Girl*, in praise of Mary Hall, 'I cannot speak too highly of her, as it has been no easy

task for a girl to go through the wet and cold we have had this winter
. . . [S]he has never missed a day or been late at any time through all
the severe weather we have had . . . I am afraid I have thought of land
girls as summertime workers, but Mary has proved to me I am wrong.'[39]

Prisoners of war also made up for the labour shortage on the farms.
British farmers preferred the work ethic of German prisoners and
complained that the Italians could not be persuaded to work without
bribes of chocolate and cigarettes. But 50,000 Italian prisoners of war
were eventually mobilized for agricultural work and they reduced the
need for the motley crew of 'soldiers, the publican, the postman', schoolchildren, and even townspeople spending their summers at agricultural
holiday camps, who in the early years of the war had joined the land
girls in the fields at harvest time.[40]

In contrast to American farmers, who came under relatively little
government control, British farmers were controlled by the County
War Agricultural Executive Committees, which mixed an anachronis-
tic feudalism with war socialism. These hierarchical, class-based
committees, appointed from the local gentry, exercised complete control
over the farmers in their areas, who had no right of appeal against
their decisions. The War Ags, as they were known, were responsible
for ensuring that government directives were carried out on the ground
and, most importantly, they administered the ploughing-up campaign
which transformed pasture into wheat- and potato-growing fields. The
majority were helpful, reasonable and effective but, as in the United
States, their prejudice in favour of large and supposedly more efficient
arable farms created an atmosphere in which industrial-style farming
was favoured over small-scale family farms.[41] The official histories of
the ploughing-up campaign, and many later historians, have ignored
those farmers who expressed doubts about the wisdom of the government's policy and resisted the orders of the War Ags. However, more
recent research shows that their fixed view of arable farming as superior led to some grave injustices. An example of this is the Hampshire
War Ags' attitude to Rex Paterson, a dairy farmer with a large modernized milk herd. Despite the fact that the Ministry of Food had prioritized
milk and was desperate to increase milk production, in a counter-
productive order Paterson's committee placed him in the second class
of farmers and forced him to plough up 800 acres of his pasture to

grow potatoes. There were also cases of corruption. Farming was a protected occupation and a number of War Ags evicted farmers unfairly, wrongly accusing them of negligent farming practices, in order to replace them with relatives or friends who could then evade conscription. By 1945 farmers' organizations held details of at least 300 cases of dubious eviction.[42]

AMERICAN DRIED EGG AND ARGENTINIAN CORNED BEEF

The British restructuring of agriculture was a modest success. However, if the government had been forced to rely solely on the food grown in Britain to feed its people then it would have been forced to impose upon them an eighteenth-century peasant-style vegetarian diet.[43] The introduction of lend-lease in March 1941 came as a great relief as it allowed Britain to import large quantities of American frozen and canned meat, especially luncheon pork and sausages, canned fish, dried egg, canned and dried milk, dried fruit, fats and oils, as well as wheat for bread flour.[44] Most of these foods were distributed not through the rationing system but through a morale-boosting points system which allowed shoppers more choice. The American imports enabled people to inject variety and flavour into their monotonous meals based on bread and potatoes. 'The outstanding buy was generally agreed to be the large tin of American sausage meat which cost a whole sixteen points, but besides providing enough meat for several main meals contained a thick layer of nearly half a pound of fat.'[45]

If American farmers benefited from Britain's need for protein and fat so too did Iceland's fishermen. The requisitioning of much of the British fishing fleet for mine-sweeping and the closure of fishing grounds led to an acute shortage of fish, and provided Iceland with a fine opportunity to reverse its economic decline. In the 1920s Icelandic fishing had been a growing industry. Farmers moved off their sheep farms and into the coastal towns to take up a life at sea. The catch of cod was dried and salted and sold to Spain. Then, in the 1930s, the Depression and the Spanish civil war wiped out the market for Icelandic salt cod. By 1939 the fishing fleet was decrepit, and the economy was in poor shape. As an island dependent on imports, with only mutton and fish as its exports, Iceland's balance of payments deficit was an insoluble problem and the country was deeply in debt.[46] British wartime demand for fish revived the industry. Icelandic ships would put out from harbour, put their catch on ice, and take it straight to the British ports. Often the vessels would then fill up their empty holds with as many black market consumer goods as they could lay their hands on, and sail back to Iceland. While in 1933 about three-quarters of Icelandic fish exports were salted, ten years later only 10 per cent were salted and about half were iced. Salting and drying factories disappeared from the Icelandic coastline, to be replaced by freezing plants, which mushroomed from two in 1930 to eighty by 1949.[47]

By the end of the war, Iceland's balance of payments problem had been reversed. Indeed, the British government constantly complained that it was being fleeced by the Icelandic fishing industry. The Ministry of Food was also charged high prices by British trawler owners, and fish, having been relatively cheap, became very expensive. Pam Ashford, a secretary in a coal-exporting firm in Glasgow, frequently complained to her Mass Observation diary that 'fish is beyond our purse. Haddock is today at 4/- per lb'.[48] By 1945 the Icelandic government had built up a healthy reserve of foreign currency which it promptly invested in British and Swedish fishing trawlers and additional freezing plants. Private entrepreneurs then used their savings, hoarded from the high wages and high prices paid for fish during the war, to set up small fishing and fish-processing businesses. Modern Icelandic prosperity rested firmly on the back of the post-war development of the fishing industry.[49]

The most important supplier of food to Britain (apart from the United States) was its empire in the form of the Commonwealth. What is most striking is the willingness of these governments to restructure their own agricultural sectors so that they could meet Britain's new import requirements. Perhaps the most extreme example of this is the case of the five Australian mutton dehydration factories which were set up in response to the British government's concern about its meat stocks. The dehydrated mutton was intended as an emergency food reserve which would take up very little shipping space. The experiment proved extremely expensive. It took nearly seven pounds of mutton at 2s. 2 ½d. per pound to produce one pound of dehydrated meat. When reconstituted, one pound made up three and a half pounds of an extremely unpleasant lumpy grey mince. The revolting reconstituted mutton was a perfect example of how to take poor-quality food and make it almost inedible. As it turned out the British never needed to resort to dehydrated mutton as a component of their meat ration. Once the 1942–43 shipping crisis was over, the Australians closed down their mutton dehydration plants and shouldered the financial loss.[50]

At the beginning and at the end of the war Australia supplied Britain with much of its frozen meat, but the United States and Canada were the main suppliers in 1943, when Australian meat was diverted to feed the United States army in the Pacific. Canadian agriculture mirrored Britain's restructuring process in reverse as the farmers switched from arable to livestock farming. On the western plains farmers were encouraged to decrease their wheat production and to start growing coarse feed grains, which were then used to fatten the country's growing herds of pigs and cattle. Canada replaced Denmark as Britain's chief supplier of bacon, providing the island with four-fifths of its bacon by the end of the war.[51] Canada's agricultural story is very similar to that of the United States. The war brought its farming sector out of depression and solved the problem of rural unemployment by siphoning surplus labour into industry. The number of farms declined, while their size increased, and farmers earned enough to buy expensive capital inputs such as machines and chemicals which greatly improved productivity.[52]

New Zealand in its turn restructured its dairy industry in order to accommodate Britain's new demands. Before the war New Zealand had supplied Britain with large quantities of butter, but butter was almost purely an energy food, providing plenty of calories but only traces of protein and minerals. Cheese, in contrast, provided protein, calcium and phosphorus as well as energy. In terms of shipping space it was more economic than meat as it contained more than twice the energy and protein per cubic foot of shipping space of frozen lamb.[53] The British government put in a request to the New Zealand Ministry of Agriculture to switch dairy production from butter to cheese. The New Zealanders obliged and reorganized their dairy factories so that by 1942 New Zealand was exporting 132,000 tons of cheese to Britain, compared to 80,000 tons in 1938–39. But then in 1942 the British changed their minds. The American supply of cheese was surprisingly good but Japanese successes in south-east Asia had cut the British off from a large proportion of their supply of vegetable oil for margarine. The co-operative New Zealanders reorganized yet again and refitted their factories so that they could once again make butter.[54] However, the poor farming season of 1942–43 meant that butter rationing had to be introduced for the first time and New Zealanders cut their annual butter consumption from 48 pounds a head to 36 pounds in 1945 in order to make butter available for the British.[55]

By 1942 the number of ships arriving at New Zealand's ports had decreased considerably but they were able to maintain their meat exports by de-boning and telescoping their beef, lamb and mutton. De-boning beef was an ingenious space-saving technique invented by the United States army. All the bones, fat and least nutritious cuts were removed from the carcasses, which were then compressed into fifty-pound boxes. It took about 60 per cent less space than meat carcasses, which had to be hung, and thus made better use of the space in the refrigerated ships, which were extremely scarce. Dehydration and canning also reduced the bulk of meat exports and the New Zealanders stepped up these industries as well. Overall, New Zealand's meat production increased by 14 per cent, but it was still necessary to introduce meat rationing in March 1944 in order to ensure a sufficient surplus to meet Britain's order.[56]

Britain's most important South American trading partner, Argentina, faced an appalling 70 per cent reduction in the amount of shipping (in tonnage) arriving at its ports. The Argentinians showed great resourcefulness in coping with the shipping shortage. Even though the volume of Argentinian exports had to be greatly reduced, they still managed to maintain the value of their food exports. The solution was to process every foodstuff before it was shipped. This not only reduced the bulk of food exports but added to their value. With the massive decline in global demand for animal feed, Argentina doubled the size of its own hog herds and processed the maize – which they would normally have exported – into canned pork. Oilseeds were pressed into vegetable oil, beef was de-boned or canned.[57] Indeed, Argentinian corned beef filled British warehouses, as it made up the bulk of the British meat reserve. Argentina eventually supplied Britain with 40 per cent of all its wartime meat requirements.[58]

The processing of meat by means of de-boning, telescoping and canning meant that Britain was able to maintain its meat imports at their pre-war level.[59] Given that half of Britain's meat was imported before the war and that domestic livestock farming was cut back during the war, these techniques played a vital role in maintaining the meat ration. If the processing of food in order to save shipping space was essential it also led to the creation of some of the most unsavoury of wartime foods. Perhaps the most detested was dried egg. The British Ministry of Food's Department of Scientific and Industrial Research developed the technique for spray-drying eggs to create a powder which took up only 20 per cent of the shipping space required for fresh eggs. The United States over-produced eggs, and there was never any shortage of the powder.[60] Every four weeks each British household was entitled to a grey packet of dried egg which was supposedly equivalent to a dozen fresh eggs.[61] But egg powder was no substitute for the real thing. No matter how much it was whipped into a froth it failed to aerate cake mixtures. The British stubbornly continued to use egg powder to make omelettes and scrambled eggs.[62] 'The two words which still make my blood run cold, are DRIED EGG,' wrote Jill Beattie, who was at a boarding school during the war. 'The very worst breakfast . . . was a two inch block of hard scrambled egg oozing with water which saturated the half slice of so-called toast beneath it – and the TASTE – ugh!'[63] Processed cheese was no better. Ernst van Someren, a chemist living in Hertfordshire, flavoured his family's omelettes (made with eggs from their own chickens) with processed 'cheese' from a tube, 'a soapy wartime product with no consistency and poor keeping quality, unfit to eat raw'.[64]

A variety of other unspeakable powders and pastes was manufactured. Doreen Laven recalled that, 'towards the end of the war dried banana powder appeared but we all thought it disgusting. It became a joke that if we children were naughty we'd be made to eat a spoonful of it.' Doreen had never tasted a banana and was bothered by the model bunches of the fruit which still hung in greengrocers' displays. She often pestered adults to describe the taste, 'an impossible question, bananas aren't like anything except bananas'.[65] The one product which processing rendered more desirable, at least in children's eyes, was milk. As a wartime child my mother would sneak into her neighbour's pantry to steal a spoonful of condensed milk from any tins that were already opened. Tins of condensed milk also became a useful commodity for barter between soldiers and civilians.

The reorganization of British agriculture was an essential element in securing the island's food supply but it was Britain's continued reliance on imports which was the real strength of the food policy. Britain's pivotal place in the world trade in commodities meant that it was able to draw on the food resources of a wide variety of countries with more productive agricultural systems, from the United States to Argentina, the Commonwealth and the colonies (which will be discussed in another chapter) to the tiny neighbouring island of Iceland.[66] Britain reduced its imports by weight but still managed to import 56 per cent of the calories consumed on the island. Thus condensing food was the key to keeping Britain fed. However, if the British did not sacrifice the energy content of their food they did sacrifice taste. The one weakness of the strategy was, of course, the fact that the ships which brought in these foodstuffs had to run the gauntlet of the German U-boats in the Atlantic. The next chapter asks whether the Battle of the Atlantic ever posed a real threat to Britain's food supplies.

6

The Battle of the Atlantic

*The stability of [food] supplies ... depended [on] a kind of
specialist diplomacy in food matters, of which the most skilled
exponents were the British Food Mission in Washington.*
(R. J. Hammond, historian of the British wartime food
administration)[1]

On New Year's Day 1940 the stationery salesman Christopher Tomlin
noted in his Mass Observation diary that he had heard the nutritionist
John Boyd Orr on the radio recommending porridge rather than bacon
for breakfast and extolling the virtues of potatoes. 'His propaganda
point is to avoid imported foods and to grow as much as we can. Me
to Mother and Father: "I don't like to suggest it, but it looks as if the
Government's scared." "How do you mean?" "They think we won't
be able to get enough food across with all these boats sunk".'[2] Churchill later recalled that 'the Battle of the Atlantic was the dominating
factor all through the war. Never for one moment could we forget that
everything happening elsewhere, on land, at sea or in the air, depended
ultimately on its outcome.'[3] The Battle of the Atlantic evokes images
of brave merchant seamen defying the U-boats and often paying with
their lives, doughty Britons withstanding the hardship of life under
siege and brilliant code-breakers at Bletchley Park cracking the German
navy's Enigma code, which enabled them to pinpoint where the U-boats
were lying in wait for the merchant marine. But the battle was not only
about German submarines, ominous menace though they were. More
decisive in the struggle to supply Britain with all its wartime needs was
the lack of shipping. It was this, combined with mismanagement at the

ports, a creaking internal British rail network, *and* the U-boats, which led to a drastic fall in total imports arriving in Britain from 68 million tons before the war to 26 million tons in 1941.[4]

The Battle of the Atlantic was also waged between the Allies themselves, in a struggle over shipping allocations. The British food supply was heavily dependent on the diplomatic skills of the men of the British Food Mission in Washington who represented Britain's food needs at the Combined Food Board and worked hard to persuade the Americans and Britain's other allies that British food requests were reasonable and that they should take priority over competing raw-material and military requirements.[5] The success of the British Food Mission meant that although the Battle of the Atlantic hampered the Allies' ability to conduct military operations, at no point in the war did it threaten the British people with hunger, let alone starvation.

THE WORST WINTER OF THE WAR

As German troops marched into Poland, Hitler ordered all submarines patrolling the ocean trade routes to attack hostile ships without warning.[6] The Germans used submarines, planes and mines to sink the British merchant marine. Throughout 1940 Admiral Karl Dönitz, head of the U-boat arm of the German navy, was able to inflict severe damage on British merchant shipping with the fifty-seven submarines under his command.[7] Without radar or sophisticated anti-submarine technology, the British navy were unable to provide ships with adequate protection from this invisible enemy. Among the U-boat crews the autumn of 1940 was known as the 'happy time'. After sinking a record number of vessels the German sailors would arrive triumphant at their French bases to flower garlands and champagne. British sailors returned to their blacked-out ports with scenes in their heads of oil tankers instantaneously bursting into flames, drowning men coated in oil and dead bodies floating in the jetsam of torpedoed ships. Nearly 6,000 British, Indian and African seamen died in 1940.[8] By February 1941 Britain was losing ships three times as fast as the shipyards could build them. Meanwhile, the Luftwaffe was bombarding Britain from the air, damaging docks, transport links and food storage warehouses.[9]

Despite the air of triumph which surrounded the submarine campaign against British merchant shipping, Germany did not direct more resources into U-boat production, which in 1940 only kept pace with losses. Neither Dönitz nor Admiral Erich Raeder, Commander-in-Chief of the German navy, could interest Hitler in their plans for naval economic warfare. Hitler still cherished unrealistic hopes of persuading Britain to ally with him, and, like the German Admiralty during the First World War, he was reluctant to provoke the United States by unleashing a ruthless campaign on its merchant marine. His priorities lay elsewhere, first with the invasion of France, and then with the attack on the Soviet Union. This meant that U-boat production was starved of the steel and labour needed to build a fleet of 300 submarines, which Döntiz argued would be necessary to have a decisive impact on Britain's imports.[10]

This was fortunate for Britain, as in the first year of the war the government discovered that it had badly miscalculated the negative impact war would have on shipping. During the First World War Britain had learned that fewer ships were sunk if they travelled together in convoys and the convoy system was introduced as soon as war broke out, but as all ships had to sail at the speed of the slowest vessel in the convoy this lengthened the journey time and meant that ships were often inconveniently re-routed. Chaos in the British ports made matters worse. The U-boats' control over the North Sea meant that all shipping activity from the eastern ports had to be diverted to the Clyde, the Mersey and the Bristol Channel. Lack of storage space meant that goods piled up on the quays.[11] Before the introduction of lend-lease Britain's shortage of foreign exchange meant that as many export goods as possible needed to be loaded on to the ships to pay for the imports Britain needed. Relations between the dock workers and their employers were poor, and disaffected workers loading and unloading the ships in a desultory fashion, with inadequate equipment, delayed the entire process. The unnecessarily long ship turn-around in British ports reduced imports by 10 per cent.[12]

This caused the first wartime food crisis. In 1939 the arrival of imports of bulk foodstuffs had already fallen far below expected levels and the government rapidly began to use up its stocks of wheat and flour. Wheat storage had been moved to the west of the country, as far out of reach of aerial bombardment as possible, but the transfer of shipping from the eastern to the western ports meant that Britain's poor east–west rail links could not cope with the volume of traffic. The Ministry of Food struggled to convey sufficient supplies to the eastern flour mills, some of which ran out of grist. This did not affect supplies of bread to the population but it made the government extremely sensitive to falling stock levels, which it blamed, wrongly, for the problem. In December 1939 the cabinet affirmed that a minimum of thirteen weeks' stock of flour was essential to ensure that the distribution of wheat did not break down. This figure failed to take into account that it was the way in which stocks were distributed around the country which had caused the problem, and was unnecessarily high. This early mistake reinforced a tendency to overestimate the necessary level of stocks and this was to be the cause of much bad feeling in the future between British and American food officials.[13]

Britain's war effort was entirely dependent on the continued arrival of imports for all of its oil, most raw materials for industry and more than half its food (in calories).[14] The sudden cut in shipping led to industrial shortages in the first year of the war, and in response planners allocated loads of steel to ships which normally carried wheat across the Atlantic. The heavy cargoes damaged many of these ships as they crossed the seas in stormy winter weather and this intensified the shipping crisis by taking ships out of action while they waited for repairs. The British shipbuilding industry had gone into decline in the 1930s and had not recovered by 1939. Lack of skilled workers, appalling relations between employers and their workers and run-down shipyards left Britain completely unable to repair these ships speedily and replace those which were sunk.[15] Thus, the German U-boats were only one factor among many which caused the shipping crisis. At the beginning of the war the disorganization at the ports, longer journeys and delays, and the inadequacy of the shipbuilding industry were far more significant in causing the shipping shortage.[16]

The crisis was compounded by military competition for shipping space. On 10 June 1940 Italy entered the Second World War and launched attacks from its colonies in Libya and Ethiopia on the British in North and East Africa. Churchill was determined to achieve victory in these campaigns and in order to do so he was prepared to compromise the quantity of civilian imports arriving in Britain. German U-boats had closed the Mediterranean to Allied shipping and all men and military supplies for the campaign had to make a 20,000-kilometre journey around the African Cape and up the Red Sea. In order to carry troops and their arms as quickly as possible, the fastest ships in the merchant fleet, the refrigerated ships, which normally carried frozen meat and dairy products, were withdrawn from carrying civilian cargoes and converted into troop carriers. Forty to fifty escort ships were also diverted from the protection of merchant shipping in the North Atlantic in order to escort them on their journey. Refrigerated ships were in extremely short supply and their diversion to military duties (combined with losses to enemy attack) resulted in a one-fifth reduction of the merchant marine's refrigerated capacity. This cut refrigerated goods coming into Britain by 30 per cent. At the end of the year dairy and fruit imports had reached only half of their target level and frozen meat imports had fallen drastically.[17] In addition, German bombing raids had 'made serious inroads into our refrigerated stocks of meat' and by January 1941 only two weeks' worth of reserve stocks of frozen meat were left in Britain's warehouses.[18] The meat allowance, which had risen in September 1940 following the slaughter of livestock as feed-grain imports were reduced, was cut back to one shilling's worth in March 1941. This amounted to about a pound of meat a week, although it could be stretched to a little more if choice cuts were avoided in favour of poorer cuts and offal.[19]

The autumn and winter of 1940–41 was the worst period for British food during the entire war. At the end of January 1941 Maggie Joy Blunt, a freelance journalist keeping a diary for Mass Observation, summed up the atmosphere of foreboding in Britain. 'It is as though we are beginning to see at last the slow subsidence of our river of wealth. We are not starving, we are not even underfed but our usually well-stocked food shops have an empty and anxious air. Cheese, eggs, onions, oranges, luxury fruits and vegetables are practically unobtainable . . . Housewives are having to queue for essential foods. We live on potatoes, carrots, sprouts, swedes, turnips, artichokes and watercress . . . the meat ration . . . was cut at the beginning of the month and now includes all the offal we could once buy without coupons . . . Prices are rising. We are warned by statesmen repeatedly that Hitler intends to invade us . . . The outlook really seems very grim indeed.'[20]

The low point in the food supply was exacerbated by initial problems in the newly created wartime administration. The Ministry of Food had not yet developed a clear strategy of how to feed the British population and in the first year and a half of the war tended to concentrate on one shortage at a time, rather than developing an all-encompassing policy. They responded to the meat shortage by encouraging consumers to stretch out the meat ration with oats. The price of oats was subsidized and an advertising campaign started. However, the Ministry failed to take into account the limited facilities for milling oatmeal and the result was a shortage of oats in the shops.[21] People were unable to eke out their protein allowance by turning to fish, as the closure of fishing grounds and military requisitions from the fleet had reduced the catch and made fish very expensive, much to everyone's dissatisfaction.[22] The public also complained vociferously about the disappearance of onions, the supply of which from continental Europe and the Channel Islands had been cut. The Ministry responded by controlling their price but this drove the few onions that were available under shop counters.[23] However, even in this difficult period it was only the meat ration which came under real threat and a solution was found. The fast refrigerated ships took the troops as far as South Africa where they transferred to slower vessels to complete their voyage to Egypt. The reefers (as refrigerated vessels were known) then sailed on to Argentina to pick up frozen meat supplies.[24] The U-boat threat was to get much worse, but the cut in the meat ration in early 1941 was the only time during the entire war that the Ministry was unable to provide the amount of food which it guaranteed the population through the ration. It was the government's failure to plan for a sudden and acute shortage of shipping, combined with the problems that surrounded the organization of the ports and transport, and, finally, the demands of the military campaign, which posed the greatest threat to civilian food supplies in the second winter of the war.

THE AMERICAN LIFELINE

In March 1941 Churchill took action. He set up the Battle of the Atlantic Committee, which concentrated its efforts on getting the docks running as efficiently as possible and released 40,000 men from the armed forces to work in the shipyards repairing the backlog of 800,000 tons of damaged ships.[25] At the same time the Americans introduced the lend-lease programme, which enabled Roosevelt to support the Allied war effort without actually taking the unpopular step of declaring war. One of the positive side-effects of this was that the British no longer needed to pay for their imports with exports and this allowed dock workers to concentrate on channelling imports into the country as quickly as possible before sending the ships on their way to pick up another cargo. Lend-lease also provided for the repair of British ships in American ports, alleviating the pressure on British shipyards.[26]

Moreover, lend-lease made plentiful supplies of American food available to the British. It enabled the Ministry to provide British civilians with sufficient quantities of meat to make the ration bearable, it provided tinned and dried foods and it supplied Britain with the cod liver oil and orange juice which allowed the government to transform the ration into an instrument of welfare provision for the needier sections of society.[27] In fact, Britain's reliance on imported foods was to turn out to be one of the strengths of the food-rationing system. Imports could generally be relied upon to arrive in the quantities that the Ministry had requested (the requests made allowance for the fact that a proportion of the imports would be sunk on their way to Britain). In contrast, the domestic food supply was often harder to manage as the yields of various crops, especially potatoes, were far harder to predict.[28] However, the reliance on American food was not without its problems. From March 1941 British food officials were caught up in endless wrangling with American officials over the quantities of food which Britain requested.

Immediately after the introduction of lend-lease the British made a mistake which would sour Anglo-American negotiations over food throughout the rest of the war. After the miserable food situation of the winter of 1940–41 Churchill decided to prioritize the import of foodstuffs over raw materials and acceded to Minister of Food Lord Woolton's request for a target of 15 million tons of food imports for 1941. This decision was definitely unwise. Churchill was often to prove a liability when he intervened in shipping allocation, and Woolton had failed to pay sufficient attention to actual food availability in America.[29]

The United States had not yet joined the war and rationing had not been imposed on the American consumer. In fact the Americans were enjoying a meat-eating bonanza. A juicy steak was the American meal of choice, regarded as perfect sustenance for a hard-working man. But rationing during the First World War, recession and inflation in the 1920s, followed by the Depression of the 1930s, meant that for several decades Americans had been denied the chance to indulge in red meat. Rising employment and wages in the war industries had given Americans the opportunity to satisfy their love of beef. The farmers responded by implementing the largest ever increase in livestock production. There was plenty of meat in the United States but American per capita consumption had risen from 126 pounds to 141 pounds a year and there were no extra supplies available to meet the increased British demands.[30]

The only foodstuff available in the United States in sufficient bulk to fill the cabinet orders to import 15 million tons of food was grain for animal feed: 276,000 tons of feed grains were duly shipped to Britain. Cabinet Office economists indignantly pointed out that beef cattle were eating shipping space while the blast furnaces of Britain were idle for lack of raw materials.[31] Feed imports were stopped but the food quota was not revised to allow for food to be replaced by raw materials. British officials feared that if they admitted that meat stock requirements had been set too high then American food officials would be discouraged from doing their utmost to find meat supplies to fill the cargo quotas. Meanwhile, those in charge of finding a cargo for the ships ended up loading the only foodstuffs that were available – wheat and sugar, neither of which the British needed in such large quantities. When the imports arrived in Britain the Ministry of Food stockpiled them. Illogically, this did not create a sense of abundance. The Ministry was always fearful that food imports might fall further and they sat on the stocks rather than distributing them, and in the end much of the food went to waste.[32] The most damaging consequence of the entire incident was that American food officials now regarded British estimates of their needs, especially their figures for necessary reserve stocks, with immense scepticism. Woolton's inflated food import quota had done nothing to improve the protein content in the British diet. This was achieved by increasing meat imports from Argentina. Instead it had created an atmosphere of mutual distrust between food officials which flourished once the Americans entered the war on 7 December 1941.[33]

FROZEN MEAT VERSUS MEN AND ARMS

As the war progressed the Ministry of Food found itself caught in a double bind. While insisting that it was doing a good job and that the people of Britain were being well fed, it needed to convince its allies that every effort must be made to supply Britain with food and that a drop in imports would be disastrous.[34] Towards the end of 1942 British food officials once again came into conflict with their counterparts in the United States over meat supplies. The dispute coincided with the worst period for Britain's shipping in the autumn and winter of 1942–43.

That summer Hitler finally prioritized the U-boat blockade of Britain, and increased submarine production meant that Admiral Dönitz took command of thirty new U-boats a month. His force was at last approaching the 300-strong mark that he had always argued was essential to success.[35] U-boat sinkings of merchant shipping began to bite deep. Meanwhile, Germany had attacked the Soviet Union and the United States had officially entered the war. Both Stalin and the American chiefs of staff were eager to open a second front against Germany on continental Europe. General George C. Marshall, the United States Army Chief of Staff, visited Britain in April 1942 to lobby for a cross-Channel offensive. This put enormous additional pressure on British shipping, as it required the build-up of American troops (and their supplies) in Britain in preparation for an assault. Each American infantry division needed a substantial 32,000 tons of scarce shipping to transport its men and all their equipment across the Atlantic.[36]

The Allies simply did not have enough ships to cope with the competing requirements to ship adequate civilian food supplies, raw materials to support the armaments industry, and enough military materiel and men to challenge German supremacy on the European continent.[37] As the German Naval War Staff smugly pointed out in October 1942: 'They *have* or *manufacture* enough, but they cannot transport enough for waging war, the economy, and their food supply.'[38] This was a limitation that American generals were unwilling to accept. Generals Marshall, B. B. Somervell, Commander of Army Service Forces, and Somervell's Chief of Transportation, C. P. Gross, were extremely unwilling to prioritize British civilian food imports over military shipping requirements. Somervell was ruthless. He would requisition shipping without any regard for civilian allocations and tried to establish his authority over the loading of all ships so that he could de-prioritize food imports whenever military needs arose.[39]

In the end it was clear to both the British and the Americans that at this stage in the war an invasion of France would have little chance of success and a compromise was reached over the question of a second front.[40] It was agreed to launch an invasion of North Africa from the west, codenamed Operation Torch. Even this smaller-scale military campaign exacted a high price in terms of civilian supplies. Cargo vessels had to be re-routed to provide military supplies, and naval escorts were diverted from merchant shipping to troop ships. It was decided that this could be compensated for by allowing the faster ships in the merchant fleet to sail fast and alone rather than in slow convoys. But this made them more vulnerable, and twenty-four ships sailing on their own were sunk that autumn. The preparations for Operation Torch cost Britain a 30 per cent reduction in imports in 1942.[41]

Between April and September 1942 Lord Woolton was forced to use stocks of canned corned beef to make up one-seventh of the meat ration. Butchers opened the large tins and then allocated portions of corned beef according to the shopper's entitlement. Editha Blaikley, who lived in Sussex with her sister and brother-in-law, commented on her corned-beef supper: 'It must go to the hearts of good butchers to weigh out tiny rations of corned beef instead of cutting up proper joints to their customers' tastes.'[42] In August the American War Shipping Administration suggested relieving some of the strain on British shipping by diverting Australian meat to feed the US troops who were building up in Australia and New Zealand ready for an attack on Japanese strongholds in the Pacific. America would compensate for Britain's loss of most of its frozen meat imports by filling the quota from American meat production. By switching meat imports on to the North Atlantic short haul, two and a half times more cargo could be carried in the same time that it took to transport one load from the southern Dominions.[43]

The Americans pledged to send an extra 263,000 tons of frozen meat and offal to Britain in 1942–43. This represented a mere 4 per cent of American frozen meat production and appeared to be a reasonable quota.[44] Meat production in the United States was at a record high. But competition for American meat had become even more intense since the Soviet Union and the United States had entered the war. In September 1941 Roosevelt's special envoy to Britain, Averell Harriman, had gone to Moscow to negotiate with Stalin over Allied assistance in the fight against Germany on the eastern front. Harriman enthusiastically supported the Soviets in their claim that they would be key in defeating the Wehrmacht and in November 1941 the United States began sending the Soviet Union 500,000 tons of lend-lease food per month. The Soviets, like the British, wanted concentrated high-calorie foods such as canned and frozen meat, cheese and eggs. Throughout 1942 the dangerous convoys through the Baltic to Murmansk and Archangel used up shipping space which would otherwise have brought imports into Britain, and was extremely costly in the long term as shipping losses on this route were almost 20 per cent.[45]

The United States army alone took 60 per cent of 'US choice' grade cuts of beef.[46] American civilians were also clamouring for meat, and voiced their dissatisfaction at the lack of high-grade meat in the shops. Catherine Renee Young complained to her husband in a letter in February 1943: 'Yesterday I didn't take any meat not because we didn't have any but because I'm sick of the same thing . . . we hardly ever see good steak anymore. And steak is the main meat that gives us strength. My Dad just came back from the store and all he could get was blood pudding and how I hate that.'[47] In the autumn of 1942 the United States government launched a 'Share the Meat' campaign. But posters depicting how the American family of Mom, Dad, Johnny and Suzy had been joined at their loaded dining table by a GI, a US marine, a Russian, a Briton and a Mexican, did little to persuade Americans to cut their meat consumption even by the small target amount of 11 pounds a year.[48] The United States failed to meet its targets for the meat exports it had promised. By January and February 1943 the Americans were delivering only half of the 40,000 tons of frozen meat a month which they had pledged.[49]

In November 1942 the British Ministry of Food began to panic. On 8 November the Allies launched Operation Torch and American and British troops landed on the shores of Morocco and Algeria. The troops needed resupplying continuously and the heavy and prolonged battle in Tunisia meant that supply requirements were unexpectedly high well into 1943.[50] Sinkings of merchant ships reached their peak in November 1942 with the loss of 700,000 tons of shipping to submarine attacks and another 160,000 tons of shipping destroyed by aircraft and mines.[51] About 9 per cent of all food shipments to Britain were sunk. Meanwhile, 155,738 cubic metres of frozen food, earmarked for export to Britain, rotted on the docks of the American east coast ports while waiting for shipping. The military cold storage warehouses were empty but Somervell would not allow them to be used for civilian export cargoes.[52] The Ministry of Food reminded both the British cabinet and United States food officials that without imports of flour, meat, fats and sugar Britain could only hold out for four to six months.[53] Lord Cherwell, Churchill's scientific adviser, warned 'we are trying with the equivalent of about one-third of normal fleet to feed this country and maintain it in full war production ... With all the extra military demands which have emerged ... it is not surprising that our imports, which have always been regarded as some sort of inverted residuary legatee, have suffered severely. But this cannot go on.'[54] In March 1943 the Ministry warned the War Cabinet that Britain was consuming three-quarters of a million tons more goods than it was importing and within two months reserves would have run dry.[55] Lord Cherwell sent a veiled threat to the United States military, who were busy planning to launch an invasion of continental Europe: 'we could hardly undertake new [military] operations, however favourable the opportunity, with stocks so near exhaustion'.[56]

Robert Brand of the British Food Mission in Washington was willing to concede to his American counterparts that Britain could manage short-term gaps in the supply. But, he argued, living under the threat of the German blockade, the British could not cope with a lack of guarantees or even the abandonment of a programme which ensured frozen and canned meat and cheese to Britain's workers. One of the strengths of relying on food imports was that in theory they were more predictable than agricultural harvests and therefore guaranteed the safety of Britain's food supply. The United States Minister of Agriculture, Claude Wickard, showed no signs of distress over the American failure to meet its meat export quotas and gave the impression, by referring to the British as 'companions in misfortune', that it was beyond his control to remedy the situation.[57] The American food administration was hampered by the fact that it did not fully control the meat trade and it had failed to build up sufficient stores of food stocks. This created repeated localized meat shortages in United States cities and meant that there were insufficient stores to draw upon to fill quotas for exports to Britain.[58] Officials were particularly worried that meat rationing might be introduced before they had managed to solve the problem of distribution and stocks in order to guarantee that they could honour the ration in the cities. But the real nub of the problem was the fact that American War Shipping Administration officials were suspicious of British claims, certain that the British were not being candid about their figures. They were firmly convinced that British meat stocks were, in fact, more than adequate. Jealous of British stocks, and distrustful of British protestations, American food officials had decided to implement a forced reduction in British reserves by refusing a certain quantity of the promised exports.[59]

There was some justification for the Americans' mistrust of British claims. A tendency to overestimate stock requirements and to err on the side of safety was built into the British food system.[60] But Wickard was cavalier when, in the face of British protests, he suggested that the meat diversion scheme with Australia should be abandoned. The British were not in a position to revert to their old sources of frozen meat. The Australians had already refocused their meat industry on canning, and a drought in South America meant that there were shortages in Argentina. Robert Brand eventually appealed directly to the White House through Harry Hopkins, Roosevelt's closest adviser and the chief administrator of lend-lease. Brand pointed out that while the amount of meat the United States had pledged to export represented just 2 per cent of what the Americans ate themselves, it represented 10 per cent of the British meat ration.[61] Hopkins agreed to divert frozen meat destined for the Soviet Union to Britain and pledged 250,000 tons in the future. The United States finally introduced meat rationing in March 1943 and this helped to ensure that this pledge was honoured and Britain was able to rebuild its stocks.[62]

Nevertheless, throughout the worst months of the Battle of the Atlantic British civilians were never confronted with the problem of hunger, let alone the spectre of starvation. In his memoirs Lord Woolton asserted that 'the country never realized how nearly we were brought to disaster by the submarine peril'. He then went on to tell the story of how five ships, all of them carrying bacon, were sunk on the same day. The Ministry of Food had to go to great lengths to make up for the losses. It diverted stock from Liverpool and sent special lorries to distribute around the country the load of the one ship which did arrive. Woolton ended the anecdote dramatically, 'We honoured the ration but it was a near thing.'[63] This is a tale of temporary shortage overcome, not catastrophe averted. In fact, the British, having become accustomed to rationing, were managing well. Laboratory technician Edward Stebbing was of the realistic opinion that although 'the first nine months of 1942 were perhaps the most depressing of the war . . . [and] some restrictions have proved irksome . . . I think we are better off than most other countries at war and that we could put up with much more inconvenience before we could be said to know what real hardship is'.[64] In January 1942, a year after concluding that the food outlook was grim, the journalist Maggie Joy Blunt reflected in her Mass Observation diary, 'we have been and are promised to be the best fed nation in Europe . . . A regular supply of butter, marg, cooking fat, cheese, bacon, sugar and tea arrives each week. As much bread and flour as I need. Custard powder and starchy things like rice, tapioca and so on can be had at intervals liberally without "points". The milk ration is helped out by tinned and powdered varieties. There are still plenty of tinned beans, carrots and soups. Potatoes, carrots and some greens at nearly normal prices. Eggs are very scarce. Meat is more difficult than it was, but there is often sausage meat and corned beef as substitutes and makeweights. Fruit is very scarce but I have had several lots of good apples from the greengrocer recently and occasionally dried fruit.'[65] In contrast to the devastating impact which the United States blockade had upon Japan, 'there was never any real likelihood that Britain would starve or even that the Allied land campaigns would be seriously handicapped, let alone halted, through losses at sea'.[66]

The most serious threat to the British food supply in 1942–43 was not the submarines but the American decision not to honour the promise to replace Australian meat supplies, combined with the US military's determination to prioritize military shipments over British civilian food cargoes. In May 1943 when, at 28 ounces a week, the newly introduced American meat ration was double that of the British, Somervell's Chief of Transportation C. P. Gross asserted that the British 'were still living "soft" and could easily stand further reductions'.[67] The British food officials in Washington usually won the arguments and managed to secure shipping space and cargoes but they never managed to convince the Americans that their requirements were legitimate.[68]

VICTORY IN THE ATLANTIC

Victory in the Atlantic was achieved through the enormous American shipbuilding programme which began to gather momentum in 1942. At his shipyards on the west coast Henry Kaiser applied the principles of mass production, learnt in the automobile industry, to ships. The Liberty ships were built to a standard design out of prefabricated pieces which were then welded together. This was much quicker than riveting.[69] Chauncey Del French and his wife Jessie moved to Vancouver, Washington, to work at the Kaiser shipyards, along with 38,000 others. They lived in makeshift housing at Ogden Meadows, one of the eight housing projects hastily constructed for the influx of workers. The cooking and bathing facilities were rudimentary, the walls so thin that they could hear their neighbours sneeze two apartments away.[70] Vancouver itself was transformed into a huge gambling den with queues of men waiting to play at the poker tables in every beer parlour. The food stores never closed.[71] Chauncey worked as a pipe fitter in the hectically busy shipyard. 'Blue prints were runoff twenty four hours a day, stopping for only a half hour for lunch and between shifts to clean the machine. The prints came off in a continuous run and then were cut, trimmed and folded to specifications. Girls on motor scooters carried folders full of blueprints to where they were needed.'[72] Jessie was a sweeper. This was a tough, dirty job, cleaning up the oil, water and bits of metal left behind by the construction teams before the painters moved in. 'Work never stopped on the ships. Early in the morning or late at night it was possible to hear the roar of construction at Ogden Meadows, five miles from the shipyard.'[73] Men and women lost their lives in accidents but Chauncey regarded their deaths as 'no different than [those experienced by] a fighting combat division in the front line'.[74]

The American shipbuilding programme is one of the most striking examples of the United States' immense productive powers, with which the Axis could not hope to compete. By the spring of 1942 it took just two months to build one ship and the average evened out at forty-two days.[75] In 1943 three ships a day were rolling out of the eighteen shipyards producing Liberty ships around the United States. Each ship represented 14,000 tons of shipping and could carry a cargo of 10,000 tons. By 1943, as fast as Dönitz and his crews could sink ships, Kaiser and his workers built them. By the beginning of 1943 new construction was producing 1.5 million tons' worth more shipping than was sunk at sea, and throughout 1944 the rate was sustained at a steady 2 million tons over and above the replacement of losses.[76]

Meanwhile, from mid-1943 the Allies began to beat back the U-boat threat in the Atlantic. The development of radar gave them a powerful new weapon, which denied the submarines their invisibility, and more up-to-date escort ships carrying better-trained crews improved the protection of convoys. The Allies learned that the most effective way of disposing of the submarines was to attack them by both sea and air as they approached their prey. Air cover from bases in Greenland and Iceland greatly improved the North Atlantic convoys' chances and the air gap was later filled by planes from aircraft carriers. The behind-the-scenes work of decoding enemy communications carried out by the team of academics at Bletchley Park meant that, bar a gap in 1941–42, the Allies always knew more or less where the U-boats were lying in wait. In October 1943 the US Admiral Ernest King relegated the U-boats to the category of a problem rather than a menace.[77]

Britain's food supply benefited. The percentage of imports lost to sinkings fell to 0.6 in the last quarter of 1943. More shipping was available for the long-haul routes to Australia and New Zealand and increased imports of mutton and lamb from the southern Dominions boosted British meat imports. By the end of the year the Ministry of Food had built up stocks of about 6.7 million tons of food (before the war stock levels had run at about 2.5 million tons). The food warehouses were so full that sugar and oilseeds had to be kept outside under tarpaulin.[78] More importantly, by the end of that year the Allies were in a position to take the military initiative and on 6 June 1944 they finally launched their attack on German forces in continental Europe and invaded France.

Despite the large food reserves which the Ministry of Food had managed to amass towards the end of 1943, British food officials were unable to relax. It could be argued that they developed a form of 'stocks hypochondria'.[79] This was inflamed by the battles they fought in the committee rooms of the Combined Food and Combined Shipping Adjustments Boards. Here discussions were guided by an unspoken hierarchy of food entitlement, which reflected the balance of power in the Allied world. The United States military effortlessly placed themselves at the pinnacle of this hierarchy. Next in line were American civilians. The United States food administration continually demonstrated its unwillingness to impose strict consumption restrictions on the American public, and even when rationing was introduced Americans received the most generous food allocations of any country in the world. It was no wonder that those responsible for feeding British civilians, who came fourth in line after their own military forces, felt that they needed to fiercely defend British civilian supplies against the encroachments of the US food officials.

In the closing years of the war it became increasingly clear that a severe food shortage threatened the world once the war was won. As the British tried to maintain supplies in order to preserve large food stocks against this contingency, Anglo-American wrangling continued. O. A. Hall of the Ministry of War Transport exclaimed in January 1944, '[the] squabbling that goes on as to how many ½ ships we have against so many ⅞ of a ship . . . simply drives one crazy, and . . . will cause us perhaps to overlook the really important things in life!'[80] Throughout 1944 the British constantly found American allocations contingent on their willingness to distribute their hard-earned food stocks to newly liberated Europeans.[81] These disputes were to continue long after victory in Europe when the Allies were indeed confronted by a worldwide food shortage of catastrophic proportions.

7

Mobilizing the British Empire

A populace three-parts starved is in no state to support armies or resist dangerous rumours. It may be a seedbed for devastating epidemics of disease which spread to the troops.

(Editorial in *The Statesman*, August 1943)[1]

Narratives of the Second World War frequently represent Britain as an island nation standing bravely alone against the Nazi domination of Europe. But Britain was by no means alone. Although the war is often represented as the beginning of the end for empire, in fact, between 1939 and 1945 the empire can be said to have come into its own as a 'formidable, efficient and effective power system, prepared to exploit its apparently limitless resources, and able to deploy large-scale fighting forces simultaneously throughout the world'.[2] The empire was presented at the time as pulling together in Britain's hour of need and there was undeniably a sense of this among its many peoples. After the fall of France, and Britain's ignominious withdrawal from Dunkirk, Australians rallied to the British cause and more than 100,000 volunteered for the armed forces between June and August 1940.[3] The chiefs of Bechuanaland drew on a deep-seated loyalty to the long-dead Queen Victoria to rally their men to fight for Britain, their traditional defender against the rapacious South Africa Company, and within six months had recruited 5,500 men for the British army.[4] Men from Canada, Australia, New Zealand, South Africa and Southern Rhodesia (now Zimbabwe) fought alongside Indians, Ceylonese, and Africans from Basutoland (now Lesotho), Bechuanaland (now Botswana), the Gambia, the Gold Coast, Kenya, Nigeria, Sierra Leone,

Swaziland, Tanganyika (now Tanzania) and Uganda. British military manpower came from as far afield as Mauritius and the Seychelles, and Britain had two important military bases in the empire, in Egypt and India, while the United States used Australia and New Zealand as their Pacific base.

There was, however, tension between this projected image of working together for a common cause and the exploitation inherent in the notion of empire. Throughout the later part of the war, for example, the Australians found themselves sacrificing lives in campaigns in New Guinea with barely any strategic significance. Yet they felt they had to continue to take an active role in the military campaign in order to claim their right to influence the post-war settlement.[5] In Britain, the Secretary of State pronounced that the colonies could contribute to the war effort by dispensing with unnecessary consumption, reducing imports and building up reserves of food. The Resident Commissioner in Bechuanaland responded that the majority of Africans were already consuming a bare subsistence diet, and that the poorer sections of society were already 'taxed to the limit'.[6] He found it difficult to see how the poor, who made up most of the African population, could find room to make extra sacrifices.

The war intensified the exploitative nature of colonialism. The British sold imperial assets to the Americans in return for lend-lease and used the empire to levy taxes and raise what amounted to forced loans. Government intervention in ordinary people's lives increased substantially. Africans were told what crops to plant and were forcibly recruited to work in tin mines in Nigeria and on white settlers' farms in Southern Rhodesia.[7] Before the war the philosophy that colonies should be self-supporting rather than a drain on the British government's budget perpetuated under-development. The financial resources to stimulate industrial growth and manufacturing were not made available. In 1940 a new attitude to colonial government was ushered in by the Colonial Development and Welfare Act which acknowledged the need for colonial administrations to facilitate the economic development of the countries in Britain's possession.[8] The under-development which the earlier policy had fostered ran counter to the needs of the war effort. First and foremost, colonial economic and industrial development during the war facilitated Britain's exploitation of its empire's resources.

War industries burgeoned in the colonies as the shipping shortage reduced the amount of imports arriving and gaps opened up in the market. Often the level of manufacturing remained basic, processing foodstuffs, providing materials for the building industry and small goods for the armed forces. In Nigeria, production of rubber, columbite (used in making metal alloys), coal, cotton, ropes, bricks and tiles, and soap all increased under the pressure of wartime shortages.[9] If industrial development was small-scale it still contributed to the greater war effort by making the colonies less of a burden on Britain. It also relieved some of the pressure on Allied shipping by supplying goods and food-stuffs to the military bases scattered across the empire. In India, industry adjusted to a war footing. The iron and steel company Tata expanded and began producing motor engines, parts for aircraft, land-ing craft and large quantities of munitions. Most of all, India produced billions of yards of cloth for the military and is said to have 'clothed the armies east of Suez', while it also supplied them with millions of blankets and tents.[10]

There were groups within colonial societies who profited greatly from the growth of these war industries. Indian industrialists and businessmen reaped phenomenal rewards as the fixed prices set by the government of India left them with a large profit margin, and many in India added to their incomes by evading taxation.[11] In some parts of the colonial world cultivators were also able to cash in as the drop in food imports created an insatiable demand for home-grown food. In the wheat-growing region of the Punjab the price of wheat rose by 300 per cent. Farmers paid off their debts, invested in irrigation and took up the high-status habit of sipping tea in the evenings. Villagers from Rampura in Mysore sold as much of their rice and sugar as they could on the black market and used their substantial gains to send their sons to school and to expand into shops and rice mills.[12] In Niumi, a district of the Gambia, women from the villages around the town of Bathurst grew extra tomatoes to sell in the market and became relatively wealthy, although the drastic cut in the import of consumer goods meant that there was little for them to buy.[13]

Throughout the colonial world the arrival of Allied troops, the recruitment of men into the armed forces, who sent remittances back to their families, and the creation of new and comparatively well-paid jobs led to unprecedented levels of cash flowing into previously impoverished economies. This increased the demand for consumer goods just as the shipping crisis led to their scarcity. Inevitably, this resulted in inflation. In Britain, strict price controls and rationing protected civilians from wartime inflation and, in particular, rising food prices. But colonial administrations showed themselves less willing to intervene to protect their more vulnerable subjects from the negative economic impact of war. The exception to this rule was the Middle East, where the Middle East Supply Centre (MESC) successfully reorganized trade and agriculture within the region and prevented food shortages from sparking off social unrest. The success of the MESC suggests that, given the political will, the British might have made a better job of harnessing the economic potential of the rest of the colonial world while at the same time protecting its inhabitants from hunger and starvation.

Elsewhere in the empire measures to stimulate domestic food production and maintain reasonable prices remained much more limited. British colonial administrations argued that it was impossible to impose rationing on food systems which were dispersed and beyond full colonial control. In Bechuanaland the British relied on a 'gentleman's agreement' with the food traders who ran the stores in the African reserves, that they would not increase prices unfairly. Of course, this was continually ignored. The purchase of items which no one wanted would be made compulsory by the traders on the purchase of a more desired foodstuff.[14] The Government Secretary wrote to the district administration in 1943 to complain that men in the armed forces were receiving letters from their wives at home complaining that they did not have enough to eat. 'In view of the allotments made to their wives by the men [out of their pay packets] it is difficult to understand this complaint unless traders in the Territory are making more profit than they should on essential foodstuffs.'[15] But the district claimed (probably fairly) that it could not afford the 'large and expert staff' which would be needed to enforce price controls.

The poor peasantry, artisans and the middle classes on fixed incomes suffer most in the face of inflation. Throughout the empire those who bought their food on a daily basis were faced by inexorable rises in the price of food, which meant that every day they were able to buy a little less to eat. For some the price rises deprived them of their ability to buy even the most basic of subsistence diets. Uncontrolled inflation in effect robbed them of their entitlement to food.[16] In the Gambia, American cracked wheat was brought in to replace imports of Burmese rice but those villagers without sufficient cash to buy ever more expensive food resorted to eating seed nuts.[17] The Scottish Livingstone hospital in Moleopolole, Bechuanaland, reported in 1945 that acute food shortages meant that the poorest people were living on roots and berries.[18] The number of the British empire's African subjects who died of wartime hunger is unknown. Starvation peaked with the arrival of drought in many areas in 1942 and there was famine in northern Nigeria and Tanganyika. Outside British Africa similar processes claimed the lives of 25,000 Cape Verde islanders and 300,000 Rwandans.[19]

The failure of colonial administrations to protect the vulnerable from the impact of wartime inflation was exacerbated by a policy which, in effect, exported food shortages to the empire. Britain was never as ruthless as Germany and Japan in its exploitation of its empire's resources, nor did it engage in deliberate acts of murder or dispossession, but its officials and politicians did act according to an unspoken food hierarchy which gave the lowest priority to the needs of the empire's colonial inhabitants. The exportation of hunger was perhaps at its most stark in tiny island colonies such as Mauritius.

For the sugar-producing island of Mauritius the shipping shortage spelled disaster. The island was left with a crop which nobody wanted and no means of making the money to buy in the food imports on which its inhabitants were completely dependent. And then in 1942, with the Japanese occupation of Burma, their main supplier of food disappeared from the world market. In exchange for buying up the bulk of the sugar crop the British government insisted that the islanders attempt to achieve some level of self-sufficiency, and stipulated that a third of the land under sugar be planted with food crops.[20] The islanders made a valiant attempt to replace their annual imports of 50,000 tons of Burmese rice with 49,000 tons of manioc, maize and sweet potatoes and some peanuts. A Nutrition Demonstration Unit toured the island showing the villagers how to make maize bread and prepare manioc flour. A combination of droughts, cyclones, a losing battle against weeds, and the despondency and malnutrition of those few labourers who were available, meant that the crops yielded far less than the islanders had hoped.[21]

The Allied shipping crisis of 1942–43 posed a real threat to the survival of the Mauritians. The fact that the United States was supplying less meat to Britain than it had promised meant that the Ministry of Food was lobbying hard for extra shipping to be sent to Argentina and Australia to replenish Britain's depleted meat reserves. The Anglo-American Torch landings in North Africa were diverting thousands of tons of shipping away from civilian to military supply. The pressure was also building up for an assault on continental Europe and this meant that yet more ships had to be allocated to the build-up of American troops in Britain. In response to these problems Churchill took the decision at the beginning of 1943 to cut by 60 per cent the amount of shipping travelling to the Indian Ocean.[22] This augmented British imports by about 2 million tons.[23] But the success of the British government in sheltering its own civilians from the worst consequences of the disruption of world trade came at a cost elsewhere in the empire. By March 1943 the cut in shipping meant that the Mauritians' food stores were virtually exhausted. The islanders were now at the mercy of the Combined Food Board of British, American and Canadian officials who controlled the allocation of food on the available ships. Shipping officials took pity on the islanders and diverted a ship carrying 3,000 tons of wheat to the island, and manioc starch from Madagascar helped eke out the food further, until later on in the year a consignment of flour arrived from Australia. In a stroke of exceptionally bad luck the ship carrying a long-awaited peanut processing plant was torpedoed when it was in sight of the island. Although the Mauritians did not starve to death, their wartime diet contained far too little fat and minuscule amounts of protein. Throughout the war Mauritius received not a single cargo of lentils and pulses, the main source of protein in the local diet. In contrast to the British who ended the war generally physically healthier, the Mauritians ended the war severely malnourished.[24] Although Britain did not set out with the explicit intention of exporting wartime hunger to their empire, this is in fact what happened.

THE MIDDLE EAST SUPPLY CENTRE

No sooner had the British finished evacuating their troops from Dunkirk on 3 June 1940 than Italy joined the war and launched attacks on the British in their African empire. Fighting in East Africa ended with British victory in Ethiopia in May 1941. But by then the Italians in Libya had been joined by the German Afrikakorps led by Lieutenant-General Erwin Rommel. Until June 1944 this was the only front on which the British and American armies engaged in combat with the Wehrmacht. The fighting ranged backwards and forwards across the western desert until Anglo-American landings in Morocco and Algeria in November 1942 helped to push the Axis forces, now under attack from the east and the west, back across the Mediterranean to Sicily.

Britain's military base for the North African campaign was Egypt, technically independent and neutral, but still treated by the British like the colony it once had been. The Middle East command based in Cairo was responsible for a vast area which encompassed the Mediterranean islands of Cyprus and Malta, and stretched from Turkey in the north down through Syria, Palestine, Iraq and Iran to the sheikhdoms of the Persian Gulf and on into the Sudan, Ethiopia and Somalia. It included six sovereign states, four British colonies, four League of Nations mandates (including two Free French regimes) and former Italian colonies, as well as the Anglo-Egyptian condominium.[25]

At the beginning of the war the supply situation in the Middle East was chaotic. Troops and equipment flooded into the area. The German U-boats had effectively closed the Mediterranean to Allied shipping and just a few convoys ran the gauntlet of air and submarine attacks in order to supply Malta. Everything was brought in around the Cape to the ports on the Red Sea, which were not equipped to deal with this level of tonnage. Their capacity was about 5.5 million tons and the military campaign alone needed at least 5 million tons of goods and equipment. To make matters worse, once the Italians in East Africa capitulated, the United States, which was not yet in the war, declared the Red Sea and the Gulf of Aden open again to American ships. In the spring of 1941 American businessmen, capitalizing on the wartime shortage of consumer goods, began sending cargoes of clothing and luxuries to the already overcrowded ports. Pyramids of crates filled with stockings, cosmetics and underwear built up on the quays next to tanks and crates filled with arms and military supplies.[26]

The military activity injected a steady flow of cash into the Middle Eastern economy, causing inflation. As food prices went up, merchants began to hoard grain, speculating on rising prices. The British could not afford to allow inflation and food shortages to spark off food riots, hunger or famine in the towns and cities behind the North African front line. Not only might this threaten the military campaign but it was politically inexpedient, given that Egypt and the rest of the Arab countries were not particularly well disposed towards the British. In the spring of 1941 the British managed to avert an Axis takeover in Iraq and were struggling to set up Free French regimes in Syria and Lebanon. There was a perpetual sense of unease surrounding Allied dealings with Egyptian officials, who it was felt would happily have swapped them for Axis masters. To make matters worse, the battle for North Africa began to go against the British. In April and May 1941 the Germans conquered first the Greek mainland and then Crete. Rommel began to drive the Allies back across the western desert. In July 1941 Oliver Lyttelton was appointed Minister of State in the Middle East. In a characteristic *tête-à-tête* dinner with Churchill – 'a small dinner table: a bottle of champagne: one servant: the Prime Minister in a boiler suit, fresh from his bath, hungry and relaxed' – the situation was made clear, and in particular it was impressed upon Lyttelton that 'the strain on our shipping was at breaking point' and a solution must be found.[27]

One of Lyttelton's most effective acts was to reanimate a modest operation known as the Middle East Supply Centre with a small office in General Headquarters, Cairo. In December 1941 he appointed a young Australian commander, Robert Jackson, to its head, having recognized in him a man of exceptional organizational talent.[28] The MESC remained an advisory body throughout the war but Jackson adopted 'an executive posture' and behaved as though he could impose his will on the various governments under the jurisdiction of Middle

East command.[29] He managed to get things done by fully exploiting his connections and good relations with his employer, Oliver Lyttelton (who in February 1942 returned to Britain as Minister of Production), General Sir Wilfred Lindsell, chief supply officer for the three armed services in Cairo, and Frederick G. Winant, who became the US representative on the Executive Committee of the Centre and facilitated co-operation in Washington.[30]

Under Jackson's direction the MESC expanded into a vast undertaking which attempted to meet the supply needs of this large but economically stagnant region from its own resources. When Lyttelton left Egypt in February to take up his new post as Minister of Production, Jackson lost no time in making good use of the gap before the next Minister arrived. He went on a tour, going from government house to embassy to cabinet chancellery to military headquarters and royal palaces, cajoling, persuading and pleading for co-operation from the various heads of the strange assortment of countries that came under the Middle East Supply Centre's purview. Jackson compensated for the Centre's lack of executive powers by fully exploiting his one sanction – control of shipping space – to pressure the various governments into accepting his suggestions.[31]

Jackson urged the various governments to co-operate with a number of initiatives, including a harvest collection scheme. Before the MESC took over there had been no central assessment of stocks and reserves for the region. Private merchants bought up local grain and then sat on stores waiting for prices to rise. The British military competed with local governments to buy as much locally produced flour as possible and all the various Middle Eastern governments competed for shipping space to bring in Australian and Canadian wheat and South African maize. Jackson set up a central body to collect the harvest and store it in a collective pool along with any other essential imports. In this way the region's entire stocks of basic foods such as grains, sugar, fats, oils, tea, coffee, canned milk, meat and fish, as well as other vital raw materials and equipment such as pharmaceuticals, coal and tyres, were controlled by the MESC. The military were included in the scheme to ensure that they no longer disrupted local markets by requisitioning food independently. Competition for shipping space between the different countries was thus eliminated and the ability of merchants to hoard goods and wait for prices to rise as they became scarce was curtailed.[32] Food and the various other goods were then allocated to those places most in need of them.

There was no time to lose in implementing Jackson's plan. From the beginning of 1942 the Middle East rapidly began heading towards a food disaster. In January 1942 the poor of Cairo stormed the bakeries and protested that the bakers were mixing sawdust with the bread flour.[33] There were food riots in Tehran, Beirut and Damascus, and workers in British camps in Iran went on strike over lack of food.[34] In January Lyttelton warned London that stocks of wheat from the poor harvest of 1941 were already running out. There were several months to be struggled through before the next harvest would again bring a flow of food into the cities. The British government took these warnings to heart and shipping was diverted to bring 350,000 tons of wheat into the area.[35] Jackson's friendship with General Sir Wilfred Lindsell, chief supply officer for the three military services in Cairo, now paid off as he was able to persuade Lindsell to cut the troops' rations and release small quantities of food from army stores on a daily basis. Rommel was approaching Cairo across the western desert and there was a mounting sense of panic among the British community. As the British prepared to evacuate to Palestine, General Headquarters began to burn their files, covering Cairo in a pall of smoke.[36] In the end, the military situation was saved by the second battle of El Alamein, which brought Rommel's advance to a halt. The risk of civilian food riots in Cairo was averted by the MESC's newly introduced food collection programme, which brought grain from that year's harvest into the city three weeks earlier than usual.[37]

The Centre created new chains of interdependence within the region which relied more upon trucks and trains than scarce ships, although for the transport of some products the Centre used the ancient sailing dhows of Zanzibar, which enjoyed an Indian summer before they were eclipsed in the post-war era by modern shipping. In Egypt rice was grown in place of cotton and fed to the Indian troops stationed in North Africa. The surplus went to Ceylon to replace Burmese rice. The reduction of cotton-growing in Egypt led to a shortage of cottonseed oil, which was instead supplied by the Sudan.[38] Australian and Canadian imports of wheat, upon which the Arabian Peninsula, Cyprus and

Palestine were dependent, were replaced by local imports of barley brought in by rail.[39] Ironically, given our present-day image of Ethiopia as a country of famine, it supplied wheat and millet to southern Arabia, Eritrea and Somalia and to the famine-stricken inhabitants of Hadhramaut in the Aden Protectorate.[40]

This alternative supply network was supplemented by attempts to innovate in agriculture, although the level of agricultural under-development in the region meant that virtually all the efforts of the Centre had to be focused on improving civilian rather than military food supplies.[41] Marshall Macduffie, an American employee of the Centre, was impressed by the ability of the British to rustle up experts whenever they were needed. The military allowed the Centre to analyse the professional qualifications of all the men and women serving in the area and, if they were likely to prove useful, re-assign them to work for the Centre. Businessmen, old colonial hands, experts in agronomy, would be tracked down and within a few days these men (and some-times women) would appear and set off to share their knowledge with the farmers of the region.[42] Irrigation schemes were set up in Syria, Lebanon and Iran, improved seed selection and the breeding and distri-bution of hybrid maize, good use of fertilizers, improvements in animal husbandry and mixed farming were all introduced under the auspices of the MESC.[43] The army was enlisted in the campaign for agricultural production and soldiers helped to bring in the harvest in Iran. In one of the Centre's most ambitious projects, troops were sent to the Sudan, southern Arabia, the Persian Gulf, upper Egypt, Ethiopia, Eritrea, Tripolitania and Kenya to lay poisoned bait in the breeding grounds of locusts. Where they were unable to deal with the locusts while they were still land-bound, the RAF and the Soviet air force (who almost never co-operated with civilian schemes), sprayed the swarms of this destructive pest from the air. In this way the 1943–44 crops were saved from the rapacious insect.[44]

Industrial production was also stimulated. Steel was made in Turkey and Egypt, Palestine made canteens and clothing for the army.[45] Every scrap of useful material was salvaged and recycled: tin from scrap metal, sulphuric acid from kerosene production for phosphate fertiliz-ers, sodium sulphide from oil refineries for use in the manufacture of leather.[46] One of the Centre's most valuable schemes to save shipping space was to convert the region's trains from coal- to diesel-powered engines. Every request for any article, from spare parts for tractors to rubber tyres, was first scrutinized by an army of office workers and checked against availability elsewhere in the region and its priority compared with a host of other requirements for imports. Macduffie recalled an MESC meeting to review import licences. 'Arrayed around a table were seven trim men in British Army uniforms. Before them were sheaves of papers . . . The meeting . . . resembled a tobacco auction held in low conversational tone. The papers were picked up and quickly passed down the line of uniforms with barely audible comments in the clipped rapid-fire speech that is characteristic for person-to-person communications among the British military.' At the end of an hour Macduffie had not understood a word of what had been said, but 'several hundred claims on Anglo-American resources, of vital importance to millions, had been processed'.[47]

The Centre succeeded in reducing the tonnage entering the region's ports by more than half.[48] A certain amount of smuggling still went on: Arab dhows took rice, fats, oils and tea from India to Iran and the sheikhdoms of the Persian Gulf. Iran was denied shipments of fats in 1942 because it was felt that this black market was supplying them with more than their fair share.[49] Even though the area was flooded with British soldiers in Egypt, Soviets and Americans in Iran and the Gulf, and French in the Levant – all with money to spend – and there was a shortage of consumer goods amid a wartime boom in demand, uncontrolled hoarding and runaway inflation were held in check. For the most part the MESC managed to protect the entitlement to food of the poor and those on fixed wages. There was famine in Hadhramaut in the Aden Protectorate and in British Somaliland, and there were bread shortages, but the food situation for most inhabitants of the region remained stable, and possibly even improved. About a third of the Egyptian rice crop was used to enrich the diet of the Egyptian population and infant mortality declined in the region during the war, which is usually an indicator of satisfactory nutrition.[50] The MESC was thus a success in that it maintained an important military region and sustained the military effort, while at the same time cutting down demands on shipping space and cushioning the indigenous population from the impact of war.

Officials within the MESC hoped that regional co-operation would continue after the war and the efforts of the Centre would provide a basis for the continued improvement of agriculture within the region. However, although the mechanization of farming continued in Iraq and Syria, and Egypt continued to show an interest in the improvement of its wheat and rice varieties, much of the work of the MESC in terms of improving fertilizers, seeds and livestock was abandoned for lack of resources. Without the pressure of war, western and local governments lost the political will to invest and co-operate.[51]

PROFITEERING IN EAST AFRICA

Although from the summer of 1941 the fighting was confined to the northernmost coastal strip of Africa, the hinterland of the British base in Egypt stretched all the way down the eastern side of Africa as far as South Africa. Throughout the war South Africa acted as a staging-post on the vital sea route around the Cape. It supplied the empire with men and gold, and the expansion of the country's industrial and manufacturing base meant that it was able to produce weapons as well as manufactured goods. South African foodstuffs were transported to Egypt through East Africa, which acted as a secondary military base. Southern Rhodesia developed an iron and steel industry and the country's industrial output tripled.[52] Rhodesian and Kenyan farmers grew maize, sisal and pyrethrum daisies. But there was no Middle East Supply Centre set up here. Instead, the war exposed the rapacious nature of colonialism. White settler farmers used the conflict to demand guaranteed prices for their food crops, and in Northern and Southern Rhodesia the settlers used unwillingly conscripted African labour to work on their farms. By 1945 the white settlers had managed to entrench themselves both on the land and in the colonial administration. But some African producers also found ways of capitalizing upon the rising demand for foodstuffs, and their post-war desire to continue to build upon their prosperity set them on a collision course with the settlers.[53] Meanwhile, measures to protect the entitlement to food of the poor and vulnerable were inadequate and in 1942 drought and crop failure resulted in localized famines in the region.

In 1939 the outlook of white settler farmers in East Africa was bleak. Every white farmer in Kenya was carrying an average debt of £2,000 and it was proving economically unviable for European settlers to establish themselves as farmers.[54] When the leader of the Kenyan settler community, Major Cavendish-Bentinck, travelled to London at the beginning of the war he was told that the Ministry of Supply might be interested in their tea and sisal but their maize and coffee crop were of no interest to Britain.[55] Nor did the government have any desire to prop up their failing enterprises. The situation was similar for white settler farmers in the Rhodesias. But when the war moved to Ethiopia in the summer of 1940 the settlers began to insist that their contribution to the war effort would be to increase agricultural production, and they began to pressurize their colonial governments to increase prices and provide them with loans. In Kenya their demands were resisted until November 1941, when the presence of British troops, Italian prisoners of war, Polish refugees, convalescent soldiers from North Africa and troops in training for Burma created a new and urgent demand for food. By 1943 the military were purchasing £1.5 million worth of meat, maize, vegetables, bacon and dairy products, virtually double what they had spent in 1941. Japan's capture of south-east Asia created demand for Kenyan sisal for rope-making and pyrethrum daisies, which were the basis for insecticides. These two crops earned plantation owners more than double the amount of money earned by sales of food to the military.[56] Sisal and pyrethrum were mainly sold to the United States, and so Kenyan farmers gained disproportionately good access to lend-lease farm machinery. Meanwhile, white settlers took advantage of the recruitment of colonial officers into the army to take over the colonial establishment, and created and ran production and supply committees, which enabled them to set the agricultural agenda within the colonies.[57] They put government loans and lend-lease equipment to good use, breaking in new land with the assistance of Italian prisoners of war and conscripted African labour, and used their new-found wealth to pay off their debts.[58]

In Northern and Southern Rhodesia European farmers struggled to find Africans to work on their farms. The Africans preferred to look for work in the towns or the South African mines, and higher wartime food prices provided those on the reserves with the incentive to farm for themselves rather than for a miserly wage. When the settlers pressed their governments to introduce African conscription for farm labourers they were told that conditions on the reserves were too precarious to justify further recruitment of men, and insisted that farmers must improve pay and conditions in order to compete for workers. The white farmers had no intention of improving working conditions on their farms and protested that the Africans were far more productive if they were working under European supervision and that African men should not be allowed to lie about on the reserves when the empire was under siege. The colonial administrators recognized these arguments as a call for exploitation dressed up as patriotism and resisted the settlers' demands until 1942, when a drought threatened food production.[59] The European farmers immediately capitalized on the administration's fear of food shortages, to insist on the implementation of wartime conscription for farm labour. The Secretary of State was told that unless Africans were recruited to bring in the harvest almost half the colony would be threatened by famine. Moreover, there were the difficulties that would arise in trying to feed the white civilians, 10,000 RAF personnel taking part in the Empire Air Training Scheme, and 6,000 internees.[60] Even before the Compulsory Native Labour Act was passed in August, the conscription process had begun. The Africans went unwillingly and it was widely reported that the approach of African messengers from the Native Department (who were used as recruiters) was 'a signal for all able-bodied men to scatter to the four winds'.[61] The farmers paid them only one shilling a day. The government paid the rest of their wages and supplied them with food. Altogether this provided white Rhodesian farmers with a subsidy worth £63,700.[62]

An indignant War Office investigator pointed out that the settlers were forcing the army to pay inflated prices for their goods. African farmers were paid substantially less for their maize. In Kenya the rate was 6s. 20 cents per bag compared to 13s. a bag for that of the settlers. White farmers argued that if the Africans were paid too much their lazy natures meant that they would reduce production. The colonial administration had been bullied out of taking the more reasonable and much cheaper course of action, which would have been to encourage peasant production rather than subsidize white-owned farms. The Native Commissioner for Mt Darwin in Southern Rhodesia 'found there was no convincing reason for compelling Africans to work on increased acreages for Europeans while their own acreage was reduced and settlers sold their maize at twice the price of African maize'.[63] In the maize- and peanut-producing region of Mrewa the commissioner wondered to 'what extent food production is being increased in European areas by removing 440 growers from the Reserves which between them sold 40,300 bags of maize and 12,700 bags of shelled nuts during the current year.'[64]

By agreeing to pay white farmers more for their crops and accepting their demands for African conscripted labour, the colonial governments reinforced labour migration and rural neglect. In the African reserves a number of factors came together to promote poverty, malnutrition and a rise in infant mortality. Concentration on the war effort meant that welfare and development schemes were neglected, the conscription of able-bodied men into the army and as farm labourers diverted too many men away from subsistence farming, while poor rains in 1942 led to crop failure on the reserves in 1943.[65] However, the Northern Rhodesian colonial administration did have some success in protecting the reserve population of women and children from hunger. In an attempt to avert hunger if millet crops should fail it was made compulsory for everyone to grow at least some extremely drought-resistant cassava. For the women on the reserves it made sense to adopt this new plant. It could be cultivated in the same fields in which they had previously grown their staple millet, and so it did not depend on scarce male labour to cut down trees and clear new land. Its drought resistance was prized and it had the added advantage that it could be grown as a cash crop. The government bought large quantities to feed the labourers it employed on road-building.[66] Those who grew cassava survived the droughts of 1942 and 1949 better than those who stuck to growing the traditional millet. But cassava's spread carried a price. The preparation of manioc flour is laborious, and as it is seen as women's work it substantially increased the workload of peasant women. Porridge made from manioc is also less nutritious than that made with millet, and in the long term the nutritional quality of the cultivators' diet declined.[67]

Elsewhere in East Africa the forced conscription of African labour to work on sisal plantations had a particularly baleful impact on the reserve populations. It is a sign of the British government's desperation but also of its cavalier attitude towards the lives of its colonial subjects that Tanganyikans were impressed into working, virtually as temporary slaves, on the sisal plantations. On at least one estate the men lived in appalling conditions with no housing, firewood or proper medical attention for the painful sores associated with sisal cutting.[68] Meanwhile, their families left behind on the reserves were reduced to hunger. Unfortunately, a government drive for more maize had persuaded the African farmers to plant corn, which is even more drought-sensitive than millet. Lack of labour and of rain in 1942 resulted in a devastating fall in the harvest. The dearth of food could not be compensated for with the usual imports of Burmese rice, and Churchill's diversion of shipping from the Indian Ocean meant there was no hope of emergency imports of food. Famine deaths were confined to the area of Ugogo but hunger was widespread. Even the workers on the sisal plantations had their ration of one kilogram of meal a day reduced to 316 grams. Children were sold in return for grain. This is remembered in Tanganyika as 'Europe's famine'.[69]

By caving in to settler demands the colonial East African governments failed to implement policies which secured the benefits of higher wartime prices for food for African farmers. Nevertheless, the official price, even for African maize, doubled, and many Africans made their own efforts to ensure that they were able to participate in the wartime bonanza. Some simply side-stepped the government and evaded controls by transporting their maize along pre-colonial trade routes at night. Black market maize fetched an even higher price than that paid to the settlers by the government purchasing boards.[70] Whether East Africans went hungry depended on the ways in which the war disrupted their local economy. In areas where there was road-building, a disproportionate number of wage labourers compared to farmers led to a tendency towards over-selling and later hunger. In other areas the peasants held back food, planning for food shortages, or found that even if they produced a surplus of food they had nowhere to sell it.[71] The herders of livestock were probably the worst hit as the army's insatiable demand for meat meant that they were forced to sell their cattle at prices well below the market value. The army sometimes paid even less than in the worst period of the Depression, and the stock routes were too well policed to allow for the growth of a substantial black market.[72]

The most fortunate were those with ready access to markets. Around East Africa's towns peasant production diversified into mixed farming.[73] In Kenya, the African districts of Nairobi were filled every day with women from Kiambu selling vegetables and charcoal for a good profit. The Kikuyu sold their vegetables to army-run vegetable-drying factories where their potatoes and beans fetched double the pre-war prices. In the districts of Nyeri and Embu 11,000 families were issued with seeds and their planting schemes were organized by the Department of Agriculture.[74] Even the famine in Kenya's Central Province in 1943 was a source of profit to the Kikuyu tribe. The starving people of Machakos had plenty of money. Each month the soldiers fighting in the war sent home large remittances and their hungry families could be seen on the roads each day, fetching food from the Kikuyu farmers. 'The District Commissioner estimated that during the three worst months the Kamba tribe of Machakos must have spent at least £100,000 each month on food in Kikuyuland and Kitui.'[75] The Kikuyu were able to make seven times the price offered by the Maize Control Board for their crops, and four and a half times more money than the white settlers. The entrepreneurial saved up their money and invested in lorries and shops, and the newly prosperous disrupted social hierarchies within the reserves as they challenged the traditional authority of chiefs and elders and sought political representation and a voice in the colonial regime.[76]

By 1945 white settlers had infiltrated the colonial bureaucracies and were the owners of fully capitalized farms. Their numbers were swelled in the immediate post-war years by the arrival of young men intent on escaping Britain under a Labour government.[77] Determined to take advantage of their new, much stronger position, the white settlers resented the economic challenge represented by the African protocapitalists thrown up by the war. As soon as hostilities had ceased Kenyan settlers reverted to the old arguments of the 1930s, claiming the African farmers were denuding the land and they began pushing for the removal of the now relatively prosperous vegetable-growing African squatters* from their farms. This set post-war Kenya on a

* The squatters were Africans who were allowed to live on and farm part of a white farmer's land in return for labour.

course towards internal conflict which came to a head seven years later with the Mau Mau conflict, when Kikuyu farmers rose in protest against repressive measures which deprived them of their land.[78] A side-effect of this conflict was the consolidation of Kikuyu land-holdings which provided the basis for the 1950s 'agricultural revolution'. Vegetable-planting schemes like the one associated with the long-closed military vegetable-drying plant were revived. African farmers were reorganized into high-productivity cash-crop farming and began growing European vegetables on a large scale. This is why Britain still imports fresh beans by air from Kenya.[79]

In the Rhodesias the political power of the settler communities had expanded to such a point that they were able to push through the creation of a Native Labour Supply Commission which recruited African labour to work on white farms right up until the 1970s, reinforcing the neglect of African farming.[80] The bitter consequences of the resentments this caused are still being felt today in Zimbabwe (as Southern Rhodesia was renamed), where Robert Mugabe's 'land reform programme' has dispossessed white farmers, and raging inflation has left the African population destitute, ravaged by hunger and a cholera epidemic in 2008.

WEST AFRICA AND THE DOLLAR DEFICIT

In 1939 West African farmers were faced with the same depressing prospect as East Africa's settler farmers: their crops (cocoa beans, palm produce and peanuts) were surplus to requirements. In 1939 America and Britain already had one year's worth of cocoa beans in storage and the farmers' third best customer, Germany, had disappeared from the market.[81] Cocoa beans came very low on the shipping officials' list of priorities and the farmers were faced with the prospect of harvesting a virtually worthless crop. In order to prevent the farmers from facing bankruptcy the British government bought up that year's supply, much of which it destroyed. In 1941 the West African Cocoa Control Board was set up to organize the bulk buying of cocoa, and from 1942 it dealt with other products and became the West African Produce Control Board.

However, the immense wartime demand for food and the Japanese capture of south-east Asia revived the demand for West African foodstuffs, which in 1942 were suddenly seen as an untapped and valuable resource, as were the region's supplies of tin, bauxite (for aluminium), iron ore, rubber, cotton and sisal.[82] A Resident Minister for West Africa was appointed and for the first time a co-ordinated economic policy was applied to Britain's four West African territories – the Gold Coast, Sierra Leone, the Gambia and Nigeria. The rising demand for foodstuffs meant that the Boards were able to sell West African produce for a good profit. But West African farmers benefited little from the revival of the food trade. The Boards continued to pay the producers low prices while the rising profits were channelled into the coffers of the British government, which used them to pay off some of Britain's debt to the United States.

Before he set off to take up his post as Resident Minister for West Africa in June 1942 Lord Swinton met with the Minister of Food. Lord Woolton told him that the nutritionists had warned him that the British could not cope with a cut in their fat ration. He added, 'It all depends on what you can do in West Africa whether we can maintain it or not.'[83] Before the war Nigeria had been governed according to the 1930s' philosophy that expensive modernization projects were not to be encouraged. Governor Sir Bernard Bourdillon had been implacably opposed to the rationalization of agricultural production and had vetoed the introduction of European-run plantations and even the import of hand-presses to ease the task of processing palm kernels. Although after 1940 he had adopted the new wartime approach and had approved the construction of a Pioneer Mill and the distribution of hand-presses for palm kernels, the backward state of the industry meant that an increase in palm oil supplies in 1942 depended entirely upon villagers stepping up production.[84]

Palm oil is obtained from a kernel inside the stone of the palm fruit. In West Africa the job of extracting the kernel was done by women and children who would crack the stone open, using a rock. In an effort to stimulate villagers into greater palm kernel production, collecting stations were set up across West Africa, and competitions were organized to see which school could crack open the most stones and extract the kernels. Lord Swinton visited one such school in a remote part of eastern Nigeria where, to help them along with the work, the teacher and pupils had invented a song with a refrain which ran along the lines that they were 'cracking Hitler on the head'.[85] Given that it took up to a million of the feather-light kernels to make a ton in weight, West Africa's wartime export of over 400,000 tons of kernels a year represented an incredible cracking effort on the part of its women and children. British housewives had West African villagers to thank for their weekly supplies of 2–3 ounces of margarine which supplemented the butter ration of 4 ounces.[86] In his memoirs Swinton proudly related that 'we won the battle of the fat ration'.[87]

The palm oil produced in Nigeria was marketed through the West African Produce Control Board, originally set up to deal with the problem of excess cocoa beans. The demand for West African oils was 'virtually bottomless' and a wartime use was found even for cocoa beans, which were sold to the United States for the production of emergency chocolate rations for the armed forces.[88] The sale of Nigerian cocoa alone yielded £2,700,068. Similar sums were made on Nigeria's other export crops, including palm oil.[89] A substantial fund accumulated in British government hands, which it used to repay American loans. The Boards had been set up at the beginning of the war in a benevolent attempt to save colonial farmers from financial ruin. They provided the merchants and farmers with stability throughout the war but at consistently low prices, which were set at a minimum below which the government might have faced political unrest. But they were far below the market prices of the later years of the war and rose much less than the cost of living.[90] Thus, the producers were cheated of the profits created by the eventual wartime boom in demand for food. This was an iniquitous way of raising a 'forced loan' from West African farmers.[91] And when the funds from the marketing boards were eventually reinvested in the region they were used to develop industry and gave little back to farmers.

The post-war decision to carry on the work of the Boards continued the exploitation of West Africa's cultivators. In post-war Gambia, where wartime shipping shortages had severely cut down the imports of consumer goods, the population were asked to carry on making reductions in imports. The Gambians had to put up with a lack of even the most basic consumer items such as cotton cloth, soap, matches and cigarettes. At the same time they were asked to increase production of their main cash crop, peanuts, which Britain sold to America to help reduce the nation's dollar deficit.[92] This pattern of using colonial cash crops to sell to the United States and solve the on-going problem of the balance of payments was replicated across Africa. This pushed Britain's post-war colonies into a position whereby cash crops became their only purchase on the world economy. At the same time post-war protectionist policies, which created trade barriers around the developed world, meant that these under-developed countries were unable to export enough of their agricultural goods to boost industrial growth.[93] When West African states inherited the marketing boards, these were an unfortunate gift to governments which tended to exercise extreme authority over their citizens.[94] A competitive produce trade in West Africa and fair payments to West African farmers were effectively stifled by this legacy, until Nigeria closed down the state marketing of cocoa in 1986.[95]

THE BENGAL FAMINE

India was for the British as important a military base as Egypt. It was the empire's only significant source of military manpower in the east and supplied a large proportion of the soldiers who fought against the Japanese on the Burma front. The only reason the Japanese advance had ground to a halt on India's eastern border was because Japan simply could not fight the Chinese, the United States and the British in India all at once.[96] Nevertheless, Japanese military commanders consistently harboured a desire to invade India and bring the British empire crashing to its knees. In 1943 India was the supply base for the Chinese Nationalists, cut off from the world by the Japanese blockade, and British preparations were under way to launch a military campaign to re-take Burma and Malaya.

Despite India's strategic importance, the Indian government made lamentably little effort to maintain economic stability within the colony, particularly in comparison to the work of the Middle East Supply Centre, which exercised far less power. Indeed, in 1942–43 the Indian government presided over the development of a nationwide food short-age, which in Bengal developed into full-scale famine. At least 1.5 million Bengalis died during 1943–44, when food scarcity was at its height. Altogether about 3 million may have died as a result of the famine as epidemics of smallpox, cholera and a particularly nasty strain of malaria which killed its victims within six hours swept through Bengal, killing those weakened by malnutrition.[97] This was a death toll greater than that for Indians in combat in both the First and Second World Wars, and it overshadows the death toll of 60,000 British civilians killed by aerial bombing.[98] If the Middle East Supply Centre was a British success story, the failure of the colonial government in India to protect the sub-continent's inhabitants from the inflationary consequences of war was, in the words of Leo Amery, Secretary of State for India, 'the worst blow we have had to our name as an Empire in our lifetime'.[99]

'No words can describe the plight of the destitute of Loharjang . . . Most of the children were mere skeletons. A young girl of 17 had lost the use of one hand and could hardly speak. The old people were incessantly crying and falling at our feet . . . In the afternoon we crossed over to the other side of the river where I saw three corpses lying uncared for: women and children were squatting or lying pell-mell in slush and mud all through the narrow streets . . . an old woman who could not walk had managed to creep to the [gruel] kitchen but she could not creep back to her hut and was lying on the road.'[100] These were the scenes that met the reporter for the *Hindustani Times*, K. Senthanam, as he toured Bengal in 1943.

The government of India, which was composed of Indian politicians as well as British officials under the Viceroy Lord Linlithgow, showed a complacency towards the problem of wartime food supplies that was both irresponsible and callous. Once tragedy had struck in Bengal in 1943 Ian Stephens lambasted the government in an editorial for the Calcutta newspaper *The Statesman*: 'Blame for the extremely grave situation rests heavily on the Government of India. We find ourselves amazed by their lack of vision . . . in this vital matter. From the knowledge in their possession risk of a food shortage and rocketing prices should have been discernible to an alert eye within their organization from the moment of Japan's belligerence

... yet a full year was allowed to elapse before a Food Department at the Centre was even set up ... [B]y mumbling that food shortage did not exist, they willed themselves into belief that the dread spectacle would vanish.'[101]

At the beginning of the war the government was naively pleased that rising food prices were benefiting the peasants, whose incomes had sunk pitifully low during the Depression. In the wheat-producing Punjab cultivators enjoyed a new prosperity. The Indian Civil Service officer Malcolm Darling noted that the increase of silver jewellery on the women's arms and ankles was a sure sign that the peasantry were growing wealthy.[102] But the greatest beneficiaries of inflation were the food merchants and traders who began to hoard grain, speculating on ever higher prices. Although pre-war India exported wheat, it imported rice from Burma. When Burma fell to the Japanese in the spring of 1942 India lost 15 per cent of its rice supply and there was a scramble for rice. Prices rose as traders competed to buy up stocks and the market then froze as speculators sat on their stores, waiting for inflation to push prices higher. Bombay, Travancore-Cochin and Bengal were worst hit by the loss of Burmese imports as they depended on them the most.[103] In 1941 the government had taken what turned out to be the 'tragic step' of handing responsibility for food administration over to each province. When Burmese rice imports dried up most provinces reacted with what Justice H. L. Braund, Regional Food Controller for the Eastern Areas, later termed 'insane provincial protectionism'.[104] The British governor of Madras banned rice exports from the province and other provinces followed suit.[105] The machinery of trade in food was strangled; in particular, flows of food from surplus to deficit areas within the country came to a halt.[106]

Throughout 1942 the government of India did not have a clear picture of the food situation and it was in any case reluctant to act decisively. The government lacked the self-confidence to impose its will on the Indian upper classes. Cautious of provoking political dissent, the government shied away from imposing heavy taxation, price ceilings and consumption restrictions on India's business and industrial classes, on whose collaboration it depended for the expansion of Indian industry and manufacturing, which were making a significant contribution to the war effort. Given that the government did not exert its powers to impose stringent price controls to clamp down on inflation, it should have done more to protect the vulnerable from its consequences and in particular to cushion them from rising food prices.[107] This was particularly important given that a considerable section of the population was already living at a bare subsistence level.[108] Rationing would have entitled the worst hit to at least a minimum of food. But Justice H. L. Braund unwisely advised the government that rationing could not be practically implemented. He argued that the administration of a complicated and largely unregulated trade would be beyond the government's capabilities.[109] By April 1942 food queues had become a feature of India's larger towns. The people would wait patiently for *days* in the hope that supplies would not run out before they reached the head of the line. Prices in Bombay rose by 25 per cent just six weeks after the declaration of war.[110] As the conflict wore on the middle-class clerks and administrators who worked for the colonial bureaucracy found they could afford less and less meat, fish and milk, despite the fact that they were spending an increasingly large proportion of their income on food.[111] In the countryside the wages of agricultural labourers and artisans remained virtually static but food prices climbed every day.

The Quit India Movement, which began in August 1942, distracted British administrators from the growing seriousness of the problem. Angered by the British government's offer of only limited self-government in return for Indian support during the war, Gandhi and the Indian National Congress called for immediate independence and for a civil disobedience campaign until it was granted. The British felt they had been stabbed in the back in their moment of greatest need and they responded harshly. The Congress leadership were imprisoned and Indian resisters encountered brutal repression. The police and army opened fire on demonstrations. In Bengal the government lost control in parts of the district of Midnapur, and army and police reprisals included burning down houses, raping women, and shooting and imprisoning troublemakers.[112] Many officials adopted an unsympathetic attitude towards Indian complaints of food shortages and blamed the problem on Congress politicians who had urged producers and merchants to withdraw their support from the government by closing their shops.[113]

It was not until December 1942 that the government of India finally woke up to the fact that they were facing an extremely serious food crisis, although they were still unaware that famine conditions were building up in Bengal. The newly created Food Department set about reviving the flow of food around the country by buying up food in surplus provinces to distribute to deficit areas. Unfortunately, the only grains available were wheat and millet, both of which rice-eating people lacked the means to prepare and which they found relatively indigestible. Therefore this did little to solve the acute rice shortage.[114] It was estimated that India as a whole was short of a million tons of food and the Viceroy, Lord Linlithgow, asked for 200,000 tons of grain to be diverted to India by April 1943, and 400,000 tons thereafter.[115] But the shipping crisis was at its height and with the failure of the United States to meet its meat import quotas, as well as Operation Torch in North Africa, Britain was struggling to maintain civilian food supplies. If Britain were to meet India's request, shipping and supplies would have to be withdrawn from either British soldiers fighting the Germans or British civilians making do on corned beef.

The immediate response to Linlithgow's request came from Lord Cherwell, scientific adviser to the British government and a friend of Churchill. He replied (incorrectly) that 'India's yearly production of seventy million tons of cereals made it self-sufficient in grains'. He could not see how 'India's larger populace would derive . . . comfort from aid that disproportionately deprived the British people of ten times the sustenance'.[116] The War Cabinet as a whole was hostile towards India and its demands, but Churchill in particular despised Indians and their independence movement. Ill, and irritable, Churchill was not inclined to be generous with India at Britain's expense. He is said to have claimed that Indians had brought these problems on themselves by breeding like rabbits and must pay the price of their own improvidence.[117] When, at the beginning of 1943, he ordered a 60 per cent cut in both military and civilian shipping to the Indian Ocean, he asserted, 'There is no reason why all parts of the British Empire should not feel the pinch in the same way as the Mother Country has done.'[118] India was ordered to live on its stocks and with this instruction Churchill exported shortages within the empire's food system to India.

The first signs of famine appeared in the Bengali province of Midnapur at the end of 1942. After the Japanese invasion of south-east Asia, boat- and rice-denial schemes had been implemented in the coastal areas. Most of the boats and rice stores in the area were removed. This was intended to deprive any invading Japanese of the means of transport and suste- nance and was an over-zealous attempt to learn the lessons of Burma when the British authorities had failed to destroy boats which were then used by the invading Japanese.[119] This had the unfortunate effect of denying the local populace both transport and sustenance. When a cyclone hit the area and destroyed the rice crops in October 1942 the people descended into misery and signs of starvation began to appear.[120]

Throughout 1942 the cost of rice in Bengal had been steadily mount- ing. Before the war the price for one maund* of rice had been 9 rupees. By March 1942 one maund of rice sold in some districts for 100 rupees.[121] The Bengali coalition government, under the leadership of the Muslim politician Fazlul Huq, proved themselves as incompetent as the central government at dealing with the problem. In an attempt to prevent further inflation they fixed rice prices in July but the price was set too low below prevailing market prices and supplies of rice disappeared from the market.[122] Tarak Candra Das, an anthropologist at Calcutta University, was visiting his home town of Brahmanberia in Tippera when the price controls were announced. 'A few petty dealers of rice were forced to part with their goods at the controlled price, either by the police or the public . . . [T]he effect of this on the market was disastrous. Petty dealers stopped coming to the market and the permanent shops had no rice. Thus a market where hundreds of maunds of rice used to be sold every day could not offer a *chatak*† even. One cannot think of it nor imagine. The consequence was that men of all positions had to go to the villages to purchase rice from the farmers and petty dealers and at once the price rose by 10 to 20 rupees in a few days.'[123] It quickly became clear to traders that the government had neither a reserve of grain with which to flood the market, thus bringing down prices, nor effective measures in place to punish those who breached the controls. Consequently, the black marketeers lost all inhibitions and the government all credibility.

* About 86 pounds or 37 kilograms.
† About 2 ounces or 50 grams.

Most economic and historical examinations of the causes of the Bengal famine take the view that there was plenty of food in Bengal safely stashed away in the village stores of landlords and traders, all of whom were waiting for inflation to push prices higher.[124] New research, using figures for the yields at the rice research stations in the province, which are the only hard figures of actual yields available, suggests, however, that the winter rice harvest of 1942 had in large measure failed. The unusually warm, humid and cloudy weather, together with the cyclone in October, had spread the spores of a fungal disease throughout the region. There may have been as little as half the usual amount of rice available in the Bengal food system. This would provide an alternative explanation as to why landlords and farmers with rice stores were in no hurry to release them, as they knew that there was a real and frightening shortage of rice in Bengal.[125] Whether it was the product of greed or anxiety, by the end of 1942 the Bengali rice trade had frozen. There was not enough food on the market and there was no hope of receiving extra supplies of food from outside India.

The provincial government focused its attention on protecting the food supply for Calcutta. The city had been bombed by the Japanese four times and the working population were nervous. Calcutta, so close to the front line with Burma, could not be allowed to go under. The stocks of the city's traders were seized and special shops were set up in factories which supplied the industrial workers with subsidized food. Industrialists, unable to get rice any other way, often bought their supplies on the black market, fuelling the price rises. Special 'control shops' sold food to the poor at low prices and government markets supplied the middle classes. In the scramble to find 20,000 tons of rice each month for the city the needs of the rural population were ignored.[126]

District officers watched helplessly as the rural population began to die of starvation. By 1943 famine had spread throughout the whole of Bengal. The schoolmaster Bisewar Chakrabati wrote to the Bengal Relief Committee describing the scenes he witnessed in his home village. 'The whole population seems to be moving silently towards death. Men have neither the capacity nor the energy even to try to live. A stupor seems to have overtaken all.'[127] The traditional strategy of selling children for food no longer worked as nobody wanted extra mouths to feed. Instead, girls were sent 'to a merchant or a Muslim *jotdar* [large tenant farmer] for a night. Thus they can procure a few annas or a few chataks of rice.'[128] In a group of villages which contained 592 families in 1942, 90 families died during the famine. All of them were labouring families dependent on cash incomes, and simply did not have enough money to buy extortionately expensive food.[129] The rural middle classes were also hard hit. The high-caste Bengali author H. K. Gupta wrote to a wealthy merchant in September 1943 explaining that his family had sold all their valuables and clothes. They were now naked and dying 'by inches', but 'on account of my position in society' he did not feel that he could 'beg from door to door [or] . . . stand on the roads with the beggars'.[130] Patronage and charity, which usually acted as a safety net, broke down. If labourers and artisans asked to be paid in rice rather than cash landlords simply stopped employing them.[131]

A few energetic district officers, wealthy Indians and charitable organizations in Calcutta began relief operations on their own initiative, but without a substantial influx of grain there were limits to what could be done. The Bengal government did not know what to do, as injecting cash into the economy did nothing to draw forth hidden stocks of food and they did not have access to sufficient quantities of food to enable them to distribute meaningful food aid. The other provinces, concerned by food shortages of their own, were reluctant to send rice supplies to Bengal. Their meagre contribution amounted to just 17,000 tons, under one month's worth of food for Calcutta.[132] Even the Punjab, which had plenty of food, showed no empathy with the plight of the Bengalis and concentrated on protecting the profits of Punjabi farmers. In June 1943, when the famine was at its height, the Revenue Minister of Punjab, Sir Chhotu Ram, instructed his farmers not to sell their grain to the government under a certain price.[133] Frustrated by their inability to open up the market, the government of Bengal persuaded the government of India to re-introduce a free market in rice and open the borders. All this succeeded in doing was spreading the problems of Bengal into the neighbouring provinces of Bihar, Orissa and Assam.[134]

In August the government of India finally began to send in trainloads of food from its central stocks and the provincial government set up gruel kitchens. These were soon surrounded by men and women too weak to walk backwards and forwards to the kitchen, who lay 'about it on the cold ground . . . without any clothes . . . death soon relieves them of all sufferings'.[135] The kitchens distributed a soup made of inferior grains such as millet, and a few vegetables, and probably did more harm than good. Doctors treating famine victims discovered that 'a gut habituated throughout life to rice, and then enfeebled by weeks of privation, when switched to a diet of the rougher "up-country" grains simply will not take them and an uncontrollable flux ensues'. This was eventually recognized as a clinical state and 'famine diarrhoea', often caused by the aid kitchen gruel, caused yet more deaths.[136]

Famine victims began pouring into Calcutta in the summer of 1943, a 'vast slow dispirited noiseless' army of apathetic skeletons.[137] They would sit and weep for food even when food was given to them. 'Bewildered, finding no help, they squatted in the by-ways and grew feebler and lay down and after a while died.'[138] Many died on streets within sight of shops stocked with food. It became apparent to Ian Stephens, editor of the Indian newspaper *The Statesman*, that the Indian and British governments were doing everything they could to use wartime censorship to suppress the news of the famine. Indignant, Stephens ran an eight-week campaign against the authorities, harassing them with attacks in editorials, letters and using photographs of the dead and dying on the streets of Calcutta to publicize the plight of the Bengalis. In October the Secretary of State for India finally acknowledged the famine in a speech in Birmingham.[139]

It was only with the appointment of Viscount Wavell as Viceroy in September 1943 that decisive action was taken. Wavell's brief was to sort out the food situation before it threatened military strategy. The military chiefs of staff had warned the War Cabinet that 'unless the necessary steps are taken to rectify this situation, the efficient prosecution of the war against Japan by forces based in India will be gravely jeopardised and may well prove impossible'.[140] The famine was causing trouble among the troops who were destined to re-take Burma, 60 per cent of whom were Indian. Bengali soldiers were receiving distressing letters from their families and, although one British tank crewman witnessed Tommies dangling bits of bacon out of a train window in the faces of starving Bengalis, many of the soldiers, British as well as Indian, were so distressed by the horrific sight of the famine victims that they were reported to be feeding the beggars with their own rations.[141] Meanwhile the Japanese sought to capitalize on the situation by spreading rumours that they were willing to send food aid from Burma.[142]

In Bengal, Wavell mobilized the military to escort deliveries of rice into the rural areas, distribute clothing and to show villagers how to prepare the unfamiliar grains used for relief. The breakdown in the transport system was tackled, and boats removed under the denial scheme salvaged, bridges repaired and river ferry crossings re-established.[143] That winter, to everyone's relief, the rice harvest was good. This revived the rice market and measures were finally taken to protect the access to food of the most vulnerable. Price controls were enforced and rationing was introduced in Calcutta. The famine victims were cleared from the city's streets and taken to camps. 'The Famine of Bengal . . . as if by magic vanished into thin air.' Many of those who were rounded up were separated from their husbands, wives or children in the process and their fate is unclear. It seems likely that the majority who were already too weak to recover simply died, out of sight.[144]

The Indian government at last implemented a programme to safeguard food supplies for the entire sub-continent. The Food Department developed what was known as the Basic Plan, which put an end to free-market trading and ensured that food surpluses were pooled and distributed where they were most needed. Rationing was introduced in the cities and towns, and by early 1945 covered 42 million urban Indians and even extended out into the countryside to cover the rural poor.[145] Although the situation in Bengal was gradually being alleviated, Wavell was concerned that famine might spread across the sub-continent. In other areas that depended on Bengali rice there had been signs of famine in 1943. A British resident on a rubber estate in Mysore had reported that it was no longer possible to walk through the estate as the starving workers posed too great a threat to safety. Many rubber estates in Travancore had closed down as they could not feed their workers, and the bodies of famished coolies were reported to be lying by the side of the roads in Coorg.[146] Wavell repeatedly telegrammed London pleading for food for India. Churchill peevishly replied that if food was so scarce in India why had Gandhi not yet died?

Given Churchill's determination to prevent the Americans from taking all the credit in the battle against the Japanese it seems strange that he was so cavalier about the food situation in India. On 17 February 1944, India Secretary Leo Amery warned him: 'once it becomes known that no supplies are coming from outside the machinery of the Governments of India will be quite incapable of preventing food going underground everywhere and famine conditions spreading with disastrous rapidity all over India. The result may well be fatal for the whole prosecution of the war, and that not only from the point of view of India as a base for further operations. I don't think you have any idea of how deeply public feeling in this country has already been stirred against the Government over the Bengal Famine.'[147] Prejudice and dislike seem to have made Churchill determined that India should not be helped. He is said to have thought the Indians were 'the beastliest population in the world next to the Germans'.[148] But Churchill was not alone in his refusal to prioritize India's food needs. A committee to look into the question of food supplies for India decided that the risk of civilian hunger in India was a lesser evil than jeopardizing British civilian food supplies or military supplies for the Indian army. In November 1943 the committee even turned down a Canadian offer of 100,000 tons of wheat for India for lack of shipping and the British government prevented the Indian legislative assembly from applying to the United Nations Relief and Rehabilitation Administration (UNRRA) for food aid.[149] 'If UNRRA operated in India in the sphere of supply and public health,' Amery pointed out, 'they would no doubt wish to send supervisors or inspectors whose operations would presumably be concentrated on Bengal and you must expect undesirable attention to be directed, e.g. on the breakdown of administration there.'[150] He was painfully aware that the spotlight of world attention would not show the British government in a good light if it were focused on India and Bengal.

In desperation Wavell transferred his attentions to Claude Auchinleck and Louis Mountbatten, respectively Commander-in-Chief of the Indian Army and Supreme Commander of the Allies in South-East Asia. They conceded that they could afford a 10 per cent cut in military supplies, which persuaded the chiefs of staff in London to divert twenty-five ships from military transports and forced the cabinet to agree to a shipment of 200,000 tons of grain. Depressed by the dreadful predictions for the

1944 harvest, Wavell continued to campaign for food for India and asked Churchill to make a personal appeal to Roosevelt for shipping. Churchill's weakly worded request meant that Roosevelt simply passed the issue on to the Joint Chiefs of Staff, who, of course, replied that no ships could be spared in the light of the forthcoming invasion of France. Wavell pronounced the British cabinet 'short-sighted and callous'.[151] His disgust left the British command unmoved and it was not until there were real fears of demoralization in the Indian army at the end of 1944 that military reinforcements were replaced by a shipment of 20,000 tons of Australian wheat.[152] When Wavell heard of the wealth of supplies airlifted in to Holland in March 1945 he remarked with bitterness, 'A very different attitude [exists] towards feeding a starving population when the starvation is in Europe.'[153]

Churchill was probably right in thinking the Indian government was sclerotic. It lacked the self-confidence 'to take a firm stand against agricultural or industrial interests' and failed to 'make Punjab provide cheap food or industrialists cheap goods'.[154] Instead it allowed businessmen and Punjabi landlords to make vast profits from the war while its efforts to protect the standard of living of workers in the cities and the countryside were ineffectual. The food situation which developed in wartime India demolished for good 'one rationalization of imperialism [which argued] . . . that British rule protected the Indian poor from the rapacity of the Indian upper class'.[155]

Despite the depth of anti-British feeling demonstrated by the Quit India Movement, the British took their position as the established rulers of India too much for granted. The Indian government's failure to secure India as a safe military base was the combined result of incompetence and complacency. Millions of Indians were allowed to die of starvation before the government was galvanized into action. In contrast, when the rice-eating people of the Persian Gulf showed signs of discontent over relief supplies of wheat, the Middle East Supply Centre scraped together a shipment of Iraqi rice to avoid the threat of political unrest.[156] Admittedly, British insecurity in the Middle East was exacerbated by the fact that in the spring of 1942 only a few hundred kilometres of desert lay between the German army and Cairo, while the Japanese in Burma were at the end of their supply lines and several hundred kilometres of jungle separated them from Calcutta. But the

Middle East was also fortunate in Lyttelton's appointment of Robert Jackson to the MESC. Jackson was a superb organizer who set up an efficient and dedicated organization. India's Food Department lacked cohesion and initiative and did not bring in effective measures until after the worst had happened and famine had struck. On the ground the Bengal government and administration lacked vision, and even when it was clear that a famine was in the offing they failed to grasp that it was not simply a matter of food supply but also of the fact that the poor had lost their purchasing power and could not afford what food was available on the markets.

'It was all too likely that . . . in upsetting the delicate mechanism of the world's food economy' the war would bring hunger to some part of the empire.[157] It is difficult to reach any conclusion other than that racism was the guiding principle which determined where hunger struck. Churchill's hatred of Indians was inflamed by what he regarded as the ingratitude and treachery of the Quit India Movement, and when it came to making decisions about where resources should be channelled India was given the lowest priority. By refusing to believe in the seriousness of India's food situation Churchill and his War Cabinet determined that India would be the part of the empire where the greatest civilian sacrifices would have to be made, and displaced hunger on to the colony.

The moral argument for British rule in India had begun to unravel long before the outbreak of the Second World War, but as Jawaharlal Nehru argued in *Discovery of India*, the fact that 'rich England and richer America' failed to come to the rescue of the Bengal famine victims placed a question mark over the sincerity of the Allies' claim that they were fighting to bring freedom from want – let alone justice, fairness and tolerance – to the world.[158] Thus, the Bengal famine gave added strength to the Congress Party's post-war demands for Indian independence. However, the Bengal famine played far less of a role in the debates about independence than one might have expected of such a devastating event. One explanation for this is that Congress politicians were in prison at the time and so had no first-hand experience of the horrors. By the time they were released at the end of the war the political focus had shifted on to the public trials of the men who had joined the Indian National Army and to the issue of partition.[159] When the Famine

Inquiry Commission reports were published in April and August 1945 they were overshadowed by the end of the war and the news of the horror of the industrialized killing of Jews in the Nazi death camps. Later, the quiet and unobtrusive deaths of the victims of starvation were again overshadowed by the violent murder of up to 10,000 Indians a day in the riots that surrounded the partition of India. Besides, it was in no one's interests to remember the Bengal famine. The British did not wish to be reminded of one of the most shameful episodes of their rule in India. Indians also felt themselves to be implicated. The provincial government of Bengal was in Indian hands at the time and while British district officers may have been incompetent in responding to the developing crisis, the old structures of welfare and charity among the Indian wealthy had also broken down. When India gained its independence in 1947 the Bengal famine faded into obscurity and was quickly forgotten.

India was lost to Britain when it gained its independence in 1947. But if colonialism was now discredited and the seeds of independence were sown in Africa, they did not yet come to fruition. The extensive wartime controls that colonial governments had adopted were re-interpreted as development programmes and Britain concentrated on the colonial production of cash crops in order to reduce the dollar deficit which the virtually bankrupted country was struggling to overcome. Thus, the exploitation of the empire's food resources was destined to become a feature of the post-war world.

8

Feeding Germany

This time we robbed the occupied countries, and our people did not have to go hungry until the end of the war.
(Elisabeth D., a German woman who lived through both the
First and Second World Wars)[1]

The National Socialist leadership, and in particular Hitler and Göring, were determined to feed the German population adequately throughout the war. By 1939 Walther Darré, the Minister for Food and Agriculture, and Herbert Backe, working within Göring's organization for the Four Year Plan, had done their best to prepare the agricultural sector. Even the schoolboy Harry Simon was aware of the need for self-sufficiency and that 'Germany must make itself independent of other countries, produce its own goods, not only farm produce, but also everything else . . . Nothing was to be wasted.'[2] The Battle for Production in agriculture had been matched by a campaign to suppress consumption and divert consumers towards home-grown foods rather than foreign imports. Nevertheless, the leadership were well aware that a long war would prove too great a drain on the country's manpower and industrial resources for agriculture to be able to maintain its impressive levels of self-sufficiency. If it were to rely on its own food supply Germany needed to fight a short war.

In the end German farmers managed to maintain production remarkably well even though the war dragged on for five and a half years and the prioritization of the war industries meant less machinery and fertilizer was available to them than to British farmers. As in Britain, the productivity of German farms rested on the hard work of agricultural labourers. But while in Britain farm labour was provided by the Women's Land Army and prisoners of war, in Germany much of the labour was made up of workers forcibly brought into the Reich from the occupied territories. In this way Germany imported the exploitation of its newly conquered empire. By the end of 1943 the foreign agricultural and industrial workforce amounted to 7 million more mouths to feed. German agriculture struggled to produce enough food to provide an adequate civilian ration, a generous ration for the military, whose share of German food production had quadrupled by May 1943, and a miserly ration for the forced labourers. Just as Britain looked to its allies and the empire for food imports, Germany looked to the occupied territories to make up the food deficit. While Britain's food policy had its darker side, in particular the War Cabinet's decision in 1943 to displace hunger on to Britain's colonial subjects rather than British civilians, Britain's exploitation of its colonies was neither so ruthless nor so openly dismissive of the value of human life as were the National Socialists in their conquered territories. At a meeting with the leaders of the occupied countries on 6 August 1942 Göring reminded them that, 'The Führer repeatedly said, and I repeat after him, if anyone has to go hungry, it shall not be the Germans but other peoples.'[3]

THE BATTLE FOR PRODUCTION

In his quest for 'nutritional freedom' Backe had directed ministerial funding into a variety of autarky-oriented research projects such as the development of protein- and oil-rich plants and the best type of potato to provide maximum quantities of vitamin C over the winter months; he had encouraged the setting-up of fish farms, the production of organic fertilizers and home production of animal feed.[4] One of the most successful of the Reich Food Corporation's autarky programmes aimed to make dairy farmers self-sufficient in feed for their cows. Before the war Germany relied on imports for about 50 to 60 per cent of its butter and margarine and 95 to 99 per cent of its vegetable oils.[5] The Allied blockade cut off Germany's access to supplies of whale oil, which was one of the main ingredients in margarine.[6] Under instruction from the Reich Food Corporation farmers extended the acreage of oilseed crops but this could not compensate for the deficits in fat imports and the Corporation looked to dairy farmers and butter production as a means of maintaining the fat content of the German ration.[7] In order to feed the cows dairy farmers were encouraged to plant root crops such as turnips and sugar beet to replace grain (which was needed for bread), and special silos were built where green stuff could be stored for long periods without losing its nutrients.[8] This allowed farmers to produce more butter, and by 1943 German dairy farms were the source of 60 per cent of the butter consumed in the Reich, up from 30 per cent at the beginning of the war. By then Germans were, of course, eating less butter and the quality had declined noticeably. Wartime butter was watery, and older Germans still make a distinction today between wartime butter (and margarine) and a higher quality product, when they redundantly refer to 'good butter'. But even though consumption levels fell considerably and the quality was marred, these efforts did ensure that fat, an essential source of energy, taste and the feeling of fullness, was still present in the German diet throughout the last two years of the war.[9]

One of the greatest challenges for German farmers was the maintenance of both potato and pig production. The German pre-war diet was heavily dependent on potatoes, and Germans displayed a marked preference for pork, consuming far more than the British, who in the 1930s ate substantially more mutton and lamb.[10] The problem with pigs is that they compete with humans for food as they are usually fattened on grains, potatoes and sugar beet. A reduction in the number of pigs has the undesirable effect of reducing the amount of animal fat in the diet as pigs produce the most fat of all farm animals out of a given amount of feed. A decline in the number of pigs leads to a vicious cycle. As meat and fat become less available humans eat more potatoes, which in turn takes fodder away from pigs.[11]

Problems had already begun in January 1940 when bad weather affected the supply of potatoes.[12] Then in 1941 German pig farmers were hit by a poor barley harvest, which meant that they needed more potatoes for their animals. In June, rationing for potatoes had to be introduced and the meat ration was cut by 25 per cent as the number of pigs began to fall.[13] The entire consumption of potatoes rose from 12 million tons a year before the war to 32 million tons during the war. If farmers had been able to grow more, the consumption would have risen even further.[14] But a poor potato harvest in 1943 meant that competition for potatoes became so intense that both human and pig potato consumption fell. By 1944 Germany's pig herds had fallen to 60 per cent of their pre-war levels and the amount of potatoes available for each pig had fallen by half.[15] This was reflected in a 10 per cent reduction in pigs' selling weight and a further fall in the supplies of pork, bacon and fat. By 1944 meat supplies had fallen to nearly one half of what had been available in 1933.[16]

German farming became caught up in a spiral of falling pork and potato production. Supply problems led to food shortages in Germany's towns and cities throughout the summer of 1941. The Swiss consul in the city of Cologne reported that this meant the townspeople had been unable to lay down sufficient stores of food for the winter. When, for two weeks in November, it became impossible to buy potatoes this became a problem because the city's inhabitants had no food in their cellars to tide them over. There were protests in the city in December which had to be controlled by the police until the supply of potatoes finally revived.[17] The scarcity of meat was made worse by the potato shortages and this problem plagued Germany's towns and cities throughout the war.

The greatest difficulty which Germany's farms faced was a shortage of labour, and this was already severe in 1939. The greatest drain on farm workers was industry. Well before Hitler's invasion of Poland millions had left behind the poor pay and miserable living conditions of the agricultural labourer in favour of more profitable work in the expanding war industries.[18] Once war was declared another 1.5 million rural workers were called up into the armed forces. Given the National Socialists' portrayal of the Germans as a 'People Without Space', the mopping-up of surplus rural labour by industry and the army should have had the same effect as it did in America, painlessly solving the problem of agricultural over-population. But the decline in labour was not accompanied by a parallel process of rationalization and capital investment, as it was in the United States. Germany began the war with a healthy agricultural research culture which was developing new seeds and plants and refining breeding techniques for livestock, but as the war swallowed up more and more of the country's resources the application of new technologies became impossible. In addition, although Germany began the war with the intention of maintaining a programme of farm mechanization, the fighting on the eastern front devoured both men and arms and the Allied bombing raids gradually began to impact on industrial capacity. Armaments production eventually overrode all other industrial priorities and by 1944 the production of agricultural equipment had fallen by over 40 per cent.[19] Fuel shortages and lack of spare parts prevented the proper use of those machines that were available. Even draught animals were in short supply as horses were requisitioned for the eastern front, where each infantry division relied on 1,200 horse-drawn wagons to transport its supplies.[20]

Military requirements also led to a drastic decline in the availability of artificial fertilizers. As the military use of nitrogen rose by 500 per cent, the amount of nitrogen-based fertilizers available to farmers fell by 60 per cent.[21] Even manure from animals became less nitrogen-rich as the amount of protein in animal feed fell.[22] Phosphorous fertilizers were import-dependent and by the last two years of the war they were only available in tiny quantities. Nevertheless, between 1939 and 1944 the bread grain harvest fell by only 3 million tons.[23] This impressive maintenance of grain farming was achieved through sheer hard work.

Much of the hard work was done by farmers' wives and daughters. In Württemberg and Bavaria, where farms tended to be small family enterprises, 60 per cent of farm labourers during the war were women. *Sicherheitsdienst* (SS intelligence service) reports from the region contain plentiful examples of small struggling farms where women had taken over from their husbands. In one of many similar cases, a farm of about 16 hectares was being run by the farmer's wife, her mother and a frail hired hand, whereas before the war it had been operated by the owner and four male labourers.[24] Once the troops invading the Soviet Union had established the occupation of fertile areas such as the Ukraine, the German agricultural labour shortage was made worse by the call-up of skilled farmers to administer and advise on the establishment of German farming in the east. While they were a loss to the farms in the Reich, these men did little good in the occupied Soviet Union where many of them met a brutal fate at the hands of partisans.[25]

Rather than mobilize the general population, including non-farming women, to fill the agricultural labour shortage (as was done in Britain), the National Socialists chose to import labour from the occupied territories in the east.[26] Even as the German army launched its attack on Poland, plans were laid to channel prisoners of war on to the East Prussian farming estates, where the root crops were ready for harvest. By the end of September 1939, 100,000 Polish prisoners of war had been rushed through medical and police checks and sent to dig up potatoes in Prussia.[27] German agriculture's appetite for workers was voracious and a labour recruitment campaign rapidly got under way in occupied Poland. When an advertising campaign yielded insufficient volunteers the campaign quickly degenerated into a violent process of forced deportation.[28] By the autumn of 1941 German farms were completely dependent on 1.3 million Polish and Ukrainian forced labourers – many of them women – as well as 1.2 million mainly French and Soviet prisoners of war.[29] Reich Food Corporation official Rudolf Peukert acknowledged in 1944 that 'without the employment of hundreds of thousands of foreign workers it would have been impossible to maintain German agricultural production at its present level'.[30] Forced labour produced about 20 per cent of the food grown within Germany during the war.[31]

The employment of foreign workers on German farms was a practical solution to Germany's manpower shortage. Their presence allowed German industry to continue recruiting rural workers, which it much preferred to using women or foreigners, and large agricultural enterprises were satisfied by the plentiful and cheap labour. However, the policy deeply offended Nazi agrarian idealists whose vision for the countryside was one of a pure Aryan peasantry tilling the soil and acting as a racial and social foundation for the nation. It was deeply worrying to such ideologues that wholesome German women might work the fields side by side with Slav *Untermenschen*.[32] Early on in the war the *Sicherheitsdienst* complained that some farmers were treating the Polish workers as members of the family. In eastern Germany there was a long tradition of Poles coming over to do seasonal work on German farms and these farmers continued to treat them as they had done before the war.[33] There were even reports of farmers, who shared the Poles' Catholic faith, attending Sunday church services together with their forced labourers.[34] In order to preserve some semblance of racial order Himmler introduced draconian laws of separation. As in the concentration camps, the forced labourers wore letters sewn on to their clothes to indicate their inferior status. They were paid a pittance, banned from social contact with Germans, even from using public transport. A romantic liaison with a German carried the risk of the death penalty.[35] Edith Hahn, an Austrian Jew who was sent to work on a German asparagus farm in 1942, observed that 'it quickly became clear that the Germans were interested in using our strength but not in preserving it . . . We were always ravenous . . . surrounded by bounty and aching with hunger.'[36] Hahn bitterly recalled how 'the farmers had grown proud and haughty . . . like Volkswagen and Siemens, they had slaves'.[37]

There were, however, plenty of farmers who could see no sense in the racial laws and simply ignored them. Hermine Schmid, who ran a large farm, commented in a letter in April 1943 that she was 'very satisfied' with her Polish and French workers. 'If they are well treated all POWs work well without needing to be watched. They eat with us together, although this is actually forbidden.'[38] Many farmers were reluctant to allow ideology to get in the way of practical considerations. Unwilling and undernourished labourers would provide little help on a farm.[39] Indeed, if they lived with a kind farmer, forced workers often received more food than German civilians living in towns, and almost all forced agricultural labourers will have eaten better than most of their fellow countrymen living under German rule in their own countries. Agricultural forced workers were therefore unusual, and fortunate, in that they subverted the National Socialist 'nutritional hierarchy', which in theory allotted them starvation rations.[40]

Agricultural forced labourers benefited from the fact that there was plenty of food in the German countryside throughout the entire war, even in 1944–45 when food shortages became increasingly pronounced in the towns and cities. Germany was still a predominantly rural society. In the 1930s more than half the population lived in small village communities or market towns. Millions of Germans grew their own food on allotments and smallholdings, many keeping pigs and chickens.[41] In 1939 about one-third of the population were classified as self-supporting and were not included in the rationing system.[42] Even many of those who were entitled to rations grew their own vegetables and fruit and kept small animals such as rabbits. Those who lived through the war in rural areas, or had friends or relations living in these circumstances, were always able to eat enough, and quite often enjoyed good food. Irmgard B recalled that her mother, who was a midwife, 'always brought milk back when she had delivered a baby for a farmer'.[43] Marie Vassiltchikov, who was well connected in the German aristocratic world, frequently benefited from the bounty of her friends' country estates, enjoying peaches and cream in March 1944 and food parcels of butter, bacon and sausage. 'After a copious lunch' on 8 April 1944, she commented, '*what* it is, these days, to own a country place!'[44]

While the rural nature of German society was to prove an advantage for a large section of Germany's civilian population, the preponderance of small-scale farmers was to prove a weak point in Germany's wartime food economy. As the National Socialist state learned to its cost, throughout Germany and the rest of occupied western and eastern Europe, it is much more difficult to exert control over farmers with smallholdings than it is over large agribusinesses and it is particularly difficult when the small farmers are disgruntled. Many German farmers were disillusioned by the failure of the regime to live up to its promises. The hoped-for rise in the rural standard of living had not materialized. Subsidies that supported prices meant that farmers were financially better off, but there were few opportunities to invest their capital in farm improvements. Indeed, National Socialist policies tended to widen the gap between rich and poor farmers.[45] Disappointed, the small farmers retreated into self-sufficiency, which meant that they produced less surplus food and the surplus which they did produce they preferred to channel on to the black market for higher prices.[46] This placed a serious limit on the state's ability to fully exploit its agricultural resources. It was both unable to stimulate production to its maximum and unable to control all of that which was produced. The National Socialists' frustration with this state of affairs is indicated by their introduction of draconian laws. In 1942 farmers who failed to relinquish their entire bread grain harvest to the state were threatened with penal servitude and hefty fines, but these coercive laws appear to have done little to increase the amount of grain the state was able to collect.[47] The British government was better protected from the development of such a situation by the greater specialization of British farms. If he was unhappy with government policy a farmer who produced solely milk or wheat could not decide to withdraw into self-sufficiency. The German mixed smallholding with a few pigs or cattle, chickens, a little wheat, and a vegetable garden, could simply scale down production and withdraw from the market.

This withdrawal into self-sufficiency was even more of a problem among farmers in the German-occupied territories. They resented receiving instructions from agricultural organizations which had been imposed upon them by the conquerors, and unfair pricing policies provided little incentive to produce for the market. This meant that in rural areas of Europe a great many farmers withdrew on to their farms and tried simply to ride out the war. Emilia Olivier lived on a farm with her parents in the hamlet of Brion in Maine et Loire in western France. Apart from the fact that some of her uncles were in Germany as prisoners of war and that an aunt's horse was requisitioned by the Germans, the war barely impinged on Emilia. The blackout, watching the fire in the sky after a bombing raid on the nearby town of Voisin, and the loud thuds, which made the doors in their house shake, as the retreating Germans blew up the Loire bridges in 1944, were as close as her small family ever came to the fighting. On the farm they did not miss any foodstuffs or ever go hungry. They kept the cream back from their milk and made butter and soft cheese. They always had 'good white bread'. Her father grew the wheat and was allowed to mill a certain quantity for his own use. He would take it to the miller using the horse and cart, and always had to carry papers in case he was stopped by a German road block. But if he was fortunate enough not to meet any checks on the first journey, he would go back and make a second trip, thus illegally doubling his allowance of wheat. The wheat was poorly milled and much of the husk was left on the grain. At the house they had a windmill and they used this to separate out the chaff and make white flour. They also processed their neighbour's wheat and the neighbour had an oven in which he baked the bread for both families. Emilia and her family never needed to turn to the black market, and it seems they did not bother to trade their own goods on the market although they did regularly sell milk, potatoes, eggs and chickens to a woman who would bicycle out to their farm from the town of Angers.[48] Emilia's memories sum up just how little the war affected the food habits of many European farmers and their families.

Even though German farmers managed to maintain a good grain harvest until 1943, the demands on grain supplies became ever greater as the war wore on. Civilians, the military and a growing number of prisoners of war and forced labourers within the Reich placed impossible demands on the productivity of the farmers. Already in August 1940 the bread ration had to be cut, only to be followed by a cut in the cereal ration in May 1941. The decline in meat and fat production meant that Germans came more and more to rely on their bread ration, and when the hard winter of 1941 damaged the grain crops Backe was forced to begin using up the country's grain reserves in order to maintain the bread ration for the German population. In the spring of 1942 bread, meat and fat rations all had to be cut again.[49] By 1943–44 an ordinary German civilian was eating 40 per cent less fat, 60 per cent less meat and 20 per cent less bread than in 1939.[50] German agriculture simply could not supply sufficient food for the civilian population, the voracious army and a growing number of prisoners of war and forced labourers. Germany looked to its occupied territories to make up the food deficit.

THE OCCUPATION OF WESTERN EUROPE

The dominant National Socialist attitude towards the countries the Wehrmacht invaded was to treat them as a source of plunder rather than as long-term supply bases. The military policy was that all troops should live off the land, and in every defeated nation the Wehrmacht ruthlessly requisitioned industrial and agricultural goods. In the winter of 1940–41 it became clear that the war was going to last longer than the leadership had hoped, and when the decision was taken to invade the Soviet Union the plan was hatched to use the east as the main source of food for the army, as well as a supplier for civilians in the Reich and possibly even to fill food deficits in western European countries such as Belgium and Norway.[51] In the summer of 1942, unable to achieve victory in the east, the National Socialist leadership realized that Germany was engaged in a long war of attrition with the Soviet Union, Britain and the United States – and, to make matters worse, the regime was faced by an internal food crisis. It was then that Göring began to insist that every morsel of food should be squeezed out of all occupied territories and to insist that hunger should be exported outside the Reich.

Despite the National Socialists' focus on the east as Germany's source of sustaining food supplies and their short-term attitude towards the resources of western Europe, the latter actually contributed more food to wartime Germany than the occupied Soviet Union. Denmark and France both exported slightly higher quantities of meat to the Reich (768,000 and 758,000 tons respectively) than was received from the Soviet areas (731,000 tons). Moreover, if the official figures for the amounts of food requisitioned by the occupying forces are counted together with the amounts exported to Germany, then Denmark, Holland and France collectively contributed 21.4 million tons of grain-equivalent, in comparison to the 14.7 million tons provided by the occupied Soviet Union.[52] Even though collectivization had modernized Ukrainian agriculture it was not as productive or as efficient as western European agriculture, which was better placed to restructure in order to withstand the disruptions of war. With hindsight, Backe would have done better to turn his attention to exploiting the food resources of western Europe rather than those of the Soviet Union.

GREEK FAMINE AND BELGIAN RESILIENCE

The National Socialist policy of plunder wreaked havoc in countries such as Greece, where agriculture was basic and peasant-based. When the German army arrived in April 1941 the officers of the high command requisitioned all the food they could lay their hands on: oranges, lemons, currants, figs, rice and olive oil. Whereas the British navy had brought in shipments of food for the Greek civilian population throughout the military campaign and even the Italians had distributed pasta and olive oil, the Wehrmacht made no attempt to feed the Greeks. To make matters worse, the German troops were expected to live off the land and many units were not even provided with a mess, eating instead in local restaurants.[53] The food situation rapidly deteriorated and in the summer of 1941 Marcel Junod, a Swiss Red Cross delegate in Athens, reported that the streets were filled with 'walking spectres.

Here and there old men, and sometimes young ones, sat on the pavement. Their lips moving as if in prayer but no sound came. They stretched out their hands for alms and let them fall back weakly. Pedestrians passed backwards and forwards before them without paying the least attention. Each one was asking himself when his own turn would come.'[54]

Although Greece was a predominantly rural country, the peasantry, especially on the islands, produced mainly cash crops such as olive oil, tobacco and currants. The population was dependent on the annual import of 450,000 tons of American grain for one-third of its food but the British blockade of occupied Europe cut Greece off from all imports.[55] The compartmentalization of the country into three zones of occupation under the Germans, the Italians and the Bulgarians prevented food from circulating, and in particular it meant that what little food there was available in the north did not get through to Athens and the south.[56] Meanwhile, the escape of the Greek merchant marine before the Germans arrived left the islands more or less cut off from the mainland.[57] In a pattern which could be observed in every economy affected by the wartime loss of imports, inflation set in and producers and retailers withdrew their food supplies from the market. They either hoarded them, speculating on further price rises, or sold them on the black market, often to German agents collecting food for the military. The Greek government therefore lost access to what little food supply was left in the country and was unable to protect the poor and the needy from spiralling food prices by giving out food aid.[58] The numbers of the poor swelled daily as the Germans requisitioned and dismantled industrial plant for transport to the Reich, leaving thousands unemployed. In Athens the government was only able to provide rations of 458 calories per person, not even half of what most people need to maintain the body's normal functions. In November this fell to a paltry 183 calories, the equivalent of one or two slices of bread a day. In August people began to drop dead in the streets of Athens.[59] By January 1942 the death rate was 2,000 per day and infant mortality had risen to over 50 per cent. Families would leave the bodies of their children in the streets, hoping to continue using their ration cards. One island in the Aegean sarcastically conveyed the message to Athens, 'send bread or coffins'.[60] Meanwhile, the health of German troops in North

Africa greatly improved that summer as small ships laden with fresh fruit and vegetables began to sail from Greece to the Libyan port of Bardia.[61]

In the summer of 1941 the Red Cross, the United States government and campaigning groups within Britain* all argued that it was imperative that the British government revise their blockade policy and allow food aid to get through to the Greeks. When he had announced the blockade in August 1940 Churchill had been adamant that there was to be no question of food aid. To send in food, even for innocent civilians, would, he argued, simply relieve the Germans of the need to feed the people, and help their war effort. Besides, the Nazis were not to be trusted – the food would most likely be diverted into German stomachs. The former American President Herbert Hoover, who had risen to prominence in public life as a self-appointed organizer of food relief during the First World War, was infuriated by Churchill's stance. He described him as 'a militarist of the extreme school who held that incidental starvation of women and children was justified'.[62]

Churchill eventually caved in to the pressure to allow relief for Greece through the blockade. The famine was on such a vast scale that it aroused American public opinion against the policy. Further rational argument came from Oliver Lyttelton, Minister of State in Cairo, the headquarters for the North African military campaign. Lyttelton was facing protests from the Greek community in Egypt where the British position was never particularly secure. He telegrammed the British government with the warning: 'History will I believe pronounce a stern judgement on our policy. I appeal not only to mercy but to expediency ... we shall undermine the resistance of an ally and lose a possible centre of successful insurrection against the Axis if we continue to starve the Greeks ... I have no doubt where the balance of advantage of winning the war lies.'[63] In January 1942 shipments of wheat were allowed through the blockade and from April regular cargoes of wheat and other foodstuffs were shipped into the Greek ports.[64] But by then at least 20,000 people had already died

---

* One of which was the Oxford Committee for Famine Relief, now known by its abbreviation Oxfam, which was set up in response to the plight of starving Europeans.

of starvation. Even after April the food brought in by the Allies was never enough. Although it halted the large-scale urban famine, the Greeks continued to die of starvation. Reinforcing Churchill's argument that the Germans were not to be trusted, relief eventually became a tool which the occupying armies used mercilessly against the guerrilla resistance fighters in the mountainous areas. Villagers in those areas where the partisans were active were denied any food aid; instead, their homes and fields were burned to the ground in an attempt to clear the area and deprive the resistance fighters of their support network. In 1943 and 1944 much of the Greek countryside starved. By the time Greece was liberated in 1944, half a million Greeks, 14 per cent of the population, had died from hunger and associated diseases.[65] This was a civilian casualty rate eight times higher than that suffered by Britain.

Food aid for Greece was the only significant exception Churchill was willing to make and the blockade against the rest of occupied Europe was enforced throughout the rest of the war. Campaigners from the relief organizations continued to plead for aid to be allowed through, arguing that if Britain stood by while Germany used starvation as a weapon of war it would call into question the humanitarian rhetoric that Churchill himself used so liberally.[66] But it was Churchill's fixed idea that no quarter could be given in the fight against Germany. Perhaps, if the defence of the strategy had been tempered by greater acknowledgement of the suffering it caused, it would not have created such a large question mark over the reputation which the Allies claimed for themselves as representatives of the forces of 'Good' over 'Evil'.[67]

In theory Belgium was in a similar position to Greece. It depended on annual imports of 1.2 million tons of grain from overseas, which came to a sudden halt with German occupation. As the Wehrmacht moved in the quartermasters, field units and individual soldiers scrambled to buy or requisition as much food as possible.[68] However, after an extremely difficult winter in 1940–41, farmers rallied and succeeded in producing enough food to provide adequate amounts for almost all the population. The Belgians did not succumb to famine like the Greeks. The usual explanation for this is that Germany was willing to support the country with food imports for the sake of its industrial goods, at least two-thirds of which were exported to the Reich. On the contrary,

Belgium did not in fact survive on food sent in from Germany but was left to feed itself. Throughout the four long years of occupation Belgium received only 849,000 tons of grain imports, enough to cover three-quarters of a year's pre-war consumption.[69] A little food was smuggled in across the French and Dutch borders but the reason the Belgian population did not starve was because its agricultural sector proved itself able to adapt to wartime circumstances.[70]

The wartime productivity of Belgian agriculture was not the result of the efforts of the Belgian version of the German Reich Food Corporation, which was set up by the occupying forces. Indeed, the Corporation Nationale de l'Alimentation et de l'Agriculture proved incapable of influencing disaffected farmers, and its collection system was only able to muster sufficient food to distribute a daily ration of between 1,000 and 1,500 calories per person. What kept the Belgians alive was the food which the farmers channelled on to the black market. Farmers in large enterprises were able to illegally siphon off only a part of their produce, but farmers with smallholdings probably sold virtually everything they produced on the black market, which eventually developed into an alternative food economy.[71] The extent of the black market is indicated by the absurd statistic that the smaller an animal and the easier it was to conceal, the fewer the number of such animals – rabbits, chickens, goats – were recorded in the official figures.[72]

Belgian agriculture was much more modern than Greek peasant farming, and the farmers were sufficiently flexible to be able to switch to crops rather than livestock, and increase grain and potato production. The high prices their goods fetched on the black market provided sufficient incentive to produce. In 1943 a kilogram of black market bread cost 49 francs compared to 2.60 on the legal market, a kilogram of meat sold for 190 francs while the official price was 34 francs. This would suggest that if the occupying administration had applied a fair pricing policy it might well have been able to gain much more from Belgium than the paltry 27,200 tons of fruits and vegetables which Belgium exported to the Reich in 1942, falling to only 7,300 tons in 1943.[73]

A similar story played itself out in France. The country's reputation for fine food and wines meant that the German occupying forces were all the more rapacious in their plunder. With the exchange rate absurdly weighted in their favour, German soldiers could afford to supplement their rations with sumptuous meals in restaurants and cafés. On a trip to Paris from Berlin in October 1942 Marie Vassiltchikov, who worked for the German Foreign Ministry, wrote to her mother: 'life is still most agreeable so long as one can afford it. This does not mean that things are particularly expensive; but to have a decent meal (say, with oysters, wine, cheese and fruit, plus a tip) you must fork out about 100 francs per person; which is, after all, only 5 marks.'[74] German officers were served beefsteaks 'imperfectly concealed under token fried eggs' and washed down with champagne. The First World War hero turned famous author, Ernst Jünger, a German officer in Paris during the war, recorded in his diary that 'to eat well and to eat a lot' while surrounded by the hungry, ragged French, 'gives a feeling of power'.[75] For occupying troops in France the Wehrmacht's policy of living off the land translated into living off the fat of the land. Even the lowliest of the German occupiers were able to afford luxuries in France. When he was doing his labour service Alois Kleinemas was billeted at the chateau in Cognac. He was able to collect a crate of brandy to take home to celebrate his parents' wedding anniversary. He also used to post them packets of butter.[76] Helmut Radssat recalled that the canteen of the Verneau barracks in Angers was particularly cherished by those soldiers who had come from the eastern front. 'The precious aroma of wine and brandy was quite new to me. In Germany such luxuries were becoming more and more scarce. It was in those barracks that I learned to know and appreciate good wines.'[77]

French agriculture was particularly badly hit by a shortage of labour. Around 50,000 of the 2 million French prisoners of war were agricultural workers who were sent to work on German rather than French farms. Altogether, about 400,000 agricultural workers were missing, leaving women and the aged to run the farms. Shortages of horses, tractors, fuel, fertilizer and pesticides led to a precipitous decline in yields. Worst hit were meat and milk, but even potatoes, sugar beet and wheat showed steep reductions, particularly in the first year of the war, after which yields stabilized.[78]

Official food prices rose only modestly but prices on the black market soared. This triggered an inflationary spiral whereby the less the food authorities were able to requisition the more the rations were reduced. In August 1942 Göring responded to internal food shortages within the Reich by calling together the various leaders of the occupied territories and insisting that they deliver more food to Germany. 'As far as France is concerned', he pronounced, 'I am positive that its soil is not cultivated to the maximum . . . also the French stuff themselves to a shameful extent . . . Collaboration from the French I see in one way only: let them deliver as much as they can.'[79] Given Göring's own notoriously extravagant eating habits and the behaviour of the German occupiers who were known to wolf down omelettes made with twelve precious eggs, this was the application of the worst possible kind of double standard. Göring demanded from France quantities of wheat, meat and butter which amounted to between 15 to 20 per cent of all available food.[80] His secretary, Paul Koerner, noted that Germany's military commander in France was so horrified by the demands that he initially refused to convey them to the authorities in Paris.[81] He feared that it would lead to further ration cuts and food riots. In the long run he concluded that it would simply be counter-productive and would further demotivate the farmers, leading to a long-term fall in production.[82] By 1944 the energy value of the French ration had fallen to 1,050 calories and, as in Belgium, the black market or connections to a rural family with food became essential for the survival of anyone living in a town or city. This in turn pushed up prices on the black market, leading to the diversion of more and more food on to the illegal market.

Germany exported wartime hunger to the countries it occupied. In Belgium and France those who suffered were the people without any or only limited access to the black market. Thus, prisoners in Belgian gaols began to die of starvation in 1942, unable to survive on the 1,550 calories a day that the ration provided and unable to supplement their rations from alternative sources. Urban office workers, clerks, civil servants and the old suffered disproportionately as they lacked the cash or the luxury goods to barter for supplementary food.[83] By 1943–44 Belgian and French families were spending 70 per cent of their income on food. Even middle-class Parisians had to make do with a dreary round of soup, a little sausage and the occasional egg with beans.[84] Tuberculosis, which is strongly associated with malnutrition, spread among the young and in France deaths from the disease doubled. Malnutrition could be read in the stunted growth of children. In 1944 French girls were 11 centimetres, and boys 7 centimetres, shorter than the height of their counterparts in 1935. By 1943, 80 per cent of urban Belgian children were suffering from rickets, caused by severe vitamin D deficiency in the diet. Parisians betrayed their lack of vitamins in their dull eyes and sallow complexions.[85]

ALLIES AND ARYANS

In theory Italy and Germany were allies but when in October 1940 Mussolini tried to assert Italy's autonomy by invading Greece without consulting Hitler all he succeeded in doing was relegating Italy to the position of a satellite state of the Reich. Italy's humiliating inability to defeat the Greeks and the need for Germany to send in its own troops to finish the job discredited Mussolini in the eyes of both the National Socialists and his own people.[86] When Mussolini was overthrown in the autumn of 1943 Italy went over to the Allies, triggering German occupation of the country.

Italy's agricultural sector should have been well prepared for war. When Mussolini seized power in 1922 one-quarter of Italy's budget for imported goods and services was spent on wheat. Mussolini could see that if his plans for a Mediterranean empire were to be realized, food self-sufficiency would be an essential element in addressing the balance of payments deficit and freeing up foreign exchange. Once these problems were solved Italy would have a far more solid economic foundation for industrial development.[87] Italy's agricultural sector was certainly in desperate need of regeneration, marked as it was by low productivity, high unemployment and poverty. The 'Battle for Wheat' was launched in July 1925 and by dint of land reclamation the area under wheat was increased. Outreach and education programmes introducing machinery, fertilizers, higher-yielding wheat varieties and irrigation were extremely effective. By 1935 Italy had increased its wheat production by 40 per cent and significantly reduced its expenditure on food imports. The only problem was that internal wheat production did not cover the gap created by cutting imports, and the annual amount of wheat available across the population declined by 14 kilograms per person.[88]

When Hitler invaded Poland, Italian officials began to panic-buy wheat from Hungary and Yugoslavia, afraid that they would be unable to feed the population with Italy's own wheat harvest, and bread and flour shortages did indeed plague wartime Italy. Meanwhile, Darré went on a tour of the country to assess future prospects for food exports to the Reich.[89] Once Italy had entered the war a general state of administrative chaos meant that Mussolini's Battle for Wheat campaign was neglected and overall agricultural yields fell. In 1943 they had fallen by 25 per cent. Once the Germans had occupied the country they sank dramatically to 63 per cent of pre-war levels.[90] Filled with contempt for their erstwhile allies and careless of its impact on the Italians' food supply, the National Socialists continued to demand wheat, rice, tobacco, cheese, fruit and vegetables in exchange for coal. Those German soldiers stationed in the country were allocated a meat ration of 750 grams a week. This represented about double the amount of calories provided by the daily Italian ration. The Italians complained that the Germans were 'eating away at Italy'.[91] In 1944 the Agriculture Minister, Edoardo Moroni, begged for Germany to send a delivery of grain or at least trucks so that food could be transported to the cities. His pleas fell on deaf ears.

The gradual worsening of the Italian food situation was reflected in the experience of the family of Giovanni Tassoni and his wife Guila. The family was very poor. They lived in a one-room shack near the gravel pit where Giovanni worked manufacturing lime in a kiln. The nearest town was Valmonte, two hours' train journey from Rome. No one in their neighbourhood possessed a radio or read newspapers, so they were only vaguely aware of the course of the war and most of their information came from rumours. In the early years the war had little effect on the family. Women, children and the elderly became increasingly dominant in the town as the young men were conscripted, and food became more difficult to acquire. By 1942 the shortage of food began to make itself felt. The ration of bread sank to 150 grams a day, and meat, oil and butter rations were all gradually reduced. Then suddenly in August 1943 Germans appeared and, as the Tassonis realized, they were now in charge. 'Food became even scarcer', and this was not helped by the demands of the occupying troops who would come to their shack and demand eggs or bread.[92]

By late 1943 at least thirteen people were living in the Tassonis' hut besides the Tassonis and their own five children. It was a struggle to feed everyone. The Germans had requisitioned the local flour mill so 'Giovanni reconstructed an old coffee mill for the milling of the flour. When properly fastened to the table, it was possible to produce four to five kilos of flour if one worked all night. At first the only wheat that was available was black, and when that ran out fava and ceci beans were ground to make the flour for bread.' The family turned their entire garden over to the production of potatoes, and 'Guila coaxed her hens to make more eggs so that she could trade some for bread, which the Germans baked in their giant ovens nearby.'[93] The Tassonis were eventually driven out of their home by Allied bombing and went to live in a cave. German soldiers fleeing from the invading Americans would occasionally turn up there and beg for civilian clothes. Then one day the Americans arrived and scattered caramels from the turrets of their tanks. 'Word spread quickly that the fields near Cisterna and Anzio where the Americans had been dug in, were full of such treasures, and so people from all over bicycled, ran, and walked in that direction to bring home whatever they might find. The scavenging was always dangerous because of the possibility of setting off a land mine. The food was as welcome as it was unfamiliar. Everything was in cans – even the spaghetti – and tasted of sugar.'[94] When the Allies liberated Italy they were shocked by the utter deprivation of the urban population. As the troops arrived in the port of Naples they were horrified to observe malnourished people, dressed in rags, picking scraps of garbage out of crevices in the pier. In the town itself a prostitute could be bought for 25 cents, the price of an American C ration can of meat and vegetable hash.[95]

Even if the Italians began the war as Germany's allies their supposed racial inferiority and military ineptitude meant that the National Socialists accorded them little respect. In contrast, the Danes were regarded as fellow Aryans. Consequently, the occupying German authorities interfered less in the agricultural administration of the country and allowed the existing pre-war institutions to remain in place.[96] This caused far less disruption to agriculture than was the case in Belgium or France and enabled the government to maintain greater control over its farmers.

The Germans had highest hopes for receiving food imports from France and Holland. It was hoped that the Dutch surpluses, which had previously gone to Britain, would simply be redirected to the Reich. But this calculation failed to allow for the impact of the loss of agricultural inputs such as fodder and fertilizer because of the blockade. The Dutch responded to this problem by quickly converting from livestock to arable farming and although they were able to send large quantities of meat and fat to the Reich in the first two years of the war, by the end they were only able to supply potatoes, feed grain, sugar and large quantities of fruit and vegetables.[97]

It was Denmark which surprised the Germans. Danish administrators adopted a pricing policy which encouraged farmers to maximize production of the commodities most desirable for Germany – beef, milk, pork and bacon – and, despite difficulties associated with the lack of imported feed and fertilizers, the farmers delivered.[98] Control over Danish consumption was left in the hands of the Danish government and was limited to no more than butter rationing and restrictions on the purchase of meat. The reasonable rations meant that the black market barely existed in Denmark and the Germans were able to cream off a surprisingly large surplus. Denmark provided the Reich with about one month's worth of butter, pork and beef a year. As food supplies in Germany decreased, this contribution became ever more important, providing perhaps as much as 20 per cent of the urban population's meat in 1944.[99]

Holland and Denmark both possessed relatively efficient agricultural sectors. In particular, scientific knowledge was integral to their agricultural processes. This meant that they were able to restructure their agricultural production, and the eating habits of their populations were sufficiently flexible to allow the substitution of one foodstuff for another. As a result their populations were the best fed in occupied western Europe. Nevertheless, there was a subtle difference between the diets of the two countries which was reflected in a rise in infectious diseases such as diphtheria and tuberculosis, measles, whooping cough, dysentery, bronchopneumonia, typhoid and flu among small children and young adults in Holland.[100] Most of the factors which could explain the spread of infectious diseases – overcrowding, the increasing mobility of populations, lack of soap and poor hygiene, illegal and possibly unsafe slaughtering of meat – were present in both countries.[101] The explanation seems to lie in the micronutrient deficiencies in the Dutch diet which have a particularly pernicious impact on the development of the immune system in the young.

Like the British, the Dutch switched to eating wholemeal bread and more vegetables and cut back on meat and fat. The poor in particular converted to a plant-based diet and swapped their meat coupons for bread on the black market. Lack of animal foods in the diet led in turn to a lack of trace elements such as iron, zinc, selenium, vitamins A, B6 and B12, which makes children more vulnerable to disease and increases the rate of child mortality.[102] This phenomenon impacted on child health throughout all of German-occupied western and eastern Europe. It was only the Danes, who managed to maintain an adequate amount of meat in their diet, who escaped this side-effect of German occupation.

Having spent the war relatively cushioned from wartime hunger, the Dutch suffered terribly at the end of the war during the battle to liberate Europe. In September 1944 the Allied operation to re-take Holland failed, and the provinces of North and South Holland and Utrecht were left in German hands. Thinking liberation was at hand, the Dutch railway workers had gone on strike, and in retaliation the Germans cut the gas, electricity, water and food supplies into these parts of Holland.[103] Throughout the cold winter of 1944–45 the situation of the Dutch trapped in this pocket became desperate. Cornelia Fuykschot recalled that without water to wash, heating or light, life became dirty, cold and joyless. Every evening her family retreated into the kitchen 'in the gathering darkness, the street empty, the curtains open since we had no light of any kind and our hands in our pockets because it was cold inside too'.[104] Here they would huddle around the stove where a pot of black market dried peas would be cooking. Fortunately her mother had laid down a store of peas early in the war in case of an emergency. 'We ate a pan full of them every day. They were our only meal and all there was. Parsley, celery, carrots and onions were finished. Even salt could no longer be bought . . . You had to chew carefully because some of the black was not pea, nor blight, but gravel, and that could cost you your tooth. Most of the peas went down unchewed; they had not even swelled up enough to become bigger, and we let our stomachs do the sorting and digesting.'[105] By March 1945 the peas were beginning to run short and Cornelia's family eked them out by limiting themselves to one cup each per day.

The Red Cross lobbied to be allowed to transport food into the area. But Churchill remained as unwilling as ever to feed European civilians trapped behind German lines. He argued that the food would just be eaten by the Germans. The American government was also concerned that the Soviets might be antagonized if any food transported into the area by the Allies fell into the hands of the Wehrmacht. The Soviets were in no mood to countenance feeding German soldiers while the Red Army was still spilling blood trying to defeat the Wehrmacht in the east. Reports began to reach Britain that the Dutch were dying in the streets of Amsterdam.[106] In the end the death toll reached 22,000.[107] The Dutch prime minister in exile informed Churchill that his people would hold him responsible for the deaths, and General Eisenhower, Supreme Commander of the Allied Forces, pointed out that he did not want to send Allied troops into an area where people were already starving.[108] Conditions generally deteriorated for the first few weeks after liberation and the already dire food situation meant that chaos and a significantly increased death-rate were likely to ensue. These arguments persuaded Churchill to relax his stand. The American food administrators in Britain released some of the United States' stocks earmarked for Germany, and the Allies began air-dropping food into the region in March 1945. Air-drops were chosen as the quickest and most effective way of getting food to the area from Britain. Once it had been decided to bring in aid, the measures were generous. From the end of April 1945, 800 Allied planes dropped 7,458 tons of food, including flour, chocolate, tea and margarine. Unfortunately many of the packages smashed, leaving a thin layer of fat all over the dropping zones. The Dutch authorities' punctiliousness in first collecting and sorting the food before attempting to distribute it as fairly as possible, meant that it took another ten days before the civilians started to receive handouts. For some this was ten days too long and the delay cost lives.[109] The Dutch were finally liberated by the Canadians in May 1945. Cornelia remembered the delight her family took in the military supplies that became available in the stores and her praise for reviled wartime foods indicates the level of deprivation the Dutch had experienced. 'The grocery stores sold powdered egg, bought from army surplus, something we had never heard of before, and it fascinated us with its possibilities. You just had to add water and you could fry an omelette! . . . Another new item was Spam . . . canned meat. That too had myriad possibilities, all of them good.'[110]

The fact that Denmark was able to export 200,000 tons of butter to the Reich between 1940 and 1943, in comparison to a paltry 49,000 tons of butter from France, demonstrates the superiority of the lenient occupational agricultural strategy adopted in Denmark.[111] The situation in Denmark showed that with the right governmental pricing policies farmers could be motivated to overcome their difficulties and maintain yields. Even in Belgium, which was hard hit by the loss of imports, farmers demonstrated this point – although in Belgium's case the motivational pricing was provided by the black market. Sensible pricing policies would also have addressed the problem of small farmers' tendency to withdraw from the market and reduce their production.

When imports are measured in quantity (rather than in monetary value) then the continental European countries delivered 40 per cent less food in 1943 than they had in peacetime.[112] The German occupiers would have had a better chance of squeezing more food out of western Europe if they had invested in restructuring agriculture rather than concentrating on plunder. If the self-sufficiency lessons learned in Germany had been transferred to the relatively modernized western European farmers this would have gone some way towards addressing the problems created by blockade. In addition, if civilian rations had been maintained at a reasonable level, as they were in Denmark, the black market would have been made superfluous to survival and thus been dampened down. In this way the authorities would have gained control over a far greater proportion of the food the farmers actually produced. Backe's insistence on looking eastwards to the less modern and adaptable Ukraine as a bread basket for the Reich revealed just how little he understood the economics and the logic of agriculture and food supply. Meanwhile, Göring's insistence on regarding the occupied countries as short-term sources of food, and the ruthless requisitioning policies which he insisted upon, meant that hunger, malnutrition and, in the case of the Greeks, famine, were exported to millions of Europeans.

9

Germany Exports Hunger
to the East

*What can one do, how to live? They probably want to give us
a slow death. Obviously it is inconvenient to shoot everybody.*
(L. Nartova, an unemployed teacher in Kiev, 25 April 1942)[1]

Early in 1941 Hitler, Göring and Backe all set their sights on the Soviet
Union as the solution to Germany's food shortages. Their intentions
were set out in the Hunger Plan – Backe's scheme to divert food from
the towns of the occupied Soviet Union, which it was estimated would
result in the death by starvation of 30 million Soviets. The plan clearly
stated that the first priority would be to feed the Wehrmacht. The
National Socialists wanted their troops to be well fed, but Backe was
adamant that over a prolonged period German agriculture would be
unable to bear the strain of feeding at least 3,000 calories per man per
day to a military force which, at its peak, numbered 9.5 million men
(about one-seventh of the total population).[2] The Wehrmacht was
particularly greedy for grain, meat and fat. By the beginning of 1943
the army was consuming 40 per cent of the total amount of grain
available to the Reich, and 62 per cent of the meat.[3] Even in 1941 it
was clear that Germany's campaign for self-sufficiency would be unable
to close the meat and fat gap for the civilian population and the extra
food to feed the army would have to be found from elsewhere. Hence
the clear statement in the Hunger Plan of 1941 that 'the war can only
be continued if the *entire* Wehrmacht is fed from Russia in the third
year of the war'.[4]

It was hoped that the Ukraine would produce enough food not only
to feed the army but to supplement the food supply within the Reich.

Within Germany memories of the First World War did much to dampen down enthusiasm for going to war. The German people were afraid that the Second World War would bring a repeat of the dreadful turnip winter of 1916–17. The *Sicherheitsdienst*, whose job it was to monitor the public mood, found that already in the summer of 1941 food shortages and the unequal distribution of rations were the most complained about issues after the resentment caused by the conscription of women.[5] The *Sicherheitsdienst* claimed that across the whole of Germany a psychosis of anxiety had developed over food.[6] They cited depressed workers in Cologne upon whom the victories in Russia appeared to have made little impression. As they stood queuing for food outside the shops they had been heard to declare that 'the alleged victories in the East were less important than the necessity of getting enough to eat'.[7]

Nutritionists fed the sense of anxiety which surrounded the issue of food. When Germany invaded Poland, Franz Wirz, campaigner for the improvement of German health, wrote to Leonardo Conti, head of the Department of Health. During the First World War, he warned, 'malnutrition prepared the ground for the poison of defeatism and revolution. In the present war the strength of the homeland and performance levels of the workers play an even greater role than ever before.'[8] In 1940 Leonardo Conti was already arguing that German rations were at the limits for maintaining health.[9] At the Institute for the Physiology of Work Heinrich Kraut had developed the idea of the 'full person', who on average needed 1,800 calories a day for his body to carry out its normal existential metabolic functions such as breathing and digestion. Kraut correctly concluded that only the number of calories which were added to this basic requirement made any difference to productivity. He calculated that a 'normal user' (*Normalverbraucher*) required an extra 230 calories to carry out everyday physical activities. A hard labourer on the other hand would need an extra 1,750 calories.[10] Kraut's calculations provided the basis for the original ration quantities allotted in 1939. These rations were, however, regarded as a minimum and many German scientists believed that fewer calories would damage health and impact upon workers' productivity.

Kraut therefore responded with alarm when cuts were made in the rations. In August 1940 the bread ration was cut by 600 grams a week, representing a drop of about 50 calories per day in workers' diets. The workers who relied on bread for their lunchtime meal were dissatisfied and Kraut's Institute for the Physiology of Work found that they had lost 2 or 3 kilograms in weight, demonstrating that their food intake was not commensurate with their energy expenditure.[11] When in May 1941 the Ministry of Food cut the meat ration by 400 grams a week Kraut drove to Berlin to warn Backe that the war could not be won on such small quantities of food. Backe received reassurances from Kraut that no lasting damage would be done if the ration was raised again in a few months. No doubt such advice made him all the more determined to put the Hunger Plan into action and extract as much food as possible from the Soviet Union.[12]

Throughout the first half of 1941 the concerns of Backe at the Ministry of Food, Conti at the Ministry of Health, the reports of the *Sicherheitsdienst* and nutritionists working for the Institute for the Physiology of Work all created a powerful sense that Germany was building towards a food crisis. But Hitler, Göring and Backe were all confident that the attack on the Soviet Union would solve the problem: 'On the endless fields of the East surge waves of wheat, enough and more than enough to feed our people and the whole of Europe . . . This is our war aim.'[13] The military and political leadership expected to defeat Russia within two or three months and Hitler, Göring and Backe thought that by September 1941 Germany would begin reaping the spoils of war and transports of Ukrainian grain would start to arrive in the Reich.

There were many within the regime who did not share their optimism. On the basis of Germany's and Austria's disappointing experience in the Ukraine in 1918 there were plenty of sceptics who thought that Russia might feed the occupying troops, but were doubtful whether the Soviet Union would provide the German Reich with useful resources, let alone food. Gebhardt von Walther, a German official in the Moscow embassy, wrote to Hasso von Etzdorf, representative of the Foreign Office in the Army High Command, warning that agricultural production would almost certainly decline. Etzdorf handed the report on to Chief of the Army General Staff, General Franz Halder.[14] Halder was himself pessimistic, judging that the army could hardly be expected soon to reach the oilfields in the Caucasus, let alone exploit them. His advisers thought, as it turned out correctly, that the Soviet Union would marshal its resources beyond the Urals, out of the Germans' reach, while the overpopulated and impoverished Ukraine would prove a disappointment.[15] The Finance Minister Lutz Graf Schwerin von Krosigk and Foreign Office official Ernst Freiherr von Weizsäcker wrote letters to Göring and the Foreign Minister Joachim von Ribbentrop respectively, warning that it was folly to expect to be able to import agricultural goods from an invaded Soviet Union.[16] Hitler and Göring remained adamant that if sufficient ruthlessness was applied in the extermination of the Soviet urban population Russia's food supply would prove bountiful.

They were to be disappointed. The Ukrainian harvest of 1941 was far lower than expected. The Hunger Plan proved difficult to implement and an administrative muddle developed in the east with the army in conflict with the occupying administration over the exploitation of Soviet food supplies. In the winter of 1941 the Wehrmacht became bogged down on the eastern front, unable to capture Moscow. The troops were hungry, as were the industrial workers in the Reich. Backe warned that there would have to be further ration cuts. Throughout its existence the National Socialist state can be described as being in a process of 'cumulative radicalisation'.[17] The National Socialist food system developed along just such a trajectory of progressive instability and extremism. Beginning in the winter of 1941 and continuing throughout the spring and summer of 1942 the regime was faced with a food crisis which pushed it towards ever more extreme acts of aggression and culminated in the massacre of the Soviet, Polish and European Jewish population.

Hitler's role in this process is obscure. It is often argued that Hitler was as afraid of a repeat of the turnip winter as the rest of the German population, but when the *Sicherheitsdienst* warned him of the disastrous impact on morale of the ration cuts in the spring of 1942 he is said to have 'insisted that the people had hidden reserves of strength which were unaffected by temporary hardships'.[18] At this stage in the war he still believed in the German people. On the other hand, he was outraged on their behalf and seriously concerned that food shortages might impact on the war effort. He was determined to take draconian measures to solve the problem. It was in the spring of 1942 that Hitler pronounced that other peoples should starve before the Germans. The response within his administration was to begin a campaign to exterminate 'useless eaters', primarily the Polish Jews. No paper evidence has ever been found which proves that Hitler ordered the extermination of the Jews to begin. However, Hitler always intended to rid Europe of its Jewish population, as he declared in a speech to the Reichstag on 30 January 1939.[19] The food problem provided his administration with a rationale for beginning a process of systematic extermination.

LIVING OFF THE LAND

It was the Wehrmacht's policy to live off the land in occupied territory but in June 1941 the unusual decision was taken to implement the policy from the very beginning of the invasion, while the fighting was still under way. Wehrmacht commanders were aware that supply lines to the eastern front would be stretched to breaking point and the few arterial roads running east would be of little use. Stalin had deliberately failed to upgrade the road system as a form of defence against attack and many of the main roads petered out into gravel tracks. The rail network offered a more viable solution for bringing in supplies of fuel and ammunition but this too had few routes running east–west and the Soviet rail gauge was (again deliberately) wider than the German. The Soviets were also expected to inflict heavy damage on the rail lines as they retreated.[20] In order to relieve the inevitable congestion on the railways the decision was taken that virtually no food should be brought in from the Reich. Army Quartermaster-General Eduard Wagner noted that 'extensive exploitation of the land' would have to be immediately implemented.[21]

Commanding officers were duly instructed to obtain as much of their food as possible from local sources. Early on in the campaign, the supply officer of the 286 security division reported that sufficient quantities of food to provide the men with the full ration had been 'extracted from the civilian population without misgivings'. He did complain, however, that the local 'flour, noodles and bread were of an unfamiliar consistency and bad quality'.[22] 'We live well,' another foot-soldier reassured his family in a letter written in July, 'even though we are sometimes cut off from the supply lines. We supply ourselves, sometimes chickens, sometimes geese, sometimes pork cutlets.'[23]

However, it quickly became evident to the German supply officers that the policy of living off the land was getting out of hand. It was never the quartermaster-general's intention that army units should routinely plunder the villages. At the planning stage he emphasized that 'the capture [of Soviet food supplies] must be tightly controlled. The country's stocks are not to be utilized through indiscriminate pillaging. But rather through seizure and collection according to a well thought out plan.'[24] But the German infantry went into action with the Barbarossa decree ringing in their ears, instructing the men to execute all Red Army political officers and energetically punish any signs of resistance on the part of the civilians.[25] In effect it gave them carte blanche to participate in atrocities against the civilian population. In all areas of the eastern front the infantry shot 'useless' villagers out of hand, stole their possessions or drove them from their homes. As part of the frenzy of killing, troops sometimes indulged in the senseless slaughter of livestock.

The quartermaster-general's office repeatedly stipulated that the collection of food should be planned and organized and that individual acts of plunder were forbidden, but the men demonstrated themselves incapable of understanding the distinction between plunder organized by the German authorities and plunder as part of the general destruction of Soviet society which the troops had been encouraged to undertake.[26] Florian Geyer of an SS cavalry brigade described in a letter home how the soldiers simply needed to shoot in the air as they entered the villages and the inhabitants would appear with eggs. An artillery man gloated over his night patrol's booty of seven sheep and numerous geese: 'Yummy, yummy say I – like in the old days.'[27] Only a few weeks into the campaign, at the end of July 1941, the 18th Panzer Division reported that the 'last remaining food reserves and livestock' had already been taken from the villagers in its area. In November the front-line troops were warned that 'the livestock population in the occupied parts of Russia has already been so frightfully reduced, that if the unsparing taking of cattle from the land by the troops continues . . . it will result in starvation among the inhabitants and cause severe problems for the German army due to the approach of winter.'[28]

The Wehrmacht was never able to extract sufficient quantities of food to cover all the food needs of the Army Groups North and Centre. Belorussia, which was the base for Army Group Centre, was expected to find lavish quantities of food to support between 1 and 1.5 million troops at the front, large numbers of troops in transit, and an occupying force in the rear of just under half a million.[29] The soldiers at the front alone ate 120 tons of meat each day and their numerous draught horses chomped through vast quantities of fodder.[30] These were not rich agricultural areas and the already backward farms now had to contend with a lack of tractors, fuel, draught animals, fertilizer and labour as forced labour requisitions for the Reich denuded the area of all able-bodied men and women. The only incentive to meet the excessively high demands placed on the collective farms was the fear of the dreadful punishments inflicted on those who failed to meet their quotas. The area was soon denuded of fodder crops and this was reflected in the slaughter weight of livestock, which fell by half. The Wehrmacht eventually moved on to eating the peasants' draught animals, three-quarters of which ended up on the plates of the German soldiers, leaving the peasant women with no alternative other than to yoke themselves to the ploughs.[31] Between September 1941 and August 1942 Belorussia provided Army Group Centre with 60 per cent of its bread grain, 90 per cent of its potatoes, 65 per cent of its meat and 10 per cent of its fat. But by January 1943 the strain on the agricultural system was beginning to show and its contribution to the army's needs had fallen and accounted for only 17 per cent of its grain and 11 per cent of its meat.[32] The deficits had to be made up by transports of food from the Ukraine or the Reich.

It was expected that Army Group South, based in the Ukraine, would not only be able to cover all its own food requirements but transport food to Army Groups North and Centre. As the Wehrmacht entered the Ukraine many of the ragged peasants welcomed the Germans as liberators, come to free them from the tyranny of Soviet rule, and took them into their homes, gave them lodging and treated the wounded. In the early 1930s Stalin had imposed collectivization on the Ukraine, abolishing the private ownership of land and forcing the peasants to work on state-run farms formed out of the consolidation of their private plots. Seven million Ukrainians had died in the famine which accompanied this process. Many took the opportunity of the German invasion to indulge in an orgy of destruction, breaking apart combine harvesters and tractors in a Luddite frenzy of rage against enforced collectivization.[33] The *Sicherheitsdienst* was astonished by the Ukrainians' faith in the German occupiers and later a leading Ukrainian nationalist Andrij Melnyk complained that Germany had missed a valuable opportunity. He asserted that the Ukrainians had been 'ready to bear even a heavy burden, if they had been certain that their right to life and national development ... would have been respected'.[34] Most peasants were hoping the Germans would dismantle the detested collectives and reintroduce private ownership of farmland.

Alfred Rosenberg, Minister for the Occupied Eastern Territories, was in favour of appeasing the peasantry and dissolving the collectives. He envisaged the Ukraine as a satellite state where the majority of peasants could be won over to German rule and persuaded to co-operate in producing as much food as possible for the Reich. In this he was supported by Otto Bräutigam, deputy head of the Eastern Ministry's Main Political Department and a specialist in Soviet agriculture. Early on in the occupation Bräutigam warned that the seizure of millions of tons of food would 'cause anxiety and hatred of Germany among the people of the occupied territories ... it cannot be good for German long-term interests'.[35] But Rosenberg and his officials were in complete disagreement with Erich Koch, Reich Commissar of the Ukraine, with Göring and with Backe. This group wanted to keep the collective farms as the most effective means of quickly implementing colonial exploitation. The military were also in favour of maintaining the collectives as they simply wanted to get as much food as quickly as possible and state-run farms seemed the best way to achieve this in the short term.[36]

However, in the summer of 1941, as the Germans took possession of the country, agriculture descended into confusion. Peasants who went into the fields to bring in the harvest were first strafed by German planes as they attacked, and then by Soviet aircraft, trying to prevent the Germans profiting from Ukrainian bounty. In many parts of the Ukraine the harvest began far too late and the results were mixed. On the west bank of the Dnieper the peasants were hit by the loss of machinery, although when the Germans offered a generous payment of one in three sheaves, which was more than they were accustomed to under the Soviets, they worked hard to bring in the crop by hand.

The Germans arrived late in the countryside north of Kiev and the peasants had already hidden away their bumper crop in attics and cellars. On the eastern bank of the Dnieper the Soviet evacuation of crops, livestock and equipment meant that there was very little left to eat and as the Germans moved in the hungry peasants were already setting to work sowing a winter crop.[37] By November the collective farms had only delivered a disappointing 1 million tons of grain, far less than the 5 million the German agricultural planners had expected, and a quarter of which had already been eaten by the Wehrmacht. A drive to bring in the rest of the crop before the winter set in was hampered by the fact that the troops supervising the harvest were called away to the front, allowing much of what was harvested to disappear into secret Ukrainian stores. A lack of sacks held up the transport and milling of the grain, and damp, mice-infested stores led to the damage of yet more of the precious harvest.[38]

Within the Wehrmacht the army quartermaster was in internal competition with the army's economy offices for a disappointingly small amount of food. The latter began to transport food back to Germany in order to build up reserves for the troops it was expecting to return to the Reich once victory had been achieved. The consequence of this was that once victory proved elusive much of the army's reserve food supplies were in the wrong place.[39] Meanwhile, the civil administration in the Ukraine was concentrating on fulfilling its food quotas for German civilians. The civil administration refused to give the Wehrmacht accurate figures for the food it had and what it expected to collect. Although it was obliged to give the Wehrmacht first refusal on all foodstuffs, it employed a tactic of offering the army quantities of grain which it knew the army would be unable to store. When the Wehrmacht refused the deliveries they were quickly sent back to Germany. In November and December the army was in the ridiculous position of watching five trains of livestock per day leave for the Reich while it did not have enough fresh meat to fill the ration for the troops at the front. It took the army weeks of protest finally to secure half of the storage space at the train stations which then enabled it to buy part of these supplies, and it was only in January that it was able to secure trains of cattle for the southern quartermaster.[40]

Even when the Wehrmacht had the foodstuffs in its possession, it lacked the means to take the food to the front. The increasingly power-ful resistance by the Red Army meant that more and more supply trains were needed to bring munitions up to the front. The shortage of rolling stock became acute as trains broke down or were destroyed. This reduced even further the means to transport food. The occupying powers were simply not sufficiently well supplied with manpower, rolling stock and equipment to fully exploit what food there was in the occupied territories. In the end single lorries kept up a daily trickle of supply.[41]

Throughout the summer Hitler, Göring, Backe and Quartermaster-General Wagner were disappointed by the amount of food the army was managing to extract from the occupied areas. The army had too few men behind the lines to stamp out the partisans or punish passive resistance on the part of the civilians, which hampered the efficiency of centralized collection efforts. The unauthorized collection of food on the part of the troops made matters worse. The Wehrmacht's supply problems were becoming acute by September 1941 when Backe inten-sified the pressure by presenting Hitler with a new food plan which made it clear that the only way to avoid reducing rations within Germany was for the Wehrmacht to take more food out of the occupied Soviet areas. In the paper he explicitly refused to supply the army with grain and meat from German farms.[42]

The department of the quartermaster, food officers and the military commanders and commandants on the ground responded to the prob-lem of the disappointing food deliveries by calling for the removal of Jewish mouths from the Soviet food chain. It is difficult to build up a precise picture of the plans for the annihilation of the Soviet Jews as the National Socialists took care not to leave incriminating written records. It is certain that 'pre-invasion there were no orders given and no written plan to wipe out *all* the Soviet Jews'.[43] It was assumed that the majority of the Soviet Jewish population would die from under-nourishment along with the rest of the inhabitants of the western towns in which they were concentrated.[44] As the Wehrmacht stormed across the Soviet Union it was followed by the *Einsatzgruppen*, who were ordered to murder all adult men identified as potential political leaders and resistance organizers. Some of their victims were Bolsheviks but most of them were Jewish. In the summer the campaign was stepped up and the SS and the police began systematically to murder *all* Soviet Jews, including women and children. The quartermaster-general reported that he expected the annihilation of the Jews in central Lithuania, which began in August, to significantly alleviate the food supply problems for Army Group North. In August, 15,000 Jews were shot in Polesje (Prijetsümpfe). Task forces moved through northern Ukraine massacring the inhabitants of village after village. Particular targets were Jews in urban areas where the civilian population was starving, especially in the towns where food and shelter were a problem for troops moving up to the front.[45] In Kharkov 15,000 Jews were murdered that winter, supposedly in order to alleviate the food situation. In Kiev the German authorities claimed that a systematic massacre of Jews on 29 and 30 September had alleviated the food and housing conditions for the rest of the civilian population.[46] By the end of 1941 there were virtually no Jews left in eastern Belorussia, northern and eastern Ukraine or any other parts of the occupied Soviet Union. Over a period of six months a total of 800,000 Soviet Jews had been murdered.[47]

IMPLEMENTING THE HUNGER PLAN

In the summer of 1941 the shortcomings of Backe's starvation policy became apparent. The designation 'plan' gives an entirely false impression that the implementation of the strategy was well thought through and organized. In fact, the bureaucrats on the ground were given no precise instructions as to how the Hunger Plan should be implemented.[48] The attack on the Soviet Union was supposed to end in victory sometime towards the end of September. This would free up plenty of troops, whom Hitler, Göring and Backe then intended to deploy in enforcing the starvation of the towns.[49] There was no contingency plan in place for the eventuality that a military campaign would be taking place while the inhabitants of the hinterland behind the front were supposed to be starving to death. For example, it was predicted in the document that livestock rearing would cease in Belorussia due to a lack of imported feed.[50] This was all very well as long as there were no longer troops at the front line relying on local food supplies.

In the first few weeks of the military campaign the principles of the Hunger Plan were followed and Soviet civilians received no food handouts and no provision was made to introduce rationing in the towns and cities. However, the army relied on the urban areas as transport and support centres for the troops. Given the small numbers of security forces, the prospect of civilian unrest in these towns was most unwelcome. In the Ukraine the Wehrmacht used the towns not only as food supply bases for the soldiers at the front but also as centres for small-scale repair workshops and armaments factories, even though this was in direct conflict with an alternative plan to shut down all eastern industry and ship the labour back to the Reich. Instead of going to work in their factories the industrial workforce spent long days trawling the countryside for food. The armaments inspector for the Ukraine, Major-General Hans Leykauf, complained in frustration, 'if we shoot dead all the Jews, allow the prisoners of war to die, dish out famine to the majority of the urban population, and in the coming year will lose a proportion of the rural population to hunger, the question remains unanswered: *Who will actually produce economic goods?*'[51]

As the realities sank in of the difficulty of controlling vast swathes of eastern territory filled with starving towns and cities, the military administration in the Ukraine changed its mind about the Hunger Plan. A local military administrator commented in October that 'ever more frequently there has been mention of the civilian food supply . . . That the Russians are still here too, we never really considered. No, that is not quite right. Following the official instructions we were . . . not supposed to consider them. But the war has taken a different turn . . . Under these circumstances we cannot afford not to consider the population in food terms. But where are we supposed to get anything from?'[52] Orders were sent out by the field commanders for the peasants to bring food into the towns.[53] It was proving impossible to close off entire towns from the countryside, and the black market was flourishing as civilians streamed into the rural areas to barter for food.[54]

Once the civil administration took over the government of the occupied areas from the military, the agricultural organization was put under the control of Backe and the hard line of the Hunger Plan was re-imposed. Exceptions were made for those sections of the population that were useful to the Germans. Railway workers, wagon drivers and colonies of road-builders were fed on the lowest ration scale of the army.[55] But the rest of the people were allocated no rations. The brutal policy swelled the ranks of the partisans and the rural population was augmented by townspeople fleeing the hunger. The military appealed for a change of policy. Field Marshal Walther von Brauchitsch suggested a new feeding hierarchy which prioritized the German army, but which placed the indigenous civilian population second in line, before German civilians in the Reich. Lieutenant-General Erich Friderici supported such a scheme, pointing out, 'This is not a humanitarian concern but a purely practical consideration in German interests.'[56]

Göring remained implacable, and doggedly repeated to military sceptics his mantra that the German administration must expect 'the greatest death rate since the Thirty Years War'.[57] Despite the Wehrmacht troops' reputation for brutality there were evidently plenty who found this too much to stomach. Not only did the quartermaster-general have to issue repeated warnings to the troops that they must not plunder indiscriminately, he also had continually to issue commands that troops were not to feed Russian civilians from the mess. Evidently, in the contradictory chaos that was the occupied Soviet Union, both were frequent occurrences. The quartermaster-general noted that the ordinary soldiers were often 'very kind' to the civilians, even though they were repeatedly told, 'every gram of bread or food that I give out of generosity to the people in the occupied territories, I take away from the German people, and my family'.[58]

Towards the end of the year, the Commander-in-Chief of the 9th Army made the bitter observation that 'if the Russian attack had been a Blitzkrieg, then we would not have needed to take the civilian population into account. But an end [to the fighting] is not foreseeable . . . in these circumstances it is not sensible to follow a course which makes the civilian population 100 per cent into an enemy.'[59] On 4 November 1941 the civil administration bowed to the reality that some townspeople were already receiving food and set a maximum ration scale for the towns in the occupied territories. However, the allocation of food simply modified the principles of the Hunger Plan and targeted more specific groups. It was stipulated that those who worked for the Germans could receive up to 1,200 calories a day, their dependants 850 calories, but the number of people receiving this ration was not to amount to more than 20 per cent of the total population. Children under fourteen and Jews were allocated the impossibly tiny amount of 420 calories, which amounts to about 500 grams of potatoes. Jews were banned from purchasing eggs, butter, milk, meat or fruit, from dealing with farmers directly or from going to the food markets. This was a death sentence by hunger rather than by shooting. Over the winter of 1941–42 tens of thousands of Jewish men, women and children died of starvation.[60] They were joined by at least 1 million Soviet prisoners of war, deliberately left to starve in the holding camps, and millions of Soviets who lived in cities which were deprived of a food supply.

In the autumn of 1941, in the area controlled by Army Group Centre and in the General Government, about 9,000 Soviet prisoners of war were dying in the German camps each month.[61] This equals the total number of British and American soldiers who died in German and Italian captivity during the entire five and a half years of the war.[62] At a meeting with the Wehrmacht, Göring clarified the National Socialist attitude to the Soviets: 'When it comes to the care of the Bolshevik prisoners, we are not, in contrast with other prisoners of war, bound by any international agreement to look after them. Their care can only be determined by their ability to work for us.'[63]

The conditions in which Soviet prisoners of war were held were appalling. The camps were nothing more than fields surrounded by fences. There were frequently no buildings, nor even tents. There was little water, the distribution of food was minimal; the Ministry of Food allocated them a ration of 1,561 calories a day but transport problems meant that supplies were erratic. While the prisoners still had some fat reserves and bodily resistance there were only one or two deaths a day in each camp. But as autumn approached and the weather conditions worsened they began to die in droves. A German officer described how anyone following a column of prisoners 'can see that all the leaves and the discarded stalks of sugar beet have been picked up from the fields with wild greed and consumed . . . In the fields if a group of prisoners approaches, the women throw sugar beet on the path and they are gathered by the prisoners as quickly as possible. It is to be expected that the sight of these weakened prisoners whose hunger stares out of their eyes, damages the reputation of the Germans in the eyes of the population.'[64] But comments such as this were not welcome. Those uneasy about the policy were told, in the language of the Hunger Plan, that they 'must realise that every unjustified or surplus amount of food that the prisoners receive, must be removed from the civilians at home or the German soldiers'.[65] By September 1941 the prisoners were so desperate with hunger they began to beg the guards to shoot them.[66]

Once it became clear that the eastern territories were not going to yield the quantities of food that had been hoped for, the policy of allowing the prisoners to slowly starve to death shifted to one of determined extermination. Backe threatened that, unless the Soviet prisoners' ration was reduced, a cut in the German civilian ration would be necessary. In one of the few statements that clearly expressed what was usually an unspoken policy, the Quartermaster-General Eduard Wagner told the army chiefs of staff in no uncertain terms that 'prisoners incapable of work in the prison camps are to starve'.[67] Even those who were selected as fit enough to work died as they laboured. A lieutenant in charge of reconstructing the Russian railways complained in October 1942 that he was 'experiencing horrible days. Every day thirty of my prisoners die, or I must allow them to be shot. It is certainly a picture of cruelty . . . The prisoners, only partially clothed, partly without coats, could no longer get dry. The food is not sufficient, and they collapse one after the other . . . When one sees what a human life really means, then an inner transformation in your own thinking happens. A bullet, a word, and a life is no more. What is a human life?'[68]

Between October 1941 and March 1942 somewhere between 500,000 and 700,000 Soviet prisoners of war starved to death. The prisoners held by Army Group Centre and in the General Government, where food-supply problems were at their worst, were the most affected. While Army Group Centre took only 47 per cent of the Soviet prisoners, 71 per cent of those for whom they were responsible died.[69] In Poland, 85 per cent of the prisoners died. By February 1942, 60 per cent of the 3.35 million Soviet prisoners were dead.[70] If the Germans were to fail to achieve their goal of starving the entire urban Soviet population to death, they applied the principles of the Hunger Plan to their Soviet captives with chilling efficacy.

The siege of Leningrad has become an iconic symbol of starvation during the Second World War. Stories abound of Leningraders boiling leather to make jellies and burning antique furniture and precious books to keep warm.[71] The desperate inhabitants of the city are known to have resorted to cannibalism, and about 1,500 people, mainly young unemployed women desperate to find food for their children, were arrested for the crime.[72] One million people died in the siege of Leningrad. The responsibility for their deaths lies largely with the German invaders, but the Soviets were also partly to blame for the plight of the city. As the German army made alarmingly fast progress across western Russia it became clear that it would reach the city, but the authorities evacuated only 636,000 people, leaving more than 2.5 million to face a long winter of hunger. In all likelihood 'the leadership did not want to appear to be abandoning the city, a symbolism that would not have been lost on the rest of the country'.[73] Stalin was prepared to sacrifice Leningrad's population ruthlessly for the sake of Soviet morale.

Disorganization and lack of preparation meant that there was too little food stored in the city for its citizens to survive a prolonged siege. The authorities failed to disperse what food there was, leaving it vulnerable to air raids. On 8 September, 3,000 tons of grain and 2,500 tons of sugar went up in flames when the Badaev warehouses were fire-bombed. Later, Alexei Bezzubov, an inventive nutritionist who worked at Leningrad's Vitamin Institute, initiated the digging-up of the 'boulders of sweet black earth' which remained at the burnt-out site, and managed to manufacture boiled sweets out of it for the energy-starved Leningraders.[74] Initially, rations were too generous and used up the meagre stores of food too quickly. Eventually the corn and rye flour that was left had to be eked out with cottonseed oil cake, which was usually used for ship fuel, edible cellulose, chaff, flour sweepings and dust from flour sacks. The resulting bread was 'black, sticky, like putty, sodden with an admixture of wood pulp and sawdust'.[75] Anna Ivanovna Likhacheva, a doctor working in the clinic of the Red Banner factory, recalled how the 'fatalities began in December, when the lack of food was coupled with the cold and loss of public transportation. Cold starving people, faithfully carrying out their duties . . . trudged tens of kilometres, often on only 125g of ersatz bread per day and soured cabbage leaves or yeast soup for dinner . . . Excruciating hunger forces a person to think and talk only about one thing – about food, to share memories of dishes that one loved or disliked.'[76]

Despite the fact that so much has been written about the siege of Leningrad, it is less well known that the Germans regarded the death by starvation of its inhabitants as only one element in a far larger plan to eliminate as many Soviet consumers – or, rather, 'useless eaters' – as possible. Even if the inhabitants had wished to surrender, explicit orders had been given forbidding the Wehrmacht from accepting. Quarter-master-General Wagner remarked, 'What are we supposed to do with a city of three and a half million which just rests itself on our supply pouch?'[77] There could be no question of diverting food from the Wehrmacht into a conquered city.[78]

If the Germans had taken the city they would still have left the population to starve, just as they did the people living in the area around the city. These civilians were so desperate that it was impossible to stop them wandering around in the front-line areas looking for something to eat. Tatiana Vassilieva was thirteen when the war stranded her family in Wyritza, a small town in the German-occupied area, about 60 kilo-metres from Leningrad. In autumn they slaughtered their goat and 'ate meat for a whole week. Everything from the garden was eaten up ages ago.' Her mother then bartered all their possessions for potatoes, but by December they had nothing left to barter. Not quite defeated, her mother made a soup out of the family cat and a gruel out of birch wood, against which their stomachs revolted. Then, in despair, Tatiana, her two-year-old sister and her mother joined her sick father on the bed and 'prepared to die'. They were saved by a German tailor who was billeted in their house in January. '"Bread . . . children" he said, and put his finger to his lips.' But then he was called up to fight on the front. Rather than watch her family fade, Tatiana set out with a sledge in search of food. On an empty stomach she walked 120 kilometres, taking several days before reaching a corn-growing area where two kind women give her a sack of grain.[79] Although she saved her family, her father was later beaten to death by the SS and she was eventually deported to the Reich as a forced labourer. At the end of the war she came home to a 'broken' mother, and to her sister, who had become partially deaf and had lost the use of her legs.

The policy of starvation was also applied against the populations of Kiev and Kharkov in the Ukraine, but because the circumstances were less dramatic in that they were not besieged the stories of these cities are less well known. Hitler ordered that Kiev be reduced to rubble by aerial bombing but his generals ignored his demand and took posses-sion of the city on 16 September 1941. Every day a large proportion of the 400,000 people still living in the city would stream out into the countryside to bargain for food. A reverse stream of farmers would later be seen driving their carts into the city to pick up the household goods they had been offered in exchange for food. Then, in October, the German authorities banned the supply of food to the city.[80] Otto Bräutigam later wrote of how the agronomists in meetings would simply state, 'Kiev must starve.'[81] Road-blocks were set up and the peasants were no longer able to trundle their carts laden with cabbages and potatoes into the city.[82] The authorities did allow a market to open two days a week where it was sometimes possible to buy a few potatoes. Mostly only potato peelings were available. They were minced to make into a flour which was fried as a sort of pancake. A survivor recalled that as a child he found these pancakes 'unbelievably nice'.[83] Bread was still sold in the city but non-workers were allocated a mere 200 grams, or one or two slices, a *week* (this was eventually raised to 400 grams in December). Even in Leningrad at that time people were receiv-ing 125 grams of bread a *day* (875 grams a week). The bread was a peculiar substitute substance made from millet mixed with barley, chestnuts and lupine (usually used as fodder for animals). It had a clay-like consistency but disintegrated as it dried out and, as one unfor-tunate consumer described, 'it was gritty to eat and had a bitter-sweet taste. It was difficult to digest.'[84] Many became ill from eating it.[85]

The only sure way of obtaining food was to work for the Germans in one of the small factories that were still functioning, on the railways or in an administrative office. A cleaning lady for the railway admin-istration recounted how she received millet soup and porridge at work, which enabled her to survive. In the winter of 1941 Kiev's Labour Office was 'besieged by hungry people'.[86] But the sick, the elderly, the young and the unemployed – among them many scientists and scholars from the universities and academic research institutes – were unable to scratch together enough food. The mayor of the city did what he could, protecting food supplies for the hospitals from the depredations of the police and distributing food to the elderly and the scholars. But people began to die. From the (probably inaccurate and low) figures of the

Sicherheitsdienst it is possible to see that the mortality rate rose steeply from 58 deaths in October 1941, to 1,120 in February 1942.[87] In November Mikhail Iakovlevich Gerenrot, a former communist official, reported that the city was deserted. The only people on the streets were 'emaciated or swollen from hunger, they roam the streets and walk from house to house in search of charity . . . I also came across people who were lying and sitting; they were so emaciated that they were unable to move.'[88] A. Anatoli Kuznetsov commented on the mood of those who were managing to survive: 'It was bitterly cold and the people walked down the streets with grim expressions on their faces, hunching themselves up from the wind, worried, in ragged clothes, in all sorts of strange footwear and threadbare coats. It was indeed a city of beggars.'[89]

In Kharkov the horror began with the Soviet scorched earth policy. By the time it became clear that the Germans were going to capture the city it was too late to evacuate the remaining 450,000 inhabitants (before the war the population was about 1 million). Instead, the authorities simply began blowing up buildings, to the surprise and shock of passers-by. In an article entitled 'Lest we forget', in the *Ukrainian Quarterly* of 1948, an anonymous 'citizen of Kharkiw' described what happened: 'The government authorities . . . took great trouble to destroy all food products. Declaring the remaining part of the population as traitors and "enemies of the nation" the authorities fully justified themselves in destroying all food stores. Long grains and vast stores of corn, flour and vegetables were destroyed, burnt or spoiled by soaking with kerosene. These enormous quantities of food if justly distributed among the people who stayed would have saved the majority of them from starvation.'[90]

Kharkov was a ruined city of bombed and burned-out houses, 'the black silhouettes of exploded and burnt factories and official buildings' stood out against the skyline, bomb craters were scattered across the city, and where once there had been bridges there was now a 'chaos of stone and iron'.[91] The infrastructure broke down and the people were left without electricity, water or a sewerage system. The anonymous citizen described how 'every kind of communication and transportation facility is totally destroyed. The entering and the leaving of the town is strictly prohibited. Communication of any kind is cut off even

between the parts of the town situated on both sides of the small river
... There are no stores, no markets, no shops of any kind.'[92] Those
who worked for the Germans received about 300 grams of bread a
day. The only way of surviving was to evade the police checks and
barter for food in the countryside.

That winter of 1941–42 'the silence of death prevail[ed] in the main
streets which only a year ago were crowded with people and traffic ...
No people are to be seen anywhere ... No sign of life is to be found.
But you can notice some window frames closed with boards and a
crooked stove-pipe emitting a faint stream of smoke. Here people live!
People who have found a miserable corner to go and hide in, a wretched
nook slowly to die in. In these very small kitchens life is pulsating still.
Here a whole family and sometimes many families have found their
poor shelter. All the inhabitants of Kharkiw live this winter in small
kitchens often with seven to ten people together. They sleep on benches,
tables and simply on the floor in dust and smoke amidst dirty dishes
and garbage. In the daytime they all crowd around the kitchen stove,
– dreary figures wrapped up in odds and ends of raiment and in old
galoshes, snow-boots, warm slippers etc. The rooms are extremely cold
because of the prevailing cold of thirty degrees below zero ... Food is
an article still more rare and consequently more expensive than fuel
... The small supplies of food stored by the population have been long
consumed. The town is void of eatables like a desert.'[93] By the end of
1942, 150,000 of the 450,000 inhabitants who had stayed in Kharkov
had died, the great majority of them from starvation.[94]

THE FOOD CRISIS OF 1941–42

The massacre of the Soviet Jews, the deaths of millions of Soviet prisoners and the agonies of the citizens of Leningrad, Kiev and Kharkov
as they slowly wasted away from hunger did nothing to alleviate the
food crisis which developed on the eastern front that winter. By the
autumn of 1941 it was clear that the Red Army was going to put up
far greater resistance than the Wehrmacht had expected and that
Germany was facing a long and immensely tough battle in the east,
which would require large amounts of equipment, men and food. The

German army was now fighting on an ever lengthening front (it grew from around 1,200 kilometres to about 2,400 kilometres) with supply lines which stretched back over more than 1,500 kilometres of mainly unpaved roads.[95]

As the winter of 1941 approached, the Wehrmacht supply officers became increasingly anxious that they had been unable to build up sufficient stocks to feed the men at the front over the cold months to follow. Army Groups North and Centre were still requesting supplementary food supplies from the Reich. Even the SS were complaining about the food their men were receiving. What was more, the German administration's grip over the areas it occupied was threatened by increasingly effective partisan action behind the lines. But the main problem was transport. The supply troops simply could not get the food through to the men at the front. When the autumn rains set in the roads turned into muddy quagmires. Most of the divisions at the front relied on horse-drawn wagons to bring up food and weapons. The commander of the 16th Army's II Corps reported that 'from my own experience I know that while walking on the roads one sinks to one's knees in the mud, and the water pours into one's boots from above . . . [Horse-drawn] panje-wagons could not get through and the number of food-carriers [on foot] did not suffice.'[96]

A couple of weeks in November brought some relief as the rains stopped and the frost set in and 'solidified the monstrous ruts leading to the east'.[97] Then the winter snows arrived and in that first unbearable winter the temperatures fell to minus 40 degrees Celsius. The motorized Panzer divisions experienced a process of demodernization as those tanks not wiped out by the Russians broke down. Wolfgang Reinhard of the 18th Panzer Division recalled that if the complicated spare parts could not be obtained then 'nothing could be done'.[98] Leo Mattowitz despaired as 'everything mechanical came to a dead halt. Nothing worked at all. Not like the Russians. They were used to it, they took proper precautions. Their machine guns worked, their motors kept running. We didn't even have anti-freeze. Just imagine it: before we left the vehicles we had to let the water run out because it would freeze overnight . . . we were totally unprepared for winter. Totally.'[99] The Germans found that even their railway locomotives were inferior. The Soviets insulated the boilers on their engines in order to prevent the heat escaping into the frosty air. The German trains, without insulation, used excessive quantities of fuel. To make matters worse, they would not run unless the low-quality coal which had been captured in the Donbas region was mixed with higher quality German coal or oil, which had to be imported.[100]

The modern war of 'quick marches and decisive encounters', which the German troops had been expecting, suddenly descended into trench warfare horrifyingly reminiscent of the First World War.[101] Having marched nearly 1,000 kilometres in five weeks the men of the 16th Army found themselves halted in a swamp east of the River Lovat. They dug in and stayed there for fourteen months.[102] Karl Meding, aged nineteen, found himself living with a comrade in a hole near Vitebsk in central Russia. 'There were wooden poles over it and on that lay hay and on top of that, snow ... One of us always had to stand outside this hole and see if the enemy was coming. We were always looking towards the east and the wind came from the east. Even the fear of death ... wasn't as terrible as this. It was undoubtedly my very worst experience in Russia. Everything froze. We used to huddle there with our feet wrapped in straw ... You couldn't make a fire and all we had to warm up our coffee was some little candles'[103] Guy Sajer claimed that 'the punishment we suffered, not at the hands of the Russian Army ... but from the cold, is almost beyond the powers of description'.[104] If the men in their fox-holes were lucky enough to be sent hot stew from the field kitchens it often arrived stone cold, sometimes frozen solid.[105]

The soldiers were a 'pitiful sight'. The Wehrmacht had not prepared for a winter war and there were not enough warm clothes. Many wore 'light coats, rags wrapped around feet or shoes' in temperatures of minus 40 degrees.[106] Frostbite claimed many victims. There were barely any washing facilities, there was nowhere that was dry, clean clothes were an unknown luxury and the soldiers became infested with lice. The tiring noise and anxiety of being hit by the artillery barrage and the disturbing nature of hand-to-hand combat combined with fatigue to induce some level of battle exhaustion in virtually every soldier. 'Now I have barely any appetite,' noted one depressed German.[107] Illness was rife. Weakened by exhaustion and malnourishment the troops fell victim to typhus, spotted fever, skin and bladder infections.

Guy Sajer began the war thinking himself 'invulnerable, filled with pride we all felt', but in the trenches on the banks of the Don river, 'we seemed like nothing, like bundles of rags which each sheltered a small, trembling creature. We were underfed and unbelievably filthy. The immensity of Russia seemed to have absorbed us.'[108]

The doctor for the 12th Infantry Division complained that there was not enough meat, potatoes or pulses, and the supply of sugar, which the men needed to provide sufficient energy to withstand the cold, was too small.[109] Transport problems were mainly responsible for the food shortages but this was exacerbated by the irresponsible plunder of the troops themselves. Along the eastern front there stretched a desolate barren zone which the Germans referred to as the *Kahlfraß*, or defoliated zone, where the villages had been stripped of food. The devastation was at its worst closest to the front line but in some places it stretched back hundreds of kilometres.[110] In December the 18th Panzer Division's quartermaster warned that any further requisition orders were unlikely to be fulfilled because the inhabitants had nothing left. Their food stores were bare, and their winter equipment – sledges, snowshoes and felt boots – had all been taken. One field commander in the south complained that the Hungarian and Romanian troops were the worst offenders, taking 'everything that was not nailed down'.[111] Their depredations around the Black Sea and Donets Basin in the autumn of 1941 left the Wehrmacht without sufficient supplies for the winter.[112] Underfed front-line troops resorted to further 'wild' actions. Lacking fodder for their horses, the soldiers fed them straw from the thatched roofs of the village houses.[113] They paid for their violence with their own hunger. In February 1942 the 18th Panzer Division's bread ration was cut in half, down to 300 grams a day.[114]

At the end of 1941 Herbert Fröbose was flown in to Kaluga, about 80 kilometres from Moscow. He went to join a division which had taken shelter in an old factory. His new comrades' first reaction was to think, 'Oh no, not more people to feed.' But the welcome was warm when it was discovered that they had brought food. Fröbose spent his time at the factory frozen, filthy and itchy with lice. Within two weeks half of his fellow replacements had been sent back with frostbite. They were sent bread, sometimes a little margarine, but no jam. At night the field kitchen was sometimes able to drive some soup over

1. (*left*) Herbert Backe, German Minister for Food and Agriculture and architect of the Hunger Plan. A typical *Schreibtischtäter* (desk perpetrator).

2. (*below*) A dispossessed Polish family, some of the thousands who were evicted from their farms to make way for the settlement of ethnic Germans.

OURS...to fight for

FREEDOM FROM WANT

3. (*above*) One of Norman Rockwell's extremely popular illustrations of Roosevelt's four freedoms, which reinforced the notion that Americans were fighting to defend their way of life.

4. (*left*) The British Ministry of Agriculture promoted potatoes as a perfect energy food by using the cheerful cartoon character Potato Pete.

5. The practice of bartering for food in the
countryside was endearingly known in German as
'hamstering'. Severe food shortages in the urban
areas meant that hamstering eventually became
a vital source of food.

6. (*left*) For occupying troops in France the Wehrmacht's policy of living off the land translated into living off the fat of the land. These German soldiers are buying cakes from a street stall in Paris in 1940.

7. (*below*) The banner on the side of the train reads, 'First foodstuffs – Ukraine/Berlin'. While food was confiscated from the east, the German blockade of Ukrainian cities and the extermination of Polish Jews was intensified in order to remove 'useless eaters' from the food chain.

8. (*left*) A Jewish man suffering mistreatment from a civilian in the Ukraine, June 1941.

9. (*below*) All over the Soviet Union hundreds of thousands of peasants and workers were reduced to living in primitive circumstances. This woman is cooking on a makeshift oven in a suburb of Stalingrad.

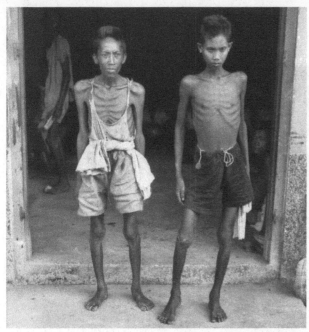

10. (*top*) Two Malayan natives at an Australian treatment centre on the island of Balikpapan, Borneo, in July 1945. These Malayans, who had been brought to Borneo as forced labourers by the Japanese, are clearly suffering from severe malnutrition. Millions of south-east Asians died of hunger as a result of Japanese policies.

11. (*right*) Japanese soldiers cooking their rations on Muchu Island, New Guinea, in September 1945. The Japanese army did not cook for its soldiers in field kitchens; instead each man lit a small fire and prepared his own meal.

12. (*left*) After having been in action for a few days in the Sanananda area of Papua, during which they survived on a diet of bully beef and biscuits, these US troops are enjoying the opportunity to cook themselves a jungle stew using fresh food.

13. (*below*) A badly emaciated Japanese soldier on Sandaken, North Borneo, awaiting transportation to a prisoner of war camp in October 1945. The American blockade of Japanese shipping meant that Japanese soldiers throughout the Pacific were left without food supplies, with devastating effect.

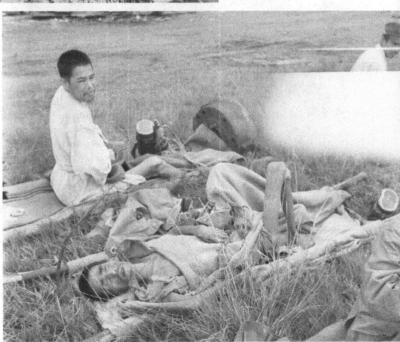

14. (*above*) Japanese civilians approach some GIs who are lunching on K rations in Tokyo in August 1945. By the end of the war the Japanese urban population was teetering on the verge of starvation, and as this picture shows the townspeople grew vegetables amid the ruins in order to survive.

15. (*left*) Australian naval personnel delighted by the soup, steak and onions, fresh peas, potatoes, bread and butter, strawberry ice cream and coffee piled up on their American mess trays. These Australians were discovering for themselves that the US military was the best fed in the world.

to them but it arrived cold. Then the supplies of food stopped coming. 'The road was just snow and mud and you could not get through any more. Even the oil was frozen.' Their one motorbike had to be pulled on skis by a horse. In February 1942 they began to retreat through an area of burned-out villages. It was chaotic, everything was frozen, there were no food supplies, and they survived for two months on horsemeat.[115]

If the civilian and military occupational administrations were unable to requisition sufficient food supplies for the soldiers on the eastern front, the Reich was not in a position to alleviate their position by sending in large quantities of German supplies. The winter was bitterly cold and collections of clothing for soldiers at the front were met with resentment by the people of Cologne, who were themselves extremely short of warm underwear and sweaters.[116] Food shortages had become commonplace in German cities. Potatoes periodically disappeared from the shops and fruit and vegetables were rarities. Nutritionists were concerned that industrial workers were still losing weight, especially miners in the Ruhr area, who were thought to have lost up to 6 kilograms.[117] It was thought that this would significantly reduce productivity, as the labour force had used up its fat reserves and was now making inroads into its muscle tissue.[118] In the spring of 1942 bread consumption began to eat into the country's grain reserves and Backe realized that he was failing in his aim to ensure that all German civilians received at least 2,300 calories a day. Conti warned that at 1,358 calories per day, the basic ration – received by non-workers – had fallen well below the minimum 1,700 calories essential for an adequate diet.[119] But grain, meat and fat shortages meant that the rations would have to be cut again. The *Sicherheitsdienst* inflamed the situation by warning that the workers and urban population were in a mood reminiscent of 1918, pessimistic about the outcome of the war and critical of the regime.[120] The National Socialist leadership was determined to distance itself from the incompetence and indecision of the German government during the First World War and decided that it was time for radical action to be taken. The occupied territories must be made to release their food stocks with no regard for the consequences for the indigenous population. It was now that the mantra that other peoples should starve before the Germans was taken up by the National Socialists. The Reich Propaganda Minister, Joseph Goebbels, made a note in his diary to this effect.[121]

In March Hitler attempted to promote the exploitation of the occupied territories by ordering that all soldiers on leave or travelling to the Reich for duty should return with packages containing as much food as they could carry. These food parcels became known as '*Führerpakete*'. It was hoped that in this way Germany would tap the food which was being siphoned off into the black markets of the occupied territories.[122] In her diary in April 1942 Maranja Mellin recorded the return of her father from Paris with a *Führerpaket*. 'He brought lots of things with him. Clothes, stockings, dried beans, writing paper, liver sausage, carrots in meat sauce, gloves, soap, belts, shoes, washing powder . . . Four pears and almonds, cinnamon and pepper. The table was full . . . wherever the men are they buy things.'[123] Another young girl, astonished by the 'mountains of booty' that her father brought home, said, 'if everyone is sending this much home, then there is nothing left in France'.[124]

Meanwhile, not disheartened by the disappointing results of the Hunger Plan, Backe and Göring returned to its logic. In order to free up more food yet more people needed to be exterminated. Attention was now turned to the Polish Jews and the Hunger Plan was reshaped into a more targeted instrument of racial genocide.[125]

THE HOLOCAUST IN POLAND

At the end of 1941 a line of demarcation existed along the old Soviet–Polish border of 1939. To the east the policy was one of total extermination, to the west only about 10 to 20 per cent of the Jews had been murdered.[126] The National Socialist precaution of keeping written documentation of inflammatory policies to a minimum means that there is still a question mark over the exact timing of the decision to murder the Polish Jews. Hitler's regime did not begin the war with a clear plan. There were various outlandish ideas floating about, including the notion that it might be possible to deport all European Jews to the island of Madagascar. Most officials seem to have expected that after the conquest of the Soviet Union the Jews in Poland and western Europe would be deported into the Siberian wasteland where they would be worked or starved to death.

The Holocaust was not just the product of an irrational ideology but the conclusion of a series of crises in the German conduct of the war. The failure to conquer the Soviet Union, the rise of partisans in the occupied zones, a dwindling food supply in the Reich – which was diminishing the productivity of workers and might provoke resistance to the regime – all created an atmosphere of crisis and the belief that extreme action was necessary to remedy the situation. This came together with the unfortunate circumstance that the organizational and military means to commit murder on a vast scale were being put into place. The appetite of the SS had been whetted by the ease with which the Soviet Jews had been eradicated. An extermination camp at Chelmo had already been built as an experimental pilot project and the systematic gassing of Jews from the Warthegau had been carried out there. It had always been the intention of Hitler and a section of the National Socialist leadership to eradicate the Jews from Europe. The food crisis of 1941–42 provided an ostensibly rational reason as to why the crime of murder should be committed. The Jews could not be allowed to continue eating the precious food which the German workers deserved: they must die in order to free up desperately needed food supplies.[127] Thus food worries gave added impetus to the Holocaust. The historian Christian Gerlach argues that without the food panic that winter, many more Jews might have survived, albeit under terrible conditions as forced workers.[128]

In December 1941 the Governor-General Hans Frank returned to the General Government of Poland, having met with Hitler. He announced that plans to deport Polish Jews to the east were no longer viable. Given that they were 'extremely damaging eaters' they needed to be removed as quickly as possible. A meeting in January would decide exactly what action should be taken.[129] The meeting he referred to was the now infamous Wannsee Conference at which plans were laid for the deportation and extermination of the European Jews. It was at this conference that the decision was taken to target first the Polish Jews in the General Government.[130] During the winter and spring of 1941–42 preparations for industrialized murder on a massive scale were made with the construction of the extermination camps at Belzec, Sobibor and Treblinka. These death camps were not extensions of the concentration camp system, but were specifically built in order to kill Jews efficiently. Most of the people who arrived at these camps were dead within twenty-four hours. They were quite different from the concentration camps, which were places of punishment where the inmates often died of hunger and overwork but were not systematically murdered. Although extermination camps were built at the concentration camps of Auschwitz and Majdanek, the death camps tended to be separate from the concentration camps and their administrators were drawn not from the camp system but from members of the euthanasia campaign who had conducted the elimination of the mentally ill within Germany.[131]

By the winter of 1941–42 the black market in the General Government had grown into a second economy over which the administration had no control. While the shops were empty, their window displays nothing but cartons of vinegar and mustard labelled 'empty boxes', the streets were alive with black market traders.[132] This was unsurprising as the ration was so inadequate that the only means of survival for the urban population was to buy food illegally. Workers were absent from work for at least two days a week while they went into the countryside to barter for food. As a consequence, factories needed to employ more people and the shortage of food led to a constant state of friction with the occupying forces.[133] German officials argued that the Jews were the fuel which kept the fire of the black market burning. Zygmunt Klukowski, the doctor in charge of the hospital in the town of Szczebrzeszyn in the district of Lublin, agreed with the German assessment. 'In Bilgoraj the Jews are allowed to buy only horsemeat. But the Jews are buying and selling everything possible. They are masters of the black market . . . Villagers sell to them freely, knowing that they will receive the highest possible price. From my window I can watch the exchanges.'[134] Indeed, the Jewish ration of somewhere between 300 and 500 calories a day left them no alternative than the black market.

In the Warsaw ghetto the black market was run by an assortment of professional racketeers who bribed the guards at the gates. Meat in the ghetto was known as *dupniki* (from the Polish *dupa* for arse). From slaughterhouses the black marketeers bought the rectums of cattle which had been discarded as waste. They were smuggled through the gates in barrels hidden under garbage and the Jewish butchers washed and ground them and sold them as minced meat. 'This was the meat – a delicacy if you could find it – of the ghetto.'[135] Another ghetto delicacy was coagulated horse blood, which was spread on bread and seasoned with salt and pepper.[136] Every day swarms of children would slip past the guards, climb over the walls or crawl through the sewers to go out and beg in the streets of Warsaw. Others would walk into the surrounding fields and dig up potatoes. They would come home, the lining of their coats bulging with potatoes, a little bread, or maybe some porridge. Those who were caught would be brutally beaten and sometimes they were shot, but if they got past the guards their efforts kept their families alive for one more day.[137] The Jews in the ghetto slowly starved to death. In March 1942 alone 290 bodies were found lying in the streets and the ultimate death toll was around 100,000, the vast majority having almost certainly succumbed to nutritional dystrophy and hunger oedema. Already in July 1941 Rolf Höppner of the *Sicherheitsdienst* in Posen calmly reasoned 'would [it] not be the more humane solution to deal with those Jews who are incapable of work by some other faster method? In any case this would be more pleasant than leaving them to starve.'[138]

In 1942 the administration of the General Government argued that if the Jews could be eliminated from the food chain then this would dampen down the black market, free up more food for the non-Jewish Polish population and improve Polish–German relations and the productivity of industry.[139] Orders were given to begin rounding up the Jews. Initially the plan was to eradicate only those incapable of work and ensure that the rest were put to good use in the factories and labouring in the concentration camps.[140] The civil administration was extremely anxious to ensure that the campaign was completed before the farmers began to bring in that summer's harvest. In preparation, no attempt was made to control the black market in Warsaw in the hopes that all the stocks from the previous year would be used up, leaving no life in the system. Then an effective collection of that year's harvest would prevent a sizeable diversion of grain into the illegal economy. Police chiefs were reminded in June 1942 that 'the successful collection of the best possible harvest is dependent upon the removal of illicit trading and the elimination of the Jews'.[141] Those who organized the murder of the Polish Jews were in no doubt that the campaign was directly linked to the problem of food.

The programme began in 1942 in the areas where the food situation was worst. It began with the shooting of Jews in Galicia, and then the extermination camps began to open. Belzec became operational in February 1942. On 25 March Klukowski noted in his diary that there were 'more and more cases of Jews being shot outside their own homes and also at the railroad stations . . . Now the Germans are transporting entire trainloads, mostly Jews, but we do not know where, maybe closer to the front for hard labour.'[142] The next day he reported that the Jews were disturbed about 'the forced movement of their population. From different areas we received information about actions against the Jews. Entire railroad trains loaded with Jews from Czechoslovakia, Germany, and lately Belgium, passed through, possibly to Belzec, where a new large camp was just organized.'[143]

On 8 April Klukowski reported in something of an understatement that 'the Jews are upset'. Their fate had become clear. He went on to describe somewhat incoherently what people had heard: 'We know for sure that every day two trains, consisting of twenty cars each, come to Belzec, one from Lublin, the other from Lwow. After being unloaded on separate tracks, all Jews are forced behind the barbed-wire enclosure. Some are killed with electricity, some with poison gases, and the bodies are burned. On the way to Belzec the Jews experience many terrible things. They are aware of what will happen to them. Some try to fight back. At the railroad station in Szczebrzeszyn a young woman gave away a gold ring in exchange for a glass of water for her dying child. In Lublin people witnessed small children being thrown through the windows of speeding trains.'[144] There was an atmosphere of panic in the town as news came from nearby Zamosc that 2,500 Jews had been evacuated by train. A few days later a mob assembled outside the Jewish homes in Szczebrzeszyn, waiting to loot them once their inhabitants had been removed. On 8 May the Gestapo began a mass shooting of Jews in the town. 'They shot people like ducks, killing them not only on the streets but also in their own houses – men, women and children, indiscriminately . . . I can still see the wagons filled with the dead, one Jewish woman walking along with her dead child in her arms.'[145] Some of the Poles responded with laughter, others looted the homes of the dead. 'The Gestapo ordered the Judenrat to pay 2,000 zloty and 3 lbs. of coffee for the ammunition used to kill the Jews.'[146] But no trains arrived at the station at Szczebrzeszyn and the remaining Jewish population continued to wait in fear. Meanwhile, in May Sobibor extermination camp opened and then in July Treblinka began to function. Regular trains from Galicia, Radom and Krakow made their way to these camps. On 23 July the daily transports of at least 5,000 Jews began from the Warsaw ghetto to Treblinka. At the beginning of August Hans Frank reported that the programme was being implemented with full force.[147] Even as the Warsaw ghetto was being cleared Goebbels travelled to the city to secure deliveries of vegetables for the Berlin population.[148]

In the summer of 1942 the Allies were told of the terrible fate of the European and Polish Jews. The information came from Gerhard Riegner, the representative of the World Jewish Congress in Switzerland. His informant was Eduard Schulte, a German industrialist who regarded the National Socialists as gangsters intent on a policy that would lead to Germany's ruin. He had a variety of unwitting sources of information, many of them high up in the army and National Socialist administration.[149] Schulte's business interests frequently took him to Switzerland and it was on a visit in July 1942 that he told his Jewish contacts that a plan was being discussed at Hitler's headquarters to deport all Jews in German-controlled territories to the east where they would be exterminated. A large crematorium was said to have been built and Zyklon B had been mentioned as the means of killing them. Riegner later passed on further reports that the plan had originated from Backe, who 'is said to have based the plan on economic reasons, as the difficult food situation would be eased by the annihilation of about four million persons who otherwise would have to be fed'.[150] This was obviously a reference to the extermination of the Polish Jews. In their book on Eduard Schulte, Walter Laqueur and Richard Breitman dismiss the idea that Schulte could have passed on the information about Backe, as this was surely wrong. 'Backe,' they argued, 'did not belong to the Nazi old guard and to Hitler's inner circle; he simply would not have been consulted on matters of high policy. He was solely an agricultural expert.'[151]

In fact, Christian Gerlach's meticulous research has demonstrated that by the summer of 1942, food, and therefore Backe, who had by now officially been appointed as Minister of Food, had come to play a central role in the decision-making process of the National Socialist regime. The 'critical food situation and its dismal future prospects' was constantly used as a justification for the course the war followed.[152] While Nazi ideology provided the 'value-rational' reason for murder, the food situation in Germany and the occupied Soviet Union provided an economic rationale.

The summer of 1942 brought no relief from the problems of food supply within the German Reich. The newly appointed Fritz Sauckel's enthusiasm for fulfilling his role as General Plenipotentiary for Labour Mobilization caused Backe yet more problems. The increasing numbers of foreign forced labourers Sauckel was bringing in to the Reich pushed the grain requirements up by about 2 million tons, and that year's harvest had been badly affected by the hard winter. Herbert Backe might well have spent his energies more profitably trying to gain greater control over the produce of German smallholdings, tackling the transport problem which caused so many shortages in the industrial towns, or overhauling the rationing system in order to equalize distribution of food. Instead, he rested all his hopes on an increased harvest in the occupied Soviet Union. Unless the Ukraine could provide more than he expected, he feared he would not be able to raise the rations in the autumn in order to help German civilians through the winter.[153] He concluded that Germany was at 'one of the most critical points in the war as far as food was concerned'.[154] In August he held a meeting with Göring and Hitler in order to discuss further reductions in the meat and fat ration. Henry Picker, an aide at Hitler's headquarters, reported that Hitler seemed unconcerned about the Ukrainian harvest. Indeed, in one of his monologues he pronounced that it was not 'a matter of whether the yields would be sufficient to provision our troops in the East, but rather whether they would be able to transport the immense surpluses to the old Reich'.[155] It was the job of the men on the ground to make sure that Hitler's wishful thinking was realized. As with so many such meetings there are no documents to record what was said, but Göring left the meeting with Hitler and Backe a nervous man.[156] He had obviously been instructed to make sure that Hitler's hopes for the Ukrainian harvest were fulfilled.

That summer each new problem brought cries for yet more food to be extracted from the occupied territories, for yet more deaths, more murders, the elimination of yet more 'useless eaters'. On 5 August Göring met with the Gauleiters of the Reich who complained vociferously about the impact of the April ration reductions on the health and morale of German civilians. The next day at a meeting with the leaders of the occupied countries Göring harangued them to deliver more food. 'God knows, you are not sent out there [to the occupied territories] to work for the welfare of the people in your charge, but to get the utmost out of them, so that the German people can live.'[157] He made it clear that Germany's policy was to export hunger. The French faced yet another painful ration cut if the demands were to be met; for the General Government it meant that any hope of improving the Polish ration had to be abandoned. Besides providing enough food for the army stationed in the territory, the General Government was ordered to deliver to the Reich 600,000 tons of grain, 150,000 tons of potatoes, 30,000 tons of meat and 5,000 tons of sugar.[158] The quartermaster for the General Government found the instructions so explosive that he would only pass them on orally to those under him. But Göring declared: 'it makes no difference to me in this connection if you say that your people will starve. Let them do so, as long as no German collapses from hunger.'[159]

Göring's policy of exporting hunger sealed the fate of the surviving Jews in the General Government. The page recording the discussion of the fate of the Jews in the occupied territories was removed from the minutes of the 6 August meeting. The only indication of what was said is Hinrich Lohse's revealing response to a question from Göring: 'I can respond to that as well. Only a small fraction of the Jews are still alive; many thousands are gone.'[160] It seems certain that Göring reiterated that the Jews must be eradicated in order to free up as much food as possible.

In ten weeks during August and September 1942, 750,000 Jews were killed in Belzec and Treblinka. On 8 August the trains, which had been expected in May, finally arrived in Szczebrzeszyn, and the Jews were rounded up and loaded on to them. The Germans claimed they were being taken to the Ukraine to work. Klukowski retorted that 'no one believes that the Jews will be moved to the Ukraine. They will all be killed. After today's events it is difficult to gain control of myself.'[161] And on 10 August he noted sadly that the trains had indeed taken the Jews of Szczebrzeszyn to Belzec. 'They have probably been killed by now.'[162] The killing was on such a scale that the gas chambers at Treblinka broke down on 28 August. The waiting deportees were left to suffer and die in the cattle wagons on the trains. In September ten more gas chambers were built at Treblinka, six more in Sobibor. By the end of 1942 another 400,000 Jews had died in the gas chambers of Belzec and Treblinka. Only 297,914 Jews were still alive in the General Government, the number that the Food and Agriculture head office had calculated would be allowed to survive as workers.[163]

In the Ukraine there were still about 330,000 Jews living in the area between the rivers Pripjet in the north and Dnjestr in the south.[164] Erich Koch returned to his capital, Rowno, after the 6 August meeting with Göring, and gathered his officials together. They were told that 'the food situation in Germany is serious . . . The raising of the bread ration is a political necessity, in order to drive the war on to victory. The missing amounts of grain must be obtained from the Ukraine . . . The feeding of the [Ukrainian] civilian population is irrelevant in view of this situation.'[165] The regional commissars were instructed to accelerate the Jewish extermination and given five weeks to complete the process. By the end of October it was over. At least a quarter of a million people had been shot.

Once areas were cleared of Jews, administrators claimed that the black market had died down. This was wishful thinking. In fact, the black market continued to thrive in Poland for the simple reason that the rations were ridiculously inadequate. As long as the black market continued to be essential for survival it would remain a feature of Polish life. The food which would have been eaten by the Jews if they had still been alive did not suddenly become available to the German administration. It stayed within the black market and was eaten instead by the starving Poles. However, it is unlikely that even the Poles were desperate enough to take up the consumption of the spare cattle rectums that would have become available after the clearing of the Warsaw ghetto. Incredibly, the General Government was nevertheless able to supply the Reich with the food that Göring had demanded. More than half the rye, oats and potatoes and more than a quarter of the barley eaten that year in Germany came from the General Government.[166] This was achieved not by the murder of millions of Jews but through the efforts of the peasantry, who brought in a surprisingly good harvest that year. This at least meant that the urban population were spared any further cuts in their absurdly small rations.[167]

FOOD CONFISCATION IN THE UKRAINE

The acceleration of the extermination of the Jews was accompanied by the reinforcement of the blockade of Ukrainian cities. Determined to prevent the harvest from disappearing into Soviet stomachs the German administration banned peasants and the inhabitants from bringing food into Kiev and Kharkov. In Kiev people had been allowed to bring in from the countryside one chicken, ten eggs or a litre of milk, and ten kilograms of potatoes. If a person was found to be carrying more than this the police confiscated the surplus. In the summer of 1942 they began confiscating everything. No food was allowed into the city. Anatoli Kutsnetsov described how he and his grandfather walked for half a day to Pushcha-Vodytsia, where they bought corn, beans and flour. Only three minutes away from home, staggering along under the weight of their purchases, having lost the feeling in their feet and shoulders, they were stopped by the police. 'My grandfather was ready to fall on his knees. The police paid no attention to him, but simply took our sacks and put them down by the post where there were several others lying already. They appeared to have set up a new checkpoint here . . . I dragged Grandpa along by the sleeve . . . he was quite beside himself.'[168] L. Nartova, an unemployed teacher, recorded in her diary the comments of the people around her: 'First they finished off the Yids, but they . . . exterminate us every day by the dozens, they're destroying us in a slow death.'[169] The *Sicherheitsdienst* recorded that people were commenting: 'We're supposed to die of starvation, to make place for the Germans.'[170] By October 1943 Kiev's population had fallen by 315,000, many of the dead having been killed by starvation.[171] The situation in Kharkov was no better. By February 1943 approximately 70 per cent of the pre-war population had succumbed to hunger.[172] People 'moved like automatons, quietly appearing and disappearing as if waiting for something. They waited for a piece of horseflesh or a cup of blood from the city slaughter-houses. They sat near ovens for hours drinking hot boiled water.'[173]

In conjunction with the blockade of the cities, an intensive food confiscation campaign was begun in the villages. The German and Ukrainian police went from village to village searching houses, back-yards, sheds, gardens and mills, confiscating every sack of grain they could find. Peasants were forced to thresh any grain they had in their stores. Those who simply could not deliver the food demanded of them were relieved of their cows or other livestock.[174] The supplies of grain, meat and fat extracted from the Soviet Union increased from 3.5 million tons to 8.78 million tons. Although most of this was eaten on the spot by the Wehrmacht, large transports of food were sent to the Reich from the Ukraine in the autumn of 1942. By the end of the year the Food and Agriculture department in the Ukraine reported with satisfaction that they had collected the entire harvest: the peasants had nothing more to give.[175]

Fritz Sauckel, in charge of the recruitment of forced labour, was amazed that 10–20 million people had not died of hunger in the Ukraine over the winter of 1941–42, as the experts had predicted.[176] But when in June 1941 Backe had drafted twelve commandments to guide future administrators in the east, the eleventh was that no 'false sympathy' was needed for the Russian, as he 'has already endured poverty, hunger and frugality for centuries. His stomach is elastic.'[177] This pronouncement had come back to haunt him. The Soviets' ability to survive was remarkable (it was equally astonishing in the unoccupied Soviet Union). Many of those alive in the winter of 1941–42 had survived the Ukrainian famine of 1932–33 and had acquired useful survival skills. For example, the Germans were sickened to discover that the civilians would dig up and eat dead horses. The *Sicherheitsdienst* reported that the Ukrainians 'got food by begging from the army; in part they had also gathered well hidden and carefully looked after reserves, and on top of this, they seem used to putting up with famine in a manner which is quite unbelievable from the German perspective and can hold on to life by making do with the most inferior food substitutes'.[178]

In the cities people found ways around the police checks. Vasyl Iablonsky, a factory worker, would often slip on to the cargo trains to nearby towns where more food was available. Announcements were made in three languages warning that anyone caught without a permit would be shot, but, 'You don't scare people like us. We hopped on and off we went. What's the difference how you're done for, you gotta eat.'[179] The rural population was saved by the inefficiency of the German civil administration. The German farmers who were put in place to administer the collective farms were too few and too under-qualified to be effective.[180] On average they were only able to visit each of the farms under their supervision once a week. This gave the Ukrainian farmers a large amount of room for manoeuvre. It allowed the peasants to indulge in petty acts of resistance, such as working slowly and frequent absenteeism. They used the time they took off from working on the collective farm to grow their own food in their garden plots. One day Oskana Iatsenko decided to stay at home to weed her garden but was filled with terror when she realized that her village chief had come to look for her, accompanied by 'the German'. 'I looked and died of fear. *I thought I had died.*' She hid among some plum trees and although they did not find her she thought: *'They will kill me, they will kill me.'*[181] A peasant caught breaking the rules might be shot or hung on the spot, receive a brutal beating or be sent to a labour camp. The harshness of German punishments was balanced by the fact that the German administrators were far less likely to find out about misdemeanours than the Soviets. The mutual surveillance, which worked as a powerful force for conformity under the Bolsheviks, evaporated in the face of the hostility felt towards the Germans.

The Ukrainian farmers used the freedom they gained in a variety of ways. Farm and brigade leaders would siphon off large amounts of produce on to the black market. Others used their new-found powers for good. Hryhorii Kariak Sova, the head of the land administration in the Novi Sanzhary district, persuaded the collective farm administrators to prepare fake records which undervalued the harvest. A second secret set of records then ensured that each peasant received more grain than they had received under the Soviet system.[182] Indeed, when Sauckel complained that the Ukrainians were eating better than the normal consumer in Germany this may not have been an exaggeration.[183] In the less fertile areas such as Polissia the peasants teetered on the verge of famine, and in the areas where the partisans were active the German reprisals left the peasants without homes or fields. But in the fertile regions many peasants recall the period of German occupation as a time of plenty, despite the summer confiscation campaign. The peasants found it much easier to hide food from the Germans and in later years there were some who reminisced that they 'ate well' and 'were not hungry', in comparison to the years of hunger under Soviet rule.[184] In a reversal of the famine caused by collectivization, it was mainly the towns and cities rather than the countryside that starved during the occupation.

The National Socialist leadership seem to have been incapable of grasping that a reign of terror is not sufficient to force people to surrender their means of existence. Hitler argued that the greater the chaos in the occupied areas the easier it would be to carry through the brutal Hunger Plan. In fact, in an under-developed agricultural area such as the occupied Soviet Union, erratic acts of violence accompanied by inadequate supervision simply resulted in the peasants retreating into self-sufficiency. They hoarded and hid away what supplies they could and directed their surplus out of the grasp of the occupiers and on to the black market. By late 1942 the civil administration was beginning to adopt a more placatory policy and there was talk of dissolving the collective farms. But it was far too late. In the spring of 1943 the Red Army began advancing towards the Ukraine, and when agricultural officials fell victim to the partisans delivery quotas remained unfulfilled. The Germans began to evacuate and took as much grain and agricultural equipment with them as they could. In a last act of spite Göring issued a secret order that all 'bases of agricultural production are to be destroyed'.[185] Backe's bread-basket slipped from his grasp.

The Wehrmacht stationed in the occupied Soviet Union never succeeded in extracting all the food it needed from the east, and the occupied Soviet Union never fed the *entire* Wehrmacht, as was the stated aim of the Hunger Plan. Even in the Ukraine the Wehrmacht still needed the Reich to provide 33 per cent of its meat and 60 per cent of its fat requirements.[186] Backe's Hunger Plan was never properly thought through and the backward nature of agriculture in much of the occupied

Soviet Union, the disruption caused by the continual fighting, the loss of agricultural labour, machines, animals and fertilizer, the contradictions of the German agricultural policy which maintained the despised collectives and simply imposed draconian collection quotas without price incentives, the growth of the black market and the Soviet peasants' ability to hide food stores from the German farm administrators, all combined to prevent the German occupiers from extracting the hoped-for quantities of food from the area. In order to gain as much food as Backe had hoped for, the agricultural administration would have had to inject capital, machinery and modern agricultural techniques into the farms. Conciliatory policies and fair prices for agricultural products would also have gone a long way towards creating an incentive for the peasantry to produce.

Despite the shortcomings of National Socialist occupation policy, the Wehrmacht and the eastern civilian administration were fed by over 7 million tons of Soviet grain and, in the Ukraine at least, 17 million cattle, 20 million pigs, 27 million sheep and goats, and more than 100 million domestic fowl disappeared into the stomachs of the German soldiers.[187] This relieved pressure on German farmers and freed up home-grown food for German civilians. Although the Soviet Union never supplemented the Reich's food supplies to the extent that Backe had hoped, Germany did receive 2 million tons of grain, large quantities of potatoes, and some meat and vegetable oils from the east.[188] Much of the food arrived in late 1942 as a result of the good Polish harvest and the concerted food collection campaign in the Ukrainian countryside. In the autumn of 1942 Backe and Göring were both relieved to conclude that their radical actions in the east had succeeded in staving off a food crisis within Germany. Goebbels announced that Germany was 'digesting' the occupied territories. In October Göring announced a welcome increase in the bread and meat rations.[189] The *Sicherheitsdienst* reported a noticeable relaxation of the tension among civilians.[190] The Christmas of 1942 was made more cheerful by imports of sugar from Hungary, wheat from the Warthegau, and sunflower oil from the Ukraine. A good potato harvest within Germany also meant that the weekly ration virtually doubled.[191]

Millions of eastern Jews and Soviet citizens died in order, supposedly, to free up food for the German occupiers. But it is doubtful that these murderous measures contributed a great deal to the collection of food in the east. Certainly, the annihilation of the Jews in the General Government did nothing to suppress the black market, and therefore what little food was freed up by their deaths was not channelled on to the plates of the Germans. In addition, much of the food that was denied the urban population in the Ukraine seems to have been eaten instead by the Ukrainian peasantry. Nevertheless, German army and civilian rations rested firmly upon the exploitation of foreign labour. Around 40 per cent of the bread and meat eaten by the Wehrmacht and the Reich population was either produced in the occupied territories, or produced within Germany using the forced labour of foreigners from these countries.[192]

It was not until after the war that the German civilian population began to suffer from inadequate rations, and this post-war experience of hunger meant that many contrasted the competence and responsibility of the Nazi government to the callous failure on the part of the victorious Allied powers to feed the civilians in their care. This attitude was expressed by Margo Nagel, a student and dentist's assistant in Berlin during the war. 'I do not recall yearning for something that was not available . . . I do not recall anyone who said they were hungry during the war. Germany was always a well-organized country and I am sure that the party authorities saw to it that food was stockpiled and well distributed. The winter after the war was quite different when I lived in Hamburg where thousands of people died of starvation and exposure to the cold.'[193] While her comments overlook the fact that the National Socialist government inflicted food shortages on urban Germans, they also show determined disregard for the fact that while Germans were well supplied between 1939 and 1945 their European neighbours were systematically plundered, murdered and deliberately starved to death for the sake of a secure food supply for German civilians.

10

Soviet Collapse

I'll never forget the little village deep in the forest where we were billeted or the atmosphere of tragedy and anxiety that permeated every word spoken, weighed upon the women drawing water at the well, and made even the children unusually reticent.

(Andrei Sakharov, a Russian physicist who spent some of the war in the countryside)[1]

When the young physicist (and later winner of the Nobel Peace Prize) Andrei Sakharov graduated from university in the autumn of 1942 his first war-work assignment was to go out into the countryside to cut wood. In the village where he stayed there were only old women and children left and the atmosphere was polluted by a 'foreboding that things would get even worse before they got better . . . the horror of war was always uppermost in people's minds'.[2] The weakest link in the Soviet wartime edifice was undoubtedly agriculture. The struggles of Soviet farmers make the problems faced by farmers in the other major combatant countries pale in comparison. With the nation's best agricultural land lost to the Germans until 1943, it was not so much a question of carefully balancing production to favour bread grains and maintain a minimum level of fats, fodder and meat, as a desperate struggle to cultivate as much of anything as possible. Throughout the war the Soviet Union struggled to feed its vast army, let alone all its citizens. The battle to produce food in the Soviet Union extracted every ounce of food from the peasantry while reducing both them and the land to a state of exhaustion.

The Soviet Union entered the war with its agricultural sector in a wretched state of disrepair. The politics of the preceding decades had caused endless disruption. The requisitioning of food, men and horses during both the First World War and the ensuing civil war led to hardship in the countryside. This was matched by food shortages in the towns.[3] Lenin's introduction of the New Economic Policy in 1921 produced a short period of relative recovery. But then, in 1926, in an attempt to release revenue for industry, the government lowered agricultural prices. The peasants reacted by holding back their food from the cities. Rationing, which had only been discontinued in 1921, had to be reintroduced. In the end rationing was in force for more than half the twenty-five years preceding the Second World War.[4]

Stalin was determined to eradicate market forces from the food economy and in 1929 he set about modernizing the agricultural sector in order to lay the foundation for his planned rejuvenation of Soviet industry.[5] He even invited Thomas Campbell, a pioneer of large-scale mechanized wheat farming in the United States, to come to the Soviet Union to give advice on the introduction of new techniques.[6] But Stalin's programme of collectivization was no neutral programme of modernization. It was a scheme designed to impose the deadly will of the state upon the peasantry. The ownership of land as private property was abolished. The kulaks, the so-called rich peasantry, whose wealth often consisted only of one or two cows, were rounded up and deported to the gulags. Between 4 and 5 million were murdered.[7] The rest of the peasantry were coerced into working for the new Party-owned farms, the *kolkhozy*, which, by consolidating peasant landholdings, were supposed to make farming more efficient.

A young Cherkessian peasant who fled the Soviet Union in 1945 expressed the views of the majority of the Soviet peasantry when he denounced collectivization as a 'slave system'. The peasants were forced to work for the collective farms for a certain number of days per year. In return they were supposed to be paid sufficient food to feed themselves and their families. However, before the collective farm could distribute food to its workers it had to deliver a quota of food to the state. These quotas were frequently set so high that the farms had virtually nothing left to feed their workers. The Cherkessian recalled that, 'There were years when you worked a whole year and got nothing, everything went to the state ... They took the butter ... the eggs ... the meat ... we had to give wool ... the food products from [our private] garden ... Collective farmers ate worse than workers ... the collective farmer worked from dawn to dusk and got nothing.'[8] His family survived on one potato and a teaspoon of corn mush a day. 'Life was horrible, life held on by a bare thread.'[9] A Ukrainian from Chernigov explained that the only way to survive was for the peasantry to cultivate the tiny plots of land which they were allowed to keep for their own use. But because 'socialist work comes first, then your private work' it was very difficult for the members of the collective to find the time to work on the private plots of land and 'in actuality, what will often happen is that his children or some grandmother in the family will work in his private lot'.[10]

In the Ukraine, where resistance to collectivization had been particularly strong, the state ruthlessly requisitioned food to the point where the villages were stripped of food, seed grain and fodder. With nothing left to feed them, the peasants slaughtered their livestock. But once the animals had been eaten there was nothing left for the people to eat either and famine spread.[11] In the Ukraine as many as 7 million peasants died of starvation. One survivor recalled how, in 1933, 'You could go into a village and see the corn standing high in the fields yet there would not be a soul in the entire village. They had planted the corn in the spring, and died during the summer, so that the corn grew untended.'[12]

The end result of collectivization was to relocate hunger to the villages rather than the towns and cities.[13] While the peasants suffered, the food situation gradually improved in the urban areas. By 1936 the government was able to abolish rationing. Emigrants interviewed by the Harvard Project on the Soviet Social System in the 1950s routinely recalled that in the towns clothing was more of a problem than food just before the outbreak of war. In the countryside collectivization did introduce new and better strains of wheat and the collective farms were mechanized, but the peasants were repressed, disillusioned and demotivated. They had no incentive to work hard on the state farms given that they were unlikely to receive a fair share of the harvest. In terms of productivity the Soviet agricultural sector continued to lag behind industry, and it was unable to provide a solid foundation upon which to build an economy, let alone to fight a war.[14]

When the German attack on Russia was announced, a disgruntled peasant in Archangel province was reported to have remarked, 'Our government fed the Germans for two years, it would have been better to have saved food for our army and for the people, but now all of us expect hunger.'[15] He was right in thinking that the Soviet people were going to go hungry. The country was living so close to its food margins that almost no surplus existed from which to create food reserves.[16] The Soviet Union lost the central black soil area, the Ukraine, parts of the Crimea and the Caucasus to German occupation. The Germans came into possession of just under half the Soviet Union's crop regions and land for beef and dairy cattle, more than half the Union's pigs and virtually all the sugar-producing land.[17] Grain and sugar beet now had to be grown in the less fertile north and east. Great efforts succeeded in expanding the cultivated area but yields were driven down by lack of technical expertise and the unsuitable climate in these areas, let alone all the usual wartime difficulties of insufficient manpower, lack of machines (or fuel to run them) and draught animals, as well as shortages of fertilizer and seed.[18]

The redirection of all energies towards maintaining the fighting at the front dealt agriculture a fundamental blow.[19] Nineteen million able-bodied peasants were called up, more than half of the male rural workforce. The tractor drivers were the first to go, leaving the collective farms without workers trained to use the machinery.[20] In 1942 the peasants were reduced to sowing and harvesting 79 per cent of the grain by hand.[21] It was not uncommon for the peasant women to resort to yoking themselves to the plough in place of draught animals. Almost the entire burden of providing food for the Soviet Union fell on women, children, the elderly and the infirm. By 1945 women made up 92 per cent of the agricultural workforce.[22] Victor Kravchenko and his fellow army recruits, walking across snowbound Tataria as they were evacuated east in November 1941, were 'amazed to see great fields of wheat, unharvested, under the snow and now and then even sheaves of harvested grain. Later a peasant gave us the explanation: "with all able-bodied men taken for the army and horses commandeered for the fronts, only women, children and cows" remained to do the harvesting and immense quantities of produce could not be carried off.'[23]

The collective farms were pushed into a vicious cycle of over-extraction, falling yields and demotivation. Decline could possibly have been reversed if the collective farms had been dismantled and the newly independent peasants motivated to increase production by high prices for agricultural produce. But this would have required large capital investment to inject much-needed equipment and livestock into the countryside. The Soviet Union in 1941 did not have the economic wherewithal to do this. Industry was overwhelmed and stretched to its limit simply trying to produce enough armaments to keep the men at the front fighting. There was absolutely no question of producing tractors or agricultural equipment. Besides, the benefits would have been felt only in the long term.

Collectivization served the government well in that it gave it a level of control over the countryside which the German occupiers across the front line would have envied. While the peasants on the collectives in the Ukraine were inadequately supervised and often able to evade and deceive their German masters, in the Soviet Union farms were treated as part of the front line. The peasants' working day was lengthened and the number of workdays they were obliged to contribute to the collective increased. Punishments for absenteeism were as harsh as they were for soldiers and industrial workers. Through the collectives the government exercised a level of control over the harvest that no other combatant government was able to achieve. Compared to the First World War, when the Russian government had to extract food from millions of landlords and small peasant producers and the food supply to the towns had dried up, the Soviets now had 200,000 collective and state farms, and an efficient working system in place for collecting the farm produce.[24] The procurements extracted during the war were ruthless. The requisition quota for each farm was calculated according to a *theoretical* biological yield rather than the actual yield. Before the war this resulted in unfair demands, during the war it became almost absurd. In Kazakhstan in 1940 the difference between the biological and actual yields was 33 per cent but by 1942 and 1943 it had risen to 100 per cent.[25] Any protest was regarded as an attempt to 'sabotage grain procurements' and carried the risk of imprisonment or hard labour.[26]

When official procurements did not yield enough food, the government would return with orders for the collectives to contribute to the Defence

Fund or the Red Army Fund. Milk was requisitioned for the Fund for the Health of the Defenders of the Motherland. In this way yet more work and food were squeezed out of the collective farmers. Despite declining agricultural yields the percentage of the collective grain harvest allocated to the military increased. By 1942 the military were consuming 24 per cent of the total grain harvest, as opposed to 9 per cent in 1940. Thus the military were fed at the expense of both the peasantry and the urban population, who received a diminished share of a smaller harvest.[27] If the peasants on the Soviet side of the eastern front were spared the murderous attentions of the *Einsatzgruppen*, the Red Army, like the Wehrmacht, also organized its own independent system of requisitioning, above and beyond the official quotas. In 1942 this was officially acknowledged when each unit was allocated 30 kilometres behind the front line from which they were allowed to requisition food directly.[28] When Lev Mischenko's volunteer regiment was sent into the fighting in defence of Moscow he was told to supply his regiment directly from the collective farms near the front, but the farmers had virtually nothing to give. They had no meat or milk and made 'bread' from potatoes rather than grain. 'Everything had been delivered to the state. It was a stark contrast to all the propaganda we had been fed about happy peasants on flourishing collective farms.'[29] He simply took whatever he could find to feed the soldiers, although his conscience troubled him.

In most countries the rural areas were better off in wartime than the urban areas. The Soviet Union was an exception. The Soviet farms were stripped of food; often the collectives had absolutely nothing to distribute to their workers, and even seed stock was taken, endangering the sowing of a new crop for the next year.[30] The principle introduced by collectivization, that the brunt of hunger should be borne by the countryside, was maintained throughout the war.

Soviet farms were simply unable to grow enough food. Figures citing the number of tons of a particular crop produced often convey little information about the amounts of food actually available, but a comparison of the Soviet production figures for 1940 and 1942 clearly demonstrates the immensity of the food crisis the Soviet Union faced. From a grain harvest of 95.6 million tons in 1940 the figure fell to 26.7 million in 1942. Potatoes fell from 76.1 million to 23.8 million tons, sugar beet from 18 million to 2.2 million tons, meats and fats from 4.7 million to 1.8 million tons.[31] The number of people entitled to rations was 61 million, rising to over 80 million in 1945.[32] Translated into the amount of food available for ordinary people these figures meant that in 1942 the official food ration could provide only about half the amount of food that had been available to Soviets in 1940 when the population was already heavily dependent on bread and potatoes and only 28 per cent of workers had felt that the food supply was adequate.[33]

In 1940 only 3 per cent of the peasantry had felt that the food supply was adequate.[34] By 1942 if they had attempted to live solely on the food they received in payment from the collective farms they would certainly have starved to death. Fortunately, Soviet peasants were accustomed to looking starvation in the face and had had years of experience of living on the edge. They knew which wild grasses were edible and how to make acorns palatable. In the forests of northern Russia the farm families supplemented their protein and vitamin intake by collecting berries, edible mushrooms and nuts, while they fed their cattle 'twig fodder', and acorns to their pigs.[35] They also stole from the collectives. A Ukrainian student who worked on a *kolkhoz* near Novosibirsk recalled that sometimes a peasant would 'go out into the field at night with a pair of scissors and snip off the ears of corn'. This was an extremely dangerous activity. 'When this was discovered, the man who did this would get eight or ten years in jail, whether he had stolen one ear or a hundred.'[36] It was even an offence to scavenge the ears of wheat missed during the harvest. Bread became a luxury and potatoes, grown in their private plots, became the peasants' staple food. They fried and boiled potatoes and made potato cakes and potato soup. During the miserable spring of 1943 the family of Andrei Sakharov's future wife used 'the rather complicated "technology"' developed by generations of starving peasants to transform 'frozen, half-rotten' potatoes into edible pancakes.[37] If they were lucky they ate some salted cucumber or pickled cabbage and drank a little milk with their potatoes.[38]

If the peasants' private plots kept them alive, they were also an important source of nutrition for the rest of the population. Throughout the war the government allowed the collective farm markets to revive, and here the peasants sold their surplus produce. In many towns and cities the farm markets were the *only* source of fresh vegetables and dairy products.[39] J. A. Alexander, an Australian diplomat in Russia during the war, described the 'dilapidated and dirty' market in Moscow where 'rows of peasants in greasy cotton padded jackets' ladled out the most repulsive-looking milk from grubby cans.[40] Although half of all food sales made during the war occurred at these markets, the overall drop in food availability meant that the quantity of food on offer declined considerably. Often thousands of potential buyers would be disappointed to find only a couple of farmers with a few sacks of potatoes.[41]

Although Soviet industry teetered on the brink of collapse in 1941–42, the industrial system eventually adapted and found inventive ways of overcoming problems. Agriculture also went to the brink of collapse, but it remained there. While the rest of the economy showed signs of recovery, in 1943 Soviet agriculture fell further into crisis and the grain harvest dropped again by a further 6 million tons.[42] The recapture of German-occupied territory made matters worse by increasing the number of mouths to feed without the compensation of regaining productive farmland. The Germans had scorched the earth as they retreated and as the Soviets retook the Ukraine they found 'no evidence of the existence of any mechanical farm machinery, work animals, or dairy herds'.[43]

If the communist government had been more enlightened in its treatment of the peasantry and in its approach to agriculture in the 1930s it might have created a healthier agricultural sector which would have been better equipped to feed the population in wartime. However, it was the loss of the most fertile agricultural regions to the Germans that made the agricultural crisis so acute. Under these circumstances, collectivization was probably what saved the Soviet Union from spiralling into an unsustainable food crisis. Collectivization enabled the government to extract virtually every crumb of food from the farms and to just about feed its army and industrial workers, although they did still go very hungry. If the peasants had been able to retreat into self-sufficiency the situation in the Soviet Union's cities would surely have become untenable. Nevertheless, agriculture remained a dangerously weak area of the Soviet economy throughout the entire war, and it was fortunate that the climate remained fairly favourable during the period

1941 to 1945. If the drought that hit the Soviet Union in 1946 had occurred a few years earlier it seems very likely that the malnourished and demotivated peasants would have toppled over the edge into famine, with a devastating impact on the Soviet war effort.[44]

I I

Japan's Journey towards Starvation

If we had breakfast, we would not eat lunch.
(Malayan commenting on food shortages under the Japanese
occupation)[1]

Japan's need for food imports was to prove one of its gravest weaknesses, and its inability to bring food into the home islands led to a steadily worsening food crisis in its cities during the last two years of the war. In contrast to pre-war Britain, which obtained half of its food (by weight) from abroad, pre-war Japan only imported 20 per cent of its food. However, while Britain was able to cope with the wartime decline in food imports by cutting down on the import of superfluous foods such as fruit and sugar, it was much more difficult for Japan to reduce imports. Although they only accounted for a small percentage of total food consumption they were vital to the Japanese diet. Japan imported nearly all of its salt, 92 per cent of its sugar, most of its soya beans and about one-third of its rice.[2] Salt, albeit in small quantities, is an essential element in regulating the functions of the human body. Manchurian soya beans were processed into miso, a soya-bean paste which was ubiquitous in Japanese cooking and a vital source of protein in farmers' diets.[3] The urban population was dependent on Korean and Formosan rice.[4] Any fall in the quantity of these imports would lead to serious deficits in the Japanese diet. The only import which Japan could cut down on relatively painlessly was sugar, and imports did decline steadily throughout the war from over 800,000 tons a year to 182,000 tons in 1945. However, as sugar accounted for 7 per cent of the already meagre calorific intake of the pre-war diet, the loss of imports led to a decline in the energy value of the Japanese diet. The lack of sugar also contributed greatly to a decline in the palatability of food.[5]

Most of the animal protein in the pre-war Japanese diet came from fish. By 1941 the fish ration mainly consisted of squid. The teacher of Saito Mutsuo, studying at a crammer in Tokyo, observed that squid lived in shallow coastal waters and that this was an ominous sign that deep-sea fishing had virtually stopped.[6] Wartime labour shortages, the requisitioning of fishing boats by the military, lack of fuel and even of cotton and hemp for the manufacture of rope and fishing nets, all contributed to a fall of more than 50 per cent in the fish catch, which led to a significant decline in the nutritional value of the wartime diet.[7] Britain compensated for the loss of grain imports by restructuring its agricultural sector and switching from livestock to arable farming. There was far less room for manoeuvre in Japan's agricultural economy. Farming was already predominantly arable and the only way to increase the rice harvest was to extend the cultivated area, but virtually every scrap of flat land and even the hillsides were already covered with paddy. Wartime labour shortages and a precipitate decline in fertilizer imports also impacted hard on agricultural productivity. This meant that while Japanese farming was unable to adjust and compensate for the fall in imports, it also produced less food, thus creating a greater dependence on imports.

RICE AND SWEET POTATOES

Strangely for a country which in its pursuit of autarky had acquired a maritime empire, Japan entered the war with a merchant fleet which only just about covered its requirements for shipping.[8] In order to survive the war it was vital that the shipbuilding industry should immediately begin constructing cargo ships, as well as a fleet of escorts to protect the vulnerable merchant marine from American submarines. Instead, shipbuilding focused on the production of battleships and in 1943 the Japanese were completely without the resources to protect themselves from a full-scale American blockade, which combined the use of submarines, aircraft and mines. This meant that from 1943 Japan was unable to bring in imports of rice from south-east Asia, and the home islands were gradually cut off from essential sources of food.[9] As imports declined and farmers struggled to maintain crop yields, the demand for food rose ever higher. Home-based military forces grew from 1 to 3.5 million between 1941 and 1945, and the amount of rice they consumed increased from 161,000 to 744,000 tons, which in 1943 equalled the entire amount of rice the merchant marine had managed to slip past the American blockade.[10] The voracious demands of the military contributed significantly to the food crisis which pushed Japan's urban inhabitants towards starvation in the summer of 1945.

By 1942 Japan had acquired an empire in China, south-east Asia and the Pacific. The Japanese military policy, like that of the Wehrmacht, was that troops should live off the land. Shipping space was too scarce and the domestic harvest too small to allow for food supplies to be sent to the armies overseas. The burden of feeding the occupying forces was therefore firmly placed on the shoulders of the farmers in the occupied territories. If there were insufficient supplies in one area, they were sent in from another part of the empire. Thus, the occupying forces in Manchuria were sent trainloads of food from Korea and the troops stationed on the Philippines were sent rice supplies from Indo-China and Siam (now Thailand), which remained independent but was allied to the Japanese. Burma, Malaya and Indo-China together represented the world's largest rice-exporting area, but mismanagement of the rice trade led to a dramatic decline in production which combined with ruthless requisitioning of supplies to create widespread hunger and, in Burma and Indo-China, famine. As the Malayan schoolteacher Chin Kee Onn commented, 'the much-publicised and rosily-painted "New Order" turned out to be the "New Disorder" and what was proclaimed to be the "Co-prosperity Sphere" was actually the "Co-poverty Fear"'.[11]

Throughout the wartime world it was women who made up the majority of the agricultural labour force and this was also the case in Japan. By 1944 more than half the Japanese rural labour force was made up of women.[12] Returning from a lecture tour in Kyushu in May of that year, the journalist Kiyosawa Kiyoshi recorded in his diary: 'when I looked out from the train, the people working in the fields were only women and children. Occasionally when I saw a man it was a really old man.'[13] It was not so much military conscription which depleted the agricultural workforce as the war industries. Even though half the population of Japan were peasants, they made up only 23 per cent of military draftees during the Pacific war. Having relied on the countryside for recruits during the early 1930s, for the war with China and America the military preferred to rely on skilled young men from the factories, who made up 43 per cent of the draft between 1937 and 1945.[14] However, large numbers of fit and active young men and women left the countryside for the towns where better wages could be earned. When she left her village to work unloading coal from ships at the docks in Niigata, the family of fifteen-year-old Toshié was delighted with her wage of 5 yen a day.[15] Between 1941 and 1945 the military and industry together swallowed up 4 million rural labourers.

One farm woman recalled how hard it was 'keeping up with the work, with so many of the men away. We had a hop field and the weeds grew shoulder-high. You almost broke your sickle on the weeds.'[16] To relieve some of the pressure on the hard-pressed women the joint labour schemes, which had been established by the rural revitalization programmes of the 1930s, expanded their activities. Not only were farm households encouraged to co-operate with each other to trans-plant, weed, harvest and thresh the rice, but 15,000 communal kitchens were set up to save everyone from having to cook for themselves and 30,000 nurseries freed up the children's mothers for long hours of work in the fields.[17] The government also exempted school-children from their studies and sent them into the countryside to help. Altogether a million students laboured in the fields. But this was not a temporary holiday, as it was in Britain or California, but a permanent release from school. Tanaka Tetsuko, a student when the war began, recalled how 'classes practically came to an end and our education became mostly volunteer work ... It was very strenuous, physical labour.' Tanaka took solace in the idea that 'we were part of a divine country centred on the Emperor. The whole Japanese race was fighting a war.'[18] So effective was the deployment of students that Japan, unlike Germany, Britain and America, barely used prisoners or forced labour in its fields.

Although the work was back-breakingly hard for those left in the countryside, Japan's problem was not so much that it did not have enough labour, but that the inefficiency of agriculture made it difficult to maximize the productivity of all the hard work.[19] Increasing efficiency through mechanization was out of the question because of the pocket-handkerchief size of the paddy fields. In the whole of Japan there were only ninety-nine tractors during the war and these would have relied on an extremely limited petrol supply. As every scrap of metal was channelled into the armaments factories, even supplies of hand implements such as ploughs, rakes, pitchforks and sickles fell by half and they became valued and scarce possessions.[20] Japanese soils are comparatively infertile but imports of materials to make artificial fertilizers, which before the war had come from Germany, France, Spain and the United States, all ceased. Although the Japanese navy captured the phosphate-mining islands of Nauru, Ocean and Christmas Island, thus depriving Australia of its main sources of raw materials for artificial fertilizers, Japanese farmers benefited little from these victories. The Allies destroyed the mines and equipment before they evacuated, and by the time the occupying Japanese had restored them the American blockade prevented most of the supplies from reaching Japan.[21] Fertilizer imports dropped from over 1 million tons in 1941 to a mere 137,000 tons in 1945.[22] Without artificial fertilizers the farmers relied on organic forms of manure, but fish and soya-bean-meal fertilizers disappeared as these were too precious as sources of human food, and the overworked labour force was obliged to invest large amounts of time and energy into collecting night soil.[23]

The government banned the cultivation of luxury crops and encouraged every farmer to grow potatoes, the ubiquitous crop of the Second World War. In the case of Japan these were sweet potatoes, which made sense as they contain 30 per cent more calories than rice and double the number of calories found in wheat. They are also less sensitive than rice to a lack of fertilizer.[24] A Japanese woman from the village of Shinohata recalled how 'we grew sweet potatoes in all the rice fields . . . as a winter crop. You cut them in strips and dried them and that was all we had for snacks.'[25] By 1945 the yield of sweet potatoes had increased by one-quarter, but the yield of virtually all other foodstuffs had fallen.[26] In particular the farmers lacked the spare capacity to cultivate fruit and vegetables, which became extremely scarce.

The government's 1930s Rural Revitalization campaign and the Manchurian resettlement plan had both tried to solve Japan's agricultural problems without impacting on the power and wealth of the rural landlords. But the circumstances of war created pressures which led the government to reform the social structure of the countryside by taking the radical – and inadvertently democratic – step of cutting landlords out of the food chain. Landlords were normally paid part of their tenants' rent in kind, which allowed them to hoard stores of rice. In an effort to ensure that the government was able to collect as much of the harvest as possible, this practice was banned by the Food Control Act of 1942 and landlords were instructed to apply for ration cards. Instead, the government now bought rice directly from the cultivators, which enabled the government to provide them with an incentive to grow more food by paying them substantially more than had the landlords.[27]

Unfortunately, the tenant farmers were unable to reap the full benefits of this positive reform until peacetime. During the war a large share of their profits was creamed off by the forced savings campaigns run by village associations, which raised what were, in effect, forced loans for the government. In addition, inflation, which pushed the prices of farm equipment and consumer goods to absurd levels, meant that even though their incomes had increased, the farmers struggled to maintain their standard of living and felt that they gained very little despite their hard work.[28] As the food situation in the cities became increasingly worrying, the government's requisition quota targets became increasingly unrealistic and the exhortations to work harder became more insistent. In reaction farmers lost their enthusiasm.[29] One farmer remarked bitterly: 'They tell us "deliver, deliver", so then they come and take away at a song the rice we sweated so hard to produce, to the point where it's hard for us to eat. I can't stand it.'[30] He concluded that it would be better if he simply grew enough food for his family and joined the swelling ranks of industrial workers in the cities who were able to earn a decent living. Following a familiar pattern for under-developed agricultural economies, where there was simply too little incentive to produce for the market, more and more Japanese farmers withdrew into subsistence cultivation as the war progressed. Kiyosawa Kiyoshi noted that because of the ever fiercer requisitioning of rice, tenants had returned almost 1,000 *tsubo** of rice fields to his parents. Rather than farm it themselves and thus make themselves liable for high delivery quotas, they had left it uncultivated. 'Thus ... farmland is steadily diminishing,' concluded Kiyosawa, 'and food become harder to obtain.'[31]

By the end of the war rice yields had fallen by half and barley yields were similarly poor. Whereas Japan's farmers produced enough rice for each person to receive 336 grams per day in 1941, by 1945 the farmers could only provide 234 grams per person per day. However, the army, on a ration double that of an ordinary civilian, had grown substantially, and peasants were allocated a share of between 600 and 450 grams of rice for every member of their family. This clearly left far too small a surplus to feed the urban population in the cities.[32] Without imports of rice from the occupied territories the Japanese cities would starve.

CHAOS AND HUNGER IN THE EMPIRE

Japan's pre-war rice supply relied heavily on imports from Korea but already in 1939 Korean rice exports were failing to live up to Japanese expectations. The war in China had boosted the country's industrial development, leading to rising food prices and farm incomes. The peasants could now afford to hold back more of their rice crop for their own consumption and Korea's export surplus shrank. A drought in 1939 resulted in a poor harvest, virtually all of which was consumed by the Japanese troops stationed in the country. A further drought in 1942 brought Korean rice supplies to Japan to a halt.[33] However, by mid-1942 the Japanese were the masters of south-east Asia, which had produced 67 per cent of the rice entering pre-war world trade.[34] This should have been the answer to Japan's rice shortage problems. By 1940 the Japanese had already begun to look to south-east Asia as an extra source of rice imports. In 1940–41 the area provided nearly 1.5 million tons for Japan, which were used to build up reserve stores on the mainland.[35] In

---

* About one acre.

1942 and 1943 three-quarters of the rice imported into Japan was coming from this area.[36] But from 1943 on, the American blockade prevented meaningful quantities of supplies reaching the home islands and the possession of an empire did nothing to alleviate the food crisis developing within Japan.

While the Japanese government presided over an ever-worsening food situation at home, as the occupying power in south-east Asia it succeeded, in an astonishingly short space of time, in running down the entire region, pushing back the progress which had been made towards modernity and re-establishing its pre-colonial isolation, undoing the process of urbanization and driving the hungry population back into the countryside to undertake subsistence farming.[37] The Japanese lacked expertise and advisers who knew the region and much of the chaos was caused by mismanagement rather than a malicious, premeditated policy.[38] In terms of managing the food supply the occupying administration's greatest mistake was to allow the rice industry to disintegrate.

Although south-east Asia was one of the world's most important rice-producing areas, the cultivation of rice was concentrated in just three areas – lower Burma, Siam and Cochin-China (the southern part of what is now Vietnam). The rest of the region – all the towns and cities, the dry northern zone of Burma, British Malaya, the Straits Settlements, the Philippines, British Borneo and the Dutch East Indies – was dependent on internal rice imports.[39] As the Japanese moved in, the transport system in the region broke down as virtually all vehicles, trains and ships were requisitioned by the military and by the Japanese trading companies that followed in their wake, dealing in the raw materials Japan had been so eager to capture, such as rubber, tin and bauxite.[40] The result was that the trade in rice was disrupted and most of the region's people lost access to essential supplies of food.

The rice trade received a further blow with the massacre of somewhere between 6,000 and 50,000 Malayan Chinese between February and March 1942. The Japanese sinisterly referred to this as the *sook ching*, or purification of the area.[41] Before the invasion of Malaya the Japanese military and civil authorities were aware that Chinese co-operation would be essential to the economic success of the occupation as they dominated the world of business and finance within the colony.

However, the Chinese Malay community supported the Nationalist government fighting the Japanese in China and also the British colonial rulers: Chinese troops fought in the defence of Singapore. The Japanese military chiefs of staff, who had experienced great difficulties countering guerrilla actions in the war in China, pushed for a programme of suppression in order to eradicate potential opposition to their rule. There were many in the military and civil administration who opposed such a policy, but in the end General Yamashita Tomoyuki, in charge of the invasion, ordered an operation to root out hostile Chinese.[42]

In practice the *sook ching* resembled the actions of the German *Einsatzgruppen* in the Soviet Union, which were initially supposed to root out political opposition but eventually became the main instruments of the extermination of Jewish men, women and children. The crucial difference was that orders for the SS to annihilate *all* the Jews came from above. In Malaya the Japanese administration did not deliberately engage in genocidal policies of extermination. The *kempeitai* (secret police) and the ordinary troops, who felt a deep-seated animosity towards the Chinese because of the brutality of the fighting they had experienced in China, took matters into their own hands and interpreted the order to root out opposition with 'severe and prompt punishment' as an excuse to wreak vengeance.[43] During the operation they killed men, women and children simply because they were Chinese, but this was not part of a concerted plan to annihilate the Chinese community. The *sook ching* was characteristic of Japanese atrocities in the occupied territories which were borne out of the ethos of senseless brutality that saturated the Japanese army. However, this behaviour ran counter to an alternative philosophy also current in the Japanese administration, which argued that Japan should 'show Asians that as an Asian power, she was a kind liberator and friend, who would treat them better than the European powers'.[44]

Those Chinese who survived the initial killing spree were ordered to collectively pay the occupation authorities $50 million, a clumsy attempt to claw revenue from the business community, which appeared to be a ransom for their lives.[45] The vindictive racial persecution alienated the entire Malayan population and reinforced the breakdown of the region's commercial networks. The conscription of labour for Japanese road-building projects, and work on the infamous Burma–Siam railway, where about 70,000 of the 200,000 indigenous slave labourers died, left the rice system without workers.[46] Draught animals became scarce, irrigation works and rice mills broke down and were never repaired.[47] Meanwhile, in the rice-producing areas of Burma and Indo-China the occupying authorities requisitioned huge quantities of rice, at a price well below its market value, in order to feed the troops and build up stores which could be shipped back to Japan.[48] Deprived of their international and inter-regional export market, the peasants were unwilling to work hard only to receive derisory payment from the Japanese and they cut back on production. In addition they made every effort to hide as much of their surplus as possible and channel it on to the black market. By 1945 southern Burma, the largest southeast Asian rice-producing area before the war, was barely cultivating enough to meet subsistence requirements.[49] Upper Burma, cut off from rice supplies from the south, succumbed to famine, but lack of documentation means that these victims of Japanese food policy have largely been forgotten, and there do not appear to be any figures for how many died.[50]

Misunderstanding the nature of the trade in food between deficit and surplus regions, the Japanese made a virtue out of the fact that inter-regional food trade had disintegrated, and introduced the catastrophic policy of 'regional autarky', banning the movement of commodities (including rice) across national and regional borders from mid-1943. Each region, they argued, should strive for self-sufficiency, supporting its own population and the Japanese troops stationed there, on food grown within its own borders.[51]

Malaya was reliant on imports for two-thirds of its food and in order to compensate for their virtual disappearance the Japanese administration launched a 'Grow More Food Campaign'. Food officers tried to introduce agricultural reforms into the countryside. In particular they introduced Formosan paddy. The Japanese not only preferred the taste but it ripened much faster, allowing double-cropping in one year. The Malayan response was mixed. In the 1990s student researchers from Singapore University interviewed farmers who could remember the occupation. They were surprised to find some who claimed that the new Japanese techniques had been a great success. The men in one village described how the governor, Lieutenant-General

Sukegawa, taught them how to introduce double-cropping by first giving a speech of encouragement and then joining the villagers in the paddy fields.[52] They felt certain that no English officer of such high rank would have contemplated wading about in the rice fields with the villagers. One even went so far as to say that it was a pity that the Japanese had not stayed longer. 'They could have taught us much more. They were not stingy like the whites . . . the British could not care less for our village.'[53]

However, the overall impression among the peasantry seems to have been that the Japanese were even worse masters than the British and, following the pattern of disillusioned peasants the world over, rather than increasing production they reduced their cultivation to subsistence levels. The officer in charge of the Kedah Agriculture Department wrote: 'I hear unpleasant rumours that many paddy planters have made up their minds to plant only sufficient for themselves and no more, and that in Kubang Pasu large areas of tenanted *bendang* (rice fields) have been returned to their owners, because cultivators were unwilling to go on with the land on account of loss of interest.'[54] When the Japanese surrendered in August 1945, 42,650 acres of *bendang* had been left abandoned.[55]

To the immense frustration of their new masters the Malayan urban population were equally unenthusiastic about growing their own food. Home gardening exhibitions and competitions did nothing to stimulate their interest. The teacher Mohd Nazir Naim and his pupils were expected to garden every morning before lessons. The songs they were expected to sing while working might well have expressed such laudable sentiments as 'Peasants are honourable people, who are loved and obey orders, forward, forward', but they failed to transform the teacher and his pupils into patriotic and dedicated farmers.[56] The Japanese administration was exasperated because the Malays seemed unaware that unless they showed more enthusiasm, when the Allies eventually imposed a blockade on Malaya they would starve.[57] The Japanese governors warned district officers that if the Malayans continued to garden with such 'an undisguised half-heartedness' their rations would be removed.[58] The Japanese governor of Pahang admonished, 'Distribution of daily necessities . . . should not be given to useless people.'[59] The schoolteacher Chin Kee Onn thought that the 1943 ration cuts of rice, sugar, salt and coconut oil were in retaliation for this lackadaisical attitude.[60]

Eventually the Malayans were forced to grow their own food in order to survive. Internal food production fell to dismal levels and when the British recaptured Burma in 1944 the trickle of rice coming in from the north ceased. Legal imports of Siamese rice came to an end and the only source of food imports was the black market with Siam. Chinese traders would load up junks and lorries with 'rice, brown sugar, onions and garlic, dried chillies', but the prices of Siamese goods were exorbitant.[61] Inflation within Malaya was fuelled by the competition between the army, navy, air force and stock companies for scarce goods, made worse by the Japanese military's practice of paying for goods with scrip (certificates which stated that the holder was entitled to a certain amount of money), which they printed indiscriminately, thus rendering them worthless.[62] Speculators and hoarders took full advantage of the situation and those who suffered were the less wealthy, who could not afford a tin of coconut oil which before the war would have cost $2.40, but by August 1944 might cost as much as $85, or $315 by February 1945.[63]

Townspeople moved into the countryside in order to find plots to cultivate and students stopped attending school and stayed at home to help in the family garden. Only eight or ten students out of forty continued to come to lessons at the Malim Nawar Malay School in Zaharah Hamzah. Those who did attend came in tattered clothing and showed signs of malnutrition and its associated diseases.[64] In mid-1943 the Japanese began destroying rubber and coconut plantations in order to found agricultural settlements. The raw materials could no longer be transported to Japan because of lack of shipping and the American blockade. Chinese, Malay and Indian Associations were instructed to find recruits to farm these projects. Many went to escape being drafted for military labour. They were given all kinds of inducements: 'rice and cloth rations; free vegetable seeds and manures; free medicines and medical services; cheap agricultural implements; subsidies and loans'.[65] But the conditions on these agricultural settlements, populated by people with barely any agricultural knowledge or experience, were appalling. In the remaining rubber plantations, where it was difficult to grow food, the children starved. When the British finally reoccupied the country in August 1945, 35 per cent of schoolchildren in Malacca were found to have anaemia and 30 per cent had vitamin deficiencies of various kinds.[66]

In Singapore tapioca noodles were substituted for the rice ration. Bread was made with a mixture of tapioca and soya flour. 'It was just like rubber, you bite, you pull, the thing stretches. Terrible!' The writer A. Samad Ismail described how an obsession with tapioca took over people's lives. 'These days everyone loves tapioca . . . nothing is talked about except tapioca; in the kitchen, in the tram, at wedding ceremonies – absorbed with tapioca, tapioca, tapioca; until dreams are sometimes about tapioca.'[67] The problem was that while tapioca provided calories, it contained no vitamins. A resident of Singapore summed up the feeling created by living on tapioca, 'We are full in tummy but we lack good substance.'[68] Tropical ulcers became common, malaria, beriberi and tuberculosis claimed thousands.[69] By 1946 the death rate in Malaya had risen to double the pre-war rate.[70]

In Indo-China the misguided agricultural policies of the Japanese and their ruthless requisitioning of rice caused one of the worst famines of the Second World War. Indo-China, nominally under French control, was designated the main supply base for the southern army operating in south-east Asia and the south Pacific.[71] The Japanese decided to use the northern area of Tonkin to compensate for jute and hemp shortages, needed for making rope and sacks. Tonkin had always been dependent on supplementary rice supplies from Cochin-China in the south but the re-allocation of land from rice to jute and hemp caused a fall in the harvest in 1943, which made the northerners more dependent than ever on southern rice imports.[72] However, by 1944 there were only five ships operating the coastal trade between the north and south, and most of the junks which provided supplementary shipping had been requisitioned by the military.[73] The region was cut off from its food imports.

Rice shortages throughout south-east Asia placed even greater pressure on Indo-China to produce rice and, even though the harvest was insufficient to feed the population, the French authorities continued to levy rice on behalf of the Japanese. To make matters worse, rather than going through the French, the Japanese army began to go out into the villages and requisition rice directly. Army representatives arrived in the village of Mieng-Ha in Ung-Hoa district with trucks. The people of Mieng-Ha only cultivated 300 hectares. When the Japanese departed they took with them 200 tons of rice. The villagers were left with nothing. Villages all over Tonkin experienced such visits and, with their stores empty, they were forced to buy rice at the market in order to fulfil their quotas for the French authorities, who bought it back from them at one-third of the price they had paid.[74]

The Tonkin peasantry began to starve. Thousands abandoned their homes and wandered about looking for food. 'They roam in long endless groups, comprising the whole family, the elderly, the children, men, women, all of whom are disfigured by poverty, skinny, shaky, almost naked, including young girls of adolescent age who should have been very shy. From time to time they stop to close the eyes of one of them who has collapsed and who would never be able to rise again or to take the piece of rag (I do not know what to call it exactly), that has covered the fallen victim. Looking at these human shadows who are uglier than the ugliest animals, seeing the shrunk corpses, with only a few straws covering them for both clothes and funeral cloth, at the side of the roads one could feel that human life was so shameful.'[75] Tran Van Mai, who wrote an account of the famine, described a couple who realized that if they continued to divide their food between themselves and their four young children they would all die. The couple decided to let the children die in the hopes that they would survive to have more offspring when the famine was over.[76]

Neither the French nor the Japanese authorities ever tried to gather accurate figures for the number of deaths. It has been estimated that between 1 and 2 million Vietnamese died.[77] New research suggests that the scale of the horror was far greater. The researchers found that in one small area some villages lost 500 inhabitants in the thirty years of war which followed the Second World War. But this was still fewer than those they lost to famine in the fifteen months between March 1944 and August 1945. There were villages which had lost as many as 40 per cent of their inhabitants during the famine. For many villages in north Vietnam, the famine rather than the Vietnam war was the worst experience of the twentieth century.[78]

The most grotesque aspect of it all was that the Japanese continued to requisition rice amidst the human tragedy. When they unseated the French colonial government on 9 March 1945, they held in storage in the country 500,000 tons of rice that was waiting to be shipped to their troops in south-east Asia and to hungry civilians in Japan.[79] But the American blockade of Japanese shipping made it almost impossible to transport the rice, and by October 1945 30,000 tons of the stores had rotted and were no longer fit for consumption. Even after the Japanese surrender, the area had been so denuded of shipping that there were not enough boats available to take the remaining stores of rice north to feed the starving.[80] When in November 1945 Chinese Nationalist troops were brought in to disarm the Japanese troops, they ransacked the area and transported as much food as possible over the border into China.[81]

In the first two years of the war a combination of overly cautious American submarine commanders and faulty torpedoes had given Japanese merchant shipping breathing space.[82] But Japanese industry spent these two years of the war in a state of disorganization. Industrialists won in the battle against the army, which wanted industry to be brought under its effective control. The result was a lack of cross-industry co-operation and collaboration essential in the making of complex armaments.[83] Added to this was the corruption and self-serving nature of the traditional industrial families, more interested in pursuing their own profits than mobilizing for war. It was not unusual for the large industrial undertakings to stockpile materials and then sell them on the black market.[84] The result was that the shipbuilding industry was disastrously under-resourced.

The navy was obsessed by the need to win a decisive battle against the enemy and ship construction concentrated on building up the battle fleet.[85] The Japanese would have been better off building as many cargo ships as possible, as well as numerous escort vessels. Energy should have been spent developing submarine detection equipment, and training the crews of escort ships and aircraft pilots in submarine surveillance and attack.[86] At the end of 1943 the state finally took effective control of industry. Aircraft production and the electronics sector were greatly improved, as was the production rate of the shipbuilding industry, which began to turn out merchant ships at some speed. The time it took to construct the new merchant ships matched the US rate of about forty days, but the quality of the vessels was inferior and they could be sunk with relative ease. Besides, these efforts were too little too late.[87] More confident US commanders, aided by intelligence (the Americans broke all the Japanese naval codes), improved torpedoes and wolf-pack tactics doubled their sinkings of Japanese tonnage that year.[88] The Japanese had absolutely no hope of building enough ships to compensate for these losses. Their only real hope was in protecting those ships that they did have. But they did not have enough escort ships and their anti-submarine tactics were obsolete and ineffective. By 1944 Japan's shipping capacity had been reduced by 60 per cent.[89]

Throughout south-east Asia the collapse of the rice trade combined with the effectiveness of the American blockade had a terrible impact. In the Philippines, Japanese attempts to introduce Formosan strains of rice and improve agriculture were as unsuccessful as in Malaya.[90] Unable to enforce a policy of self-sufficiency the Japanese reluctantly continued to import rice from Indo-China, but as the Americans stepped up their submarine campaign against Japanese shipping much of it sank to the bottom of the ocean. The price of black market rice in Manila tracks the growing severity of the food shortage. In 1941 rice cost 6 or 7 pesos per cavan;* by late 1942 the price was 30 pesos; and 70 pesos by mid-1943. Then the crisis escalated, and a year later a cavan of rice cost 250 pesos; six months later the price stood at 3,000 to 5,000 pesos, and by 1945 it had risen to 12,000 pesos. The wages for unskilled labour rose from about 1.30 pesos a day to 3 or 4 pesos in 1944.[91] The wealthy went out into the countryside to barter jewellery, clothes and furniture for rice; the poor were so desperate that they ate foul-smelling rice recovered from the polluted bottom of Manila Bay. By 1944 it was common to see the corpses of those who had starved lying in the street.[92]

In contrast, in the rice-growing area of central Luzon the Hukbalahap guerrillas were in control and the peasants lived well. Landlords, afraid of the guerrilla bands, withdrew from the region and failed to collect their rent in cash or kind. From the end of 1942 to late 1943 the Japanese, wary of conflict, kept to the coastal roads and towns and did not come into the area to requisition rice. Good weather ensured a bumper rice crop and many recall the period 1942 to 1947 as the period in their lives when food was most plentiful.[93] Ironically,

* About 56 kilograms.

when left to their own devices, the Filipinos adopted the policy of self-sufficiency which the Japanese were so unsuccessful in imposing upon their Malayan subjects. Artisan crafts were revived and villagers made soap from lime, ashes and coconut oil, wove cloth, used tree bark to make baskets, extracted salt from seawater and brewed soft drinks from ginger and coconuts.[94] A resident of Manila who moved out to southern Luzon reminisced: 'Manila was gloomy and depressing. People were suffering. They were hungry. There were many beggars. There was despair. People just wondered when the bad dreams would be over. When I moved away, though, to be with relatives, I found people in the barrios were more confident. They were living better, more organized, more positive about things, more light-hearted, freer. It's because there we were far away from the Japanese and we were part of the guerrillas.'[95] However, in late 1943 the troops on the islands were reinforced and Japanese patrols moved into the region along the back trails. A priest who was a member of a guerrilla band recalled how the Japanese 'raped, tortured, bayoneted, burned houses and crops, drove off animals and carried away clothing, food, even the agricultural equipment. In their wake they left hunger, malnutrition and starvation.'[96]

On the island of Java in the Dutch East Indies the Japanese followed a desperate strategy similar to the one they adopted in Malaya and gutted the plantations in order to grow subsistence crops. Over 2 million men were conscripted to work as forced labourers on these newly created farms, but the lack of rice imports meant that the Japanese were unable to feed them properly and they were struck down by dysentery and yaws. Meanwhile, their families in the villages struggled to grow food without their labour. Rather than alleviating the food shortage the Japanese policy spread hunger, and a drought in 1944 made matters worse. Although Javan officials colluded in allowing the villagers to squirrel much of their harvest away, hiding it from the greedy requisitioning Japanese, the occupying forces were able to collect a large share of the much-diminished harvest.[97] The food was stored away in order to supply naval ships which came to the island to pick up stores. The loss of increasing numbers of ships to submarine attacks meant that they came back again and again to requisition yet more rice from the dwindling stores.[98] By 1944 thousands could be seen along the sides of the road, dressed in sacking and rags, 'waiting for death'.[99]

Caught up in the chaos of the ever-worsening food situation in the Japanese empire were hundreds of thousands of Allied prisoners of war. On average, prisoners during the Second World War lost 38 pounds in captivity. Allied prisoners of the Japanese lost an average of 61 pounds. Many of those who survived never fully recovered and suffered from poor health for the rest of their lives.[100] The staple ration in the prison camps was white rice, which meant that the diet was seriously deficient in vitamin B. In Changi jail in Singapore the prisoners set up a 'grass soup factory' to alleviate the problem. The soup made of crushed grass tasted 'like nothing on earth' but it provided the men with essential vitamins.[101] But by the end of the war beriberi in varying degrees of severity afflicted virtually all the prisoners of the Japanese. Forrest Knox, captured on Bataan at the beginning of the war, recalled that by 1945 he had turned into 'a human balloon full of fluid'. The guards would periodically turn him over so that they could amuse themselves watching alternate sides of his face filling up with fluid.[102]

H. E. Jessup, an Australian officer imprisoned in Changi, recorded in his diary the worsening condition of his fellow prisoners as the food situation in Malaya deteriorated throughout 1944. In July he noted that the only available source of protein was a tiny quantity of dried fish which was often inedible.[103] The rice and salt rations were cut in October and the Japanese announced that they would no longer be issuing vegetables.[104] Despite the grass soup, many of the men began to go blind, a symptom of vitamin B deficiency.[105] By February 1945 Jessup was worried that the men would soon begin to die of starvation. In March he recorded that 'food is our main preoccupation these days. We get up hungry from each meal, and barely exist until the next. The nights are the worst, with our stomachs an aching void. All sorts of things are being eaten, snails from the garden, sparrows, doves (if we can catch them) and even quite a few rats have found themselves in the cooking pots. Of course all cats and dogs disappeared long ago.'[106] Jessup managed to hold out until August, and after the Japanese surrender the commandant of the jail was persuaded to release a stock of Red Cross parcels which the Japanese had been hoarding in warehouses in Singapore. The parcels tided the men over until they were liberated – on this diet Jessup even began to regain weight.[107]

The American submarines gradually drew in a net around the home islands of Japan. In 1944 and 1945 the Japanese government abandoned all hope of using the wider empire as a source of food and concentrated its efforts on extracting as much food as possible from Manchuria, accessible via the shorter and initially less dangerous shipping routes across the Sea of Japan.

In Manchuria the Japanese continued to live well. Teruko Blair spent fourteen months in Manchuria between May 1944 and July 1945. Back at home, food shortages were becoming painful but here she revelled in the fact that only sugar was scarce.[108] The picture was very different among the Chinese population. Tsukui Shin'ya, an agricultural officer in Manchuria, recalled that 'the year that the Pacific War broke out . . . the demands of the military administration increased sharply. The forwarding of agricultural produce and the commandeering of labourers shot up proportionately to the expansion of the war itself. The situation in foodstuffs ultimately brought on starvation for a group of poor farmers within the county.'[109] In the early years of the war the failure of the Korean harvest increased the pressure on Manchuria's farmers as coarse grains were sent to Korea in order to free up more rice for export to Japan. As the war wore on, Japan compensated for its own diminishing rice crop by importing Manchurian sweet potatoes, soya beans and barley. By 1945 as much as half or even three-quarters of the ration of 'rice' was made up of foodstuffs from Manchuria.[110]

An article produced by the Allied Air Headquarters, India, observed, 'The Nazis said that if anybody starves in Europe, they would be the last to starve, and the same principle seems to be applied by the Japanese in Manchuria.'[111] The article outlined that even though the Vice-Minister for Agriculture in Manchuria had admitted that there had been a serious drought and locust damage to the harvest he had reiterated, 'Whatever happens, the planned quota for export must be fulfilled.'[112] The author was astonished to find that Japanese-occupied central China, an area which was itself suffering from a food crisis, was sending wheat to Manchuria. Meanwhile, Manchuria was sending Japan record amounts of soya beans. The Japanese had reportedly stripped Shanghai of its reserve food stocks (mainly food imported before the war from Canada and Australia) and sent them to Japan. 'What is this great city going to eat?' asked the report. The price of rice was said to have increased 240–fold.[113] Tsuchiya Yoshio, a member of the Japanese military police in Manchuria, described the misery which resulted from the requisition of more and more foodstuffs. In the winter of 1944 he visited Lindian County, Heilongjiang Province. 'There were homes in the area without clothing and bedding. There were even children living there naked.'[114] Tsuchiya wondered how the children survived the cold. In the area along the Great Wall in Rehe Province, half of the residents lived without clothing, in utter despair. 'Without any assistance, they will simply flicker out of existence.'[115]

The Japanese leadership may not have constructed elaborate plans to starve to death the people whose countries they occupied. However, their callous disregard for the well-being of the indigenous population, and their ruthless requisitioning of foodstuffs, were guided by a principle similar to that applied by the National Socialists: the indigenous population in the empire should go hungry before the Japanese. But while the Japanese proved themselves to be remarkably successful at exporting chaos and hunger to their empire, they demonstrated an extraordinary inability to reap the benefits and maintain food imports to the home islands.

12

China Divided

Ultimately all things, whether military or political, resolved themselves into a peasant, dressed in torn blue or grey gown, straining to supply the raw energy of resistance.
(American journalists Theodore White and Annalee Jacoby
commenting on Nationalist China's war effort)[1]

When the Japanese attack on Pearl Harbor on 7 December 1941 cata-pulted the United States into the Second World War the people of China had already been fighting the Japanese invaders for four years. Although a deep divide ran between the communists and the Nationalists they had made an uneasy alliance in 1936 in order to form a united front against their common enemy, the Japanese. In the struggle between the two parties America had always supported the Nationalists (the *Guomindang*), and now President Roosevelt looked to their leader Chiang Kaishek as a key ally. While the colonial powers of France, Britain and the Netherlands crumbled in the face of Japanese attack, the Chinese, he told Congress in January 1942, 'had already withstood [four and a half years of] bombs and starvation and have whipped the invaders time and again in spite of superior Japanese equipment and arms'.[2] The United States provided funding and supplies to the Nationalist government throughout the war but the US administration became increasingly disillusioned by their Chinese ally and were disappointed by the fact that the Nationalists were never strong enough to launch a counter-offensive against the Japanese. In 1945 the US government condemned their erstwhile allies as corrupt and militarily incompetent. It cannot be denied that corruption was rife in the

Nationalist bureaucracy by the end of the war. The Chinese government had presided over a fiscal and bureaucratic meltdown, lost control of much of its army, which had become a scourge upon the Chinese countryside, and helplessly stood by while millions of its citizens had starved to death. If the faults in the Nationalist government played a major contributory role in the development of this situation it was also attributable to the fact that China in 1937 lacked the economic, industrial, agricultural and political fabric to withstand the assault of total war.[3]

NATIONALIST COLLAPSE

When Chiang Kaishek established the Nationalist government of China in 1928 he had fought his way to power alongside members of the Soviet-funded Communist Party. But, distrustful of the Soviets' motives and suspecting that they would oust him from his position as soon as they were able, he rounded on his former allies and murdered thousands of party activists.[4] The remnants of the Communist Party retreated into the countryside in Jiangxi province in central China until, in 1934, Mao Zedong and 80,000 of his comrades set off on the Long March to settle in the north of the country, out of reach of Nationalist persecution.[5]

Once in power, the Nationalist government set about creating a strong, centralized state to counter the political chaos and turmoil of the preceding decades, and finally modernize China. They hoped to achieve this by encouraging industrial development and, with technical assistance from the League of Nations, they built 32,000 kilometres of highways and invested in industrial and development programmes.[6] When the Japanese occupied Manchuria in 1931 the Nationalists were forced to begin to prepare for war and Chiang Kaishek concentrated on developing a strong state apparatus by building up an efficient administrative bureaucracy, which it was intended would preside over an integrated economic, fiscal and political base, with a modernized army at its core.[7] But when the war eventually came in July 1937 the Nationalists had only been in power for nine years and much of what they had managed to build up was destroyed.

In 1937 the Nationalists faced a situation comparable to that in the

Soviet Union in 1941. Forced into retreat, they abandoned their capital in Nanjing and fled to the city of Chongqing in the south-western
province of Sichuan. By 1938 the Japanese had occupied the eastern
portion of China, including the country's wealthiest region along the
eastern seaboard, and the Nationalists lost a major source of revenue
in the form of the maritime customs service.[8] In 1940 the Japanese
captured the fertile Hubei plains, and free China lost 20 per cent of its
rice-growing and 60 per cent of its wheat-growing regions.[9] Like the
Soviets, in a heroic effort they evacuated some heavy industrial plant,
much of which was floated down the Yangtze river on barges, under
heavy bombardment. But they had to abandon most textile plants and
the majority of factories producing consumer goods.[10] In the south-west
they were never able to rebuild their industrial base to a level which
could supply their troops with sufficient arms. The factories were only
able to produce 15 million bullets per month, which amounted to five
per soldier.[11] At least 50 million refugees flooded into the Nationalist
area, fleeing the savagery of the Japanese invaders, and this pushed the
population in the unoccupied area up from 180 to 239 million (or
about 60 per cent of China's population).[12]

Chiang Kaishek made the mistake of thinking that because 'China
is an agricultural country and her agrarian foundation is resilient' it
would withstand the strains of war better than the highly industrialized
countries 'whose economies are more easily affected by war'.[13] He was
to be proved wrong. In order to withstand the strains of the Second
World War a nation required a large and well-equipped army which
could be fed with a steady stream of food, medicines and arms. It
therefore needed a strong industrial base in order to produce these
supplies and a flexible capitalized agricultural sector which could adapt
to wartime difficulties and still produce increased quantities of nutritious food for the army and the industrial population. An infrastructure
and logistical apparatus which could deliver the goods to the front was
essential and on the home front a nation required a robust civilian
economy, an efficient administration and a reasonably united population. Moreover, the government needed the money to finance the war
effort. Free China had none of these things.[14]

During the first three years of war the Nationalists coped relatively
well. Rather than placing the burden of financing the conflict on the

rural population, they raised taxes on salaries and property and borrowed and printed money. To counter the inflationary effects of this strategy they cut down on state expenditure and tried to boost trade and commerce. In order to ensure a flow of goods around the country they carried on with their programme of highway construction and made strenuous efforts to ensure that the infrastructure of rail and river transport continued to function.[15] They did look to the rural population for military manpower and, in the initial phases, men were impressed into the army, which caused a great deal of rural unrest. But by 1938 this had been brought under control and, in order to safeguard agricultural production, recruitment officers were ordered to apply the principle that no family should be left without sufficient labour to grow enough food to support itself. Attempts were made to make service in the army relatively attractive. War family support committees were set up, financed by local elites, and these provided grain and welfare for the poorer families with men away in the army. Soldiers' wages were raised to enable them to send money home and in the first years of the war the Nationalists managed to recruit 2 million men a year to face an army of just over 1 million Japanese.[16]

Efforts were made to ensure that agricultural productivity improved. The area under cultivation was extended, winter ploughing was introduced and potatoes were grown as a winter crop. The peasants were encouraged to plant new, more resilient rice varieties and they were shown how to use bonemeal fertilizers and pesticides. Despite labour shortages, a lack of chemical fertilizers and transportation difficulties, the climate was kind and yields of wheat, potatoes, peanuts and rape seed all improved. In the three years between 1937 and 1940 the agricultural sector managed well and food was quite plentiful.[17]

Then, in 1940, the Japanese occupied Yichang, a strategic town which linked Sichuan to the war zones. It was now difficult to get food and armaments through to the troops on the front line. In the south the Japanese invaded Guangxi and cut the railroad link between the southern province of Yunnan and northern Indo-China, which was used to import rice. They also cut off the major ports in the province of Fujian which supplied food to the southern province Guangdong, which did not grow enough food to feed its population. Free China's link to international grain imports was now severed. In the south more than 2 million people were immediately threatened with starvation.[18] Until late 1941 the blockade was surprisingly porous. An organized ring of Chinese smugglers bought gasoline, cloth and medicines from the Japanese army. In return they sold them tungsten and tin for the manufacture of Japanese arms. The Chinese communists were able to buy weapons in Japanese garrison towns, and the *Guomindang* army stationed on the border with Indo-China was fed with rice bought from Japanese dealers.[19] However, the only official route by which international support and supplies could now enter Nationalist China was the Burma road, a tortuous single track along which lorries began to lumber day and night, carrying 30,000 tons of goods per day into beleaguered China.[20] Despite laxity along their own border with China, the Japanese were determined to close this last lifeline to the Allies and achieved their aim when they captured Burma in early 1942. From then on China's only source of Allied aid was by air over the 'hump' of the eastern Himalayas. This was a dangerous route over high mountains and deep gorges, and with unpredictable weather. The airlift brought into China 685,000 tons of war materiel and American foodstuffs between January 1943 and August 1945, but this was used mainly as a supply line for the US air bases which were established in China in order to launch bombing raids on Japan's cities.[21]

Burmese road and 'hump' supplies made little difference to ordinary Chinese people and, to make matters worse, just as food imports ceased, the weather turned and it became clear that the harvest of 1940 was going to be much smaller than in previous years. The rice harvest only fell by 18 per cent but the wheat harvest was down by 40 per cent.[22] A food panic ensued, in which the government participated. Chiang Kaishek made money available so that the government could buy up grain in Sichuan, and as prices began to rise landlords and speculators responded by hoarding rice.[23] Just over half of all farmers were tenants and the payment of rent in kind meant that landlords, who before the war had hoarded opium, were well placed to speculate in rice. Tsunghan Shen, deputy head of a food division within the Nationalist government, was living in a rented house in the countryside. He observed that his landlord bought the rice he needed for his family's daily consumption on the open market, while he put the rice he had been paid by his tenants into storage, waiting for further price rises.[24]

In 1941–42, as the Japanese launched their war against the United States, refugees from Shanghai and Hong Kong began to stream into Chongqing. They used the large quantities of cash which they brought with them to buy up as much food and as many consumer goods as possible, further fuelling inflation. Food prices in Chongqing rose by 1,400 per cent. The government was now irrevocably caught up in an inflationary spiral which lasted for the rest of their period in government.[25] When, in 1945, Chester Ronning arrived in Nationalist China as the First Secretary to the Canadian Ambassador, he found that even though millions of Chinese were starving, speculators were still hoarding rice and that they would even allow part of their rice hoard to rot while they waited for the prices to rise.[26]

The white-collar workers in the vast civil bureaucracy, including thousands of lecturers, teachers and students who had accompanied their universities as they were evacuated from the Japanese-occupied areas, found themselves unable to buy food. By 1941 the purchasing power of their wages had fallen to less than 15 per cent of their pre-war level. The students survived on a diet of bean curd and noodles from cheap teashops, and many fell sick with tuberculosis.[27] The government introduced rationing and subsidized the price of grain. But it now faced the problem that, with the price of food at astronomical levels, it simply did not have sufficient money to pay for the food it needed to feed the military and its civil service dependants. From July 1941 the government was forced to collect the land tax from the peasantry in food rather than cash. In July 1943 the government was sufficiently desperate to introduce 'compulsory borrowing' of food, an additional tax on top of the normal land tax, also to be paid in kind, but the reimbursement was to be deferred until a later date.[28] These measures did slow down inflation as they meant that the government could acquire food without printing yet more money and, although it was extreme, the inflation of food prices remained lower than it was for other scarce items such as clothing and fuel.[29] In this way the civil administration in the cities was fed, but the price was paid in the villages.

The decision to collect the land tax in kind shifted the burden of financing the war on to the peasantry. Indeed, the entire war effort came to rest on the peasantry, who provided the two essentials:

manpower and food. 'With the food [the peasant] raised, the government fed the army . . . the arsenal workers and the bureaucracy. With the manpower the peasant supplied, the government kept recruits trudging to the front, built the roads, moved essential tonnages . . . The building of an American airfield for B-29s, the construction of shelter, the organization of supply, all could be reduced to the number of peasant hands available and the number of sacks of rice they could produce to meet the crisis.'[30] What placed an impossible strain on the countryside was not so much the food needs of the urban population as the voracious demands of the military. Throughout the years of the War of Resistance (1937–45) the *Guomindang* army grew from 420,000 soldiers to over 5.5 million in 1944.[31] They ate between one-half and two-thirds of all the food the government was able to requisition, on a ration of 750 grams of rice per day.[32] From 1939 the government had made efforts to accumulate grain reserves, and storage granaries had been built in the rear areas. A great effort had been made to sustain food production in Sichuan, which provided supplementary supplies for the front line. But, after the capture of Yichang, the northern war zones were effectively cut off from the capital. The now derelict transport system was incapable of bringing meaningful quantities of supplies in to the northern front along rutted cart tracks over the few mountainous routes that were still open.[33]

The army was forced to live off the land in its own country. In September 1942 Chiang Kaishek urged the troops to grow their own food, herd animals and even to weave their own cloth.[34] In effect the centre lost control of the provinces and army commanders took over the administration of the districts where they were stationed, levying taxes and passing laws.[35] Under these chaotic conditions the army command reverted to the corrupt practices which had been commonplace in the decades of warlordism and in-fighting before the Nationalist takeover. At the Xi'an Military Conference of 1942 Chiang Kaishek devoted a large part of his speech to a host of problems which had clearly become widespread throughout the army: 'smuggling, opium consumption, engagement in commerce, joining secret societies, dependants of officers living close to army units, new soldiers beating Escort Officers, [and] mutinies among recruits'.[36] On top of the official land taxes, the military commanders imposed extra incidental levies on the peasantry, demanding 'food, animal feed, draft animals, wood, coal, clothing, transport equipment, and cooking utensils'.[37] In addition, the locals were press-ganged into working as porters and cooks. In Henan more than a million farmers were conscripted to find fodder for the army's animals, build roads, dig anti-tank trenches and construct dykes along the banks of the Yellow River. They were not paid and they were expected to provide their own food.[38] Meanwhile, the local bureaucracies descended into corruption and at every level officials would siphon off a proportion of the food payment for themselves, which they would then hoard. The social divisions which characterized rural China intensified as landlords and rich peasants found ways of evading taxes, while an increasing number of tenant and small farmers were driven to bankruptcy and hunger.[39] Agricultural production, which was already under an immense strain due to the drafting of able-bodied men into the army, began to collapse.[40]

In Henan in 1942 the peasants were assailed by a series of biblical afflictions. Drought was followed by frost and hail and then by a plague of locusts. The harvest fell to three-quarters of its normal level.[41] The peasantry might well have been able to tighten their belts and withstand these misfortunes if it had not been for at least 300,000 Nationalist troops garrisoned in the province.[42] The commanders in the neighbouring provinces of Shaanxi and Hubei refused to release food from their own stocks to alleviate the food shortage. In order to meet their collection quotas tax officials relentlessly requisitioned food in the face of the peasants' evident distress. 'As they died the government continued to wring from them the last possible ounce of tax ... Peasants who were eating elm bark and dried leaves had to haul their last sack of seed grain to the tax collector's office.'[43] Much of what they collected disappeared into the officials' personal hoards. American relief organizations found themselves buying food from these bureaucrats to distribute back to the same peasants from whom it had been unfairly extorted.[44] Three million fled the area. Others sold their land at discount prices to merchants, army officers and government officials, who mercilessly gained in wealth at their expense. Some peasants sold or murdered their children.[45] Mr Jingguan lost his father to starvation in 1942. By 1944 his family were so desperate that they sold his sister, then aged fifteen, to an older man, but she too died.[46] When the American journalist Theodore White visited the province in February 1943 he saw corpses by the sides of the roads. The desperate ate leaves, peanut husks, 'the green slime' from pools of water and even each other. 'A doctor told us of a woman caught boiling her baby; she was not molested, because she insisted that the child had died before she started to cook it.'[47] In the spring of 1943 the desperate harvested the wheat too early and ground the unripened wheat kernels to eat. Their bodies bloated and they died. Theodore White estimated in March 1943 that about 5 million people were dead or dying.[48]

One of the cruellest aspects of the hunger and famine imposed on the peasantry in the name of feeding the army was that the troops themselves were frequently weak and malnourished. By 1942 the recruitment process had degenerated into a process of impressment. Gangs would forcibly round up peasants and sell them to the army. Many would die of starvation before they reached the military camp. 'Of 40,000 conscripts arriving at a camp near Chengdu during one conscription drive, no more than 8,000 remained alive by drive's end.'[49] The officers would siphon off food to sell on the black market, leaving the soldiers with inadequate rations. It was said that 'some units could not go even a short distance without many dying alongside of the road from disease or starvation'.[50] In 1942 troops in the south were reported to be living on low-quality rice without vegetables, and one cup of boiled water per day. A second-class soldier's pay of 50 yuan per month bought very little supplementary food, given that a pound of cabbage cost 30 yuan.[51] Hunger increased the ferocity of the army's wild requisitioning of food. In Hubei province in May 1943 troops evacuated an entire town and then set about plundering everything of value which the inhabitants had left behind. The elderly who had remained in their houses were murdered.[52] In the province of Guangdong the army created a famine in which 1.5 million peasants died. Meanwhile, the rice which the army officers had requisitioned from the starving peasants was smuggled across the front line and sold to the Japanese at great personal profit.[53]

The army felt the peasants' rage in the spring of 1944 when the Japanese launched their Ichigo offensive. The Japanese aim was to capture the air bases from which the Americans were launching bombing attacks on Japanese cities and to open a land route through to south-east Asia.

As they advanced, army officials in Henan began evacuating their families, along with cartloads of goods extorted from the peasantry. They even began to round up the locals' oxen in order to pull the carts. The peasants responded with fury, at first disarming individual soldiers and then moving on to ferociously attacking the retreating Chinese troops with ancient guns and farm implements. As many as 50,000 Nationalist soldiers were disarmed by their own countrymen. About one-fifth of these were murdered, some buried alive by the peasants.[54]

The Japanese captured Henan, Hunan and Jiangxi with ease. Pressure intensified on the population of Sichuan but the situation was irretrievable. The Chinese paid the price of an Allied strategy which prioritized other areas of conflict. When the Ichigo offensive began, Nationalist China's best divisions were away in Burma fighting for the British in order to retake Rangoon. In 1945, Albert Wedemeyer, the US Chief of Staff in China, refused to divert Chinese troops to recapture the valuable agricultural areas on the northern front and insisted that Nationalist forces should be concentrated in the south, it being a priority for the Americans that Japanese troops from south-east Asia should be prevented from retreating overland into China.[55]

The death toll reveals which groups in Chinese society bore the burden of the struggle against the Japanese. Two million Nationalist soldiers died and at least 15 million civilians, 85 per cent of them peasants, and virtually all of them the victims of deprivation and starvation.[56] In allowing corruption and wild requisitioning to spiral out of control the Nationalist government could not have aided the communists more effectively. On returning from Henan, Theodore White commented, 'We knew that there was a fury, as cold and relentless as death itself, in the bosom of the peasants of Honan [sic], that their loyalty had been hollowed to nothingness by the extortion of the government.'[57] Throughout the Nationalist-controlled areas the seeds of bitterness and resentment had been sown among the peasantry.

COMMUNIST SURVIVAL

The War of Resistance destroyed the Nationalist government. It had the opposite effect on the communists, who were able to use the war to renew their energies, consolidate their base in the north and expand the areas under their influence. The 4,000 survivors of the Long March established a base in the Shaan-Gan-Ning (Shaanxi-Gansu-Ningxia) border region, with their headquarters at Yan an in northern Shaanxi. During the war they expanded their influence further into northern and eastern central China. The Japanese did not have a firm grip on rural China and the communists would set up base areas behind the Japanese lines, surrounding the Japanese garrison towns with a communist countryside. These areas were widely scattered and varied from relatively well-consolidated control to guerrilla zones.[58]

The communists were by no means firmly established as a ruling power. They were thus in a position of trying to live off the land like an army of occupation rather than an army based in its own country. An additional disadvantage was that their base area was under-developed, agriculturally poor and prone to natural disasters such as earthquakes, floods and droughts.[59] In the early years of its existence the Communist Party had adopted an aggressive policy of land reform which confiscated land from rich peasants and landlords. During the war, it seemed politic to adopt a more conciliatory approach which minimized the extent of social and economic disruption.[60] Thus, rather than evicting landlords, they set about redistributing wealth by reducing the amount of rent landlords could demand and the interest which could be charged on loans. By giving the peasantry greater access to potential profits these measures provided them with an incentive to work hard and produce more food. A number of schemes which introduced labour teams, crop rotation, increased manuring of crops, as well as irrigation projects, all improved agricultural productivity. The great achievement of the communists was to use their only resource – labour – most effectively within the limits of agricultural under-development.[61] Like the Nationalists, the communists relied on the villages for manpower for the army but they took care to minimize the potential alienation and labour shortages which were caused by military recruitment. Soldiers' families were given special assistance during the harvest and the Red Army routinely helped to bring in the crops, reducing the harvest time by as much as half in Shaanxi in 1938.[62]

The 1936 truce with the Nationalists meant that they were able to bring in supplementary supplies from Nationalist-held regions in the first plentiful two years of the war. General Peng Dehuai, deputy commander of the Communist Eighth Route Army, bought up large quantities of grain during the bountiful harvest of 1937 and sent it north for storage in the remote mountain areas.[63] The co-operation between the two parties came to an end in 1941 after a clash between Nationalist and communist troops, and from then on the Nationalists imposed a blockade on the communist-held areas. Inflation in Yan an sky-rocketed and the food situation among the communist troops deteriorated to the point where it threatened their survival. Supplies were limited to black soya bean and even this frequently did not get through. The soldiers improvised and ate melons, tree leaves, grass roots and wild herbs.[64]

Mao, in a manner reminiscent of his Japanese opponents, championed the strategy of self-sufficiency. The communists would have to take up farming and feed themselves.[65] For the purposes of propaganda Mao even tilled the soil himself and his farming exploits were held up as an inspiration, not only to the ordinary people, but to the soldiers and the bureaucracy. Party and government offices, schools, factories and army units were all encouraged to set up their own farms.[66] Mr Changzheng, a teenager when he went on the Long March to Yan an, recalled how, 'Every morning, the troops went off up into the mountains with their hoes to clear the land for planting. The ground was very hard, and some of the vegetation needed two people to dig it out. By day we prepared the ground, and by night we spun and wove cotton. We had a song which went: Till the wastelands, till the wastelands; The front-line soldiers need food. Weave cloth, weave cloth; The front-line soldiers need clothing.'[67] By 1944 the army had reclaimed, and was productively farming, about 830,000 *mu* of land, producing an impressive 13.5 million tons of grain, more than the 9 million tons of grain the Germans were able to squeeze out of the more fertile Ukraine. The communist Shaan-Gan-Ning region was able to achieve an impressive level of self-sufficiency.[68]

Attempts were made to extend the self-sufficiency programme to the rest of the Red Army in other communist-held areas. This had great propaganda value. When communist propaganda units travelled through the villages, urging the peasants to participate in the production movement, their job was made easier by the fact that the soldiers were themselves participating in the drive to increase the food supply.[69] It was, however, still necessary to requisition food from the peasantry. In the secure communist areas the military requisitions were referred to as 'national salvation grain levies'; in the less-established areas the communists preferred to ask for loans and contributions rather than demand taxes.[70] The party administrators were aware that they were not in a strong enough position to extract food ruthlessly from the peasantry, and army officers were exhorted to pay for supplies with scrip tickets. The Fourth Brigade was issued with strict instructions that it was to abide by three principles when requisitioning food. Firstly, the soldiers should take whatever the peasants chose to give them, without complaint. Secondly, political officers should, if possible, investigate the ability of different villagers to pay food taxes, and food should not be requisitioned from the poor peasants. Finally, they were to confine them- selves to taking only what they needed. Anything left over should be distributed before the troops left the area.[71] The communists were certainly better at restraining wild requisitioning of food on the part of their forces, but after the vicious Japanese attacks on communist groups in 1942 the soldiers became more desperate and unofficial levies more common. There is no doubt that communist soldiers were as capable as the *Guomindang* army of behaving like 'bandits' in the villages.[72] However, for the most part, they succeeded in maintaining the goodwill of the peasantry and, when the war against the Japanese came to an end and the civil war between the communists and the Nationalists began, while the peasantry did not rise up in support of the communists they were willing to co-operate with them.[73]

When the war came to an end the corruption of the Nationalists acted as a foil, heightening the positive aspects of communist policies. The food crisis continued and the government responded by printing money, fuelling inflation and deepening the crisis.[74] When the Nationalists moved back into the occupied areas they behaved like a colonial power and treated the locals with contempt as collaborators. One woman, who was a student in Shanghai at the time, recalled how 'carpet-bagging officials sent by the *Guomindang* to take over from the Japanese had arrived from Chongqing, and appropriated all the wealth for them- selves, and then they used galloping inflation to fleece ordinary people'.[75]

As soon as her father, a university lecturer, was paid, the family had to hurry round with heavy bags of money buying as much food as possible before inflation meant that the food prices rose again beyond their means. The Nationalists quickly lost the goodwill of the liberated population, and the rural population in the Nationalist areas were already disaffected.[76]

Meanwhile the communists, armed by the Soviets with weapons left behind by the Japanese, projected an air of 'purpose and morale' which meant that many welcomed their victory simply because they retained a level of political credibility which the Nationalists had lost.[77] In 1949 the communists won the civil war and founded the People's Republic of China, while the Nationalist leadership fled to Formosa (Taiwan). In many ways the outcome of the civil war was determined by the way in which the two parties ran their respective campaigns against the Japanese.[78] However, the reasons why this was the case have since been lost in a concerted rewriting of history. Rather than acknowledging that the communists had won the goodwill of the peasantry through the conciliatory measures which they were forced to adopt under the pressure of war, communist propaganda argued that the party had gained popular support as a result of the Red Army's heroic guerrilla warfare against the Japanese.[79] Meanwhile, the American administration's defence against right-wing outrage in the US that the communists had won in China, led those US administrators who had decided to withdraw American support for the Nationalists during the civil war to present the Nationalist government as irredeemably corrupt.[80] In the process the Nationalists' earlier, more honourable aims and successes were forgotten. In addition, the wholesale destruction of China's agricultural and industrial fabric by the Japanese was rarely acknowledged as a problem which virtually any government would have found insurmountable, let alone in the conditions of civil war.[81]

During the Second World War only the United States had sufficient resources to produce record quantities of food in wartime. However, the ability of western European countries to withstand occupation and a drastic reduction in agricultural inputs demonstrated that countries with developed economies and relatively efficient agricultural sectors were far better at weathering the difficulties created by war than those which were predominantly rural.[82] In Japan the arable nature of farming meant that there was no flexibility within the system which would allow farmers to switch from meat to grain cultivation and this made it virtually impossible to increase food production. In under-developed India and China, where the peasant-based agricultural systems were labour-intensive, and where a large section of the population was already living at the margins of subsistence, the pressures of war pushed these nations into a food crisis.

Western industrialized countries also held up better in terms of food collection. With the notable exceptions of the Soviet Union and China, farmers were relatively well fed in all the combatant nations as they were able, legally or illegally, to hold back adequate and often ample quantities of food. However, in many countries the ability of farmers to withdraw into self-sufficiency made it difficult to collect enough food to feed the cities. In Germany and France the large number of smallholdings meant that while the rural population ate relatively well, urban dwellers frequently suffered from food shortages, vegetables and fruit in particular disappearing from grocers' shelves. In the more rural parts of the world, in the occupied Soviet Union, Japan and south-east Asia, not only did the disillusion of farmers with the governing authorities, and their withdrawal from the open market, cause food production to fall dramatically, a large part of what was produced was channelled on to the black market. Only in the Soviet Union was the government able to prevent this from happening as collectivization proved to be a powerful instrument, allowing the government control over virtually all the food farmers were able to grow.

All the combatant nations, bar the United States and China, remained reliant to a greater or lesser extent on food imports. Britain benefited greatly from its dominant position within pre-war world trade. It was able to command the manpower, raw materials, clothing and food resources of its empire as well as of traditional trading partners such as Argentina and the United States. Germany was pitted against not just a small island but the sum of its empire and influence. The United States was able to feed itself and its huge army, as well as British civilians and the Soviet Red Army. Thus, agrarian resources were a powerful Allied asset. It is unsurprising that Germany and Japan wanted their own empires. They benefited greatly from their occupied territories but they were to discover that the more exploitative their policies the less effective they were. This was exemplified by Denmark, which surprised Germany with the abundance of its exports, while the Ukraine ultimately proved a disappointment.

By virtue of the fact that they were importing foodstuffs from countries suffering from food scarcity, Japan and Germany were exporting hunger. The National Socialists applied their distorted racial ideologies to their empire and, although they were determined that all nations should go hungry before Germany, they viewed the Slavs in particular as sub-human and carried through a brutal programme of starvation and extermination in the east. In the Japanese empire it was the Chinese who found themselves at the bottom of the East Asian hierarchy. But, even in the more benign sphere of the Allies, race was still a deciding factor in determining who was well fed, who went hungry and who starved. By prioritizing food imports for British civilians, the British government unashamedly transferred the problem of food shortages to its colonies, most notably India. Colonial governments then compounded the problem by failing to protect the entitlement of the vulnerable to food in the face of rampant wartime inflation. The Soviets and the Nationalist Chinese, unable to export hunger to other parts of the world, transferred it within their own countries to the peasantry, who bore much of the burden of the war effort.

During the Second World War the National Socialists discovered that it was an unexpectedly slow and difficult process to starve people to death. While laying plans for the starvation policy to be inflicted upon the Polish Jews, German physicians calculated that as long as the inhabitants of the Warsaw ghetto received no more than 800 calories of low-protein food per day it should take nine months for them to die. But again and again the National Socialists' plans to starve the Soviet and Jewish population to death came up against the ingenuity and determination of their intended victims. The Jews of Warsaw survived partly by eating the ground rectums of cattle, the Ukrainians smuggled food into the blockaded cities, and in the countryside hid stores of food, dug up dead horses and collected famine foods. All displayed a steely determination to live. In Leningrad the besieged inhabitants demonstrated that it was possible to survive without sufficient food for far longer than any of the German physicians would have thought possible. A doctor who survived the siege noted that although adults were not supposed to be able to live for more than a month on a daily diet consisting of fewer than 1,300 calories a day, Leningraders survived on far less than this for up to two or three months.[83] Valentina Grigorevna Burakova, a district doctor in Leningrad, asserted that 'in practice . . . it was not only nutrition that was conducive to survival, but also high morale'.[84] After the siege Leningraders often attributed their survival to their refusal to 'lie down and wait' for death.[85] Women tend to survive famine better than men. This was the case in the European famines of the Second World War and in the Bengal famine. The female physique gives women a slight advantage as they tend to have more body fat and a slower metabolism than men, but observers thought that, in addition, women were more determined to survive for the sake of their children.[86] The National Socialists eventually learned that only those who could be denied all access to supplementary food supplies, such as Soviet prisoners of war, could be starved to death with ease. In the case of the Warsaw Jews, rather than allow them to continue as a burden on the Polish food supply, the Nazis murdered them in the extermination camp of Treblinka in 1942.

It was during the Second World War that scientists really began to explore and understand the impact of starvation on the human body. The most disturbing and ground-breaking of these studies was conducted by twenty-eight Jewish physicians in the Warsaw ghetto. This was the first research project to look into the effects of hunger on metabolism and circulation. Over five months, doctors in the ghetto hospitals, themselves suffering from hunger and malnutrition, carefully measured the effect of starvation on their patients using sophisticated equipment smuggled in from Warsaw's other hospitals. They documented the way in which the body goes into a form of hibernation, slowing down and becoming very cold, while gradually breaking down muscle tissue in order to maintain the organism. They also discovered that recovery from starvation is uneven and that the effect of hunger on the metabolism can be reversed quite quickly, while the circulation and the heart take much longer to recover. Hence the concentration camp victims who ate large quantities of food after liberation killed themselves by placing too great a strain upon their circulation and their already weakened hearts.[87] The Warsaw doctors' report was smuggled out of the ghetto and left in the care of a Polish doctor until one of the few survivors reclaimed it after 1945 and had the work published.

Since the war, doctors have run a number of long-term studies on the survivors of the Leningrad siege and the Dutch Hunger Winter. Their findings suggest that the foetus of a woman exposed to famine, especially in the first and second trimesters of pregnancy, will be adversely affected in later life. Dutch adults with a genetic predisposition to suffer from mental disease were more likely to suffer from schizophrenia and psychotic depression if they had been in the womb of a woman starved in the winter of 1944–45. [88] Children born to women who had experienced the Dutch famine were also likely to have smaller birth weights than normal. This is unsurprising, but, more importantly, their own children tended to have lower than normal birth weights, demonstrating that it is not only the mother's but the grandmother's environment which affects the development of the foetus. This biological mechanism allows for humans to adapt to environmental conditions over generations but it also means that mothers who suffer from unusually severe conditions will pass on the impact of their experience over two generations. [89] There is some suggestion that children with smaller than average birth weights due to lack of *in utero* nutrition are more likely to develop chronic heart disease, non-insulin-dependent diabetes and other associated diseases. [90] Studies of victims of the Leningrad siege have found it difficult to filter out other factors affecting these diseases, such as social class and adult diet, in order to produce conclusive evidence that the children of famine are more likely to develop such life-threatening conditions. [91] However, there is sufficient medical evidence to confirm that the physical repercussions of the famines of the Second World War are still echoing down through the generations, into the present day.

One of the most revolutionary effects of the Second World War was that it effectively dismantled peasant societies in the United States, western Europe and Japan. After 1945 the majority of rural men mobilized for wartime purposes never returned to the land. As many as two-thirds of the pre-war western European rural population were released from the drudgery and poverty of a farming life. [92] In Japan, farmers as a percentage of the population fell from 52.4 per cent in 1947 to 9 per cent in 1985. [93] These men were diverted into industry, where their labour helped to stimulate economic recovery. This reduction in the farming population was made possible by the technological advances in agricultural productivity which were unleashed during the Second World War. The United States was the only country able to increase agricultural productivity during the conflict, but between 1945 and 1965 European agricultural 'output grew more rapidly than in any twentieth-century period before or since'.[94] In the 1960s Japan's agricultural productivity had risen to the point where the country began to export, rather than import, rice.[95] Rather than acting as a drag on economic development, as it had been in the 1930s, farming became profitable, while at the same time its political influence was reduced.[96] Extreme agricultural conservatives, who saw agriculture as a bastion against the pernicious effects of modernization, were resoundingly defeated.[97] The revolution in agricultural productivity allowed the developed world to achieve its pre-war goal of producing plenty of affordable food. Thus, it was agricultural science that provided the solution to Germany's and Japan's food dilemma of the 1930s, which neither the new *Lebensraum* nor the Greater East Asian Co-Prosperity Sphere had been able to deliver. Ironically, in the post-war world both Germany and Japan were able to achieve the prosperity to which they had aspired precisely by following the course which in the 1930s they had spurned: American aid and 'successful incorporation into world trade resting upon capitalist competition and market economies'.[98]

PART III

The Politics of Food

In his role as head of the Department of War Engineering Armament in Russia, Victor Kravchenko 'constantly had to telephone factories and pressurize them to work faster and meet their targets . . . This was largely futile as they were working as hard as they could already . . . To speed up output I drafted plans for supplying workers in certain plants with bread and hot meals, and they were put into effect when Stalin signed them.'[1] In the wars of the twentieth century military success was intimately linked to the ability of industrial workers to produce tanks, aircraft, artillery and heavy ammunition. Under these conditions of total war the industrial working population became cogs in a vast war machine. Every combatant government looked to scientists, engineers and factory managers to develop new weaponry and to organize its manufacture as effectively as possible. In the same way they looked to nutritionists as the new engineers of the human body, to advise on the use of food as a means to maximize the productivity of workers.

The late nineteenth-century understanding that foods were made up of proteins, carbohydrates and fats had given rise to this new group of scientists, drawn mainly from the disciplines of biochemistry and medicine, who sought to understand the way in which the body processed food. By the late 1930s it was understood that the number and type of calories required by humans differed according to age, sex and levels of exertion, but the scientists were uncertain as to exactly how many calories were needed for different activities. In the early twentieth century the discovery of vitamins had added a new dimension to knowledge about the body's nutritional needs. It was not yet fully understood how vitamins and trace minerals worked to maintain health, but the late 1930s nutritional consensus prioritized animal over plant proteins and argued that meat, milk and dairy products, vegetables and fruit were all essential foods which protected the body from disease. A new concept was beginning to develop of the balanced diet which included a wide range of foodstuffs.

During the 1930s Japan and Germany drew extensively upon the new science of nutrition in order to help prepare their nations for war. In Japan nutritionists reformed the diet of the armed services and then turned their attention to the civilian population. In Germany scientists were enlisted in Herbert Backe's campaign for nutritional freedom, which sought to cut food imports by shifting German consumption towards a more austere diet. In Britain nutritionists had a different agenda. Professor Edward Mellanby, one of the scientists who had discovered vitamins, argued that if the government were to ensure that every citizen had access to nutritious food this would have an impact on public health as revolutionary as the nineteenth-century introduction of clean water and a functioning sewage system.[2] But the British government was reluctant to take on such an expensive commitment and it was not until the war that, by introducing rationing, the government was forced to take responsibility for the food its citizens ate.

All combatant nations introduced rationing during the war. This allowed the government to distribute shortages fairly across the population and to channel food to those who contributed most to the war effort. But rationing systems also embodied ideas about entitlement. While it was accepted in every country that the military should receive food as a first priority, the question of how to allot extra rations to those engaged in heavy physical labour such as miners, steel workers and armaments workers was answered differently by the different regimes. In Britain the idea of equality of sacrifice was made concrete in the distribution of equal rations across the adult population. In the Soviet Union the acute shortage of food made the idea that there should be any equality of sacrifice academic, as the government struggled to provide its army, let alone its industrial workforce, with enough to eat. The Soviets were faced with the situation which the National Socialists in Germany most feared, fighting a brutal war on their own territory while the civilian population went hungry and came close to starvation. The Soviet Union was probably the combatant with the least food per capita. The level of hunger in the Soviet Union made a mockery of the argument, so often propounded by the British and the German governments, that an adequate food supply was a cornerstone of success in the circumstances of total war. Despite desperate hunger and starvation the Soviet Union did the most of all the combatant nations in the European theatre to defeat Germany. Even after the Allied invasion of France the great majority of the Wehrmacht's fighting capacity was concentrated on the eastern front, with 156 German divisions in the east, compared to 59 in France and 27 in Italy. The Red Army was responsible for 80 per cent of Germany's total battle casualties.[3]

All the major combatants fought the Second World War in the name of a better future. This was usually expressed through grand notions such as the triumph of democracy and freedom, the realization of a strong and powerful Greater Germany or the harmonious collaboration of Asian peoples in a Greater East Asian Co-Prosperity Sphere. However, the details that filled in these sketches of an ideal world were often more prosaic and focused on material possessions and good food. In the United States the idea of a society where consumption fuelled prosperity and everyone could afford to eat steak became a powerful vision of the future. In Germany, Hitler held out the promise that the National Socialists would build a shiny modern mass consumer society to rival America's.[4] In Britain politicians from both ends of the political spectrum acknowledged that the prospect of social reconstruction which involved the creation of a welfare state where everyone had a house and enough to eat, gave the people 'something worth fighting for'.[5] The Soviet focus was on the defeat of the fascist invader but on another level many were fighting for a better future, whether it was the realization of the ideals of communism or the amelioration of the repression of the regime. As the war progressed, the idea of achieving a happy and prosperous life faded into a tantalizing fantasy for the Germans and the Japanese. But for the British and, most of all, the Americans, the possibility of realizing prosperity for all became a tangible goal.

A crude division emerged during the war between democratic and non-democratic countries. The former attempted to safeguard the rights of citizens, even in a time of war. The latter, especially Stalinist Russia and Imperial Japan, treated civilians and soldiers as expendable tools in a battle that was above the consideration of individual lives. The democratic nations' view of their soldiers as civilians in uniform meant that British and American military commanders went to some lengths to minimize the human cost of warfare and preferred to use superior firepower in order to reduce the number of casualties.[6] The difference in attitude was revealed most glaringly in the logistics of military supply. The United States, Britain and Japan shared the problem that 'all the principal avenues of advance lay over water', extending for thousands of kilometres across the Atlantic and Pacific oceans.[7] The space allocated to rations and service personnel on the ships of these supply lines is a good indication of the extent to which troop welfare was considered central to each military's ethos.

The amount of equipment needed by the Americans was particularly stunning. An American infantry division of between 10,000 and 13,000 men needed 32,000 tons of shipping to move to Britain, and this was once their requirements had been stripped down to a minimum.[8] As a result the Allied armies developed particularly long tails of non-combatant service personnel, averaging out at four service troops for every soldier, but rising to eighteen US service personnel for every infantryman in the Pacific, compared to somewhere between one and two to one in the Soviet and German armies.[9] The length of the American tail was in large part made up of medical staff and battalions of construction personnel who were needed to build airstrips, ports, roads and temporary harbours. But the numbers also reflected the fact that American, British and Commonwealth troops were accompanied by catering corps who made meals and baked bread, even for the front-line troops.

The most frugal of all the armies was the Japanese. They required fewer arms and less equipment, and the principle of self-sufficiency was paramount. The troops were issued with the minimum of creature comforts and rarely supplied with new clothes.[10] Before embarking for Malaya in 1941 soldiers were issued with a pamphlet entitled *Read this alone – and the war will be won*. The author informed them that 'since it is no small matter to transport supplies by sea all the way from Japan, you should fight and live on a bare minimum'.[11] The men were instructed to use their ingenuity, and if food were short they should supplement their diet with anything that came to hand, including wild grasses, a common famine food among the peasant families from which many of the army recruits were drawn.[12]

These different expectations meant that different food crisis points existed within each country's army and civilian population, ranging from the anxiety caused in Britain by the sight of empty grocers' shelves in the winter of 1940–41 to the indifference shown by passers-by in the streets of Moscow towards the corpses of people who had died of starvation in the winter of 1942. While GIs would have expressed great dissatisfaction at a meal consisting of a handful of rice, soup made from miso powder, and a can of tinned fish, the Japanese found this an adequate meal. Indeed, the Japanese high command began the war thinking that it was possible for 'the Japanese army [to] . . . continue fighting without food, if they had strong moral[e]'.[13]

The following chapters examine how well the major combatant nations fed their armies and their civilian populations. Beginning with Japan, which was brought to its knees by food shortages, and ending with the United States, which was the only nation to enjoy an abundance of food in wartime, they ask to what extent the adequacy of the food supply affected these nations' ability to wage war.

13

Japan – Starving for the Emperor

Here's what I learned: Men killed in real combat are a very small part of those who die in war. Men died of starvation, all kinds of disease.

(Ogawa Tamotsu who was stationed on New Britain for
three years)[1]

'Two years from now we will have no petroleum for military use. Ships will stop moving. When I think about the strengthening of American defences in the south-west Pacific, the expansion of the American fleet, the unfinished China Incident, and so on, I see no end to difficulties. We can talk about austerity and suffering, but can our people endure such a life for a long time?'[2] Japan's Prime Minister Tojo Hideki asked this question on 5 November 1941. The vision he conjured up of a defeated Japan was used to justify the government's decision to go to war with the United States. However, in the four years of the Pacific war the American blockade steadily eroded Japan's sea communications with its empire until its supply of oil ran out, its ships had been sunk or immobilized, and the Japanese administration was faced with the question of how much suffering the Japanese people could endure. By attacking the United States the Japanese government brought upon itself the very state of affairs which it feared.

During the course of its war with China and America the Japanese military went from being one of the best-fed armed forces in the world to a state of miserable starvation. By focusing on the need to fight a decisive battle with the United States, in the misguided conviction that this would persuade the Americans to come to the negotiating table, the military leadership demonstrated their failure to grasp the nature of the new modern war of attrition.

An Englishman living in Japan in the late 1930s noticed, 'the Japanese have something of a genius for austerity ... They can be called upon by their government to subsist for long periods on a diet so frugal that no European people would put up with it.'[3] Accustomed to this austere civilian diet Japanese soldiers were prepared to accept levels of rationing which British Commonwealth, German and American soldiers would have considered unbearable. Many Japanese soldiers took pride in their ability to survive with minimal support and poured scorn on the decadent and pampered GIs. Despite having just lost the island of Biak (off the northern coast of New Guinea) to the Americans in September 1944, one anonymous Japanese diarist declared, 'spiritually, we are the winners of this battle ... Americans cannot live in a jungle subsisting on leaves and grasses; only Japanese can. The "Have" nations like America, could afford to throw away food and equipment. It is simply wasteful ... Japan will surely reoccupy this island.'[4]

New recruits into the Japanese army were subjected to a brutal training programme which indoctrinated them with a belief in *bushido* (fighting spirit), the idea that self-discipline and willpower could overcome all obstacles. Military commanders firmly believed that Japanese soldiers could be expected to continue fighting in the most impossible circumstances. This attitude was exemplified by Lieutenant-General Mutaguchi Renya, the commander in charge of the Japanese attack on India in April 1944. When the Japanese became bogged down at Imphal he stubbornly repeated the mantra, 'drummed into [Japanese officers] from their cadet days, that because the difference between victory and defeat was razor thin, the most tenacious side would be the victor'.[5] From the safe distance of Burma he instructed his troops: 'The struggle has developed into a fight between the material strength of the enemy and our spiritual strength. Continue in the task until all your ammunition is expended. If your hands are broken fight with your feet. If your hands and feet are broken use your teeth. If there is no breath left in your body, fight with your spirit. Lack of weapons [and he might well have added lack of food] is no excuse for defeat.'[6]

The fervent belief that spirit would prevail despite the overwhelmingly superior resources of their enemies was the central principle of the Japanese war effort. The ultimate expression of this belief was the use of kamikaze pilots in the last desperate months of the war when 'human lives were substituted for material substance'.[7] However, the Japanese military command was eventually to discover that there were limits to *bushido*. Starving Japanese troops on Guadalcanal, too weak to stand up for lack of food, were said to have brandished their bayonets at any American soldiers who approached them, demonstrating their continued fighting spirit. But when the Japanese commander Imamura Hitoshi witnessed the pitiful state of the troops on the island, he admitted that *bushido* was useless in the face of starvation.[8] In August 1945 the Japanese government faced the decision of whether to make their civilian population, teetering on the edge of famine, suffer the same fate as their soldiers. Their dilemma was resolved by the United States dropping atomic bombs on the cities of Hiroshima and Nagasaki, thus bringing about the Japanese surrender.

HEALTHY EATING AS A PATRIOTIC VIRTUE

Before the war the Japanese military were far in advance of the other combatant nations' armed forces in terms of their attitude towards, and application of, the newly developing science of nutrition. The Meiji government, which came to power in 1868, was determined to create a strong modern Japanese army and navy modelled on those of the European powers. But in the 1870s Japanese sailors were plagued by ill health and routinely fell sick with beriberi. This was caused by an over-reliance on vitamin B-deficient polished white rice as the staple naval food. A research committee was set up to look into the matter. One of its members was Takaki Kanehiro, director of the Tokyo Naval Hospital, who had studied at St Thomas's Hospital in London. Vitamins were not yet understood but he suggested that one ship's company should try the experiment of living on a high-protein British naval diet of bread, ship's biscuit, salted meat and beans. When the experimental crew arrived fit and well in Hawaii the Japanese navy decided to adopt a western diet for its sailors.[9] Although the reasons for the improvement in the sailors' health were not fully understood, this was an important development. Firstly, it predisposed military caterers to look

275

to foreign diets as a way of reforming the eating habits of the Japanese military. Secondly, it established a strong link between physicians and the Japanese quartermaster, which was a crucial factor in facilitating the application of the discoveries of nutritional science to military rations. This placed Japanese military catering far in advance of the European and American armed services, in which this medical-catering connection was not established until the Second World War.

Co-operation was established between army caterers and doctors in 1921 when a Military Diet Research Committee was set up to investigate the nutritional value of meat and fish. The army was beset by the problem that most of its rural recruits, drawn from a countryside in crisis and many having grown up in desperately poor farming households, were malnourished and physically weak. The committee concluded that the customary Japanese diet of rice, miso soup, a little fish, a few vegetables and pickles was not suited to the creation of robust warriors. The physical prowess of westerners had long been attributed to their meat-based diet, and it was decided to increase the amount of meat in the ration. In the 1920s Japanese soldiers were fed about 13 kilograms of beef a year. In comparison to the European annual consumption of about 50 kilograms this seems a paltry amount, but it was vastly more than the 1 kilogram a year consumed by the Japanese civilian population.[10]

Under the direction of Marumoto Shozo, First Army Accountant at the Army Provisions Depot, army meals were transformed. In order to integrate meat into the soldiers' diet Marumoto copied dishes from the inexpensive Chinese eateries and western-style restaurants which had sprung up in Japanese cities in the 1920s. Japanese servicemen were introduced to curries and stews, stir-fries, wheat noodles, pork cutlets, pan-fried chicken and breaded meats, none of which they would have encountered in their rural homes. The advantage of these western and Chinese dishes was that while they were relatively inexpensive they substantially increased the protein and fat content of army rations. Stewing, deep- and stir-frying were all novel culinary methods in 1920s Japan and a training school for army cooks was established to initiate them in the practices of foreign cookery. Mess kitchens were provided with newfangled equipment such as meat grinders and vegetable cutters. Marumoto gathered together a team of catering instructors who were sent throughout the Japanese empire re-educating army cooks. To help in this process he published a series of military cookbooks packed with information on high-calorie, low-budget meals.[11]

The strategy of reforming the army diet using Chinese and western dishes was boldly innovative. Most military caterers go to great lengths to avoid serving unfamiliar foods to servicemen, who are renowned for their conservative taste buds. However, it was easier to produce meals that pleased the majority if the army cooks avoided Japanese dishes. Each region had its own distinctive cuisine and preferred a mixture of flavours, which made it extremely difficult to create even a simple miso soup which all the men liked. The taste of home-made miso varied from household to household, while different regions preferred miso with varying levels of saltiness or sweetness. An army catering reformer who conducted experiments with soldiers serving in China in 1936–37, found that while the majority liked the miso soup they were served, 22 per cent found it too sweet and 10 per cent too salty.[12] The adoption of foreign dishes flattened out these taste differences and accustomed all the men to the same set of standardized tastes. This was reinforced by the use of factory-produced and thus standardized soya sauce as the predominant flavouring instead of miso.[13] No matter which region the men came from, they all liked the meat-based and deep-fried dishes.[14] The fact that Japanese servicemen took to these foreign dishes was, without doubt, aided by the military practice of serving white rice (mixed with barley to provide vitamin B) with breakfast, lunch and dinner. Many rural recruits, used to a frugal diet based on brown rice mixed with barley or millet and eked out with radish leaves, had never eaten so well. For conscripts of the 1920s and 1930s the experience of eating plentiful and unusual food appears to have been one of the dominant memories of their time in the military.[15]

In 1925 the army extended its efforts to improve Japanese health into the general population. The Army Provisions Depot set up the Provisions Friends' Association which set about introducing the military principles of mass catering into schools, hospitals and work-place canteens. The Home Ministry provided funding for school canteens, of which there were more than 12,000 by 1940. Training academies for dieticians were founded. The army proselytized the strange arts of boiling and deep-frying and unusual ingredients such as potatoes and lard, through exhibitions and talks, radio broadcasts and cooking demonstrations.[16] The aim was that every home in Japan would adopt the economical and nourishing military diet. Women's magazines, aimed at both farming households and the urban middle classes, all included menus and recipes detailing how to prepare the high-calorie dishes that were by now standard military fare.[17]

The propagation of the image of the ideal housewife feeding her family military-style meals was integral to the on-going militarization of daily life in Japan during the 1920s and 1930s. Propaganda emphasized that it was the responsibility of Japanese women to improve the physical strength and fighting-power of the nation. The Japanese government was far more willing to take on the responsibility for disseminating nutritional knowledge than the British government in the 1930s. However, in return, the Japanese were expected to make their best efforts to apply this information in their daily lives as part of their role as loyal subjects. This expectation was heightened by war when government propaganda 'elevated . . . eating healthily at a low cost to the level of a patriotic virtue'.[18]

The war with China seriously undermined these reforming efforts within both the military and the civilian population. By the late 1930s the war with China was making it increasingly difficult for the state to supply sufficient good-quality food to Japan's urban population. A labour shortage on Japan's farms, as a result of conscription of rural workers into the armed forces to fight in China, as well as a drop in imports from Korea and Formosa, due to a war-related increase in domestic demand and a poor harvest, resulted in a rice shortage.[19] Mary Kimoto Tomita was the daughter of Japanese immigrants to America. In 1939 she arrived in Tokyo to learn something of her parents' culture. In November she wrote to her friend Miye, 'Japan's general population is just beginning to feel the pinch of war. Until this summer they said that everything was the same as before the war. But now rice is scarce and the price is the highest it has been since 1918. There is a scarcity of all materials . . . Everything is so expensive. I wonder how the poor people live.'[20] Tokyoites particularly disliked eating the long-grained *gaimai*, or foreign rice, which the government imported from Korea and Formosa. A rice-saving campaign tried to persuade reluctant urbanites to eat noodles and barley.[21] Despite the oft-repeated claims that the patriotic Japanese were willing to make sacrifices for the 'life-or-death struggle' in China, Mary remarked that people actually complained heartily about the foreign rice and high prices.[22] When a friend sent a parcel of American food she generously shared out the booty among her Japanese friends. 'Food takes on so much importance in underfed Japan. Just to look around in a streetcar, one can readily see how true it is that Japan is an undernourished nation! And about half of the people have stomach trouble. Their everyday food is so frugal, so when they get a treat they soon overeat and . . . get indigestion.'[23]

The queues in front of the rice traders' stores lengthened each week. In April 1941, even before the Japanese government declared war on the United States, rationing had to be introduced. The different food-stuffs on the ration card were sold in a variety of retail outlets and queuing for many hours a day became a feature of Japanese life. It could sometimes take one member of a family a whole five days queuing at shop after shop to procure enough food for a week.[24] John Morris, a lecturer in English at Tokyo University between 1938 and 1941, recalled that in order to avoid the queues 'those who could afford it [made] . . . even more frequent use of restaurants . . . The number of courses remained much the same . . . but the quality rapidly deteriorated. Beef, which in normal times is both plentiful and excellent in Japan, practically disappeared, its place on the menu being taken more often than not by whale meat . . . But quite often there would be no meat of any sort available, even in the better restaurants, for days at a time.'[25] As Morris rightly noted, the disappearance of meat impacted mainly upon the wealthy. Despite the nutritional campaigns of the 1920s and 1930s meat consumption had not become established among the general population. In fact, for many the whale meat which they ate during the war was their first experience of affordable meat.[26]

When Morris returned to Britain in December 1941 he was struck by 'the abundance of food. For months past I had been reading in the Japanese press about the terrible food shortage in England, so that it came as almost a shock, though an exceedingly pleasant one, to find how well we were being rationed.'[27] Morris's observation indicates just how tight Japan's food situation was even before it entered the world-wide conflict. The diet provided by Japanese rations was austere. Each person was allowed 330 grams of rice per day, which amounted to approximately 1,160 calories.[28] This was adequate as long as different cereals such as barley, sweet potatoes and pumpkins were available to supplement the rice and make filling meals. Due to the concentration of all the farmers' energies on the cultivation of staple crops, fruit and vegetables became extremely scarce. These were the main source of essential vitamins and minerals and their disappearance opened a serious nutritional gap in the diet.[29] Even before the attack on Pearl Harbor the urban population was living close to the margins of adequate nutrition.

In order to address the problem of endless queues the government eventually placed food distribution in the hands of neighbourhood associations, which transferred the work of queuing from individual families to the head of the association. Senoh Kappa, a well-known stage-set designer, wrote a semi-fictional autobiography in which he told of his experiences as a boy, called 'H', during the war. His family were something of an oddity because they were Christian, and in an attempt to deflect criticism his mother took on the job of head of their neighbourhood association. 'Even though she had expected the work to keep her very busy, Toshiko was astonished at the way it went on increasing from day to day . . . In the morning she would go to lectures on air raid drill, and in the afternoon she would gather the neighbours together to share with them what she'd learned; then the evenings would be occupied with the pick-up and distribution of rations.'[30] She had to be very careful how she divided up the portions of dried fish and vegetables to avoid accusations of unfairness.

In Japanese society, where membership of a 'voluntary' association was virtually compulsory, the neighbourhood associations were the urban equivalent of the Rural Revitalization associations in the countryside. Initially conceived as instruments of social indoctrination, during the war they became increasingly important as economic and organizational institutions. They set up air and fire defence groups, kept an eye out for thieves and illicit activities, and encouraged their members to put their money into savings.[31] The workings of the associations reveal the double-sided nature of the Japanese state's dealings with its citizens. On the one hand they provided an instrument by which the government could intrude into the private lives of ordinary people. Government nutritionists used the associations to influence eating habits, often directing which meals people should cook by tailoring the rations so that they provided the ingredients for a specific meal, the recipe for which was provided along with the food. Nutritionists taught the association heads how to cook with unfamiliar foods and gave them tips on how to save food, all of which they were expected to pass on to the women in their associations. The associations were used to convey the government message to its citizens that it expected them to make the best of their frugal rations as part of their sacrifice for the war effort.[32] By reinforcing social control and mutual surveillance, they deepened the repressive nature of Japanese society. But they also satisfied the Japanese preference for social harmony. Rather than dealing with a large, faceless, centralized institution, the ordinary civilian encountered an old-fashioned replacement for the extended family. Those urban citizens without relatives to turn to could admit their need for aid to the association. When they worked as intended, the associations provided urban inhabitants with an extended and supportive community in a time of need.[33]

Rice and food shortages also impacted on military rations. In 1929 army meals provided each soldier with 4,000 calories a day.[34] This was nearly double the average civilian consumption of 2,200 calories and far richer in protein and fat.[35] But in 1941 the military ration was halved. At 600 grams of rice a day it was still double that received by civilians but it meant that Japanese soldiers, who in the 1930s had been fed almost as well as US servicemen, now received a ration which equated to only half the food eaten by a GI.[36] The army catering service continued to demonstrate high levels of innovation and expertise in their creation of sophisticated ration packs. Indeed, American ration-pack developers considered the emergency rations of Japanese airmen particularly good, and issued instructions on how to work out what was in the packs so that US soldiers could consume any they found.[37] But the sophisticated mess menus of Chinese noodles, curries and western pork cutlets were abandoned out in the field.

Each Japanese infantryman carried his personal ration of 600 grams of rice per day in his own rucksack along with packs of miso powder or soya sauce. If he was fortunate he was also issued with some tinned or pickled vegetables, tea, salt and sugar. Rice was not an easy food to use as a field ration. It tended to spoil in the humid heat of the Pacific islands and it had to be prepared before dawn or after sunset lest the smoke from the numerous cooking fires gave away the unit's position. Unlike canned meat it could not be eaten raw in an emergency. But the men preferred it to bread or hard biscuits.[38] If supplies were maintained and the rice was mixed with barley or wheat and supplemented by other ration components, it provided an adequate, if frugal, field ration.

Altogether the food in a Japanese soldier's rucksack weighed about four pounds – two-thirds of the weight of a US infantryman's ration pack – but often less, as rice was perennially short in the field.[39] Each soldier boiled his own rice in his mess tin, allowing the army to dispense with field kitchens. The ideal ratio of service troops to fighting men was one to one compared to the American ratio in the Pacific of eighteen service troops for every combat soldier.[40]

CHURCHILL'S RATIONS

The imperial army's policy that as little energy as possible should be spent on the logistics of food supply meant that Japanese commanders generally issued soldiers going into battle with only enough food for a few days. General Slim, Allied Commander-in-Chief of the defensive campaign in Burma, was astonished to find that the Japanese would provide only nine days' supply for campaigns which were clearly likely to last for weeks. 'If it was Heaven's will that they would win then something would turn up – like the supply dumps of their enemies.'[41] Indeed, rather than considering the capture of enemy stocks of food as a welcome bonus, Japanese commanders regarded this as integral to supply plans. In the early campaigns of 1941–42 in Malaya and Burma the Allied shock and lack of preparation for invasion worked to the advantage of the Japanese. However, the stunning success of these Japanese victories masked the weaknesses of Japanese logistics. The problems involved with feeding the troops were solved by Allied incompetence rather than by efficient Japanese organization.

In Malaya the Japanese surprised the British commanders by skirting round their carefully constructed road-blocks and driving their light tanks and bicycles right through the supposedly impenetrable rubber-tree plantations. Japanese troops charging into the British rear areas, bayonets at the ready, created an unrealistic assessment among the Allies that the Japanese were spectacularly adept at jungle warfare.[42] In the chaos and disorganization of the retreat, the Allies left behind them large quantities of abandoned supplies. At the aerodrome in Jitra, in northern Malaya, the Japanese found fuel and bombs which they then put to good use bombarding Allied positions. They nicknamed it the 'Churchill airfield'. The food stores and boxes of rations the Allies left behind them became known as 'Churchill's rations'.[43] Colonel Tsuji Masanobu, the author of the pamphlet *Read this alone*, which warned the troops not to rely on food supplies from the home country, later proudly recalled that 'each man had been moved to the front with dry bread and rice sufficient for only a few days in accordance with the plan ... Owing to the availability of Churchill supplies there was no necessity for us to transport even one bag of rice or tin of gasoline.'[44] This was gleeful overstatement but it was certainly true that the Japanese relied heavily on British and Australian food dumps throughout the Malayan campaign. As the soldiers began to filter over on to Singapore island they had completely outrun their own supply lines.[45]

When he turned his attention to Burma, General Yamashita continued to implement the policy. The troops detailed to move across the Burmese border were told 'if food is not enough, get it from the enemy'.[46] Lance Corporal Kawamata Koji recalled that this was exactly what the troops did. As his infantry regiment fought its way into Burma on a meagre diet of boiled rice, thin miso soup and wild grasses, they discovered an abandoned gun emplacement stocked with boxes of food filled with tins of corned beef, cheese, butter, coffee and tea. The soldiers 'grabbed the food and filled their stomachs'. Later that night they moved on towards the River Sitang, 'refreshed by the present from Mr Churchill'.[47] Corporal Nakai Buhachiro's regiment was not as fortunate. Having sacrificed food in order to carry more ammunition, they crossed the Siam–Burmese border with only one week's rations and two packets of biscuits as an emergency reserve. As they hauled their heavy horse-drawn guns through the jungle, struggling to keep up with the fast-moving infantry, their rice ran out. They made a porridge from the skin of the paddy they carried for the horses and eventually killed a pack-ox, only to discover that Siamese oxen were much tougher than the Japanese variety. Nakai's gums ached so badly from chewing on the meat that he was reduced to sipping ox soup.[48]

The Japanese captured Rangoon in March 1942. Here they discovered storehouses crammed with whisky, canned food, coffee, cocoa, milk, butter, cheese, corned beef, jam and cigarettes.[49] The Japanese enthusiasm for western rations did, however, lead to some unfortunate incidents. Second Lieutenant Yoshino Suichiro's 'gift ration from Mr Churchill' contained an unpleasant surprise. Besides whisky and chocolate, each man in the lieutenant's water-supply unit was issued with two packs of chewing gum. Before long all the soldiers were afflicted by diarrhoea. The chewing gum was 'not a candy at all but a medicinal chewing gum for children containing a laxative!'[50]

Food shortages on the home islands meant that the idea that the army abroad should not become a drain on the homeland was a first principle for the Japanese, just as it was for the Germans. Like the Wehrmacht in the Soviet Union, the Japanese army requisitioned food from local farmers and indulged in wild and unofficial plunder. In China troops often raided granaries. Indeed, Kiyosawa Kiyoshi met a journalist who had worked in China and told him that the Chinese 'attach the insect radical to the "Imperial" character in the phrase "Imperial Army"', transforming it into the 'locust army'.[51] Where the imperial army differed from the Wehrmacht was in its application of the principle of self-sufficiency. If there was not enough local food the soldiers were supposed to grow it themselves. In Malaya the Grow More Food campaign was not just aimed at the indigenous population. Japanese officials in the administration, businessmen running the stock companies that arrived to extract south-east Asian raw materials, and the army of occupation, officers and men alike, were also expected to put several hours a week into growing vegetables.[52]

Those stationed in more remote areas were sent minimal supplies and expected to fend for themselves. It would have been impossible to send Allied troops into the jungles of south-east Asia and demand that they organize their own provisions. Firstly, this would have been seen by them as a dereliction of the army's duty to supply them with food. Secondly, the soldiers of western countries had sophisticated tastes and (even if they were farmers) led civilian lives which meant that they were unused to subsistence farming and foraging. Japanese soldiers had no such high expectations of their army commanders and had simple needs. They demonstrated great ingenuity in finding themselves something to eat.

Abe Hiroshi, supervising the building of the Burmese railway in the remote border area between Siam and Burma, recalled that the elephants which brought in their food would often fail to arrive. 'When lunchtime approached, about ten men would be assigned to chase down lizards. They were real big and you caught them by hitting them on the head with a stick. The beautiful pink meat was delicious.'[53] In Burma Sergeant Aihara Isawo's company commander devised an ingenious means of catching fish. Each night the river was diverted so that it flowed on to the grasslands around the army camp. The next morning the water was drained away, leaving catfish and snakehead stranded. The soldiers would eat them fresh and then salt down the surplus. 'Dried fish proved very useful later on our long march in the first Arakan operation, as our only source of protein.'[54]

If this strategy of living off the land, combined with self-sufficiency farming and foraging projects, was successful on mainland south-east Asia it was much more difficult to employ on the islands of the Pacific. In August 1941 the Vice-Chief of Staff, Lieutenant-General Tsukada Osamu, warned that the policy of dotting small numbers of troops about the Pacific on isolated islands was 'like sowing salt in the sea'.[55] But, with a characteristic determination to avoid unwelcome truths, the army command transferred him from his post just before the war got underway. Most of the Pacific islands which Japan occupied were populated by subsistence farmers who supplemented their small gardens with hunting and gathering. This was quite different from Burma's or Indo-China's rice-producing agricultural economies. It was unrealistic to expect islanders to produce large surpluses of food to feed armies of Japanese troops. To some extent the army command acknowledged this and made provision for supplies to be brought in from elsewhere. Rabaul on New Britain was chosen as a forward supply base for the south-west Pacific; here regular deliveries from Japan and south-east Asia were collected and then sent out to troops on other islands. It was planned to maintain stores on Rabaul at a level sufficient to supply three divisions (about 80,000 men) for two months.[56] Initially things went well. In September 1942, 180 tons of fresh vegetables, 60 tons of fresh meats, 25 tons of soya sauce, 9 tons of sugar, 100 tons of rice, 2 million cigarettes and bottles of soft drinks, 20,000 bottles of beer and about 5 tons of candy were unloaded from the refrigerated *Taiko Maru*.[57] A number of self-sufficiency projects were set up, a bakery, a miso paste factory and a tobacco factory were constructed alongside a copra oil mill and two ice plants. Until 1943 Rabaul functioned as an effective, partly self-sufficient base for operations in the south-west Pacific but then the American blockade of Japanese shipping began to take effect and, after the successes of 1941–42, the Japanese campaign went into reverse.

THE AMERICAN BLOCKADE

One of the fatal flaws in the Japanese military command's conduct of the war was their woefully inadequate preparation for anti-submarine warfare. Given that Japan's war economy was absolutely dependent on merchant shipping, this was utterly irresponsible. On the home islands Japan's war industries were unable to function without imports of steel, aluminium, iron ore and oil.[58] The arms and equipment then had to be shipped out to the soldiers throughout the empire. Japan's cities were dependent on rice imports from abroad, and even the internal distribution of the domestic rice crop was dependent on shipping. A large proportion of the urban population lived on the island of Honshu, while much of Japan's food was grown on the islands of Hokkaido and Kyushu. Shipping was needed to take the rice from one island to another. The mountainous terrain of Japan's islands meant that even if the rice crop was destined to remain on the island where it was grown, it was easier to transport it by rail to the nearest port and then ship it around the coast to the cities. Japan's sea communications were steadily eroded throughout the war. Even by November 1942, before the American submarine campaign had reached its full force, Japanese shipping capacity had been severely reduced with the sinking of 285 merchant ships.[59] The concentration on building battleships for the chimerical decisive battle with the United States meant that Japan had neither sufficient shipping nor enough escort vessels to withstand the onslaught when it began in earnest in 1943. Japan's merchant marine could not have been expected to withstand a concerted attack, even if there had been an efficient allocation of resources and no incompetence. From 1943 Japan's shipping capacity melted away, leaving its troops stranded across the Pacific, and the home islands shut off from essential supplies.

In 1943 the food supply in Japan reached a critical turning-point. The 3.5 million servicemen stationed on the home islands were eating about half of the domestically grown rice crop.[60] The peasants were allowed to keep back around 400–600 grams of rice a day for each member of the family before handing over the rest to the government.[61] This left the urban population with a very small share of an ever-diminishing harvest, and then rice imports from south-east Asia more or less ceased. The government was forced to eke out the rice supply to the cities and towns with substitute foods. In 1943, between 10 and 20 per cent of the rice ration consisted of substitutes such as Manchurian wheat and barley. The ration rice became known as 'Five Colour Rice' because of its 'mixture of white rice, yellow (old) rice, green beans, red grains and brown insects'.[62] Once a week the urban population were issued with noodles. In his semi-fictional autobiography, Senoh Kappa's alter ego, 'H', recalled some soldiers who came to train at his school, and at lunchtime sat and ate white rice while the boys contented themselves with 'meals of "substitute rice" . . . pieces of pumpkin and sweet potato'.[63] In the first year of the Pacific war it had been possible to supplement the ration rice with unrationed pumpkin and sweet potato. When the government began to monopolize these foodstuffs in order to distribute them instead of rice, it became much more difficult to find extra food and meals became increasingly inadequate. Meat 'was almost unknown' and fish was strictly limited and expensive. Milk was only available for the sick and for children. Even supplies of soya sauce and miso paste were running short.[64] The amount of protein and calcium in the diet began to fall, while palatability was much reduced by the lack of sugar and edible oils.[65]

Each time Iida Momo returned home from his boarding school he could see 'how the war was eating away at the vitality of Tokyo. One week the sake shop down the road was shuttered and silent: supplies of alcohol had dried up. The next week the nearby geisha house had vanished, its occupants packed off to provide consolation to soldiers on the battle front.'[66] The restaurants too began to close. Arakawa Hiroyo and her husband owned a bakery shop in Tokyo. They made *katsutera*, a sort of sponge cake made with flour, eggs and sugar. The decline of their business reflected the dwindling food supply in Japan. At first, as a food business, they were supplied with flour and sugar, and customers would bring them vegetables in exchange for *katsutera*.[67] Eventually the supply of their ingredients declined and they were only able to bake every two or three days. Then the police would drop by. 'Oh, today you're baking?' they would comment innocently. 'This house sure smells good.' And then Arakawa would have to give them some cakes. The grocers in her street suffered from the same problem. Police and soldiers would simply pocket the food and refuse to pay.[68] Eggs were the first of their ingredients to disappear altogether. For a while they had a supply of powdered egg from Shanghai but eventually this became unavailable, as did sugar. Arakawa changed the business to making sandwiches, but even these they had to fill with whale ham because there was no pork to be had. Then bread and whale ham became unavailable. Undaunted they changed to making 'cut bread' for the army, which meant that supplies of the necessary ingredients were guaranteed. Cut bread was a dough filled with bean paste. Then the military laid claim to their bread-making machine for the iron and they had to close their business. By this time the air raids had become so bad in Tokyo that they were glad to leave and Arakawa and her son went to live in the countryside.[69]

The black market became rife in Japan, which, despite its outward appearance of social conformism, had its fair share of spivs who rejected the rules. Iida Momo's father, Iida Toshifumi was one of them. As a young man Iida Toshifumi had eloped with a girl from his neighbourhood the night before her wedding (to another man). The couple travelled through Korea and Manchuria, eventually reaching Siberia, supporting themselves with a scam. Iida would pretend to sell his partner to the local brothel and then, having pocketed the money, help her to escape. He returned to Tokyo in the 1920s and lived by various dubious schemes until he set up a small company making ultraviolet lamps. During the war he converted to making valves for X-ray equipment to be used by the armed forces, and made good money selling a portion of his raw materials on the black market to businesses without army contracts. Iida Momo recalled that his 'father had absolutely no ideological feeling about the war whatsoever. His war was all about how to cheat war: how to get enough food for his family; how to keep his business going; how to prevent his son from being conscripted . . . He'd spent much of his life as a virtual outlaw, and he had learnt not to pay any attention to what the authorities told him.'[70]

By mid-1943 even generally law-abiding citizens were resorting to the black market in order to buy food. A survey of 2,000 urban families found that more than half regularly bought food on the black market. Even though they did not feel they could afford it, they felt they had little choice.[71] This was a sure sign that the food supplied on the ration was insufficient. At this point in the war urban Japanese felt the lack of fruit and vegetables most keenly. A secret government inquiry into the rationing system in 1943 found that the number of vegetables actually distributed was 30 per cent below the amounts stated on the ration cards; fruit availability was 60 per cent less than the stated ration.[72] Kiyosawa Kiyoshi was a journalist and historian who kept a wartime diary in which he frequently expressed his disgust with the hypocrisy and stupidity of the various governments which came and went throughout the conflict. The diary was kept at great danger to himself and his family. If the *kempeitai* had found it he would certainly have been accused of un-Japanese defeatism and faced imprisonment. Kiyosawa first began to comment on the lack of vegetables in December 1943, when only two (large white Japanese) radishes were available for each family in his neighbourhood association.[73] By March 1944 'half a radish must last a family of four two days'. In April 'the rationing of vegetables, of late it is said to be one sen a person for one day. But one sen is not worth one green onion.'[74] Fruit was unobtainable in the towns, and when he visited Hakone in the spring of 1944 he was shocked to discover that persimmons were unaffordable even in the countryside.[75] A report on food conditions in Japan based on information collected from enemy sources for the New Zealand intelligence department reported that the entire apple crop was 'reserved for hospital patients and soldiers'.[76] Kiyosawa heard that a nutritionist examining families in Hayama who were living entirely on the ration without any black market purchases found that they were suffering from night-blindness (a symptom of vitamin A and B deficiencies).[77] Thus, by the end of 1943 the declining ration was beginning to cause serious malnutrition among the Japanese population.

If the health of Japan's urban population was beginning to be affected by the blockade in 1943, its impact on the imperial army's troops scattered across the Pacific islands was devastating. In the spring the flow of food from Japan and south-east Asia to Rabaul was seriously disrupted, and stocks of rice, barley, canned vegetables, oranges, meat, fish, miso paste, soya sauce, beer and *sake* all ran low. Stores were frequently 'insufficient to allow a satisfactory food issue to all'.[78] The military high command's answer to such problems was that the campaign for self-sufficiency must be intensified. Divisions based on the Solomon Islands and New Britain were instructed that total self-sufficiency must be achieved by the end of 1943. On Bougainville in April troops stationed in the south-west of the island were instructed: 'The regiment will confidently complete its mission even if its supply line is cut in the rear by bravely establishing a self-supporting status in the present location . . . Direct the main effort towards the development of agricultural areas and the securing of staple food with which to make the place self-sufficient.'[79] Each unit was ordered to employ half their men in farming. The locals were also employed in intensive gardening activities.[80] On New Guinea the troops stationed around Madang and Wewak were ordered to cover 50 per cent of their food needs with crops which they were to requisition or grow themselves, while the rest of the troops on the island were instructed to supply themselves with 25 per cent of their food. Even the front-line troops on New Guinea were told that Allied air attacks on communication lines meant that despite the fact that they were engaged in combat they would have to purchase, requisition and confiscate their food from the locals or cultivate their own vegetable gardens.[81]

The commanding officer on Rabaul, Imamura Hitoshi, responded by starting a farming initiative. The men at the base began to lead a strange semi-agrarian, semi-military existence. Each soldier planted up about 500 square metres with green stuff, sweet potatoes and aubergines. The unit commanders even held competitive exhibitions of the men's crops as an incentive to intensive gardening.[82] One Japanese diarist recorded that 'beautiful [vegetable gardens] just like in Japan' covered the area.[83] The men also kept chickens, cultivated edible snails and made great efforts to catch lizards and snakes.[84] The soldiers began to divide their time equally between self-sufficiency, construction of an underground fortress, and training, with a small amount of time allotted to sanitation and rest. In addition, the locals were urged by the military police to cultivate as much food as possible. They were told that 'there is nothing else for you to do, except for the whole village to strive for that one thing [to grow as much taro, bananas, and papayas as possible]'.[85] The Eighth Fleet military supplies section noted that 'fresh provisions at Rabaul were unexpectedly favourable'.[86] Indeed, they calculated that the men on the island were producing approximately 12 tons of food a day in June 1943. Even in 1945, although a disillusioned military diarist complained that his unbalanced diet of rice, barley, pumpkin and soya sauce was making him skinny, the death toll from starvation was low.[87] While the policy of self-sufficiency was reasonably successful on Rabaul itself, the soldiers-turned-farmers at the base could not possibly hope to produce enough food to continue to provide adequate supplies for troops stationed elsewhere on dependent islands.

GUADALCANAL

Meanwhile, on Guadalcanal in the Solomons, Japanese soldiers paid the price for the navy's inability to protect the sea lines of communication and provide adequate food supplies for troops engaged in combat. Japanese troops were in the process of building an air base on Guadalcanal when US marines attacked on 7 August 1942. By 18 August the Americans had captured and finished the airfield, which they named Henderson Field. It became the focus of six months of bitter fighting. Under the cover of darkness, the Japanese ran troops, food and ammunition from Rabaul past Bougainville and along a channel between New Georgia and Santa Isabel known as the Slot, a supply line which the Americans referred to as the 'Tokyo Express'. The Japanese continued to land reinforcements on the island until November, but their position became increasingly hopeless. The transports were unable to carry enough food supplies, as well as men and equipment, and the rations on the island were reduced to one-third of their normal quantity. Then the Americans began to attack the destroyers that accompanied the supply barges and, not wishing to lose vital ships, the Japanese adopted a method of dropping barrels of supplies from ships sailing past at a safe distance. The barrels were attached to rubber bales and tied together with rope and floated in to shore where the soldiers could collect them. But one private, who recalled stuffing oil drums with rice, powdered miso, matches and candles for the men on Guadalcanal, commented that the soldiers were too weak from hunger to go out to the shore and retrieve them.[88]

Japanese divisions made three attacks on Henderson Field. Each one ended in wholesale slaughter. The few men who survived were then faced with hiding out on the island with nothing to eat. As each new Japanese unit arrived for a fresh attack it met the starving remnants of the previous force. Making their way up to the airfield, Major-General Kawaguchi Kiyotake's second assault team met a few stragglers from the first – Colonel Ichiki Kiyonoa's unit. 'They were so much skin and bone ... clothes torn and boots falling to pieces; some had no footwear at all. They bowed repeatedly and asked for food.'[89] The third assault team of the 2nd Division were met by those few of Kawaguchi's men who had not been mown down by concentrated machine-gun fire on the Bloody Ridge. Skinny from starvation, they exhibited the symptoms of severe vitamin deficiency and malnutrition. 'Their ribs protruded. Their black hair had turned a dirty brown and could be pulled out in patches. Their eyebrows and eyelashes were dropping off and their teeth were loose. For almost three weeks no one had had a bowel movement and their bodies were so starved of salt that the sea water tasted sweet.'[90]

By December 1942 the fact that the Japanese were having trouble getting supplies of ammunition through to the island became irrelevant in the face of the death of 120–30 soldiers from starvation each day. Two staff officers, sent to investigate conditions on what had become known as the 'starvation island', reported back to Imamura Hitoshi on Rabaul that the soldiers were so weak that each man on patrol needed the food of four men.[91] By January 1943 the death toll had risen to 200 a day. Lieutenant-General Hyakutake Harukichi (now in charge on the island) drew up a timetable of death in which he calculated that a man who could still rise to his feet had about thirty days left to live, while a prone man who could nevertheless still speak might last for only two.[92]

Finally admitting defeat, the Japanese evacuated about 13,000 survivors in January. They were barely able to walk the 30 kilometres to the evacuation point. Unusually for a Japanese commander, used to keeping his emotions under control, Imamura, visiting the survivors on Bougainville, was moved to tears by the men, 'thin as thread, their faces ... blistered in blue ... staggering ... unable to stand ... ill-fed they were dejected'.[93] Imamura estimated that 15,000 Japanese soldiers had starved to death on Guadalcanal while only 5,000 had been lost in combat.[94] It was this experience which shook Imamura's, until then, unshakeable faith in the Japanese fighting spirit.[95]

NEW GUINEA

For the troops fighting on New Guinea, the high command's policies on the provisioning of troops proved disastrous from beginning to end. The capture of the capital settlement of Port Moresby on the southeastern tip of the island was considered to be crucial to Japanese plans. It was seen as a gateway to Australia, and by controlling the island of New Guinea they hoped to prevent the Allies from establishing a bridgehead from which to attack their base at Rabaul on New Britain. The battle of the Coral Sea in May 1942 prevented the landing force from achieving their goal of attacking Port Moresby from the sea, so the Japanese decided to attack by land. In July 1942 they began landing troops in the north-eastern area of the island around Buna. From here they planned to travel by means of the Kokoda Trail over the Owen Stanley range of mountains to Port Moresby.

The Japanese arrived on New Guinea without having carried out any serious investigations into the geography or climate of the island. It quickly became clear to the commanding officer Major-General Horii Tomitaro that the route over the mountains would present a challenge to bringing supplies up to the front line. The men would require about 3 tons of food and equipment each day, which would have to be taken 20 kilometres along a treacherously slippery log road, subject to Allied air attack, before the supplies were transferred to the heads of native porters for the journey along the trail. This was a narrow, single-track jungle path which zigzagged its way through thick forest, losing 180 metres for every 300 gained, so jagged were the mountains. At high altitudes it was bitterly cold; down in the valleys the humidity was unbearable. 'The fringes of the forest [were] interwoven from ground to treetop level with vines and creepers to form an almost solid mat of vegetation which has to be cut by the machete ... before progress is possible.'[96] Tramped over by an army of soldiers in the pouring tropical rain the track turned into 'boot-sucking porridge'.[97] As the Japanese advanced, Horii worked out that the number of porters needed to make what would eventually become a twenty-day round trip would increase to 4,600. To compound the problem, as the journey lengthened, the carriers themselves would need to consume more and more of the provisions they were carrying.[98]

In a manner characteristic of Japanese commanders, Horii gambled on quick advances and the capture of enemy food stores. One prisoner of war later claimed his unit had been issued with as few as seven days' rations, another that they were only given fourteen days' worth of food for the march across the 350-kilometre trail.[99] By the time they reached the Iorabaiwa Ridge, which was the furthest point of their advance, the soldiers were more interested in capturing food than in defeating the Australians. They swarmed on to the ridge and began crazily searching for ration dumps. Distressed to discover that the Australians had taken most of their food with them, they struggled with each other over the remnants. 'In the scramble for punctured tins and mud-stained rice, the warrior spirit evaporated. The Australian rearguard went unmolested.'[100] The Australians had by now adopted the cruel policy of contaminating any food that had to be left behind in a retreat. One Australian soldier recalled taking great delight in bayoneting the tins of food and scattering the sacks and meat over the muddy ground before withdrawing.[101] After eating everything they could find, the Japanese were afflicted by horrible gastric complaints.[102] In a last-ditch attempt to motivate their troops, the Japanese officers promised them plentiful Allied food stores if they captured Port Moresby itself.[103] But then in September 1942 the Japanese high command prioritized the battle of Guadalcanal. Even though they could see the lights of Port Moresby shining in the distance, Horii's troops retreated and dug in, back where they had started, at Buna.

Here malaria and amoebic dysentery swept through the troops. Malnutrition meant that their resistance to malaria was 'nil' and this was a particularly nasty strain which attacked the mucous membranes in the nose and stomach. A side-effect was severe diarrhoea and if this and a fever continued for more than four days the result was death.[104] The Japanese, sitting in their foxholes 'like mummies', began to suffer from shell-shock.[105] The Allies forced them out of their bridgeheads and they retreated back along the northern coast of the island. A Japanese army report entitled 'Lessons learned from battles at Buna and Giruwa and intelligence on future offensives' attempted to analyse why they were unable to hold their positions. Malnutrition was identified as the main reason for defeat. Lack of food, the report concluded, had led to a loss of morale, even despair, and the breakdown of military discipline. The absurd aspect of the report was that rather than identifying Allied destruction of Japanese shipping as the cause of the supply problem, it focused on the fact that New Guinea was a 'barren wasteland' with a harsh climate and an environment in which it was virtually impossible to cultivate additional provisions. Lack of supplementary produce, in other words failure to achieve self-sufficiency, was held to blame.[106]

However, the idea that troops on New Guinea could achieve even 50 or 25 per cent food self-sufficiency was ludicrous and the failure of the supply lines in 1943 meant that they received far less than half of the food they needed. The system of dropping oil drums stuffed with supplies was employed in New Guinea as well as at Guadalcanal. Unfortunately, the rocket the ship fired to alert the soldiers to the bales of supplies drifting in on the tide also caught the attention of the enemy. 'Suicide squads' were sent out to gather in as much as they could under a heavy barrage from the Allied soldiers.[107] Eventually there were too few ships left to continue with these so-called 'rat' runs. The Americans had systematically torpedoed them, claiming fifty-eight which had been on supply missions. The Japanese switched to the 'mole' system. Now it was submarines that towed in the rubber bales and set them free without surfacing. Each submarine could drag enough supplies to feed 30,000 men for two days but the soldiers were only able to recover perhaps as few as one-third of the drums. Then in August 1943 Imperial Headquarters announced that New Guinea would now be self-sustaining. No more supplies would be brought in. The Japanese forces on the island were abandoned to starvation.

In an effort to conserve what food supplies there were on the island the commanding officers warned the troops in September that they must not carry out wild acts of plunder on the villagers' gardens. The natives 'are are to be pacified', the troops were told, 'and we are planning thereby to increase our supplies especially fresh vegetables'.[108] But the inhabitants of Loboda village near Milne Bay recalled that the Japanese constantly pilfered from their gardens, killed their pigs and even ate raw taro they were so hungry. Others would go from hamlet to hamlet begging for gifts of food in exchange for a compass or clothing.[109] About a third of the 20th Division stationed at Finschhafen were allocated gardening tasks, while about one-sixth of the men went out foraging for food in the local area. Japanese troops became more preoccupied with finding their next meal than fighting to hold on to territory, and the Allies found that they fought hardest to maintain their occupancy of areas where they controlled native gardens. If the gardens were eaten out then they might fight to gain ground in areas where there was more food, and they were so hungry that they would sometimes raid native vegetable gardens behind the Allied lines.[110] A significant number of ambushes and attacks were carried out with the express purpose of stealing Allied rations.[111] For the natives, 1944–45 was a period of terror. Their buildings, cooking fires and gardens all attracted Allied bombing. On the ground the Japanese foraging parties were brutal and vindictive.[112] But even when the Australians arrived, conditions did not improve greatly as their soldiers raped the women without fear of being disciplined. One senior Australian officer was said to have commented that 'after all, "the Marys raped very easily"'.[113]

Allied interrogations of Japanese prisoners revealed an army slowly disintegrating from hunger.[114] An Allied Intelligence Research Report concluded, 'officers and men alike, in forward areas, are preoccupied almost to the exclusion of everything else with the shortage of food

... Bitterness and resentment, reaching at times a homicidal level, are generated by this life or death competition, especially towards officers who are, or appear to be abusing the privileges of their rank ... Comparison of their own plight with the enemy's comparative affluence, especially brought home by the capture of our parachute dropped supplies or one of our ration dumps, reminds the Japanese soldier again of the extent of his abandonment.'[115] Superior Private Nakata Motoo told his interrogators that he had decided to surrender after his officers had ordered the men into the fields to collect potatoes during mortar and air attacks and then had taken the best food for themselves.[116]

By the summer of 1944 the Japanese were reduced to eating *sacsac*, a tasteless, brown starch made from sago palms. Water was passed through the fibre hollowed out of the palm trunks to produce a glutinous mass which was wrapped in leaves and cooked. The sticky mess was even sent up to feed the front-line troops. At first they mixed it with rice or wheat but eventually they ate plain *sacsac*, which did little to assuage hunger pangs or provide energy or nutrition. In the Sepak river area the men in combat were given dried grasses to eat.[117] Well aware of how hungry the Japanese were, the Allies bombed supply bases, and even strafed the palm trees to deny them coconuts and *sacsac*.[118]

On 10 December 1944 the commander of the 18th Army on New Guinea, General Adachi Hatazo, issued an order that 'while troops were permitted to eat the flesh of the Allied dead, they must not eat their own'.[119] This admission of cannibalism among Japanese troops is supported by a number of Australian War Crimes Section reports as well as by US army documents which indicate that the Japanese on New Guinea ate each other, members of the local population, Asian prisoners of war who had been brought to the islands as forced labourers and Allied soldiers. The reports contain eyewitness accounts by soldiers who discovered the mutilated bodies of their comrades, as well as evidence that their flesh had been eaten. On 20 May 1945 an Australian soldier recovered the body of one of his battalion. He had been stripped, and both his arms were cut off at the shoulder. 'The stomach had been cut out, and the heart, liver and other entrails had been removed, all fleshy parts of the body had been cut away ... A Japanese mess tin which appeared to contain human flesh was lying four to five yards away . . . between two dead Japanese soldiers.'[120] Hatam Ali, an Indian soldier taken prisoner by the Japanese, was sent to New Guinea as part of a labour force to build an airfield in 1943. He later recounted that when the Japanese ran out of food in 1944 the guards would select one prisoner each day who 'was taken out and killed and eaten . . . I personally saw this happen.'[121] The prisoners had been transformed from a workforce into a food supply.

By failing to provision their troops the Japanese high command not only displayed a criminal contempt for the value of their soldiers' lives, they handed the Allies an excruciatingly effective weapon to use against their soldiers. As the Pacific fleet under the command of Admiral Nimitz moved through the Marshall, Caroline and Mariana islands, capturing only those islands of strategic interest, the US navy left the remaining Japanese garrisons to 'wither on the vine'.[122] The islands became floating prison camps and the starving Japanese resorted to eating any living thing: 'pigs, dogs, possum, mice, bats, kangaroos, snakes, lizards, frogs, leeches, earthworms, centipedes, all sorts of insects (butterflies, caterpillars), maggots (in some cases they even took maggots from the latrines), crocodiles, fish, lobsters, crabs, shells, birds'.[123] They dug up any edible vegetable matter, collected wild grasses and ate water lilies and duck weed. Australian soldiers moving into areas that had once been held by the Japanese found that they had completely cleared these regions of food.

The Americans did supply food to those islands which were cut off from supplies but where there were no occupying Japanese. But the term 'wither on the vine' was a euphemism worthy of the National Socialists, who spoke of 'resettlement' rather than 'mass murder'. The indigenous islanders 'withered' alongside the Japanese, like the Greeks who died as a result of the British blockade of occupied Europe, incidental victims of a wider military strategy. In the Caroline Islands, the Japanese on Kosrae turned into 'stick men', and they and many of the 179 labourers who had been brought in from Pohnpei died of malnutrition, unable to survive on potato leaves.[124] The last Japanese supply ship reached Ocean Island in 1943. After that a few submarines dropped off bales of food. The islanders ate *ren ruku* (pawpaw leaves) while the Japanese grew pumpkins in barrels of night soil. The islanders began to die of starvation* and a few were executed for stealing rice. Eventually the Japanese evacuated the survivors to Kusaie where they were set to work growing food for the Japanese while surviving on a diet of soup made from leaves.[125] One islander commented, 'It would be better to be a soldier than a civilian prisoner. Soldiers have weapons and have a chance. We had no chance, we were slaves. We were the same as pigs: we had no human rights.'[126]

Allied prisoners of war also withered on the vine. Kasayama Yoshi-kichi was a Korean guard for a prisoner of war camp on an island off the coast of New Guinea where they were supposed to be constructing an airfield. Here the guards, like the prisoners, slept in blankets with-out shelter. When it rained, guards and prisoners alike caught cold and came down with dysentery.[127] 'Demands for food and medical supplies came from the prisoners, but we didn't have any "main course" either. We had only rice and the leaves of the tapioca plant. We made some soup with those leaves, a little garlic, salt and a bit of butter. Our superiors were in the same shape. There was nothing to eat and noth-ing to give. Japanese army regulations specified that we were to feed the Japanese first, then the locals, and what was left was for the prison-ers.'[128] He described how the prisoners would first become emaciated, then their lips would dry out, their eyesight blur and then they would die. 'At the end it wasn't a matter of giving food to the prisoners or not giving it. There wasn't any food even for the Japanese soldiers.'[129] As the guards and prisoners attempted to escape by sailing to Java, they drank water contaminated by corpses and contracted beriberi. Their flesh swelled and their legs became heavy. The guards began to die alongside their prisoners. Only 800 of the original 2,000 prisoners made it back to Java.[130]

Desperate hunger prevailed throughout the Pacific and south-east Asia. In a letter to the newspaper *Asahi Shimbun*, the veteran Nishi-hara Takamaro, then in his seventies, recalled how on Luzon in the Philippines 'a fellow soldier whose name I didn't know came crawl-ing over to me. Taking off his clothes, he bared his pointed rear end. It had become dark bluish-green. "Buddy, if I die, go ahead and eat this part," he said, touching his scrawny rear end with his bony finger.

* Of the 923 islanders 130 died.

I said, "Idiot, how could I eat a war buddy?" But I couldn't take my eyes off the flesh on his rear.' Nishihara claimed that he was saved by the discovery of a dog, which he killed and ate along with some salt he found stored on a dead comrade's body.[131] In Ooka Shohei's autobiographical novel *Fires on the Plain* he described how the remnants of Japanese regiments were left wandering the islands looking for something to eat. Ooka's novel describes how the soldiers descended into cannibalism. His protagonist would occasionally meet another soldier. They would both let out 'an inhuman cry' and avoid each other: 'I was not interested in them; I was on the lookout for immobile people – for fresh corpses that still retained human lineaments.'[132]

Although they may have descended to an unimaginable level of hunger and misery the majority of Japanese soldiers appear to have clung on to a remnant of their initial fighting spirit. The ethos of *bushido* taught that when a Japanese soldier went into battle he had two options: to fight and win, or to die fighting. Surrender was not considered an option, and the majority of Japanese soldiers eventually chose to commit suicide or to die of starvation rather than surrender.

BURMA

While the Japanese troops in the Pacific degenerated into starvation, in Burma the military command demonstrated their inability to learn lessons from previous mistakes. In April 1944 Lieutenant-General Mutaguchi Renya launched an attack on India. He had been charged with preventing the Americans from reopening the Burma road and the supply line to Nationalist China. However, he had a much grander vision, supported in Japan by War Minister Tojo Hideki. Mutaguchi was under the illusion that he was about to lead a triumphant march on India which would take the British out of the war and persuade the United States to negotiate with Japan.[133] The idea was to capture Imphal, the key logistical town in Assam, and cut off the supply route by capturing Kohima. The Japanese could then move on to Dimapur, a key British supply base in the Brahmaputra river valley.

The route into Assam from Burma was along narrow tracks through thick, hot, steamy, muddy jungle. The only way to move supplies up the line was by pack animal. This was obviously a re-run of the Kokoda Trail: half of the supplies which left the supply base would have been consumed by service personnel before they reached the combat troops.[134] Major-General Inada Masazumi, Vice-Chief of General Staff of the Southern Army, expressed his reservations about the feasibility of the plan and was consequently levered out of his position.[135] The division commanders for the attack on Kohima were also dubious and thought that it would be impossible to maintain the supply routes. Lieutenant Sato Kotoku was said to have told his staff that they would most probably all starve to death. However, the campaign went ahead and the supply services mustered a herd of 15,000 cows to double as meat on the hoof and pack animals (despite the fact that cows are unsuited to carrying heavy loads). The usual orders were issued to the commanders that they must capture enemy stocks.[136]

This time the British had no intention of feeding their enemies, and as his regiment approached Kohima Captain Kameyama Shosaku was disappointed to discover 'the enemy had destroyed all their food and supplies' as they retreated.[137] His regiment was forced to attack enemy positions at night in order to plunder their supplies of 'rations, bullets and grenades'.[138] When Senior Private Wada Manabu's transport section moved on to the northern ridge at Kohima they found the 'British had burned their food and supply depots so that not even a grain of rice or a round of ammunition was left for us. The best my comrades and I could do was to find three tins of corned beef in the enemy positions.'[139] Not only were the Allies now better at evacuating their positions without leaving presents from Mr Churchill for the Japanese, their supply logistics had advanced considerably by 1944. The Japanese laid siege to British and Indian troops at Kohima, but throughout the seventeen-day siege air supply flew in 3,000 tons of stores, including food, drinking water and ammunition.[140] In 1942 an Air Dispatch Depot had been set up at Chaklala in India where pilots were trained how to drop supplies packed into carefully designed containers attached to special parachutes.[141] This enabled the British and Indian troops to keep fighting, albeit on half rations, while the Japanese, unable to supply themselves from Allied food dumps, starved. The British also managed to blockade Japanese communication lines and by April the Japanese were so short of shells that they could only fire at the enemy for a few hours a day. Reduced to boiling 'vegetable matter' to stave off 'our terrible hunger', they watched the British through their telescopes as they took their afternoon tea break.[142]

A similar story was played out at Imphal, where the Japanese besieged the British for two months. Unable to get their hands on enemy stores, they could only watch as American Dakotas flew in 40 tons of food and ammunition a day.[143] Under orders from their new Supreme Allied Commander, Mountbatten, the British held on, despite the onset of the monsoon.[144] In contrast, stuck in their 'octopus holes', up to their armpits in water, the Japanese 'felt [they] had arrived at the very limit of [their] endurance'.[145] Despite Lieutenant-General Mutaguchi's repeated exhortations that the troops should continue fighting, Lieutenant Sato stated to Mutaguchi's chief of staff that before his men could do anything else 'first we must eat' and he decided to withdraw.[146] The retreat was a horror of mud and death. The medical orderlies constantly slipped and fell and the wounded on the stretchers groaned and complained. The path was littered with rain-sodden corpses, stinking of decomposition and crawling with maggots.[147] Emaciated or crippled soldiers were given hand grenades and encouraged 'to sort themselves out'.[148] The survivors arriving in the field hospitals looked like 'living skeletons', in uniforms 'worn to shreds'. Presented with rice in their mess tins they would pitifully ask Nurse Nagai Hideko, 'May I eat all of this?'[149] The 'defeated stragglers' felt great bitterness towards their commanders who, having issued orders for the men to fight on regardless of the fact that they had no ammunition or food, had either committed suicide or escaped.[150] The fighting was vicious on both sides. At Kohima and Imphal 17,587 Allied soldiers were killed or wounded. The final death toll on the Japanese side was far higher. More than 60,000 Japanese died during this campaign but almost half of them did not die from injuries incurred in battle but from starvation and associated diseases.[151]

The key to success in battle in such under-developed areas was technical and logistical superiority. As they pressed on into Burma in 1945 the Allies were in a position to support their troops with 58,725 tons of airborne supplies, move 48,900 personnel into the area by air and evacuate 11,580 casualties by plane.[152] The Japanese were still relying on obsolete tactics such as rounding up draught cattle and attempting to capture enemy supplies. In a mirror image of the reversal of fortunes on the eastern front, the British, like the Soviets, were now well equipped and able to command superior logistical techniques. The Japanese, like the Germans, fought on bravely but were utterly lacking in the technical resources to secure victory.

Official figures for exactly how many Japanese soldiers died of starvation do not exist, but a Japanese scholar has produced estimates based on careful examination of the conditions in each battle theatre. He confirms Imamura's estimate that 15,000 of the 20,000 who died on Guadalcanal starved to death. Only 6 per cent of the 157,646 troops sent to New Guinea survived. Almost all of those who died were killed by starvation and tropical diseases. In the Philippines, where the Japanese retreat was extremely disorganized, he estimates that 400,000 of the 498,000 Japanese deaths were caused by starvation. Altogether it would appear that 60 per cent, or more than 1 million, of the total 1.74 million Japanese military deaths between 1941 and 1945 were caused by starvation and diseases associated with malnutrition.[153] The Tokyo War Crimes Tribunal did not prosecute the Japanese war leadership for crimes against their own people. The men at Imperial Headquarters were never held to account for their decision to abandon the New Guinea garrison and a host of other Japanese soldiers to 'self-sufficiency', which by the end of the war had become a euphemism for leaving them to die of starvation.[154]

HUNGER ON THE HOME ISLANDS

Ordinary Japanese civilians never received clear information about the events of the war. They had to piece together a picture of what was really going on from rumour and obscure and incomplete references in the newspapers and on the radio. Reports of 'brilliant continental [Chinese] campaigns unknown in the history of war' were a sure indication that the conflict in the Pacific was going badly. But rumours did filter through to Japan that the blockade was having a terrible impact on the troops fighting on the Pacific islands. In May 1943 the secret diarist Kiyosawa attended a lecture at the Japan Club given by a Commander Akiyama where the fighting on the island of Attu was discussed. He reported that the commander described the Japanese army as 'falling into isolated helplessness . . . it is a fact that the destruction en route by submarines is considerable, and the soldiers occupying the island have only the military equipment they brought at the beginning. I sympathize with the desperateness of their fight.'[155] In November 1944 Kiyosawa heard 'a story at the barbershop' that the soldiers 'did not have food and ate human flesh . . . they killed prisoners of war. It is said they were placed in a large cauldron, the oil was skimmed, and they were eaten . . . They were probably exaggerating, but I think to a certain extent it might be true.'[156]

While rumours reached the home islands of the hungry plight of the soldiers, for urban civilians the discomforts of war turned into privation. In March 1944 Kiyosawa noted that 'everywhere one goes, the core of discussion is the inadequacy of food supplies'.[157] At his daughter's school the girls no longer warmed their lunches on the stove. 'This is because they were immediately stolen.'[158] Visiting Hokkaido, he was told by his guide that his family of seven children had nothing to eat but gruel and they had all lost between 6 and 9 kilograms in weight.[159] Kiyosawa noted that 'of late everybody is extremely emaciated. When I encountered Ohata of the Foreign Ministry after an absence of one month, he was completely emaciated. When I met my neighbour Koike on the street he was so thin I didn't recognize him. It seems that everybody is like this.'[160] Between the spring and summer of 1944 Kiyosawa himself lost more than 5 kilograms.[161]

The Japanese government placed an inordinate amount of faith in food science as a way of overcoming food shortages. During the war ten new training establishments for dieticians were founded, where the students were taught how to maintain a healthy diet despite food shortages. The knowledge was then passed on to the neighbourhood associations.[162] However, there were limits to what inventive cookery could achieve without ingredients. The Provisions Friends' Association which had begun life in the 1920s, spreading the benefits of the cheap and nutritious western dishes advocated by the military, was reduced to publishing posters and pamphlets advertising the benefits of chewing rice more carefully. It also devised a variety of chemical dietary supplements and a sinister-sounding cooking activator, which was advertised as softening fibres and disguising bad smells and thus appeared to promote the consumption of stale and indigestible foods.[163] Indeed, many of the substitute foods which the government's nutritionists invented were fairly indigestible. In *A Boy Called H*, Senoh Kappa described how a series of articles began appearing in the newspapers in 1943, entitled 'How to Make Do on "Decisive Battle" Food'. Although H and his schoolfriends were so hungry they 'manfully tried anything that seemed remotely edible', they were irritated by the way in which the propaganda tried to divert attention away from the shortcomings of the government. Slogans which declared, 'Shortages of foodstuffs mean shortage of ingenuity!' seemed to imply that the fault lay with the general population's lack of initiative. The cheerful exhortation, 'Let's get by on "decisive battle" food!' encapsulated the government's helpless response to a failing strategy: the Japanese must try harder. One such article recommended a variety of 'nourishing' edible insects, in particular the grubs of bees, dobsonflies, dragonflies and long-horned beetles. It suggested boiling them in soya sauce or roasting them in a little oil. Another set of suggestions gave substitutes for rice such as the skins of sweet potatoes, pumpkins or mandarin oranges, dried and then ground to make a flour out of which dumplings could be made. The same article emphasized that the straw of the rice plant was also edible and when ground and mixed with powdered *hijiki* (a type of seaweed) and flour and kneaded into a dough was said to make excellent noodles. 'H had eaten bee grubs and locusts, but resolved on no account to eat rice straw.'[164]

Matsumoto Nakako recalled that these *kai somen* (sea treasure noodles) were on sale in the markets at a very cheap price when she was living in rural Hakata in 1946. At the time there was nothing much else to eat except pumpkin, and her family ate the *kai somen* in order to 'feel full'. Her memory of them was of 'a wonderful food'. In 1970, when she became a professor of food and nutrition, she met a man who had worked as an expert for the government in the wartime agricultural department. He told her they had been made from seaweed mixed with rice straw. They made some for themselves and tried them, and she realized how very hungry she must have been as a child. They tasted horrible.[165]

By the end of 1944 Kiyosawa reported that the dominant topic of conversation in the cities was no longer food but 'amateur farming. Everybody is doing this.'[166] Government advisers instructed the neighbourhood associations on the cultivation of vegetables, and gardening tips were broadcast on the radio.[167] 'The newspapers talk of nothing but vegetables.' As usual the government promoted strategies without providing the means to employ them. Kiyosawa was frustrated. 'We we are told to plant leeks, even I searched everywhere for leek seeds, but in vain. I merely planted what was given to me by a neighbour.'[168] He reported the appearance of posters saying 'Plant more pumpkins at any cost' but he despaired that this was only propaganda and 'nothing is done . . . From this one probably understands how unproductive bureaucratism is.'[169]

The food shortages adversely affected the productivity of workers in the war industries. In 1943 rations for industrial workers provided a spare 2,000 calories for men and 1,474 calories for women. The food intake of Japanese workers was therefore comparable to that of Soviet workers in the early years of the war. The government made an effort to boost productivity by delivering extra rations to industrial plants. Male heavy manual workers received an extra 730 grams of food, women doing the same work an extra 560 grams. Many factory managers bought food on the black market to distribute to their employees.[170] Kiyosawa heard 'that people like night-shift work in factories because they can have a meal at night'.[171] There were signs of hunger and desperation as workers went absent from their factories more and more frequently. They travelled into the countryside to barter with the peasants for food. By 1945 the process of progressively stripping away one's clothes, jewellery and other valuables in return for food was referred to as *takenoko seikatsu* or the 'bamboo-shoot existence', as bamboo shoots peel away in layers, much like onions. In the countryside a new breed of criminal appeared. The 'vegetable thief' crept into the fields at night and stole the food before it could be harvested. In 1944 nearly half the economic crimes committed in the Osaka prefecture involved food.[172]

In the last half of 1944 the Japanese made one last effort to sustain the war effort and substantially increased the production of war goods, using up stocks of raw materials in the process and employing all available labour.[173] On 4 July 1944 Kiyosawa heard with despair that 'those in middle school and above the third year level in elementary school are sent to munitions factories and made to work . . . with this, Japanese scholarship will be completely eliminated . . . If Japan goes on just as it is, it will plunge into darkness.'[174] By October of that year nearly 2 million students over the age of ten had been put to work in Japanese industry. By February 1945 the ranks of student workers had swelled to 3 million, two-thirds of all children of that age.[175] Kiyosawa's daughter Eiko went to work at the Japan Steel Pipe factory. The one advantage was that she was given a lunch of 'rice and soup in which two or three pieces of vegetables have been added'.[176] For H, lunchtime was the highlight of his day working at the school factory. The students were given bread rolls which tasted as though they were made with sawdust, or rice-balls leavened with sorghum, which gave them an unappealing 'pinkish hue . . . the sorghum rice didn't just taste unpleasant, it had a dreadful smell too, which combined with the smell of the bakelite container so that when you took the lid off you were overcome by a stale, warm odour'. There might also be a stew of dried herrings or a pickled radish leaf. It all tasted awful but they 'devoured the stuff ravenously even while they complained'.[177]

The desperation of the Japanese government can be measured by the misery they were prepared to inflict on the young. Tanaka Tetsuko, who had been helping the peasants in the fields, was sent to a factory where they manufactured one of the most ineffective weapons of the war. These were papier mâché balloons designed to carry anti-personnel bombs. The idea was to fill them with hydrogen and then release them into the jet stream over the Pacific. The Japanese hoped they would float over to the west coast of America and cause havoc. They are known to have caused only one set of fatalities, among a family picnicking on the American west coast.[178]

Tanaka and her classmates worked twelve-hour shifts without a break. In the factory 'the floor was muddy with the extra paste that always streamed off the drying boards. From above, steam condensed into water droplets fell on us. Each person was in charge of two drying boards. The paper dried very quickly, so you shuttled back and forth between them like a crab. If it got too dry it would crack and fail the quality test. That was unforgivable, so we ran barefoot across the pasty floor.'[179] After their shift they had a meal of rice mixed with black, foul-smelling sweet potatoes, had a bath and went to bed shivering under one blanket. Sunday was their day off and they slept all day 'like corpses'.[180] They were all so hungry that when they were sent food by their families they could not bring themselves to share. 'Girls would put their heads into the closet and start eating. You just stopped caring about other people.'[181] Some of the girls thought the small white pills they were given were nourishment pills but in fact they were probably amphetamines, designed to keep pilots awake.

On Christmas Day 1944 Kiyosawa observed that the dominant wartime topic was no longer food or farming but bombs and incendiaries. The American aerial bombing campaign now dominated urban life. Two days later he wrote of the enemy coming 'in rows of silvery wings' and in February 1945 he noticed that the B-29s had been joined by carrier-based planes, which he took as a sign that the 'navy has been completely destroyed'.[182] Tokyo was devastated. 'What is unbearable to see is large numbers of old ladies and the sick . . . people carrying in one hand bedding left from the fire, people carrying buckets that have been scorched. These people hobble aimlessly down Ginza Street. The eyes of each and every one are reddened. It is probably because of the smoke and heat.'[183] The government set up dining halls where workers received a thin porridge 'garnished with potato fragments, a radish leaf, a bit of snail, or a few grains of rice'. The demand was enormous. In the Shinjuku district of Tokyo people began queuing as early as nine in the morning for the lunch at noon. If the dining halls were bombed, bags of dried biscuits were distributed as a substitute.[184] Kiyosawa's nephew and his family were left homeless. All the aid that they received was 'a five-day ration of rice and soya sauce' and a free train ride out of the city.[185]

SURRENDER

Long before August 1945 it was clear to the Japanese leadership that the country was defeated. During the summer of 1945 the Allied strategy against the home islands consisted of a mix of blockade and bombardment. The aerial bombing campaign had flattened Tokyo,

Osaka, Nagoya, Yokohama, Kobe and Kawasaki.[186] The planes then went on to disable Korea's rail network, shutting down supplies of raw materials for plane manufacture. The inter-island rail and sea connection between Honshu and Hokkaido was smashed in July.[187] In order to reinforce the blockade the US air force had diverted a substantial number of B-29 bombers from the bombing campaign to lay extensive minefields around Japan's shores. 'Operation Starvation', as the mining campaign was known, was an extremely cost-effective form of attack. At a loss of very few planes the mines sank over a million tons of shipping. By August half of the 1.5 million tons that remained of the merchant marine was damaged and the rest of the ships were marooned in their harbours, barely able to move due to the net of mines spread around Japan.[188]

Japanese industry had ground to a halt for lack of raw materials.[189] Hashimoto Yukio was working on a project to manufacture a special type of aluminium. 'The quality of material used for airplanes had declined to the lowest level. The collection of pots and pans (which were melted down to make planes) was totally inadequate to meet our needs.' When his team began to salvage materials from downed B-29 bombers he realized the odds which Japan was up against. 'I had thought that since Japan was under such duress, the quality of American materials would naturally have suffered as well. But the components we analysed met the normal standards, and the surface of the propellers shone brightly like silver. I won't forget the chill I felt at the strength of American production capabilities.'[190] His team worked many long nights to get the metal ready in time to contribute to the war but were overtaken by Japan's surrender. 'When I saw the duraluminium, its material label still on, used for dustpans and ladles lined up in black markets right after the War's end, I felt my energies seep from my body.'[191]

The metal for Japanese fighter planes was so inferior that Hashimoto heard that the engines cracked if they were flown at full throttle. This was rapidly becoming irrelevant as the country ran out of aviation fuel. Despite having rebuilt the oil industry in the Dutch East Indies the Japanese could not take advantage of their success as the shipping blockade had cut them off from their supplies. 'No [oil] tanker reached Japan after March 1945.'[192]

In May the government abandoned the attempt to bring in raw

materials for the war industry and concentrated on importing food. By now between half and three-quarters of the rice ration was distributed in the form of sweet potatoes and soya beans.[193] The government had never officially acknowledged that the progressive substitution of other foods for rice amounted to a reduction in the ration, but in July it finally admitted that it could not fill the ration quotas and the cabinet issued a statement announcing a 10 per cent reduction in the staple ration. The loss of imports meant that the level of salt in the urban population's diet was close to the minimum for survival.[194] Piles of Manchurian soya beans, millet, peanut oil and salt lay rotting on the quays of the Korean ports but there was too little shipping to bring much across the mine-strewn Sea of Japan. Even those few ships that ran the blockade did so in vain. Coastal transport within Japan had been brought to a halt by the American mines and this placed intense pressure on the inadequate rail system. This and a lack of labour at the docks meant that the food ended up rotting in the holds of the ships and on Japanese quays instead. Fearful that localized famines would develop which would lead to civil disorder, in characteristic fashion the government called on farmers 'to double production by assuming the "special attack spirit"'.[195]

Nutritionists were still trying to find ways of feeding the urban population with substitute foods and these became increasingly bizarre. At some point in 1945 a substitute flour was distributed, suspiciously named the 'pulverized diet'. It contained a powder of acorns, sweet potato vines and mulberry leaves and was not only revolting but potentially damaging to human health. Suto Ryosaku recalled that her mother made dumplings with this flour but the children in the family simply could not eat them. 'Even when we told them to shut their eyes and eat, it was no good.'[196] In Osaka a broadcast explained to the civilians that used tea-leaves, the blossoms and leaves of roses, silkworm cocoons, worms, grasshoppers, mice, rats, moles, snails, snakes, and a powder made of the dried blood of cows, horses and pigs, made useful supplementary foods. The Osakan authorities even claimed that a fermenting agent could be used to break down sawdust and render it edible.[197]

The Americans were unaware of the full impact of Operation Starvation. In June a US assessment of the situation asserted that the country would not experience a 'serious overall food shortage in 1945'.[198] Certainly, the Japanese were not yet dying of starvation in large numbers but average calorie consumption in the cities had fallen to 1,680 and was thus hovering around the starvation level. Kiyosawa was one of the early victims of the blockade. He died in May 1945, aged fifty-six, of pneumonia, brought on by his malnourished and emaciated condition. The urban population was steadily losing weight and around a quarter of townspeople were suffering from malnutrition. Tuberculosis, beriberi, digestive, skin and vitamin-deficiency diseases were rife. The birth-rate had fallen and infant mortality had risen. Post-war studies of children's heights show that the growth of the youth of Japan was seriously stunted.[199]

In the summer of 1945 Japan's fate lay in the hands of just eight men: the six members of the Supreme Council for the Direction of the War, the Lord Keeper of the Privy Seal, Marquis Kido Koichi, and the Emperor.[200] Three representatives of the military within the council – Army Minister Anami Korechika, Army Chief of Staff Umezu Yoshijiro and Navy Chief of Staff Toyoda Soemu – maintained a firm line, right up until 6 August and the dropping of the first atomic bomb, on Hiroshima, that Japan should never surrender. In July 1944 Kiyosawa noted in his diary that no matter how unrealistic, the Japanese military seemed to hope against hope that they would be able to lure the American battleships closer and closer and then 'deliver a devastating blow when the enemy approaches'.[201] When, in August 1944, it became apparent that the government were preparing for an American invasion of the home islands he concluded that they still believed 'in a final divine wind and that the war will end with a great victory'.[202]

Kiyosawa's assessment of the militarists' thinking was correct. Their plan was to continue to inflict devastating casualties on the Americans until they were forced to negotiate. After Germany's unconditional surrender on 8 May 1945 they correctly assessed that the American public and soldiers had little stomach for yet more fighting and bloodshed, and were eager to bring the war to a speedy end. What the Japanese leadership failed to grasp was that the Allies would never accept the terms on which the militarists wished to surrender, which included that there should be no change in the government, no occupation of the Japanese home islands, that Japanese troops should be allowed to disarm themselves, and that any war crimes trials would be conducted by the Japanese.[203] The Allies were fully committed to achieving an unconditional surrender. They saw the final defeat of the German and Japanese armies, and the imposition of social reforms during a period of occupation, as essential to achieving a lasting peace.[204] On 26 July 1945 the Allied leaders held out an olive branch in the form of the Potsdam Declaration, which specified that they were looking for the unconditional surrender of the armed forces (rather than the entire nation) and that the Japanese would eventually be allowed to set up their own government.[205]

A group had emerged within the Japanese government which was in favour of negotiating a peace, and the civilian members of the council, Foreign Minister Togo Shigenori and Prime Minister Suzuki Kantaro, welcomed the Potsdam Declaration, at least as a basis for further negotiations. During a post-war interview with members of the US Strategic Bombing Survey a former Japanese prime minister, Prince Konoe Fumimaro acknowledged that the upper-class members of the council and the Marquis Kido Koichi were afraid of 'a sort of communistic revolution'.[206] Unlike the militarists, who saw foreign occupation as the worst possible fate that could befall Japan, the noble elite were afraid that the destruction of Japan's cities and its economy would undermine the social fabric of the nation to the extent that the masses would rise up in protest against the suffering and trigger a social revolution which would undermine the Imperial institution and bring the feudal structure of Japanese society tumbling down. After the dropping of the atomic bombs, one of the reasons the Emperor gave for his decision to surrender was the fear of domestic upheaval.[207]

It is impossible now to tell whether this would have happened. The food situation after the surrender in August gives some indication of the extent to which the situation would have worsened if Japan had continued fighting and the American blockade had continued. The harvest of 1945 was affected by wet, cold weather followed by typhoons and floods in the autumn. In November the government calculated that they only had enough food to provide a ration of 1,325 calories per person, and the inefficiencies of the delivery system meant that the ration sometimes provided only one-third of the calories needed to survive.[208] The government began a campaign to redistribute more effectively what little food was available. This staved off a serious food crisis until mid-1946. However, this would almost certainly have been impossible to achieve if the war had still been going on. Japan would not have been able to use shipping to move food between the islands and the Americans were planning to begin the systematic destruction of the Japanese rail network in August. This would have immobilized the Japanese transport system. If the war had continued, famine would almost certainly have occurred in Japan's major cities and many thousands of Japanese would have starved to death, beginning with infants, children, the elderly and the infirm.[209] There were protests over the incompetence of the government's food policy in 1946 and, while they were never likely to lead to revolution while the Americans were occupying the country, it is possible that if the war had continued the increasingly desperate urban population might well have risen up to demand peace.

After the war, Paul Nitze of the United States Strategic Bombing Survey (USSBS) team argued that Japan was already on its knees in August 1945 and that surrender would only have been a matter of time. Nitze confidently gave a date when Japan would have been ready to accept defeat: 1 November 1945.[210] What Nitze failed to take into account was that the military leadership was prepared to sacrifice any number of Japanese civilians in the final battle. Prince Konoe Fumimaro, along with most of the other Japanese leadership interviewed by the USSBS, pointed out that although Japan was 'of course . . . nearing the limit . . . the army would not admit it. They wouldn't admit they were near the end . . . The army had dug themselves caves in the mountains and their idea of fighting on was fighting from every little hole or rock in the mountains.'[211] In March 1945 the government began to organize the civilian population into a Patriotic Citizens Fighting Corps.[212] Young boys were issued with bamboo spears, and H was described as being filled with dread when he read an article in the newspaper in 1945 which spoke of 'officers and men of the Imperial forces . . . throwing themselves into the fray with no concern for themselves, standing in the vanguard of their one hundred million compatriots'.[213] It was clear that the military applied its own principles to the civilian population and expected them to die fighting rather than surrender.

In late July 1945 Emperor Hirohito, with whom lay the final decision to surrender, and the 'peace party' within the government were still wavering. They thought that there was some merit in the militarists' argument that Japan would be able to force the Allies into a negotiated peace settlement superior to that offered at Potsdam if the Japanese first inflicted thousands of casualties on an American invasion force. In any case, even if they had wanted to surrender immediately, they were unable to prevail over the fixed determination of the militarists to continue fighting. To persuade these men of the need to surrender unconditionally, and to strengthen their position against the entrenched 'war party', would require a dramatic display of American power. A number of possible strategies were open to the United States, none of them particularly appealing. They could continue the bombardment and mass destruction of Japanese cities and the nation's infrastructure and combine this with the continuation of the blockade in order to starve the Japanese people into submission. They could launch an invasion of Japan and take the country by force, or they could use their new weapon, the atomic bomb, and demonstrate the overwhelming force which the United States was prepared to use in order to bring the war to an end.

United States analysts thought that a strategy of blockade and bombardment would be slow and painful. The American public would have had to wait patiently for an end to the war, while thousands of Japanese civilians starved to death. In addition the Allies would have had to stand idly by while Allied prisoners of war, civilian internees and indigenous slave labourers in the Japanese empire died at an estimated rate of somewhere between 100,000 and 250,000 a month. When the prisoners of war in the Dutch East Indies were finally liberated they were found to be 'absolutely at their last gasp'.[214] It seems likely that if a policy of blockade had been chosen there would have been no prisoners of war or European civilian internees left to liberate.

The American government was reluctant to wait for Japan to come to such an agonizing end. General Marshall and army planners were certain that disillusionment would set in among the American public long before it set in among the Japanese militarists. The overriding aim of the US government was to end the war in the Pacific within twelve months from May 1945.[215] General MacArthur, eager to lead the biggest amphibious assault in the history of warfare, was pushing for an invasion of the home islands. However, throughout the summer American commanders became increasingly concerned about the defences the Japanese had constructed on the island of Kyushu, where the invasion was planned to take place. By now the Americans had learned the lesson that the Japanese would fight to the death and that, once they were dug into defensive positions, they would have to be eradicated cave by cave, foxhole by foxhole, often in hand-to-hand combat. Throughout the first half of 1945 American soldiers had paid heavily for the capture of Iwo Jima and Okinawa. At Okinawa kamikaze planes had sunk thirty-six American ships and damaged 368 more. The Japanese soldiers, dug into a network of caves, had fought to the bitter end, and while only 7,401 had been captured, 92,000 died. American casualties had also been high: 12,520 dead, 36,613 wounded. The one battle for Okinawa accounted for 17 per cent of the total US marine and naval losses during the entire war.[216] On Okinawa the Americans had also witnessed the way in which the Japanese soldiers drew civilians into the battle. Soldiers and civilians had taken refuge in a complex of cave systems in the south of the island. The soldiers would send the civilians out to fetch them food and water and eventually persuaded many of them to commit suicide rather than be captured. Higa Tomiko, aged seven, wandering around the battlefield in search of her older sisters was invited to join one such group of soldiers and civilians intent on suicide. Having sunk down on her haunches to rest at the mouth of a cave 'someone spoke from the back of the cave. "Little girl, if you want to escape, now's the time. We're going to seal the entrance and blow ourselves up with a bomb. Of course, you can die along with us if you like." A shiver went right through me. I sprang out of the cave and slid down the cliff, trying to get as far away as I could. Presently, there was a loud explosion behind me.'[217] Between 62,000 and 100,000 civilians died during the battle for Okinawa.[218]

The battle for Kyushu promised to be far more bloody. Japanese commanders had taken new heart from Okinawa and were confident that they could inflict a terrible death toll upon the Americans. The army made extensive and chilling preparations for this, their final 'decisive' battle. After the surrender, Edmund J. Winslett, officer in charge of Sixth Army photographic intelligence, toured the defences of Kyushu and found a 'maze of caves' and communicating passageways, not just for supply and ammunition dumps, but for everything, including messes. There were also 12,275 kamikaze planes ready and waiting to inflict damage on the United States fleet.[219] By August 1945, 900,000 Japanese soldiers outnumbered the American invasion force of 766,700.[220] The highest estimate of casualty figures ever given to Truman for the invasion appears to have been a quarter of a million. But the estimate of W. B. Shockley, an expert on Secretary Henry Stimson's staff, seems more realistic. On 21 July 1945 he pointed out that, given the pattern of Japanese fighting behaviour so far, 'the Japanese dead and ineffectives at the time of defeat will exceed the corresponding number for the Germans. In other words, we shall probably have to kill at least five to ten million Japanese. This might cost us between 1.7 and four million casualties including 400,000 to 800,000 killed.'[221] In the end these casualty predictions were never put to the test. On 6 August the centre of the city of Hiroshima was wiped out within just a few seconds by an atomic bomb. This was the American version of the 'divine wind', and it was this that finally shocked Emperor Hirohito into taking the decision to surrender. Initially, the military refused to believe that the war was over. Anami argued that the Americans would not have enough material for more than one bomb. Hirohito appears to have wavered.[222] On 8 August the Soviets invaded Manchuria. On 9 August the citizens of Nagasaki followed those of Hiroshima into the dust. Somewhere between 100,000 and 200,000 civilians died in the atomic explosions.[223] Given the overwhelming destructive power of the new weapon, Japanese hopes for a decisive battle of attrition on Kyushu disappeared. This time the shock was great enough for the Emperor to carry the hotheads in the government with him. On 15 August 1945 the Emperor announced the Japanese surrender to his nation.

Takezawa Shoji, then a young girl, came in from the fields where she had been catching frogs. Her schoolteacher had instructed the class to catch as many as they could and then 'dry them in preparation for the decisive battle on the mainland'. She was tired and dispirited, having caught only six of the creatures. At her home she found scores of people listening to the Emperor's speech of surrender on the radio. 'To be truthful, his voice sounded as weak as I felt. I wondered if the Emperor, like us, hadn't yet eaten his lunch.' As she listened she found herself thinking about 'pumpkins, potatoes, and sweet-potato-flour cakes'.[224]

14

The Soviet Union – Fighting on Empty

Hunger and cold held our people in their merciless grip.
(Victor Kravchenko, head of the Department of War Engineering Armament for Russia)[1]

For every Briton or American that died as a result of the war, eighty-five Soviet citizens lost their lives. The Soviet Union suffered by far the highest death toll of all the combatant nations. The Japanese, in comparison, lost seven people to every Briton or American, the Germans lost twenty. The total Soviet death toll is estimated to have been somewhere between 28 and 30 million – a total which would have satisfied the Nazi architects of the Hunger Plan who intended to starve this number of Soviets to death. It represents 15 per cent of the pre-war Soviet population and about a third of all the people who died worldwide during the war. The human price the Soviets paid for victory was colossal.[2]

Of the 28–30 million dead 9 million were military, which leaves a figure of 19–21 million civilian casualties.[3] The evidence is simply not available to give a breakdown of the causes of civilian deaths. A large proportion will have been starved or shot in the German-occupied areas. But conditions in the unoccupied Soviet civilian rear were also harsh; 'food was in extremely short supply and sickness was rife'.[4] If 1 million Soviet citizens starved in Leningrad alone, then another 1–2 million Soviet deaths are almost certainly attributable to starvation. It is known that tens of thousands of prisoners starved in the Soviet gulags where the wartime decline in the food supply subjected the inmates to famine conditions.[5] In the countryside the peasants were living on the very margins of existence and a proportion of the young, the old and infirm will have succumbed to hunger. Circumstantial evidence suggests that even if famine conditions were not reached, large numbers of the vulnerable starved in the towns and cities. In Moscow in 1942 'the sight of men and women falling dead of starvation on [the] streets became too commonplace to attract crowds'.[6] Even valuable industrial workers starved. A worker in an aviation plant in Kuibyshev described how 'there were cases when people fell over from hunger' on the assembly lines. 'Some people died on the job. I personally saw two people die because of hunger.'[7] James R. Miller, writing about the impact of the Second World War on the Soviet Union, argues that the figure of 30 million war deaths does not even include 'war-related physical consequences such as those caused by chronic malnutrition'.[8] The disintegration of the agricultural sector and the food supply system meant that all but the most privileged Soviets were affected by hunger and malnutrition. This chapter asks to what extent the critical food situation in the Soviet Union threatened its ability to fight.

FEEDING THE RED ARMY

The Red Army was unprepared for the German attack on 22 June 1941. The Wehrmacht pushed its way across the Soviet Union at terrifying speed. Soldiers and civilians retreated before them in disorder, bombed by German aircraft as they fled. The soldiers ran out of ammunition, and as thousands were killed or captured still holding their guns the army began to run out of rifles. Even spades were in short supply and men had to dig trenches with their helmets.[9] In the disorganization of the retreat units were forced to abandon their cooking equipment, and about 60 per cent of the troops were left without mobile field canteens. Some divisions left their food supplies behind as they fled; in others cases the evacuation of food to the rear was so efficient that the troops in combat had nothing to eat. German soldiers described the Red Army troops that emerged from the Vyazama region as 'wild-eyed' with hunger. Caught up in the bogs of that area with no supplies they had been reduced to gnawing the bones of dead horses.[10]

A Ukrainian who was called up on the second day of the war described the chaos and lack of preparation to an interviewer for the Harvard Project on the Soviet Social System. The men were initially buoyant, confident that the Soviet Union had been preparing for the war for so long that surely everything would be well organized. But after only one or two days in the army, their morale plummeted. They were given no mattresses, and slept on the bare floorboards of the barracks. The food was abysmal and insufficient and they had to eat sitting on the floor. Having been called up in the summer they had left their warm clothes behind at home for their families to sell. But they were not even issued with uniforms. Within a few days of training their clothes were in rags.[11] They were hopelessly under-equipped and were given virtually no weapons. When they went into battle they 'lost 200 men (about 70 per cent of the battalion) in the first days of fighting, mostly because they had no weapons'. The Georgian troops broke down and cried. 'They were just like sheep.'[12]

By the end of 1941 the army had lost 4.5 million men (over half of them captured) and the Soviet Union had lost most of its fertile agricultural regions, as well as a large proportion of livestock.[13] The country faced a food crisis of immense proportions. The centralized food distribution system focused all its energies on feeding the 12–13 million men in the armed forces.[14] Red Army soldiers were allocated a frugal 2,954 calories a day on active duty. In normal circumstances this would support a moderately active man. In combat, the rations were supposed to increase to 3,450 calories a day, a good 700 calories short of what a soldier needs to eat when fighting in cold conditions. Even the relatively modest British army ration contained 5,300 calories when the men were fighting in cold climates.[15] If the stipulated amounts were too little, the actual food which they received usually contained far fewer calories. For the first year and a half of the war, the infantry's rations were only slightly better than the dismal food eaten by the civilian population. Meals for the front-line troops consisted of *kascha* (porridge) for breakfast, *borscht* (soup) for lunch, and bread and cucumber pickle for supper.[16] The Red Army field kitchens were elementary, producing meals out of buckwheat, dried fish, potatoes and as much fat as possible as this helped to keep out the cold. But in the first years of the war, it was rare for Red Army soldiers to be supplied with hot meals from a field kitchen and many survived on dry rations of bread and dried fish for weeks on end.[17] A Ukrainian drafted into the army at age sixteen went with 'great enthusiasm', eager to fight the despised Germans but he was shocked by the terrible conditions. 'The uniforms we got were used. Instead of shoes we got some kind of rags. How about food? Also bad. 700 grams of bread a day. Little fat. For the rest we got cabbage and frozen potatoes. That's all. Many got sick. Only when we got a blanket we could exchange it for food. But this was punished.'[18] Some soldiers were so desperately hungry that, despite draconian punishments if they were caught, they would sell pieces of their uniform in the markets.

The soldiers lived in *zemlyanki*, which were holes in the ground boarded up with wooden planks and roofed with turf. Sometimes divided by curtains they could be tiny, or large enough to hold as many as 400 men. At least the crowd warmed the space up a little although the air generally became rank.[19] Padded jackets and trousers, fur gloves and warm hats were sometimes available but winter boots were in short supply and some Soviet soldiers had absolutely nothing to put on their feet.[20]

For the first year chaos prevailed. The Soviets struggled with the same problems the Wehrmacht was encountering in the occupied parts of the country: poor east–west connections, inadequate roads, and an overburdened rail system. A large proportion of the rail network had been lost to the Germans, and what was left was single-track lines which caused long delays. The slow-moving trains came under constant air attack and congestion was made worse by the operation to evacuate thousands of factories. Trains filled with new recruits and supplies for the front line had to wait while the trains evacuating the factories passed in the other direction. Most of the rail lines radiated out from Moscow, which meant that supplies had to be sent first to Moscow and then out to their destination. The return journey was made with empty wagons. This severely hampered the movement of food from surplus areas to the towns and to sections of the front line where it was needed. By 1942 the turn-around time for freight cars had increased from seven to thirteen days.[21] Later that year the Germans cut the rail line running from Moscow to Stalingrad; the only connection left was a fragile line that ran close to the front line, or a much longer detour via Astrakhan and the Caspian Sea.[22]

A Ukrainian soldier recalled that the unreliability of the overburdened transport system meant that 'sometimes the unit would be fairly well fed and sometimes it would be hungry but there was always enough vodka and cheap tobacco . . . About twenty or thirty kilometres in the rear food was not so bad at all but the supply of food was very irregular.'[23] At the Volkhov front near Leningrad during 1942–43 a doctor described how sometimes the food supply would dry up completely for two days.[24] Corruption aggravated the supply problems. In March 1942 a journalist for the *Krasnaya Zvezda* reported that soldiers on the Kalinin front north of Moscow were starving. The quartermaster, General Andrei Khrulev, went to investigate and to his disgust found the report to be true. The officers were using the transport problems to mask the fact that they were selling off the food on the black market. The culprits were sent to penal battalions. Despite such harsh punishment it was a common practice for officers to siphon off meat and vegetables to sell on the black market.[25]

The failure of the centralized food distribution system to provide a consistent and balanced food supply across the Red Army is exemplified by the disparities to be found in the food stocks of the 64th, 57th and 51st Armies, all of which were on the south-eastern front, defending Stalingrad in the summer of 1942. The 64th Army was in the worst position and was virtually out of food, with barely three days' worth of flour and bread, just over three days' worth of meat and no fish or fats. The situation of the 51st Army was not much better but they did have a ridiculously large reserve store of fifty-nine days' worth of fat. Neither of these armies had any sugar. In contrast, the 57th was comparatively well off with a month's worth of stocks of sugar, and about a week's worth of flour, bread, cereals, meat, fish and fats. Reflecting the administrative disorganization behind these shortages, plans to bring food up to the front line were only formulated by the Chief Administration of Food Supplies of the Soviet Army (*Glavprodsnab*) a week after the Germans had captured the outer suburbs of the city. Food stocks were stored on the left bank of the River Volga, which meant that they had to be brought across on barges under a barrage of German bombs.[26]

The city of Stalingrad was reduced to 'an enormous cloud of burning, blinding smoke; it is a vast furnace lit by the reflection of the flames'.[27] The fighting took place in heaps of rubble amid ruined buildings. A German Panzer division lieutenant described how in the house-to-house battles, 'The front is a corridor between burnt-out rooms: it is the thin ceiling between two floors ... eighty days and eighty nights of hand-to-hand struggles. The street is no longer measured in metres, but in corpses.'[28] Even once the food was across the river it was virtually impossible to bring meals up to soldiers engaged in this sort of battle. The brave cook of one Soviet anti-tank detachment would strap a large army thermos to his back and crawl up to the point where the troops were under fire to bring them soup or warming tea.[29] But more often than not the hungry soldiers had to forage in cellars for whatever food the civilians had left behind. One Soviet veteran recalled, 'Whatever we saw we ate. There was no regular supply of food. In Stalingrad I ate horses and dogs.'[30]

In the end, however, it was the encircled Germans who starved. The Red Army caught General Paulus's 6th Army in what became known as the Kessel, or cauldron, in late November 1942. The German high command instructed Paulus to hold out and he was told that the Luftwaffe would fly supplies in to the men. But the plan to airlift food and arms was never feasible given the weather conditions and the number of available planes.[31] Infantryman Heinz Pfennig recalled that, 'Bread was doled out. There was rarely any extra food. Our potatoes were just dried potato flakes.'[32] The soup was hot water with a few pieces of horsemeat floating in it. A fellow soldier, Wilhelm Hoffmann, recorded in his diary, 'The horses have already been eaten. I would eat a cat, they say its meat is also tasty. The soldiers look like corpses or lunatics, looking for something to put in their mouths.'[33] At Hitler's headquarters General Kurt Zeitzler confined himself to the same rations as were available for the men caught in the cauldron and lost 11 kilograms in two weeks. Irritated, Hitler ordered him to eat properly. He did not wish to be reminded of the reality of the situation.[34] When General Paulus surrendered to the Soviets, who had pressed into the city and finally retaken it, Hitler was furious.

Stalingrad was a psychological turning-point on the eastern front as both sides felt that the tide had turned and that the Red Army had finally gained the upper hand in the conflict. But the winter of 1942–43 did not mark a turning-point in the Red Army's food situation. A theatre manager, who was an officer during the war, explained to his Harvard interviewer, 'after Stalingrad, we had no products or food for our men ... Our soldiers had only cabbage to eat. I decided to permit them to steal food.'[35] He was reported and taken before the commander of the division. 'He asked me why I had permitted this, and I replied that my soldiers were hungry, that everyone was hungry, and that the hunger of my soldiers was none of his affair. I was sentenced to go to a penal battalion.'[36] Incredibly, he survived the punishment and was released just as the Red Army retook Kharkov. 'I started everything anew ... I finished the war as a senior lieutenant.'[37] The theatre manager's decision was not unusual. Red Army units horribly abused the slogan 'everything for the front'.[38] They would go into the villages and round up horses, commandeer food from the collective farms and raid peasants' private supplies of honey and potatoes.

The soldiers became expert foragers. One veteran recalled how he would collect nettles with his comrades. They picked goosefoot (*lebeda*) and gathered frozen potatoes abandoned by fleeing civilians. In the fields they dug up garlic and onions and made green soup, motivated by an 'intuitive belief ... that they could get important nutrients from these foods'.[39] Soviet soldiers would often stave off scurvy by making a foul brew of boiled pine needles, rich in vitamin C. Vera Vladimirovna Milutina, a survivor of the Leningrad siege, recalled trucks driving through the streets of besieged Leningrad carrying soldiers who had been out in the countryside collecting pine and spruce branches. 'They were extracting vitamins from the pine needles, and this infusion, I had heard, worked miracles on the starving wounded in the hospitals.'[40] The soldiers once tossed her a heap of branches and she gnawed on them all the way home. 'I totally devoured their tender bark and needles ... we had neither the strength nor the time to cut needles and put them into boiling water.'[41] Red Army soldiers usually carried a bag with them into which they could stuff any chance booty. These were a military extension of the 'just in case' bags which Soviet civilians began to carry around with them in the 1930s on the off-chance that they might come across some rare household goods or food.[42] Helmut Geidel, a German who fought with the 14th Panzer Division on the eastern front, recalled that after one battle he found a dead Russian with the head of a dog in his bag which he obviously intended to eat when the opportunity to cook it arose.[43]

The pre-war years of turmoil, poverty and deprivation had inured the Soviet people to low standards of care. This would have helped the soldiers to endure the appalling wartime conditions. For those who believed in the communist project, the promise of a brighter future may well have motivated them to fight. But on both sides of the eastern front repressive discipline and fear of the draconian punishments for cowardice and desertion were also powerful factors which kept the hungry men at their posts. For the Soviets a further powerful preventative against desertion was the severe punishment inflicted on the families of those men who went missing in action (and were thus not confirmed dead) as well as on the families of men taken prisoner.[44]

The fighting on the eastern front descended into an orgy of brutality which gave the conflict a powerful internal momentum.[45] Tales spread through the Red Army of the murderous actions of both the Wehrmacht and the SS within occupied territory, and Soviet soldiers gradually became aware that Red Army prisoners of war were being deliberately starved to death. In response, the Soviets became frighteningly vengeful, which, in turn, escalated the brutality of the Germans. Hans-Ulrich Greffrath, an officer in the Wehrmacht, claimed, 'we fought with ever-increasing defiance and bitterness not because we were Nazis, but because of the terrible experiences we had at the front. We saw mutilated soldiers who had fallen into the hands of the Russians – soldiers without noses, without eyes . . . We knew we had to keep on fighting if we wanted to prevent this sort of thing from happening to our families at home.'[46] His sentiments were shared by the Soviets, who were united in a hatred and horror of the Germans and fear of the annihilation of their society, which would surely result from a German victory. It was the conviction among ordinary soldiers that the consequences of failure in battle would be apocalyptic that gave Red Army soldiers every reason to fight, with or without adequate food rations. It is a testament to their determination that they eventually proved such a formidable force despite the fact that well into 1943 they were fighting on empty stomachs.

FEEDING THE CITIES

In the years leading up to the Second World War the people of the Soviet Union had faced one disruption to normal life after another. The First World War, the Bolshevik revolution, and the civil war had cost about 15 million lives and steadily lowered the standard of living.[47] One Russian recalled how 'from the time of the Revolution in 1917 . . . the people have become more reticent, sullen . . . Every person tries to protect his own interests. For him, his food is everything.'[48] By 1920 Russian workers were eating about half the amount of food they had consumed just before the First World War.[49] Then, at the end of the 1920s, private enterprise was outlawed by the communist regime and almost overnight the state became the only distributor of goods. The result was the intensification of shortages and the growth of queues and waiting lists for everything from food and clothes to housing and medical care. Government stores were often bare and the Russian diet became yet more limited, with poor-quality foods such as horsemeat and ersatz tea made of apples the norm.[50]

The 1930s were worse than the 1920s. The reverberations of poor harvests, collectivization and famine in the countryside were felt in the cities as refugees from rural hunger flooded into the urban areas. Urban life was characterized by intensely overcrowded housing, a shaky electricity and fuel supply and a lack of the most basic essentials such as shoes, clothes, pots and pans. Life developed into a constant struggle to acquire basic necessities and people would spend hours standing in queues hoping to buy tiny quantities of substandard food.[51] By 1933 Soviets were consuming one-fifth of the amount of meat and fish that they would have eaten around 1900.[52] The promise that after the class struggle communism would deliver a far higher quality of life slipped ever further into the future. But in the end the deprivations of these years stood the Soviet population in good stead, inuring them to the much worse conditions which prevailed during the Second World War.

In the first year of the war, industry disintegrated into a state of disarray similar to that of the Red Army. Much of the country's industrial capacity was in the west. Throughout the summer and autumn of 1941, 1,500 factories were taken apart and, along with many of the workers, were sent on a laborious journey to the Urals, central Asia and Siberia, where they were reassembled.[53] On arrival in the new location, parts were often missing, tools and equipment scarce, power supplies low and the labour force was usually below full strength. There was often nowhere for the workers to live, and at one tank factory in the east more than 8,000 women workers lived in earth bunkers, dug into the ground. Despite the confusion and hardship the saving of these plants was a major feat which contributed a great deal to Soviet industrial survival.[54] Nevertheless, the Wehrmacht overran factories with a total annual capacity of 13 million shells. Only one-third of the target number of shells was produced in 1941 and tank production could not keep up with the heavy losses at the front.[55] Just to sustain the most basic defence against the German onslaught, let alone attempt to mount a counter-offensive, the Soviets had to pour all their energies into producing arms.

In the drive to supply the troops with weapons, *everything* else fell by the wayside. Even subsidiary industries such as iron and steel, coal and oil were neglected. In 1941–42 the civilian sector of the economy virtually collapsed. The clothing industry produced only half its normal quantity of goods, but most of these were uniforms and woollens for the military. Ordinary people found it almost impossible to get hold of new clothes or shoes.[56] The transport systems in the towns and cities began to falter for lack of fuel and people were forced to walk to work. Electricity was reserved for the armaments factories, and ordinary homes were only supplied for a few hours at a time. There was a severe shortage of fuel for heating or cooking; there were no new pots and pans to replace those that were worn out; there was virtually no soap for washing of clothes or bodies. In these extreme circumstances it became increasingly difficult to sustain even the most basic daily life.[57]

Victor Kravchenko, an industrial party official who was to defect to the United States at the end of the war, described how in the first winter, as the Germans approached Moscow, the city, 'like an individual . . . suffer[ed] a nervous breakdown . . . The blacked-out capital to which I returned was hungry, frostbitten, pockmarked by enemy bombs. It seemed broken in spirit and almost too weary to despair. Its people . . . dragged themselves from frozen homes to labour long hours in under-heated plants and offices . . . the official rations were barely enough to sustain life but the shops could rarely meet these pitiful food requirements.'[58] The physicist Andrei Sakharov recalled that among all the privations of daily life, 'the worst thing was the continual hunger'.[59] Irene Rush, an Australian teacher of English who lived through the war in Moscow, described how the 'food pinch' began in August with the issue of milk cards for children. 'Very little sugar was being given on the ration cards. There was no salt; and potatoes were getting scarce. Everyone was on the trail to buy a little extra food at the "commercial" shops, especially oil or clarified butter . . . Word would fly round: "there's oil at such and such shop", and people would seize their billies and hasten there, joining a queue that already contained perhaps hundreds of people . . . On entering the shop after hours of waiting people became more tense and silent: all feared to hear the dreaded words: "The oil (or what have you) is finished, go home citizens!"'[60] By the end of the winter every dog, cat and crow in the capital had been caught and eaten.

Irene Rush and her friends scraped by on a peculiar assortment of substitute foods. A friend made up food packages of throat pastilles, cough drops and 'some horrible "sea cabbage" that looked like grey-green chaff and tasted like concentrated iodine' from the chemist shops.[61] There was no longer any point in queuing up for cooking oil, and they took to frying their food in Vaseline or paraffin oil. Doctors warned that the old and the young were beginning to display the signs of serious vitamin deficiency.[62] 'Hunger and cold became more of a threat than the Luftwaffe.' The Muscovites sat huddled in their apartments, wrapped up in coats and shawls, even gloves, in total darkness behind their blacked-out windows. 'Life was difficult and joyless.'[63] The bodies of people who had collapsed from hunger began to appear on the streets.

This breakdown in ordinary civilian life was replicated 'in a small-scale episodic, yet widespread fashion . . . across the whole country through all the years of war'.[64] When the power supply broke down, the lights went out and the factories and shops closed, people retreated to their freezing apartments. Exhausted by long walks to work, the

awful struggle to wash and cook, far too little poor-quality and innutritious food, they despairingly chopped up and burned their furniture
and books to keep warm, and many died quietly of hunger. These
sporadic and dispersed crises will have accounted for a large number
of the Soviet civilian deaths from starvation which went almost un-
noticed and unrecorded.[65] The collapse of ordinary civilian life was a
serious threat to the war effort. It was essential to keep the metal
industries running, which supplied the munitions factories with their
raw materials. When fuel was in short supply and the transport sector
collapsed, workers struggled to get to their factories. Most crucially of
all, it was vital to supply the food rations which kept the workers in
the munitions factories alive. Without a civilian economy the entire
war industry was in danger of grinding to a halt.[66]

Before the war almost the entire calorific intake of the Soviet urban
population was supplied by state-run shops. When the Germans
attacked in June 1941 the communist system of central planning
could not cope with the demands of prioritizing *everything* at once
and food officials concentrated on feeding the army.[67] A semblance
of a rationing system was adopted but the idea that this was in order
to distribute shortages equally across the population was meaning-
less in the Soviet context. Workers and townspeople were provided
with ration cards but the entitlements stated on them represented a
set of aspirations. If they had received the amounts of bread, flour,
cereals, sugar, fats, meat and fish allocated by their ration cards,
Soviets would have been eating about a half of the caloric consumption of American citizens.[68] Even this would have been a meagre diet
for people engaged in hard manual labour, living and working in
cold houses and factories (keeping warm uses up calories), with a
daily life which included many arduous household tasks. But the
system could rarely provide the foods on the card in anything like
the stated quantities. A Ukrainian military cartographer, who escaped
from the Soviet Union after the war, told his American interviewer
in the 1950s a joke which summed up the Soviet wartime experience
of food. 'One Muscovite meets another and asks, "How are you
doing?" "Like Lenin." "What do you mean like Lenin?" "That is
simple: they have not buried me, but they are not giving me anything
to eat."'[69]

Nevertheless, disillusion with the government did not set in to the same extent as it had done during the First World War. People's faith in the government was sustained by the fact that Stalin's regime made it clear that it was committed to feeding the cities even at the expense of the countryside.[70] The extreme food shortages were not caused by the fact that the peasants were being allowed to hoard stores of food, but because there simply was not enough food. The only item on the ration card which the state did guarantee to provide was bread. It was poor quality and black, made with inferior grains, but four-fifths of the calories and proteins that people obtained from their rations came from this bread. After the Red Army, industrial workers received priority in terms of food supply, and the greatest advantage they had over other citizens was their entitlement to a larger ration of bread. Those working in the heaviest industries received four or five times as much as those at the bottom of the scale.[71] In Rostov the women working in heavy industrial factories were there because the work entitled them to a 'first- or second-category food ration card, that is to say eight hundred or six hundred grams of bread'.[72] One former worker recalled, '[I did] not underestimate the six hundred grams of bread that came with my job.'[73]

By the end of the war, women made up just over half the heavy industrial workforce, and 80 per cent of the workers in light industry.[74] Alongside the women, worked many young boys and teenagers. Agrippina Mikhailovna Khromova, who worked as a lathe turner in an electromechanical plant in Moscow, recalled that as the men were called up to the front, 'schoolboys and teenagers arrived at the plant. I worked as a machinist and instructed these boys and girls. You know, they couldn't even reach the machines!'[75] Teenagers were drawn to war work by the food. Once they reached the age of twelve, adolescents lost the extra rations they had received as children and were reclassified as dependants. This group received the lowest rations despite the fact that they required a highly calorific diet in order to grow. Indeed, they were at an extremely high risk of starving to death if they tried to survive on a dependant's ration. In Leningrad a fifteen-year-old machine operator remarked: 'It is no secret that . . . boys tried every means possible to get into the factory, because at the factory canteen you could get three bowls of hot yeast soup and a bottle of soya milk in exchange for a ration coupon for 12 and a half grams of groats.'[76] Throughout the country teenagers sought out factory work as a survival strategy.

If their higher bread ration was a blessing, it was also held over workers' heads as a threat. Absenteeism could be punished by the withdrawal of a proportion of the ration. Manual workers could lose as much as a quarter of their daily bread, an office worker one-fifth. Since ration bread was virtually the only source of protein and energy, this was a real incentive not to break the rules.[77] Andrei Sakharov, having graduated from university in the autumn of 1942, was sent to work in a cartridge factory in Ulyanovsk. He described the working conditions for the women at his factory: 'They sat at the deafening machines hour after hour, in huge, dimly lit rooms, hunched over and perched cross-legged on their stools to keep their wooden shoes off the cold floor, which was flooded with water and lubricants. Their faces were hidden by kerchiefs but when I caught a glimpse of them, I could see that they were lifeless, drained by fatigue.' Many of the women from the countryside had left children behind at home and worried about them but it was impossible to get leave to visit them and if they went absent they risked five years in a labour camp. 'The only escape was to get pregnant.'[78]

At the cartridge factory Sakharov discovered that even obtaining the bread ration was not always easy. The deliveries were irregular and 'a worker from the night shift might have to stand in line from eight a.m. till the middle of the afternoon before getting his ration. Since he had to be back at work by eight p.m. he had practically no time to sleep. And you couldn't leave the line for a moment – try it, and you'd never get your place back in the silent, unyielding queue.'[79] While in Germany or Britain food queues were a tiring annoyance, in the Soviet Union they drained the energy and used up precious time which could have been spent sleeping. A second problem was how to 'cash in' the rest of the ration cards. 'Coupons for groats, butter, and sugar were often wasted, having expired by the end of the month, unless they were traded for bread coupons or were spent in the canteen, since most of the time nothing of the kind could be found in the stores.'[80] Frequently one food substituted for another. Instead of meat, eggs might be distributed, or a little honey rather than sugar. An inhabitant of Rostov recalled that nothing could ever be relied upon and a mysterious law appeared to govern these substitutions. At times they could be heartbreaking. A worker at a defence plant in Kuibyshev remembered that in the winter of 1941–42 they were given chocolate as a substitute for everything, even meat and bread. Even many years after the end of the war she still could not 'look at chocolate'.[81]

At the beginning of 1942 the fate of the Soviet Union looked bleak. No contemporary observer would have confidently predicted that the Soviets would not only hold out against the Germans but eventually be crucial in bringing about their defeat. Foreign Minister Vyacheslav Molotov conceded to the American embassy that 'non-essential workers were "living on [a] restricted ration, one which provides them with a bare subsistence level of nutrition"'.[82] The officials in the food offices, who had to make decisions about the quantity of food which would be distributed to the different types of consumer, were in the unenviable position of deciding who they should abandon to starvation.[83] Desperate hunger caused a wave of crime to sweep across the Soviet Union as the hungry raided gardens and food stores.[84] Those at the margins of society, the elderly and the infirm, were dying of hunger. One Russian émigré remembered the *dokhodiagi* (people on the verge of death) who lurked at the edges of a dining room for sick children in Chernikovsk, licking the plates once the children had finished eating.[85] US naval intelligence officer Kemp Tolley was haunted by the spectacle of little knots of 'starved wretches' who gathered on the docks at Molotovsk near Archangel where shipments of lend-lease food were being unloaded. They would scoop up and wolf down by the fistful 'raw meat, and scraps or steaming chicken guts thrown out with the [American] ship's galley garbage'.[86] This grisly feast was made at great risk of the guards seizing them. Under one ship's slop chute lay a body covered by a blanket of snow; he or she had been shot down by the guards while hunting for scraps.[87]

Even as late as August 1943 American analysts were worried that 'the present stringencies in food and manpower' would 'by the summer of 1944 ... prove a serious impairment to Russia's military capabilities'.[88] Given that the Soviets were doing most of the fighting against the Wehrmacht, holding down 189 German divisions on the eastern front, in contrast to just fourteen against the Allied forces in Italy, this was a source of real concern.[89] However, beginning in the spring of 1942, the Soviets managed to restructure and initiate recovery, first in the armaments industries and the military and then in 1943 in the civilian economy. Years of unreasonable quotas and demands from above meant that industrial managers had become adept at concealing spare capacity from their superiors so that their targets would not be raised to impossible heights. During the war they used this slack to increase productivity.[90] The imposition of communist rule had suppressed individual ingenuity but in the special circumstances of war the controls over management eased. Once officials realized that taking responsibility would not necessarily have fatal repercussions, they demonstrated great resourcefulness.[91] With the transportation system stretched to its limits central distribution no longer worked and as a consequence self-sufficiency flourished. Factories began producing their own raw materials, machine tools and components, some industrial plants set up their own steelworks and trained their workers to repair as well as run the machinery.[92] Even in the gulags the factories producing uniforms manufactured their own needles, thread and parts for sewing machines.[93]

While managers were afforded greater freedom, controls over the workers tightened. The Soviet war machine maintained the communist principle that an atmosphere of terror would force people to find a way of meeting impossible demands. The factories were treated as part of the front line. From September 1942 leaving employment without permission was regarded as a form of desertion. Holidays were banned, working hours were extended, slackers or absentees risked being sent to a labour camp. On occasion soldiers escorted the workers to the factories.[94] A senior Russian engineer who worked in munitions factories throughout the war recalled that the tired and hungry workers were fearful. They lived at the mercy of the director, who could withdraw their status as essential war workers (bronya) at his whim and turn them over to the military committee.[95] But as Victor Kravchenko discovered, there were physical limits to what under-fed workers could achieve.

In May 1942 Kravchenko was made head of the Department of War

Engineering Armament for the Sovnarkom.* In effect he was put in charge of armaments factories throughout Russia. 'In line of duty I visited a great many factories where output was lagging. Invariably I found that food shortage was one of the main reasons.'[96] In the winter of 1942–43 he was horrified to see that the workers in the factories were 'gaunt with hunger'.[97] This was having a disastrous impact on productivity. 'Neither Stalin's terse commands nor Beria's "strong measures"', he commented sourly, 'could squeeze adequate equipment from factories lacking raw materials and operated by workers on a starvation diet.'[98] He noted that where factories were able to provide their employees with one fairly nourishing meal this speeded up the tempo of production. '"Give us more food and we'll give you more goods," the executives always pleaded. "Our people haven't the strength to meet your deadlines".'[99] But when Kravchenko presented his superior with a plan to increase production in a particular factory by providing the workers with 500 grams of bread a day, he was told, 'Look here. Are you a social worker or a Bolshevik? Humanitarianism is a bad guide in making state decisions. Learn from comrade Stalin – love the people but sacrifice their needs when essential!'[100]

Yet at the Kremlin Kravchenko found himself 'among men who could eat ample and dainty food in full view of starving people not only with a clear conscience but with a feeling of righteousness, as if they were performing a duty to history'.[101] Kravchenko was surprised to discover that breakfast at the Kremlin consisted of eggs, stewed meat, white bread, and tea with sugar and biscuits. After he had eaten his fill he would still have enough left over to pass on some food to his secretary, his waitress and her two children.[102] Stalin certainly did not stint himself during the war. At Kremlin banquets caviar, fish and meat were all washed down with liberal quantities of vodka, wine and cognac.[103] It was a bitter reality that during these years of terrible privation the communist elite was cushioned from the suffering, just as they had always been. When the state monopoly on the distribution of goods was introduced in the 1920s a system of closed stores was set up which were only open to the employees of certain factories or offices. In theory they were supposed to protect the working population

* RSFSR – Russian Federation Council of People's Commissars.

from shortages but in effect they created elites with privileged access to scarce goods.[104] As a member of the Sovnarkom, Kravchenko was entitled to shop at closed stores which stocked 'bacon, canned goods, butter, sugar, flour, salt pork – all brought in from the United States – as well as Soviet fish, fowl, smoked fish, vegetables, vodka, wine, cigarettes . . . Not one Russian in a thousand suspected that such abundant shops existed and, indeed, the authorities operated them discreetly, as far as possible out of sight of the masses. There was usually a line-up of elegant motorcars outside our "closed" food store, for instance, but few passers-by knew what they were there for. No ordinary Muscovite got a glimpse, let alone a taste, of the lend-lease and home-made luxury piled up in that shop.'[105]

Meanwhile, many factory administrators took the initiative and tried to remedy the dire food situation of their workers by applying the principle of self-sufficiency to the rationing system as well as to industrial production. Allotments were dug and in the new industrial area based in the Urals–Volga–Siberia heartland, 7 million gardens sprang up beside the newly reassembled factories. The cabbages and potatoes which they grew were used to supplement the workers' canteen meals. It has been estimated that factory gardens contributed about 250 calories a day to each worker's diet.[106] Given the low ration, this was not a negligible contribution and by 1944 this source of food was vital to about 25 million people.[107]

Despite their important contribution to workers' diets, factory meals were not particularly impressive. One Russian worker recalled that her factory served 'a thin soup made of gritts [corn porridge], or beet leaves, or nettles, or rarely cabbage. The second dish is gritts or potatoes, (or rarely) meat – little fresh meat, mostly herring or hard coarse sausage made of meat scraps'.[108] This supplemented her 600 grams of ration bread. War workers in a factory in Kuibyshev were given watery soup and an occasional glass of milk made from milk powder.[109] At Sakharov's factory, for lunch each worker was given 'a few spoonfuls of millet porridge mixed with American powdered eggs'. The porridge was served on 'sheets of paper and eaten on the spot, washed down with ersatz tea'. There were no utensils available. Demonstrating the ingenuity of the wartime factories, their shop 'eventually managed to stamp out spoons' for all the workers.[110]

The principle of privilege was maintained even under these grievous circumstances. Directors, managers and engineers ate in separate canteens where more and higher-quality food was served. In Leningrad during the siege, bread, sugar, cutlets and small pies were said to have been available at the canteen for the party headquarters at Smolny.[111] Agrippina Khromova recalled how at her plant in Moscow, 'when I worked as a forewoman, they gave me special food rations. We ate in a dining hall and then went home. But the rations weren't given out to everybody. It was a terrible thing. You sat, you ate, and people were standing behind you and waiting; maybe something would be left, and they could eat.'[112]

Miners, defence industry workers labouring under particularly difficult conditions, and a number of selected factories were eventually given extra bread rations.[113] But despite the advantages of a bigger bread ration and supplementary soups made from vegetables grown in the factory gardens, many workers would only have been eating somewhere around 2,000 calories a day, which was insufficient to maintain the health of a person undertaking strenuous physical activity who really needed between 3,500 and 4,000 calories.[114] If German workers on their more generous rations lost weight, the Soviet workers must also have lost a considerable amount of weight over the course of the war. The evidence for the rest of the Soviet Union is scanty, but in Leningrad it was common for workers who were *not* emaciated and who appeared to feel well to suddenly collapse and die, afflicted by a metabolic crisis induced by starvation.[115] Aviation workers in Kuibyshev were also recorded as having collapsed on the assembly line.[116] There are no records of how many workers died from hunger and exhaustion at their workplace but it does not seem improbable that there would have been thousands of such deaths.

It is incredible that Soviet workers managed to put in a gruelling working day of between twelve and sixteen hours and 'in the middle years of the war . . . produced three aircraft for every two German, and almost double the number of tanks'.[117] In 1942 the concentration on armaments production, which had put such enormous strain on the entire system, began to pay off. In this year the factories began to supply not only enough ammunition to keep the soldiers fighting but also better equipment and this was channelled into a restructured army.

Stalin conceded that the military command was better off in the hands of his more competent generals. New tank corps, using the formidable T-34 tanks, were joined by fast-moving armed units which deployed the Katyusha rockets, greatly feared by the Germans.[118] By the end of 1942 the Soviets could concentrate seventy to eighty tanks along a kilometre of the front line, whereas in 1941 they had been able to muster only three.[119] The Red Army first matched and then overtook the Wehrmacht in terms of firepower, and the balance shifted from manpower to weaponry. Indeed, it was the sheer amount of Soviet firepower which eventually defeated the Germans.[120] In the autumn of 1943, Guy Sajer, 'plodding . . . at the rate of three miles an hour' along the Konotop–Kiev road in flight from the Red Army, recalled 'our mobility, which had always given us an advantage over the vast but slow Soviet formations, was now only a memory, and the disproportion of numbers made even flight a doubtful prospect. Moreover, the equipment of the Red Army was constantly improving, and we often found ourselves pitted against extremely mobile motorized regiments of fresh troops.'[121] Lend-lease equipment from America also helped. American-supplied radios and telephones improved communications. American trucks liberated the Soviets from the limitations of their network of rail and horse-drawn wagons while freeing up Soviet factories to concentrate on tank manufacture.[122] Then, in July 1943, the tank battle at Kursk 'ended any realistic prospect of German victory in the east' and the Red Army began the long slow battle to push the Wehrmacht back towards the German border.[123]

By 1943 the supplementary industries – producing coal, steel and other raw materials as well as power – and the railways, were no longer lurching from crisis to crisis and had recovered to some extent.[124] The civilian economy was running again in most places, even if at a low ebb. Breakdowns continued to occur but in isolation. The likelihood of complete collapse across the entire nation was no longer imminent. Soviet central planning eventually proved itself amazingly effective in organizing the industrial economy but it remained entirely inadequate when it came to feeding the general population.[125]

In 1942 the communist government, which before the war had tried to take responsibility for every crumb of food eaten by the urban population, now openly changed its tactics and devolved responsibility for finding food on to the individual. President Mikhail Kalinin told the Soviet people, 'if you wish to take part in the victory over the German fascist invaders, then you must plant as many potatoes as possible'.[126] In Britain digging for victory provided people with supplementary vitamins and variety in the diet, whereas in the Soviet Union it made a real difference to people's chances of survival. Margaret Wettlin, an American married to a Russian theatre director, recalled that it took time for people's gardening efforts to bear fruit and it was not until 1943 that the gardening campaign really made an impact on people's diets. 'All Russia was gripped by the garden campaign. Plots were distributed to individuals and groups through factories and institutions. Posters reminded that potatoes were a substitute for bread. Newspapers and magazines were full of articles teaching and advising amateur gardeners how to get a crop. There was a nightly and especially a week-end exodus to the suburbs, with travellers on the trams armed with spades and hoes neatly wrapped up to avoid injury to fellow passengers.'[127] The number of private gardens tripled between 1942 and 1944.[128] Irene Rush recalled that in the summer of 1943 Moscow 'floated in a green sea of potato plants. Even rubbish tips had been cleared of rubbish, levelled out and neatly planted.'[129] Rush and her friends fried the potatoes in a 'smelly kind of greenish oil that people dubbed American machine oil'.[130] Potatoes became known as the 'second bread'.[131] If food became bland and monotonous in Britain or Germany, it was far worse in the Soviet Union where the meals often consisted only of potatoes. 'People cooked nothing but potatoes. They boiled potatoes, fried potatoes, roasted potatoes. They made potato cakes, potato soup, potato fritters. But every effort to disguise the outer form left the soul of the potato unchanged. You could see this when people paled on biting into the latest deception.'[132]

In a rather more desperate effort to extend food supplies the Soviet Academy of Sciences gathered together a commission to assess the suitability for human consumption of a range of wild meats. The list included foxes, gophers and mice, and a pamphlet on feral meat was produced which advised that squirrel meat contained more calories than pork. Leaflets were also printed detailing how to cook nettles, which are rich in protein and vitamins.[133] It seems quite likely that the hungry Soviets took the nutritionists' advice. Lydia Usova recalled sitting in a park during the siege of Leningrad, 'watching sparrows hopping about, and I found I had purely felt instincts – if only I could catch one of the sparrows and make soup of it! . . . there were the weeds we began to eat. In the mornings I would get up at about four o'clock and go to any refuse dump and pick nettles. If I managed to collect a handkerchief full it was wonderful!'[134]

In the extreme conditions of the war, the communist regime allowed the revival of the system of collective farm markets which it had long been trying to suppress. In effect it legitimized, or at least turned a blind eye to, the black market. The farm markets were the only places where milk and vegetables were sold.[135] The Australian diplomat J. A. Alexander noted that at the government store where he bought his food 'there were no eggs, fresh milk, fruit or vegetables to be bought at any price'.[136] The peasants were struggling to feed themselves, and as the quantity of food sold at these markets fell significantly the scarcity of food meant that collective market prices were astronomical.[137] In the 1930s a kilogram of potatoes on the collective farm market cost one rouble, compared to 18 kopeks in the state-run stores. In August 1944 Alexander noted that in the Moscow markets 'half a dozen lbs [2.7 kg] of potatoes costs 20 roubles'.[138] Only those with wealth, in the form of either cash or good-quality clothes and other household goods, were able to benefit fully from the markets. Nikolai Novikov, a middle-ranking Soviet diplomat who was evacuated to Kuibyshev, complained bitterly that his family's ration was insufficient to feed even the children. He was fortunate to be able to barter the family's clothes for butter, meat and milk.[139] Margaret Wettlin observed that the Soviets were willing to barter anything they had for food. 'People had developed the most absolute indifference to things . . . Only life was important . . . Dresses could go, furs could go, watches could go, shoes could go, everything formerly cherished could go without so much as a hanging on with the eyes. People would come in naked to the finish. And they did not care.'[140] But many Soviets had neither money nor spare clothes. For those without such capital, bread became an alternative currency. It was forbidden to exchange ration bread for any other foodstuff, but in the collective farm market in Kuibyshev one kilogram of black bread, or about two days' ration for a worker in the defence industry, could buy 300 grams of meat, or

160 grams of butter, perhaps six eggs, or 2 litres of milk, or 2 kilograms of potatoes.[141]

Irene Rush, who struggled through the war on the minuscule ration allowance of a non-industrial worker, could not really afford the collective farm markets. By the winter of 1942 her diet was reduced to soup made from dried potato peelings and the ration bread of 400 grams a day, supplemented by a little horseradish or mustard, 'a little lump of sugar for our faintly coloured hot water (tea)', and an occasional half pint of milk or half a cabbage bought at the peasant market for twenty times the normal price.[142] She and her friends, with their clothes hanging off their bodies, had begun to look like 'waxworks figures that had started to melt'.[143] Instead of bartering at the markets she would (illegally) go out into the countryside along with vast numbers of Muscovites with rucksacks packed with 'lace curtains, needles, combs, dress materials and shoes . . . and even hand sewing machines and gramophones'.[144] If they were fortunate, they returned with them stuffed full of potatoes and cabbages. Irene and her friends would also try to find work on the collective farms so that they would have access to vegetables. Nevertheless, their 'faces grew puffy with dropsy and lack of vitamins'.[145] Like the Red Army soldiers she and her flatmate used to make a bitter vitamin C brew out of pine needles steeped in water.[146]

THE AMERICAN LIFELINE

In 1943 the Soviet Union overtook Britain as the principal recipient of American lend-lease food. Shipments of lend-lease equipment and food began arriving in the Soviet Union in November 1941. But between 1941 and 1943 the Soviet Union only received about 30 per cent of the amount of food sent to Britain.[147] In 1943 this shifted and it is estimated that lend-lease foodstuffs increased the availability of sugar and vegetables in the Soviet Union by as much as a half, and the availability of meat by one-fifth, while it probably doubled the amount of fats in the country.[148] Without the American supplies of food many more Soviet civilians would undoubtedly have starved to death.

Food made up only 14 per cent of the total lend-lease tonnage but, apart from cereals and grains, it consisted of highly concentrated foods, such as dehydrated vegetables and eggs, canned meat, milk, butter and fruits and vegetables, dried fruits and nuts.[149] Soviet documentation, which would help to assess exactly how significant lend-lease food was, is lacking, but its important contribution to the war effort is indicated by the fact that food and raw materials were the two items for which Stalin always pressed the hardest.[150] Lend-lease food would have been sufficient to provide one pound (or just under half a kilogram) of high-quality, high-calorie food per day for 6 million soldiers.[151] As they opened American cans, Soviet soldiers are said to have joked, 'Well boys, here is the opening of the Second Front.'[152] Canned meat may have been a poor substitute for military intervention in the west but the soldiers were grateful for the copious tins of Spam. These replaced the dried fish which had been virtually the only source of protein in the front-line ration. Dried fish had two distinct disadvantages. It did little to satisfy hunger and it made the soldiers very thirsty. Drinking to relieve the thirst was no trivial matter for a rifleman in a foxhole within range of German snipers as it meant that he needed to urinate frequently. Spam solved this problem while it also satisfied the stomach, was far higher in calories, and was immune to the depredations of rats while in storage.[153]

Most of the American food probably went to feed the army but workers in key defence plants were allocated some of the supplies. The egg and milk powder and the chocolate that industrial workers remember being given was all probably American lend-lease food. While in Britain dried egg was among the most reviled of wartime foods, in the Soviet Union its protein and energy were extremely valuable to workers surviving on a fare of watery soups. Ordinary Russians probably did not see much of the American bounty, although late in the war Irene Rush did mention supplementing her home-grown potatoes 'with American supplies of condensed milk and fat pork'.[154] Even though the great majority of Soviets never had a chance to savour American tinned goods, by filling some of the army and industrial workers' rations the lend-lease supplies took some of the pressure off the home-grown Soviet food stocks, leaving a little more to go round for the ordinary civilian. It certainly provided some relief for the broken peasantry who were at the limits of their capabilities and simply could not release more food without starving themselves.[155] In addition, the thousands of tons of vegetable seeds which the Americans sent to the Soviet Union aided the setting up of kitchen gardens and allotments.[156] Towards the end of the war lend-lease food may even have supported as much as one-third of the average civilian calorie consumption.[157] A Russian lathe operator who defected after the war may have been buttering up his American interviewer but he claimed that 'we soldiers realized that our boots, jackets, trousers, food, every-thing – came from the Americans. Every soldier understood that, if it were not for America's help, we would not have won. For we had no food, no clothing.'[158]

In 1943 pressure on the peasants to supply ever larger quantities of food for the fighting forces was further relieved by the application of the principle of self-sufficiency to the Red Army's own food supply. That year the military set up 5,000 farms producing meat and fish, milk, eggs, potatoes, mushrooms and green vegetables. By 1944 these were able to cover a good proportion of the protein requirements of the standard military ration.[159] In combination with lend-lease the farms meant that, in the last two years of the war, Red Army soldiers were finally guaranteed a ration that contained more calories and a better quality of food than the civilian ration. In 1944 and 1945 Red Army soldiers consumed, per capita, 39.7 pounds of fat a year, more than double the amount allotted to civilians.[160] For many who joined the army in the last years of the war it was the first time they had eaten two meals a day since 1941. One recruit, who joined the army in November 1943, remembered how fortunate he felt to be eating potatoes: 'I had no meat, but I got potatoes. You were lucky if you got to peel potatoes. You could keep the skins. To go to the kitchen was like a holiday.'[161] The improvements did not eradicate hunger from the Red Army ranks. A soldier sent to guard a warehouse of lend-lease food in Archangel in 1944 was overcome by temptation: 'I was so hungry and there was so much food. I decided to take a box . . . I took a whole case of *tushonka* [canned meat], sugar and dried bread. I realized that I shouldn't do this but I opened a can of *tushonka* and ate it. Then I left my post and went to my superior and told him I had the food. He kissed me. We went and ate a couple of cans'.[162]

In 1943 the Red Army began to push the Wehrmacht out of occupied territory and was able to requisition large quantities of food from the previously occupied peasants. The liberated areas provided the soldiers moving through with half of their flour requirements, almost all the vegetables and meat they needed, as well as fodder. This indicates just how ineffective the German occupation forces had been in requisitioning food from the peasantry. The Soviets were equally ruthless in their policy of feeding the army at the expense of their own people and far more efficient in extracting food. When the Red Army occupied other countries it proved itself as pitiless as the Wehrmacht. As the Soviets moved through Hungary and Romania the military ration was increased, first by 15 and then by 34 per cent.[163]

Once the Red Army reached East Prussia its vengeance was unleashed on the German civilian population in an orgy of rape and plunder. In many towns Soviet soldiers raped every German woman, regardless of her age. Confronted with the comparative wealth, even of wartime Germany, the Soviets were at a loss to understand why the Germans had invaded the Soviet Union. What could such a prosperous nation have hoped to gain from such a poor one?[164] When a Ukrainian rail engineer first arrived in Germany with the Red Army he was amazed. 'We would walk into an apartment and there would be some old man there. We would look around and see how he was living and we would say, "You must be a bourgeois!" And he would say, quite timidly, "No, I am just an ordinary worker; I have been working all my life." And here the fellow was living in three or four rooms! When the young people in the army saw this sort of thing, they became convinced by the evidence of their own eyes that the Soviet propaganda had been giving them great lies.'[165] The Ukrainian took part in the looting of German homes. Mirroring the 'Führerpakete', which encouraged German troops to bring home as much food as they could carry when they went on leave from the occupied territories, Soviet troops were given permission 'to send packages home, ten kilograms a month', but the shops were empty. 'So we would go into a German's apartment together and simply clear out the place and send everything that we took home. We were especially interested in getting clothes, because we knew that in the Soviet Union all the people had were rags. Of course, the order did not say that we were permitted to loot the

Germans' houses, but it was really implied in it. Anyway, no one ever stopped us.'[166]

PERSEVERANCE DESPITE HUNGER

A Soviet citizen's average daily intake of calories between 1942 and 1943 is estimated to have been 2,555 calories. In 1944, the amount is thought to have increased to 2,810 calories. This was a sign that the war had turned a corner.[167] This quantity of food would be perfectly sufficient to sustain relatively sedentary contemporary lives but it was far below what was necessary to sustain health and energy in the tough everyday life of the Soviet citizen in wartime. The Soviets survived on far less food than all other combatant nations except the Japanese. They consumed at least 500 calories less than the average British or German civilian, while Americans were, on average, consuming at least 1,000 more calories a day than a Soviet. However, the picture conveyed by averages fails to convey the unreliability of the food supply, the periods of shortages and severe lack of food, the fact that food was distributed unequally across the population, so that while the communist elite might stuff themselves on stewed meat for breakfast, the dispossessed and hungry were reduced to licking the plates after others had finished their meal. A dependant's or non-manual worker's ration of 200 to 400 grams of sub-standard bread meant that it took great ingenuity to scrape together enough to eat. Irene Rush recalled, 'how we hungered for and enjoyed that meagre food! We were always hungry an hour or two before it was time to eat; and by meal time, a piece of dry bread tasted like manna from heaven.'[168] This is not the statement of a person living comfortably on 2,555 calories a day. From the evidence which fills in the picture of averages it is safe to conclude that only a tiny minority of the privileged were eating the actual number of calories that their bodies required. The majority of Soviet civilians were severely undernourished.

Apart from the problem that the food did not fill the Soviets' energy requirements, it was nutritionally sub-standard. The Soviet Union was the only European nation to suffer from an outbreak of scurvy during the Second World War. The irregular and deficient diet caused gastritis, stomach ulcers, dysentery, diarrhoea and vitamin C, K and A deficiencies.[169] Even the Australian diplomat J. A. Alexander, who had privileged access to food, suffered from his virtually vitamin-free diet. Only one month after his arrival in the country in August 1944 he had 'lost a good deal of weight . . . We are finding our urgent food needs here to maintain health are milk, vegetables, fruit and fruit juices.' In October he complained that he had not had 'a fresh egg or any fresh milk since I arrived'.[170] The Soviet birth-rate fell by half during the war and disease flourished. Typhus, a sickness which goes hand in hand with malnourishment and poor hygiene, increased greatly, although the government did manage to implement effective measures, including disinfecting every train passenger before a journey, which prevented a raging epidemic.[171]

The breakdown of ordinary civilian life was a serious threat to the war effort. But the appalling food situation was never so bad that there were not enough soldiers to fight on the front line or workers to struggle on the industrial assembly line. The impressive wartime achievements of the Soviet Union were, however, achieved at a terrible cost. The lives of the entire population were reduced to nagging hunger and grinding drudgery. Daily life was a perpetual misery. Kemp Tolley, sent to Komsomolsk to check on the use of lend-lease equipment, was filled with sadness 'that fellow humans should have to exist in such hardship, without a shred of beauty, no control over their private destiny – in effect, human manure that will hopefully fertilize and improve the lives of succeeding generations'.[172]

Once the war was over, starvation was never mentioned by Stalin. Indeed, wishing to disguise the weaknesses of the post-war Soviet Union, he was only prepared to admit to 7 million war deaths, a figure which does not even cover the 9 million military casualties.[173] The starvation of the besieged Leningraders received no official acknowledgement. When the Leningrad poet Olga Berggolts visited Moscow at the end of 1942 she was shocked to find that while the Muscovites talked of the people of Leningrad as heroes they had no idea that they had starved to death defending their city. Berggolts was in Moscow to give a radio interview. She was told, 'no recollections of the starvation. None, none. On the courage, on the heroism of the Leningraders, that's what we need . . . But not a word about hunger.'[174] The unacknowledged loss of millions of Soviet civilians to starvation could only be imposed upon a population by a dictatorship at ease with the notion that the lives of the majority of its people were expendable. However, given the pressing circumstances of the war, the Soviet government could probably not have fed its people much better. The Soviets had little room for manoeuvre. Admittedly, the problems of the agricultural system were partially self-imposed but there was no time or spare capacity to address them during the war. And in order to make as much food available to the urban population as possible the communist regime did abandon its principles and re-open the free market in food.

Germany and Britain feared that hunger, let alone starvation, would undermine morale to such an extent that this would bring the war effort to a halt. No such collapse in morale appears to have occurred in the Soviet Union. The people were used to shortages and difficult living conditions, and the fact that it was clear that the government was prepared to sacrifice the peasantry to hunger before the urban population contributed to the morale of the urban civilians, who kept the economy running. Moreover, the youth of the Soviet Union had been brought up to believe in the communist struggle. A sincere belief in collectivism and the political conviction that communism would bring about a better future undoubtedly motivated many of the young. Vladimir Ivanovich Mikhailov was nineteen when the war began. When he first went to the front his sincere belief in the 'spirit of internationalism' made it hard for him to fight the Germans. 'I thought, these are probably the workers of the Ruhr, the dockers of Hamburg . . . how on earth can this be?'[175] Once he realized that the National Socialists were intent on destroying the Soviet Union he fought with fervour despite suffering from terrible hunger pangs. 'We endured. But I remember what a human turns into, consumed by this terrible feeling of hunger.'[176] Many in the generation born in the 1920s seem to have been imbued with this spirit of sacrifice. For them the war was one more test of the Soviet people on the road toward the triumphant attainment of the communist ideal.[177]

The spirit of sacrifice which undoubtedly permeated the entire wartime Soviet population was not, however, always directed towards the support of communism but was inspired by more personal motives. Victor Kravchenko admired the sense of purpose and motivation among the workers. When there was a rush order they would 'remain in their factories for many days without a break, snatching some sleep on the premises . . . I watched them working in one shop when the shop next-door had been turned into a blazing hell by a direct bomb hit. I know that these plain people were the real heroes and the real strength of the Russian war . . . They were struggling to give all possible support to their sons and brothers and fathers at the fighting fronts.'[178] In addition, fear should not be underestimated as a motivating factor in the Soviet Union. The purges of the 1930s had created an atmosphere of terror within society, and the labour camp was a tangible and horrible prospect which kept workers and peasants at their posts and discouraged open expressions of discontent. However, many Soviets felt that the cloud of repression lifted slightly during the war. Andrei Sakharov noted a temporary release from 'the daily grind of a totalitarian, bureaucratic society' which allowed the workers a measure of pride and dignity, which they relished.[179] There was certainly a widespread although misplaced hope that after the war the regime would soften and life would improve.

The strongest motivational force which kept the Soviets going through the war was fear and hatred of the Germans. This was shared by virtually every Soviet no matter what their position with regard to the communist regime. Once civilians realized that labour camps, execution and starvation were the lot of Soviets in the occupied areas, a hatred of the Germans and a determination not to come under their rule became a driving force in the war effort. Victor Kravchenko explained that although he detested Stalin's regime he nurtured a 'passionate hatred for the invader'. This, he argued, was 'the key to the mystery why the Russians fought and in the end conquered. They did not fight *for* Stalin but *despite* Stalin.'[180] The Second World War was of a completely different nature from the First World War, when capitulation was an option. The Soviets were faced with 'national extermination' and they saw the conflict as a fight to the very end.[181] Thus, under certain conditions, the Soviets demonstrated that hunger, malnutrition and deaths from starvation do not necessarily prevent a nation from fighting, and indeed winning, a total war.

15

Germany and Britain – Two Approaches to Entitlement

As the army marches on its stomach ... so does the industrial worker produce his best work when his stomach is well looked after.
(Noel Curtis-Bennett, author of a book on feeding British industrial workers during the war)[1]

The fighting won't stop until Göring fits into Goebbels' trousers.
(Popular Berlin saying in early 1945)[2]

When the war began in September 1939 the National Socialists had already accomplished the difficult task of switching the German population's diet to a wartime footing. Throughout the 1930s, as part of Herbert Backe's campaign for 'nutritional freedom', strenuous efforts had been made to guide consumption away from scarce, high-quality foods towards lower-quality substitutes. Germans had been encouraged to eat fish instead of meat, margarine rather than butter, and to base their meals on potatoes and brown bread. In 1940 British nutritionists envied the Germans their frugal diet of autarky. Ernest Graham-Little, a member of the Food Education Society and an MP, attributed the Germans' military successes of that year to the fact that their diet was 'more scientific and effective than ours'.[3] In the *British Medical Journal*, Jack Drummond, Scientific Adviser to the Ministry of Food, explained: 'The present German rations are based on the simple but sound principle that a "peasant diet" of "high extraction" or wholemeal bread, plenty of vegetables and potatoes, and some dairy produce in the form of cheese or separated milk, provides all the essentials of sound nutrition.'[4]

British politicians throughout the 1930s had, in contrast, determinedly resisted all efforts by nutritionists to persuade them to interfere in the nation's eating habits. This meant that the British had to make the painful adjustment to a diet of austerity in the first two years of the war. However, after the difficult winter of 1940–41, the food system stabilized and in the end the public's belief that the Ministry of Food was doing a good job in sharing out shortages fairly across the population transformed food into one of the factors that positively contributed to maintaining morale among the British.[5]

The fact that the German Aryan population was adequately fed between 1939 and 1945 is often identified as one of the successes of the National Socialist regime. Indeed, both governments were successful in creating food supply and distribution systems which avoided the mistakes of the First World War and used food effectively to support, rather than undermine, the war effort. Throughout the war, average consumption of calories in Britain and Germany ranged between an adequate 2,500 to 3,000 calories. The British wartime diet was of a slightly better quality in that it contained more meat while the Germans relied more heavily on bread and potatoes, but the British and the Germans survived the war on a comparable diet. Despite many similarities, the two rationing systems were marked by telling ideological and material differences. The British Ministry of Food placed a great deal of emphasis on the argument that the British rationing system ensured equality of sacrifice across the population. In Germany, where the food supply was tighter, greater emphasis was placed on the efficient and effective distribution of food. Although the entitlement of certain sections of society to food was entirely disregarded, arguably this resulted in a rationing system which (within its limitations) was more just in that it allocated the most food to those expending the greatest physical effort.

Although food consumption averages create a picture of a very similar food situation in both countries, the story of the German food supply followed a different trajectory from that of Britain. An initial period of stability was followed by a crisis in the winter and spring of 1941–42, which was relieved by the exploitation of the occupied territories. Then in 1943 the strain of war began to impact hard upon agriculture. Falling harvests combined with the intensification of the aerial bombing campaign to result in worsening food shortages in Germany's cities until, in the last months before the Allied victory, the supply system broke down.

1930S BRITAIN — A NUTRITIONAL DIVIDE

Throughout the 1930s the Conservative-dominated national coalition governments which held power determinedly upheld the view that the social welfare measures introduced since 1918 had provided the working population with adequate protection against the economic vicissitudes that marked the period. Indeed, government expenditure on social welfare increased significantly in the inter-war years. After the First World War the insurance scheme to cover unemployment was extended to cover nearly all of the working population, and their dependent wives and children. In 1919 the Ministry of Health was created and the national health insurance scheme was supplemented by child welfare clinics and a school health service. In 1925 the pension scheme was extended and provision was made for widows and orphans.[6] However, a number of scientific investigations found that the government's picture of Britain as a healthier and less impoverished nation required substantial qualification. In fact, the country was marked by deep regional and class inequalities. Death-rates in the industrial centres were sometimes half as high again as the average death-rate, while in affluent Buckinghamshire, Hertfordshire and Surrey death-rates were 20 per cent lower than the average.[7] The main cause of deprivation was Depression-related unemployment. In the north of England, Scotland and South Wales, decline in the coal, textile and shipbuilding industries had created pockets of abject poverty.[8] Medical officers estimated that as many as 80 per cent of the working-class families in Jarrow and Stockton were living in appalling conditions caused by unemployment.[9] The health of women and children was particularly hard hit by poverty, as was indicated by the rising maternal mortality rate, which increased by 22 per cent between 1922 and 1933.[10]

Studies showed again and again that ill-health among women and children could be traced back to inadequate diets. Surveys in Durham and London found that the majority of children were showing early signs of rickets, caused by vitamin D deficiency. R. A. McCance, who was later to influence wartime nutrition policies, linked the high incidence of anaemia among working-class women to a lack of iron and protein in the diet.[11] Lady Rhys Williams, working with expectant mothers in the Rhondda valley, found that all it took to reduce maternal death-rates from 11.29 per thousand to 4.77 was to feed pregnant women nourishing foods.[12] It was clear that ill-health among the poor was directly related to deficient family income. The poor quite simply could not afford to buy enough good-quality food.

British government ministers and their advisers were reluctant to admit that the much trumpeted health insurance scheme was failing to provide for those who needed health care the most: the wives and children of working men and the unemployed.[13] The Ministry of Health dismissed Lady Rhys Williams's findings as 'speculations' and asserted that ignorance, not income, was the root of the problem. Poor diet and ill-health were the result of 'bad cooking, bad marketing, [and] bad household economy'.[14] This shifted responsibility firmly on to the shoulders of the poor. The question of responsibility was at the heart of the matter. It was not in the government's financial interest to accept responsibility for ensuring that everyone could afford an adequate diet, and the government was wary of acknowledging a problem which it felt that it could not resolve. The Chief Medical Officer, Sir George Newman, regarded an inquiry into the question of poor health among working-class women as inadvisable for the very reason that he was certain that it would reveal 'a great mass of sickness and impairment attributable to childbirth, which would create a demand for organized treatment by the state'. He believed that a positive relief programme which addressed health problems on such a scale was beyond the capacity even of 'modern civilized nations'.[15]

If the government thought that improving the nutrition of the deprived would require a programme of assistance which was beyond its capabilities, the findings of two studies by the Rowett Institute and the British Medical Association, announced in 1936, were even more unwelcome. Using a set of minimum dietary standards developed by a League of Nations committee of twelve physiologists and biochemists, the studies found that the problem of malnutrition was much more widespread throughout the British population than had been thought.

In the inter-war years the League of Nations acted as a driving force for nutritional research, and doctors, teachers, health officials and campaigners applied the League of Nations minimum dietary standards in a series of surveys conducted in different countries throughout the world. The surveys revealed the depressing fact that even in the 'civilized' nations the great majority of the urban working classes existed in a state of hidden malnourishment because they could not afford to buy nourishing foodstuffs. In Australia, the Advisory Council on Nutrition found that while Australians ate enough calories, urban children in particular showed signs of rickets and vitamin-deficiency diseases.[16] Even on the tiny island of Iceland nutritionists despaired of the health of the urban working classes, who were cut off from the farms and the traditional diet of mutton, butter and skyr (skimmed milk mixed with rennet), and instead derived sufficient energy but not enough vitamins from their diet of low-cost calories from rye bread, margarine, a little fish, coffee and sugar.[17]

In Britain, the Rowett Institute survey uncovered a yawning dietary gap between the rich and the poor. The wealthy were shown to be consuming 70 per cent more iron, 90 per cent more phosphorus, and 260 per cent more calcium than the bottom third of society.[18] The survey by the British Medical Association confirmed these findings. The wealthy were consuming the lion's share of the nation's meat, fish, butter, cheese, fruit and vegetables, while the bottom third of the nation were scraping along on a thoroughly innutritious diet of cheap white bread, margarine, jam, a little bacon and copious quantities of tea. The causes were lack of proper kitchens in which to prepare hot meals, lack of time and, predominantly, lack of money. While they appeared to be adequately fed, in that they consumed a sufficient number of calories, about one-third of the nation did not earn enough to buy adequate quantities of the so-called protective foods such as milk, fruit and vegetables. Thus, they were denied access to vital sources of the vitamins and minerals which strengthened the body's immune system and were a prerequisite for good health.[19]

Despite the fact that the Rowett Institute's survey had been conducted in co-operation with civil servants at the Ministry of Agriculture, the

British government did everything in its power to prevent the publication of its findings. The director of the institute, John Boyd Orr, was called in to see the Health Minister, Sir Kingsley Wood, who 'wanted to know why I was making such a fuss about poverty when, with old age pensions and unemployment insurance, there was no poverty in this country. This extraordinary illusion was genuinely believed by Mr Wood who held the out-of-date opinion that if people were not actually dying of starvation there could be no food deficit. He knew nothing about the results of the research on vitamin and protein requirements and had never visited the slums to see things for himself.'[20] When Orr and another doctor decided to talk about the survey's findings on a radio broadcast they were warned that if they went ahead they might well be struck off the Medical Register.[21] Orr was infuriated by the government's attitude and the monstrous injustice that at the same time as 'mothers and children [were] suffering malnutrition because they were too poor to afford the more expensive health foods . . . these foods were so abundant that the government was taking measures to reduce production so as to raise retail prices'.[22] Although his fellow participant was sufficiently intimidated to withdraw from the radio programme, Orr, as a research scientist who had no intention of practising as a doctor again, went ahead, undeterred by government threats. He also decided to publish the Rowett Report under his own name, and *Food, Health and Income* was published in 1937 by Harold Macmillan, publisher and at that time MP for Newcastle.[23]

In response to the revelations of widespread malnutrition, the League of Nations argued that rather than cutting back production in order to avoid the creation of surpluses, farmers needed to produce more of the protective foods. Governments, in turn, needed to take responsibility for their citizens' well-being and ensure through a variety of measures that the poorer sections of society were able to gain access to these foodstuffs.[24] These were radical and provocative suggestions which the British government preferred to ignore until the Second World War forced the issue. Then, in the circumstances of total war, where every aspect of the food production and distribution system was controlled by the Ministry of Food, it was no longer possible, nor was it in the government's interest, to abdicate responsibility for the nation's health. Many of those researchers whose work had been spurned by the government in the 1930s were drawn in to give advice to the Ministry of Food and found themselves able to exert a level of influence over the government decision-making process that was unprecedented, even if it was limited.

1930S GERMANY – THE CAMPAIGN FOR NUTRITIONAL FREEDOM

The National Socialists came to power in 1933 determined to reduce unemployment and pull Germany out of economic decline. They held out the promise of a gleaming future, with new houses filled with modern consumer goods such as refrigerators, radios and washing machines. There would be affordable family cars and relaxing holidays for all members of the regenerated and united community of racially pure Germans (the *Volksgemeinschaft*).[25] However, the regime's more immediate aims were at odds with this vision of plenty. A growing economy and rising wages generally lead to increasing demand for food and consumer goods. The National Socialists were determined to suppress these inflationary pressures, cap the demand for imports (especially food imports) and overcome the pressing problem of the balance of payments. Hitler wanted to spend precious foreign exchange not on cattle and butter from Denmark but on iron from Sweden.[26] The rise in the German GDP was not going to be channelled into improving the diet of the nation's citizens, but into re-industrialization and rearmament. Göring was in earnest when he announced to the German population in Hamburg in December 1935 that the National Socialist leadership had chosen guns over butter.[27]

In order to achieve their aims the National Socialists would have to change the German nation's eating habits and suppress demand for imported foods such as coffee and oranges, and all those foods dependent on imports of fodder for their production such as meat and butter. Despite the dictatorial nature of the regime the National Socialists proceeded with caution, unwilling to provoke food protests.[28] The campaign for nutritional freedom was conducted through persistent persuasion and was given credibility by an array of scientists, nutritionists, doctors and social reformers, all of whom promoted the health benefits of the foods of autarky. In 1938 Franz Wirz, a member of the NSDAP's Committee on Public Health, published a book on *Healthy and Secure Nutrition* in which he argued that since the end of the nineteenth century the German people had been consuming excessive quantities of meat, sugar and fat and this had led to 'nervous ailments, infertility, stomach and digestive disorders ... heart and vascular disease'.[29] A reduction in these foods would not only free Germany from its dependence on food imports but also create a strong and healthy people ready to face the physical rigours of war.

Wholemeal bread was presented as the backbone of the frugal diet of autarky. Since the beginning of the twentieth century German bread reformers had been campaigning against the spread of white bread. It was demonized as a manifestation of the corruption of the modern world. The reformers argued that by removing the protein, fat and minerals along with the bran and husk of the wheat, the newly invented milling process robbed people of their rightful nutrition.[30] One reformer came up with the slogan: 'Anaemic bread causes anaemic blood.'[31] For the National Socialists white bread was a wasteful way of using expensive imports and precious home-grown wheat, as more of the grain was discarded in the process of making white flour. In the south and west of the country, where the people showed a marked preference for the degenerate luxury of white rolls, a campaign was launched in 1937 to promote wholemeal bread. Millers were instructed how to produce wholemeal flour and bakers taught how to use it to make edible bread.[32] Advertising proclaimed, 'Wholemeal bread is healthier and more nutritious and filling!' and a quality label was attached to the loaves. Wholemeal bread was presented as the food of the *Volksgemeinschaft*: it was the most appropriate staple food for a healthy Aryan race which used its resources efficiently.[33] By 1939 consumption of the patriotic loaf had risen by 50 per cent.[34]

The German Women's Enterprise (*Deutsches Frauenwerk*) was another enthusiastic promoter of autarkic foods and they ran cookery classes which taught women how to make filling meals using fewer calories.[35] The promotion of quark was possibly their greatest success. Invented in the 1920s, quark was a cross between yoghurt and cream cheese. It was made from the sour milk which was a by-product of butter production and which had previously been fed to animals. Quark was the perfect food in the quest for autarky. It diverted food from animals to humans, it was nutritious – containing fats, calcium and protein – and it was a substitute for scarce foodstuffs as it could be used to replace butter or cream. The German Women's Enterprise held demonstrations on how to use quark and lobbied grocers to stock it in their stores. Quark consumption rose dramatically in the 1930s, possibly by as much as 60 per cent, and it is still popular in Germany today.[36]

But the ultimate Nazi food was the *Eintopf* or casserole. The *Eintopf* rendered poor-quality cuts of meat tasty through slow cooking, while eking out small quantities of (preferably left-over) meat with vegetables. Cooked, as its name implies, in one pot, it used less cooking fuel. It was thus the epitome of a thrifty and virtuous meal. Sarah Collins, an Englishwoman living in Berlin in 1938, recalled how 'the first Sunday of the month was designated as "Eintopf" Sunday'.[37] Every family was supposed to make a hot-pot and 'the amounts saved by this frugality contributed to the Winter Help Fund'.[38] Goebbels, as propaganda minister, was aware that the ordinary people's trust in the regime rested upon a belief in the probity of the leadership. As early as 1935 he began to create an image of the National Socialist leaders as men with simple tastes, and officials in his ministry were instructed not to publish pictures of the NS leadership seated at groaning dining tables littered with bottles of wine.[39] On *Eintopf* Sundays 'field kitchens appeared ... at midday on Unter den Linden, and photographs were taken of the Party hierarchy eating their Eintopf alfresco'.[40] The dish 'was served in all restaurants, whilst uniformed jack-booted collectors rattled collecting tins in the faces of the guests'.[41] This transformed the drive for autarky into a social ritual which was supposed to unite and strengthen the *Volksgemeinschaft* through sacrifice.[42]

Changes in eating habits were less the result of the internalization of National Socialist propaganda about the racial health benefits of German-grown food, than the product of necessity and lack of choice. One of the first foods to disappear as a result of the National Socialists' attempt to reduce food imports was cheap margarine, a staple of the poorer sections of society. Alfred Hugenberg, Hitler's first Minister of Agriculture, decided to stimulate German butter production by making it compulsory to mix a certain amount of butter into margarine. The result was to make margarine more expensive, and an increasing number of consumers were forced to switch to cheaper, lower-grade margarine.[43] However, margarine production was dependent on falling imports of whale and vegetable oils, and there was simply not enough to go around. Shopkeepers reported that they could only cover about two-thirds of the demand for cheap margarine.[44] In Brandenburg the state police reported ugly scenes among frustrated customers, and women fainted, exhausted from standing for hours in queues waiting to buy tiny quantities of fat. 'The question of food is at the moment the most pressing,' the police warned. 'A general tendency toward price rises is noticeable. Some goods have risen by 40 per cent in price. Especially threatened is fat, meat, potatoes and textiles. In conjunction with this, hoarding has begun which creates a war-psychosis. Margarine as the people's fat cost 24 Pf in 1932, today [1934] about 98 Pf is normal.'[45]

Reductions in fodder imports led to pork, bacon and beef shortages.[46] The number of domestic pigs and cattle fell by over a million, while the number of live cattle being imported into the coastal regions in the north-west also dropped significantly.[47] Coastal areas and the northern industrial towns began to run out of meat. In 1935 and 1936 butchers in the Ruhr area were forced to close from time to time for lack of meat to sell.[48] Eggs, an alternative source of animal protein, also became scarce and Sarah Collins noted that one had to 'go from one shop to another buying all sorts of things which were unnecessary, in order to be given two eggs.'[49]

The living standards of workers declined. Official government statistics show workers' wages rising back to their pre-Depression levels by 1937 and the regime argued that this was because it had managed to prevent excessive price rises in food. In fact, food prices rose by much more than government figures suggest and the cost of food was also adversely affected by the emergence of a black market. National Socialist statistics did not take into account the impact of food shortages, the decline in the quality of food, the new and hefty deductions from workers wages for social insurance, the Labour Front and Winter Relief, and the impact of the housing shortage, all of which bit deep into the living standards of the workers.[50] By 1936

German working-class families were spending somewhere between 43 and 50 per cent of their income on food, in comparison to only 30 per cent in British working-class families.[51] The United States Ministry of Agriculture calculated that in the decade ending in 1937 the meat consumption of German workers fell by 17 per cent, milk by 21 per cent and eggs by 46 per cent.[52] These figures are probably slightly inflated, but the general effect of the National Socialists' militarism was to suppress consumption and deny many Germans the foods they would have preferred.[53]

Throughout the 1930s the National Socialists redefined their policy of denying Germans meat, butter, white bread and coffee as a drive to achieve racial fitness. The frugal diet of autarky was supposed to create a revitalized nation of fertile, vigorous workers and soldiers. While the government prepared for war by building tanks, aeroplanes and weapons, the German people must prepare by readying their bodies to withstand the demands of war as soldiers, workers or mothers of the future generation. The state intruded deep into the private space of German citizens. Propaganda reminded the members of the Hitler Youth, 'Nutrition is not a private matter!' The German citizen was the property of the state, embodied in the person of the Führer. It did not seem strange in this context to assert, 'Your body belongs to the Führer!'[54] It was the duty of every good German to comply with the diet of autarky. An embittered German émigré in 1939 observed that 'Germans today . . . consider hunger almost as a moral duty.'[55] Anyone who grumbled about the regime was accused of missing superfluous luxuries such as butter or coffee. As a result, more honourable complaints tended to be suppressed 'for rather than be thought to be complaining out of mere greed, most Germans prefer to suffer in silence'.[56]

Research into the biological standard of living in 1930s Germany indicates that the populations of the large cities were the worst affected by food shortages. The mortality rate in large cities was 18 per cent higher than in small towns. In particular, the cities saw a rise in the incidence of diphtheria, which is associated with a lack of protein in the diet. The worst hit were children between five and fifteen, whose mortality rate rose by 13 per cent.[57] This would seem to suggest that the children of the German working classes were suffering from the micronutrient deficiencies associated with a lack of animal protein in the diet which the German occupation was later to inflict upon the children of occupied Holland. Although the autarkic diet based on wholemeal bread and reduced quantities of meat and fat could credibly be presented as a healthy diet, in fact it denied the poorer sections of German society protective foods – meat, butter, milk – in sufficient quantities to ensure health. A by no means unbiased émigré doctor writing in 1939 argued that 'there is not today in Germany a definite, specific state of hunger such as reigned in the days of the World War blockade. But there does reign, instead, the much more treacherous and incomplete state of hunger which is a continuous and chronic state of under nourishment – the result of a self-blockade arising from the idea of agricultural autarky.'[58]

Food deficiencies in Germany in the 1930s should not be blamed on the policy of food autarky alone. At least in part they were also attributable to class-based inequalities which skewed the distribution of foods in all European societies. Given the National Socialists' dislike of criticism, independent investigators did not challenge the official statistics by surveying the nutritional standards of the German poor and underprivileged.[59] However, Germany, like Britain, certainly had urban slums, and a stubborn sector of long-term unemployed existed at least until 1936. Ethnologists who went into the rural districts in search of healthy settlers for the conquered eastern territories also uncovered depressing levels of poverty. The policy of food autarky will have done nothing to alleviate the class-based problem of poverty and malnutrition.

THE POLITICS OF RATIONING

Once the war began, the British and German governments both aimed to feed their populations as well as possible and thus fend off the problems of low morale and discontent which they anticipated as a result of wartime food shortages. Both governments sought to distribute their limited food resources efficiently, and at the same time be seen to do so fairly. They took different routes in order to achieve these common goals.

The National Socialists had no intention of repeating the mistake of the First World War, when rationing was introduced too late and disillusion with the government and its ability to feed its people was already widespread. There was to be no delay this time. Rationing was introduced in Germany in August 1939 even before the Wehrmacht had marched into Poland. The German ration was both comprehensive, covering foodstuffs such as bread, and highly differentiated. The nutritionist Heinrich Kraut from the Institute for the Physiology of Work worked out a system which allocated those undertaking heavy and ultra-heavy work substantially more food (3,600 and 4,200 calories respectively) than a 'normal user', who received a basic ration which amounted to 2,400 calories.[60] Children and young adults were allocated smaller quantities of food but pregnant women and nursing mothers were given supplementary rations.[61] The aim was to distribute a limited supply of food across the population as efficiently and fairly as possible, while at the same time securing the loyalty of the working classes.[62]

What made the German food system distinctive was that while the entitlement of every 'good' German citizen to a decent ration was held as sacrosanct, the non-productive and racially undesirable were not accorded the same right to food. Below the normal rationing system, there operated a second tier of food allocation for non-Aryans. From August 1939 Jews were allowed to shop only at designated stores, which often charged them an extra 10 per cent. The time when they could go shopping was limited to one hour each day, after four o'clock, by which time many stores had run out of most goods.[63] Lucia Seidel, who ran a grocery store in Kassel, took pity on her Jewish customers and would often package up their shopping before the day's supplies ran out and send her young son to deliver it to their houses.[64] When food shortages began to occur in the towns, signs went up in shop windows warning that scarce foods would not be sold to Jews. Those Jews who were forced into heavy labour were able to obtain a tiny quantity of meat, but by 1941 meat, fruit and butter were virtually unobtainable for most Jewish shoppers, who were also forbidden to buy tinned food, coffee and most vegetables.[65] Only those with tiny children were able to buy milk. Their neighbours sometimes policed the restrictions. When one Jewish woman sent her small son to buy milk, the other shoppers protested so loudly that the shopkeepers stopped serving him. The neighbour of another little Jewish girl would stand in front of her to prevent her from going out into the street with her shopping bag until the clock struck four.[66]

Refugees in their own country, forced to move house continually, shunned in the bomb shelters, unable to buy clothes or shoes, and banned from public laundries, many Jews worried most that they might starve to death.[67] Even if they were able to obtain food on the black market the frequent Gestapo raids on Jewish homes meant that it was dangerous to store illegally acquired foodstuffs. By 1942 the deportations to the east were well under way. In the autumn of that year, just as the food situation in Germany was improving, a new rule ominously announced that those Jews still living in the Reich were no longer allowed to buy meat, eggs or milk, and that Jewish children were no longer entitled to special supplements.[68] As the Jews were loaded on to the trains which took them to the extermination camps many were already gaunt with hunger.

The mentally ill and disabled, defined as a burden on society, were also victims of this starvation policy. In 1940 the director of a large mental hospital, Dr Valentin Falthauser, came up with the idea that his young charges could be fed a diet of potatoes, turnips and boiled cabbage, which was devoid of fats and very low in protein. After about three months they starved to death. He argued that this was a practical solution to the problem of disposing of these unproductive members of German society, as it allowed the doctors to feel that they were simply allowing their charges to die rather than actually murdering them.[69] Nevertheless, the asylum prohibited the ringing of church bells at the funerals of the six or seven people buried each day so that the local inhabitants would not become aware of the suspicious death-rate in the asylum.[70] The Falthauser diet spread to other institutions and 'deliberate starvation based upon differential diets was practised in asylums throughout the length and breadth of Germany'.[71] Hermann Pfannmüller introduced two special 'hunger houses' into his asylum at Eglfing-Haar where 429 patients died between 1943 and 1945. Pfannmüller would frequently visit the kitchens to taste the food and check that it was devoid of protein, while the cook did her best to subvert his efforts and slip nourishing ingredients into the gruel.[72] It is unclear how many of the 200,000 people commonly labelled as victims of the 'euthanasia' programme in fact starved slowly to death.[73]

The British government, unlike the National Socialists, did not spring into action on the food front as soon as the war began. Lulled into a false sense of security by the first few months of phoney war, the cabinet was surprisingly reluctant to introduce rationing. Plans were in place, which the Ministry of Food was keen to implement, but Churchill* was reluctant to restrict the liberty of British citizens and he especially disliked placing limitations on people's eating habits.[74] Butter, bacon and sugar were eventually rationed in January 1940 and meat followed in March.[75] Unlike the German ration, the initial British ration was worked out without any reference to nutritional advisers. It was very similar to the one that had been in place during the First World War and it reflected the limitations imposed by British agricultural production and the fall of imports due to the shipping crisis. There was no pretence that this would necessarily provide a nutritionally balanced diet.[76]

The system worked according to two principles. Firstly, the amount of food stated on the coupons represented a minimum amount of food which the government guaranteed to distribute to each person. Secondly, everyone, from miners and steel-workers, engaged in the heaviest work, to the sedentary office worker and housewife, received the same 4 ounces of bacon or ham, 4 ounces of butter, 2 or 3 ounces of margarine, 1 ounce of cheese, 12 ounces of sugar, one shilling's worth of meat (or 14–16 ounces), 2 pints of milk and 2 ounces of tea a week.[77] Children were allocated less food, but among adults there was no differentiation according to gender, class or the contribution of one's work to the war effort. Even those members of the military who were stationed in Britain with a desk job, and who could hardly justify a bigger ration on the grounds of physical exertion, were given the same rations as the rest of the civilian population. Food Minister Lord Woolton commented in his memoirs: 'This was not only right and just, but it was good for the morale of the civilian population, who otherwise would have been critical and justifiably envious of the armed forces.'[78]

---

* At this point in the war he was First Lord of the Admiralty.

The British government was aware that in a planned economy every transaction took on an aura of purpose and thus social inequalities, which in peacetime appeared to be the 'neutral' result of an impersonal market, would, if reinforced by rationing, take on the appearance of having been consciously created by government.[79] The British working classes were deeply suspicious and believed that if there were sacrifices to be made they would end up making them while the rich sidestepped the rules.[80] The British food rationing system was designed to avoid deepening social rifts, and instead to foster social consensus. Lord Woolton explained: 'I believed that if food control were to be readily accepted by British people it had to remain essentially simple and have the appearance of justice.'[81] By allocating everyone the same amount of food it emphasized its purpose as the equitable distribution of food and scarce goods across the entire population. This distribution of food resources, which apparently privileged no section of civilian society, is one of the characteristics of government wartime policy which earned it the title of 'war socialism'.

In fact, while giving the ration the appearance of equity, this principle made it deeply inequitable. In the first two years of the war the British underwent a painful period of adjustment to wartime conditions. Food prices rose and the poorest families and those in low-priority occupations were worst affected. Christopher Tomlin, a stationery salesman whose family's weekly income amounted to £3 15s., declared himself 'white hot with fury at recent price increases . . . We can't afford to pay the extras on milk and eggs. It's a good thing for munitions workers who earn £5 a week . . . it's a bloody disgrace for families in circumstances like mine.'[82] Pam Ashford in Glasgow recorded shortages of eggs, fish, onions and milk in the city. It was working-class women who initially bore the brunt of rationing. They tended to sacrifice a large share of their meals to their husbands or children. Those families with adolescents struggled the hardest as the young adult ration was often too small for a growing teenager. Families with small children did better, as the children's ration was generous and could be shared out among the rest of the family.[83] In 1941 the sugar ration was cut by 4 ounces. This was felt hardest by the poorer families, who relied on sugar as a primary source of energy. Air raids during the Battle of Britain made matters worse, as women often did not bother to cook an evening meal, instead taking sandwiches and cocoa into the shelters. Government surveys in 1940 and 1941 found that the energy level of the British diet had fallen by 7 to 10 per cent, and the diet of the poorest third of the population remained deficient in vitamins and calcium.[84] In particular, the government was concerned the population was not eating enough to sustain the longer and harder working hours which were called for by wartime mobilization.

FEEDING THE BRITISH WORKING CLASSES

The British Ministry of Food's thinking was that bread and potatoes should not be rationed as they were the main energy-giving foods in the wartime diet. In theory, this meant that British workers did not need supplementary rations because they could boost their energy intake with unrationed foods.[85] However, it is much harder to consume the 4,000 calories a day required by a man engaged in heavy physical labour if most of the energy is supplied by bulky foods. Men working in heavy industry regarded meat as an essential source of nutrition and complained bitterly that the ration provided insufficient quantities for working men. The wartime social survey of 1942 found that 42 per cent of men in heavy industry and 45 per cent of those in light industry did not feel that they were getting enough food to stay fit and healthy. The equal ration for everyone demonstrably disadvantaged miners, steelworkers, dockers and shipyard workers, who were found by the survey to be significantly less well nourished than the middle classes.[86] It was clear to the Ministry of Food that action needed to be taken to provide workers with more food. Rather than introducing a complex system of differentiated rations, the Ministry decided to provide workers with canteens where they could buy extra meals. In 1943 it became compulsory for all firms employing more than 250 people to set up a canteen. Working men's canteens served double the meat allowance permitted in an ordinary restaurant. By the end of that year there were 10,577 factory canteens and 958 on docks and building sites and at mining pit-heads, supplying the men with hot, meat-based meals for one shilling or less.[87]

The needs of manual workers in the countryside, who were too dispersed to congregate in canteens, were addressed by the Rural Pie Scheme. Food manufacturers, including a subsidiary of Lyons, made meat pies and delivered them to the Women's Voluntary Service, who then distributed them to farm workers. The demand for pies grew so large that Lyons had to set up satellite pie plants in their provincial bakeries.[88] Agricultural workers also received an extra cheese ration as this made for a portable lunch, but many land girls complained that the cheese disappeared into their landlady's larder, never to emerge in their sandwiches.

Supplementary to the factory canteens was a network of what were originally termed 'communal feeding centres'. Despite presiding over the administration of 'war socialism' it is said that Churchill could not stomach the communist image evoked by the name, and instead christened them British Restaurants, which he felt had a more patriotic ring.[89] They were set up partly in order to maintain social harmony. A middle-class housewife writing for Mass Observation in October 1941 registered her resentment that the air raid protection workers and police had their own canteens run by the Women's Voluntary Service, where they were provided with hot meals at midday. While she agreed that 'it's only right that miners, blastfurnace men, dockers, shipyard workers, agricultural workers etc. should have the lion's share of meat, cheese, sugar and butter', these men, who in Bradford had nothing to do but sit about playing cards, were able to eat egg, sausage or fish and chips, scones, biscuits and jam tarts off the ration 'at jolly low prices'.[90] At the other end of the scale there were the rich and privileged, who were able to evade food restrictions and eat well at fancy restaurants. Even though a maximum charge of 5 shillings was imposed on restaurant meals in June 1942, the real cost of the meal was covered by phenomenally high prices for wine or a fee for using the dance floor. Anthony Weymouth, a middle-class professional, only ate in restaurants if someone else was paying.[91]

British Restaurants appeased these resentments by providing the entire population with affordable opportunities to eat off the ration. In September 1942 the laboratory technician Edward Stebbing 'paid [his] first visit to a British restaurant and had a very good lunch; stuffed lamb, potatoes and cabbage, date roll and custard, and a cup of tea, at the very modest price of 11d.'.[92] Much has been made of the significance of British Restaurants. In fact, only 5 per cent of the population ate in them on a regular basis, choosing to go to one only if they could not get home for lunch.[93] However, taken as a whole, the system of canteens, restaurants and the pie scheme proved an efficient way of ensuring that extra food was channelled into the stomachs of the working population. Don Joseph, an apprentice at an aircraft factory in London during the war, recalled, 'many families had double the official ration because they ate at their place of work'.[94] Every day he ate lunch, as well as sandwiches during his two tea breaks, at his work's canteen, and three times a week he ate his supper at the technical college canteen where he attended evening classes.

Factory canteens and British Restaurants provided the teams of food experts and nutritional advisers who were appointed to oversee the kitchens with an excellent opportunity to try to improve working-class diets. But their efforts did not always meet with enthusiasm. A former hotel chef sent to manage a factory canteen in Birmingham despaired at the workers' resistance to his attempts to provide them with healthy, productivity-boosting meals. When he tried to cheer up a dish of boiled beef and carrots with a white sauce, there were protests. Salads and savouries were refused. The men wanted 'fish and chips, cream cakes, bread and butter, and brown gravy over everything'. Sadly, he concluded that 'Birmingham people do not understand food.'[95]

A particularly knotty problem for the Ministry of Food was the question of how to distribute fairly foodstuffs which suffered from an erratic supply, such as tinned meat, fish and fruit, dried fruits, tapioca, rice, biscuits, dried peas, beans, breakfast cereals, suet and jellies. None of these was imported in sufficient quantities or in a steady enough flow to be able to guarantee their supply and put them on the ration. M. P. Roseveare, Principal Assistant Secretary at the Ministry of Food, came up with the ingenious points system.[96] The foods were given a price in points as well as pounds, shillings and pence, and each person was allocated a certain number of points each week. The Ministry would adjust the points price of foods according to the quantities available. If they were in short supply the number of points they were worth would rise, and as they became more widely available their points value would decline. In this way consumer demand could be steered away from foods in short supply. At Christmas the number of points would be adjusted to allow for a little luxury, and Doreen Laven can remember 'my mother and aunt sitting in the fading light either side of the living room boiler, listening intently to the radio as these increases were announced and making comments like "half a pound of sultanas, that's not bad Grace," or, "I'd hoped there might be more margarine."'[97] By the end of the war British households were spending about 11 per cent of their food budget using points. Given that about 30 per cent of the budget went on rationed food, another 15 per cent on 'controlled distribution' foods such as onions, and the rest on unregulated foods such as bread, flour, oatmeal, potatoes, fish, fresh vegetables and fruit other than oranges, a psychologically beneficial illusion of control and choice was present in the system.[98] As Lord Woolton remarked somewhat condescendingly, 'for the women it became "shopping" instead of "collecting the rations", and this gave them a little pleasure in their harassed lives'.[99]

By the beginning of 1942 the British Ministry of Food had succeeded in creating a stable system which distributed food relatively evenly across the civilian population. A Mass Observation survey of 'food tensions' found that 77 per cent thought that the situation was better than they had expected and a Gallup poll of the same year reported that 79 per cent of its respondents thought Lord Woolton was doing a good job.[100] The high degree of satisfaction with the government was in large part attributable to the fact that it was very rare that people felt they were unable to obtain their full share of what was available. Owing to the fact that not all calories consumed were covered by the rationing system, it is only possible to arrive at estimates, but after a low point in the second winter of the war, the average British person's calorie consumption appears to have recovered to about 3,000 calories a day.[101] This was a generous amount of food to allocate to every person in the country and indicates the fact that, despite U-boats, the shipping shortage and wrangling with US officials, the British were able to maintain a satisfactory level of food supply throughout the war. The sense that the food supply could be relied upon and that on the whole shortages were being shared out across the population appears to have made food one of the factors that contributed to good morale among the British.[102]

FEEDING THE GERMAN WAR MACHINE

The initial German ration was generous and appears to have initiated a process of levelling up, whereby the poorer families gained access to more and better food. In 1939 the Research Institute of the German Labour Front calculated that 42 per cent of working families were entitled to more food than they had eaten before the war.[103] Elisabeth E. recalled that children-rich mothers had so many more sugar coupons than they needed that they were happy to give them away to others.[104] Nevertheless, price rises and food shortages affected the cities, and meat, poultry, game, eggs, oil and fats all became increasingly difficult to find in the shops despite the fact that they were on the ration.[105] Price-capping policies demotivated farmers from growing fruit and vegetables and grocers passed on to their customers the cost of the hefty bribes they were forced to pay wholesalers in order to persuade them to release their limited stocks of vegetables.[106] Working women, who could only go shopping after work, arrived in the evenings to find empty shelves, and there was much resentment that shopkeepers held back the best foodstuffs under the counter for their wealthiest customers.[107]

German workers were resentful of the fact that they were now expected to work overtime without supplementary pay, and those whose jobs were classed as heavy campaigned to have their work reclassified as ultra-heavy so that they could receive a larger ration.[108] Like industrial workers in Britain, German working men felt that they did not receive enough meat and they looked on enviously as soldiers, who were not in what might be termed 'action', manning anti-aircraft batteries in the cities, were fed substantial front-line rations. One of the things military recruits most enjoyed was their generous meat ration. Fritz Harenberg recalled, 'I liked the military period in the barracks. We received very good food. Cutlets . . . as big as a toilet lid . . . salad, potatoes, gravy and everything. And not once a week, many times in a week.'[109] Compared to the heavy workers' daily 171 grams of meat, the field ration of 250 grams seemed excessive for soldiers who were not engaged in actual combat. But the Wehrmacht was jealous of its privileges and resisted any attempts to cut rations among troops stationed within the Reich.[110] Workers began to demand the same rations as the Wehrmacht.[111]

The German rationing system was equitable in that it acknowledged the need of physical labourers for larger quantities of food but, despite the best efforts of Kraut to calculate the nutritional needs of each ration class, the rations were too low for heavy workers in the physically demanding war industries. In the first year of the war, workers began to lose weight.[112] Göring recognized that the high-calorie needs of miners, upon whom so much of the war effort depended, were not being met by the ration, and he issued a decree which stipulated that miners working overtime should be provided with a warm meal. Here, as so often, the German government was not speaking with one voice. Backe was adamant that the German food budget was too tight to free up extra food at Göring's whim, and the Ministry of Food only stopped demanding food coupons in return for the extra meal after the capture of France guaranteed that the German food supply would be augmented. More often than not, the warm meal miners were supposed to receive turned out to be just some extra bread, and miners in the Ruhr area derisorily referred to the supplementary food as the 'Göring sandwich'.[113] Eventually, under pressure from employers as well as workers, the Ministry of Food created a further category of workers. Night workers and those who worked a particularly long day, either because of exceptionally long hours or because they had to walk a considerable distance to the factory, received more food.[114] Overtime was often rewarded with bowls of soup, and workers who put in more than sixty hours a week or worked shifts of more than twelve hours were rewarded by 250 grams of tinned fish in oil, or tomatoes.[115]

But the Ministry of Food did not feel sufficient food could be made available to increase ration quantities significantly (rather the ration was progressively cut over time) and it certainly did not feel that enough food was available to allow workers to supplement their diet off the ration. The German Labour Front tried to solve the problem of hungry workers by attempting to persuade them to eat in factory canteens. This was seen as a way of preventing the men from sharing their extra ration allocations with their wives and children. If the extra food at the canteens had been provided off the ration, as it was in Britain, no doubt the men would have been willing to eat in them. But the workers were required to surrender some of their ration coupons in return for canteen meals and they distrusted such a system, fearing the kitchen workers would cheat them of their full food entitlement.[116] Given that their food intake was limited, it was natural that they preferred their wives to control how the food was cooked and eaten. In the face of entrenched resistance many factories eventually capitulated and instead provided the men with the means to warm up their own food.[117]

In the winter of 1941–42 the Wehrmacht on the eastern front were bogged down, cold and hungry, the Ukrainian harvest had been disappointing and the farmers within Germany were struggling to grow enough potatoes and produce sufficient pork. Ration cuts in the spring of 1942 roused the regime's worst fears that they were facing a protracted war without sufficient food supplies. To make matters worse, over a million German soldiers had been killed or gone missing on the eastern front. The war in the Soviet Union was proving a voracious consumer of men and materiel. From the autumn of 1941 the military began drafting industrial workers into the army, despite the fact that there was no one to replace them on the assembly lines.[118] The Reich was facing serious food and manpower shortages. Nutritional research shifted its emphasis from the health benefits of an autarkic diet to research into food as a tool for maximizing physical efficiency. Robert Ley, head of the Labour Front, pronounced that 'it was the highest social achievement to preserve the health, and thus the ability to work, of the productive people'.[119] In 1942 the academic journal of the Institute for the Physiology of Work published the findings of investigations which calculated the precise amounts of calories required for a range of jobs, from foundry workers and carpenters to concentration camp guards.[120] Another study examined the impact of glucose and a glucose–vitamin B1 preparation on the performance of workers in hot working conditions, and a further paper published findings on a study of 'the impact of warm meals on the productivity of women doing night work'.[121] It was found that the women's productivity actually sank by 16 per cent if they were given a cup of warm tea, in contrast to a warm meal, which made them 10 per cent more productive.[122] These nutritional studies were a rational attempt to find ways to expend every gram of food as efficiently as possible and use food and manpower resources as effectively as possible. However, when it came to feeding foreign workers the idea of using food resources efficiently was obscured by a mass of ideological principles.

In early 1942 Hitler sought to overcome the manpower shortage by appointing Fritz Sauckel as the General Plenipotentiary for Labour Mobilization. In the same reshuffle he appointed Albert Speer as Minister of Armaments and War Production and Herbert Backe, who had long overridden Walther Darré in matters of food, was confirmed in his position as acting Minister for Food and Agriculture. Hitler looked to these three men to revitalize the war effort. Sauckel immediately set about solving the manpower shortage by importing foreign workers from the east at the rate of 34,000 a week. By the summer of 1943 there were 6.5 million foreign workers in the Reich.[123]

In contrast to western European forced labourers, who received only marginally less food than German workers, the eastern workers were given completely inadequate rations. The watery soups which they were fed contained agonizingly little fat and protein, and the bread they were allocated was virtually inedible. Known as 'Russian' bread it was made of a mixture of rye, sugar beet waste and straw.[124] The work by physiologist Nathan Zuntz during the First World War had demonstrated that it was possible for a human on an inadequate diet to continue physical work right up to the point where starvation caused the failure of the vital organs.[125] But in following this principle with the Soviet forced labourers the National Socialists came up against the limits of the human basic metabolic rate. They discovered that feeding one worker 3,000 calories was more effective than feeding 1,500 calories to two workers. The two workers on 1,500 calories each used up all the energy simply staying alive. The well-fed worker could stay alive *and* expend the surplus energy on productive physical activity. The military administration complained, 'It is illusory to believe that one can achieve the same performance from 200 inadequately fed people as with 100 properly fed workers . . . the minimum rations distributed simply to keep people alive, since they are not matched by any equivalent performance, must be regarded from the point of view of the national war economy as a pure loss, which is further increased by transport costs and administration.'[126] At the IG Farben factory in Landsberg only 158 of the 500 eastern workers employed at the factory were fit enough to work. A manager at a screw factory in Nuremberg was concerned that his German employees might start to sympathize with the Russian women labourers who sat in the workrooms crying with hunger.[127]

The regime was divided over the matter of eastern workers' rations. Speer and the Wehrmacht wanted the rations to be improved. They were motivated by practical, not humanitarian concerns. The German armament industry was by then reliant on Soviet forced labour and Speer was struggling to rescue the failing war effort. However, he came up against the Foreign Department of the Reich Security Head Office (RSHA) which represented the interests of the ideologues in the party. For them the sizeable population of eastern workers within the Reich represented an unsavoury pool of contamination.[128] It would be politically unthinkable to improve the diet of these sub-humans until the civilian ration, which had been cut in the spring, was again raised. They insisted that, rather than following a 'goal-rational' logic, the feeding policy for eastern foreign workers follow a 'value-rational' logic.[129]

In the autumn the plunder of the food supplies of the occupied territories eased the food situation within the Reich, and the civilian ration was raised. Even then the forced labourers' diet was only improved by a 10 per cent increase in calories and it was rare for eastern workers to receive their full food allocation. Often much of the food that arrived at the camps was rotten and had to be thrown away.[130] Olga Fjodorowna Sch., a Pole who worked for IG Farben, recalled that she and her fellow workers supplemented their diet with 'grasses and leaves . . . but they gave us cramps and pains in the heart. When the Americans freed us I could not even drink a glass of milk. I was eighteen years old and weighed thirty-one kilos.'[131]

In 1942 the manpower shortage led the pragmatic wing of the National Socialist regime to look to the concentration camps as a possible source of labour. Until this crisis point in the war the hard labour of concentration camp inmates was regarded merely as a form of punishment and was not supposed to be productive. In fact, according to Himmler, 'the more physically exhausting and senseless the work was, the more success-ful the measure'.[132] For the political opponents of the regime, the Polish and eastern European intelligentsia, communists, homosexuals, Jehovah's witnesses, Catholics, members of the resistance, common criminals and Jews in the concentration camps, hunger was so overwhelming that all other desires faded away, leaving only an obsession with food. 'Sigi is seventeen years old and is hungrier than everybody,' wrote Primo Levi in a description of his time in the work camp of Buna (a sub-camp of Auschwitz). '[Sigi] slipped on to the subject of food and now he talks endlessly about some marriage luncheon . . . everyone tells him to keep quiet but within ten minutes Béla is describing . . . a recipe to make meat-pies with corncobs and lard and spices . . . and he is cursed, sworn at and a third one begins to describe . . .'[133] In Auschwitz these conversa-tions were known as 'stomach masturbation'.[134]

In 1942 concentration camp prisoners were transferred to undertake productive work in the aircraft and rocket industries. The most notori-ous of such projects was Dora Mittelbau in the Harz mountains, where concentration camp inmates constructed an underground factory for the production of the V2 rockets which were to menace Londoners in the final months of the war. They had to sleep inside the tunnels amid the noise and dust of the work, and saw daylight only once a week. The sanitation was rudimentary and they never had enough water to drink. One third (20,000) of the workers died. The tunnels were littered with the dead bodies of prisoners who had collapsed from overwork and malnutrition, and corpses swung from the ceilings overhead, placed there to remind the workers of the fate of recalcitrants. When Speer and his staff visited on a tour of inspection some of his team were so distressed by what they saw that they 'had to take extra leave'.[135]

Himmler began to look for cheap ways of feeding the concentration camp prisoners so that they would have enough energy to work like 'Egyptian slaves' for the regime.[136] The SS Brigadier Walter Schieber of the Armaments Supply Office invented a sausage made from the waste products of cellulose production. It was flavoured with a liver aroma and looked and smelt like liver sausage, and was christened 'eastern food'. Himmler was delighted with the sausage and described it as an 'unbelievably nourishing, tasty, sausage-like paste, that made an excellent foodstuff'.[137] It was given to inmates at Mauthausen and the guards described the prisoners as enthusiastically spreading it on their bread. But Ernst Martin, an inmate who worked as a clerk in the clinic there, secretly examined the paste under a microscope and found it was crawling with bacteria. He recalled that even the guard dogs would not touch it. Soon after its distribution the incidence of stomach and intestinal disorders increased and killed 116 of the prisoners. Nevertheless, a production centre for the sausage was set up and 100,000 of the prisoners at Dachau, Buchenwald and Sachsenhausen were fed the revolting paste with unknown consequences for their health and mortality.[138]

Although the National Socialists did acknowledge that western Allied prisoners of war were protected by the rules of the Geneva Convention, and officers were exempted from labour, the ordinary soldiers were also put to work for the regime on a minimal diet. R. P. Evans, captured in France in 1940, was sent to Stalag VIII B in Upper Silesia, where he worked alongside Poles, Czechs, Bulgarians, Italians and Jews. The British prisoners cleared tree stumps and constructed roads on a site which was destined to become a plant for extracting petrol from coal. 'After a twelve hour working day, we were absolutely exhausted when we returned to camp. After a wash with ersatz soap . . . we were then issued with our food. This consisted of about a pint of watery vegetable soup, usually mangold or sauerkraut . . . three potatoes boiled in their jackets, and a loaf of black bread between twelve men, and sometimes a minute piece of ersatz margarine.'[139] Often the men could not resist eating the bread, intended for their breakfast, which meant that, apart from an early morning cup of ersatz coffee, they frequently had to wait another twenty-four hours for their next meal. Comradeship among the men weakened in the face of hunger: 'it became a case of each man for himself, and devil take the hindmost'.[140]

It was only when Red Cross parcels began to arrive in the camp about eighteen months after their imprisonment that the food situation improved. From then on they received a steady supply until just before the end of the war. The survival of British, French, Canadian and American prisoners of the Germans was good, only 4 per cent dying in captivity. R. P. Evans was convinced that the Red Cross parcels were the key to their survival. When the first parcels arrived 'we carried them back to our rooms and sat and gloated over them . . . The first cup of tea was like drinking nectar . . . Some chaps started eating, and kept right on until it was all gone. True to my nature, I rationed mine, and had a little each day to supplement the German rations.'[141]

THE BLACK MARKET

The level of black market activity in any country during the war can be read as an indicator of the level of acceptance of the food rationing system among the population. It also acts as an indicator of whether rationing was providing people with sufficient food. By its very nature black market activity is difficult to measure, but what evidence there is suggests that although the German and British black markets did not approach the size of those in occupied Europe, there was a black sector in both countries.

Farmers, food processors and food retailers acted as the main generative source of black market dealings. In Germany, small farmers had resisted government controls since the Reich Food Corporation was founded in 1934. In particular, they disliked the centralized collection of milk which denied them the ability to make good profits selling home-made butter in the local urban markets.[142] Evasion of centralized controls continued into the war when they became particularly common in the meat market. There was a variety of tricks that could be employed, such as simply failing to register livestock, sending healthy animals to the knacker's yard, and failing to weigh the carcasses with the heads so that the equivalent of the weight of the heads could be kept back in good meat for illegal sale.[143] In Britain and Germany farmers and slaughterhouses used all these ploys. However, the amount of black market meat emerging from the slaughterhouses in Britain appears to have consisted of a tiny proportion of the legal total, while in Germany, perhaps because of the greater number of smallholders, it seems to have been more prevalent. In Germany, the special courts set up to prosecute black marketeering dealt most often with charges of illegal slaughter.

In 1942 the mayor of the commune of Rottweil, near Stuttgart, his son, two clerks and an official from the Reich Food Corporation were tried for a scam which they had been operating with the farmers since 1939. Slaughtered pigs were weighed without their heads or trotters and the equivalent weight in meat was withheld. The conspirators were accused of removing 5,080 kilograms of pork (equivalent to 2,500 weekly basic ration portions) from the system. The mayor and the Food Corporation official were lucky to escape the death penalty and received a prison sentence instead.[144] The magistrate argued that use of the death sentence would create an undesirable atmosphere of conflict with the farmers in the region. This tendency towards leniency in the courts, and the National Socialists' reluctance to prosecute prominent officials for fear of publicizing the disreputable behaviour of party members, meant that the threat of the death penalty did little to discourage this kind of activity. Besides, the state lacked the manpower to monitor the actions of every official and it seems that many took the risk, calculating that the chances that they would be found out were relatively low.[145]

In wartime Britain the term black market conjured up images of an underworld of organized crime run by suspiciously well-dressed men known as spivs. It was seen as having little to do with ordinary, respectable people.[146] In fact, most black market transactions were petty infringements, like the exchange which took place between Vere Hodgson and her grocer in February 1941. 'Went for my bacon ration and while he was cutting it had a word with the man about the Cubic Inch of Cheese. He got rid of the other customers and then whispered, "Wait a mo." I found half a pound of cheese being thrust into my bag with great secrecy and speed!'[147] Shopkeepers would process their wares carefully and build up a surplus of under-the-counter stock which they could slip into the shopping baskets of their favoured customers. In Germany, Inge Deutschkron, a Jew living underground with a couple who ran a bookshop, recalled that the husband expected his wife Grete to put meals on the table that were just as in normal times. In her effort to provide sumptuous meals Grete was sucked into a complicated, network of transactions. Her parents ran a food shop and she got as much butter as she wanted from them. Then there was Frau Marsch, who worked in a butcher's. She would smuggle meat out and swap it for real coffee, or swap butter for coffee, coffee for meat, meat for soap. In the end, 'Grete was so wrapped up in her black marketing that she could hardly think about anything else.'[148]

Too much has probably been made of the idea that the British pulled together during the war, but the Ministry of Food did manage to cultivate a sense of social justice which seems to have been shared by the population at large. Those who admitted to a Mass Observation survey conducted after the war that they had dabbled in black marketeering looked back on their behaviour with a mixture of guilt or self-justification.[149] The great majority of black market users were conscious that they were taking more than they were entitled to and thus disrupting a system which they accepted did a relatively good job of equitably sharing out the hardships of war.[150] The greatest danger to the Ministry of Food's carefully constructed image of fairness was the 'luxury feeding' of the rich. A Home Intelligence report from March 1942 warned that a sense of inequality of sacrifice was being fuelled by 'the resort of the rich to expensive restaurants'.[151] Even after the regulation of restaurant meals in June, chefs were still able to commandeer plentiful supplies of unrationed meats such as fish, lobster, chicken and rabbit, and there was no denying that the rich could still eat well if they paid for it. However, aristocratic indulgence does not seem to have thoroughly undermined the sense of common sacrifice which developed within British society during the war years. George Orwell, who in the 1930s refused to believe that Britain's 'bitterly class-ridden society' would be able to unite over a war, was as early as December 1940 surprised to find that 'patriotism is finally stronger than class-hatred'.[152] The British working classes expected the British aristocracy to indulge, and it seems that the general consensus was that despite their fine dining habits they were held sufficiently in check, while at the same time the government did enough to protect the interests of the working people.

In Germany there was certainly plenty of luxury feeding in Berlin restaurants. In February 1941 Marie Vassiltchikov, who worked in the Information Department of the Foreign Ministry, 'lunched at Horcher's and simply gorged. As the best restaurant in town, they scorn the very idea of food coupons.'[153] Horcher's was one of Göring's favourite restaurants and he is said to have regularly indulged in meals which consumed a week's worth of an ordinary German's rations. Since the early days of the regime Goebbels had been trying hard to build up a public sense of the German people as a *Volksgemeinschaft* or a society of equals. Göring's flamboyant lifestyle, drinking, eating and partying to excess at the various castles and hunting lodges which he built for himself, consistently undermined the propaganda and destroyed the idea of the National Socialists as restrained and upright leaders. While Göring might greet supper guests at his palatial residence at Carinhall wearing a 'blue or violet kimono with fur-trimmed bedroom slippers' and a girdle set with jewels, guests dining at the house of Goebbels would be met by liveried footmen who would collect their ration coupons on silver trays. Goebbels' guests were frequently disappointed to discover that their coupons had earned them a meagre dinner of herring with boiled potatoes.[154] Hitler himself ate a peculiar vegetarian diet and generally served austere and execrable food at his dining table. A typical meal might consist of 'a horrible grey barley broth – with crackers and some butter with Gervais-cheese as pudding'.[155] His weakness was sugar. Hitler loved fancy cakes and chocolate bars and could eat as much as 2 pounds of chocolate in one day.[156] In 1943 after Goebbels had announced that Germany must now invest every ounce of energy in waging total war, he was so incensed by Göring's continued extravagance that he arranged for an angry mob to attack Horcher's. In defence of his right to luxurious meals Göring posted a contingent from the Luftwaffe to guard the restaurant. He eventually lost this particular battle when the restaurant was forced to close for lack of foodstuffs. (The family and their staff relocated to Madrid.) But to Goebbels' despair many Nazi potentates followed Göring's example and sought to capitalize on their positions of power.

The public's awareness that corruption was entrenched among the 'upper ten thousand' of the National Socialist administration undermined Goebbels' rhetoric about the need for full mobilization and sacrifice. Hitler issued a decree in March 1942, and again in May 1943, calling on those in top positions to set a good example under the present conditions of total war, but this was to little avail as self-serving corruption appears to have been the norm.[157] In 1942 a long-standing arrangement between a Berlin delicatessen trader called August Nöthling and an array of members of the Nazi elite to supply rationed goods without taking payment in coupons was exposed. Among his customers were Foreign Minister Joachim von Ribbentrop, Minister of Food and Agriculture Walther Darré, the Chief of Police Wilhelm von Grolman, Field Marshals Walther von Brauchitsch and Wilhelm Keitel and the Interior Minister Wilhelm Frick, who was listed as having received off the ration, 'ham (smoked and tinned), tins of corned beef and sausage, venison, butter, fat, poultry, chocolates, tea, cocoa, sugar, oil, sweets, honey and fruit'.[158] The report on Nöthling's activities was written by the Police President

Wolf-Heinrich Graf von Helldorf, who failed to mention that he had himself bought spirits, wines and Cognac from the shopkeeper.[159] When the affair came to Goebbels' attention and he confronted the culprits they came up with an array of what Goebbels dismissed as 'soggy' excuses, the most common being that the food shopping was handled entirely by their wives, who had not realized that they were doing anything wrong.[160] Goebbels' determination to make an example of these men at a public trial was frustrated by Nöthling, who, it was claimed, committed suicide in his cell.

It was perhaps the awareness of the prevalence of high-level corruption which made Hitler and Göring (to Goebbels' annoyance) reluctant to punish small-scale black marketeers who went out from the towns to barter in the countryside for food, a practice endearingly known in German as 'hamstering'.[161] Henry Picker, an adjutant at Hitler's head-quarters, reported that at lunchtime on 23 June 1942 Hitler held forth on the subject of hamstering, arguing that the police should not search people coming into the cities from the countryside for a few eggs. He demonstrated his failure to grasp the economics of agricultural supply by arguing that as long as the farmers filled their quotas this sort of traditional trade did no harm. Goebbels pointed out that 'the end result is that there are absolutely no fruit or vegetables in the shops'.[162] He was put down by Hitler, who argued that too much transportation of vegetables meant that they spoiled and this, in fact, was a more efficient way of ensuring that the towns were fed by their hinterlands. This was not a view which would have been shared by the townspeople who were bartering away their Persian rugs, table linen and children's toys in exchange for potatoes, a little milk, a few green vegetables or fruit. The growth of a black market of barter in Germany indicated the seriousness of food shortages within the industrial cities. It was a disturbing signal that the ration was failing to ensure all German civilians an adequate diet.

THE GERMAN CITIES – HUNGRY BUT NOT STARVING

In Britain the food situation had stabilized by the end of 1941, and even if meals were monotonous and not particularly tasty, the food supply remained stable and adequate throughout the rest of the war. In Germany, in contrast, the food situation in the cities progressively worsened until a crisis was reached in the winter and spring of 1941–42. Potato shortages had begun to impact upon urban dwellers in the summer of 1941, but by the time the exceptionally cold winter months set in there were serious problems with the potato supply to the cities and shortages were reported in Cologne, Frankfurt am Main and Berlin. Wilhelm Kiel, a social democrat living in the northern industrial area, described how he had to 'literally go begging to the farmers, from house to house, in order to obtain, pound by pound, the quantity of potatoes we need, in order to eke out a bare existence until the autumn'.[163] Women tried to disguise the lack of meat on the menu by making 'false meatballs and cutlets' out of potatoes, lentils, turnips and white cabbage, but with a shortage of potatoes and vegetables it became increasingly difficult to make filling meals.[164] Berliners were so starved of greens that nettles and sugar beet leaves sold for high prices in the markets.[165]

A further depressing development was the progressive decline in the quality of bread, the other mainstay of the diet.[166] Over the months and years of the war the milling grade of wheat was continually increased until by April 1942 virtually none of the bran was removed. Gradually, more and more barley, potato and rye flour was mixed in with the wheat flour. This did not necessarily affect the nutritional value of the loaves but food offices began to complain that the bread was causing digestive problems and diarrhoea. In 1942 a report from Regensburg complained, 'a good bread for labouring people is half the meaning of life and has a tremendous impact on productivity as well as morale'.[167]

The decline in the quality and quantity of staple foods was accompanied by a Ministry of Food campaign to encourage people to find substitute foods. Teachers were instructed to take their classes out into the fields to gather weeds and grasses such as yarrow, goat's rue and stinging nettles as replacements for cabbage. Even the roots of carnations were recommended.[168] In the autumn of 1942 the Württemberg Milk and Fats Trade Association encouraged people to go out into the woods and collect beechnuts, from which a valuable edible oil could be extracted. For every kilogram delivered to them they promised to issue a voucher for 200 grams of margarine or oil.[169] Unfortunately, the beechnut crop was poor that year and these exhortations to find substitute foods did nothing but remind civilians of the hunger winters of the First World War, when people were so desperate they too went out into the fields to gather wild foods.

In the autumn and winter of 1942 the intensive exploitation of the occupied territories brought temporary relief and rations were raised. But the relief did not last long. The year 1943 brought yet more food shortages to Germany's cities. In Essen bread and potatoes made up 90 per cent of what most people ate and the industrial towns were once more hard hit by an unsatisfactory potato harvest in the summer.[170] The Ministry of Food began to make plans to distribute swedes and turnips, and Italian rice and lentils were brought in to eke out the supplies of staple foods.[171] The basic meat and fat ration had to be cut yet again in May.[172] Even though military rations were cut by 20 per cent, the army was too large a burden on the system. All this was exacerbated by the 7 million foreign workers in the Reich and the fact that local officials began to distribute generous rations to the homeless in the bombed-out cities.[173]

In the spring of 1943 Sybil Bannister, an Englishwoman married to a German gynaecologist, discovered how serious the food situation in the towns was in comparison with the comparatively plentiful food supply in the countryside. Sybil spent the first years of the war living in Bromberg, a town in the annexed part of Poland. Here she missed cheese and sauces but felt that she 'could not grumble. We were always able to buy a winter store of potatoes . . . in the summer we had ample fruit and vegetables to bottle for the winter months.'[174] Then she took her baby son to stay with his grandfather in Wuppertal-Barmen. Here everyday life was much more difficult. 'Besides the war in general, there were two things which were obviously lowering their vitality; one was the food shortage, and the other the continued air-raids . . . The food shortage was as yet not desperately acute. There were enough goods in the shops to supply the full complement on the ration cards, but this was just *not* enough. It is easy to go short for a few days or a few weeks without noticing many ill effects, but when it runs into months, the need accumulates until a permanent state of hunger and enervation ensues . . . in May 1943, coming straight from the country in the East where we had unlimited supplies of milk, potatoes and vegetables, into a town in an industrial centre in the West, it was remarkable to notice what a difference the deficiency in these foods made to the possibility of varying the menu and still more of satisfying appetites . . . In Barmen there was not only no full milk for adults, but potatoes were rationed and vegetables in short supply. As it was impossible to "fill up" with these commodities, the bread ration also proved inadequate . . . It was a constant worry to know how to fill the hungry mouths.'[175]

It is not necessary to be actually starving in order for food deprivation to cause psychological and physical distress. Women used up a great deal of mental and physical energy thinking up different ways of preparing the same foods and producing something edible out of a few potatoes and lentils, with barely any fat or green vegetables. Long and tiring food queues, anxiety about where the next meal would come from, interspersed with periods of real deprivation, all combined to cause great stress. Then the Allied aerial bombing campaign began to hit the industrial areas in earnest and the inhabitants of the cities were reduced to a state of misery.

Sybil Bannister was unlucky enough to experience the first bombing raid to hit Wuppertal-Barmen while she was visiting her father-in-law. The family's home was destroyed. They were given chits which allowed them to buy food in the shops. As the air raids in Wuppertal had only just begun, the shops were still stocked but, 'Later on . . . there were no goods available in the shops.'[176] The bombing raids took their toll on food warehouses and household stores. More and more food had to come out of the regular rationing system to set up emergency kitchens for the homeless.[177] In the city of Cologne, the last two years of the war were appalling. Lengthening food queues were matched by long walks to work as the public transport system broke down. Lack of fuel for cooking and heating, combined with frequent air raids, made home life debilitating, and the shabby clothing and worn shoes gave the civilian population a depressing air. There were no work shoes to be had or rubber boots. Washing was difficult with the tiny piece of inferior soap which was allocated on the monthly ration.[178] The deaths of friends and neighbours from the bombing campaign, and the increasing loss of men at the front to death and injury and military defeats – first at Stalingrad, then North Africa, Italy, on the Atlantic in the submarine war, and over and over again on the eastern front – all wore down civilian morale.[179]

Under these circumstances of increasing hardship industrial workers began to turn to factory canteens. Workers' families were evacuated and the men were left with no one at home to cook for them. Others were bombed out and had no alternative but to eat at the factory canteen. The numbers using them rose from 800,000 to almost 5 million.[180] Sybil Bannister was extremely glad of her canteen meals. After visiting Wuppertal she had returned to Bromberg, only to flee before the Russians in January 1945. She ended up in Hamburg working as a nurse for sick workers at a factory, where 'there was a canteen ... where they served up a wholesome hot-pot with very little meat in it, but certainly as much as the number of coupons they asked for, added to which (thrown in, coupon free) there was a good helping of potatoes and vegetables, which were rationed and in short supply. We lined up to fetch the soup-plate full of steaming stew.'[181]

In Britain, as the next chapter will discuss, the diet of the working classes improved despite the exigencies of war. In Germany, even though the regime intended to spare the workers from hunger, it was the industrial working population which bore the brunt of wartime food shortages. Germany simply did not have enough food and too much of what was grown stayed in the countryside rather than being transported into the cities. By 1944 German townspeople were eating barley grits rather than meat and potatoes, and shortages in the cities had become the norm.[182] The loss of the Ukraine intensified the meat and fat shortages and led to a drastic cut in sugar supplies.[183] Nevertheless, at no time did the food situation reach the disastrous levels of the last two winters of the First World War. When food shortages were at their worst between 1914 and 1919, the meat supply afforded each person only a paltry 14 grams of meat per day, while in 1944–45 Germany had enough meat to allocate each citizen a still meagre but more adequate 48 grams a day.[184] There was no question of famine or mass starvation even in the urban areas. Nor was there ever any question of social unrest or worker revolt as a result of hunger, although the Sicherheitsdienst constantly warned that the workers were in a dangerously critical mood. The National Socialists had so effectively destroyed the social democratic, communist and trade union leadership during the 1930s that an organized opposition to the National Socialist government no longer existed. Ration cuts were accepted with grumbles and complaints. Those who acknowledged that working to the bitter end would help to prop up a government they detested resigned themselves to the situation, concentrated on getting on with their lives, and quietly made a concerted effort to obtain food on the black market.

As the war came to a close in late 1944 and early 1945, the black market became an increasingly important source of food. Those with possessions to barter occupied a position of privilege. Ruth P., a child at the time, recalled with sadness how her beautiful white doll's bed, her doll Christel, and a marionette with a black pony 'were all given away for barter for a goose and a duck, a rabbit or something. All for something to eat.'[185] Those with neither possessions to barter nor useful social connections, including many families who had fled their homes in the east or lost them to bombing, found themselves at the bottom of the social order. In a letter to her husband, written at the very end of 1944, Mathilde Wolff-Mönckeberg wrote, 'We sometimes have *very* little and don't look exactly blooming. Especially at the end of each rationing period [of 4 weeks] we have virtually nothing. We get only ¾ lb of butter *each month*, a disappearingly small piece of cheese, very little meat, each only ½ lb . . . Even the bread is insufficient . . . sometimes I spend hours wishing for lots of good fat things to eat! And sweet things.'[186] In contrast, her landlady seemed to be faring quite well and her Christmas celebrations included real coffee made with beans, and Christmas cakes. There was still good food to be had if one had the means to acquire it. Despite a great deal of misery and some deprivation, even the least well-off in German society were still far better off than most of the rest of continental Europe. Maria H. recalled, 'We were hungry, actually we were always hungry, but it was not as though we suffered from starvation.'[187]

16

The British Empire – War as Welfare

> *I was determined to use the powers I possessed to stamp out the diseases that arose from malnutrition, especially those among children.*
>
> (Lord Woolton looking back on his term as Minister of Food, April 1940 to November 1943)[1]

> *From my own investigations I became convinced that 'cowardice in the face of the enemy' could be traced to nothing less than malnutrition . . . sufficient to undermine stamina and morale.*
>
> (Stanton Hicks, founder of the Australian Army Catering Corps)[2]

In 1945 the British Ministry of Health announced that from the beginning of the war it had used all available nutritional knowledge to create a 'general policy laid down . . . on sound lines' and which made it 'possible to arrange for a balanced diet for all'.[3] This, argues the food historian Derek Oddy, was an audacious claim and one that sits oddly with the history of the British government's attitude to nutritional reform in the 1930s. Britain entered the war with a government which had, over the previous decade, consistently resisted the idea that the state should take responsibility for the nation's health. In contrast to Germany and Japan, where vigorous efforts were made to change and improve the population's eating habits, the pre-war British government demonstrated an aversion to making a potentially expensive commitment to ensuring that every citizen ate well. Nevertheless, the dominant story told about rationing in Britain between 1939 and 1945 is a heroic tale of a government seizing the opportunity presented by war to improve the nutritional lot of working people. It has also become commonplace to refer to the Second World War as the period during the twentieth century when the British people were at their healthiest. Britain certainly ended the war with a population which was eating a healthier diet than in the 1930s, and the nutritional divide between the wealthy and the poor had begun to close. A social consensus had evolved, accepted by some members of the government (but by no means all), that states must take responsibility for their citizens' diet, health and welfare. Although the government certainly did not enter the war intending to bring about such a change, the war conferred on reformers and nutritionists a level of influence which enabled them to bring about a revolution in attitudes to food and its connection to well-being.

A similar revolution took place within the British and Commonwealth armies. In 1939 the standard of cookery in British and Australian military messes was abysmal: the cooks were poorly trained, underpaid and took little pride in their work. During the war the dreadful food undermined military morale. In the field the British empire's troops were still reliant on an innutritious diet of bully beef (corned beef) and biscuits, just as they had been during the First World War. The nutritional research of the inter-war years had made it possible to recognize vitamin deficiency diseases, and the emergence of symptoms of vitamin deficiencies in British, Australian, African and Indian troops fighting in North Africa, Burma and the Pacific created pressure to reform army diets. There was a new sense among the British and Commonwealth governments that men called upon to sacrifice their lives for their country had a right to expect a decent level of care in return. Medical officers and quartermasters began to ask themselves what soldiers *should* be eating, rather than concentrating on simply sending them what food was available. The quartermasters of the empire's various armies were stimulated into researching new ways of supplying soldiers, at their bases and on the front line, with nutritious food.

DR CARROT – GUARDING THE BRITISH NATION'S HEALTH

The ration which was introduced in Britain in 1940 had been calculated without any reference to nutritional advice. Despite the version of events which the Ministry of Health was to present as the official narrative at the end of the war, neither the Ministry of Health nor the Ministry of Food consulted the emerging group of nutritional scientists in order to draw up a ration which was nutritionally balanced. The ration simply reflected the food that was available.[4] However, the British population was being asked to expend far more energy than in peacetime. In the war industries shifts of ten to twelve hours became the norm, and people were asked to take on extra wartime duties which made for an arduous working week.[5] A worker in Portsmouth described how his life had become far harder: 'Take last weekend. I was at work all day. I did 'Ome Guard till four in the morning. Then I had to start work again at six!'[6] There were concerns that the austere diet would provide too little energy and nutrition to maintain the war effort. It was only as these anxieties began to emerge that the government turned for expert advice to the nutritionists, whose work they had for so long ignored.

In fact, on their own initiative, the intrepid biochemists Elsie Widdowson and R. A. McCance had already set about testing 'how far food produced in Britain could meet the needs of the population and enable them to fare well'.[7] McCance recalled that 'this was fun' even though the diet the scientists put themselves on in the autumn of 1939 contained such small quantities of meat, cheese and sugar that it was 'considered intolerable by our critics'.[8] They filled up on unrestricted amounts of wholemeal bread and potatoes, and after three months on the diet, over the Christmas holidays of 1939–40, they subjected themselves to fitness tests which included bicycling to the Lake District from London and long hikes with weights in their rucksacks. They concluded that a minimal wartime diet was adequate to maintain health and fitness in all respects except the calcium intake, and immediately began a series of experiments to work out how the calcium deficiency in the diet could be remedied.[9]

Meanwhile, in June 1940, the government finally convened a Scientific Sub-Committee on Food Policy, six months after rationing had been introduced. The committee was dominated by agricultural scientists, whose main concern was food production rather than consumption, but it also included Britain's leading nutritionists – Professor E. P. Cathcart, Professor Sir Edward Mellanby and Sir John Boyd Orr – all of whom had conducted research into the deprived diet of Britain's poor.[10] Jack Drummond, a nutritional biochemist at University College London, was appointed as the Chief Scientific Adviser. It was only now that a long-term plan was drawn up by the scientists, who tried to ensure the ration diet was nutritionally balanced.[11]

The influence of the Scientific Sub-Committee was felt most by the officials in charge of the food import programme within the Ministry of Food. They were instructed to consult with Drummond on the types of food to prioritize. It took about a year for the scientists and administrators to work out a satisfactory system for the consultation process, but from the middle of 1941 it began to work well. It was through this diffuse influence that nutritionists probably had the most powerful impact on the British wartime diet. The Ministry of Food used bread as the staple food. This was a more efficient use of food resources, as feeding wheat directly to humans maximized its energy-giving potential, while feeding wheat to animals wasted much of the energy in the grain. During the First World War the government had prioritized total calories and had relied almost entirely on bread to feed the population. In the 1940s, however, the new nutritional knowledge emphasized the need for protective foods and recognized the importance of animal proteins in the diet. The nutritionists on the sub-committee recommended that frozen and canned meat and calcium-rich condensed dairy products should be given priority for importation. This ensured that during the Second World War the entire population was able to supplement its bread intake with these protective foods.[12]

Nutritionists by no means exercised unlimited influence over government food policy. In the first two years of the war they tried in vain to persuade the Ministry of Food to switch from white to wholemeal bread. It was ironic that in its reliance on bread as the wartime staple, the British government adopted the strategy of the much-criticized working-class housewife of the 1930s. In *The Road to Wigan Pier*

George Orwell described how the poor in pre-war Britain filled up on bread and margarine. 'For breakfast you got two rashers of bacon and a pale fried egg, and bread and butter ... for tea there was more bread and butter and frayed-looking sweet cakes which were probably bought as "stales" from the baker.'[13] While the middle classes in the 1930s spent just 3 per cent of their food budget on bread, it absorbed 12 per cent of the working-class budget.[14] Unsympathetic observers condescendingly pointed out that this was a reflection of the ignorance of housewives who spent their food budget unwisely. In fact, working-class women had discovered that filling up on bread was the most effective way of staving off hunger when faced with poor cooking facilities and a very small amount of money.[15] During the war the government followed the same principle and at its highest point wartime consumption of bread per person reached 1.8 kilograms a week, in comparison to the consumption of about 650 grams a week in the 1990s.[16] The problem was that the bread, which formed the substance of both the 1930s working-class and the initial wartime diet, was white.

White flour was one of the first modern industrial foods. It was produced in the late nineteenth century in the United States, where rollers were used to grind the hard American wheat. The new method produced a fine, soft, white flour. However, because the process removed the wheat germ (which is the source of the vitamins, iron and protein) it also produced a flour severely lacking in nutritional value. Thus, the entire British nation ran the risk in wartime of falling into the working-class nutritional trap of the 1930s by relying on a foodstuff which was deficient in essential nutrients. Nutritionists were in agreement that the introduction of wheat-germ-rich wholemeal bread was essential to ensure the health of the British people. When Widdowson and McCance concluded that on the whole the wartime diet was sufficient to maintain health, they had been eating wholemeal not white bread. A wholemeal loaf was made available in 1940 but it only accounted for 9 per cent of the bread which was sold. The nutritionists recommended that the extraction rate of wheat should be raised from around 70 to 85 per cent.*[17] But they came up against powerful interests in the form of the Millers'

---

* An extraction rate of 70–75 per cent removes the bran and the wheat germ (containing fats and minerals). An extraction rate of 85–90 per cent removes only the bran and makes for a more nutritious, if browner, flour.

Mutual Trade Association and the livestock feed suppliers, who bought the waste from wheat processing as animal feed. Both groups brought pressure to bear on the civil service not to increase the extraction rate of wheat. Industry's objections were not the government's only concern. Even the nutritionists acknowledged in their report that wholemeal bread went stale more quickly and that British people did not really like it.[18] Less mindful of the health consequences than of public opinion, the government was unwilling to undermine food morale by making something that was greatly disliked the basis of the British wartime diet. It was not until the shipping crisis became acute in 1942 that the government was forced to outlaw white bread, the wheat extraction rate was raised and the loathed beige National Loaf became the only available bread.[19] This saved one million tons of shipping space a year.[20]

In the meantime Widdowson and McCance had been exploring the problem of calcium deficiency in the ration. A long series of experiments, which involved weighing and analysing everything they, and a group of their friends, ate and excreted, proved their hypothesis that the phytic acid in wholemeal flour hindered the body's ability to absorb calcium. They found that the problem could be solved by adding calcium carbonate or phosphate to wholemeal flour. It was on the basis of their work that the decision was taken to add 120 milligrams of calcium to every 100 grams of National wholemeal flour.[21] Jack Drummond, who had worked on butter substitutes before the war, also insisted that margarine should be fortified with imported concentrates of vitamins A and D in order to compensate for the reduction of butter and eggs in the diet.[22] The fortification of foods with vitamins and minerals was a novel measure which benefited the health of all members of society. In fact, the diet of austerity inadvertently improved the entire nation's health in a number of ways. Although the National Loaf may have been disliked, its high iron and vitamin B content meant that the nutritional value of the working-class diet greatly improved.[23] The switch to arable farming not only increased the importance of bread but also greatly increased the availability of potatoes and the reliance on these for starchy energy boosted the amount of vitamin C in people's diets. The enforced reduction in the consumption of fats and sugars may have been painful but it was far healthier to use the plant carbohydrates in wholemeal bread as a source of energy, rather than sugar. Another beneficial side-effect of the war was the dig for victory campaign which meant that in order to add substance and variety to their meals ordinary people took to growing and eating more vegetables.

By 1943 there were about 1.5 million allotments in Britain.[24] In many of them amateur gardeners struggled to grow onions. These were probably the most missed vegetable of the war. When imports from the continent ceased, they disappeared from the shops. The loss of onions was keenly felt as they were an essential flavouring ingredient in British cookery, particularly in dishes based on the ubiquitous potato. In the winter of 1940 a father writing to his daughter Anne (who had been evacuated to Canada) complained, 'What I would like more than anything I think for lunch today would be bread, lashings of butter, cheese and onions. Of that menu all I could get would be bread.'[25] Anne's father suggested to the manager of the hotel where he was living that they should plant a vegetable garden together and grow onions. Throughout the war, it was the case that anyone who missed onions tended to try and grow their own because the Ministry of Food's attempt to encourage the commercial cultivation of onions was something of a fiasco.

Onion cultivation was placed under the administration of the newly established Vegetable Marketing Company. In 1941 the first large-scale commercial crop was eagerly awaited and the company set up a scheme whereby consumers could reserve their share of the onion harvest at their local grocers' shops. The process of reservation began in September but there were protests as many people were away on holiday and missed their chance to claim a share of the onions. The reservation period was extended but with disastrous consequences. That August had been wet and chilly and this does not suit onions. The 1941 crop was not only meagre but much of it was unfit for storage. While the Company dithered, not allowing farmers to start distributing the crop until the reservation process was complete, the onions began to rot. Farmers were furious and consumers were bitterly disappointed to find that their especially reserved share amounted to a derisorily small bag of onions.[26] Commercial onion cultivation improved in 1942 but there were never plenty of onions and those grown by amateur gardeners often fell victim to a blight which killed the plants or made the onions inedible.[27] Onions were so prized during the war that they were given away in raffles and as birthday presents.[28] On 18 March 1941 Maggie Joy Blunt, a freelance journalist keeping a diary for Mass Observation, recorded that 'Lady A was given an onion yesterday for her birthday. Her cook flavoured bread sauce with it and then used it for something else'.[29]

Gardeners had more success with other vegetables and, in particular, Britain's gardens filled with neat rows of potatoes. If the rationing system was designed to smooth over class distinctions, when it came to gardening class differentials emerged. Virginia Potter, an American who had married an upper-middle-class Englishman, turned her one acre of garden into a smallholding where, with the help of her domestic staff, her husband and a land girl, she grew eighteen sorts of vegetables, including much-coveted onions, five different types of fruit, and kept ducks, geese, hens, rabbits and pigs. Her garden was so productive she was able to sell some of her produce to the local British Restaurant.[30] This was a different order of digging for victory from the working-class family's small plot where they might tend potatoes, a few runner beans and some tomatoes. The middle classes ate a greater variety of greenstuff, while the working classes relied more on root vegetables.[31] Nevertheless, more than half the manual workers in Britain kept a garden or an allotment, and every class increased its vegetable and thus its vitamin consumption.[32]

The Ministry of Food made every effort to educate the British public in the principles of the new science of nutrition and, in particular, the propaganda explained the sources and importance of the newly discovered vitamins. Housewives were given instruction in how to cook vegetables so as not to destroy their precious vitamin content. Carrots and potatoes were proselytized by the cartoon characters Dr Carrot 'the children's best friend' and Potato Pete the 'energy food'. On posters Potato Pete announced that he made a good soup and Dr Carrot that he guarded your health. Carrots, it was explained, contained vitamin A which helped you to see in the dark of the blackout. They were also supposed to contain sugar, and therefore they were often suggested as a replacement for fruit.[33] One Ministry of Food recipe used grated carrots, plum jam and almond flavouring to make a 'mock apricot tart'.[34] The comical characters Gert and Daisy, charladies whose husbands were in the forces, featured on the radio programme *The*

Kitchen Front, broadcast at 8.15 every morning. They conveyed a variety of nutritional messages through humour.[35] Lord Woolton himself would often speak on the radio. Woolton's great talent was for propaganda and he exhibited an aptitude for informing without cajoling and always in a light-hearted fashion.[36] These techniques may sound childish and somewhat condescending to modern ears but now that the idea of a balanced diet and knowledge about the benefits of vitamins are commonplace it is difficult to imagine how much these campaigns changed British people's understanding of food.

The wartime diet may have been good for health but bread and potatoes in large quantities eventually palled. On 23 March 1943 Pam Ashford complained, 'How I grow sick of never-ending starch – bread, bread, bread.'[37] The small quantities of butter and cheese in the ration meant that there was little to add to the bread or potatoes to make them more interesting. Europeans were used to a high proportion of fat in their food and without it dishes seemed tasteless. Even though it was relatively energy-inefficient to import, the nutritionists recommended that bacon should be a staple of the ration as it added flavour to food.[38] Without onions, and with the disappearance of many condiments such as anchovies and lemons, it became increasingly difficult to produce palatable meals.[39] For the British, eating became a matter of filling up on fuel rather than a pleasure. By 1946 they were so fed up with their dull, flavourless food that, although there was no need for anyone to go hungry, many people were in danger of eating too little of even the essential foods because they simply had no further appetite for plain fare.[40]

The Ministry of Food made efforts to address the problem of monotony and lack of flavour but their inventive recipes for 'mock' foods seem more likely to have made meals taste worse rather than better. A mixture of margarine, dried egg, cheese, salad dressing, vinegar, salt and pepper was recommended to make up an uninviting-sounding mock crab. Mock cream could be whipped up using margarine, sugar, dried milk powder and a tablespoon of precious fresh milk.[41] It would probably have been better just to do without cream. R. J. Hammond, the official historian of Britain's food campaign, who had lived through the imposition of such dishes on the public's taste buds, was of the opinion that 'gastronomically speaking, nothing could be more pathetic' than the 'Victory Dishes' which the Ministry of Food devised with 'potatoes, dried egg, salt cod and the like'.[42] British housewives do not appear to have shown a great deal of enthusiasm for experimenting with these outlandish dishes and most of the population got by on Spam, soya-based sausages, meat pies, tinned and powdered soup, fish paste, Bovril and cocoa.[43] Hammond suggested that 'a nation possessed of a more resourceful culinary tradition' would have been able to do better.[44] Indeed, Italian prisoners of war seem to have been able to create tasty dishes with their rations. Doree Griffin, who worked as a land girl on farms in Oxfordshire, commented enviously that a 'gorgeous smell' would waft from the hedgerow when the prisoners' cook was preparing their meal. In contrast, the land girls' staple lunch tended to be beetroot sandwiches.[45]

It was the upper and middle classes who complained the most about wartime food. Evelyn Waugh wrote *Brideshead Revisited* in 1943–44 while recovering from a minor parachuting injury. He later explained that 'it was a bleak period of . . . privation and threatening disaster – the period of soya beans and Basic English – and in consequence the book is infused with a kind of gluttony, for food and wine, for the splendours of the recent past'.[46] Waugh was not alone in longing for a luncheon of plovers' eggs and Lobster Newburg, and it was those sections of society who were used to lavish quantities of good food who suffered the most acute sense of deprivation. As a Cambridge regional food officer put it, while the poor had always had to struggle to come by food, the wealthy were, often for the first time in their lives, faced with the fact that they could not buy all the food that they wanted. In addition, they had to learn to cook in the basement kitchens which had once been the preserve of their servants. During the war it was the middle classes who talked endlessly about food.[47]

While the eating habits of the upper and middle classes were levelled downwards, the working-class diet was levelled upwards. A friend of the journalist J. L. Hodson remarked, 'our rationing of foods has, willy-nilly, achieved some levelling up of the nation; fewer folk have gone hungry and fewer have gorged themselves'.[48] The idea, which was widespread at the time, that the war had brought about a social, cultural and economic levelling of society was largely illusory. The income gap between the working and middle classes remained as wide as ever.

However, reduced unemployment and higher wages greatly improved the purchasing power of working-class families. The real income of a man in industry rose by 46 per cent during the war.[49] It was this rise in purchasing power, combined with price controls and the guarantee of the ration, which gave the working classes access to adequate quantities of meat, eggs (albeit dried), butter and milk products. More than any action by nutritionists or government-directed policy it was full employment and the fairer distribution of food brought about by the need for food rationing which had a revolutionary impact on the nation's health and gave the poorest third of society access to animal protein, vitamins and calcium. The huge gap that had previously existed between the nutritional value of the diet of the wealthy and the poor was substantially narrowed during the war. Nutritionists delightedly pronounced that the bottom third of British society had been pulled out of misery and were finally eating an adequate diet.[50]

This nutritional levelling-up of the lower classes was a by-product of rising wages and planned food economies across the world. Throughout the 1930s nutritionists had argued that all it would take to improve the health of the lower classes would be for governments to step in and implement policies which gave people access to better food. They were vindicated by the positive effect of wartime rationing systems on the diet and health of the working classes across the globe. In Sweden a coupon system was introduced which ensured that the poorest could afford butter and milk.[51] In Australia, although per capita consumption of meat was cut by half, a greater share of the reduced total went to the working classes.[52] In 1945 urban families were found to have increased their milk consumption by a third and their cheese consumption by a quarter.[53] Although competition for fruit and vegetables was fierce between American army suppliers and Australian civilians, in 1944 the Australian working classes were eating 17 per cent more fresh fruit and substantially more fresh tomatoes than before the war.[54] In Canada, where workers' wages rose, they were found to be consuming increased quantities of protein, iron and calcium and, when the government discovered that the Canadian diet was hopelessly deficient in vitamin C, it imported, at great expense, oranges and grapefruit juice from the United States.[55] Even in Iceland, work constructing camps, roads and airfields for the British and the Americans meant that the urban working classes were finally able to buy adequate quantities of milk, meat and vegetables.[56]

CLOSING THE NUTRITIONAL GAP

The nutritionists' influence on government food policy may have been restricted but a number of measures were introduced into the rationing system which, rather than aiming to increase the productivity of the working population, set out specifically to address the malnutrition and health problems of the deprived. This welfare policy was the result of the interests of specific personalities within the government.

In 1938 the Scottish Unionist MP Walter Elliot was appointed to the position of Minister of Health. His training as a doctor made him aware of the new research into the impact of diet on health and as Minister of Agriculture he had already introduced free school milk. In 1939 the rising cost of milk caused him great concern. For the poor, milk was already unaffordable. In the 1930s the dependant's allowance for a man on the dole was 4s.11d. and the amount of milk recommended for a pregnant woman by the government's own Medical Officer cost 4s.1d.[57] Elliot began work on setting up a wartime scheme to provide nursing mothers and young children with subsidized milk. But before he could implement it he fell from favour in May 1940, along with Neville Chamberlain, and Churchill removed him from office.[58]

However, in April 1940 Lord Woolton had been appointed to the position of Minister of Food and he survived Churchill's rise to the position of prime minister. He took over the departing Elliot's milk scheme with enthusiasm. Like the government's nutritional advisers, Woolton had witnessed the misery of urban poverty and in him the poor found an ally. Woolton was a businessman, formerly chairman of Lewis's in Liverpool, and later to become chairman of the Conservative Party. But he and his wife were also philanthropists. As a young man he had lived among the poor as the warden of a philanthropic society for the poor and needy of Liverpool, and during the First World War his wife had helped to run a feeding programme for the distressed wives and children of absent servicemen.[59] He was as aware as the scientists that malnutrition took its greatest toll on women during their childbearing years, and that it was the inability of poor women to buy more and better-quality food to meet their greater nutritional needs during pregnancy which left working-class women and their children vulnerable to death, disablement and disease. Woolton's timing was good. The sense that Britain was under siege was created by the British army's withdrawal from France at Dunkirk in June and the Treasury was persuaded to be generous.[60] Pregnant and nursing women were given priority access to a pint of milk a day at the cost of 2d. Their children were also allocated two pints of milk a day under the age of one, and a pint a day subsequently.[61] This was an extremely successful initiative. By September 1940, 70 per cent of those eligible were participating.[62]

The poor showed less enthusiasm for the Ministry of Food's vitamin scheme, which was also designed to address the problem of poverty-related malnutrition. In December 1941 all children under two (all children under five from February 1942) were given an allowance of blackcurrant juice and Icelandic cod liver oil. When Britain ran out of blackcurrants the juice was replaced by lend-lease orange juice from the United States. But in January 1943 only one-fifth of those eligible were collecting their allocations. The lack of enthusiasm perhaps had something to do with the taste of the cod liver oil, which according to a Ministry official was 'horrible'. An aggressive advertising campaign eventually pushed up the acceptance of orange juice to nearly half of those entitled to it.[63] However, the children's orange juice ration did not always find its way to its intended beneficiaries. The upper-middle-class Maggie Hay recalled mischievously that it tasted very good as a mixer with gin.[64]

Two further measures aimed to improve children's health more generally. In October 1941 *The Times* reported Woolton as having said, 'I want to see elementary school children as well fed as children going to Eton or Harrow. I am determined that we shall organise our food front that at the end of the war ... we shall have preserved and even improved the health and physique of the nation.'[65] The Milk in Schools scheme was now extended to all schoolchildren. School dinners were also introduced, providing about 1,000 calories, or a third of the children's daily energy needs. By the end of the war, more than 1.5 million children, 40 per cent of the school population, were eating school dinners and 46 per cent drinking school milk.[66] The circumstances of war removed the stigma of charity which had surrounded the school milk scheme in the 1930s. By 1945 it was considered perfectly natural that all children should eat school meals and drink free bottles of milk. It was only with the appointment of Margaret Thatcher as Education Minister that free school milk for children over seven was brought to an end in 1971.

Between 1939 and 1945 maternal and infant mortality rates among the working classes declined. The incidence of tuberculosis rose during the difficult early years of the war, but the disease went into decline again in 1942 and the rate of infection continued to drop. The School Medical Officer for the London County Council claimed that any height and weight differences between children of different social classes had virtually disappeared by the end of the war. A more nuanced picture emerged from Liverpool, Sheffield and Newcastle where it was still possible to differentiate between children at 'good' and 'bad' schools, but the height and weight of the children at the 'bad' schools had improved. In the poorest pockets of Britain, such as Jarrow, the number of children who could be classed in the worst health category of 'D' had virtually vanished.[67] Deficiency diseases such as rickets were essentially eradicated. The nutritionists concluded that besides winning the war with Germany, Britain had also won the war against malnutrition.

Throughout the western world the wartime introduction of planned economies, which accepted responsibility for the health and welfare of all a nation's citizens, marked a decisive break with the past. In post-war Britain it would no longer be possible for a government, whether Conservative or Labour, to turn away from abject misery, declaring that it was the result of ignorance and, by implication, beyond the means of the government to rectify. The Ministry of Food had demonstrated that it was possible for the government to tackle these issues, and even if certain politicians were reluctant to accept that the state's relationship to its people should change, the public's expectations had shifted. This was demonstrated by the British people's response to the Beveridge Report.

In 1941, William Beveridge was asked to chair a minor government committee on insurance benefits, but the report that he published in

December 1942 was more far-reaching and called for a comprehensive system of social security based on subsistence-rate benefits, a new health service, and measures to ensure full employment. The cabinet response to the report was divided. The Labour Ministers – Ernest Bevin, Herbert Morrison, Hugh Dalton – were all in favour of reform, although not necessarily in the shape that Beveridge had suggested. But they were not in a position within the coalition government to direct social policy. For the most part the Conservatives maintained their pre-war attitude to the poor and remained resistant to welfare, which they insisted would reduce initiative. They had no desire to engage in any attempt to redistribute wealth. Lord Beaverbrook and Kingsley Wood – who had once tried to intimidate John Boyd Orr and who was now Chancellor of the Exchequer – were both unenthusiastic. Churchill himself 'was said to be "allergic to post-war policy"'.[68] The Conservatives did their best to tone down Beveridge's recommendations and obstruct radical reform.

If the report did not exactly galvanize Churchill's coalition government into action, it caught the imagination of the British public. Within two weeks of publication 635,000 copies of the report had been sold. One week later, nine out of ten people interviewed for a Gallup poll believed that its proposals should be adopted.[69] The British public's enthusiasm indicated that the war had stimulated the desire for a fairer society where everyone had work, a decent house and enough nutritious food to eat. The government could not completely ignore public enthusiasm and, in response, the Ministry of Reconstruction was set up in November 1943, headed by the popular Lord Woolton. Family allowances and educational reform were introduced before the war came to an end and the benefits of the wartime provision of school meals were extended into the post-war world by R. A. Butler's Education Act (1944).[70] By the general election of 1945 the British people were ready to vote for a Labour government, which they felt would strive to construct a fairer society.[71] Welfare was no longer seen as a special service for the needy but as a social service for all. Thus, the statutory fortification of foods, such as bread, which was continued after the war, applied a protective policy across society.[72] However, the egalitarian notion that everyone should receive the same share, which Woolton had applied to food rationing, animated much of the thinking behind the development of the measures introduced by the welfare state. The unfortunate result was that the fundamental inequality of the food rationing system came back to haunt post-war welfare measures and pensions, in particular, were set too low to really lift the most needy among the aged out of impoverishment. Nevertheless, the war marked a decisive break with the past in that, after 1945, 'government . . . never recovered from the wartime expectation that it should continually "do something" in all spheres', and that it was right and proper for the state to take responsibility for its citizens' health and well-being.[73]

HEALTH AND MORALE - THE ARMY CATERING CORPS

The stimulus for the British army to improve military catering was the negative impact that dismal food had upon the morale of the troops. 'When it started out the food was good . . . by the time it reached us it was not very appetising. To anyone nurtured in comparative comfort . . . the conditions, particularly in the mess, were appalling.'[74] This was the opinion of R. P. Evans, a Bren-gun operator in the 8th Battalion Worcestershire Regiment. Military cooks took little pride in their work, which was hardly surprising given that they were poorly paid and allocating kitchen duty to an ordinary private was used as a mild form of punishment. Having agreed to train as a navy cook in 1940, the nineteen-year-old brewery worker R. B. Buckle was indignant to discover that the instruction consisted of being used as a dogsbody, peeling potatoes and cleaning up the kitchens. When he came to take his cook's examination he still had no idea how to make Yorkshire pudding or pastry for an apple pie. An obliging Wren* made most of his meal for him. As the paymaster tasted 'a small spoonful from my plates and pronounced me a cook it crossed my mind, if this was how other departments were trained I wondered how we expected to win the war'.[75]

In the first years of the war the dreadful army food was a major

* Member of the Women's Royal Naval Service.

source of discontent among servicemen stationed in Britain. After the British army was driven out of France in June 1940, well over half of the 3 million strong British armed forces were stationed in the home country. In theory this should have made it easier to feed them, but the miserable food situation in the winter of 1940–41 was reflected in the military rations. In his Mass Observation diary for 9 February 1941, the reluctant recruit Edward Stebbing complained: 'Tea today: one piece of bread and jam, a piece of cake and a cup of tea.'[76] A typical day's fare would be, for breakfast, a small piece of bacon or liver, porridge and two slices of bread. Lunch at noon would be meat, potatoes, cabbage and carrots, followed by semolina. Spotted dick (a suet pudding with currants) and custard was more popular but less frequently served. Tea was bread and butter, cheese, and possibly a slice of cake, followed by a supper of cold pudding or bread and butter and cocoa.[77] It was recognized that hard physical training meant that soldiers required extra meat, but the home service ration of 3,300 calories allocated British soldiers only 6 ounces a day.[78] Canadian troops stationed in Britain, used to far higher standards at home, were horrified by the British army food. It was one of the main topics in letters home, and in two Canadian camps in August 1941 there were sit-down strikes over the fact that there were only two cooked meals a day.[79]

For the British soldiers the food was one among many discontents. The army was made up of conscripts who saw themselves not as soldiers but as civilians in uniform. In contrast to the conscript army of the First World War, which was mainly made up of men who had been servants and farm labourers and who were accustomed to a culture of deference, the conscripts in the Second World War were better educated and less deferential towards the upper classes.[80] These men resented high-handed upper-class officers, chafed against what they saw as pointless army discipline, the low pay, the sack-like uniforms and the public's low regard for the ordinary squaddie. Leaky tents and damp barracks, disagreeable food, cheerless NAAFI* canteens serving revolting tea, all took their toll on morale.[81] Stebbing reported, 'All the time one hears grumbles about the stupidity of the military authorities,

---

* Navy, Army and Air Force Institutes.

the red tape, the habit of doing things in the most awkward and round-about way, the silly trivial things we are made to do, the shortage of food'.[82]

The army realized that something would have to be done. Ordinary men who had been called upon to risk sacrificing their lives for their country had a right to expect a decent level of care in return. In the sphere of food, in 1938 the army had already appointed Isidore Salmon of the J. Lyons Company to advise the quartermaster. He initiated the building of a new army cookery school at Aldershot and lobbied hard for the creation of a new catering corps. He pointed out that unless the cooks were better paid and properly trained they could hardly be expected to take pride in their work and produce appetizing meals. An Army Catering Corps was set up in March 1941 with Richard Byford, catering manager of Trust Houses, as its director. Byford put together a team of managers from the catering industry and the food in army messes gradually improved.[83] The level of improvement can be seen in the cookery notebook which Fusilier H. Simons kept while attending his course at Aldershot in 1944. He was taught how to use a variety of different field ovens and how to build one out of scrap if no oven was available. The cookery lessons gave instructions on how to make a roux, salmon and potato cakes, a variety of stews and hotpots and how to prepare dehydrated foods so that they would at least be edible.[84] By mid-1943 food seems to have faded as a source of discontent in the army stationed in Britain.[85]

The men who supervised food reform within the British army were drawn from the catering industry, and their focus was on improving the standard of cookery. In the Australian army the man appointed to shake up the army messes was Cedric Stanton Hicks, Professor of Physiology and Pharmacology at the University of Adelaide and one of the growing body of new scientists of nutrition. Hicks had supervised the South Australian League of Nations' nutritional survey and was, therefore, very much alive to the issue of nutritional deficiencies in the Australian diet. He brought a quite different quality of commitment – it might be described as a crusading zeal – to the effort to improve not only the taste but also the nutritional value of army meals.

During his tour of inspection as the newly appointed catering adviser to the Australian army, Hicks found the cooks as incompetent and

uninterested in their job as the ones in the British army. He was astonished to discover that they were still cooking with Soyer stoves, invented
by the famous Victorian chef Alexis Soyer during the Crimean war
(1853–56). The stoves routinely burned the porridge, soups and stews
and they reduced cabbage to a sludge-like mush. Hicks claimed that
the local farmers were benefiting greatly because the soldiers left most
of their food on their plates uneaten and he calculated that about 40
per cent of the army food supply ended up as pig slops.[86] Not only did
the Soyer stoves produce inedible food, they were, Hicks expostulated,
'the most efficient destructor of Vitamin C that could be devised'.[87] He
began a concerted campaign to outlaw the stoves and eventually
persuaded the Australian army to adopt the Wiles' steam cooker, a
mobile oven which could cook a meal in twenty minutes while a convoy
was on the move. It used less fuel than the Soyer stove and Hicks was
later to demonstrate, with the help of a scientist from CSIRO,* that
vegetables steamed in this way retained 75 per cent of their vitamins,
a huge improvement on the 80–85 per cent vitamin depletion rate in
a Soyer stove. When the 4th Military District tried out the new stoves
Hicks's efforts were vindicated as the troops actually returned for
second helpings of their vegetables.[88] These mobile steam cookers were
eventually adopted by the British army in 1944, to much praise.

Having installed better ovens Hicks devised a balanced mess ration
which contained a generous 3,944 calories, but he thought it likely
that the existing cooks would continue to ruin the food. His 'growing
realisation that food might well be a deciding factor' in determining
the performance of troops fortified his resolve, and 'at fever heat' he
pushed for the better instruction of army cooks. '"Fighting with food"
became our slogan.'[89] Hicks pulled in First World War veterans who
were now in the catering trade managing hotels and restaurants and
set them to work reforming army cookery. In March 1943 Hicks finally
won his battle to set up an Australian Army Catering Corps. By this
time the main focus of Australian fighting was on New Guinea, and
Major N. M. Gutteridge was appointed as the liaison officer between
the Medical Directorate and the Quartermaster Nutrition Branch on
the island. From then on medical officers were in constant contact with

---

* Commonwealth Scientific and Industrial Research Organization.

the catering advisory staff and a process was set in motion whereby continuous inquiries about food and health in the field were relayed back to nutritional headquarters, which then adjusted methods and supplies. This system worked well in improving the skills of the cooks and raising awareness among the troops as to the benefits of eating the right sorts of food.

FIGHTING ON BULLY BEEF AND BISCUITS

The influence of the new army catering corps on field rations was not to be felt until well into the conflict. In the early campaigns the food rations received by the British empire's combat troops were little different from those the soldiers ate in the trenches during the First World War. In 1941 the British 8th Army in Egypt was one-quarter British and three-quarters imperial. Three Australian divisions, as well as Australian Air Force squadrons, were joined by the Indian army and a huge force of pioneer soldiers mainly drawn from the African colonies, who dug tank traps, manned anti-aircraft batteries, constructed railways, put up telegraph lines and loaded and unloaded the ships bringing supplies into the Red Sea ports.[90] The staple diet of all of these soldiers was bully beef and hard biscuits. Gerald Page, an army cook who served in the North African desert, described these biscuits as 'a cross between Cream Crackers and Dog Biscuits' – the ones made in Australia were reputed to taste like 'dry, solid, soap'.[91]

In his diary in September 1941, R. L. Crimp, a soldier in a British motorized platoon, described the process of distributing desert rations. 'At 6 o'clock, armed with sacks, canisters and empty water cans, we accompany the corporal to platoon HQ for rations. The sergeant's already built "basic" piles on the ground – four cans of bully, a tin of milk, a tin of cheese, and six oranges – for each section [of half a dozen men] . . . Jam and margarine, in 7 lb tins, come once a week and go round in rotation.' The men fought over the tinned potatoes as they particularly disliked the yellow sweet potatoes grown in Egypt. 'For once, the fresh is not preferred.'[92] The monotonous and unpalatable diet was made worse by the quality of the water, heavily chlorinated and so saline that the tea curdled. The troops in North Africa created a brew known as 'char', very strong tea drunk with condensed milk and as much sugar as possible.[93] Crimp described how brewing 'desert char' was a consoling ritual. The 'desert army [was made up of] thousands and thousands of little groups whose very core was a fire tin and a brew can'. The men would gather around, the 'section mugs ... marshalled on the ground' ready with tinned milk and sugar already added.[94] The German troops fighting in the desert subsisted on an equally unimaginative diet of canned sausage meat, cream cheese in tubes, sardines, dried peas, salted vegetables, greasy margarine and jam and a moist black rye bread known as *Dauerbrot* (long-lasting bread). This was washed down with ersatz coffee, which the soldiers thought was execrable.[95] It was joked that it was this heavy diet, inappropriate for the climate, that defeated Rommel's troops in North Africa, but the joke would have held for either side.[96]

The men were supposed to live on such basic rations for only short periods of time. But in Egypt the supply of fresh foods was extremely limited, and without fresh meat or vegetables the troops fell ill. Julius Segano, a recruit from Bechuanaland, recalled that constant bully beef and biscuits caused chronic constipation. His anti-aircraft unit was issued with purgatives to alleviate the problem but these did little to get their stomachs moving. They discovered that the best remedy was the fear induced by a German aerial bombing raid.[97] More seriously, the troops began to suffer from vitamin deficiency diseases, and Axis and Allied troops alike fell ill with jaundice and dysentery. Gerald Page recalled that huge consignments of tinned fruit were brought up from South Africa to provide the soldiers with much-needed vitamins and fibre.[98] Similarly, the Wehrmacht brought in shipments of fresh fruit and vegetables from Italy and Greece even while the famine in Athens was at its height. In Egypt, Palestine, Cyprus, Syria and Iraq the British army started potato-growing schemes. It provided the farmers with the seed potatoes and guaranteed the price at which they would buy back the potato crop. Merchant seaman Roy Bayly recalled bringing in a shipment of seed potatoes for the scheme. They were a tricky cargo, as the potatoes required ventilation or they began to rot. Potato growing continued after the war in Egypt, Palestine, Syria and Cyprus, where they became a staple crop. Bayly liked to 'think that the potatoes imported from Egypt today are the direct descendants of "my" potatoes of 1943'.[99] The army also set up special vegetable farms, cultivated by African pioneer troops.[100]

These measures alleviated the health problems of men stationed behind the front line, but for those in combat a prolonged period on bully beef and biscuits caused debilitating side-effects which affected their ability to fight. In January 1942, after seven weeks of fighting around Benghazi, Allied troops began to show signs of serious ill-health. The limited transport capacity of the supply lines and the absolute priority placed on petrol to sustain the campaign, meant that it was out of the question to send up bulky fresh meat and vegetables. The men were urged to take their vitamin B and C tablets along with the salt pills which were issued to counteract the effects of the heat. More condensed margarine, bacon and oatmeal were supplied with onions and chutney to add some flavour to the food.[101] It was situations such as this which stimulated the British army quartermaster to research new ways of feeding front-line troops with nutritious food. Towards the end of the North African campaign the quartermaster came up with a marked improvement on the endless bully beef and biscuits: the composite ration. This was rations for fourteen men for a day, packed into one box. According to Gerald Page, 'we all thought they were very good'. Inside the box were 'Tinned Steak and Kidney Puddings, Steam Puddings, Soup, Chocolate, Sweets and English Brand Cigarettes and Tobacco . . . luxuries we had forgotten about in the desert.'[102] The composite ration packs provided variety and more nutritious meals, and 'compo rations', as they were known, became standard British issue during the campaigns in Italy and north-west Europe. Nevertheless, there was no substitute for fresh food, and once the Allies captured parts of Italy in 1943 they were able, like the Germans before them, to supplement their tins with fresh fruit and vegetables. 'Grapes were issued, and we were able to gather tomatoes from the fields and buy eggs from the local farmers.'[103]

PORRIDGE, PEAS AND VITAMINS

The impact of a bully beef and biscuit diet on the health of troops fighting in the tropics was far worse than it was in North Africa. In this climate vitamin deficiencies made the men susceptible to a host of unpleasant tropical diseases from skin rashes and ulcers to malaria. This could seriously impact on the fighting capacity of an army. When the Australians on New Guinea began to push the Japanese back along the Kokoda Trail towards their bridgehead at Buna they crossed the Owen Stanley range of mountains and entered the malarial zone of the island. For every man who was wounded, seven were incapacitated by sickness.[104] The response of the Australian army medical corps and quartermaster to the problems of ill-health and malnutrition faced by the troops on New Guinea provides a case study of the way in which attitudes towards the health and diet of soldiers within the armies of the British Commonwealth changed during the Second World War.

On the Kokoda Trail the Australian army ran into the same problems as the Japanese. The Australian high command appear to have been almost as ill informed about conditions on New Guinea as were the Japanese generals. Lieutenant H. T. Kienzle was detailed to build a supply road along the trail. He replied to the commanding officer, Major-General Basil Morris, in Port Moresby that this was utterly implausible. He went on to warn Morris that in the eight days it took for the native porters to walk the track to the front-line troops, they consumed more than half the food they could carry. He outlined that simply bringing in sufficient food supplies left no room for arms, ammunition, medical supplies or any other of the dozens of 'items needed to wage war . . . the maintenance of supplies is a physical impossibility without large-scale co-operation of plane droppings'.[105] But Morris did not have sufficient air capacity to use planes to bring in supplies and for months all the Australians had to rely on were native carriers.

Conditions on the Kokoda Trail were exhausting. The jungle was like a second enemy, 'a constant, wet, muddy, malarial and thoroughly disagreeable presence'.[106] It always seemed to be raining and at night the Australians stood in their weapon pits, soaked to the skin, shivering but awake, silent and struggling to stay alert. Their feet turned pulpy and began to rot in their boots.[107] The supply problems meant that, like the Japanese, the Australians were soon very hungry.[108] Lieutenant Hugh Dalby recounted, 'Once you get up into the high altitudes, it's cold, it's enervating; you have a tin of bully a day. Sometimes if you were lucky you might get a tin of peaches between about ten. We later got some rice at Isurava. I had a batman called Kennedy. He was a wizard . . . he cooked the rice. We all got a Dixie full of it. By the Lord living Moses! . . . I was the last one to get fed. I could have eaten twice the quantity. A solid something in your stomach!'[109] Eventually the United States air force began to make air drops of food but their aim was not always accurate. Warrant Officer Wilkinson described how when their supply plane missed its target his unit was forced to raid the Japanese lines to reclaim their supplies of food. He cut his tongue licking out a tin of salmon. 'Hell, I was hungry.'[110] Medical reports noted that the men who returned from fighting on the trail were 'not only fatigued and worn out by the hard conditions and disease, but by subnutrition as well'.[111]

At the beginning of 1943 the Japanese were dug in at Buna in heavily fortified bunkers made out of coconut logs and oil drums. The Australians were unable to skirt round them because of 'neck-deep swamps of black, sucking mud'.[112] Although the Japanese were suffering from night blindness caused by vitamin deficiencies, dysentery and malaria, the Australians had to oust them one by one from their strongholds.[113] The medics reported that the Australian troops fighting in these difficult circumstances were showing signs of avitaminosis, including weight loss, muscular weakness, sensory disturbances, oedema of the extremities of the body and lesions on their mouths, lips and tongues.[114] Army medics complained that the troops' diet did not contain enough of vitamins B and C.

During the course of 1943 Australian and American infantrymen, with US air support, forced the Japanese back along the coast and into the valleys of the northern part of the island. As the battle for New Guinea progressed, Australian rations slowly improved. The food situation improved, firstly because it was possible to bring supplies into the northern coast of the island by boat. A cold store was built at Finschhafen which meant that the quartermaster was able to bring in more frozen food, although quantities were always limited by the shortage of refrigerated ships.[115] While the logistics of supply became easier, the quartermaster nevertheless acknowledged the deficiencies of the basic ration based on six items – tinned meat, salt, biscuit, tea, sugar and dried milk. It was abundantly clear that this provided an insufficiently nutritious diet and the number of basic items in the field ration was raised to thirty-three, including dehydrated and tinned vegetables.[116] At first the vegetables did little to improve the men's health, as the system of blanching the produce before it was canned or dried destroyed its vitamin C content. It was Hicks who introduced a new method by which the vegetables were soaked in a sodium sulphite bath before they were processed. This preserved the vitamin C, and the nutritional value of canned and dehydrated vegetables increased.[117]

Meanwhile Hicks had come up with two simple ways of remedying the lack of vitamins in the ration: the addition of porridge and peas, both easily transportable. His solution was born out of experiments conducted with the Northern Observation Force on patrol in the Kimberleys region west of Darwin in northern Australia. These men suffered from sores known as Barcoo Rot which was a sign of vitamin deficiencies. Hicks persuaded the men on patrol to take packages of wheat with them into the outback. They ground the wheat themselves and made porridge, eaten with dried milk. This, along with dried yeast and dried apricots, substantially increased the men's vitamin B intake. When the dried milk cans were empty they were tied to the soldiers' belts and filled with a little water and a handful of Tasmanian field peas, which grew shoots within twenty-four hours. The shoots were then transferred to muslin bags, the tins were scalded and the process begun again. The pea sprouts were high in vitamin C and could be eaten raw if necessary. The men came back from their six-week patrol fit and healthy. Hicks was vindicated and wheat porridge and Tasmanian field peas were incorporated into field rations.[118]

The porridge element of his campaign to improve army nutrition was largely unsuccessful. Men in the tropics did not want to eat a hot and stodgy breakfast and the portable wheat gristers, which were supplied to the soldiers on New Guinea, tended to break. The catering adviser on the island, Lieutenant W. H. M. Schultze, surveying the eating habits of the 7th and 9th Divisions at the end of 1943 found the gristers to be useless.[119] However, the doctors did agree that wheatmeal greatly improved the vitamin B intake of the men and it was incorporated into the bread flour.[120] Schultze was also critical of the Tasmanian peas, complaining that many arrived mouldy and fermenting.[121] The Quarter-master-General anticipated a lack of enthusiasm for the peas, and a note was sent out to the units explaining that they provided 'in a convenient and transportable form' the vitamins normally found in vegetables. It was stressed that, in order to be effective, the peas had to be germinated and an explanation was given of how this was to be achieved between layers of sacking. Knowing that cooks would be reluctant to take on such a laborious task, the memo warned that 'wastage of this special ration issue will be regarded as a serious breach of discipline'.[122]

Confronted with the difficulties of actually preparing the peas in field kitchens the cooks naturally found inventive shortcuts. G. T. Martin, cooking for the 2nd/6th Australian Field Ambulance in New Guinea, never had time to soak any of the dehydrated vegetables before cooking them. 'With those big four gallon dixies and up the Ramu Valley, we were cooking for about 800 men . . . what we found out was to get the water boiling and put all these dehydrated vegetables in them, without soaking them and boiling them for three or four minutes. And then put the lid on them and put the fire out and let it steam and they went alright then . . . And just before you were ready to serve you put on the butter, salt and pepper, milk or whatever you had in with it.'[123] Martin applied his boiling technique to the 'rock hard' peas and when Hicks paid a visit to Martin's unit 'he saw what we were doing and oh Jesus, he played up merry hell!! . . . We said to him, "Are you stopping for dinner?" and he said "Yeh". "Well pass us your remarks then." And he came back after dinner and he said they are very good – and the next thing we get is a big screed on how to cook! Oh after he tasted it, tried what we were doing, he went back to headquarters somewhere and put out this big screed on how to cook dehydrated vegetables.'[124] Hicks was undoubtedly concerned that Martin's rather aggressive cooking method was reducing the vitamin content. His screed was part of an on-going educational offensive: the catering advisory staff constantly reiterated that more needed to be done to teach the cooks how to prepare the field ration properly.

Reception of the peas was mixed. At an army hospital one cook went to a great deal of trouble to sprout the peas in order to provide the invalided soldiers with vitamins. But the soldiers mistook the bean sprouts for maggots and could not be induced to eat the stew.[125] However, the 7th Division in New Guinea appear to have been better informed about the reasons for issuing the special rations and the soldiers actually went to the trouble of sprouting the peas themselves and ate them raw. The 2/6th Cavalry Commando Squadron even adopted the Northern Territory technique of sprouting the peas in tins while they were on the move.[126]

One of the unqualified successes of Hicks's newly created Army Catering Corps was its special field bakery units. The bakers proved ingenious in difficult circumstances and improvised ovens out of old oil drums and, despite difficulties with waterlogged fuel, they were able to produce 1,450 rolls in two hours. They also baked an array of tempting treats such as jam puffs and cream horns. The soldiers were appreciative and would even eat mouldy week-old bread in preference to the despised 'dog' biscuits.[127]

The work of the Army Catering Corps undoubtedly improved the taste and nutritional value of the food provided in the base areas. But the complexities of jungle warfare, where lines of communication were difficult, meant that the forward troops on the front line were still eating poorly for weeks at a time. Hicks and his team responded by developing the operational ration. A tin of meat and vegetables, a pack of biscuits, dried egg, oatmeal, a bar of fortified chocolate and tea and cocoa provided 4,000 calories' worth of energy and a dose of vitamins D and B. This was supplemented by an emergency ration which squeezed 3,900 calories into a fruit bar, a pack of dried meat and vegetables and milk tablets.[128] From mid-1943, an Australian infantryman carried an emergency ration in the left pocket of his uniform, and the operational ration in his haversack.[129] G. C. Lloyd remembered getting operational rations for the first time in the Finisterre Ranges of New Guinea. 'We thought they were marvellous when we first got them.'[130] But after seven days on patrol Lloyd and his companions found that they 'could hardly look at ... [the] little packets full of lollies and chewing gum and dried fruit bars and chocolate and also stuff like Maggi soups and that sort of thing.'[131] However, exhausted and tense, soldiers quickly tire of any food and men in combat routinely grouch about their rations no matter what their quality. Although sweetness was the element in the operational and emergency rations which the men complained about the most, it had been introduced in response to oft-repeated requests from the soldiers.[132] On the whole, Schultze found that once the men had been educated in the correct use of the operational ration it worked well, and allowed for the 'economical use of the regular standard ration, avoided monotony, and prevented wastage'.[133] The fortified chocolate was found to be a real 'morale builder'.[134]

When Lieutenant H. E. Young, a field research officer in nutrition attached to the Medical Directorate, carried out nutritional surveys of the 7th and 9th Divisions in New Guinea at the beginning of 1944, he found that the 'hard work [which] had been put into the question of feeding the soldier', and the co-operation between medics, quartermasters and nutritional advisers, had produced a better, more balanced and also more palatable ration. In addition, the effort to transport these rations to troops in combat had improved.[135] Although the men hated the tinned cabbage, they liked the dehydrated carrots and onions. They were eating the Tasmanian pea sprouts raw and greatly enjoying the three bread rolls issued to them daily. The nutritional value of the bread had been improved by the addition of 6 per cent wheatgerm to the flour. The men were drinking their supplies of fruit juice and enjoyed the chocolate bars in the operational ration. Even though native porters were scarce, the field kitchens were managing to take two hot meals a day up to the forward troops on the front line.[136] The troops continued to show signs of mild vitamin deficiencies, but the experience of contemporary soldiers shows that, no matter how high the quality of the rations, this is a normal by-product of living on dried food fortified with artificial vitamins. Ration packs can never act as a completely satisfactory substitute for fresh food, and Australian soldiers today suffer a decline in their immune status and lower vitamin levels in their blood when performing manoeuvres while subsisting on today's more sophisticated ration packs.[137] While their Japanese opponents on the other side of the front line had been abandoned to hunger by their high command, by 1944 Australian sick rates in New Guinea had fallen and the morale of the troops had greatly improved.[138]

NUTRITIONAL RECONDITIONING – THE INDIAN ARMY

If malnutrition became a problem among British and Australian troops after living on field rations for too long, among the troops recruited from the colonies army doctors and quartermasters were confronted by a far more deep-seated problem of endemic malnutrition. The Bechuanaland recruit, Robert Kgasa, recalled that quite a lot of the men who arrived at the training camp in Lobatsi were sick. However, a few weeks on an army diet transformed them. 'Oh it was a change! All of those who looked elderly, in about three to nine months, they were young, and could even play football. Men would put on weight.'[139]

Selogwe Pilane, who was among the first intake of recruits, reported 'we were fat and healthy by the time we left Botswana'.[140]

In India the problem required more than a few weeks of good food in a training camp. During the first Burma campaign in 1941–42 both British and Indian troops suffered from malnutrition and vitamin B deficiency. This was unsurprising given the disorganization of the supply lines and the chaos of the retreat. However, once the men were back at their bases on a remedial diet high in protein and protective foods, the Indian troops took far longer to recover, suggesting that they were already malnourished before the exigencies of the military campaign made them physically unwell. Part of the problem was the poverty of the ration allocated to the Indian troops. British soldiers in the Indian army did not receive a generous weekly ration, but their 16 ounces of bread, beef and milk, 8 ounces of vegetables, 10 ounces of potatoes and 4 ounces of onions, plus sugar, salt and tea was generous in comparison to the Indians' miserly 24 ounces of atta (ground wheat for chappatis) or rice, 3 ounces of lentils, 2 ounces of potatoes and ghee (clarified butter for cooking), sugar and salt. In October 1942 the British troops were put on to full field service rations which provided a far more generous 4,500 calories a day, including significantly more bread, meat and milk. But the food shortages in India meant that the Indian government was reluctant to increase the food rations for Indian troops.[141]

By this time the Indian army had swollen by 2 million to around 3 million men. The military need for manpower meant that recruitment practices changed, and rather than concentrating on drawing men from the traditional 'martial races' in the north-west, the army enlisted men from all regions of the sub-continent. The economic situation in India was so dire that many artisans and labourers, who had been badly hit by the inflation of food prices, volunteered in search of regular pay and food.[142] The rules were relaxed to allow men who were underweight to join the army. As a result, the army collected together a ragged assortment of men who clearly required 'thorough nutritional reconditioning' before they could be transformed into a fighting force.[143] An anaemia investigation team was set up which fed the men on a variety of experimental diets and took regular measurements of their weight. Even on the meagre standard army ration the men gained 2–5 kilograms within four months of enlisting in the army.[144] Despite the new recruits' weight gain on the standard ration, malnutrition and vitamin deficiency diseases remained a problem across the army and it became clear to the medics that the ration system was desperately in need of reform, and that it was essential to introduce animal protein and protective foods into the Indian soldiers' diet.

The commanding officers in the Indian army were, however, extremely reluctant to tamper with the ration scales. They were steeped in the old ways of the Raj, which scrupulously respected caste prejudices and food taboos. This outdated approach harked back to the shock of 1857 when a violation of dietary taboos was supposed to have sparked off a mutiny among Indian troops, who rose up against their officers and British rule.[145] The exaggerated respect for food taboos resulted in a ration system which was divided into a formidable number of caste-appropriate diets. Hindus could not be served beef or Muslims pork, and both often ended up with rather tough goat meat. In addition, the British Indian army was joined on the sub-continent by American airmen, a small American infantry force known as Merrill's Marauders, who trained two divisions of Chinese troops stuck in India after the retreat from Burma, and Middle Eastern and West and East African troops. The foreign troops required specialized foods such as mealie meal for the South Africans and burghal (a sort of lentil) for Trans-Jordanian troops.[146] As a consequence, the Indian quartermaster became bogged down by an overly complex system which worked with 198 different ration scales.[147] The various restrictions were printed on the backs of the ration forms in 'microscopic type', and during the audits the harassed food officials found themselves accused of over-provisioning because they had missed details such as that the issue of cans of meat and vegetables required a cut in the fresh vegetable ration.[148]

The prejudices of the old guard were finally overcome in 1943 when India began to mobilize for a push into Burma and south-east Asia. An Indian army catering corps was formed and the field service ration was improved. Mutton, carefully labelled as *halal* for the Muslims and *jhatka* for the Hindus and Sikhs, was introduced. Fresh vegetables, fruits and marmite, rich in vitamin B, were added to the menu. An emergency ration pack suitable for use by any Indian no matter what caste was developed, containing a chocolate bar fortified with vitamins which provided 1,350 calories. A twenty-four-hour operational 2,700-calorie ration contained biscuits, chocolate, cheese, a tin of sardines, sugar, milk powder, tea and salt. Eight-man composite ration packs provided a hearty 4,400 calories and incorporated tins of mutton.[149] Like the British and the Common-wealth armies, the Indian army underwent a revolution in provisioning techniques which acknowledged the necessity of a ration which not only gave the soldier energy but also protected his health.

Britain and the Dominions ended the war with healthier populations and an expectation among the general population that the state was respon-sible for ensuring the health of its people. A similar process occurred within the British and Commonwealth armies. This co-operation between the state and scientists and, in the armies, between medics and quarter-masters, allowed the discoveries of nutritional science to be applied to the diet of civilians and soldiers, with beneficial effect. These developments were extended into the post-war civilian and military culture. In 1944 the British Army Council decided to extend the life of the Army Catering Corps.[150] It was no longer seen as a temporary answer to a wartime problem but as an integral part of the regular army. In Australia the work of Stanton Hicks was continued at a laboratory at Scottsdale in northern Tasmania, set up by the Australian Defence Science and Technology Organization to work on the application of food technology to the nutri-tional improvement of military rations.[151] After independence the Indian army eventually set up its own Defence Food Research Laboratory at Mysore in 1961. Post-war soldiers throughout the world could expect their rations not only to be as flavoursome as possible under the circum-stances but also to maintain their health. However, this apparently positive side-effect of war also helped to create a less constructive post-war view of eating as a means solely to achieve a narrowly defined idea of physical health.[152] This has promoted nutritional scientists to a position of power over food choices in western societies which many would argue is beyond their capabilities. In the post-war world nutritionists have been allowed to define which foods are healthy or unhealthy and to dictate which foods people should and should not eat.

17

The United States – Out of Depression and into Abundance

The war gave a lot of people jobs. It led them to expect more than they had before . . . We were gonna reach the end of the rainbow.
(Peggy Terry, from Kentucky, who worked in a munitions factory in Michigan during the war)[1]

When America fed us, men ate but couldn't finish it all.
(Labour corps worker from Tanna, Vanuatu)[2]

'How those dough boys do feed, porridge and cream and peaches, white bread and jam, pancakes, and syrup, and bacon and pukka coffee.'[3] The newly liberated British prisoner of war, Eric Barrington, was treated to American hospitality when he managed to cross the Elbe river out of the Russian zone of Germany into the area held by the United States. 'The sergeant brought out a parcel of cookies from home and the captain a pound box of chocolate creams . . . a packet of Camels was handed round and we were "gang" happy again.'[4] Dinner was meat stew, mashed potatoes, sweet rice and stewed plums. 'No wonder Yankee POWs miss their rations, a far cry from the bully biscuits', which Barrington recalled were the predominant foods when he was fighting in North Africa.[5]

American soldiers were the best fed in the world during the Second World War. As the only country to experience an agricultural as well as an industrial boom, the United States was able to meet the food requirements of its 11.5 million servicemen with ease, and rationing in America had less impact on the structure and content of meals than in any other country. American soldiers and civilians alike consumed significantly more food than their allies or their enemies. But, if the United States was in an enviable position with regard to its military and economic strength, the government faced the problem that its people had little reason to fight. Lofty ideals such as freedom and democracy and the need to defeat fascism in its German and Japanese forms had little meaning on an everyday level for most Americans. At no point in the war were they fighting to defend their homeland from invasion, unlike the British and Soviets at the beginning of the conflict, or the Germans and Japanese at the end. The natural reluctance of the American government to interfere with the civil liberties of its citizens combined with this vague definition of war aims made it much harder for the US government to mobilize an army and impose restrictions on its civilian population. In the end, most Americans felt that they were fighting to preserve the American way of life and one of the most powerful symbols of this lifestyle came to be the abundance of American food. The superior rations which US troops and ordinary civilians received thus became a powerful signifier of American strength and superiority, not only for the Americans themselves but also for their allies and enemies.

THE 'GOOD WAR'

In the early 1940s the effects of the Depression could still be seen in the American working population. Raging unemployment in the 1930s had swelled the numbers of the destitute and marginalized. America's commitment to the philosophy of individualism meant that there was no welfare system in place to cushion the fall of the 15 million unemployed men and their families.[6] Millions sold their possessions to make ends meet and millions more were evicted from their homes after failing to pay the rent. Hunger ravaged these families, and when unemployment was at its height in 1933 it became commonplace for people to collapse from hunger in the streets of Chicago.[7] In 1941 Paul McNutt, director of the newly created Office of Defense Health and Welfare Services, claimed that as many as 45 million Americans 'do not have enough to eat of the foods we know are essential to good health'.[8] As preparations for war got under way, the head of the Draft Board, Lewis B. Hershey, asserted that two out of every five men called up were unfit for military service due to disabilities which were linked to poor nutrition. The Surgeon-General, Thomas Parran, warned that poor health due to poor diet would not only pose a threat to the country's military strength but would also slow down industrial production and lower 'the morale of millions'.[9]

The Second World War lifted the United States out of the Depression and into a period of economic boom.[10] The growth in the war industries brought an end to the plague of unemployment, and between 1941 and 1944 the lowest-earning families doubled their wages.[11] Helen Studer and her husband had been hard hit by the Depression. Their hog-raising business collapsed and the only work her husband was able to find was digging ditches for pipes in Colorado, where the family lived in a tent. When the war came she and her husband moved to California and they both found work in the Douglas aircraft factory. 'People didn't know what to do with their money when they were making so much. 'Course I came from the ridiculous to the sublime, 'cause we went through a depression in the thirties and we were in debt when we came out here. Between my husband and I, within a year we were out of debt.'[12] Helen Studer's story was replicated across the United States. During the war, Peggy Terry from Paducah, Kentucky, first found work in a shell factory close to home and then moved to Michigan to work in a factory testing aeroplane radios. Her wage increased from $32 to $90. 'We had a lotta good times and we had money and we had food on the table and the rent was paid. Which had never happened to us before.'[13]

It was this growth in prosperity which earned the Second World War the title 'the good war' in the United States. Lee Ormont, who had a partnership in a supermarket chain, acknowledged, 'Those of us who lost nobody at the front had a pretty good time . . . We suddenly found ourselves relatively prosperous. We really didn't suffer.'[14] The rise in wages had an extremely beneficial impact on the nutritional well-being of the working classes. American workers now had the means to eat well. The war did not redistribute American wealth. In fact, the income gap between rich and poor widened, but wage increases had the same levelling-up effect as in Britain and the dietary gap between the rich and poor began to close. Before the war the richest third of the American population had spent double the amount that the poorest third spent on food. In 1944 the rich were spending only a third more on food than the poor.[15]

In particular, the working classes increased their consumption of the protective foods – meat, dairy products, fruit and vegetables – which had been under-represented in their pre-war diet. The animal protein gap between the classes was narrowed as the working classes increased their consumption of meat by 17 per cent, while the wealthiest section of society ate 4 per cent less.[16] 'Customers, who have never enjoyed the luxury of club steaks, are now requesting them in five-pound cuts for roasts', reported the manager of the Great Eastern supermarket chain.[17] In 1948 a survey of urban families found that three-quarters of them were consuming the recommended amount of calcium compared with one-half in the spring of 1942, and only one-third in 1936.[18] The 20 million Victory Gardens that were planted across America added interesting new tastes and vitamins to working-class menus.[19] Salads, squash and baked aubergine all found their way into the dishes of people used to a more conservative diet. In Mississippi, two-thirds of the new foods which people discovered during the war were vegetables, mainly home grown.[20] In 1943 a team surveying the diets of New York schoolchildren were pleasantly surprised to find that the children were now eating not only fresh fruit, but also green vegetables such as spinach. A survey of 400 Texan families from all sections of society showed them to be eating more milk, eggs and butter and twice as many green vegetables than in 1927–29 when a similar survey had been conducted.[21]

As in Britain, many Americans ate a healthier diet during the war than they had done in the 1930s. In contrast to the British, they also ate more. The supermarket owner Lee Ormont recalled that people 'splurged on food'.[22] With the shortage of consumer goods and strict petrol rationing, there was little else to buy. While the British reduced their expenditure on food by about 11 per cent, in America expenditure on food increased by 8 per cent and rationing had to be introduced in order to restrict civilian consumption of high-quality and condensed foods which were needed by the military and America's allies.[23] More than half the supply of some foodstuffs and a large proportion of the best-quality food disappeared into the storehouses of the military quartermasters. In addition, large amounts of canned foods, especially canned meats, had to be withheld from the American public so that the United States could honour its commitment to supply lend-lease food to its British, Soviet and Chinese allies.[24] By 1943 sugar, sweets, coffee, butter, cheese, canned goods, frozen and dried vegetables and fruits, and red meat were all rationed.

The United States government exhibited a characteristically laissez-faire approach to the mobilization of the economy and society for war. The energies of private business and industry were harnessed, but they were not brought under direct government control. William Knusden, head of the Office of Production Management, initiated the redirection of industry into the construction of military equipment simply by calling together America's leading businessmen and presenting them with a list of military requirements which they then volunteered to supply.[25] Secretary for War Henry Stimson summed up the approach: 'If you are going to try to go to war . . . in a capitalist country you have got to let business make money out of the process, or business won't work.'[26] This strategy was remarkably successful in a climate in which businessmen disliked being told what to do but presided over an industry with 'widespread experience of mass-production . . . great depth of technical and organisational skill, the willingness to "think big", [and an] ethos of hustling competition'.[27] When the United States entered the war its economy was still essentially geared to civilian production, and military expenditure was minimal.[28] But by the end of 1942 America had developed a military economy which out-produced the Axis, and by the end of the four years of war America had doubled its industrial production. 'Two-thirds of all the Allied military equipment produced during the war' was manufactured in America.[29]

In spheres such as food production and supply, where it was necessary for the state to take control and cut out the free market, the American government exhibited a cautious distrust of its own interventionist measures. Rationing was introduced in order to spread shortages fairly across the different socio-economic groups within the population. This was the motivating force behind most rationing systems. However, in other countries rationing was also used as a tool to direct eating habits. In Britain the food system pushed the population towards a higher consumption of bread and potatoes; in Japan the population were given noodles in order to save rice. The United States government was unique in the wartime world in its adamant declaration that in the sphere of food it had no wish to undermine the 'initiative and democratic habits of American citizens', and the public were told that rationing had been introduced in order to protect people's ability to make their *own* food choices. The government was remarkably tentative in its attempts to direct consumption, even towards healthier foodstuffs.[30] This was partly a reflection of the public's hostility towards government intervention in the private areas of everyday life and partly a consequence of the abundance of food within the system. During the war American farmers produced 50 per cent more food per person than before the war, and even with the voracious demands of the military and America's allies this meant that there was still plenty of food in the system, the government having no need to intervene in order to ensure that those supporting the war effort got enough to eat.[31] Thus, the United States allowed itself the luxury of retaining the ideology of individual liberty during wartime. American resources were so plentiful that the country could afford the wastage of energies that resulted from allowing the individual and the market as free a rein as possible.

One of the consequences of this laissez-faire approach to food consumption was that the influence of nutritionists on government food policy was limited while, despite wartime restrictions, the food industry retained its power to protect its commercial interests. In 1940 the National Research Council created two boards to develop a national food policy. The Food and Nutrition Board was given the task of collating the latest scientific research and developing nutritional standards, while the Committee on Food Habits was supposed to translate its findings into concrete recommendations for meals. In May 1941 the Food and Nutrition Board presented its most influential piece of work at the National Nutrition Conference. This was a table of recommended daily allowances which addressed a serious gap in scientific knowledge by clearly stating 'how much of each of the known nutrients a person needed to maintain good health'.[32] The table provided the military, the government and a variety of private agencies with an authoritative measure against which to judge the diets of soldiers, workers and their families. However, in drawing up the table the nutritionists erred on the side of caution. The recommendations were about 30 per cent above what they considered to be average requirements. This created a tendency for American rations to be overly generous and, conversely, for various menus and diets to be deemed insufficiently nutritious when they were, in fact, more than adequate.[33] The influence of the food industry could also be seen in the phrasing of the recommendations, which repeatedly asserted that a wide variety of foods could meet each particular nutritional requirement. This was an attempt to placate the different farm and food interest groups which protested vigorously if nutritional advice appeared to favour one foodstuff over another. For example, the beef industry was apt to protest loudly at any suggestion that beans or eggs made good substitutes for meat.[34]

The Food and Nutrition Board's recommended daily allowances were widely publicized in newspapers, magazines and radio broadcasts. In 1943 the Department of Agriculture printed them in its most widely circulated pamphlet, the *National Wartime Nutritional Guide*. By the end of the war the American public, a large proportion of whom in 1941 had been unable to distinguish between vitamins and calories, understood the need for a healthy diet and balanced meals.[35] However, this was a diffuse level of influence. Nutritionists were never able actively to direct civilian eating habits in the most effective way, by manipulating pricing, as they were unable to gain executive powers within the Office of Price Administration where the price of foodstuffs was regulated. They achieved a minor success in that they persuaded the government to implement the fortification of basic foodstuffs such as bread, milk and margarine with iron, the various B vitamins and vitamins A and D.[36] This was a health measure which benefited the population across the board. But even the propaganda of healthy eating was more efficiently exploited by the food industry than by the scientists. The War Advertising Council was attended by representatives from advertising agencies, corporate advisers, the media and officials from various interested government departments such as the Office of War Information. Together they agreed on the outlines of public information campaigns. In this way the government co-opted the food industry to do the work of spreading healthy-eating propaganda while still allowing them to make money, or at least keep their brands in the public eye, guaranteeing them future – if not always present – sales.[37] The problem was that the food industry tended to use the language of the new science of nutrition to sell its products, regardless of their real health benefits. Thus, the American public were urged to eat grapefruit because it was rich in 'Victory Vitamin C', but they were also told that Nestlé's cocoa was a 'concentrated energizing food', and children's love of sweets was encouraged by campaigns which promoted the benefits of sugar by pointing out that it was an essential part of a combat soldier's diet.[38]

In Germany, Britain and the Soviet Union every effort was made to maintain industrial productivity by channelling food to workers by means of extra rations, special canteens or bigger bread rations. In the United States a programme for improving industrial workers' nutrition was set up by the Nutrition Division of the Office of Defense Health and Welfare Services.* However, Paul McNutt and his team found themselves unable to exert any real influence on government policy. Roosevelt's refusal to appoint one person to co-ordinate food policy meant that the division's attempts to improve the food provided for workers became bogged down in a mass of bureaucratic negotiations. In order to push their policies through they had to argue their case within the multiplicity of ministries and departments governing food production, distribution and sale. The nutritionists were given no executive powers over industry and had to content themselves with giving industrial plants advice on how to set up and run canteens and what sort of food to serve, without being able to require them to adopt these measures.[39] In the United States the feeding of workers was left largely to the discretion of private employers.

In the huge and hastily constructed war plants this tended to result in the inadequate provision of eating facilities. At Ford's Willow Run plant, where bombers were made in an enormous hall, there was one cafeteria for more than 10,000 people. Most of the workers could not get there and back in their half-an-hour lunch break. Luncheon wagons provided food but the workers complained that the sandwiches were often made with inferior luncheon meat, the coffee was like dishwater

* Later the division was transferred to the War Food Administration and renamed the Industrial Feeding Programs Division of the School Lunch and Distribution Branch, Commodity Credit Corporation.

and the lukewarm food was slopped unappetizingly on to paper plates.[40] Chauncey Del French, who worked at the Kaiser shipyards in Vancouver, Washington, recalled that 'two of the greatest causes of dissatisfaction among workers were the high prices and the minute portions of meals served at Hudson House [dormitory] and the shipyard cafeteria'.[41] The prices were listed as having been approved by the Office of Price Administration, 'but OPA took no interest in the size of the portions' and the men felt cheated. 'A welder who worked with our crew voiced the thought of the hundreds who quit on that account alone: "Whenever I eat a meal that costs me $2.35 and I'm still hungry, I know I've been gypped. I can do war work at home, and that's where I'm going."'[42] Given that it cost $225 to recruit and train each worker, it would have been cheaper to force the contractor to improve the meals but, even though the yard's counsellors were aware of the problem, nothing was done.

The United States government had no incentive to irritate employers by forcing changes in the provision of food for workers or by interfering in the profit-making activities of catering contractors. The food provision at some of the larger war plants might have been substandard, but on the whole workers could afford to feed themselves well. American workers were in no danger of going hungry; on the contrary, they were extremely well nourished. The Nutrition Division was assigned the task of assessing the nutritional quality of factory cafeteria lunches. A survey of an Illinois canteen classed 71 per cent of the meals as poor, but this was because they were judged against the Food and Nutrition Board's recommended daily allowances and thus the assessors applied absurdly high standards. The meals were classed as poor if they were missing two out of a list of foodstuffs which included an 8-ounce glass of milk or some other dairy food; a cup of green or yellow vegetables; meat, cheese, fish or eggs; two slices of wholegrain bread; butter or fortified margarine; fruit juice; or citrus fruits.[43] The list in itself was an indication of the generous quantities of fresh and nutritious food American wartime workers were accustomed to eating. A Soviet worker, existing on watery soups, would have been grateful for a meal made up of just one of the items on the list, while British workers would have been delighted by the meat or a fresh egg.

Even when there was compelling evidence of a need for state intervention, as in the soaring industrial accident rate, the government remained reluctant to intervene. In the first year of the war it was more dangerous to work in an American factory than it was to be a soldier. By June 1942 more workers had died in industrial accidents than had been killed in action.[44] Inexperienced 'green' workers, new to their jobs, working unfamiliar machines and overcome by fatigue, all contributed to the problem. Most of the injurious or fatal mistakes were made on the graveyard shifts when the workers were tired and physically low. This should have provided ammunition for the Nutrition Board to insist that night workers should be served fortifying warm meals, which were proven to help workers remain alert.[45] The federal government did step in and organize a safety campaign, followed by the setting-up of a committee on health and safety in 1943. But here again the government limited itself to offering advice and did not empower the committee to enforce regulations.[46]

Meanwhile the Coca-Cola company used the war to infiltrate the workplace. The company was the only soft drinks manufacturer exempt from sugar rationing because it was the main supplier of sodas for military bases. The company produced a pamphlet for the government entitled *The Importance of the Rest-Pause in Maximum War Effort*. It outlined at great length the argument that workers were more efficient if they were given regular breaks. It was only at the end, once the case had been made, that it was suggested that Coca-Cola should be the rest-break drink.[47] The utility of Coca-Cola as a drink for improving productivity was somewhat dubious. As the Germans discovered, a hot meal rather than a drink was of far more benefit to tired workers.[48] Nevertheless, Coca-Cola appears to have succeeded in its campaign. Peggy Terry, who worked in a shell factory in Viola, Kentucky, complained that 'Coca-Cola and Dr. Pepper were allowed in every building, but not a drop of water. You could only get a drink of water if you went to the cafeteria, which was about two city blocks away. Of course you couldn't leave your machine long enough to go get a drink. I drank Coke and Dr. Pepper and I hated 'em . . . We had to buy it, of course.'[49]

If the nutritional gap between the classes began to close during the war, a deep racial divide continued to mark American society. Black

Americans were actively excluded from the economic boom sparked by the growth of the war industries. Many war plants refused to employ blacks and by the end of the war only 8 per cent of all jobs in the war industries were held by blacks. Many of these were southerners who had left the poverty of a rural life, and women who had escaped the drudgery of domestic service.[50] This was an improvement on their share of only 3 per cent of war industry jobs in 1942, but they were nevertheless under-represented and frequently employed in the most dangerous jobs – handling ammunition, gunpowder or poisonous chemicals.[51] Many war plants would only employ blacks in menial positions as porters, janitors and cleaners.[52]

Those black men willing to sacrifice their lives for America found the armed forces also unwilling to admit them, and when they were enlisted they tended to be assigned to menial positions, as cooks or in service battalions. In the army and in many southern states segregation was still in force. Blacks were required to use separate washrooms in factories, they were denied access to parks and pool halls and expected to ride in the back of buses and streetcars, well away from the white passengers.[53] One campaigner pointed out that the United States government made itself sound pretty foolish when it declared itself 'to be against park benches marked JUDE in Berlin, but to be *for* park benches marked COLORED in Tallahassee, Florida. It was grim, not foolish, to have a young black man in uniform get an orientation in the morning on wiping out Nazi bigotry and that same evening be told he could buy a soft drink only in the "colored" post exchange.'[54]

One of the major sources of disruption to the war effort was racial unrest. In 1943 there were 242 racial confrontations in forty-seven cities and the worst disruption was concentrated in war-production centres such as Mobile, Detroit and Philadelphia, where white protests against the employment or promotion of blacks led to wildcat strikes, the paralysis of transport systems and riots in which blacks were killed.[55] In the one month of March 1943 the US Labor Department concluded that 101,955 work days had been lost as a result of racial bigotry.[56] Throughout the black community there was great bitterness that while America claimed to be fighting to defend democracy abroad the government did not apply democratic principles to its treatment of blacks at home.

Blacks were doubly disadvantaged in that their difficulties in finding employment in the war industries excluded them from the benefits of rising wartime wages, while at the same time they were less protected from wartime inflation. In the black areas of America's cities astronomical rents were charged for broken-down and overcrowded housing and the local stores charged outrageously high prices for foodstuffs of inferior quality. In theory, price controls should have held this problem in check but the Office of Price Administration had few volunteers checking up on the prices storekeepers charged in the black areas of the cities, and on average blacks paid more than whites for their food.[57] In August 1942 a survey conducted by the National Association for the Advancement of Colored People found that the black population of New York was paying 6 per cent more for their food than other inhabitants of the city. Although the Association asked OPA to address the problem in the black neighbourhoods, nothing was done.[58] The bitterness culminated in the August of 1943 when a 'commodity riot' broke out in Harlem and the white-owned stores which overcharged the community were looted and destroyed. After the Harlem riot, action was at last taken in New York, and within a week the OPA had set up an office in the area and appointed black administrators to oversee food-pricing in the area.[59] But throughout the war Roosevelt and his administration remained reluctant to address the real grievances of the black community and it was not until the civil rights movement of the 1960s that the United States government finally accepted the need to protect the basic democratic rights of all its citizens.

There were those within the administration who were eager to use the war to improve the system of poor relief set up during the Depression. The report of the Conference on National Nutrition for Defense (1941) argued for the continued use of the food stamp plan and school lunches, both of which had been introduced in the 1930s, in order to 'bring nourishing, adequate meals to those who could not otherwise afford them'.[60] However, the New Deal food relief programmes had been seen by both their chief administrator, Harry Hopkins, and the Secretary of Agriculture, Henry Wallace, primarily as ways of off-loading agricultural surpluses and maintaining farm incomes, rather than as the means of improving the nutritional quality of the diet of the poor.[61] Thus, although by 1942 the school lunch programme was benefiting 5 million children (about one-quarter of the total school population) it had also improved farm incomes to the tune of at least $16 million and the school kitchens had been inundated with farm surpluses of eggs, grapefruit, onions, apples, apricots and almonds. The food donations were so unbalanced that the schools often had to buy in extra foods in order to make balanced meals and the children became so sick of many of the donated foods that they refused to eat them.[62]

By 1943 the enormous wartime demand for food had solved the problem of food surpluses and most of the New Deal relief programmes were phased out. Federal funding was withdrawn from the food points and relief schemes, and states which wished to continue participating were required to find the funding themselves. As a result the poorest states, with the largest populations in the greatest need, withdrew from the relief schemes.[63] This meant that a stubborn residue of the impoverished, who had not been pulled out of poverty by the wartime boom, lost their access to food aid. This was particularly the case in the farming belt, which stretched from the mid-Atlantic coast to the south and west through Virginia and West Virginia, South Carolina, Kentucky, Tennessee, Alabama, Mississippi and Arkansas to Louisiana. Poor land, outdated machinery and a lack of capital to invest in new technologies meant that farms in these areas were left untouched by the wave of wartime prosperity which washed over America's farming community.[64] In these areas living standards actually fell as there was an exodus of doctors, dentists and teachers who went to the army and the more prosperous towns, leaving hungry and malnourished women and children with virtually no health care and a sub-standard education.[65]

The one New Deal relief programme to be saved was the school lunch programme. A concerted campaign by nutritionists at the Bureau of Home Economics managed to secure continued federal funding for the scheme. The senator for Georgia, Richard Russell, reminded the government that these meals were more important than ever to schoolchildren now that their mothers were engaged in war work and could not be expected to come home at noon to prepare a hot meal. 'At a time when England is enlarging her school lunch program I do not see how we in this country could justify curtailment here.'[66] Indeed, the scheme expanded until, by the end of the war, it was feeding 8 million children while another 2 million received milk at school.[67]

The school lunch programme was the one area of wartime food policy where nutritionists gained real power. Each state was required to hire dieticians and nutritionists to supervise the scheme, and the recommended daily allowances were used to measure whether the lunches were 'of optimum nutritional value'.[68] The Committee on Food Habits, under the direction of the anthropologist Margaret Mead, devoted its efforts to creating suggested menus which would provide meals that were not only healthy but which fostered a sense of national unity. Mead argued that school lunches should avoid offending the tastes of the many ethnic groups within America's diverse population. For this reason she argued that spicy seasonings, which would alienate one group or another, should be avoided and suggested that salt should be the only flavouring used. By trying to please all tastes Mead succeeded in promoting the insipid. The committee produced a set of menus which reduced the ethnic and regional diversity represented within the culinary repertoire of the United States to a bland array of soups, meat pies, broiled fish and plain boiled vegetables. School lunches acted as a powerful force for homogenizing the American diet, subtly creating preferences for innocuous meals which all Americans could share. In Chicago the school lunch programme was praised as a force which Americanized immigrant children. The Polish, Lithuanian, Mexican, Italian, Catholic, Protestant or Jewish children who sat down to consume these meals were described as 'eating democracy'.[69]

If they helped to create a unified American diet, school lunches did little to actually feed the poor. The programme did stipulate that all children from low-income families and those on welfare should receive a free meal. But federal funding only covered the cost of the food and the states had to find the money to provide new lunchrooms and kitchens, and to pay for helpers. This meant that the poorest states had the fewest participating schools and not very many school meals ended up in the stomachs of the needy.[70] The laissez-faire attitude of the government, the bureaucratic muddle of the food administration, and the failure of American nutritionists to find a powerful government minister, like the British Lord Woolton, to champion their cause, ensured that the American rationing system was far less effective as an instrument of welfare than rationing was in Britain.

FUTURE HOPES

The new-found prosperity of American workers allowed them to buy goods which had previously been out of their reach. Peggy Terry overheard 'a woman saying on the bus that she hoped the war didn't end until she got her refrigerator paid for. An old man hit her over the head with an umbrella.'[71] But the desires generated by wealth were thwarted by shortages of every imaginable consumable as industry focused its energies on armaments. Instead, consumers were urged to save and, to encourage them, a vision of a post-war world of plenty was disseminated through advertising campaigns which spread the government's propaganda messages while maintaining a brand presence in the eyes of potential consumers. The relentless advertising created an absurd sense that the only thing Americans were fighting for was for the right to consume. A Royal typewriter advertisement captured the tone of the great majority of wartime American advertisements: 'WHAT THIS WAR IS ALL ABOUT . . . [is the right to] once more walk into any store in the land and buy anything you want.'[72]

Eileen Barth, a social worker whose husband was in the army, explained, 'I remember an ad in which people were shown as pigs because they seemed to want so much. To me, it was wanting to have things for the first time in their lives. They were able to enjoy life a little more, even get a house in the suburbs. These were people who lived through the Depression, as children, many of them. I guess you'd say a new middle class came into being. Perhaps they concentrated a little too much on the material life. The war did it.'[73] The privations Americans had put up with during the Depression and now during the war shaped their post-war desires.

What most Americans wanted was their own home. Given the overcrowding in the cities and the state of disrepair of both urban and rural housing stock, it was hardly surprising. Jean Muller Pearson married a pilot in the 120th Observation Squadron and followed him to his base in Boise, Idaho. The housing shortage meant that people would rent virtually any habitable space, and she and her husband squeezed into the top floor of a house with another couple, sharing a bathroom, kitchen and a sitting room on the landing. Then her husband was posted to Tonopah, Nevada, where they ended up living in what had been a miner's shack. They had an old iron stove in the kitchen which was both oven and water heater, and the '"refrigerator" was a wooden crate attached to the outside of the kitchen accessible through a window that opened inward. On very cold nights milk and produce froze.'[74] They were fortunate in that they had a bathroom in a lean-to built on the side of the shack. Theirs was one of only thirty bathtubs in the whole town and Jean would invite the other wives over for a bath.

After such living conditions, a detached suburban home with its own yard and, most importantly, a sense of privacy, seemed very appealing, as did numerous labour-saving appliances such as washing machines.[75] A vital element in this new world was not only a new refrigerator standing proudly in the kitchen of the ideal suburban home but one that was filled to the brim with food. A public service advertisement for Macy's in the *New York Daily News* in September 1943 listed 'defending Democracy' and 'a better world' as things Americans were fighting for, but it also included 'a steak for every frying pan'.[76]

In May 1943 an opinion poll found that rationing and wartime food shortages had barely made any impact on American meals. Two-thirds of the women surveyed asserted that their diet had changed very little since the introduction of rationing, and three-quarters of the women acknowledged that the size of their meals had stayed the same.[77] The minimal impact that rationing had on American eating habits is revealed by the passing comment of a woman from New York, who noted that coffee rationing, which cut consumption from three cups to one a day, was 'the wartime measure to have affected one the most'.[78] The food privations inflicted on American civilians by the war were minimal compared to those suffered by civilians in all other combatant nations. As one US soldier acknowledged to his English hostess: 'if American women had had to put up with half as much as we have they would have made a terrific fuss'. As it was they still complained a great deal.[79]

The overriding problem was that Americans had no particular emotional investment in the war. Before Pearl Harbor American public opinion had been adamantly opposed to involvement in another European conflict. After the Japanese attack there was outrage and anger and a sense that the United States had to win. But there was ambivalence about the sacrifices American civilians were willing to make. Many could see that agriculture was booming and food was plentiful and they did not believe that rationing was really necessary. The Americans' natural suspicion of state intervention made them question the government's motives for implementing the system. One soldier's wife commented sourly that she thought it 'was a patriotic ploy to keep our enthusiasm at fever pitch'.[80]

Housewives resented the favourable distribution of sugar to commercial bakeries. This made them more reliant on bought cakes and denied them the homely activity of baking.[81] Intermittent shortages of foodstuffs followed by sudden gluts of the same foods shook housewives' faith in the rationing system. In the spring of 1943 potatoes disappeared from city shops. The army had used up the winter reserve stocks. A few weeks later there were so many potatoes no one knew what to do with them.[82] Eggs followed a similar pattern in the autumn – disappearing, only to return in the spring of 1944 in excess.[83] These food shortages were certainly not serious, as they were in Germany's cities where staple foods became unavailable, leaving the inhabitants with insufficient food to sustain their energy and health. But they were unsettling and inconvenient.[84] In addition, half the black women employed as maids and cooks deserted their employers for better paid war work, leaving their mistresses to cope with only the assistance of recipe books and filled with the resentful sense that the proper order of life had been thoroughly upset.[85]

The food around which American civilians' dissatisfaction with rationing centred was red meat. Red meat, preferably beef, was highly valued as a prime source of energy, especially for the working man, and its presence on a plate helped to define the food as a proper meal. But during the war most red meat, and especially steak, disappeared into the army bases. Butchers continued to stock lower-quality cuts of red meat, pork, poultry and fish, and during the war Americans ate at least 2.5 pounds of meat per person per week. This was a generous quantity and it represented a per capita increase of at least 10 pounds a year.[86] In comparison, Soviet workers were lucky to find a scrap of sausage in their canteen's cabbage soup and the British had to get by on less than half the American ration. Moreover, a proportion of the pound of meat per week which British civilians ate was often made up of corned beef or offal. American women did not take kindly to offal and few took the advice of a recipe book designed to assist the 'gallant soldier on the home front . . . in making the most of her meat purchases during the present emergency' by beginning resolutely to jelly tongues, Creole kidneys, fry liver like the French, and apply the cooking of Maryland to tripe.[87] Instead, they preferred to use 'stretchers' to make their meat go further and reduced waste by religiously using up leftovers.[88]

There was plenty of meat available but it was not the kind American civilians craved. It is therefore unsurprising that the black market in food was most active in the meat trade. During the war a large number of small slaughterhouses sprang up which traded locally and were able to evade the inspectors from the Office of Price Administration. They would buy livestock for slaughter above the ceiling price and then sell it on to black market distributors.[89] Butchers would sell favoured customers high quality steaks in the guise of 'pre-ground' hamburger which used up fewer ration points. In an attempt to persuade Americans to abide by the rules, Eleanor Roosevelt took the Home Front Pledge to always pay ration points in full.[90] The food at the White House, which under the Roosevelts had never been good, was now used to set an example, and although the 'New York Times sympathised with the President for having to lunch on salt fish four days in a row' Eleanor insisted that this was only fitting in a time of war.[91] In sympathy with the American public's dismay over coffee rationing Eleanor also cut the demitasse of coffee from the White House after-dinner ritual.[92]

The American black market never got so out of hand that it was a threat to the economy, but the illegal meat trade was sufficiently active for it to threaten the Department of Agriculture's ability to meet its supply commitments to Britain. It grew in size throughout 1943 as enthusiasm for the war waned once the public realized that a speedy victory was beyond the reach of the Allies.[93] The attitude of Americans towards the black market signalled that both a consensus and social cohesion were weaker in wartime America. In contrast to Britain, where petty pilfering was justified with guilty defensiveness, many Americans viewed it with the triumphant sense that they had beaten the system.

Others simply did not question it at all, taking small under-the-counter transactions for granted. When Helen Studer was working as a riveter at the Douglas aircraft factory in California, she recalled, without any apparent guilt, how the friendly woman at the grocery store would slip extra goods into her bag. 'When I'd get home, I'd have three or four things on my bill that wasn't said out loud. I'd have a carton of cigarettes . . . There might have been a couple of pounds of oleo [margarine] or there may have been five pounds of sugar. I never knew what I was going to have.'[94]

The advertising images generated during the war created an image of the meaning of victory as the freedom to indulge in all those luxuries which Americans had been denied during the war. In 1943 Norman Rockwell in the *Saturday Evening Post* illustrated the four freedoms which Roosevelt stated that he hoped the war would achieve for the world in his State of the Union address to Congress on 6 January 1941. Rockwell depicted the freedom from fear, freedom of speech, freedom of worship, and freedom from want, with images of ordinary Americans going about their everyday lives: parents checking on their sleeping children, a man speaking at a town meeting, a congregation at prayer in a church and a family seated around a table laden with food. The private, homely nature of the paintings reinforced the widespread notion that the grand ideals of freedom and democracy which Americans were fighting to defend were embodied in the details of the American way of life.[95] Most particularly they appeared to be symbolized by an American family sitting down to eat a huge Thanksgiving turkey. Rockwell noted in his autobiography that this picture of abundance caused a certain amount of resentment among Europeans living in conditions of austerity, who were able to read the message of American superiority encoded in the image of plentiful food.[96]

That these ideas and images were internalized by ordinary Americans is illustrated by a letter Phil Aquila wrote to his sister in October 1944. Posted to Kentucky during the war, Phil kept in touch with his family in Buffalo. His family, of Italian descent, was poor, and every summer his mother used to take all nine children out to the farms around New York to work in the seasonal harvesting of the vegetable crop. 'I hope by now Ma's finished canning,' he wrote, 'although she still can buy a lot of stuff at the market of Bailey & Clinton Streets to can if she feels she needs more food for this winter. Yep, people in this country are sure lucky, to be able to stock up as much food as they want. That's what us guys are fighting for, so tell Ma to stock up.'[97]

During the Depression years the idea emerged of the consumer as the saviour of the American economy. The working man who bought himself goods such as radios and refrigerators by means of hire purchase was the key to generating industrial production. Not only was he improving his standard of living but the demand for consumables would increase productivity and keep working men in jobs.[98] At the end of the war, the government returned to this argument and encouraged purchasing without restraint as a way of preventing the expected post-war economic slump. The 'former head of the Office of Price Administration, Chester Bowles, told his former colleagues in advertising, the resulting mass markets, where "the janitor's appetite for a sirloin steak is as profitable as the banker's," would democratize the benefits of prosperity'.[99] Consumerism was the American answer to Britain's Beveridge Report which symbolized the hope for a better world to be achieved through the creation of a welfare state. Americans believed that if the masses were able to gain access to the fruits of economic abundance, political and economic equality would follow.[100]

TROOP WELFARE

The daily meals of American soldiers revealed the influence of the Food and Nutrition Board's overly generous recommended daily allowances. The standard ration provided on military bases contained a staggering 4,300 calories, about 800 calories more than is strictly necessary for a soldier in training.[101] Men at the front were allocated 4,758 calories a day, and American soldiers were fortunate to receive sufficient food to sustain a man in combat in cold or tropical conditions. The German combat rations at 4,000 calories came close to competing with American standards but the Japanese opposing them in the tropical conditions of the Pacific were fighting on an official ration which contained fewer than half this number of calories, and the soldiers rarely received their full allocation.[102]

The United States military zealously applied the new knowledge of protective foods to the meals of the armed forces. Every meal contained meat and each serviceman ate a gargantuan 234 pounds per year, just under double the 140 pounds per head for civilians. This was the main cause of red meat shortages in American butchers' shops.[103] In December 1940 R. B. Buckle, a nineteen-year-old British brewery worker from Norfolk, found himself living at an American navy receiving station in Seattle, waiting to board the battleship *Warspite*. He was amazed by the food: 'We sat down in a huge dining hall and were waited on by coloured sailors who wore dazzling white uniforms . . . The meal was excellent. Steak, mark you! Real steak with onions, creamed and French fried potatoes, green beans and a delicious sauce. Sweet was apple crumble and cream. A huge mug of coffee completed the meal.'[104] When Buckle was savouring American food, it would still be another year before the United States joined the war. Even once America had been drawn into the conflict the boom in agriculture meant that the armed forces were always well supplied. Indeed, in terms of food, the United States armed forces were in a league of their own. As one British officer commented, their rations were 'lavish to the point of extravagance'.[105]

Generous meals were one of General George Marshall's strategies for dealing with an army of drafted men who preserved a strong civilian mentality. Few American recruits felt they were under an obligation to serve their country. On the contrary, they felt that while they sacrificed their liberty and possibly their lives, their country was under a powerful debt of obligation to them.[106] They expected to be well looked after in the armed forces, and soldiers and their families formed a powerful pressure group within the United States. Even minor expressions of discontent over rations led to outspoken criticism in the forces' newspaper, the *Stars and Stripes*.[107] The military was so sensitive to discontent among the new recruits that it set up a polling organization specifically to track the mood among its soldiers. The polls found that the men chafed a great deal against the conformity and petty restrictions of army life but their biggest gripes were food and pay.[108] In response Marshall adopted a placatory policy which made 'troop welfare . . . an essential part of modern warfare'.[109] The result was that the United States military went to great lengths to ensure that soldiers in the field had the means to wash, good-quality field hospitals backed up by an efficient evacuation system, regular mail deliveries, recreation facilities and, most importantly, good food.[110]

A book for worried mothers entitled *When Your Son Goes to War* (1943) assured anxious women that the army was aware that 'this generation of boys had been brought up on milk as a definite item of diet', and men in the armed forces were plied with the liquid.[111] In army camps 'each soldier has a separate half-pint bottle [of milk]; or [a] one quart bottle is placed on the table for each four or five men'. As a consequence, civilians living near military bases suffered from milk shortages.[112] Besides meat and milk, draftees were provided with a surfeit of vitamin-rich vegetables. After a breakfast of 'fruit, dry cereals, broiled bacon, eggs, French toast and syrup, toast and butter, coffee or milk', the trainees at Randolph Field air base in Texas were given for lunch 'heart of celery, green olives, head of lettuce, roast turkey and cranberry jam, mashed potatoes, raisin dressing, giblet gravy, buttered jumbo asparagus tips, creamed cauliflower, lemon custard or ice cream, rolls and butter, layer cake, preserves, coffee or tea'. If the men were still hungry, at supper time they could round off their day with 'fresh celery, smothered round steak, escalloped potatoes, frosted peas, strawberry ice cream, layer cake, bread and butter, coffee or milk'.[113] The idea that most recruits were used to this quality and quantity of food in their own homes was absurd. Draftees, particularly in the infantry, which was disproportionately made up of 'the depression drop outs, the slum kids, the backwoods boys from Appalachia and the deep South', had never eaten so well.[114] Despite vigorous training, the airmen at Randolph Field found themselves gaining 10 or 20 pounds (4–9 kilograms) in weight each month.[115]

In the US army, as in the British and Commonwealth armies, medical officers and quartermasters were beginning to liaise and pay greater attention to standards of nutrition as a means to maintain soldiers' health. But the American policy of maintaining morale through welfare gave extra impetus to the new awareness of the need to supply soldiers, at their bases and on the front line, with nutritious food. The US Surgeon-General's office made every effort to ensure that field rations were the next best thing to a proper mess meal. A director of nutrition was employed to devise a balanced B ration for field kitchens. The B ration aimed to include three different sorts of meat, four vegetables, a dessert and canned fruit or fruit juice in the five pounds of food allocated to each man for a day.[116] If the B ration could be prepared with fresh food this was ideal but many field kitchens had to rely on canned meat and dehydrated vegetables. However, it was possible to liven these up with the wide range of supplementary ingredients and condiments which were provided with the B ration (in theory it consisted of 100 different elements), such as rice, macaroni, oats, jam, syrup, peanut butter, pickles, pepper, vinegar, tomato sauce and a variety of flavourings.[117] From this range of ingredients the director of nutrition created dietician-formulated master menus which were sent out to all army cooks. This, the Surgeon-General claimed, ensured that wherever they were in the world, in 'England, Italy, North Africa, Egypt, Persia, India and China', all United States troops were eating the same nutritionally balanced meals.[118]

B ration meals were far superior to anything produced in the field by the US military's allies or enemies. Stan Tutt, part of an Australian air maintenance crew at Milne Bay on New Guinea, felt like a second-class soldier in comparison with the Americans who lived in a camp across the road. They had proper beds, a mosquito-proof recreation hut, regular deliveries of mail, and oranges which they generously shared with their Australian neighbours. Stan and his fellow soldiers felt bitter as, with empty stomachs, they unloaded trucks one December morning, tantalized by the aroma of bacon and eggs frying in the American camp across the road. 'We [had] not eaten a fresh egg since coming to New Guinea.'[119] The components of the German field ration were much more basic, centred on rye bread, meat, fat and vegetables, with pudding powder, condensed milk and a few spices to add a little variety and flavour.[120] The *Gulaschkanone*, as the Wehrmacht's field kitchens were known, provided simple meals of soup or stew. The Soviets' field kitchens were even more elementary, producing meals out of buckwheat, dried fish, potatoes and as much fat as possible, as this helped to keep out the cold. In the first years of the war it was rare for Red Army soldiers to be supplied with hot meals from a field kitchen and many survived on dry rations of bread and dried fish for weeks on end.[121] The Japanese, at the other end of the spectrum, dispensed with the bother of field kitchens and left their troops to cook their own rice.

The menus devised for the US military followed the same principle as that applied to school lunches, in that they sought to avoid offending regional or ethnic tastes. Rather than acting as a forum for learning about the culinary diversity of the United States, army canteens acted as a powerful homogenizing force. Many young recruits had little experience of other Americans outside their own region, or of their different food habits. William Bauer, an aviation cadet from New Jersey, recalled 'how provincial we were, how provincial all of us were ... I had only been to New York, Pennsylvania and Delaware.' During his training in the south he discovered fried chicken and soft ice cream and he felt that his experiences of other parts of America and the world made him 'a much broader person and a much better person'.[122] But it was not in army messes that he found out about other Americans' food habits. The bland (if filling) canteen meals were based on the Anglo-Saxon model of meat and two vegetables.[123] Like American schoolchildren, the recruits from diverse regional, religious and ethnic backgrounds found themselves eating the innocuous food of democracy.[124] Their taste buds were moulded into conformity, and Margaret Mead and the other members of the Committee on Food Habits would have been delighted by a post-war poll in which the majority of Americans described their perfect meal as an elaborate version of one of their menus: a fruit or shrimp cocktail followed by vegetable or chicken soup, a steak for the main course with mashed potatoes or chips and peas, with a side salad, roll and butter, and apple pie for dessert followed by hot coffee.[125]

On American bases throughout the world Post Exchange (PX) stores were kept well supplied with a stock of small treats: American candies, cigarettes and drinks. This was part of Marshall's troop welfare policy. These supplies of small luxuries were supposed to ensure that the soldiers felt that they had a little piece of home with them in the foreign countries where they were fighting. The PX stores became a powerful force in establishing Coca-Cola as the archetypal American beverage. In the 1920s and 1930s Coca-Cola was not yet established as *the* American drink, although a vigorous advertising campaign had helped to make it popular, especially in the south. But when America entered the war the company saw the conflict as a huge advertising opportunity, and it immediately began to lobby the government to be allowed to carry on manufacturing the drink. It produced hundreds of letters from military bases and defence plants to prove that there was a bottomless demand for the drink among those who were crucial to the war effort.[126] The Quartermaster-General, Somervell, was persuaded, and in 1942 Coca-Cola was exempted from sugar rationing when supplying military bases.[127] In all, 148 plant technicians from the company were given the military title of technical observer (TO) and sent out to open sixty-four bottling plants across the world: in North Africa, India, the remote Pacific on the Mariana island group and New Guinea and, after the war, in occupied Germany and Japan.[128] Thus, Coca-Cola monopolized the soft drinks market for US servicemen; 95 per cent of all the drinks available in PX stores were made by Coca-Cola and, wherever they were stationed, US troops could be observed drinking the beverage by the local inhabitants.[129] Advertisements back in the United States proclaimed that Coca-Cola had become a 'symbol of our way of living'.[130] This was not an idle boast. The drink 'turned out to be a nearly perfect symbolic repository' for American culture for both the servicemen and their observers.[131] 'To have this drink is just like having home brought nearer to you,' wrote one homesick soldier. 'It's things such as this that all of us are fighting for.'[132] Another claimed that he was fighting 'as much to help keep the custom of drinking Cokes as I am to help preserve the million other benefits our country blesses its citizens with'.[133] Once the war was over Coca-Cola was firmly established as 'a sublimated essence of all that America stands for'.[134]

The policy of making troop welfare central to the conduct of the war meant that the US army was unusual in that it accorded food virtually equal weight with the rest of the equipment US troops needed in order to fight. In their summary of quartermaster operations in the war against Germany, William Ross and Charles Romanus noted that 'rations were probably the best-handled category of Quartermaster supplies on the European continent . . . A food shortage in any US military unit, no matter how small, was regarded as a major emergency, to be corrected by whatever action necessary.'[135] Indeed, they argued that by the time the Allies landed in France in June 1944 a 'subsistence philosophy' had developed among the US service technicians, who saw it as their duty to ensure that the combat soldiers received hot, tasty and nutritious meals whenever possible. This 'subsistence philosophy' gradually developed over the two years of American combat experience in North Africa and Italy, beginning with the Torch landings in North Africa in November 1942.

The US troops who waded ashore in Morocco carried in their rucksacks two awkward cylindrical C ration canisters, each weighing 5 pounds. This contributed greatly to the overall weight of the men's backpacks, which came to 132 pounds altogether. When waterlogged, the packs became far too heavy and some men drowned trying to wade ashore. As a consequence, the shape and weight of the canisters was altered. Each C ration pack consisted of three tins, containing beef stew, pork and beans and meat hash, an issue of 'C square biscuits', coffee and sugar.[136] The C rations had been developed in the Subsistence Research Laboratory in Chicago in the 1930s and this was the first time that they were put into use in the field. In theory, the troops were only supposed to live on C rations for a week, at most a month, before the B ration was reintroduced, and after sixty to ninety days the men could expect refrigerated supplies of fresh foods to start arriving.[137] However, the logistics of supply were chaotic in North Africa and the troops quite often ended up living on C rations for several weeks at a time. This was unpopular, one commander complaining that after only three or four days of C rations his men 'suffered spells of nausea and digestive disturbances'.[138] This reaction was understandable given that when an exhausted infantryman, nerves stretched to breaking point, opened a C ration tin of meat he was confronted by a layer of reddish grease which tended to collect at the top of the can. Even when field kitchens were eventually set up in North Africa their meat issue was supplied by C ration meat cans and the men began to feel as though they only ever ate stew or hash.[139] Although the GIs thought the tins of mutton stew and steak and kidney pie in the British composite ration packs were repulsive, they envied the Tommies the variety. Suggestions were sent back to the Research Laboratory from North Africa. Larger chunks of meat, which could be chewed, were requested, a better opening mechanism for the cans so that the grease gathered at the top did not spill out on to hands and clothes, and, because the C rations were tasteless when eaten cold, a demand for canned heat, from which the British and Germans benefited. This was a can with a wick leading to a heating element in the centre of the tin which heated the food within seconds. They also asked for a few extras to be added such as chocolate, soap, cigarettes and toilet paper.[140]

In response, the Subsistence Research Laboratory came up with the five-in-one, which the quartermaster began to issue to troops at the end of the North African campaign. This provided variety in the canned meat options: roast beef, meatballs and spaghetti, and canned bacon. It also contained dehydrated potatoes, onions and vegetable soups, and dried milk. The GIs did not think much of cabbage flakes, the tomato juice cocktail or the greasy substitute for butter known as Carter's spread, but they did think the five-in-ones were a huge improvement and in 1943 the ten-in-one, which was similar but for ten men, was added to the ration options at the quartermaster's disposal.[141]

The American equivalent of the operational pack which Stanton Hicks developed for soldiers right on the front line was the K ration. It provided 3,000 calories in three meals – veal for breakfast, Spam for lunch and dried sausage for dinner. There was also a fruit bar, crackers, which had a tendency to turn rancid in the tropics, cheese, a bouillon cube, malt-dextrose tablets, and a packet of lemon crystals to dissolve in water; in addition there was chewing gum (the taste of which used to permeate everything else if exposed to heat), cigarettes, toilet paper, soap, water purification tablets and a can opener.[142] In comparison, their enemies in the Wehrmacht were still going into battle equipped with an iron ration which had barely changed since the days of the First World War. The German half 'iron ration' consisted of a packet of hard biscuits and a can of meat, while the full iron ration included an additional issue of preserved vegetables, coffee and salt.[143] The Japanese quartermaster developed impressive emergency ration packs but in practice Japanese soldiers went into battle without such luxuries and were fortunate to be issued with their full allocation of rice before an assault. When they took Americans prisoner they were staggered by the K ration packs, particularly their inclusion of toilet paper and soap. The Japanese only received some low-grade soap, toilet paper and toothpaste once a month in their meagre 'comfort' kits.[144]

Despite the superiority of C and K rations to anything issued to the Axis troops, Allied soldiers complained a great deal about them. British troops were often issued with K rations, and William Woodruff, in a field near Anzio, wrote, 'Dammit it's a wonder we haven't lost the war eating that Yank stuff. It's all wrapping and bull. When you've swallowed the spearmint and the fags and the glucose candy and dehydrated muck that goes with it, your guts feel empty. Gives you wind it does. It's got nothing on British treacle and duff.'[145] Wherever the Americans fought, they left behind them a trail of discarded ration containers. In Italy enemy reconnaissance planes were sometimes able to spot bivouacs and hideouts by looking for the glint of gold C ration cans catching the sunlight. In order to prevent this, the cans were eventually given a coat of green paint.[146] Alongside the cans would be a litter of rejected cabbage flakes and the cellophane packages of lemon crystals, which came with the K ration. The GIs would not touch the crystals, and even the Subsistence Laboratory finally had to admit that they 'were characterised by a biting acidity' which could only be countered by vast amounts of sugar.[147] The soldiers' practice of discarding half of their ration packs because they disliked or were simply bored to tears by the food in them frustrated the Subsistence Laboratory researchers, as it meant that the carefully balanced diet and the correct quantities of calories for combat, which the rations were supposed to contain, were not actually consumed by the troops. During the Italian campaign in 1943 surgeons reported that the men lost weight, were physically exhausted and the appearance of 'skin lesions, lassitude, and neuritis' indicated vitamin deficiencies in their diet.[148]

The fatigue and nervous tension of combat are often accompanied by a loss of appetite. Soldiers in stressful situations may force themselves to eat in order to maintain their energy levels. Under these conditions almost any food, no matter how appetizing, tends to induce nausea and revulsion. Soldiers frequently became caught up in a vicious circle of lack of appetite, revulsion in the face of tinned rations, undernourishment, repeated combat and further nervous exhaustion. During the Second World War the new attention paid to health and nutrition meant that medics and quartermasters learned that hunger and exhaustion among the troops would eventually contribute significantly to the development of combat fatigue and that an important contributory factor in all of this was a monotonous and unpalatable diet.[149] Although immediately after the war the historians of the quartermaster corps claimed that 'the development of packaged rations for combat will probably stand as a landmark in the history of food preparation', the real lesson the United States army learned during the conflict was to prioritize the preparation and delivery of freshly prepared hot food to men in combat.[150] In January 1944 the US army conducted a feeding experiment at Monte Cassino, using equipment borrowed from a battalion bakery. Ham, egg and cheese sandwiches, hamburgers, cakes and cookies were prepared and then delivered to the troops at the front by means of mules and jeeps. These fresh foods supplemented the C rations and were enthusiastically welcomed by the troops.[151] Their response confirmed that soldiers needed to be fed freshly prepared food whenever possible and throughout the campaigns in Europe during the summer and winter of 1944 the quartermaster made a determined effort to reduce the use of ration packs wherever possible. Only 21 per cent of all the food provided in western Europe was given out in the form of operational ration packs, while 79 per cent of the soldiers' meals were cooked in mess and field kitchens.[152] This was a lesson which the quartermaster applied during the Americans' next war, in Korea (1950–53), when as much of the troops' food as possible was prepared in field kitchens.[153]

AUSTRALIA – FOOD PROCESSING FOR VICTORY

Histories of Australia's part in the Second World War focus on its military contribution in Greece, Crete, Syria and North Africa, and the fact that thousands of Australian lives were wasted in ignominious mopping-up operations in New Guinea between 1943 and 1945. No matter how valiant Australian efforts in battle, these campaigns were peripheral in the defeat of both Germany and Japan.[154] The more effective, and less publicized, Australian contribution to the war effort was to supply American troops in the Pacific with 420,000 pairs of trousers, well over a million knitted shirts, 270,000 battle jackets, 11 million pairs of socks, 1.5 million blankets and 1.8 million boots and shoes – not to mention vehicles, petrol, building materials for housing, telegraph equipment, ammunition and hospital treatment.[155] Most importantly, over half of the supplies the United States took from Australia came in the form of food. In 1943 Australia and New Zealand provided the 1 million US servicemen serving in the Pacific with 95 per

cent of their food: tens of thousands of tons of canned meat and vegetables, biscuits, dehydrated vegetables and processed milk. Indeed,
Australia 'supplied more food per head of population to the Allied
larder than did any other country'.[156] The United States quartermaster
corps referred to Australia 'as a zone of interior for the South West
Pacific', in other words as an extension of the United States.[157] During
the war Australia was transformed into a vast food-processing plant
for the United States army.

However, when war broke out in 1939 food was certainly not seen
as the most important contribution Australia could make to the war.
Unable to ship all but the most concentrated foods to the country's
main market, in Britain, Australians were faced with gluts of unwanted
wheat and apples. Scientists desperately searched for new ways of
protecting large stores of grain from weevils and mice.[158] Agricultural
machinery plants converted to munitions production.[159] Farm workers
hurried to join up or left the countryside for better-paid jobs in industry. The number of people employed in agriculture fell by 120,000.[160]
By the time the United States and Japan entered the war in December
1941 Australian agriculture was in decline.

From January 1942 the Americans began to build up troops in
Australia in preparation for military action against Japan. The United
States divided the Pacific war zone into two military domains: the
South-West Pacific under the army command of General Douglas
MacArthur, with his base in Australia, and the South and Central Pacific
under the naval command of Admiral Chester Nimitz, based in New
Zealand. As well as feeding its own civilians and military forces,
Australia now had to supply Britain with as much frozen meat as
possible, feed the 100,000 US troops stationed in Australia and the 1
million US servicemen fighting on Pacific islands, as well as tens of
thousands of Japanese prisoners of war. This amounted to an additional
5 million hungry mouths.[161] The economy was turned on its head and
the food industry, which had been neglected, was now of the utmost
importance. Agricultural machinery plants were converted back to
producing tractors and other agricultural devices and men were called
back from the army to fight on the wheat and vegetable fields, rather
than in the jungles of the Pacific and deserts of the Middle East.

The US army authorities discovered that the Australian food industry was antiquated, and vegetable production barely mechanized.[162] It was clear that it would be unable to cope with feeding hundreds of thousands of soldiers. The US military responded by bringing in a division of experts, hastily promoted into the army for the duration. One of them was Major Belford Seabrook from the pioneering Seabrook Farms in New Jersey, who set about teaching the Australians the art of agribusiness. He introduced new varieties of vegetables which were more amenable to mechanized harvesting such as 'tomatoes with fruit that grew on accessible parts of the plant, [and] stringless beans'.[163] Farmers were taught how to stagger the planting of peas so that as each successive field matured they could be fed through the canning factory.[164] Seabrook introduced scientific methods for testing the starch content of the vegetables, to predict precisely when the crop should be picked for processing.[165] Factories were sent pattern machines from America so that they could manufacture power-operated potato diggers, rotary weeders, and bean and pea harvesters.[166] Using a pea harvester, a crop which used to take 1,500 pickers two weeks to harvest could be processed by fifteen men in days.[167] Major Seabrook was praised by one contemporary historian for having 'effected an agricultural revolution in this land', without which 'Australia could not have met the demands made upon her'.[168]

To complement the introduction of new vegetable-growing techniques, American experts overhauled the canning industry. Faulty end and side seams on the Australian cans had a tendency to let in bacteria. In May 1942 the GI Stan Tutt was horrified by the tins of tomatoes he had to unload in northern Queensland. The tomatoes were 'so fermented the contents were trickling from the cases – vile'.[169] The revolting brew had spoiled the bags of flour placed underneath the tins. In November that year thirty-two US airmen developed botulism as a result of eating Australian canned beetroot. Eight of them died.[170] Major C. R. Fellers, head of the Department of Food Technology of the University of Massachusetts at Amherst, was drafted in to improve canning technology. He set up the US Quartermaster's Laboratory in Tooth's Brewery, Sydney, which tested the quality and safety of food supplied to the army. A Captain C. E. Norton used lend-lease money to build four factories to supply the equipment for can-making and he and his team visited the canning factories to make sure that the sealing equipment was working and that the cans were heated up long enough to kill bacteria.[171] The American team of skilled management and technicians accomplished in months what might have taken years without the stimulus of the war.[172]

The amount of land used to grow vegetables doubled. By 1944 Australia was producing more than a million tons of vegetables and 50 million pounds of them disappeared into cans destined for US servicemen on Pacific islands.[173] Seventeen newly constructed dehydration plants around the country transformed much of the rest of the crop into dried vegetables. Despite being far less palatable, they were invaluable for transporting to troops along lengthy supply chains as they weighed only one-eighth of their original weight. In addition they did not require valuable tinplate, which had to be imported from the States. Dried potato soon became a staple of both American and Australian servicemen in the Pacific. Australia produced over 21 million pounds in 1945 alone.[174]

Australian farming's efforts were impressive. The only problem was that Australian and American tastes differed greatly. When US servicemen lived on Australian military rations they were horrified. Thomas St George, stationed in South Australia, was expecting ham and eggs for breakfast. He was disgusted by the mutton stew which he was served out of an oil drum, 'like cold glue full of unidentifiable vegetables, and with all the delicious appeal of a soggy snow bank'.[175] The stewed coffee made with chicory which arrived in the other oil drum was equally unpleasant. What was more, the garbage was carried away in the same drums that brought the food. American annual consumption of mutton was a mere 6.5 pounds per head. It was regarded as a poor man's meat. But it was an Australian staple, each Australian consuming a substantial 70 pounds of mutton per person per year.[176]

Moreover, there was a discrepancy between the ration for the Australian troops which was made up of only twenty-four basic items, while the GIs were used to thirty-nine staple items and 814 more calories per day. The US army quickly took over the provisioning of its troops within Australia and fed them according to US ration scales. The Americans were provided with fresh eggs, macaroni, spaghetti, rice and coffee, all of which were denied Australian soldiers. An extra sixpence per man per day for their maintenance supplied their canteens with fresh fruit, fruit juices, vegetables, breakfast cereals, saltines, cocoa, baking-soda, cornflour and cornmeal, *and* an extra four ounces of beef and three ounces of bacon a week per man.[177] Given that virtually all this extra food was grown and processed in Australia, this seemed doubly unfair. The inequality was replicated in the field. R. Palmer, who served in the Australian navy, once made a trip on an American supply ship from Port Moresby to Milne Bay, New Guinea. Stowed away below the hatches were 'crates of fresh apples and there was butter, boxes and boxes of butter, and there was beef hanging up . . . All come from Australia you see . . . The supply ship used to come up from Australia with all this fresh fruit on and fresh food which we never got.'[178] The Australians on New Guinea used to joke that US amphibious operations were carried out in two waves: first the marines, then a consignment of refrigerators.[179]

By September 1942 ordinary Australians were feeling the effect of feeding the Americans and the resentment among Australian troops was matched by some civilian bitterness. Wartime prosperity meant that Australians, like the Americans, had more money to spend on better-quality food and they resented shortages, especially given that the American servicemen seemed to 'eat about three times as much as the average Australian in a day'.[180] In particular, the Australians could not get over the fact that grown men chose to drink milk. A mother in Brisbane complained sourly to the *Brisbane Courier Mail* that her two small children could not get a taste of ice cream because the milk bars reserved their supplies for GIs, who would also drink several milk shakes at one sitting. Although their official allowance was 8 ounces (which was already double the Australian), it was estimated that GIs drank about 24 ounces of milk a day.[181] The Americans' taste for fried chicken had made poultry unaffordable and eggs were scarce.[182] Tinned foods, especially canned meat, had just about disappeared from the shops. Virtually all the biscuits produced in the Perth area went to Western Command. Only a small supply of milk and arrowroot biscuits was set aside for small children.[183] Rationing was gradually extended to cover tea (½ pound for five weeks from July 1942), sugar (1 pound a week from October 1942), butter (8 ounces, reduced to 6 ounces a week in 1944) and meat (2¼ pounds in 1944).[184]

Worst hit were the isolated northern towns, closest to large military

THE POLITICS OF FOOD

camps, which were never well supplied with foodstuffs, even in peace-time. In Townsville, northern Queensland, the frustrated inhabitants looked on as all the fresh food, ice and beer disappeared behind the gates of the US army base.[185] Marion Houldsworth, a young girl living in Townsville during the war, recalled how 'milk . . . became almost unobtainable. Meat was scarce.'[186] Toothbrushes, butchers' wrapping paper and shoes were all in short supply and it became 'harder and harder to get ice for the kitchen ice-box. Often the ice-works had run out by seven o'clock in the morning.'[187] Marion's brother Barry would set off at five in the morning to queue for ice but 'the Yanks' would often drive up and push in ahead of the queue. 'Without the supply of ice, food went off quickly in the heat.'[188] At Christmas in 1943 there were no vegetables or fruit in the shops and even bread could not be bought because the bakeries had run out of flour. The town's limited water supply was also running very low, unable to cover the needs of both the town and the army base. 'Sometimes water was only available for two hours a day, and looked like mud.'[189] In 1944 typhoid fever broke out in the southern part of the town and Marion's mother boiled both the drinking water and the milk. The town descended into squalor. There was broken glass everywhere as the 'troops made a habit of pelting [drinks bottles] out of trucks'.[190] When John B. Chandler, Lord Mayor of Brisbane, visited in March 1944 he was horrified to find the place 'filthy', and stinking of 'every imaginable and unimaginable odour'.[191]

The Australian government complained that American food demands were unsustainable. MacArthur was implacable. He refused to reduce the American ration or to compromise on quality. He argued that if the government wished to address Australian servicemen's resentments then it should spend the extra £10 million and upgrade their own troops' food. In order to prevent the Australians calculating the required supplies according to Australian standards, the United States army representatives would never divulge exactly how many troops they needed to feed in the South-West Pacific, nor how large their reserve food stocks were.[192] Canberra grudgingly acknowledged in February 1944 'that if the present United States scale is maintained some increase in the Australian scale for forward areas will have to be conceded'.[193] The British government met with the same American stubbornness when it came to feeding the 228,000 US troops stationed in Britain. The British mess ration at 3,300 calories a day was considered too meagre for American servicemen and General Somervell refused to countenance the idea that the British should 'impose their standard of living on our troops'.[194] (This was the same man who did everything in his power to prevent Britain from building up what he considered to be excessive stocks of civilian supplies.) Americans stationed in Britain received an extra 600 calories a day and, although they were fed by the US supply services, the fresh food such as meat, dairy products, fruit and vegetables all had to be procured locally and this put a strain on the British food supply system. It seemed unfair that US soldiers should scoff 12 ounces of meat per day, while British soldiers ate half this amount and civilians only one-third.[195] But British protests were in vain. Although Marshall admitted that the meat ration was excessive, he was not willing to face the negative publicity in the United States if cuts were made in the men's ration. The only concession which the British were able to wring from the US supply services was that the GIs' bread should be made with British national wholemeal flour. This was unpopular, but here the British government also played the card of public opinion and argued that British civilian morale would be too adversely affected if the US troops received crusty white rolls as well as the lion's share of meat.[196]

On the one hand Australia felt that US demands were excessive, on the other the Americans were often unhappy with the foodstuffs which the Australians supplied. In August 1942 the British and the Americans reached an agreement that Australia would divert its meat exports to feed the US forces in the south-west Pacific. America would compensate for Britain's loss by increasing the amount of frozen meat it exported across the Atlantic. This turned out to be an unsatisfactory arrangement for all sides. The Americans failed to fulfil their quotas to Britain while the Australians were not forthcoming with the types of supplies which the Americans favoured. Boneless beef was an ingenious invention which saved shipping but Australian meat packers did not want to invest in the new equipment they needed to produce it and were never able to fill the quotas the Americans set for this product.[197] Consequently, the American field kitchens had to use canned rather than fresh meat and even the canned meat was unsatisfactory. Major George

Hallman, head of the meat section of the Food Production Division of the Subsistence Depot, showed Australian canners how to make American dishes such as chilli con carne, luncheon meat (Spam), Vienna sausage, pork sausage, pork and beans, and roast beef with gravy. But the canners were hampered by the small scale of pork farming in Australia and reluctant to branch out into lines which would surely decline as soon as the war was over. To the annoyance of the American troops, Australian meat canners continued to churn out corned beef, corned mutton and minced beef loaf, all of which the GIs loathed.[198] American and Australian tastes in vegetables also differed greatly. The Americans preferred tinned tomatoes, peas, corn, string beans and asparagus, and they hated the canned beets, carrots, cabbage, parsnips and pumpkins that prevailed in Australia. To the US quartermaster's disgust, 40 per cent of the canned vegetables the US supply services received in 1943 were beets, cabbages and carrots: double the amount agreed.[199]

It was extremely difficult for the quartermaster to sustain a 'subsistence philosophy' in the circumstances which prevailed in the Pacific combat arena. On their base island of Pavuvu in the Solomon Islands, E. B. Sledge and his companions from the 1st Marines Division lived on a diet of 'dehydrated eggs, dehydrated potatoes, and that detestable canned meat Spam'.[200] Even the fresh bread was 'so heavy that when you held a slice by one side, the rest of the slice broke away of its own weight. The flour was so massively infested with weevils that each slice of bread had more of the little beetles than there are seeds in a slice of rye bread.'[201]

Storage proved an enormous headache in the Pacific islands. By 1944 MacArthur's troops had leapfrogged their way along the northern coast of New Guinea and supply bases had been established at Port Moresby, Milne Bay, Oro Bay, Finschhafen and, after MacArthur's 900-kilometre leapfrog in April 1944, at Hollandia. At each of these bases the service corps had to carve a port and storage space out of virgin jungle.[202] There was no time to create proper warehouses. Food and equipment containers were simply stacked, often directly on to the mud, and covered with canvas. Tents or shacks were sometimes available but the protection they afforded was minimal. The heat, humidity and torrential rain took a heavy toll. The corrugated cardboard which packaged much of the food disintegrated, and flimsy wooden food cases fell apart under the heavy and frequent handling they experienced along the way. Food in cloth bags spoiled very quickly, but even tin cans went rusty or were punctured and the contents festered. In 1942 and 1943 it was estimated that 40 per cent of the rations in the South-West Pacific Area were spoilt or rotten by the time they reached the field kitchens. At Port Moresby one inspection of the stores found that more than half the cans of food inspected were 'unsuitable for issue'.[203]

In response the quartermaster research laboratories devised special bags, which had an asphalt moisture barrier integrated into the cloth, for dry goods such as flour, salt, sugar, powdered milk, rice, dry beans and peas. American companies invented a new sort of cardboard called V-Board made out of fibre and sisal, and Australian food processors began to package dry as well as wet goods in specially lacquered cans.[204] By 1944 wastage of food was down to about 13.6 per cent but it was never as low as in Europe, where wastage from all sources was in the region of 9.5 per cent.[205]

The result was that in the Pacific the US troops went through frustrating cycles of feast and 'famine'. Rather than following the carefully balanced menus sent out by the Surgeon-General's headquarters, in New Guinea as soon as a reefer arrived with fresh food the cooks allowed the men to gorge themselves. For two days in November the troops at Oro Bay each ate nineteen eggs a day as well as mounds of butter and beef. The cooks argued that the reason for their failure to behave responsibly and carefully husband these foods was the lack of refrigerated storage.[206] However, once the fresh supplies were consumed the men were forced to revert to a diet of corned beef hash and dehydrated vegetables. In March 1944 the quartermasters at Lae complained that they had twenty-six days' worth of the detested corned beef and corned beef hash and plenty of canned carrots, cabbage and beets but no one wanted to eat them. In contrast, their canned fruit supply was down to one day's worth, and their canned milk would only last another two days. Milne Bay was in a similar situation with a 'hopeless excess' of corned beef and C ration tins of meat, but no dehydrated potatoes and onions, coffee, sugar or cheese.[207] Major-General Innis P. Swift, commander of the 1st Cavalry Division on New Guinea, reported that his men were 'sick and tired of corned beef and . . . say that dehydrated foods are all right for about a week, but after that they are nauseating'.[208]

If the American troops got fed up with their cans of stew, at least they still had plenty to eat, in contrast to their Japanese opponents. 'For every *four tons* of supplies the United States shipped to its ground forces in the Pacific, Japan was able to transport to its own men just *two pounds*.'[209] Onoda Hiroo, holding out against the Americans on the Philippines in 1945, found discarded chewing gum on one of the leaves which he had picked for his dinner. 'Here we were holding on for dear life,' he commented, 'and these characters were chewing gum while they fought!'[210] Ogawa Tamotsu, a doctor on New Britain, retreating through the jungle suffering from dysentery and starvation recalled that 'sometimes at night a smell of coffee drifted through the jungle. That was a scent I will never forget. The enemy sentries having coffee from some kind of portable coffee pot.'[211] Sergeant Funasaka Hiroshi, stuck in a cave on the island of Palau, observed the American camp below him. 'I could imagine the Americans sleeping soundly inside those tents . . . And in the morning, they'd rise leisurely, shave, eat a hearty breakfast, then come after us again as usual. That sea of shining electric lights was a powerful, silent commentary on their "battle of abundance" . . . I had an image of the island divided in half with heaven and hell lying next to each other, separated by only a few hundred metres.'[212]

FEEDING PACIFIC ISLANDERS

Early in the morning of 2 October 1942 the islanders on the atoll of Funafuti in the British colony of the Ellice Islands* spotted what looked to them like 'a huge group of crabs . . . crawling across the ocean towards us'.[213] By 8 a.m. the convoy of two cruisers, five destroyers, a cargo ship, three supply ships and at least three other large vessels was lined up, waiting to sail into the lagoon. Seaplanes were busily flying around, dropping smoke bombs to indicate the dangerous reefs. Once inside the shelter of the lagoon, barges and landing craft were unloaded

* In the central Pacific Ocean, now called Tuvalu.

and the sea was soon full of vessels, bringing 853 marines, 122 naval construction personnel and 113 miscellaneous medical, aviation and administrative staff up on to the tiny island of a few square kilometres, along with a mountain of stores, trucks, bulldozers, mobile cranes, dozens of freezer containers, guns and artillery shells, water desalinators, and more than 4,000 drums of gasoline. One hundred kilometres away the coast-watchers on the island of Nukufetau observed a black cloud of exhaust fumes rising up into the sky and sent a coded message inquiring what was happening. They received no reply so as not to alert the Japanese to the covert American activity.[214]

Although Admiral Nimitz used New Zealand as his main regional base, the US navy also built a chain of airfields and naval bases across the south and central Pacific. Until the Second World War Pacific islands were 'isolated on the colonial fringe'.[215] Their experience of westerners was limited to contact with traders, missionaries, planters and colonial officials. By the middle of 1942 there were tens of thousands of Americans stationed across the islands from Fiji and Samoa to New Caledonia. Three of the Ellice Islands' six atolls were transformed into 'anchored aircraft carriers' and sheltered harbours for ships and seaplanes.[216] From here the Americans launched their central Pacific offensive towards the Gilbert, Marshall, Mariana and Caroline islands. Western Samoa played host to between 25,000 and 30,000 American troops at any one time. This amounted to the equivalent of about one-third of the entire Western Samoan population. Tongatapu was swamped by around 8,000 soldiers and sailors in contrast to the entire native population of around 35,000 spread across the three Tongan island groups.[217] The presence of the Americans had a huge impact on the lives of Pacific islanders. They brought with them military installations, incredible quantities of equipment and plenty of cash. In the Pacific the military power which the Americans employed to dislodge the Japanese from their island strongholds is still recalled with awe but, most of all, the Americans are remembered by Pacific islanders for their food.[218]

The lives of the approximately 4,000 Ellice Islanders were changed for ever by the arrival of that convoy of ships on the morning of 2 October 1942. Until that date the only ships which had visited the islands had been small, but now the islanders were confronted by the sight of enormous battleships and a lagoon covered with hundreds of boats. Most of the islanders had never seen a car and for a few days after the American landing they stopped walking along the paths on the island until they overcame their fear of the speed at which the heavy trucks, bulldozers, cranes and graders moved.[219] The Americans made no attempt to live off the land on the Ellice Islands as the Japanese might have done. Instead they destroyed the islanders' means of growing food. In order to make space for an airstrip for fighter aircraft, thousands of food-bearing coconut and bread fruit trees were felled. The islanders' ancient *pulaka* garden pits, dug by hand over centuries, and painstakingly filled with rich compost, took only five weeks to fill in and level.[220] The Tuvaluans were now completely dependent on the stores of rice, biscuits and flour brought in from the United States and sold in a special government store. Those with GI friends also gained access to the foods sold exclusively to the troops in the PX store. Pole O'Brien, a nineteen-year-old nurse at a government clinic, tasted ice cream for the first time at a dance. '"Ask for ice cream," said one of the girls. They had never eaten anything so cold in their lives. I told them, "swallow it, don't hold it in your mouths like that, the Americans are watching us. Eat it! Finish it!"'[221] The Funafutians shared their bounty with friends and relatives. Parcels were sent off regularly on the cargo ships visiting the outer Ellice Islands. In exchange for the Americans' generosity the Tuvaluans would go fishing and give their catch to Colonel Good, the island's commander.[222]

Throughout the Pacific, Japanese and Americans alike employed thousands of islanders as labourers and porters. The Americans fed them more food than they had ever seen before. Isaac Gafu, a Solomon Islander working in a labour gang on Guadalcanal, recalled 'those big shipments of food, my goodness! The food made us enjoy working very much. Because of the fact that we ate good food, we did not tire easily.' The only danger was that 'we might get tired from eating!'[223] Another Solomon Islander was delighted when some Americans invited him and his fellow workers inside their tents to sit on their beds and share their food. They even provided their guests with glasses, plates and spoons. 'That was the first we had seen of that kind of thing.'[224] In Pacific island cultures the sharing of food is of immense social importance. The giver demonstrates his ability to command the resources to acquire food and cements his ties of kinship and community with those with whom he shares.[225] Since their first contact with Europeans, Pacific islanders have been interested in western foods. By the 1930s canned meat, usually corned beef, was a normal part of islanders' diets. But when the Americans arrived Pacific islanders were surprised and pleased by their generosity and open-handedness with food. The Americans' willingness to share food made the islanders feel as if they were being treated as friends and equals. This unthinking distribution of abundance cast the more distanced colonial authorities in a poor light.[226]

However, the Pacific islanders frequently misread these small acts of personal friendliness and interpreted them as gestures indicating a wider and more meaningful shift towards greater political equality. Sadly, the islanders were mistaken if they thought that the United States government was in any way committed to ensuring their long-term welfare. While the Americans were present, spreading their largesse, allowing the islanders access to the wonders of ice cream and Coca-Cola, the environmental devastation of the Ellice Islands was not too worrying. But when the Americans had packed up and gone the Tuvaluans were left unable to re-establish their gardens. On Funafuti they rebuilt their huts out of ugly corrugated iron left behind by the Americans and hoped for compensation from the British government.[227] The people of Vaitapu, demoralized by the devastation of their home island, moved to a fertile island in Fiji which they bought with their combined savings and compensation money.[228] The Americans could not be accused of plunder: they took responsibility for the feeding of the islanders while they were stationed there. But they were careless both of the negative impact the military campaign had upon the lives of the islanders and of the fact that after the war they would be completely unable to feed themselves. The Ellice Islanders' traditional way of life was wiped out without a backward glance.

The Americans were more careful in the five easternmost Samoan islands, which had been a United States colony since 1899. They did not want their own colony to become food-dependent. Agriculture on the islands was sufficiently well developed for it to be realistic to hope that the Samoans would continue to feed themselves. However, the plan to establish a naval base at Pago Pago Bay, and the inevitable influx of almost as many Americans as there were Samoans, was obviously likely to place a strain on the islanders' food resources.[229] In 1940 Captain A. R. Pefley arrived on the island with, among other things, the brief to set up an agricultural programme to increase food production. However, Pefley's companion, G. K. Brodie, explained in a frustrated memorandum that the Samoans were completely unreceptive to their advice. Demonstrating an attitude to farming which was typical of Pacific islanders, and which had frustrated colonial officials for decades, he explained that 'as long as they have sufficient food in the ground for their needs, they are satisfied. They do not entirely grasp that when we take most of their men for labour they will have to rely on the women, old men, and children for their plantation work. We are making every attempt to encourage or force them to keep planting in excess . . . If their food supply fails we will have to take over the task of feeding the island by the importation of rice.'[230] This was exactly what happened.

The Second World War accelerated American Samoa's integration into the modern world. Ships began putting in at Pago Pago in increasing numbers throughout 1942 until by March 1943 shipping arrivals had risen from 3 to 121 a month.[231] 'The pouring of American troops into Samoa is something I will never forget,' reminisced an islander. 'The ships kept coming in, ships moving round the island, and ships anchored at the mouth of the harbour ready to come in. As soon as they finished unloading they moved out, the next one came in, dropping off marines and supplies.'[232] Frenetic activity continued until March 1944 when the base was demoted back to the rank of naval station. But from January 1942 to the beginning of 1944 there was enough work to provide virtually every man on the island with a relatively well-paid job. One Samoan described how before the war he had worked for the Public Works Department as a general labourer, for 15 cents an hour. In 1942 he was a heavy equipment operator on 37 cents an hour. 'When I got my pay check, I thought it was gonna kill me; it was so much money. I immediately turned it into liquid and did a little gambling.'[233]

The children of American Samoa had a bonanza. They would 'attach themselves to soldiers or sailors and thereby get to eat in the mess hall and gain access to sweets and sodas that the troops could buy at the [post] exchange. Once they learned the appetites for these foods, the children never lost them.'[234] Dental caries among Samoan children sky-rocketed from a virtually unknown problem to an affliction which affected 72 per cent of American Samoan children in 1954, not helped by the absolute refusal of the Samoans to brush their teeth.[235] The position of American Samoa as a colony meant that it was always likely that it would eventually adopt an Americanized diet, but the war speeded up the process. By 1942 bread and butter had replaced plantains for breakfast; coffee, sweetened with lots of sugar, was the most popular drink; and rice and chicken or canned meats such as corned beef had replaced taro and fish.[236] By 1948, despite the fact that most of the American navy personnel had been moved to Hawaii, American Samoa was importing 1.8 million pounds of canned meat, 388,252 pounds of canned fish, and similarly staggering quantities of flour, biscuits, canned fruit and sugar to feed a tiny population of about 40,000 people, who before the war had been largely self-sufficient.[237] A survey for the South Pacific Commission in 1952 confirmed that so many islanders had abandoned farming and fishing during the conflict (and refused to return to it once hostilities ceased) that the islanders were now dependent on imported food.[238]

The American approach to feeding Pacific islanders stood out in contrast to the treatment they received at the hands of the Japanese. As one Tuvaluan islander on Tarawa put it, 'We fed the Japanese, the Americans fed us.'[239] The contrast was exemplified on the islands of Palau. This previously German colony had been occupied by the Japanese during the First World War. By 1935 Palau was at the heart of the Japanese South Seas empire, with more Japanese living in the four Japanese farming villages on the island of Babeldoab than there were islanders. Relations with the colonial masters were not necessarily bad. There were mixed Japanese–Palauan families and personal bonds were strong enough for the islanders to give shelter to Japanese women and children during the war.[240] However, the relationship deteriorated in 1944 when the Americans cut the supply lines and began bombing the island, reducing the capital of Koror to rubble. At the end of March, the Americans attacked and captured Peleliu and Angaur in one of the bloodiest and most useless battles of the Pacific. The Americans then built an airstrip and bases on these islands and left the rest of Palau to 'wither on the vine'.

Although the Americans evacuated some of the islanders by boat, many were trapped by the conflict and 50,000 Japanese soldiers and 5,000 islanders were left on Babeldoab to try and feed themselves despite constant strafing attacks, which prevented farming or fishing.[241] The bombing forced the islanders to retreat to makeshift shelters in the woods. One Palauan recalled how he lived in 'a hole. Covered with leaves. Rain came in.'[242] Now the islanders encountered the harsh face of hungry Japanese who requisitioned the islanders' pigs, took over their taro gardens and sent them out to gather food but refused to share any of it with the Palauans. One islander, whose younger brothers were 'so weak, they couldn't move', was forced to forage for food for a Japanese soldier. He took his revenge by placing poisonous wild taro on top of the basket. The soldier was tortured for weeks afterwards by a sore and swollen mouth.[243]

When Japan surrendered in August 1945, the frightened villagers emerged from the woods. Every two weeks the Americans would arrive with supplies of food. The villagers were astonished. 'We would say, "These are very kind people, very rich, like Santa Claus." And it was a very awesome thing, you know. All the Japanese were telling lies, these people were like angels come from heaven, with these candies, food, everything, produce. We were no longer frightened of the Americans. We looked at them as an easy source of food, of abundance.'[244] However, the Americans' post-war behaviour as colonial rulers soon lost them their reputation for being Santa Claus. Unlike the Japanese, who had invested in their colony, the new American masters viewed Palau as an underdeveloped backwater and adopted the attitude that the islanders should be given no more than their means of production could earn them. This left them living in primitive conditions. Koror, which under the Japanese had been a thriving town with electricity, pavements, restaurants, theatres and shops, was never rebuilt. In the 1980s the best buildings in the town were dilapidated Japanese ones which the islanders had patched up. The Americans drove out the Japanese with amazing military might, lazily distributed largesse, and then appear to have lost interest.[245]

In the opinion of one Palauan 'the United States [was] . . . the worst thing that ever happened to the people of Palau'.[246] Like many islanders all over the Pacific the Palauans regarded the Americans as 'all-powerful, magnanimous new benefactors'.[247] During the war islanders made unheard-of amounts of money from selling goods and services to the US military. On Western Samoa the natives sold the troops bunches of bananas worth a few pence for five dollars. Crude distilled alcohol sold for over three Samoan pounds a bottle.[248] The enterprising Tongans opened laundries, sold coconuts at extortionate rates, and were surprised to find that Americans would pay 400 per cent above the usual price for souvenirs.[249] Thousands of islanders had earned good wages, well above the usual rates paid by the British or the Australians, constructing airfields, roads and docks, unloading ships and simply carrying supplies from one place to another. By 1945 they had begun to take American largesse for granted. On Palau 'it began to be "Give me this, and give me this, and give me this." And then came the reality.'[250] The Americans departed, uninterested in developing tiny remote island economies, and left in their wake high expectations and expensive tastes, and a group of disappointed wartime entrepreneurs who were unwilling to slip back into a quiet and extremely basic life of subsistence farming.

After the war Pacific islanders were restless and the war stimulated migration to the United States, New Zealand and Australia, which in turn increased contact with the wider world. The wartime construction of an infrastructure of airfields and roads allowed an inward flow of outside influences and some of the islands became tourist destinations.[251] The islanders were often more critical of colonial or indigenous governments and the power structures within society shifted as traditional sources of power were usurped. In American Samoa, for example, the chiefs derived power from determining who could farm land. As young men moved away from farming into wage labour they lost their grip on this social group. The most powerful wartime legacy in the Pacific was a new interest in cash and the goods it could buy. The war had created unrealistic hopes and expectations of prosperity.[252] Thousands of islanders switched from farming to wage labour in order to be able to afford western commodities. This led the Kilenge on New Guinea to switch from subsistence farming to copra production, with a devastating environmental impact which has led to the disappearance of traditional sources of food. As food gardens disappeared the wild game birds and animals grew fewer, and as the streams grew muddy, as a result of copra production, the fish moved further from the shore.[253] Overall this meant that island economies became less agriculturally self-sufficient and more and more dependent on foreign exchange to buy in imports of food. This had the pernicious side-effect of drawing island economies into the under-developed world's cycle of debt and dependency.[254]

Perhaps the most pervasive and damaging legacy of the war in the Pacific was to inflame the islanders' passion for western imported foods such as pasta, wheat bread, ice cream and Coca-Cola. As Paul Madden, a technical observer running a Coca-Cola bottling factory on New Guinea, commented in 1945, 'many of the smaller children had never tasted Coca-Cola before . . . but they'll certainly be steady customers from now on'.[255] The adoption of western foods had a powerful and mainly negative nutritional impact. The rice and fried flour balls which were used to replace the starchy element in Pacific meals, usually made up of taro or plantain, were far less nutritious. Instead of fresh fish islanders would often eat canned meat, and most meals were now accompanied by Coca-Cola or some other sugary soda. While western Europe emerged from the Second World War having shaken off the problem of malnutrition and vitamin deficiencies among its population, the war brought these problems to the Pacific.[256] These non-traditional meals are packed with fat, sucrose and salt, and today Polynesians are afflicted by an epidemic of the modern diseases of obesity, diabetes and heart disease.[257] Without the Second World War Pacific islands would eventually have been drawn into the global marketplace but the war accelerated the process and often made it a painful experience.

Wherever they went during the Second World War, Americans had more food than anyone else. It was thus that food became central to the Americans' view of themselves. The majority of US servicemen had only the haziest notion as to why the United States was fighting the Second World War. In the end many fixed on the idea that they were fighting to preserve the American lifestyle. GIs interviewed by the *Saturday Evening Post* for a series on 'What I am Fighting for' cited the President and their relatives, but many claimed they were fighting for a home and a future: 'the big house with the bright green roof and the big front lawn'.[258] Soldiers stationed abroad aspired to the suburban lifestyle just as much as the civilians back home. The idealization of the American way of life sustained many homesick soldiers, and for many of them all that was good about their country was summed up by its bountiful and good food.[259] When the journalist John Hersey asked American troops at Guadalcanal 'What are you fighting for?' it was unsurprising, given the Pacific combat diet of corned beef hash and dehydrated vegetables, that a faraway look came into their eyes and one of them 'whispered: "Jesus, what I'd give for a piece of blueberry pie"'.[260] If good and plentiful food came to symbolize America for the Americans, it also became central to other nationalities' view of the United States. To those whose countries America used as a base, liberated or defeated, plentiful American food became a symbol of the United States' economic superiority.

The Panzer grenadier, Helmut Geidel, recalled that 'when the bags of the wounded were loaded on to carts to be taken away, the other soldiers would go through them looking for the emergency ration and eat it'.[261] Allied and German troops carried fortified chocolate bars as emergency rations. In contrast, Japanese soldiers created their own more basic emergency kits. Sumeragi Mutsuo, who survived four months in the jungles of the Philippines, listed the three items which he considered essential to survival: 'salt, matches, and a mess tin'.[262] Rice went mouldy too quickly to make it worthwhile to transport. Tinned food was an item of such rarity it would have been laughable to try to find some. Salt, however, was vital; without it the feet swelled up and it was impossible to make palatable the field grasses which were the main food. A mess tin was useful for cooking the grasses, and, even more importantly, for boiling water, which was essential to avoid dysentery. The matches, of course, made these two activities possible. 'Death', he concluded, 'awaited the soldiers who lacked these three items.'[263]

Despite promising beginnings in the 1920s and 1930s, Japanese army rations were not only far worse than those of any other armies, they were at times non-existent. The US marines, appalled by the weevil-ridden bread and the lack of shower facilities on Pavuvu, would surely have been in revolt if asked to live and fight under the same conditions as the Japanese soldiers.[264] The armed forces of all the combatant countries understood that it was not always possible to bring supplies up to the front line and would fight on bravely through temporary starvation.

On the other hand, each army had a different breaking point at which lack of food led to either withdrawal, surrender or defeat. In April 1942, once it became clear to the besieged Americans on Bataan in the Philippines that neither food supplies nor reinforcements would be arriving, they surrendered. Their food supplies had run out and many of the Filipino and American troops were emaciated with hunger.[265] The Americans recognized that their position was hopeless and there seemed no point in fighting to the death to hold a position which would inevitably fall to the enemy. If they had known their fate as captives of the Japanese they might have considered fighting a little harder: 34.5 per cent of American prisoners of the Japanese died in captivity as a result of senseless acts of violence, disease and starvation.[266]

For a Soviet soldier the understanding that death probably awaited him as a prisoner of the Germans helped him to fight on through hunger and against the odds, when British and American soldiers might well have fallen back. The response to food shortages and adversity was also determined by the level of discipline within each army, whether it was enforced externally, as it was in the Red Army and the Wehrmacht, or internalized as in the imperial army.[267] The ethos of victory or suicide was so thoroughly instilled in Japanese soldiers that they would often continue to offer resistance even when they were too weak from emaciation to stand. However, this did little for the Japanese war effort. The complete breakdown of the Japanese supply lines meant that even if their fighting spirit was not broken by the experience of extreme hunger, without the fundamental necessities of life, the soldiers could not achieve victory and instead starved to death.

Allied troops, bar the Soviets, possessed a more developed sense of entitlement and their rations reflected the high standards of personal comfort which they were used to in civilian life. The ability to fulfil their soldiers' higher expectations was crucial to the success of the democratic armies. Fortunately for the Americans, they had the resources to pump seemingly endless quantities of food into their supply lines, and the military might to protect them. By 1945 the generous food rations distributed to US troops symbolized the immense power of the United States, not only for the miserable Japanese starving on the Pacific islands, but also for their envious comrades in arms, the British, Commonwealth and Soviet armies.

Different levels of expectation within the civilian populations of the combatant countries also determined how far each nation could be pushed before it collapsed. Soviet and Japanese civilians were more likely to continue in a state of misery, when American, British and German civilians might well have begun to protest.[268] One of the most vital elements in motivating civilian populations seems to have been whether it was a war that the people believed in. The United States was hampered by a weak emotional investment in the war among its civilian population, which made them resentful and likely to grumble over hardships and shortages. Fortunately, the superior resources of the United States meant that the commitment of American civilians to winning the war was never too severely tested. In Britain there was 'an extraordinary degree of unanimous and single-minded commitment to unqualified resistance to Hitler'.[269] The British were held together by a determination that they could not and would not live under Nazi rule and somehow the war must and would be won. A crucial difference from the situation during the First World War was that in Britain there was political consensus that this was the right and only course. The anti-war voices of the pacifists and communists faded away as the war progressed, and between 1939 and 1945 political consensus was maintained by a coalition government.

In Germany political opposition had been effectively silenced during the 1930s. The only group in a position to attempt a putsch or coup was the old conservative elite in the army and their attempt to assassinate Hitler failed in July 1944. Even if they were not committed National Socialists, the majority of the German population did not relish a repeat of the humiliation they had suffered at the hands of the Allies in 1918. There were many who were aware of the crimes the regime had committed in the east and they feared the revenge which the Red Army would wreak upon them if it invaded – as Hitler had told his people in 1943, at the end of the war there would be only 'survivors and annihilated'.[270] War-weary or not, Germans had little choice other than to put their hopes in the *Endsieg* or final victory.

In Britain and Germany, therefore, surrender was not a readily available option. Although British and German morale would probably have collapsed under circumstances similar to those endured by the Soviets, their governments almost certainly underestimated how much their civilians would have been prepared to put up with. In any case, both the

British and the German governments were so acutely aware of the dangers of civilian discontent as a consequence of the mismanagement of the food supply that they organized the food system to ensure that food could not become a decisive factor in the outcome of the war. Although British and German civilians grumbled about their monotonous diet they were never threatened with real hunger, let alone starvation. In Britain the perception that the food supply was well organized and fair even seems to have buoyed morale. It seems likely that the British and the Germans would have held out against much worse food hardships.

Political opposition had been silenced in Japan in the 1930s. Even when a 'peace party' emerged within the ruling elite in the summer of 1945 its members found it almost impossible to prevail over the militarists within the government, who insisted that Japan would never surrender. The Japanese leadership may not have been willing to admit that they were defeated but, as the urban population teetered on the verge of famine, there were those in the government who feared that urban civilians might rise up in protest. The inability to protect the food supply lines was a significant factor in bringing about the defeat of Japan. Although the American atomic bombs were decisive in persuading the Emperor to accept defeat, he also acknowledged that fear of a popular uprising was a contributory factor in his decision to surrender.[271]

In contrast, virtually the entire Soviet population was hungry throughout the Second World War. Both rural and urban civilians suffered from malnutrition, hunger and starvation. At times lack of food came close to collapsing the economy and the war effort, but it did not break Soviet morale. The Soviets stayed at the assembly lines and continued to yoke themselves to their ploughs in the face of appalling food hardship. It is true that Stalin's purges of the 1930s had spread fear and repression, and the lack of political alternatives meant that they simply had to keep going. However, the knowledge that German victory would bring about the annihilation of their homes and families meant that the Soviets were determined to defeat the invaders and they did so *despite* hunger and starvation. In contrast to the First World War, when Germany ran out of bread, potatoes and the will to fight, the outcome of the Second World War in Europe was not determined by food.

PART IV

The Aftermath

18

A Hungry World

After the war? ... Now it is more difficult ... There are no living-quarters ... there are no homes ... It is like it was at the front during the war: the people live in the ground – the workers and peasants. The food is bad and is difficult to get ... The conditions were bad before the war; now they are worse.
(A Russian veteran describing conditions in the Soviet Union in 1948)[1]

The aftermath of the Second World War was a hungry world. The end of hostilities did not bring to an end the misery and starvation which the war had engendered. The overall amount of food available worldwide had fallen by 12 per cent per person since 1939, but the scarcity was unevenly distributed. Many millions of people were living on less than half the amount of food they would have eaten in 1939.[2] For the Japanese, defeat intensified the hunger of the last months of the war and the urban population survived on watery rice gruel and a wheat bran that was usually fed to horses. In the three months after the surrender, about 100,000 starved to death in Tokyo, and the situation was similar in other cities across the country.[3] In Germany the population only began to experience hunger *after* May 1945. The country was divided into four zones, governed by the French, British, Americans and Soviets, and the four powers could not agree over the question of reparations or the level of industrial development Germany should be allowed to regain.[4] Germany's run-down agricultural sector was able to produce only enough food to provide the urban areas with 1,000 calories per person per day and hunger raged in the cities of occupied Germany.

The Allies reluctantly imported some food, but the official ration in the American zone provided only 1,135 calories a day, rising to 1,550 calories in January 1946. The United Nations recommended minimum was 2,300 calories a day.[5] In March 1946, rations in the British zone provided just 1,014 calories, which in food terms translated into 'two slices of bread a day spread thinly with margarine, a spoonful of porridge, and two potatoes – except that potatoes were often unavailable'.[6] In Hamburg, one of the most devastated cities, the population began to lose weight at the alarming rate of 1 kilo a day. The hospitals were inundated with horrific cases of hunger oedema. The population survived by buying food on the black market. Rampant inflation had created a barter economy in which American cigarettes and chocolate were the main currency. Widespread malnutrition was reflected in a rising mortality rate, as hunger-related diseases such as diphtheria, typhoid and tuberculosis took hold among the population. The birth weight of babies fell.[7] The miserable state of the defeated Germans made something of a mockery of Churchill's speech of 20 August 1940 in which he defended the European blockade by arguing that the Allies would 'build up reserves of food all over the world so that these will always be held up before the eyes of the people of Europe – I say it deliberately – the German and Austrian peoples, the certainty that the shattering of the Nazi power will bring them all immediate food, freedom and peace'.[8]

The food misery was compounded by homelessness. Many of the world's cities had been reduced to rubble. Half of Germany's housing stock had been lost to bomb damage and in Japan 40 per cent of the urban areas had been destroyed. In Germany 13 million were homeless, in Japan 15 million.[9] Willy Brandt, later to become German chancellor, described the state of German cities: 'Craters, caves, mountains of rubble, debris-covered fields, ruins that hardly allowed one to imagine that they had once been houses, cables and water pipes projecting from the ground like the mangled bowels of antediluvian monsters, no fuel, no light, every little garden a graveyard and, above all this, like an immovable cloud, the stink of putrefaction. In this no-man's land lived human beings.'[10] Even in Hiroshima survivors continued to live among the ruins. About two weeks after the atomic bomb was dropped Teruko Blair and her family returned to the remains of their home in the city.

'The bathtub was still there, surrounded by an iron wall. The rice cooker and a battered saucepan which father had thrown in the bath had also survived. The toilet was there and the tiles around it. There was no roof.' Despite suppurating radiation burns on his hands and face, Teruko's father cleared away the rubble from the space where the house had been and her sisters and mother (who was suffering from radiation sickness) went in search of a roof. When they returned with a piece of sheet metal balanced on their heads, 'you could see them coming for miles as the whole place was flattened'. They secured the sheet of metal to the gate posts, which were still standing, and slept under this makeshift shelter 'like sardines in a tin'. Their life, she recalled, was 'worse than animals'. Despite the fact that they had been told that nothing would grow in the city for seventy-five years, her mother discovered new buds unfurling and so they cleared the spaces where their neighbours' houses had stood and 'grew wheat in the middle of the city – well there was lots of space, lots of people never came back'.[11]

If defeated Germany and Japan were now hungry, their erstwhile empires were in a dire state of deprivation. In Europe, where food production had fallen to 36 per cent of the pre-war level, the fortunate were able to secure 1,900 calories a day. But millions were living on the edge, able to obtain only 1,000 calories or less per day. Malnutrition and tuberculosis had reached epidemic proportions among children in Czechoslovakia, Greece and Italy.[12] In south-east Asia, which had once produced almost 70 per cent of the rice traded on the world market, the population were barely surviving on as little as 250 grams of food daily. The death-rate had almost doubled.[13] Korea was slipping into starvation and millions were dying on Java.[14] In the British empire, India was slowly recovering from the chaos of the mismanagement of the food supply system but only 9.5 ounces (269 grams) of grain were available per person each day.[15] Even in Latin America, which had remained comparatively remote from the conflict, inflation meant that poorer Mexicans were spending almost their entire income to buy less food than they had consumed in 1939.[16] But the situation was worst in China, which was devastated by the war. Farmers in the province of Hunan, who had fled from the invading Japanese in 1944, returned to their villages to find their seed grain had been eaten, their draught animals and livestock slaughtered, their tools stripped for metal and their homes burned to the ground. Many Chinese in the central and southern provinces were surviving on 'grass, roots, tree bark, and even clay'.[17] At least 30 million were suffering from the effects of undernourishment, and in 1946 the United Nations estimated that 7 million Chinese faced starvation within a couple of months.[18]

The situation was little better in the victorious Soviet Union. The peasants in the liberated western areas were still barely surviving on a famine diet of wild grasses and frozen potatoes, foraged from the fields. The dishes were execrable as was indicated by their names, such as *toshnota* from the Russian word for nausea, an ironic word play on *toshnoiki*, meaning food.[19] On a visit to the Soviet Union in December 1945, Foreign Secretary Ernest Bevin was not allowed to see the full extent of the wartime destruction. But he 'understood' that 1,700 towns and 60,000 villages had been 'completely knocked down'. He concluded, 'we have no measure at all [of the terrible conditions] under which her people are living'.[20] In the liberated areas of the Soviet Union, at least half of the peasantry and many of the townspeople were dwelling, like the soldiers had done at the front, in miserable damp holes in the ground, roofed over with whatever materials they could find.[21]

A respondent to the Harvard Project explained that although they were the victors 'the Russian people looked and acted like defeated people . . . They looked as if a stone were in their heart. (Respondent touches the left side of his chest, with his right hand.)' When he returned to Rostov for a visit in 1948 he saw 'several people still living in the ground', and found his aunt surviving on maize bread and soya bean soup, a little cabbage, potatoes, tea and sugar. Four years after the Germans had departed, she was still wearing the clothes the soldiers had sold to her before they retreated. There were beggars everywhere. Many were disabled veterans missing an arm or a leg. The railway stations were infested with orphaned children, singing for a rouble.[22]

In northern Russia there were many villages to which no men ever returned.[23] Without machines or fuel, women continued to yoke themselves to the ploughs.[24] Repatriated Soviets who had been prisoners of war and forced labourers in the Reich were diverted from the gulags and work battalions to which they were normally sent and used to alleviate the labour problem on the collective farms, which became miserable places of forced exile.[25] All hopes that the war would soften the Stalinist regime and that life would improve were cruelly dashed. In September 1946 Stalin reinstated central planning and the state distribution of food. The peasants' private plots, the kitchen gardens and allotments set up by factories and city dwellers were all outlawed. It was announced that an earlier decree of May 1939, which prevented collective land from being put to such uses, had been 'forgotten'. The fact that the government itself had actively encouraged people to ignore this decree was also conveniently forgotten.[26]

In the summer of 1946 a drought in the steppe regions of southern Russia and the Ukraine caused the harvest to fail. But Stalin needed more, not less, grain. Food exports to the new satellite states in eastern Europe were designed to cement Soviet control in these countries. Stalin ruthlessly implemented his usual policy of sacrificing the countryside to hunger. The state requisitioned almost the entire harvest, leaving the peasants with a few potatoes.[27] Party provincial committees warned the Central Committee in Moscow that the collective farmers were starving. The city of Kalach in Voronezh district reported that they were living in 'frightful conditions. We have absolutely nothing, we eat only acorns, and we can scarcely drag our feet. We will die from hunger this year.'[28] 'A human head and the soles of feet' were found under a bridge near the town of Vasilkovov, outside Kiev. 'Apparently a corpse had been eaten.'[29] Groups of bandits, many veterans without education or employment, began to wander the countryside stealing food. Units from the Ministry of State Security were sent to wipe them out.[30] Food was so short that Stalin was unable to cushion the urban areas, and a campaign to 'economize on bread' was announced in September just as private allotments were banned. The number of people entitled to ration cards was cut. Those who were still entitled to bread received an inferior product with oats, barley and corn mixed in with the wheat. V. F. Zima, a Soviet historian who calculated the impact of the drought and famine of 1946–47, estimated that in the entire Soviet Union about 100 million people were already suffering from malnutrition as a result of the war, and through the famine years of 1946–47 at least 2 million died of starvation and associated diseases.[31]

In Britain the joy of victory was followed by a disappointing period of increasing austerity. In 1945 the electorate voted in a Labour government in the hope that they would begin constructing the more equitable society for which a great majority of the British people felt they had been fighting. The National Health Service was established in 1948, a concrete expression of government's new willingness to take responsibility for the nation's health. However, the Labour government was faced with economic bankruptcy, and rather than ushering in a new age of prosperity it presided over a period of increasing food regulation and worsening shortages.

Rationing had to be kept in place, as with the abrupt and unexpected end to American lend-lease aid in September 1945 Britain was now in a position similar to that of Germany in the 1930s. The government lacked the foreign exchange to be able to allow an unlimited flow of food imports into the country. It even found itself using up precious gold and dollar reserves to buy food for its erstwhile enemies in Germany.[32] The British people were forced to adopt a National Socialist-style diet of autarky. In July 1946 bread was rationed for the first time and a special system was introduced to control the sale of potatoes.[33] The two staple foods that the Ministry of Food had made a principle of allowing in unlimited quantities were now restricted. The actual consumption of these two items did not fall substantially, but it was a blow to morale. The Labour government planned to produce its way out of its economic difficulties. It was essential that British workers laboured hard to produce goods for export which would finance food imports. This required yet more hard work amid a continued atmosphere of frugality and self-sacrifice.[34]

The war-weary British people were, however, sick of self-sacrifice and bread and potatoes. After the war the amount of fat and meat in the British diet fell and average calorie consumption dropped to 2,300, which was about two-thirds of American post-war consumption. Jack Drummond, the government's nutritional adviser, who resigned when bread rationing was introduced, warned that 'meals have become so much more unattractive that people will not eat sufficient', and he was anxious that they would begin to lose weight.[35] It was in this post-war period that the government began to import what to the public were bizarre and revolting substitute foods. Lack of foreign exchange, problems with securing Argentinian beef, and the drain on canned meat stocks by liberated Europe led the Ministry of Food to look for meat alternatives: whale meat and snoek. Lyons Corner Houses marinated the whale meat in vinegar and water for twenty-four hours and managed to sell quite a few whale steaks, but British housewives were reluctant to buy them. Although they could be cooked with fried onions to look like steak, they had a nasty fishy aftertaste.[36] In 1950, 4,000 tons of whale meat languished at Tyne docks.[37] In 1948 10 million tins of snoek were imported from South Africa where the fish was prized by the Asian community, who cooked it with onions and potatoes or smeared it with apricot jam and grilled it.[38] Unfortunately, the oily and bony fish, which tastes a little like mackerel, was not very well canned, and despite the best efforts of the Ministry of Food to promote it with recipes such as 'snoek *piquante*', the British refused to eat it. Probably, very few people even tried it. The unwanted tins of snoek were soon joined by a pile of 9 million tins of Australian barracuda, and sold off as cat food.[39]

Subsidies, welfare benefits and employment meant that the wartime improvements in the working-class diet were sustained. For the working classes it did seem as though Labour would eventually deliver on its promise of a better life. But the middle classes, whose lifestyle had been levelled down by the war, felt as though they had been defeated. They found themselves spending a far higher proportion of their food budget on necessities as opposed to luxuries, and their calorie and protein intake had fallen to a boringly healthy level of moderation.[40] The perception that their lifestyle was quietly being eroded is exquisitely described by Molly Panter-Downes in her novel *One Fine Day* (1947). Stephen Marshall and his wife Laura find themselves 'saddled with a house which, all those pleasant years, had really been supported and nourished' by its staff of servants. Now the gardener, the cook, the maids and the nanny have left, the house is subsiding into a state of 'shabbiness and defeat'.[41] Laura struggles ineptly with the domestic chores, spending her mornings queuing for food outside near-empty shops, failing to make palatable meals in a kitchen she barely knows how to use. Stephen can hardly believe that he now spends his evenings doing the washing up.

Over the years middle-class discontent translated into dissatisfaction with the Labour Party. The British Housewives' League organized protests against bread rationing and in 1951 Labour was defeated in the general election by the Conservatives, who had campaigned on the platform that they would bring an end to austerity.[42]

The United States was the only combatant nation to end the war in a healthy economic state. Indeed its economic expansion during the war had transformed it into 'a giant on the world scene'.[43] Almost two-thirds of the world's industrial production now took place in the United States. The American gross national product had doubled and incomes had risen. Its workers were the most productive in the world; its farmers produced the highest yields per acre of any country.[44] Amid the destruction and shabbiness of post-war Europe and Japan, US military bases stood out as islands of affluence. The economic resources of the United States, which had been so powerfully demonstrated by the firepower at the disposal of its soldiers, were now made manifest to the defeated civilian populations by their bountiful supplies of food. In Germany, children would beg outside the US army camps and the troops would pass out the remains of their amazing meals of soup, vegetables, steak and salad.[45] One of the commonest memories of liberation is that of American soldiers doling out sweets and chewing gum to children as they drove through the towns and villages. In Japan children greeted American servicemen with the salutation, 'Give me chocolate.'[46] European children were also eager to gain access to the Coca-Cola sold in the PX stores on the bases, and in Austria children could be lured to attend youth activities by the promise of free Coca-Cola. Although the company was not supposed to use its monopoly as a supplier of sodas to the troops as a marketing scheme, the sale of the drink to American soldiers acted as 'the greatest sampling program in the history of the world'.[47] By 1950 when the GI Coke bottling programme came to an end Coca-Cola had established itself as a preferred drink among veterans returning to the United States as well as among the youth of Europe, who saw anything enjoyed by American soldiers as desirable.[48]

The physique of the Americans in comparison to the thin, grubby, malnourished bodies of the Europeans and the Japanese made an enormous impression.[49] Miura Akira recalled how 'well-fed and well-dressed [the Americans were], so healthy. In contrast to us, who were all emaciated. That was the first thing that hit us so hard. We said to ourselves,

Why did we fight these people? We couldn't have won. (Laughs.)' Even their food was outsized. 'We sometimes received American potatoes and we couldn't believe how huge they were. (Laughs.) Japanese potatoes are much, much smaller. These were two, three times as large. The canned goods may not have been great by American standards, but to us everything tasted great.'[50] The contents of CARE packages, arriving in Europe from America, were marvelled at by their recipients. Over 100 million of these packages were sent to Europe (and from 1948 to Japan). As Reinhold Wagenleitner put it, the 'relief packages in a starving Europe became equated with an overflowing shop window, which displayed the overwhelming achievements of the American economic system'.[51]

19

A World of Plenty

Food will win the war and write the peace.
(Slogan of the US Department of Agriculture)[1]

Disaster struck the hungry post-war world in 1946 in the form of a drought which affected Europe, the Soviet Union, Australia, parts of South America, parts of Africa, India, China and the rest of Asia.[2] The run-down state of global agriculture meant that the world supply of meat, milk and fats was already inadequate. Now the harvest of staple foods (wheat and rice) was jeopardized. 'The realisation of staggering shortages in the very cereals which had been expected to ensure an ample filler for deficit diets ... transformed what had been contemplated with comparative equanimity as a shortage of preferred but not absolutely necessary foodstuffs into the threat of widespread and desperate suffering.'[3] It was estimated that one-third of the world's population, around 800 million people, were facing starvation.[4] The only country in the world which had a bumper harvest in 1945 was the United States. The rest of the world looked to America to provide the food supplies to alleviate its misery. It was in the crucial years from 1944 to 1946 that Roosevelt's stirring pronouncement that Americans were fighting for 'freedom from want', not just for America but for the whole world, was tested.[5] In these initial post-war years the United States was caught in an internal conflict between self-interest and altruism. The government and its people were torn between the desire to at last reap the benefits of the wealth generated by the war or to continue to make sacrifices in the name of freedom and international co-operation, and thus take an honourable lead in shaping post-war policies. The

United States' Food Administration strongly favoured the course of self-interest and determinedly worked to ensure plenty for American citizens.

AMERICAN PLENTY VERSUS EUROPEAN RELIEF

American agronomists had been anxious since the beginning of hostilities that the end of the conflict would bring about a sudden drop in demand for food, which, with America's food production at unprecedented levels, would trigger a return to the economic depression, unemployment and food surpluses of the 1930s. Throughout 1944 the War Food Administration was dominated by officials drawn from the food industry for whom this was a particular concern. The pessimistic predictions of European analysts, who warned that liberated Europe would be faced with an immense food shortage, made little impression on them.[6]

As the Allies drove the Wehrmacht out of Europe, the military were allocated the initial task of distributing food to the liberated populations. Behind them came the United Nations Relief and Rehabilitation Administration (UNRRA), which had been set up in November 1943 to assist the people of the Allied countries.* Brigadier-General William O'Dwyer, Chief of the Economic Section of the Allied Control Commission for Italy, was shocked by the utter deprivation the US army found in Italy. The basic ration in Rome provided only 665 calories and the infant mortality rate had risen to 438 per 1,000 live births. As the Allies moved through France, Belgium and Greece they were in the distressing position of distributing less food to the people than the people had been receiving under the German occupation.[7] Based on this experience, UNRRA and the US military called for America to increase food production and begin stockpiling in preparation for victory. Instead, the United States Department of Agriculture concentrated on decreasing surpluses and cut harvest targets for 1945. They stockpiled only 280 million bushels of wheat, compared with 630 million in 1942. This so-called 'bare shelves policy' aimed to have disposed of every

* It was not charged with feeding or providing relief for the people of Germany or Japan.

surplus 'GI' potato, pat of butter and slice of bread exactly as the war came to an end.[8]

The actions of the Department of Agriculture in 1944 ensured that America would have difficulty meeting the needs of UNRRA in 1945. But it was the Food Administration's response to a pork shortage in American cities at the beginning of the year that ensured that wheat, supposedly earmarked for liberated Europeans, ended up in the stomachs of America's pigs and chickens. Sequestered from the realities of starvation and food shortages in the rest of the world, the American public particularly disliked meat rationing. They had more money in their pay packets than ever before and now that the war was drawing to a close they wanted to buy choice cuts of meat. Complaints about the pork shortages were vociferous and in response Harry Truman* appointed Clinton P. Anderson, the leading critic of the government's management of food supplies, to the position of Food Administrator. Anderson's main interest was the defence of the American consumer. He immediately set about revitalizing American meat production, in particular he promised to keep feed-corn prices low and hog prices high in order to encourage farmers to produce more pork.[9]

Throughout 1945 the Under-Secretary of State, the American Federation of Labor and President Truman himself made various statements to the effect that Americans were willing and *must* share their food in order to avert misery and politically undesirable unrest in newly liberated Europe. A public opinion survey found that 70 per cent of Americans claimed they would be prepared to put up with food cuts in order to help the starving in Europe, including their former enemies the Germans. Their sincerity was indicated by the millions of CARE packages sent to Europe.[10] But the government implemented no policies to ensure that there would be sufficient food to spare. The day after the Japanese surrender rationing was lifted and in 1945, even though food production fell, civilian consumption rose. The Americans were eating more meat, butter and milk than ever before in the twentieth century. Average daily calorie consumption rose to 3,300.[11] The amount of food allocated to commercial shipments, government-financed aid and, crucially, the armed forces who were responsible for the initial task of feeding liberated

* President since April 1945 after Roosevelt's death.

civilians, all fell. In September Truman explained the problem in terms
of the need to work out financial credit schemes with European governments and UNRRA.[12] But the real problem was that American pigs,
chicken and cattle were devouring grain at an unprecedented rate.

That year a shortage of good-quality corn had meant that those
poultry and dairy farmers who did not grow their own fodder had
bought in wheat to feed their livestock. In addition, farmers with
surplus grain were keeping it back on their farms, waiting for prices
to rise. The consequence of all this was that the amount of wheat available for relief shipments was below expectations and the quantities
kept on falling throughout the winter of 1945–46. It was then that the
repercussions of the poor worldwide harvest began to show among
the cold and hungry Europeans. Grace Miller, from Montana, was
posted to Belgium in the Women's Army Auxiliary Corps (WAAC). She
described the horror felt by the US army cooks when they had to take
'a truckload of kitchen garbage to the dumps . . . [there] a crowd of
people always waited to grab anything remotely edible. People with
their cups and pans, people who had once been well off, fought to get
right under the garbage being spilled out so they could be sure to get
something to eat. Every little bone or wilted vegetable was treasured.
A mouldy loaf of bread could cause a vicious, clawing fight . . . "Those
people are really desperate," one cook told me, trying to hide his
emotion. "Makes you want to cry," he added softly, looking away.'[13]

In January 1946 the US Department of Agriculture discovered that
in the last quarter of 1945 a record quantity of wheat had been consumed
in America, mainly by livestock. Thus, they entered the year with a much
smaller surplus than usual and higher commitments than ever to export
wheat to needy countries. The Truman administration dithered. The
longer it prevaricated the more farmers held back their wheat.[14] In
the end, wheat-saving measures were imposed on industry. The extraction rate of flour was raised to 80 per cent which resulted, to the
bakers' irritation, in a dirty grey loaf. Limits were imposed on the use
of wheat to make alcohol, and as feed.[15] But Truman and Clinton
Anderson, his Food Administrator, decided that rationing should not
be re-introduced. Despite public opinion surveys to the contrary,
Anderson judged the American public were in no mood to embrace
austerity measures with enthusiasm. He was probably right in thinking

that this would have made the administration unpopular. Instead, heart-rending appeals were made to the American public to voluntarily restrict their consumption. In a radio broadcast Truman declared, 'we will not turn our backs on the millions of human beings begging for just a crust of bread. The warm heart of America will respond to the greatest threat of mass starvation in the history of mankind.'[16] In the spring of 1946 Herbert Hoover was sent on a whistle-stop Famine Survey, visiting thirty countries in fifty-seven days.[17] From Cairo he sent a broadcast to the States in which he compared the generous amounts of food eaten by Americans to the devastating hunger of millions. He urged the American public to give the gift of food and 'return the lamp of compassion to the world'.[18] Appeals of this nature made no impact on American eating habits and by March the United States was 10 per cent down on its agreed food aid targets.[19]

Hoover used his world tour to increase pressure on Britain, the Soviet Union and Latin America to provide more food. In March 1945 General Eisenhower had already had to request extra supplies from Britain for Belgium, owing to deficits in the American cargoes.[20] During 1945 Britain had released over 1 million tons of its carefully husbanded food reserves for relief for Europe.[21] Rationing was extended to bread in order to enable the government to meet Britain's aid commitments. Canada, struggling with the effects of a poor grain crop, a shortage of fruit and vegetables and a sharp decline in hog production, also demonstrated the political will to ensure that its relief commitments were met, and re-introduced meat rationing in September 1945. Throughout 1946 and 1947 Canadian meat processors produced canned meats, meat pastes, spreads and blood sausage for Europe. The mechanization of the prairie provinces also freed up 40,000 draught horses which were sent to farmers in Poland, Czechoslovakia and France.[22] In contrast, throughout the entire period of crisis the United States government proved itself unwilling to act in any way that would disadvantage American agribusiness and the American consumer. On 2 May 1946 Truman pronounced that 'the heart of the American people will have to solve the world food crisis without resort to compulsion'.[23] That year the United States fell short of the grain they had agreed to provide for relief by over 27 million bushels. Between mid-1942 and mid-1946 two-thirds of surplus wheat went to feed livestock. Only one-third was

used to provide food relief. If the use of wheat as feed had been maintained at pre-war levels then enough wheat could have been released
to export three times as much for food aid. Meanwhile, the increase
in civilian food consumption since 1943 accounted for more than the
total amount of food sent to UNRRA.[24]

In the end the world's hungry had to make do with less. They scraped
along on rations which, as 'one Italian worker said, were not enough
to live on and not enough to die on'.[25] Infant mortality rates continued
rising in Hungary, Italy, Poland, Austria, Greece and Yugoslavia. In
Vienna the rations were reduced to 867 calories a day and the Poles
were forced to divert seed grain to human consumption with the inevitable result that spring planting would be reduced.[26] Dr Tingfu Tsiang,
permanent chairman of the UNRRA Council, complained that China
was receiving an inadequate trickle of rice. The 42,800 tons it had been
sent in the first quarter of 1946 did not come close to meeting the relief
needs of the starving population.[27]

A VISION FOR THE FUTURE

As dispiriting as America's failure to meet its food aid targets was,
the US State Department's sabotage of plans to co-ordinate a global
food policy for the future was possibly even more depressing. The
first conference of the Food and Agriculture Organization (FAO) was
held in May 1945. The FAO was the product of pre-war planning
for reconstruction and arose out of the Hot Springs Conference of
1943. During the war, Roosevelt, keen to find common ground on
which the Allies could make positive plans for post-war reconstruction, called for a Conference of the United Nations.* In May 1943
technicians and experts in the areas of agriculture, nutrition, public
administration and economics from forty-four of the Allied nations
gathered at Hot Springs, Virginia, to set out a post-war agenda for
food and agriculture. Many of the delegates feared they had been
brought together merely to rubber-stamp policies that had already
been decided. But once it became clear that they were being asked to

---

* This was how the Allies referred to themselves after the Atlantic Charter of 1942.

set the agenda, they threw themselves into the conference with enthusiasm.

Although the nutritionist John Boyd Orr did not attend the conference because the British government still regarded his views as unorthodox, his film *World of Plenty* was given its first public screening. When at the end of the film Boyd Orr took up Roosevelt's line and declared that the Allies were fighting 'a war against want starting with the want of food', the delegates, many of whom had high hopes for the development of a new attitude to food and agriculture in the post-war world, rose to their feet and cheered.[28] Nutritional science had come a long way during the war. By widening the definition of hunger to encompass dietary deficiencies, the nutritionists had widened the social group to which hunger could be applied. Indeed, the whole of society was now implicated in that it had been shown that in order to maintain health it was necessary for everyone to eat healthily. It is difficult to imagine how novel this idea was then because it has become so commonplace now. The conference stated that a new contract had come into being between the citizen, who was expected to eat properly in order to stay healthy, and the state, which was expected to provide its citizens with the *means* to eat healthily.[29]

In *World of Plenty* Boyd Orr set out his vision for the future. He argued that the food lessons and agricultural techniques learned during the war should be taken and applied to the entire post-war world. The first lesson was that science had made impressive advances and it should now be fully harnessed in order to increase farm yields, particularly in the area of protective foods. The announcer in the film declared: 'Science has the answer! . . . Munitions factories must be changed over to make farm machinery. Experts can say what kinds of seeds should be sown; what kinds of fertilizers should be used. And today we have artificial aids for the breeding of animals.'[30] War had taught Allied governments how to manage and direct agricultural production and control farm and food prices, while it had also developed equitable distribution schemes.[31] These strategies should be applied not simply on a national but on an international scale. The effective, if at times somewhat fractious, workings of such intra-government organizations as the Combined Food Board had proven that the Allies were able to co-operate over the production and distribution of food. A similar structure should be put in place to co-ordinate post-war international co-operation, which would ensure that 'every man, woman and child . . . shall have enough of the right kind of food to enable them to develop their full and inherited capacity for health and well-being'.[32] The Norwegian delegate K. Evang reported delightedly that both the United States and the Soviet Union had voted for post-war co-operation. Evang summed up the conference: 'If the UN continue their co-operation in peace, the foundation has been laid for well being and health, as well as peace and security. The Hot Springs Conference will then go down in history as a door of hope for mankind.'[33]

When the FAO met for the first time in May 1945 John Boyd Orr was elected its first director-general. A year later he announced the Organization's plan to set up a World Food Board. The idea was to overcome the problem of surpluses, which had dogged pre-war agriculture, by buying up foodstuffs when they were cheap and stockpiling them. This would help to stabilize world food prices and create a food pool from which food aid could be distributed to needy countries.[34] The details of the plan still had to be resolved, but, given that the prospect of continued international co-operation seemed feasible, it was an ambitious attempt to 'reconfigure the world's political economy by organizing it scientifically, according to human need, not profit'.[35] Orr had no intention of stifling the free market. On the contrary, he set out the arguments that the League of Nations had used in the 1930s, that if the world's industrial productivity were ensured, and people were in employment and could afford to eat well, or, in other words, nutritiously, then this would in turn stimulate demand for the right agricultural products – protective foods such as meat and milk, rather than unwanted mounds of grain – and would guarantee farmers a good income.[36] Orr was awarded the Nobel Peace Prize in 1949, and he believed that his plan was a counter to the atomic bomb in that it might help to create 'a cosmopolitan world of plenty and social stability'.[37]

Orr's vision was somewhat Utopian but the idea of world government, of which he was a leading proponent, did not seem unrealistic in the world of the 1940s, when democratic countries were just emerging from the imposition of unprecedented levels of governmental control. At the second FAO conference, held in Copenhagen in September 1946, Britain's Minister of Food, John Strachey, gave half-hearted support to the scheme. The idea that Britain might have to pay foreign farmers a fair price for their produce threatened the nation's reliance on cheap food imports.

But at this meeting Strachey's reservations were over-ridden by the enthusiasm of the US delegates. There was disagreement within the American administration over the appropriate response to the plan. While the Department of Agriculture was in favour, the State Department fiercely advocated the preservation of free trade and argued against the proposal. Norris E. Dodd, Under-Secretary for Agriculture, disobeyed his government's instructions and announced that he would support the setting-up of a World Food Board. Fiorello La Guardia, Director-General of UNRRA, passionately advocated the Board and the conference hurriedly set up a commission to meet in Washington in November to consider the details.[38] But at this next meeting Dodd was placed in the embarrassing position of withdrawing American support. Officials in the State Department had worked behind the scenes to ensure that there would be no high-level government support for the proposal. The 'door of hope', which had opened at Hot Springs, Virginia, was firmly shut in the face of the nutritionists. The *Nation* condemned the State Department for its narrow-minded inability to see that there was a difference between 'restrictive nationalistic controls and international controls which have as their aim stimulation of production and trade'.[39]

After months of haggling, the State Department's preferred strategy of negotiating a reduction in trade barriers through the International Trade Organization eventually fell flat. The one agreement on wheat prices which they were able to negotiate also failed to prevent the accumulation of surpluses. Individual governments, which constantly had to adjust to short-term problems and crises, proved unable to deal both with the problem of over-production and with the distribution of surpluses as aid. By stifling Boyd Orr's plan, the United States and Great Britain deprived the world of the chance to attempt at least to implement an imaginative solution to the problem of malnutrition and hunger in a world with plenty of food.

THE SHAPE OF THE POST-WAR FOOD WORLD

The end of the Second World War was a unique moment when it seemed possible that the international co-operation between the Allies which had been so effective during the war might be maintained and built upon. But the moment quickly passed as the political considerations of the Cold War came to dominate decision-making, and the United States, the clear victor, set the agenda. In post-war America politicians of most political persuasions were united behind the idea that reconversion to a thriving peacetime economy was dependent on the American people going on a spending spree. This would stimulate the economy, maintain employment and incomes, and thus spread the benefits of mass consumerism to the entire society. The success of this strategy was dependent on a world trading structure which opened up global markets to American goods.[40] In post-war Europe it became increasingly clear that this model of a new world was in direct competition with that of the communist Soviet Union. Food quickly became a weapon in the new Cold War. In May 1946 the *Washington Post* reported that non-communist French politicians had approached the British asking for a wheat loan so that no cut in the bread ration would have to be made before the elections to the provisional National Assembly in June. In a counter-measure, designed to increase support for the communists, Stalin offered France 500,000 tons of grain. In 1947 the United States decided to channel food aid to Europe through grants rather than UNRRA, and this was seen as a sign of their reluctance to continue funding the feeding of eastern European populations under Soviet influence.[41]

By 1947, hungry, chaotic Germany was a political and economic vacuum in the centre of Europe and it was apparent that the country's fate would decide the speed of general European economic recovery.[42] Few Germans realized that they were suffering only a fraction of the misery the National Socialists had inflicted on occupied peoples in their name. They felt despair and also resentment that the occupying powers were failing to provide them with enough food. In February 1947 hunger protests began in the Ruhr area and spread to the Rhineland and the towns of Westphalia. On 3 April, 300,000 miners protested because of hunger, and sporadic unrest continued into the summer.[43] After another hard winter the protests began again in early 1948, starting in the Ruhr area and spreading to Hamburg, where thousands of dock workers went on strike. In Bavaria workers held a one-day general strike. The protests were becoming increasingly well organized and co-ordinated. In May 1948, 100,000 workers in Lower Saxony went on strike for two weeks.[44] In fact, the strikes were 'less a sign of political mobilization than of grave demoralization', but the Americans grew increasingly worried that the German population was becoming radicalized and open to communism.[45]

General Lucius Clay, military governor of the US zone, argued that 'unless we could restore some sort of economic opportunity to the German people, there was nothing we could do to prevent Communism from taking over'.[46] The German economy was crippled by inflation, which made money worthless, and a series of price controls which meant that there was very little incentive for farmers or industry to produce food and goods. Workers spent many hours out in the countryside bartering for food rather than at work in the factories. Clay was persuaded by Ludwig Erhard, a member of the anti-Nazi social free-market school of economics at the University of Freiberg, and adviser to the US administration in occupied Germany, to introduce a number of monetary reforms to address these problems. On 20 June 1948 the French, British and American zones introduced currency reform. The amount of money in the economic system was reduced and the new German marks retained their value. Many of the old National Socialist price controls were also eliminated and, with the price caps lifted on foodstuffs such as vegetables, fruit and eggs, it was now worth the farmers' while to produce for the wider market. Overnight, foodstuffs which shopkeepers had been hoarding in anticipation of the currency reform appeared in the shops and the barter economy was stifled. In July Erhard exceeded his authority and abolished rationing. When reprimanded, he is said to have responded, 'henceforth the only rationing ticket the people will need will be the German mark. And they will work hard to get these German marks, just wait and see.'[47] He was proved right, as absenteeism rates in the factories declined. The workers no longer needed to spend long days searching for food in the countryside and it was now worthwhile to work for a wage. Money had been restored as the medium of exchange and as the motivational force for economic activity and this established a firm foundation for economic recovery. In 1949 Erhard was appointed Minister of Economics in Konrad Adenauer's new government.

Erhard's economic policies are now generally recognized as having played a more important role in initiating German economic recovery than the American aid programme known as the Marshall Plan. In 1947 the food protests in Germany persuaded the US Congress that European distress threatened to translate into support for communism and it voted in favour of Secretary of State George Marshall's aid programme for the whole of western Europe.[48] The aid began to arrive a year later, in April 1948. It gave the recipient countries access to scarce foreign exchange and was spent mainly on American foodstuffs, fuel and equipment. Although the Marshall Plan may not have been entirely responsible for European recovery, it certainly helped to provide a basis from which the European nations could generate their own economic momentum.[49] In the area of food and agriculture, $3.192 billion were pumped into food, feed and fertilizers.[50] This went some way towards finally eradicating post-war hunger and helped to regenerate farming, particularly livestock farming. For the first time in over a decade sufficient quantities of meat and fat were available to the German people. With the exception of Germany, Austria and Greece, European farming had regained its pre-war levels of production by 1949–50.[51]

The Marshall Plan was as much a political and ideological tool as an economic one. A proportion of the money loaned to each European country had to be set aside to pay for a concerted propaganda exercise which sought to demonstrate the benefits of the American way of life to western Europeans. Exhibitions, films, pamphlets, radio shows and concerts all spread the message of the promise of a new society which re-cast citizens as consumers rather than as workers and producers. The French were treated to images of American workers who worked reduced hours but still had enough money to spend in well-stocked supermarkets, and whiled away their leisure time in their comfortable homes, equipped with refrigerators, washing machines and televisions. Mass consumerism and capitalism were, the Marshall Plan propaganda promised, the means to the stable, comfortable life longed for by most survivors of the war.[52]

This blatant exercise in spreading the American blueprint for prosperity and abundance to Europe was resisted by the British Labour government.[53] In the exhibition 'On Our Way', which opened in London in 1949, the images were almost entirely of workers rather than consumers. One of the displays summed up the British government's attitude.

A blackboard propped outside a mock-up of a grocer's shop carried a message warning that Marshall Aid would end in 1952 and when it did the British government would only be able to import food for which it could pay.[54] Therefore British workers needed to see themselves as producers rather than consumers and continue to work hard to manufacture export goods. If Britain did not embrace the American ideology, its economic position was nevertheless shaped by its relationship with the United States. Britain's austerity measures were a direct result of the ending of lend-lease and of the nation's need to earn foreign exchange to buy imports of food and pay off its debt to the United States. This in turn shaped Britain's new post-war relationship with its empire. Although Britain lost India in 1947 its relationship with its African colonies intensified as they were assigned the role of cash-crop producers to help clear the British debt.

In the post-war world the United States used its unrivalled power to erode the trading sphere of the British empire and lever countries into a new international economic system oriented towards the needs of America.[55] In Australia a distinct shift towards the United States had taken place. The terms of lend-lease, mutual aid arrangements, wartime trade agreements and recovery loans all meant that economically Australia was now less affiliated to Britain and more closely bound to America. Even before the war large American companies such as Coca-Cola, Johnson and Johnson and Heinz had established themselves in the country. Post-war, with the American determination to break down trade barriers, two-thirds of Australia's imports came from the US.[56] However, the relationship was not one of equals. Australia's contribution to the Second World War meant that in the plans for a Third World War, which the western governments expected at some point in the 1950s, Australia was once more firmly cast in a supporting supply role. Britain's war plan designated Australia as a 'main support area', which would supply western Europe and south Asia with wool, grain and other foodstuffs. The Americans expected the country to be able to provide food for 1 million US soldiers. Given that the Australian government was excluded from the NATO discussions where these decisions were made, it was a humiliating and frustrating position in which to be placed. It was agreed, however, that, in order to meet this projected demand, Australian agriculture would need to expand. When the Third World War failed to happen, Australia was left with an un-necessarily over-active agricultural sector and the problem of food surpluses.[57]

In terms of agricultural development and food availability the post-war world divided into three. The first world consisted of the developed countries of North America, western Europe, the southern Dominions and Japan. In these countries the wartime advances in science which John Boyd Orr identified as the key to worldwide plenty enabled them to produce more food than ever with fewer people working on the land. In fact, they all ended up producing too much food. Their food surpluses were sent in the form of aid to the under-developed countries in Latin America, Asia, Africa and the Pacific, which became known as the Third World. This view of under-developed countries as useful recipients for food surpluses reinforced a growing culture of dependency.[58] In the 1960s the Third World experienced a green revolution of its own which enabled these countries to feed their rapidly expanding populations. However, protectionist policies within Europe and the United States created trade barriers which prevented the under-developed world from exporting enough of their agricultural produce to boost their economies or to branch out into more lucrative areas of trade.[59] Meanwhile, the dependence on cash crops as exports made these countries particularly vulnerable to price fluctuations in the world market. South and east Asia and sub-Saharan Africa retained a large and under-nourished peasantry, scraping a minimal living from the land.

The second world of the Soviet Union, eastern Europe and China retreated into the closed world of communism. Stalin turned the Soviet Union into a superpower, despite the country's run-down agricultural sector. In the Soviet Union the 'average yield for most crops in the years 1949–53 was under what it had been in 1913', and it took decades for Soviet farms to recover from the deprivations of the war.[60] They were not aided by the influence of the charlatan scientist Trofim Lysenko. As director of the Institute of Genetics, Lysenko wielded sufficient political power to ensure that any scientist who challenged his scientific claims would suffer persecution. As a result his pseudo-scientific agricultural techniques were imposed on the collective farms, which continued to suffer from unrealistic sowing plans and ever-increasing food collection quotas.[61] Lysenko succeeded in persuading Stalin's successor, Nikita Khrushchev, that the steppe lands could be made fertile. The project ended in a disastrous dust bowl.[62] It was not until Lysenko was denounced during a political thaw in 1962 that Soviet farming was released from his noxious influence. While the west achieved prosperity, the east armed and industrialized at its peoples' expense. The Soviet eastern bloc continued to be characterized by a lack of consumer goods, poor-quality food and shortages.

Having won the civil war in 1949 the Chinese Communist Party was now ready to implement its land reform policies. Wary of provoking hostility from the peasantry during the war against Japan, the communists had softened their approach. Now that they were in power they pursued class warfare with vigour and during the land reform programme of 1949–50 one million 'rich' peasants were murdered. Then, in the 1950s, Mao decided to push China's modernization forward with a vigorous programme for industrialization and agricultural reform. Ignoring the lesson of the disastrous famines caused by collectivization in the Soviet Union in the 1930s, huge communal farms were formed where the labourers ate in common dining halls. They were urged to eat their fill as China would soon be overflowing with food. Minister of Agriculture Tan Zhenlin asked, 'After all, what does Communism mean? . . . First, taking good food and not merely eating one's fill. At each meal one enjoys a meat diet, eating chicken, pork, fish, eggs.'[63] Instead, the application of poor farming techniques, disorganization, impossible food quotas and failed harvests led to famine and the death of around 30 million peasants.[64]

THE RISE OF THE NEW CONSUMER

It was only the western developed countries of the first world that achieved the wartime goal of freedom from want. In these countries a new consumer emerged. This was a profoundly democratic development. From some point in the mid-1950s virtually the entire population in developed countries could afford to eat as much as they wanted. The new post-war consumers ate plenty of the protective foods such as meat, milk, vegetables and fruit and they also ate an increasing quantity of processed and packaged foods. These new patterns of consumption rested upon a series of developments which arose out of the Second World War.

The first precondition for the development of the new eating habits was the agricultural revolution which began in the United States during the war and spread to the rest of the developed world in the course of the 1950s. After 1945 heavy plant factories switched from making tanks to tractors and combine harvesters, munitions factories from making explosives to manufacturing chemical fertilizers.[65] Higher farm incomes meant that farmers were now sufficiently capitalized to apply techniques which had been around since the 1930s, as well as innovations which developed out of research conducted during the war. The development of DDT as part of wartime research into nerve gas allowed farmers to protect cereals planted on newly ploughed grassland from wireworm, which before the war had defeated many farmers' attempts to convert pasture to arable land. The chemical was used as a coating for the seeds before they were planted. By 1944 scientists had developed sixty-five approved pesticide products.[66] Machines, artificial fertilizers, herbicides, pesticides and selective plant and livestock breeding made an extraordinary impact on post-war agricultural productivity.[67] By 1959 American farm production had grown by 60 per cent of the pre-war average. In 1963 one farm worker could feed thirty people, whereas in 1940 he had been able to feed only eleven.[68]

In Europe between 1945 and 1965 agriculture underwent its own revolution in productivity. 'Output grew more rapidly than in any twentieth-century period before or since.'[69] Wheat yields in Britain rose by 75 per cent. By the 1980s grain production in Europe had outstripped population growth and the region became an exporter of grain for the first time since the Industrial Revolution.[70] Dairy cows and chickens doubled the amount of milk and eggs produced. In the 1940s roast chicken was a luxury meal and the bird on the table had normally come to the end of its life as a layer of eggs. But in the 1950s a crossbreed of chicken types introduced a new large-breasted bird which matured quickly and was bred to be eaten. This transformed chicken into a cheap and widely available alternative to red meat.[71] As a result of this agricultural revolution, food, and in particular the protective foods which had been beyond the economic grasp of the poorer sections of pre-war western societies, became plentiful and affordable. Vitamin-deficiency diseases became a thing of the past.

This productivity revolution came at a price. In 1967 Tim Swift, the veterinary surgeon for a Suffolk village, recalled the long-since-vanished farm landscape of 1947 with great pasturelands dotted with cows. Each farmer had grown some corn, kept cows for milk, and pigs which produced meat with 'four inches of fat on it'.[72] Now the pastures were ploughed over and the cows 'no longer graze under the sky. They will be in herring-boned sheds all their lives'.[73] It was the same with the pigs. But what horrified him the most were the chickens. 'They hardly bear thinking about . . . They are all deranged. Once you get such a fantastic number of birds together in one big room a kind of mass nervousness sets in . . . They eat each other . . . The only answer to this is de-beaking – taking off the top part of the beak . . . we have a new broiler house at the top of the village . . . the broilers are ready for the fried chicken trade in twelve weeks.'[74]

In 1962 Rachel Carson published *Silent Spring*, a study into the pernicious environmental impact of pesticides, in particular DDT. Her work prompted the growth of an environmental movement which has tried to ameliorate the negative impact which intensive farming has had upon the land. It is perhaps only now, when the post-war agricultural revolution appears to have run its course and technological innovations no longer hold out the hope of further increases in agricultural yields, that governments are beginning to acknowledge that while industrial agriculture produces cheap and plentiful food it also leads to the long-term destruction of the environment and the land upon which farming depends.[75]

The war also stimulated advances in food science and the processing, packaging and transportation of foods, which laid the foundations for the explosion of processed and packaged foods in the late 1950s and 1960s. In 1939 the Institute of Food Technologists, the first professional society for food scientists, was founded in the United States. American technology and know-how was transferred to Australia during the war when the country was turned into a major supplier of canned and dehydrated foods for the US forces in the south-west Pacific.[76] By 1945 Australia's scientists were at the cutting edge of food science and in the following decade the industry built on the knowledge and skills they had acquired in wartime. The dehydrated vegetables produced for the troops had been 'rather less than satisfactory, they looked, smelt and tasted pretty bad', but after the war the dehydration of potatoes was perfected and powdered mashed potato found its way into the domestic kitchen cupboards of the developed world.[77] Before the war, vegetable oils were unpalatable and unstable but by the late 1950s the processing of vegetable oil had improved to the extent that firms were able to produce high-quality salad dressings and bottled mayonnaise.[78]

During the war the American quartermaster developed a technique which reduced milk to dehydrated butterfat and skim milk powder. These powders were easily transported over long distances and could be recombined to produce butter. Once the hostilities were over, Australian companies adopted the method to manufacture a variety of dairy products in various Asian countries where there was a growing market. A by-product of the research into this technique was a method to precipitate* casein and whey. Both these products are now widely used in processed foods.[79] American farmers were already growing acre upon acre of soya beans, which are ubiquitous in processed foods, masquerading as bacon bits or used as a flour high in fat and protein. Seabrook Farms in New Jersey had already perfected the art of freezing vegetables. In Germany a freezing industry quickly grew out of the German army's wartime freezing enterprises, which included a mobile freezing ship operating off the coast of Norway.[80] Camp coffee essence, which had been produced for the troops during the war, quickly became popular as an easy way to make coffee.

Thus, the war paved the way for, and accelerated the development of, technological processes which made possible the bags of frozen vegetables, canned fruit juices, packets of dried soup powders, powdered pudding and custard mixes, jars of instant coffee, salad oils, meat pastes, and ready meals which we now take for granted. The new food science also helped to boost the rise of junk food, as the principles of the mass assembly line were applied to food. By the 1930s Lyons Corner Houses had bought the franchise for Wimpy Grills from America, where they were established in Chicago. Eventually, special areas known as Wimpy

* To cause these substances to be deposited in solid form out of liquid.

bars were set up in the Corner Houses. After the war these bars were emulated by a string of fast-food chains.[81]

The post-war agricultural revolution, and the revolution in food processing which accompanied it, both made a greater variety of food-stuffs widely available. Economic recovery, which saw the whole of Europe achieve full employment by the 1960s, meant that disposable incomes rose. An indicator of how affordable food had become is the falling proportion of household income which was spent on food. This was most dramatic in the United States where the proportion of the total household budget allocated for food dropped from 33 per cent in the 1930s to 13 per cent in the 1980s. In Britain it declined from 33 per cent to 25 per cent over the same period.[82] Governments now took responsibility for a series of programmes designed to protect the health of the entire nation, from the fortification with vitamins of staple foods such as bread, to programmes providing school meals and milk. In the post-war decades the nutritional gap between the wealthy and the poor, which had so worried the League of Nations in the 1930s, was firmly closed in the developed world.

However, mass consumption has not delivered all that its advocates promised. The lower classes did have more money to spend and they closed the dietary class gap, but spending money and consuming did not pull the lower classes up the social hierarchy. In fact, the income gap between the rich and the poor has widened since the end of the Second World War. And in the United States the myth that the working classes could spend their way into prosperity left them without the protection of socially progressive government policies and resulted in a divided and segregated suburban America.[83]

One of the most powerful impacts of the war was to intensify the American obsession with plenty which, as soon as hostilities ended, manifested itself in an immediate increase in the consumption of meat and dairy products. Thus, the war gave impetus to the development of an American culture of over-eating. The phenomenon was not confined to the United States. The explosion of consumption was replicated throughout the developed world as soon as economic recovery allowed. Many Europeans spent the war years craving red meat, white bread spread generously with butter, sweet cakes and biscuits, and when in the 1950s they were able to satisfy these desires a wave of consumption swept over western Europe. People bought themselves new appliances such as fridges and then filled them with food.[84] In Germany the post-war years of hunger were followed by a period of guzzling.[85] In Britain rationing finally came to an end in 1954. Amid the immediate flurry of consumption there was little sign that the war had drastically changed people's tastes. Instead, they satisfied their cravings for the fats and sugars which they had missed and rapidly undid much of the good done by the wartime diet. Once butter was freely available the British doubled their consumption. By 1953 each person was eating 173 grams (nearly an entire packet) a week. There was a similar orgy of cake- and biscuit-eating which meant that fat accounted for an unhealthy 45 per cent of the energy in the diet. British sugar consumption had always been exceptionally high and it rose to a poisonous 500 grams a week. Conversely, the consumption of green vegetables, which the war had promoted, fell by 100 grams a week. Deficiency diseases and susceptibility to diseases of malnourishment such as tuberculosis and diphtheria were replaced by the diseases of affluence. In Britain the incidence of dental caries in children's teeth soared. The death-rate from coronary heart disease grew alarmingly throughout the western world.[86]

If anything, palates appear to have been coarsened and tastes homo-genized by the monotony of wartime diets. This was particularly noticeable where governments controlled what people ate. Endless bland meals in army messes, factory canteens and British Restaurants habituated people to insipid dishes designed to neither offend nor excite the taste buds. This tendency was particularly noticeable among young American and Japanese men, whose army diets deliberately avoided regional dishes and sought to create a uniform cuisine.

It has been argued that war is one of the most powerful forces of globalization, and millions of young men, who would never otherwise have ventured far from home, travelled the globe in the armed forces during the Second World War.[87] The adventurous discovered new foods and new ways of eating. Anthony Lamb recalled that during his train-ing in the use of artillery at Deolali near Bombay the lunches were 'appetizing curries with all the trimmings, iced limeade, delightful Indian sweets'.[88] In his prison camp in Egypt Richard Eickelmann, a captive German, learned how to make 'desert char': extremely strong tea, flavoured with condensed milk and lots of sugar. Even in the 1990s he still prepared tea for English guests in this fashion.[89] Fred Watt, a black GI in a service corps, also enjoyed the British teatime tradition of 'little flavoured cakes and a pot of tea' every day at three in the afternoon. He concluded that the opportunity the war gave him to live abroad 'was one of the greatest experiences that I have ever had ... By me not being able to go to college, I still consider myself as knowledgeable as anyone else because of all my knowledge from travelling.'[90] But in most of the countries occupied or visited by soldiers, rationing and the scarcity of food meant that few were able to sample the best dishes in the local cuisine's repertoire. Rather, it was the soldiers who had access to superior foods. The Allied armies' reliance on canned goods from America ensured that virtually every part of the globe acquired a taste for Coca-Cola and Spam. American military food probably had the most profound impact on the diet of Pacific islanders but the taste for American foodstuffs spread throughout the globe. The Australians acquired the habit of eating packaged breakfast cereals and a fondness for sweetcorn, which had been introduced to satisfy the tastes of American servicemen.[91] The actress and cook Madhur Jaffrey recalled that after the war Delhi was swamped by US army 'leftovers in the form of mysterious boxes known as K-Rations ... my cousins and I tore them open as if they were Christmas presents, pulling out each carefully fitted tin or package with the greatest glee. Thus I was introduced to my first olive, my first fruit cocktail and my first taste of Spam. I rolled mouthfuls slowly around my tongue and pronounced each of them to be exotic and wonderful. I had never eaten tinned fruit or meat before.'[92] Thus, the war acted as a powerful vehicle for spreading the American way of eating across the globe.

Nevertheless, even though the war forced a large proportion of the world's population to give up rice, it did not instigate a widespread conversion to bread. The occupation of most of the world's rice-exporting countries by the Japanese meant that rice-eating peoples throughout the British empire were confronted with wheat as a substitute. This was a deeply unpopular development, as rice-eaters claim that a switch to wheat causes stomach problems. The inability of rice-eaters to digest other, coarser grains when weakened by malnutrition was tragically demonstrated by the victims of the Bengal famine. But wheat poses all sorts of other problems even for those who have not been weakened by hunger. Rice-eating countries often lacked mills to make wheat flour, or commercial bakeries or domestic ovens in which to bake it into bread. Ceylon had to build flour mills and bakeries to process the Australian wheat which went some way to replacing Burmese rice imports. Schools, health officers and government officials had to campaign hard, using a mix of lectures, demonstrations and posters, to persuade the Ceylonese to eat bread.[93] After the war the Ceylonese immediately reverted to rice. This was the case in virtually every rice-eating country which had been forced to eat wheat during wartime, including Bengal and Mauritius. Only in Somalia did the younger generation develop a taste for wheat bread, which they continued to eat after the war, while the older generation reverted to their preferred millet and rice.[94]

In the post-war years it was the Japanese who were forced to eat bread. The initial American policy towards defeated Japan was that they were only prepared to give sufficient aid to the country to prevent disease and social unrest. The United States had no intention of paying for the reconstruction of the Japanese economy. But the miserable state of the Japanese food system and the disastrous harvest of 1945 meant that over the period of American occupation (August 1945 to April 1952) the United States ended up spending about $2 billion, mainly on food aid.[95] However, the food which the United States provided gave no quarter to Japanese eating habits. The influx of wheat flour from America forced the Japanese to acquire the habit of eating bread and in 1946 it was announced that 'the era of flour has arrived'.[96] An electric company in Osaka even began producing bread-making machines which baked a corn- or wheatmeal batter into loaves.[97] In 1947 the occupation authorities introduced school lunches in an attempt to improve the nutrition of the children. These included small white bread rolls served alongside whatever was available from army stores, perhaps a stew or soup, some vegetables and often a drink of milk. Oki Chiyo's son recalled the introduction of American food to his school. Before this he and his sister brought a lunch from home of rice, pickled plum and a few fish flakes. He and his classmates suffered from runny noses due to the lack of protein in their diet. Over time the American lunches cured them, while at the same time they appear to have encouraged among this generation of Japanese an eclectic attitude towards unusual combinations of western foods which is still common today.[98]

Economic recovery really began in Japan after 1950, when the Korean war brought in an injection of American cash. As incomes rose the Japanese continued to eat bread at breakfast time but quickly reverted to rice for lunch and dinner. The massive recruitment of peasants into the army from the 1930s onwards had changed the rural view of rice. In the military the recruits grew accustomed to eating rice as the basic staple around which every meal was structured. When they returned to civilian life they were no longer content to revert to the peasant habit of eating millet or barley, or to mix their rice with other grains. The wartime rationing system had a similar impact on the urban poor. The fact that the basic ration was rice gave the grain the status of the staple food to which every Japanese was entitled. The fact that the rice in the ration was gradually replaced by substitute foods reinforced rather than undermined the sense that rice was the central element of the Japanese diet.[99] Once they could afford it, all Japanese, rural and urban dwellers, chose to eat rice with their meals. It was the Second World War which transformed white rice into the staple of the entire Japanese population.

Alongside food abundance and food processing, a further factor which helped to shape the new consumer was the influence which the new science of nutrition gained during the Second World War. The science of nutrition which developed out of the wartime study of the most beneficial diets for different types of physical activity tended to redefine food as the sum of different nutrients which influence bodily health. This approach to food has led to a restless search to identify those foodstuffs which are unhealthy, and those which are the key to good health. Hence the demonization of saturated fats and the recent celebration of omega-3 fatty oils. Perversely, this view of food as solely the sum of nutrients also allows us, or rather food scientists, to declare highly processed foods healthy. Thus a conglomeration of hydrogenated oils, guar gum and corn starch masquerading as yoghurt, can be defined as healthy as it is low in fat and high in calcium. This has diverted the modern consumer's attention away from natural foods and from food as a source of pleasure, while at the same time it has accorded nutritional science an authority which it does not deserve. The scientific understanding of nutrition is extremely imprecise and scientists still have only the haziest notion of how the different foods which make up a varied diet work together within the body to impact upon health.[100]

One thing is clear, however. The western diet which emerged out of the post-war agricultural and food-processing revolution is not particularly healthy. Soil repeatedly made artificially fertile, yields less nutritious food, and intensive, industrial agriculture produces foodstuffs which contain traces of harmful chemicals. The modern western diet is also over-reliant on processed foods, particularly refined carbohydrates, and provides far too many cheap and empty sugary calories. It is this diet, created out of the processes set in motion by the Second World War, which tends to make the western world overweight, at times obese, and most certainly less healthy. While the disadvantages of the western diet are now widely recognized this has done nothing to prevent the newly developing world from adopting it.

As soon as the Iron Curtain was lifted in 1989 eastern Europeans displayed a desire for abundance and plenty to equal that enjoyed by western Europeans in the 1950s. Communism in the Soviet Union and eastern Europe had never fulfilled its promise of making a life for its people better than that experienced in the capitalist west. During the aftermath of the German post-unification elections of 1990, Otto Schily, then a candidate for the Green Party and later Interior Minister for the Social Democrats, was asked on television to explain the overwhelming success of the Conservative Christian Democrats in the East. He presented the interviewer with a banana. His stunt offended many East Germans but its wordless message was clear to everyone. A banana, a rare and prized luxury because of the communist regime's lack of foreign exchange, had come to symbolize the material abundance of the capitalist west. In their first free election since 1933, East Germans had voted, not for a reformed version of socialism, as was offered by some of the other parties, but for mass consumerism: for affordable cars, holidays and plenty of good food.

Mass consumerism and good food have proved equally alluring in an economically flourishing China. The promise of Mao's agricultural minister, that communism would provide plenty of good food, is finally being realized as the urban middle classes feast on meat, fish and eggs.[101]

The Second World War provides a powerful illustration of the way in which rising incomes substantially increase the demand for food. John Beddington, the British government's chief scientific adviser, speaking to a conference on sustainable development, described how a rise in wages from £1 to £5 a day leads to an exponential increase in the demand for meat and dairy products. Once wages rise above £5 a day, a market for processed and packaged foods emerges. Other developing countries such as India, Indonesia and Brazil are following China's lead and increasing their consumption of energy-intensive foods. The food affluence, which the developed world achieved in the 1950s and 1960s, is spreading across the globe.

However, the uneven distribution of purchasing power means that as sections of the world's population improve their diet, the number of hungry people in the world is also increasing. 'If all the cereals grown in 2007 had magically been spread equally among earth's 6.6 billion persons *and used directly as food* . . . [they] could have supplied everyone with the required amounts of calories and proteins, with about 30 per cent left over.'[102] In fact, an estimated 923 million people (many of them concentrated in sub-Saharan Africa and south-east Asia) were chronically hungry and undernourished while millions more suffered from 'the hidden hungers of iron deficiency, vitamin A and iodine deficiency disorders'.[103] Even if the problem of unequal distribution were solved, the combined impact of a world population which is continuing to grow and the increasing demand for energy-intensive foods such as meat and milk products means that pressure on the world's food resources is increasing. If demand continues to rise with growing affluence, there will simply not be enough food and certainly not enough energy-intensive food to go around. The world's agriculture cannot sustain a global population where everyone eats as many calories and as much meat and dairy produce as the average American.

There is pressure on the world's food supply from other directions too. In developing economies more and more agricultural land is disappearing, as cities, industries and transport networks spread out into the countryside. The rising demand for biofuels is also beginning to impact upon the amount of grain available for food. In 2009 enough US grain to feed 330 million people was channelled into the petrol tanks of American cars. The World Bank concluded that American and European production of grain for biofuels had dramatically pushed up world food prices.[104] In addition, the environmental consequences of the industrialization of agriculture are becoming apparent. Many areas, such as the Punjab, which experienced a green revolution in the 1960s, are now facing a fall in productivity due to pesticide and fertilizer pollution, nutritionally depleted, fertilizer-dependent soils, and increased soil salinity in combination with a dangerous lowering of water tables.[105] Most worryingly of all, climate change threatens to significantly reduce the availability of agricultural land. Rising sea levels and desertification threaten rich agricultural areas such as Bengal, the Mediterranean and California. Agricultural scientists warn that research is not about to produce a new technological revolution to boost agricultural production. The optimistic post-war period when food was abundant and cheap appears to be drawing to a close and it seems likely that in the future food will become increasingly scarce and expensive.

The First World War taught governments that a free market could not be relied upon both to mobilize a nation's resources and to protect the population's access to the necessities of life. High food prices in Britain in 1916 led to industrial unrest, in Russia severe food shortages lit the spark of revolution in 1917. When they entered the Second World War most countries applied the lessons of 1914–19 and almost immediately introduced regulatory economic controls and rationing in order to ensure equitable distribution of foodstuffs. A world with less food will once again increase the pressure on governments to act to safeguard social cohesion and the sustainability of their food supplies. It is unlikely that something like Second World War ration coupons will return. Instead, it is more likely that governments will adopt the kind of mechanisms which are currently evolving to tackle the effects of global warming, such as carbon-trading schemes and international treaties like the Kyoto Protocol. Pressure will mount to create an international body such as Boyd Orr's World Food Board to co-ordinate and regulate global food production and trade. The drive to implement energy-saving measures and preserve fossil fuels will eventually extend to farming and food-trading practices and the world's population may once again be pushed towards a greater reliance on less energy-intensive and more efficient foods, the staples of wartime: bread and potatoes.

A Selective Chronology of the
Second World War

1920–21

November–February: Washington Naval Conference.

1921

Lenin introduces New Economic Policy in Soviet Union, rationing discontinued.
Japanese army sets up a Military Diet Research Committee.

1922

28 October: Mussolini becomes Italian Prime Minister.

1925

July: Mussolini launches the Battle for Wheat in Italy.
July: In Japan the Army Provisions Depot sets up the Provisions Friends' Association to spread the principles of military mass-catering to the public.

1926

Rationing re-introduced in Soviet Union.

1927

April: Chiang Kaishek orders purges of his former communist allies.

1928

Chiang Kaishek establishes Nationalist government of China with a capital in Nanjing.

1929–33

The Great Depression.
Collectivization in the Soviet Union.

1931

18 September: Japan occupies Manchuria.

1932

15 May: Japanese Prime Minister Inukai Tsuyoshi assassinated. Parliamentary government in Japan replaced by a cabinet of 'national unity'.
August: Ottawa Trade Agreement.

1932–33

Ukrainian famine.

1933

30 January: Hitler appointed Reich Chancellor.
March: National Socialists win a parliamentary majority. Japan leaves League of Nations.
June: Walther Darré appointed Minister of Food and Agriculture in Germany. The Reich Food Corporation is created and Germany launches Battle for Production.

1933–36

Roosevelt's New Deal implemented in US.

1934

Famine in the northern provinces of Japan.
October: Communists in China begin the Long March to Yan an.

1935–36

October–May: Italy invades Ethiopia and founds colony of Italian East Africa.

1936

Naval Limitations Conference, London.

Soviet Union ends rationing.

June: Prince Konoe Fumimaro becomes Japanese Prime Minister and appoints Hirota Koki as Foreign Minister.

October: Herbert Backe appointed as agricultural representative on the German Council of the Four Year Plan.

December: Chinese Nationalists and communists form uneasy alliance.

1937

Japanese Ministry of Agriculture announces Plan for the Settlement of One Million Households in Manchuria.

7 July: Japan invades China.

1937–38

December–January: the Japanese sack Nanjing.

1938

Italy sends peasant families to Libya to found agricultural settlements.

1939

30 January: Hitler declares to the Reichstag his intention of ridding Europe of its Jewish population.

June: Britain sets up the Women's Land Army.

August: Germany introduces food rationing.

23 August: Germany and Soviet Union sign Treaty of Non-Aggression.

1 September: Germany invades Poland.

3 September: Britain, India, Australia, New Zealand and France declare war on Germany.

September: British troops begin to land in France.

1939–1940

Germans evict Poles from their homes in the Warthegau and deport them to the General Government.

1940

8 January: Britain introduces food rationing (butter, sugar and bacon).

March: Britain rations meat.

April: Lord Woolton appointed British Minister of Food.

10 April: Denmark surrenders to Germany.

10 May: British Prime Minister Neville Chamberlain resigns and is replaced by Winston Churchill.

15 May: British butter ration reduced from 8 to 4 ounces a week. Holland surrenders to Germany.

27 May: British sugar ration reduced from 12 to 8 ounces a week.

28 May: Belgium surrenders to Germany.

30 May–3 June: evacuation of British and French soldiers from Dunkirk.

June: British government subsidizes milk for nursing mothers and children under 5. Japanese close Yunnan rail link between China and French Indo-China, capture Chinese town of Yichang and begin blockade of Nationalist China.

10 June: Italy enters the war and launches attack on British in North and East Africa. Norway surrenders to Germany.

25 June: France surrenders to Germany.

26 June: US imposes embargo on shipments of scrap metal to Japan.

30 June: German occupation of the Channel Islands begins.

July: British parliament passes Colonial Development and Welfare Act.

17 July: Germany announces total blockade of Britain by sea and air.

27 July: Japanese government announces plans for the creation of a Greater East Asian Co-Prosperity Sphere.

29 July: German weekly bread ration cut by 600 grams.

July–September: Battle of Britain.

10 August: Churchill announces total blockade of Germany and occupied countries.

29 August: Japan stations troops in northern Indo-China.

September: British launch counter-offensive against Italians in East Africa.

September–December: Germans begin Saybusch action as part of the General Plan for the East.

September–May 1941: the Blitz.

16 September: US brings in the draft.

27 September: Germany, Italy and Japan sign Tripartite Pact.

28 October: Italy invades Greece.

29 October: conscription begins in the US.

1941

British set up West African Cocoa Control Board.

January: co-operation between Chinese Nationalists and communists ends. Nationalists blockade communist China.

6 January: President Roosevelt makes his 'four freedoms' speech to Congress.

February: Rommel's Afrika korps arrives in North Africa.

March: British meat ration cut to 1s. a week (about 1 lb). British set up Army Catering Corps. Churchill sets up the Battle of the Atlantic Committee.

11 March: US House of Representatives passes Lend-Lease Bill.

April: Japanese government introduces food rationing and military ration halved to 660 grams of rice a day.

16 April: first lend-lease food shipments arrive in Britain from America.

May: British withdraw from Burma. Germans, Italians and Bulgarians occupy Greece. Hunger Plan discussed at a meeting of German State Secretaries. German cereal ration cut by 125 grams. US Food and Nutrition Board publishes table of Recommended Daily Allowances.

18 May: Italy surrenders to British in East Africa.

Summer–April 1942: Greek famine.

June: German weekly meat ration cut by 400 grams.

1 June: Allied forces on Crete surrender to the Germans.

6 June: Hitler announces Barbarossa decree.

22 June: Germany invades the Soviet Union in Operation Barbarossa.

July: Oliver Lyttelton appointed as Minister of State in the Middle East.

23 July: Japan occupies the whole of Indo-China.

August: German campaign against the Soviet Jews intensifies and the *Einsatzgruppen* begin to murder women and children.

1 August: US places embargo on oil exports to Japan.

September: Averell Harriman visits Moscow to negotiate with Stalin over Allied assistance in the fight against Germany.

15 September: siege of Leningrad begins.

19 September: German forces capture Kiev.

29 and 30 September: German authorities claim the massacre of Jews in Kiev has eased the food and housing situation.

October: Germans impose a blockade on the city of Kiev.

16 October: Soviet government and diplomatic corps evacuate Moscow for Kuibyshev, Stalin stays in Moscow.

18 October: General Tojo replaces Prince Konoe as Japanese Prime Minister.

24 October: German forces capture Kharkov.

4 November: German civil administration introduces food rations for Soviet urban population.

6 November: lend-lease aid introduced for Soviet Union.

December: Robert Jackson appointed head of Middle East Supply Centre. British government introduces vitamin scheme. Japanese advance into Burma.

December–April 1943: Chelmno extermination camp functions.

7 December: Japanese attack Pearl Harbor and US bases in Hawaii, Wake Island, Midway and the Philippines. Japanese invade Malaya, Shanghai and Hong Kong.

8 December: the United States, Britain and the Dominions declare war on Japan.

11 December: Germany and Italy declare war on the United States.

12 December: Propaganda Minister Joseph Goebbels appeals for winter clothing for German troops on the eastern front.

14 December: Siam formally allies itself with Japan. German troops begin to withdraw from the area around Moscow.

15 December: Stalin orders Soviet government to return to Moscow.

16 December: Japanese land on Borneo.

22 December: Japanese land on the Philippines.

December–January 1942: Arcadia conference between Churchill and Roosevelt in Washington – sets up the Combined Food Board and the Combined Shipping Adjustments Board.

1942

Famine in northern Nigeria and Tanganyika. British West African Cocoa Control Board becomes West African Produce Control Board.

January: Wannsee Conference. British allow shipments of wheat through the blockade into Greece.

5 January: American and Filipino troops withdraw to Bataan Peninsula.

12 January: Japan declares war on the Dutch East Indies. US introduces coffee rationing.

23 January: Japanese land at Rabaul, New Britain, and on Bougainville Island, the Solomons.

25 January: Japanese begin landing troops at Lae, New Guinea.

February: Oliver Lyttelton appointed British Minister of Production. Germans retreat from Kaluga.

February–December: Belzec extermination camp functions.

15 February: British garrison at Singapore surrenders to Japanese.

28 February: Japanese land on Java.

February–March: Japanese massacre Malayan Chinese community.

March: Hitler gives orders for soldiers coming home on leave from the occupied territories to bring food parcels. US interns Japanese-Americans.

8 March: Japanese capture Rangoon, Burma.

14 March: US troops begin arriving in Australia in force.

21 March: Fritz Sauckel appointed General Plenipotentiary for Labour Mobilization.

30 March: Allies divide Pacific theatre into the South-West Pacific (the Philippines, New Guinea, Bismarck Archipelago and Dutch East Indies) under General MacArthur and the South and Central Pacific Ocean Command under Admiral Nimitz.

April: German bread, meat and fat rations reduced. British make National Wholemeal Flour compulsory. Regular relief shipments begin arriving in Greece.

8 April: US delegation led by General George Marshall arrives in Britain to discuss US–British strategy on the opening of a Second Front against Germany.

9 April: US–Filipino forces on Bataan Peninsula, Philippines, surrender to the Japanese.

29 April: Japanese close Burma Road to China.

May: British withdraw from Burma. Battle of the Coral Sea.

10 May: all US–Filipino forces on the Philippines surrender to the Japanese.

15 May: US introduces petrol rationing.

21 May: Herbert Backe appointed Acting Minister of Food and Agriculture.

May–October 1943: Sobibor extermination camp functions.

June: Lord Swinton appointed British Resident Minister in West Africa. Maximum charge of 5s. imposed on restaurant meals in Britain.

July: Australia introduces tea rationing. First Battle of El Alamein.

21 July: Japanese force to attack Port Moresby lands at Buna, New Guinea.

23 July: transports begin taking Jews from Warsaw ghetto to Treblinka.

July–October 1943: Treblinka extermination camp functions.

August: Compulsory Native Labour Act passed in Southern Rhodesia. Quit India Movement. The Australians agree to divert meat from Britain to feed US troops in Pacific and in return US agrees to increase meat exports to Britain. Japanese Food Control Act.

5 August: Göring meets with the Gauleiters of the Reich, who complain about ration cuts.

6 August: Göring meets with the leaders of the occupied territories and demands more food for Germany.

7 August: US troops land on Guadalcanal.

8 August: US marines capture Henderson airfield on Guadalcanal.

26 August: Japanese begin to advance up the Kokoda Trail, New Guinea.

September: ten more gas chambers built at Treblinka, six more built at Sobibor.

September–July 1944: Auschwitz functions as an extermination camp.

1 September: Battle of Stalingrad begins.

11 September: Japanese advance up Kokoda Trail stops at Iorabaiwa, 51 kilometres from Port Moresby.

October: German bread and meat rations increased. Cyclone hits district of Midnapur in Bengal. Australia introduces sugar rationing.

2 October: US marines land on Ellice Islands (Tuvalu).

October–November: second battle of El Alamein.

October–July 1944: Majdanek functions as an extermination camp.

November: sinkings of British merchant fleet reach their peak. General Plan for the East put into practice in the Polish district of Lublin.

2 November: Australians recapture Kokoda.

8 November: Operation Torch begins with Allied landings in Morocco and Algeria.

13 November: Tydings amendment to the Selective Service Law allows for more farmers to be made exempt from the US draft.

16 November: US and Australian troops begin assault on Japanese at Buna-Gona bridgehead, New Guinea.

19 November: Red Army launches counter-attack to retake Stalingrad.

22 November: German 6th Army in Stalingrad is encircled by the Soviets.

December: German plans for the General Plan for the East calculate that 70 million people will be deported. Beveridge Report published in Britain.

10 December: Australians capture Gona area, New Guinea.

1942–43

Bengal famine, Henan famine.

1943

US intensifies submarine blockade of Japan.

January: Churchill announces 60 per cent reduction in British shipping in the Indian Ocean.

2 January: Allies capture Buna, New Guinea.

18 January: Red Army breaks through to relieve Leningrad from the east.

31 January: German 6th Army surrenders to the Soviets at Stalingrad.

8 February: Japanese complete the evacuation of their forces from Guadalcanal.

18 February: in Germany Goebbels announces the implementation of total war.

March: Australians set up Army Catering Corps.

29 March: US introduces meat rationing at 28 ounces a week.

1 April: US introduces rationing for canned goods, fats and cheese.

May: Basic (Food) Plan introduced in India. German meat and fat ration cut.

May–June: Hot Springs Food Conference.

29 June: Operation Cartwheel, the Allied offensive to retake the south-west Pacific, begins.

July: Battle of Kursk.

25 July: Italian coup, Mussolini arrested.

August: Japanese high command announce that troops on New Guinea will now be self-sustaining. Harlem Riot.

23 August: Soviets recapture Kharkov.

September: Allied landings in Italy.

3 September: Italy signs armistice with Allies.

12 September: Germans rescue Mussolini and set up puppet government in northern Italy.

13 September: Italy declares war on Germany.

15 September: Australians capture Lae, New Guinea.

27 September: Germans begin to evacuate the Ukraine.

2 October: Australians capture Finschhafen, New Guinea.

November: Allies set up UNRRA.

6 November: Soviets recapture Kiev.

15 December: US troops begin landing on New Britain.

1943–44

Tonkin famine in Indo-China.

1944

January–May: Battle of Monte Cassino.

26 January: British launch Arakan attack in Burma.

27 January: the siege of Leningrad ends.

8 February: Australians capture Huon Peninsula, New Guinea.

14 February: US announces that remaining Japanese forces in the Solomons are now trapped.

27 February: US reports about 60,000 Japanese troops now trapped in New Britain and New Ireland.

March: Soviets recapture the Ukraine.

7 March: Japanese launch Imphal–Kohima offensive in Burma.

April–December: Japanese Ichigo offensive in China.

April: Soviets enter Romania.

24 April: US troops secure Hollandia and Aitape, New Guinea, leaving 200,000 Japanese trapped in the area.

3 May: meat rationing lifted in US except on selected cuts of meat.

27 May: MacArthur declares New Guinea campaign over.

3 June: Japanese retreat from Kohima.

20 June: Japanese retreat from Imphal.

6 June: D-Day, Allied landings in Normandy.

15 June: US forces land on Saipan.

18 July: Tojo resigns as Prime Minister of Japan, replaced by Koiso.

20 July: German officers attempt to assassinate Hitler.

September: Allied operation to retake Holland fails and the Dutch Hunger Winter begins. Viscount Wavell appointed Viceroy of India.

September–November: battle for Peleliu.

October: US Admiral King relegates German U-boats to threat rather than menace.

16 October: Secretary of State for India, Leo Amery, publicly acknowledges the Bengal famine in a speech in Birmingham. Soviet Red Army enters German territory.

20 October: US forces begin landing in the Philippines.

November: Lord Woolton appointed Minister of Reconstruction.

1945

28 January: Burma Road to China reopens.

February–March: Battle of Iwo Jima.

March: Allies begin air-dropping food into Holland.

9 March: US begins firebombing Japan's major cities from the newly conquered Mariannas. Japanese seize control of Indo-China.

5 April: Koiso resigns as Japanese Prime Minister, replaced by Suzuki.

12 April: President Roosevelt dies and Harry Truman becomes President.

30 April: Hitler commits suicide.

April–June: battle of Okinawa.

8 May: Victory in Europe day.

May: first conference of the Food and Agriculture Organization (FAO), John Boyd Orr elected Director-General.

18 June: US begins firebombing Japan's smaller cities.

5 July: MacArthur announces the liberation of the Philippines.

17 July: Allied summit meeting at Potsdam.

26 July: Clement Atlee elected Prime Minister in Britain.

6 August: US drops first atomic bomb, on Hiroshima.

8 August: Soviet Union declares war on Japan and invades Manchuria.

9 August: US drop second atomic bomb, on Nagasaki.

15 August: Japan surrenders.

16 August: US ends food rationing.

30 August: US occupation of Japan begins.

September: Canada reintroduces meat rationing.

1945–46

Worldwide drought.

1946

Civil war in China.

Spring: Herbert Hoover conducts a worldwide Famine Survey.

July: British government introduces bread rationing.
August–September: famine in Soviet Union.
September: Stalin reinstates central planning and the state distribution of food.
    Second FAO conference.
November: third meeting of FAO when US sabotages plan for World Food Board.

1947

April: Marshall Plan accepted by US Congress.
6 April: Herbert Backe commits suicide.

1947–48

Hunger protests in occupied Germany.

1948

April: Marshall Plan aid begins to arrive in Europe.
20 June: German currency reform.

1949

1 October: Mao Zedong founds the People's Republic of China.

Notes

1. Introduction: War and Food

1 Stephens, *Monsoon Morning*, p. 184.

2 Furuta, 'A survey of village conditions', p. 237.

3 Adamovich and Granin, *A Book of the Blockade*, pp. 53, 31.

4 Ibid., p. 60.

5 Ellis, *The World War II Databook*, pp. 253–4. Statistics for the Second World War are unreliable. The figure of 19.5 million military deaths is a lower estimate and it includes many soldiers who died of malnutrition, associated diseases and starvation while fighting. It does not include the many Chinese prisoners of the Japanese and Soviet prisoners in German hands who died of starvation while in captivity. The millions of civilians who died of starvation in Africa and Asia are frequently not included in civilian wartime casualty figures. If they are included then the figure of total deaths caused by the Second World War rises from about 50 to about 70 million.

6 'More wealth, more meat. How China's rise spells trouble', *Guardian*, 30 May 2008; Naylor and Falcon, 'Our daily bread', p. 13.

7 Rosenberger, 'The strategic importance of the world food supply', n.p.

8 Naylor and Falcon, 'Our daily bread', p. 13.

9 Ibid., p. 16.

10 Ibid., p. 18; Timmer, 'The threat of global food shortages', n.p.

11 Rosenberger, 'The strategic importance of the world food supply', n.p.

12 Food and Agriculture Organization, 'Assessment of the world food security and nutrition situation', Committee on World Food Security, Thirty-fourth Session, Rome, 14–17 October 2008. Agenda Item II, http//ftp.fao.org/docrep/fao/meeting/014/k3175e.pdf, p. 5.

13 'Bread shortages, hunger and unrest', *Guardian*, 27 May 2008.

14 Overy, *Russia's War*, p. 134.

15 18,000 deaths between 1940 and 1942 are recorded as having been due to starvation but most of the victims of hunger will not have been counted. Roland, *Courage*, p. 102.

16 Voglis, 'Surviving hunger', p. 25.
17 Proctor, *The Nazi War on Cancer*, p. 171; Boog et al., *Der Angriff*, p. 1019.
18 Levi, *If This Is a Man*, pp. 66–7, 79–80.
19 Simmons and Perlina, *Writing the Siege of Leningrad*, p. 59.
20 Magee, 'Some effects of inanition', pp. 55–7.
21 Magaeva, 'Physiological and psychosomatic prerequisites for survival', pp. 132–5.
22 Black, *A Cause for Our Times*, pp. 7–8; Voglis, 'Surviving hunger', pp. 22, 36–7.
23 Bacon, *The Gulag at War*, p. 139.
24 Frank, *Downfall*, p. 160.
25 Bix, *Hirohito*, p. 360.
26 Offer, *The First World War*, pp. 23–4.
27 Kravchenko, *I Chose Freedom*, p. 388.
28 Goldberg, 'Intake and energy requirements', p. 2096.
29 Vinen, *A History in Fragments*, p. 229.
30 Ellis, *The World War II Databook*, p. 253; Fujiwara, *Uejini shita eireitachi*, pp. 135–8.
31 White and Jacoby, *Thunder out of China*, pp. 169; Rummel, *China's Bloody Century*, p. 118.
32 Greenough, *Prosperity and Misery*, p. 140.
33 Harvard Project on the Soviet Social System, Schedule A, Vol. 15, Case 305, pp. 44–5.
34 Ibid., pp. 45–6.
35 Davidson and Eastwood, *Human Nutrition*, p. 67.
36 Jean Legas, notes on wartime memories.
37 Davidson and Eastwood, *Human Nutrition*, p. 67; Lüdtke, 'Hunger, Essens-"Genuß" und Politik', pp. 122–3.
38 Davidson and Eastwood, *Human Nutrition*, p. 68.
39 Offer, *The First World War*, pp. 51–2.
40 Dörr, *"Wer die Zeit nicht miterlebt hat . . ."*, II, p. 27.
41 Rama and Narasimham, 'The root crop and its uses', p. 4663.
42 Grover, *Incidents in the Life of a B-25 Pilot*, n.p.
43 Ibid.; Potts and Potts, *Yanks*, p. 88; Wettlin, *Russian Road*, p. 87.

PART I FOOD – AN ENGINE OF WAR

2. Germany's Quest for Empire

1 Kay, *Exploitation*, p. 80.
2 Eden, *The State of the Poor*, pp. 264–5; see also Davies, *The Case of Labourers in Husbandry*; Teuteberg, *Der Wandel der Nahrungsgewohnheiten*, pp. 66–7.

3 Ibid., p. 65; Davis, *Home Fires Burning*, p. 69. Modern Europeans now eat about 77 kilograms of meat per capita per year.
4 Turner, *About Myself*, pp. 45–7; see also Standish, *A Life Apart*, p. 78.
5 Trentmann, 'Coping with shortage', p. 15.
6 Tooze, *The Wages of Destruction*, p. 191; Belcham, *Industrialization and the Working Class*, pp. 207–9.
7 Offer, *The First World War*, pp. 3, 39–40, 168.
8 Belcham, *Industrialization and the Working Class*, p. 208; Offer, *The First World War*, pp. 100–101.
9 Teuteberg, *Der Wandel der Nahrungsgewohnheiten*, pp. 68, 131; Belcham, *Industrialization and the Working Class*, p. 208; Standish, *A Life Apart*, p. 81.
10 Trentmann, 'Coping with shortage', pp. 17–18.
11 Offer, *The First World War*, pp. 85–6.
12 Ibid., pp. 86, 90.
13 Trentmann, 'Coping with shortage', pp. 19–20.
14 Tracy, *Government and Agriculture*, p. 30.
15 Trentmann, 'Coping with shortage', p. 21.
16 Tracy, *Government and Agriculture*, pp. 20–21.
17 Offer, *The First World War*, pp. 86, 230, 324, 331.
18 Trentmann, 'Coping with shortage', p. 19.
19 Offer, *The First World War*, p. 331.
20 Ibid., p. 321.
21 Ibid., pp. 333–4; Zilliacus, 'Economic and social causes of the war', pp. 28–9; Fischer, *World Power*, pp. 17–19; Kershaw, *Hitler*, p. 79.
22 Offer, *The First World War*, pp. 270–1.
23 Davis and Engerman, *Naval Blockades*, p. 211.
24 Hernández-Sandoica and Moradiellos, 'Spain and the Second World War', p. 253.
25 Davis and Engerman, *Naval Blockades*, pp. 159, 173.
26 Vat, *The Atlantic Campaign*, p. 34.
27 Ibid., p. 13.
28 Offer, *The First World War*, pp. 366–7.
29 Davis and Engerman, *Naval Blockades*, p. 201.
30 Offer, *The First World War*, pp. 336–7; Vat, *The Atlantic Campaign*, p. 30.
31 Cited by Vincent, *The Politics of Hunger*, p. 45.
32 Cited by Offer, *The First World War*, p. 28.
33 Ibid.
34 Vincent, *The Politics of Hunger*, p. 143; Kershaw, *Hitler. 1889–1936*, p. 99.
35 Vincent, *The Politics of Hunger*, p. 131.
36 Ibid., p. 50; Howard, 'The social and political consequences', pp. 163, 166, 172.
37 Offer, *The First World War*, pp. 74–8.

38 Kershaw, *Hitler*, pp. 97, 109.

39 Offer, *The First World War*, p. 400.

40 Kutz, 'Kriegserfahrung und Kriegsvorbereitung', p. 73.

41 Corni, *Hitler and the Peasants*, pp. xv, 5–7; Farquharson, 'The agrarian policy', p. 235.

42 Trentmann, 'Coping with shortage', p. 26; Staples, *The Birth of Development*, p. 72.

43 Kutz, 'Kriegserfahrung und Kriegsvorbereitung', pp. 73–4.

44 They were linked to the conservative Catholic Centre Party (Zentrum), the right-wing German National People's Party (Deutschnationale Volkspartei) and the centre-right German People's Party (Deutsche Volkspartei).

45 Reagin, *Sweeping the German Nation*, pp. 93–9; Spiekermann, 'Brown bread', p. 148.

46 Kutz, 'Kriegserfahrung und Kriegsvorbereitung', pp. 73–4.

47 Ibid., p. 76; Lehman, 'Agrarpolitik und Landwirtschaft', p. 29.

48 Wehler, *Deutsche Gesellschaftsgeschichte*, pp. 700–702; Lovin, 'Agricultural reorganization', p. 457.

49 Ibid., p. 461.

50 Farquharson, 'The agrarian policy', p. 234.

51 Huegel, *Kriegsernährungswirtschaft Deutschlands*, p. 22; Lovin, 'Blut und Boden', pp. 282; Corni, *Hitler and the Peasants*, p. 23.

52 Bramwell, *Blood and Soil*, p. 108.

53 Corni, *Hitler and the Peasants*, pp. xv–xvi; Farquharson, 'The agrarian policy', p. 233.

54 Huegel, *Kriegsernährungswirtschaft Deutschlands*, pp. 279–80; Wehler, *Deutsche Gesellschaftsgeschichte*, p. 705.

55 Kay, *Exploitation*, p. 14.

56 Farquharson, 'The agrarian policy', pp. 244–5.

57 Corni, *Hitler and the Peasants*, p. 249; Huegel, *Kriegsernährungswirtschaft Deutschlands*, p. 286.

58 Müller, 'Die Mobilisierung der deutschen Wirtschaft', p. 397.

59 Tooze, *The Wages of Destruction*, p. 658.

60 Ibid., p. 197.

61 Corni and Gies, *Brot, Butter, Kanonen*, p. 19.

62 Schleiermacher, 'Begleitende Forschung zum "Generalplan Ost"', p. 339.

63 Corni, *Hitler and the Peasants*, pp. 27–8.

64 Picker, *Hitlers Tischgespräche*, p. 495. Italics in original.

65 Mai, *"Rasse und Raum"*, p. 2.

66 Young, *Japan's Total Empire*, p. 309.

67 Helstosky, *Garlic and Oil*, p. 96.

68 Betts, *Uncertain Dimensions*, p. 50; Moore, *Fourth Shore*, p. 13.

69 Young, *Japan's Total Empire*, p. 309.

70 Laqueur and Breitman, *Breaking the Silence*, p. 130.
71 Bramwell, *Blood and Soil*, pp. 92–3.
72 Tooze, *The Wages of Destruction*, p. 180; Bramwell, *Blood and Soil*, pp. 94–8.
73 Ibid., pp. 99–100, 110.
74 Backe, *Um die Nahrungsfreiheit Europas*, p. 238.
75 Lehmann, 'Herbert Backe', p. 9; Bramwell, *Blood and Soil*, p. 114.
76 Huegel, *Kriegsernährungswirtschaft Deutschlands*, p. 287.
77 Kay, *Exploitation*, p. 54.
78 Keegan, *The Second World War*, pp. 94–102.
79 Kay, *Exploitation*, p. 145.
80 Ibid., p. 123.
81 Tooze, *The Wages of Destruction*, pp. 418–19.
82 Beaumont, 'Starving for democracy', pp. 58, 78–9; Rahn, 'The war at sea', p. 330.
83 Kay, *Exploitation*, p. 39.
84 Ibid., p. 42; Gerlach, *Krieg, Ernährung, Völkermord*, p. 16.
85 Gerlach, *Kalkulierte Morde*, p. 48.
86 Ibid., p. 47.
87 Ibid., p. 48; Kay, *Exploitation*, pp. 123–5.
88 Kay, *Exploitation*, p. 50.
89 Ibid., pp. 39–40.
90 Gerlach, *Kalkulierte Morde*, p. 48; Overy, *Russia's War*, p. 17.
91 Gerlach, *Kalkulierte Morde*, p. 46.
92 Ibid., p. 49.
93 Moskoff, *The Bread of Affliction*, p. 42.
94 Tooze, *The Wages of Destruction*, p. 180.
95 Kay, *Exploitation*, pp. 4, 47.
96 Ibid., pp. 57, 127. In fact the German Achilles heel was oil: Mazower, *Hitler's Empire*, p. 290.
97 Kay, *Exploitation*, pp. 180–1.
98 Gerlach, *Kalkulierte Morde*, p. 261.
99 Gerlach, *Krieg, Ernährung, Völkermord*, pp. 17–19.
100 Kay, *Exploitation*, pp. 206–7.
101 Cited by Gerlach, *Kalkulierte Morde*, p. 53.
102 Rössler and Schleiermacher, 'Der "Generalplan Ost"', p. 10.
103 Grönung, 'Die "Allgemeine Anordnung"', pp. 133–4.
104 Wolschke-Bulmahn, 'Gewalt als Grundlage', pp. 335–6.
105 Grönung, 'Die "Allgemeine Anordnung"', p. 132.
106 Wolschke-Bulmahn, 'Gewalt als Grundlage', pp. 335–6.
107 Madajzyk, 'Vom "Generalplan Ost" zum "Generalsiedlungsplan"', p.16; Roth, '"Generalplan Ost"', p. 41.
108 Roth, '"Generalplan Ost"', p. 40.

109 Tooze, *The Wages of Destruction*, pp. 467–8, 491.

110 Roth, '"Generalplan Ost"', pp. 34, 36, 39.

111 Evans, *The Third Reich at War*, p. 36.

112 Gerlach, *Krieg, Ernährung, Völkermord*, p. 177.

113 Roth, '"Generalplan Ost"', pp. 33–4.

114 Klukowski, *Diary*, p. 88.

115 Ibid., p. 104.

116 Ibid.

117 Ibid.

118 Ibid.

119 Tooze, *The Wages of Destruction*, p. 464; Madajzyk, 'Vom "Generalplan Ost" zum "Generalsiedlungsplan"', p. 12.

120 Wolschke-Bulmahn, 'Gewalt als Grundlage', p. 332; Roth, '"Generalplan Ost"', p. 35.

121 Luczak, 'Landwirtschaft und Ernährung in Polen', p. 122.

122 Wasser, 'Die "Germanisierung" im Distrikt Lublin', p. 272.

123 Klukowski, *Diary*, p. 227.

124 Ibid., pp. 274–5.

125 Harvey, *Women and the Nazi East*, p. 240.

126 Klukowski, *Diary*, pp. 227–9.

127 Luczak, 'Landwirtschaft und Ernährung in Polen', p. 120; Tooze, *The Wages of Destruction*, p. 464.

128 Klukowski, *Diary*, p. 230.

129 Harvey, *Women and the Nazi East*, p. 270.

130 Ibid., p. 266.

131 Mai, *"Rasse und Raum"*, pp. 189, 319, 323.

132 Bosma, 'Verbindungen zwischen Ost- und Westkolonisation', pp. 199–200.

133 Schleiermacher, 'Begleitende Forschung zum "Generalplan Ost"', p. 344.

134 Harvey, *Women and the Nazi East*, p. 246; Madajzyk, 'Vom "Generalplan Ost" zum "Generalsiedlungsplan"', pp. 14–16; Roth, '"Generalplan Ost"', p. 43.

135 Harvey, *Women and the Nazi East*, p. 246.

136 Wasser, 'Die "Germanisierung" im Distrikt Lublin', pp. 288–90; Madajzyk, 'Vom "Generalplan Ost" zum "Generalsiedlungsplan"', pp. 15–16.

137 Bramwell, *Blood and Soil*, p. 127.

138 Lehmann, 'Herbert Backe', p. 10.

139 Wildt, *Generation des Unbedingten*, pp. 843–4.

140 Rössler, 'Konrad Meyer', p. 362.

141 Wolschke-Bulmahn and Gröning, 'The National Socialist Garden', p. 93; Heinemann, 'Wissenschaft und Homogenisierungsplanungen', p. 70; Wolschke-Bulmahn, 'Gewalt als Grundlage', p. 336. Meyer's publication was entitled *Nahrungsraum und Überbevolkerung*.

3. Japan's Quest for Empire

1 Shin'ichi, *Manchuria*, p. 16.

2 Kershaw, *Fateful Choices*, p. 92.

3 Mitter, *Modern China*, p. 32.

4 Barnhart, *Japan Prepares*, p. 18; Martin, *Japan and Germany*, p. 82; Kershaw, *Fateful Choices*, pp. 100, 126; Gann, 'Reflections', pp. 337, 352.

5 Iriye, *Origins of the Second World War in Asia*, pp. 3, 5–6.

6 Wilson, *The Manchurian Crisis*, pp. 225–6.

7 Kershaw, *Fateful Choices*, pp. 93, 97.

8 Martin, *Japan and Germany*, p. 82.

9 Myers and Saburo, 'Agricultural development in the Empire', p. 448.

10 Ishige, 'Japan', p. 1182.

11 Johnston, *Japanese Food Management*, pp. 84–5.

12 Ibid., pp. 75–6.

13 Ibid., p. 76.

14 Ibid., pp. 56–7; Myers and Saburo, 'Agricultural development in the Empire', pp. 432–3, 440.

15 Hane, *Peasants, Rebels and Outcastes*, p. 160; Duus, 'Introduction. Japan's wartime empire', p. xv.

16 Lewis, *Rioters and Citizens*, p. 245.

17 Ibid., p. 246.

18 Beasley, *Japanese Imperialism*, p. 149; Duus, 'Economic dimensions of Meiji imperialism', p. 159; Johnston, *Japanese Food Management*, pp. 54–5.

19 Cook and Cook, *Japan at War*, p. 193.

20 Martin, *Japan and Germany*, pp. 86–7; Eckert, 'Total war', p. 7; Myers and Saburo, 'Agricultural development in the Empire', p. 437; Dore and Ouchi, 'Rural origins', p. 189.

21 Wilson, *The Manchurian Crisis*, p. 126.

22 Dore, *Shinohata*, p. 44.

23 Hane, *Peasants, Rebels and Outcastes*, pp. 40–41, 113; Martin, *Japan and Germany*, p. 87.

24 Smith, *A Time of Crisis*, pp. 59, 64.

25 Ibid., p. 72.

26 Shin'ichi, *Manchuria*, p. 129.

27 Hane, *Peasants, Rebels and Outcastes*, pp. 40–41.

28 Smith, *A Time of Crisis*, p. 242.

29 Hane, *Peasants, Rebels and Outcastes*, pp. 134–5.

30 Young, *Japan's Total Empire*, p. 324.

31 Wilson, *The Manchurian Crisis*, p. 64.

32 Shin'ichi, *Manchuria*, pp. 18–20; Barnhart, *Japan Prepares*, p. 27.

33 Kershaw, *Fateful Choices*, p. 94.

34 Young, 'Imagined empire', p. 77.

35 Peattie, 'Japanese attitudes towards colonialism', pp. 120–3.

36 Iriye, *Origins of the Second World War in Asia*, p. 6.

37 Wilson, *The Manchurian Crisis*, pp. 118, 130.

38 Smith, *A Time of Crisis*, p. 81.

39 Wilson, *The Manchurian Crisis*, pp. 63–5; Beasley, *Japanese Imperialism*, p. 177.

40 Kershaw, *Fateful Choices*, pp. 103–4.

41 Dore and Ouchi, 'Rural origins', p. 196; Iriye, *Origins of the Second World War in Asia*, pp. 38–9; Frank, *Downfall*, pp. 86–7.

42 Kershaw, *Fateful Choices*, p. 105.

43 Barnhart, *Japan Prepares*, p. 71.

44 Dore and Ouchi, 'Rural origins', pp. 197–9; Wilson, *The Manchurian Crisis*, pp. 130–1.

45 Lewis, *Rioters and Citizens*, pp. 245–6.

46 Dore and Ouchi, 'Rural origins', p. 207.

47 Ibid., p. 209.

48 Smith, *A Time of Crisis*, p. 324.

49 Ibid., pp. 222–3, 327–8.

50 Wilson, *The Manchurian Crisis*, pp. 66–7.

51 Smith, *A Time of Crisis*, pp. 270–1, 334–5.

52 Young, *Japan's Total Empire*, pp. 326–8, 335, 341.

53 Wilson, *The Manchurian Crisis*, p. 58.

54 Ibid.

55 Duus, *The Abacus*, p. 368; Peattie, 'Japanese attitudes towards colonialism', p. 89.

56 Duus, *The Abacus*, pp. 306–7, 309–10.

57 Ibid., p. 312; Tennant, *A History of Korea*, p. 242; Peattie, 'Japanese attitudes towards colonialism', pp. 100–101.

58 Young, *Japan's Total Empire*, p. 316; Duus, 'Economic dimensions of Meiji imperialism', pp. 141, 159.

59 Young, *Japan's Total Empire*, pp. 336–9.

60 Ibid., pp. 309, 351; Shin'ichi, *Manchuria*, pp. 268–9.

61 Young, *Japan's Total Empire*, pp. 401–2.

62 Shin'ichi, *Manchuria*, p. 203.

63 Ibid.

64 Young, *Japan's Total Empire*, pp. 342–6.

65 Ibid., pp. 404–5; Shin'ichi, *Manchuria*, pp. 268–9.

66 Young, *Japan's Total Empire*, pp. 330–1.

67 Ibid., pp. 392–5, 429.

68 Shin'ichi, *Manchuria*, pp. 273–5.

69 Kuramoto, *Manchurian Legacy*, p. 39.

70 Ibid., p. 92.

71 Young, *Japan's Total Empire*, p. 411; slightly higher figures are given in Shin'ichi, *Manchuria*, pp. 282–3.

72 Kershaw, *Fateful Choices*, p. 333.

73 Barnhart, *Japan Prepares*, pp. 101–2.

74 Kershaw, *Fateful Choices*, p. 99.

75 Duus, 'Introduction. Japan's wartime empire', p. xvii.

76 Peattie, '*Nanshin*', pp. 210–15; Hatano and Asada, 'The Japanese decision to move south', pp. 387, 390.

77 Ibid., pp. 399–402.

78 Iriye, *Origins of the Second World War in Asia*, p. 171; Kershaw, *Fateful Choices*, p. 127.

79 Young, *Japan's Total Empire*, p. 351.

PART II THE BATTLE FOR FOOD

1 Adams, *Farm Problems*, p. 12; Vat, *The Atlantic Campaign*, p. 8; Russell, *Sea Shepherds*, p. 177; Hammond, *Food and Agriculture*, p. 230.

2 Tinley, *Wartime Transportation*, p. 15.

3 Doreen Laven, notes on wartime memories.

4 Jackson, *The British Empire*, p. 133.

5 Bosworth, 'Eating for the nation', pp. 228–9; Crawford et al., *Wartime Agriculture in Australia*, pp. 131, 155; Milward, *War, Economy and Society*, p. 247.

6 Bannister, *I Lived Under Hitler*, p. 104.

7 Wickizer, *Coffee, Tea and Cocoa*, pp. 90–105.

8 Roll, *The Combined Food Board*, p. 47.

9 Milward, *War, Economy and Society*, p. 278.

10 Corni, *Hitler and the Peasants*, pp. 210–11.

11 Moskoff, *The Bread of Affliction*, p. 13.

12 Peattie, 'Japanese attitudes towards colonialism', p. 126.

13 Milward, *War, Economy and Society*, p. 247.

14 Smith, *A Time of Crisis*, p. 72.

15 Blythe, *Akenfield*, p. 202.

16 Bengelsdorf, *Die Landwirtschaft der Vereinigten Staaten*, p. 199.

17 Ibid., pp. 201–3.

18 Patterson, *Grand Expectations*, p. 10; Wilcox, *The Farmer*, p. 19.

19 Huegel, *Kriegsernährungswirtschaft Deutschlands*, p. 281; Stephenson, *Hitler's Home Front*, p. 7.

20 Hall, *Land Girl*, p. 59; Stephenson, *Hitler's Home Front*, p. 14.

21 Hall, *Land Girl*, p. 59.

22 Martin, 'The structural transformation', pp. 17–18.
23 Dore, *Shinohata*, p. 44.
24 Cherrington, *On the Smell of an Oily Rag*, p. 126.
25 Huegel, *Kriegsernährungswirtschaft Deutschlands*, p. 281.
26 Amrith, 'The United Nations', pp. 35–6.
27 White and Jacoby, *Thunder out of China*, pp. 30–31.
28 Becker, *Hungry Ghosts*, p. 16.
29 Hurt, *Problems of Plenty*, p. 83.
30 Brassley, 'British farming', p. 199.
31 Lehman, 'Agrarpolitik und Landwirtschaft', pp. 39–40; Huegel, *Kriegsernährungswirtschaft Deutschlands*, p. 300.
32 Foot, 'The impact of the military', p. 132; Martin, 'Agriculture and food supply', p. 191; Evans, *The Third Reich in Power*, p. 347.

4. American Boom

1 Bengelsdorf, *Die Landwirtschaft der Vereinigten Staaten*, p. 263.
2 Ibid., pp. 161, 302–4.
3 Ibid., pp. 309, 312.
4 Hurt, *Problems of Plenty*, p. 99.
5 Wilcox, *The Farmer*, p. 157.
6 Kennedy, 'Herbert Hoover', p. 87.
7 Bengelsdorf, *Die Landwirtschaft der Vereinigten Staaten*, pp. 110–34.
8 Wilcox, *The Farmer*, p. 63.
9 Ibid., p. 159.
10 Danbom, *Born in the Country*, p. 231.
11 Jeffries, *Wartime America*, p. 61.
12 Flynn, *The Mess in Washington*, p. 132.
13 Bengelsdorf, *Die Landwirtschaft der Vereinigten Staaten*, p. 88.
14 Jeffries, *Wartime America*, p. 71.
15 Bengelsdorf, *Die Landwirtschaft der Vereinigten Staaten*, p. 88.
16 Flynn, *The Mess in Washington*, pp. 136, 142.
17 Carpenter, *On the Farm Front*, p. 27.
18 Ibid., pp. 28, 122.
19 Ibid., p. 105.
20 Bengelsdorf, *Die Landwirtschaft der Vereinigten Staaten*, p. 91.
21 Ibid., p. 229.
22 Ibid., p. 230.
23 Ibid., p. 233.
24 Ibid., p. 230.
25 Flynn, *The Mess in Washington*, p. 144; Carpenter, *On the Farm Front*, p. 113; Hurt, *American Agriculture*, p. 308.

26 Bengelsdorf, *Die Landwirtschaft der Vereinigten Staaten*, p. 214.

27 Ibid., p. 219.

28 Danbom, *Born in the Country*, p. 236.

29 Hurt, *Problems of Plenty*, p. 115.

30 Pollard, *The Development of the British Economy*, p. 167; Lamer, *The World Fertilizer Economy*, pp. 198–201, 214–16; Wilcox, *The Farmer*, pp. 53–7; Lonsdale, 'The Depression', p. 121.

31 Hurt, *American Agriculture*, p. 32; Bengelsdorf, *Die Landwirtschaft der Vereinigten Staaten*, p. 351.

32 Offer, *The First World War*, p. 151.

33 Bengelsdorf, *Die Landwirtschaft der Vereinigten Staaten*, p. 83; Jeffries, *Wartime America*, p. 45.

34 Hurt, *Problems of Plenty*, p. 74.

35 Jeffries, *Wartime America*, pp. 21, 52–3.

36 Hurt, *Problems of Plenty*, p. 90.

37 Bengelsdorf, *Die Landwirtschaft der Vereinigten Staaten*, p. 70.

38 Jeffries, *Wartime America*, p. 77.

39 Harrison, *Growing a Global Village*, pp. 3–4, 20.

40 Ibid., pp. 29, 32.

41 Cramp, 'Food – the first munition of war', p. 76.

42 Harrison, *Growing a Global Village*, pp. 6–7, 42–4.

43 Wilcox, *The Farmer*, pp. 51, 76.

44 Harrison, *Growing a Global Village*, pp. 47–8, 50.

45 Ibid., pp. 56–8, 71.

46 Ibid., p. 13.

47 Seabrook Farms, New Jersey, http://www.usgennet.org/usa/nj/state/seabrook_farms_nj.htm.

48 Danbom, *Born in the Country*, p. 234.

49 Hurt, *Problems of Plenty*, pp. 124–5; Hurt, *American Agriculture*, p. 306.

50 Hodgson, *Few Eggs*, p. 380.

51 Bayly and Harper, *Forgotten Armies*, p. 368.

52 Bengelsdorf, *Die Landwirtschaft der Vereinigten Staaten*, p. 107; Lawrence, *Eat Your Heart Out*, p. 255.

53 Wilcox, *The Farmer*, p. 198.

54 Gratzer, *Terrors of the Table*, pp. 105–6.

55 Lovin, 'Agricultural reorganization', p. 460; Wehler, *Deutsche Gesellschaftsgeschichte*, p. 705; Von der Decken, 'Die Ernährung in England und Deutschland', p. 179.

56 Watters, *Illinois in the Second World War*, p. 348.

57 Campbell, *Women at War*, p. 181.

58 Watters, *Illinois in the Second World War*, pp. 348–9.

59 Bengelsdorf, *Die Landwirtschaft der Vereinigten Staaten*, pp. 107–8.

60 Lawrence, *Eat Your Heart Out*, p. 255.
61 Rankine, *Soya*, p. 1.
62 Pollan, *In Defence of Food*, p. 117.
63 Rankine, *Soya*, p. 9; Lawrence, *Eat Your Heart Out*, pp. 286–8.
64 Wilcox, *The Farmer*, p. 198.
65 Rankine, *Soya*, p. 3.
66 Bengelsdorf, *Die Landwirtschaft der Vereinigten Staaten*, p. 109.
67 Ibid., p. 301.

5. Feeding Britain

1 Cherrington, *On the Smell of an Oily Rag*, p. 161.
2 Calder, *The People's War*, p. 418; Murray, *Agriculture*, p. 340.
3 Wilt, *Food for War*, p. 225.
4 Ibid., p. 187.
5 Brassley, 'Wartime productivity', pp. 37, 48, 54.
6 Wilt, *Food for War*, p. 224.
7 Vat, *The Atlantic Campaign*, p. 223; Hammond, *Food and Agriculture*, p. 49.
8 Ibid., p. 230.
9 Adams, *Farm Problems*, p. 12.
10 Pollard, *British Economy*, p. 67.
11 Hurd, *A Farmer in Whitehall*, p. 22.
12 Wilt, *Food for War*, p. 189.
13 Hammond, *Food and Agriculture*, p. 35.
14 Smith, *Conflict over Convoys*, pp. 45–6.
15 56,200 in 1939 to 203,000 tractors by 1946. Wilt, *Food for War*, pp. 16, 226.
16 Hurd, *A Farmer in Whitehall*, pp. 22–3.
17 Dewey, 'The supply of tractors', pp. 99–100.
18 Wilt, *Food for War*, p. 189.
19 Brassley, 'Wartime productivity', p. 53.
20 Lamer, *The World Fertilizer Economy*, pp. 214–15.
21 Ibid., p. 216.
22 Ibid., p. 211.
23 Ibid., pp. 209–10, 231.
24 Pollard, *British Economy*, p. 167.
25 Harman, *Seventy Summers*, p. 177.
26 Hammond, *Food and Agriculture*, p. 89.
27 Martin, 'The structural transformation of British agriculture', p. 34.
28 Hammond, *Food and Agriculture*, p. 83.
29 Ibid., pp. 85–6.
30 Martin, 'The structural transformation of British agriculture', p. 34.
31 Brassley, 'Wartime productivity', p. 54.

32 Martin, 'The structural transformation of British agriculture', p. 34.
33 This was the peak number of land girls, reached in June 1944.
34 Mant, *All Muck*, p. 37.
35 Tyrer, *They Fought in the Fields*, p. 108.
36 Joseph, *If Their Mothers Only Knew*, p. 117.
37 Hall, *Land Girl*, p. 61.
38 Tyrer, *They Fought in the Fields*, p. 115.
39 Ibid., pp. 120–1.
40 Graham, *Oxfordshire at War*, p. 117.
41 Martin, 'The structural transformation of British agriculture', p. 27.
42 Ibid., pp. 31–2; Short, 'The dispossession of farmers', pp. 159–60.
43 Hammond, *Food and Agriculture*, p. 231.
44 Bengelsdorf, *Die Landwirtschaft der Vereinigten Staaten*, p. 327.
45 Longmate, *How We Lived Then*, p. 142.
46 Chamberlin, *Economic Development of Iceland*, p. 85.
47 Arnason, *The Icelandic Fisheries*, p. 34.
48 Garfield, *Private Battles*, p. 51.
49 Arnason, *The Icelandic Fisheries*, pp. 78–9; Tomasson, *Iceland*, pp. 37–8.
50 Crawford et al., *Wartime Agriculture in Australia*, p. 151.
51 Britnell and Voake, *Canadian Agriculture*, pp. 248, 268.
52 Ibid., pp. 407–9.
53 Baker, *The New Zealand People*, p. 199.
54 Ibid., p. 201.
55 Ibid., p. 204.
56 Ibid., pp. 204–5.
57 Milward, *War, Economy and* Society, pp. 277–8.
58 Jackson, *The British Empire*, p. 94.
59 Baker, *The New Zealand People*, p. 187.
60 Wilcox, *The Farmer*, p. 157.
61 Longmate, *How We Lived Then*, p. 147.
62 Driver, *The British at Table*, p. 29.
63 Jill Beattie, notes on wartime memories.
64 Garfield, *Private Battles*, p. 145.
65 Doreen Laven, notes on wartime memories.
66 Holland, 'Mobilization', p. 169.

6. The Battle of the Atlantic

1 Hammond, *Food and Agriculture*, pp. 187–8.
2 Garfield, *We Are at War*, p. 142.
3 Costello and Hughes, *The Battle of the Atlantic*, p. 209.
4 Overy, *Why the Allies Won*, p. 31.

5 Hammond, *Food and Agriculture*, pp. 177–8.
6 Behrens, *Merchant Shipping*, p. 43.
7 Costello and Hughes, *The Battle of the Atlantic*, p. 95.
8 Ibid., p. 109.
9 Ibid., p. 121.
10 Ibid., p. 40; Rahn, 'The war at sea', p. 301.
11 Doughty, *Merchant Shipping and War*, pp. 157–9.
12 Behrens, *Merchant Shipping*, p. 128.
13 Hammond, *Food and Agriculture*, pp. 27–9.
14 Vat, *The Atlantic Campaign*, p. 81.
15 Hammond, *Food and Agriculture*, p. 49; Behrens, *Merchant Shipping*, p. 145.
16 Hammond, *Food and Agriculture*, p. 49.
17 Smith, *Conflict over Convoys*, p. 41.
18 Woolton, *Memoirs*, p. 207.
19 Gardiner, *The 1940s House*, p. 125.
20 Garfield, *Private Battles*, p. 56.
21 Hammond, *Food and Agriculture*, pp. 155–6.
22 Ibid., p. 64.
23 Ibid., p. 53.
24 Smith, *Conflict over Convoys*, p. 42.
25 Costello and Hughes, *The Battle of the Atlantic*, pp. 124, 167.
26 Smith, *Conflict over Convoys*, pp. 231–2.
27 Hammond, *Food and Agriculture*, p. 231.
28 Ibid., p. 86.
29 Smith, *Conflict over Convoys*, p. 44.
30 Bentley, *Eating for Victory*, pp. 92–3.
31 Smith, *Conflict over Convoys*, p. 45.
32 Ibid., pp. 45–7.
33 Ibid., pp. 42, 47.
34 Hammond, *Food and Agriculture*, p. 158.
35 Costello and Hughes, *The Battle of the Atlantic*, p. 222.
36 Reynolds, *Rich Relations*, p. 86.
37 Smith, *Conflict over Convoys*, p. 43.
38 Rahn, 'The war at sea', p. 337. Italics in original.
39 Smith, *Conflict over Convoys*, pp. 76–7.
40 Jenkins, *Churchill*, pp. 691–2.
41 Smith, *Conflict over Convoys*, pp. 79–80, 155.
42 The Papers of Miss E. Blaikley, Department of Documents, IWM, 86/46/1, p. 18.
43 Roll, *The Combined Food Board*, p. 130.
44 Smith, *Conflict over Convoys*, p. 185.
45 Ibid., p. 71.

46 Bentley, *Eating for Victory*, p. 91.
47 Litoff and Smith, *Since You Went Away*, pp. 84–5.
48 Bentley, *Eating for Victory*, pp. 74, 91–2; Roll, *The Combined Food Board*, p. 132.
49 Smith, *Conflict over Convoys*, p. 187.
50 Ibid., p. 156.
51 Costello and Hughes, *The Battle of the Atlantic*, p. 230.
52 Bengelsdorf, *Die Landwirtschaft der Vereinigten Staaten*, p. 333.
53 Costello and Hughes, *The Battle of the Atlantic*, p. 213.
54 Smith, *Conflict over Convoys*, p. 152.
55 Baer, *One Hundred Years*, p. 201; Behrens, *Merchant Shipping*, p. 263.
56 Smith, *Conflict over Convoys*, p. 152.
57 Ibid., p. 188.
58 Wilcox, *The Farmer*, p. 276.
59 Smith, *Conflict over Convoys*, pp. 188, 205.
60 Hammond, *Food and Agriculture*, pp. 186–7.
61 Smith, *Conflict over Convoys*, p. 188.
62 Ibid., p. 190.
63 Woolton, *Memoirs*, p. 207.
64 Garfield, *Private Battles*, p. 316.
65 Ibid., p. 201.
66 Davis and Engerman, *Naval Blockades*, p. 286.
67 Smith, *Conflict over Convoys*, p. 177.
68 Hammond, *Food and Agriculture*, p. 187.
69 Costello and Hughes, *The Battle of the Atlantic*, p. 215.
70 French, *Waging War*, p. 51.
71 Ibid., pp. 21–2.
72 Ibid., p. 61.
73 Ibid., p. 113.
74 Ibid., p. 139.
75 Costello and Hughes, *The Battle of the Atlantic*, p. 215.
76 Ibid., p. 216.
77 Rahn, 'The war at sea', p. 341.
78 Hammond, *Food and Agriculture*, p. 185.
79 Ibid., p. 187.
80 Smith, *Conflict over Convoys*, p. 177.
81 Ibid., p. 154.

7. Mobilizing the British Empire

1 Stephens, *Monsoon Morning*, p. 180.
2 Jackson, *The British Empire*, p. 22.

3 Beaumont, 'Australia's war: Europe and the Middle East', p. 9.

4 Jackson, *Botswana*, pp. 36, 40.

5 Beaumont, 'Australia's war: Asia and the Pacific', p. 47.

6 Jackson, *Botswana*, pp. 132–3.

7 Kerslake, *Time and the Hour*, p. 163.

8 Crowder, 'The 1939–45 war', pp. 596, 611.

9 Pearce, 'The colonial economy', p. 276.

10 Kamtekar, 'A different war dance', p. 195; Bayly and Harper, *Forgotten Armies*, p. 301.

11 Kamtekar, 'A different war dance', p. 204.

12 Ibid., pp. 206–7.

13 Wright, *The World and a Very Small Place in Africa*, p. 196.

14 Jackson, *Botswana*, pp. 138–41.

15 Ibid., pp. 143–4.

16 Sen, *Poverty and Famines*, pp. 155–6.

17 Wright, *The World and a Very Small Place in Africa*, p. 195.

18 Jackson, *Botswana*, p. 156.

19 Killingray, 'African civilians', p. 141.

20 28 per cent of land in Mauritius was turned over to food crops. The same thing happened in Barbados where 35 per cent of the land was reallocated for growing food. Jackson, *The British Empire*, pp. 49, 86.

21 *The Production of Food Crops*, p. 6.

22 Tunzelmann, *Indian Summer*, p. 138.

23 Smith, *Conflict over Convoys*, p. 156.

24 *The Production of Food Crops*, pp. 7, 8, 11.

25 Wilmington, *The Middle East Supply Centre*, p. 50.

26 Ibid., p. 16; Lloyd, *Food and Inflation*, p. 91.

27 Chandos, *The Memoirs*, pp. 222–3.

28 Ibid., p. 238.

29 Wilmington, *The Middle East Supply Centre*, p. 83.

30 Ibid., pp. 81, 83.

31 Ibid., p. 45.

32 Lloyd, *Food and Inflation*, p. 89.

33 Cooper, *Cairo*, p. 162.

34 Wilmington, *The Middle East Supply Centre*, p. 25.

35 Lloyd, *Food and Inflation*, p. 129.

36 Ibid., p. 88.

37 Wilmington, *The Middle East Supply Centre*, p. 117.

38 Jackson, *The British Empire*, pp. 120–1; Lloyd, *Food and Inflation*, p. 30.

39 Jackson, *The British Empire*, pp. 166, 198.

40 Lloyd, *Food and Inflation*, pp. 55, 58, 65.

41 Milward, *War, Economy and Society*, p. 280.

42 Wilmington, *The Middle East Supply Centre*, p. 81.

43 Ibid., p. 121.

44 Ibid., p. 124.

45 Ibid., p. 106.

46 Ibid., p. 112.

47 Ibid., p. 84.

48 50.8 million to 19.4 million net registered tons. Ibid., p. 127.

49 Lloyd, *Food and Inflation*, pp. 66–7, 263, 283.

50 Ibid., pp. 327–9; Milward, *War, Economy and Society*, p. 280.

51 Wilmington, *The Middle East Supply Centre*, p. 158; Lloyd, *Food and Inflation*, p. 334.

52 Gann and Duigan, 'Introduction', pp. 19–20.

53 Anderson and Throup, 'Africans and agricultural production', p. 345.

54 Spencer, 'Settler dominance', p. 504.

55 Ibid., p. 499; Lonsdale, 'The depression', p. 120.

56 Spencer, 'Settler dominance', p. 502; Lonsdale, 'The depression', p. 121.

57 Ibid., p. 123; Holland, 'Mobilization', p. 189.

58 Spencer, 'Settler dominance', p. 504.

59 Johnson, 'Settler farmers', pp. 116–17.

60 Ibid., p. 120.

61 Ibid., p. 122.

62 Vickery, 'The Second World War', pp. 433–5.

63 Johnson, 'Settler farmers', pp. 122–3.

64 Anderson and Throup, 'Africans and agricultural production', p. 337.

65 Spencer, 'Settler dominance', pp. 507–8, 512.

66 Vaughan and Moore, *Cutting Down Trees*, p. 87.

67 Ibid., pp. 95–6.

68 Iliffe, *A Modern History of Tanganyika*, p. 371.

69 Ibid., pp. 351–2.

70 Anderson and Throup, 'Africans and agricultural production', pp. 337–8.

71 Vaughan and Moore, *Cutting Down Trees*, pp. 106–7.

72 Lonsdale, 'The depression', p. 125.

73 Vaughan and Moore, *Cutting Down Trees*, p. 96.

74 Lonsdale, 'The depression', p. 125.

75 Anderson and Throup, 'Africans and agricultural production', p. 340.

76 Ibid., pp. 343–4.

77 Bennett, 'British settlers', p. 70.

78 Anderson and Throup, 'Africans and agricultural production', pp. 343–4.

79 Bennett, 'British settlers', p. 86.

80 Johnson, 'Settler farmers', p. 128.

81 Wickizer, *Coffee, Tea and Cocoa*, pp. 328–39.

82 Jackson, *The British Empire*, p. 7.

83 Swinton, *I Remember*, p. 192.
84 Pearce, 'The colonial economy', pp. 269–71.
85 Swinton, *I Remember*, p. 207.
86 Gardiner, *The 1940s House*, p. 125.
87 Swinton, *I Remember*, p. 206.
88 Pearce, 'The colonial economy', p. 271.
89 Ibid., p. 272.
90 Meredith, 'State controlled marketing', p. 82.
91 Westcott, 'The slippery slope', p. 8.
92 Wright, *The World and a Very Small Place in Africa*, pp. 201–2.
93 Tracy, *Government and Agriculture*, pp. 230, 238.
94 Gann and Duigan, 'Introduction', pp. 22–3.
95 Fieldhouse, 'War and the Gold Coast Cocoa Marketing Board', pp. 178–9.
96 Bayly and Harper, *Forgotten Armies*, pp. 74, 269.
97 Greenough, *Prosperity and Misery*, p. 140.
98 Keay, *India*, p. 504.
99 Tunzelmann, *Indian Summer*, p. 391.
100 Stevenson, *Bengal Tiger*, p. 136.
101 Stephens, *Monsoon Morning*, p. 179.
102 Kamtekar, 'A different war dance', p. 207.
103 Knight, *Food Administration in India*, pp. 27, 47; Bayly and Harper, *Forgotten Armies*, p. 252.
104 Voigt, *India*, p. 205.
105 Rothermund, *An Economic History*, p. 120.
106 Chopra, *Evolution of Food Policy*, p. 24.
107 Kamtekar, 'A different war dance', p. 215.
108 Chopra, *Evolution of Food Policy*, p. 22; Knight, *Food Administration in India*, p. 24; Tomlinson, 'The historical roots', p. 132.
109 Voigt, *India*, p. 205.
110 Knight, *Food Administration in India*, p. 37.
111 Kamtekar, 'A different war dance', p. 209.
112 Greenough, *Prosperity and Misery*, pp. 90–2; Sarkar, *Modern India*, pp. 395–6.
113 Bayly and Harper, *Forgotten Armies*, p. 251.
114 Knight, *Food Administration in India*, p. 28.
115 Bayly and Harper, *Forgotten Armies*, p. 253; Sen, *Poverty and Famines*, p. 83.
116 Smith, *Conflict over Convoys*, p. 159.
117 'The things we forgot to remember', BBC Radio 4, 7 January 2008, http://www.opennet/thingsweforgot/bengalfamine_programme.html.
118 Smith, *Conflict over Convoys*, p. 159.
119 Bayly and Harper, *Forgotten Armies*, p. 163.
120 Greenough, *Poverty and Misery*, p. 94.
121 Bose, 'Starvation amidst plenty', p. 716.

122 Greenough, *Poverty and Misery*, p. 105.

123 Ibid., p. 164.

124 The most notable exponent of this view is Amartya Sen. See *Poverty and Famines*.

125 Tauger, 'Entitlement', pp. 65–6.

126 Greenough, *Poverty and Misery*, pp. 109–11.

127 Ibid., p. 168.

128 Ibid.

129 Sen, *Poverty and Famines*, pp. 71–2.

130 Greenough, *Poverty and Misery*, pp. 173–4.

131 Ibid., pp. 118–19.

132 Ibid., pp. 109–12.

133 Voigt, *India*, p. 206.

134 Knight, *Food Administration in India*, p. 63.

135 Greenough, *Poverty and Misery*, p. 186.

136 Stephens, *Monsoon Morning*, pp. 194–5.

137 Ibid., p. 184.

138 Ibid., p. 170.

139 Ibid., pp. 185–7, 193.

140 Stevenson, *Bengal Tiger*, p. 149.

141 Barkawi, *Globalization and War*, pp. 84–5; Hastings, *Nemesis*, pp. 64–5, 15.

142 Bayly and Harper, *Forgotten Armies*, p. 305.

143 Knight, *Food Administration in India*, p. 101; Greenough, *Poverty and Misery*, pp. 136–7.

144 Stevenson, *Bengal Tiger*, pp. 153–4.

145 Voigt, *India*, p. 207; Rothermund, *An Economic History*, p. 122; Knight, *Food Administration in India*, pp. 187–8, 190.

146 Stevenson, *Bengal Tiger*, p. 150.

147 Tunzelmann, *Indian Summer*, p. 391.

148 'The things we forgot to remember', BBC Radio 4, 7 January 2008.

149 Voigt, *India*, p. 207; Amrith, 'The United Nations', p. 61.

150 Ibid.

151 Voigt, *India*, p. 208.

152 Ibid., p. 209.

153 Cited by Sarkar, *Modern India*, p. 406.

154 Kamtekar, 'A different war dance', pp. 215, 217.

155 Ibid., p. 218.

156 Lloyd, *Food and Inflation*, pp. 66–7.

157 Milward, *War, Economy and Society*, p. 281.

158 Amrith, 'The United Nations', pp. 62–3.

159 Stevenson, *Bengal Tiger*, p. 157.

8. Feeding Germany

1 Dörr, "*Wer die Zeit nicht miterlebt hat...*", II, p. 22.
2 Simon, Memoirs, NLA MS7514, I, p. 75.
3 Tooze, *The Wages of Destruction*, p. 547.
4 Neumann, 'Nutritional physiology', p. 52; Heim, *Kalorien, Kautschuk, Karrieren*, pp. 27, 32, 39.
5 Huegel, *Kriegsernährungswirtschaft Deutschlands*, p. 261.
6 Farquharson, *The Plough*, p. 227.
7 Lehmann, 'Agrarpolitik und Landwirtschaft', p. 43.
8 Kutz, 'Kriegserfahrung und Kriegsvorbereitung', pp. 146–7.
9 Lehmann, 'Agrarpolitik und Landwirtschaft', p. 44.
10 The British ate thirty times more mutton than the Germans. Von der Decken, 'Die Ernährung in England und Deutschland', p. 179.
11 Lehmann, 'Agrarpolitik und Landwirtschaft', p. 46.
12 Corni and Gies, *Brot, Butter, Kanonen*, p. 558.
13 Farquharson, *The Plough*, pp. 224–5; Corni and Gies, *Brot, Butter, Kanonen*, p. 561.
14 Ibid., p. 572.
15 Huegel, *Kriegsernährungswirtschaft Deutschlands*, pp. 308–9.
16 Lehmann, 'Agrarpolitik und Landwirtschaft', p. 45.
17 Rüther, *Köln*, pp. 118–19.
18 Corni, *Hitler and the Peasants*, pp. 237–8.
19 Lehman, 'Agrarpolitik und Landwirtschaft', pp. 39–40; Huegel, *Kriegsernährungswirtschaft Deutschlands*, p. 300.
20 Van Creveld, *Supplying War*, p. 144.
21 Lehmann, 'Agrarpolitik und Landwirtschaft', p. 40.
22 Huegel, *Kriegsernährungswirtschaft Deutschlands*, p. 302.
23 Ibid., p. 303.
24 Stephenson, *Hitler's Home Front*, p. 198.
25 Farquharson, *The Plough*, p. 238.
26 Lehmann, 'Agrarpolitik und Landwirtschaft', pp. 36–8.
27 Herbert, *Hitler's Foreign Workers*, p. 62.
28 Tooze, *The Wages of Destruction*, pp. 362, 364; Huegel, *Kriegsernährungswirtschaft Deutschlands*, p. 340.
29 Herbert, *Hitler's Foreign Workers*, p. 1.
30 Huegel, *Kriegsernährungswirtschaft Deutschlands*, p. 313.
31 Burchardt, 'The impact of the war economy', p. 53.
32 Herbert, *Hitler's Foreign Workers*, pp. 64, 385.
33 Ibid., p. 65.
34 Huegel, *Kriegsernährungswirtschaft Deutschlands*, p. 315.

35 Tooze, *The Wages of Destruction*, p. 364.

36 Beer, *The Nazi Officer's Wife*, pp. 84–5.

37 Ibid., p. 92.

38 Dörr, "*Wer die Zeit nicht miterlebt hat ...*", III, p. 273.

39 Stephenson, 'Nazism, modern war and rural society', p. 352.

40 Stephenson, *Hitler's Home Front*, p. 286.

41 Tooze, *The Wages of Destruction*, p. 167; Corni, *Hitler and the Peasants*, p. xv.

42 Müller, 'Die Mobilisierung der deutschen Wirtschaft', p. 399.

43 Dörr, "*Wer die Zeit nicht miterlebt hat ...*", II, p. 19.

44 Vassiltchikov, *The Berlin Diaries*, pp. 153, 240.

45 Erker, *Ernährungskrise und Nachkriegsgesellschaft*, p. 29.

46 Stephenson, 'Nazism, modern war and rural society', p. 354.

47 Farquharson, *The Plough*, p. 229.

48 Emilia Olivier, interviewed September 2006.

49 Corni and Gies, *Brot, Butter, Kanonen*, p. 562.

50 Erker, *Ernährungskrise und Nachkriegsgesellschaft*, p. 24.

51 Voglis, 'Surviving hunger', p. 18.

52 Brandt, *Management of Agriculture*, pp. 611–12.

53 Mazower, *Inside Hitler's Greece*, pp. 23–4.

54 Black, *A Cause for Our Times*, p. 6.

55 Voglis, 'Surviving hunger', p. 23.

56 Black, *A Cause for Our Times*, p. 6; Hionidou, '"Send us either food or coffins"', p. 182.

57 Beaumont, 'Starving for democracy', p. 66.

58 Mazower, *Inside Hitler's Greece*, p. 27.

59 Hionidou, '"Send us either food or coffins"', pp. 183–4.

60 Ibid., p. 189.

61 Collier, 'Logistics', p. 137.

62 Kennedy, 'Herbert Hoover', p. 91.

63 Beaumont, 'Starving for democracy', p. 67.

64 Black, *A Cause for Our Times*, p. 7.

65 Ibid., pp. 7–8; Voglis, 'Surviving hunger', pp. 36–7.

66 Black, *A Cause for Our Times*, pp. 11, 17.

67 Davies, *Europe at War*, p. 71.

68 Gillingham, 'How Belgium survived', p. 74.

69 Ibid., p. 70.

70 About 10 per cent of the total food available was smuggled. Ibid., p. 84.

71 Ibid., p. 76.

72 Ibid., p. 83.

73 Ibid., p. 73.

74 Vassiltchikov, *The Berlin Diaries*, p. 73.

75 Ousby, *Occupation*, pp. 137–8.
76 Alois Kleinemas, interviewed February 2004.
77 Gildea, *Marianne in Chains*, p. 71.
78 Barral, 'Agriculture and food supply in France', pp. 90–91. Grain from 7.3 million tons in 1939 to 5.1 million tons in 1940, meat from 1.5 million to 1 million tons. Voglis, 'Surviving hunger', p. 21.
79 Barral, 'Agriculture and food supply in France', p. 93.
80 Ibid., p. 94.
81 Tooze, *The Wages of Destruction*, p. 547.
82 Brandt, *Management of Agriculture*, pp. 562–3; Barral, 'Agriculture and food supply in France', p. 94.
83 Ibid., pp. 99–100.
84 Ousby, *Occupation*, p. 119.
85 Gillingham, 'How Belgium survived', p. 85; Ousby, *Occupation*, pp. 124–5; Voglis, 'Surviving hunger', pp. 28, 31; Black, *A Cause for Our Times*, p. 17.
86 Kershaw, *Fateful Choices*, pp. 129–30.
87 Nützenadel, 'Dictating food', pp. 88–9.
88 Ibid., pp. 92–4; Corner, 'Fascist agrarian policy', p. 253.
89 Helstosky, *Garlic and Oil*, p. 105.
90 Ibid., p. 106.
91 Ibid., p. 122.
92 Pitkin, *The House that Giacomo Built*, p. 51.
93 Ibid., p. 57.
94 Ibid., pp. 59–60.
95 Kennett, *G.I.*, p. 204.
96 Nissen, 'Danish food production', pp. 173–4.
97 Brandt, *Management of Agriculture*, pp. 396, 423.
98 Nissen, 'Danish food production', p. 177.
99 Ibid., pp. 184–5.
100 Futselaar, 'The mystery of the dying Dutch', pp. 195–6.
101 Ibid., p. 201.
102 Ibid., p. 212.
103 Moore, 'The western Allies', pp. 94–5.
104 Fuykschot, *Hunger in Holland*, p. 129.
105 Ibid., p. 130.
106 Moore, 'The western Allies', p. 102.
107 Voglis, 'Surviving hunger', p. 22.
108 Moore, 'The western Allies', p. 105.
109 Zee, *The Hunger Winter*, pp. 252–7.
110 Fuykschot, *Hunger in Holland*, p. 153.
111 Nissen, 'Danish food production', p. 185.
112 Kutz, 'Kriegserfahrung und Kriegsvorbereitung', p. 154.

9. Germany Exports Hunger to the East

1 Berkhoff, *Harvest of Despair*, p. 183.
2 Ellis, *The World War II Databook*, p. 227.
3 Müller, 'Albert Speer und die Rüstungspolitik', p. 490.
4 Gerlach, *Kalkulierte Morde*, p. 46.
5 Stephenson, *Hitler's Home Front*, pp. 167, 171.
6 Corni and Gies, *Brot, Butter, Kanonen*, pp. 560–61.
7 Rüther, *Köln*, p. 120.
8 Neumann, 'Nutritional physiology', p. 55.
9 Müller, 'Die Mobilisierung der deutschen Wirtschaft', p. 402.
10 Heim, *Kalorien, Kautschuk, Karrieren*, pp. 108–10.
11 Werner, *"Bleib übrig!"*, p. 56.
12 Ibid., p. 210.
13 Bartov, *Hitler's Army*, p. 74.
14 Kay, *Exploitation*, p. 35.
15 Tooze, *The Wages of Destruction*, p. 458.
16 Kay, *Exploitation*, p. 35.
17 Fulbrook, 'Hitler's willing robbers', p. 205.
18 Kitchen, *Nazi Germany*, pp. 49–50.
19 Haffner, *Anmerkungen zu Hitler*, p. 158.
20 Dunn, *The Soviet Economy*, p. 209.
21 Kay, *Exploitation*, pp. 131–2.
22 Gerlach, *Kalkulierte Morde*, pp. 255–6.
23 Humburg, *Das Gesicht des Krieges*, p. 163.
24 Kay, *Exploitation*, pp. 131–2.
25 Gerlach, 'Militärische "Versorgungszwänge"', pp. 184–5; Bartov, *Germany's War*, pp. 5–6.
26 Bartov, *Hitler's Army*, p. 61.
27 Gerlach, *Kalkulierte Morde*, pp. 262–4.
28 Bartov, *Hitler's Army*, pp. 77–8.
29 Gerlach, *Kalkulierte Morde*, p. 256.
30 Ibid., p. 259.
31 Ibid., pp. 259–60.
32 Ibid., p. 257.
33 Berkhoff, *Harvest of Despair*, pp. 114, 119.
34 Dlugoborski, 'Die Landwirtschaft in der Sowjetunion', pp. 150–51.
35 Boog et al., *Der Angriff*, p. 995; Dallin, *German Rule in Russia*, p. 324.
36 Ibid., pp. 322–5.
37 Berkhoff, *Harvest of Despair*, p. 119.
38 Boog et al., *Der Angriff*, p. 1000.

39 Ibid., p. 991.
40 Ibid., p. 1001.
41 Ibid.; Gerlach, 'Militärische "Versorgungszwänge"', pp. 189–90.
42 Gerlach, *Krieg, Ernährung, Völkermord*, p. 38.
43 Kay, *Exploitation*, p. 108.
44 Gerlach, *Krieg, Ernährung, Völkermord*, pp. 26–7; Boog et al., *Der Angriff*, p. 991.
45 Gerlach, *Krieg, Ernährung, Völkermord*, p. 70.
46 Ibid., p. 72.
47 Ibid., p. 68.
48 Kay, *Exploitation*, p. 207.
49 Gerlach, *Krieg, Ernährung, Völkermord*, p. 29.
50 Gerlach, *Kalkulierte Morde*, p. 49.
51 Boog et al., *Der Angriff*, pp. 1010–11.
52 Tooze, *The Wages of Destruction*, p. 483.
53 Boog et al., *Der Angriff*, p. 1003.
54 Gerlach, *Krieg, Ernährung, Völkermord*, pp. 31–2.
55 Boog et al., *Der Angriff*, p. 1004.
56 Ibid., p. 1006.
57 Ibid., p. 1007.
58 Ibid., p. 1009.
59 Ibid., p. 1015.
60 Tooze, *The Wages of Destruction*, p. 482.
61 Gerlach, *Krieg, Ernährung, Völkermord*, p. 34.
62 Tanaka, *Hidden Horrors*, p. 2.
63 Boog et al., *Der Angriff*, p. 996.
64 Ibid., pp. 1018–19.
65 Gerlach, *Krieg, Ernährung, Völkermord*, p. 39.
66 Ibid., pp. 33–4.
67 Ibid., p. 42.
68 Fritz, *Frontsoldaten*, pp. 51–2.
69 Gerlach, *Krieg, Ernährung, Völkermord*, pp. 46–7.
70 Boog et al., *Der Angriff*, p. 1019.
71 Adamovich and Granin, *A Book of the Blockade*, p. 47.
72 Bidlack, 'Survival strategies in Leningrad', p. 99.
73 Moskoff, *The Bread of Affliction*, p. 205.
74 Adamovich and Granin, *A Book of the Blockade*, pp. 40–41.
75 Moskoff, *The Bread of Affliction*, p. 193.
76 Simmons and Perlina, *Writing the Siege of Leningrad*, p. 59.
77 Kay, *Exploitation*, p. 186.
78 Gerlach, 'Militärische "Versorgungszwänge"', p. 197.
79 Vassilieva, *A Hostage to War*, pp. 13–15.

80 Boog et al., *Der Angriff*, pp. 1010–11.
81 Berkhoff, *Harvest of Despair*, p. 165.
82 Ibid., p. 169.
83 Ibid., p. 172.
84 Moskoff, *The Bread of Affliction*, p. 55.
85 Berkhoff, *Harvest of Despair*, pp. 171–2.
86 Ibid., p. 144.
87 Ibid., p. 173.
88 Ibid., p. 172.
89 Ibid., p. 173.
90 Citizen of Kharkiw, 'Lest we forget', pp. 74–5.
91 Ibid., p. 72.
92 Ibid., p. 73.
93 Ibid., p. 73.
94 Ibid., p. 76.
95 Bartov, *Hitler's Army*, p. 17.
96 Ibid., pp. 15–18, 25.
97 Sajer, *The Forgotten Soldier*, p. 27.
98 Carruthers, *Servants of Evil*, p. 43.
99 Ibid., p. 53.
100 Dunn, *The Soviet Economy*, p. 198.
101 Bartov, *Hitler's Army*, pp. 15, 25.
102 Ibid., pp. 17–18.
103 Carruthers, *Servants of Evil*, p. 57.
104 Sajer, *The Forgotten Soldier*, p. 27.
105 Lucas, *The War on the Eastern Front*, p. 79.
106 Steinhoff et al., *Voices*, p. 114.
107 Humburg, *Das Gesicht des Krieges*, p. 161.
108 Sajer, *The Forgotten Soldier*, p. 85.
109 Bartov, *The Eastern Front*, p. 24.
110 Gerlach, *Krieg, Ernährung, Völkermord*, p. 70.
111 Schulte, *The German Army*, p. 113.
112 Boog et al., *Der Angriff*, p. 999.
113 Ibid., p. 1000.
114 Bartov, *The Eastern Front*, p. 25.
115 Herbert Froböse, interviewed January 2007.
116 Rüther, *Köln*, p. 120.
117 Müller, 'Albert Speer und die Rüstungspolitik', p. 486; Corni and Gies, *Brot, Butter, Kanonen*, p. 561.
118 Tooze, *The Wages of Destruction*, p. 542.
119 Corni and Gies, *Brot, Butter, Kanonen*, p. 562.
120 Ibid., p. 563.

121 Tooze, *The Wages of Destruction*, p. 544.
122 Müller, 'Albert Speer und die Rüstungspolitik', pp. 487, 495.
123 Dörr, "*Wer die Zeit nicht miterlebt hat . . .*", II, p. 20.
124 Ibid., II, p. 21.
125 Tooze, *The Wages of Destruction*, p. 544.
126 Gerlach, *Krieg, Ernährung, Völkermord*, p. 68.
127 Ibid., p. 297.
128 Ibid., p. 168.
129 Ibid., pp. 131–2.
130 Ibid., p. 168.
131 Bartov, *Germany's War*, p. 108.
132 Brzeska, *Through a Woman's Eyes*, pp. 26–7, 30.
133 Gerlach, *Krieg, Ernährung, Völkermord*, pp. 172–3.
134 Klukowski, *Diary*, p. 189.
135 Roland, *Courage under Siege*, p. 112.
136 Ibid., p. 99.
137 Ibid., pp. 111–12, 175.
138 Gerlach, *Krieg, Ernährung, Völkermord*, pp. 176–7.
139 Ibid., p. 186.
140 Ibid., p. 183.
141 Ibid., pp. 198, 200.
142 Klukowski, *Diary*, p. 188.
143 Ibid., p. 189.
144 Ibid., p. 191.
145 Ibid., p. 196.
146 Ibid., p. 197.
147 Gerlach, *Krieg, Ernährung, Völkermord*, pp. 209–10.
148 Ibid., p. 246.
149 Laqueur and Breitman, *Breaking the Silence*, pp. 37, 75; 'Eduard Schulte', US Holocaust Memorial Museum, http://www.ushmm.org/wlc/article.php?lang=en&ModulId=10005682.
150 Laqueur and Breitman, *Breaking the Silence*, p. 105.
151 Ibid., p. 130; Gerlach, *Krieg, Ernährung, Völkermord*, p. 255.
152 Müller, 'Die Mobilisierung der deutschen Wirtschaft', p. 397.
153 Corni and Gies, *Brot, Butter, Kanonen*, p. 564.
154 Gerlach, *Krieg, Ernährung, Völkermord*, p. 212.
155 Picker, *Hitlers Tischgespräche*, p. 432.
156 Gerlach, *Krieg, Ernährung, Völkermord*, pp. 212–14.
157 Tooze, *The Wages of Destruction*, p. 546.
158 Gerlach, *Krieg, Ernährung, Völkermord*, pp. 215–16.
159 Tooze, *The Wages of Destruction*, pp. 546–7.
160 Ibid.; Gerlach, *Krieg, Ernährung, Völkermord*, p. 217.

161 Klukowski, *Diary*, p. 210.

162 Ibid.

163 Gerlach, *Krieg, Ernährung, Völkermord*, pp. 220, 231–2.

164 Ibid., p. 237.

165 Ibid., p. 241.

166 Luczak, 'Landwirtschaft und Ernährung in Polen', pp. 126–7. He gives different figures for potatoes: 500,200 tons of potatoes. 50.9% of rye, 28% of barley, 65.6% of oats and 51.8% of potatoes.

167 Gerlach, *Krieg, Ernährung, Völkermord*, pp. 248, 227.

168 Berkhoff, *Harvest of Despair*, pp. 176–7.

169 Ibid., p. 184.

170 Ibid.

171 Mazower, *Hitler's Empire*, p. 164.

172 Moskoff, *The Bread of Affliction*, pp. 55–6.

173 Citizen of Kharkiw, 'Lest we forget', p. 79.

174 Berkhoff, *Harvest of Despair*, p. 122.

175 Corni and Gies, *Brot, Butter, Kanonen*, p. 564.

176 Müller, 'Albert Speer und die Rüstungspolitik', p. 488.

177 Kay, *Exploitation*, p. 167; Mazower, *Hitler's Empire*, p. 147.

178 Boog et al., *Der Angriff*, p. 1014.

179 Berkhoff, *Harvest of Despair*, p. 176.

180 Boog et al., *Der Angriff*, pp. 1020–1.

181 Berkhoff, *Harvest of Despair*, p. 134.

182 Ibid., pp. 128–9.

183 Müller, 'Albert Speer und die Rüstungspolitik', p. 488.

184 Berkhoff, *Harvest of Despair*, pp. 130–31.

185 Dallin, *German Rule in Russia*, pp. 363–4.

186 Gerlach, *Kalkulierte Morde*, p. 257.

187 Moskoff, *The Bread of Affliction*, p. 48.

188 Schulte, *The German Army*, p. 88.

189 Tooze, *The Wages of Destruction*, p. 548.

190 Corni and Gies, *Brot, Butter, Kanonen*, p. 564.

191 Beck, *Under the Bombs*, p. 19.

192 Burchardt, 'The impact of the war economy', p. 53.

193 McDermott, *Women Recall the War Years*, p. 240.

10. Soviet Collapse

1 Sakharov, *Memoirs*, pp. 51–2.

2 Ibid.

3 Service, *A History of Twentieth-Century Russia*, pp. 31, 109–10.

4 Moskoff, *The Bread of Affliction*, p. 136.

5 Taugar, 'Stalin, Soviet agriculture, and collectivisation', pp. 110–11.

6 Ibid., p. 130.

7 Service, *A History of Twentieth-Century Russia*, pp. 163–4, 181.

8 Harvard Project on the Soviet Social System, Schedule A, Vol. 18, Case 344, pp. 5–6.

9 Ibid.

10 Harvard Project on the Soviet Social System, Schedule A, Vol. 15, Case 305, pp. 23–4.

11 Service, *A History of Twentieth-Century Russia*, pp. 180–81.

12 Harvard Project on the Soviet Social System, Schedule A, Vol. 15, Case 305, p. 48.

13 Service, *A History of Twentieth-Century Russia*, p. 182.

14 Barber and Harrison, *The Soviet Home Front*, p. 6.

15 Bordiugov, 'The popular mood', p. 59.

16 Volin, *A Century*, p. 281.

17 Ibid., p. 275; Dunn, *The Soviet Economy*, p. 43. The Germans occupied about 40 per cent of crop land, 84 per cent of sugar-producing land, and captured about 40 per cent of beef and dairy cattle, and 60 per cent of the Soviet Union's pigs.

18 Volin, *A Century*, pp. 276–9; Barber and Harrison, *The Soviet Home Front*, pp. 187–8.

19 Miller, 'Impact and aftermath of World War II', p. 286.

20 Service, *A History of Twentieth-Century Russia*, p. 286.

21 Nove, 'Soviet peasantry in World War II', pp. 82–3.

22 In comparison women made up 40 per cent of the agricultural labour force in 1940. Erickson, 'Soviet women at war', p. 56; Barber and Harrison, *The Soviet Home Front*, p. 149.

23 Kravchenko, *I Chose Freedom*, p. 382.

24 Volin, *A Century*, p. 288.

25 Ibid., p. 285.

26 Nove, 'Soviet peasantry in World War II', pp. 82–3.

27 Moskoff, *The Bread of Affliction*, p. 118.

28 Ibid., p. 126.

29 Braithwaite, *Moscow 1941*, pp. 123–4.

30 Volin, *A Century*, p. 285; Barber and Harrison, *The Soviet Home Front*, p. 102.

31 Dunn, *The Soviet Economy*, p. 43.

32 Linz, 'World War II and Soviet economic growth', p. 21; Barber and Harrison, *The Soviet Home Front*, p. 80.

33 Moskoff, *The Bread of Affliction*, p. 10.

34 Ibid.

35 Medvedev, *Soviet Agriculture*, p. 135.

36 Harvard Project on the Soviet Social System, Schedule A, Vol. 15, Case 305, p. 17.

37 Sakharov, *Memoirs*, p. 57.
38 Barber and Harrison, *The Soviet Home Front*, pp. 85–6.
39 Ibid., pp. 83–4.
40 14 October 1944, J. A. Alexander Papers 1892–1983, NLA, MS2389.
41 Nove, 'Soviet peasantry in World War II', p. 85.
42 Barber and Harrison, *The Soviet Home Front*, pp. 101, 178.
43 Tuyll, *Feeding the Bear*, p. 138.
44 Service, *A History of Twentieth-Century Russia*, p. 276.

11. Japan's Journey towards Starvation

1 Talib, 'Memory and its historical context', p. 131.
2 Dower, *Embracing Defeat*, p. 91.
3 Johnston, *Japanese Food Management*, pp. 43, 87.
4 Ibid., p. 47; Dower, *Embracing Defeat*, p. 91.
5 Johnston, *Japanese Food Management*, pp. 42, 89, 160–62.
6 Morris-Suzuki, *Showa*, pp. 40–41.
7 Johnston, *Japanese Food Management*, pp. 129–30.
8 Ibid., p. 135.
9 Ibid., p. 169.
10 Ibid., pp. 140, 152; Cwiertka, 'Popularizing a military diet', pp. 7, 14–15; Cwiertka, *Modern Japanese Cuisine*, pp. 77, 129.
11 Onn, *Malaya Upside Down*, p. 175.
12 Milward, *War, Economy and Society*, pp. 258–9.
13 Soviak, *A Diary of Darkness*, p. 202.
14 Martin, 'Agriculture and food supply', pp. 189–90.
15 Partner, 'Daily life', p. 154.
16 Dore, *Shinohata*, p. 54.
17 Johnston, *Japanese Food Management*, pp. 98–101.
18 Cook and Cook, *Japan at War*, p. 188.
19 Martin, 'Agriculture and food supply', p. 190.
20 Ibid., pp. 185, 191.
21 Lamer, *The World Fertilizer Economy*, pp. 547–54; Milward, *War, Economy and Society*, p. 277.
22 Frank, *Downfall*, p. 81.
23 Johnston, *Japanese Food Management*, p. 109.
24 Ibid., p. 126.
25 Dore, *Shinohata*, p. 54.
26 Johnston, *Japanese Food Management*, pp. 126–7.
27 Havens, *Valley of Darkness*, pp. 100–101.
28 Ibid.
29 Johnston, *Japanese Food Management*, p. 123.

30 Havens, *Valley of Darkness*, pp. 99–100.

31 Soviak, *Diary of Darkness*, p. 338.

32 Johnston states that rice yields fell by only 4 per cent but Martin, the more modern scholar, gives figures of total production in millions of metric tons of rice falling between 1939 and 1945 from 11.5 to 6.6, wheat from 1.7 to 0.9 and barley from 0.8 to 0.5. Martin, 'Agriculture and food supply', p. 192; Johnston, *Japanese Food Management*, p. 128.

33 Johnston, *Japanese Food Management*, p. 137.

34 Kratoska, 'The impact of the Second World War', p. 9.

35 Ibid., p. 18.

36 Johnston, *Japanese Food Management*, pp. 135, 137.

37 Scott, 'The problems of food supply', pp. 270–71.

38 Peattie, '*Nanshin*', pp. 239–40.

39 Kratoska, 'The impact of the Second World War', p. 9.

40 Scott, 'The problems of food supply', p. 275.

41 Kheng, 'Memory as history', p. 32.

42 Akashi, 'Japanese policy towards the Malayan Chinese', pp. 66–7.

43 Ibid., pp. 67–9.

44 Kheng, 'Memory as history', p. 33; Duus, 'Introduction. Japan's wartime empire', pp. xxv–vi.

45 Akashi, 'Japanese policy towards the Malayan Chinese', p. 71.

46 Frank, *Downfall*, p. 161.

47 Kratoska, 'The impact of the Second World War', pp. 18, 22.

48 Kurasawa, 'Transportation and rice distribution', p. 33.

49 Kratoska, 'The impact of the Second World War', p. 22.

50 Scott, 'The problems of food supply', p. 280.

51 Kurasawa, 'Transportation and rice distribution', p. 33.

52 Ahmad, 'The Malay community', p. 70.

53 Ibid., p. 78.

54 Ibid., p. 73.

55 Ibid.

56 Ibid., pp. 48–9, 51.

57 Ibid., pp. 60–61.

58 Onn, *Malaya Upside Down*, p. 46.

59 Kratoska, *The Japanese Occupation*, pp. 265–6.

60 Onn, *Malaya Upside Down*, p. 44.

61 Ibid., p. 35.

62 Ibid., p. 44; Scott, 'The problems of food supply', p. 275.

63 Onn, *Malaya Upside Down*, pp. 35, 44; Kratoska, 'Introduction', p. 6.

64 Ahmad, 'The Malay community', p. 49.

65 Onn, *Malaya Upside Down*, pp. 48–9.

66 Harper, *The End of Empire*, p. 43.

67 Kratoska, *The Japanese Occupation*, p. 262.

68 Ibid., p. 255.

69 Onn, *Malaya Upside Down*, pp. 176–7.

70 Kratoska, 'Malayan food shortages', p. 109.

71 Dung, 'Japan's role in the Vietnamese starvation', p. 587.

72 Ibid., pp. 589–92.

73 Scott, 'The problems of food supply', p. 280.

74 Dung, 'Japan's role in the Vietnamese starvation', p. 607.

75 Ibid., p. 575.

76 Bose, 'Starvation amidst plenty', p. 724.

77 Dung, 'Japan's role in the Vietnamese starvation', p. 576.

78 Furuta, 'A survey of village conditions', p. 237.

79 Dung, 'Japan's role in the Vietnamese starvation', pp. 613–14.

80 Kratoska, 'The impact of the Second World War', p. 24.

81 Anh, 'Japanese food policies', p. 223.

82 Parillo, *The Japanese Merchant Marine*, p. 204.

83 Martin, 'Japans Kriegswirtschaft', pp. 261–2.

84 Martin, *Japan and Germany*, pp. 143–4.

85 Parillo, *The Japanese Merchant Marine*, pp. 9–10.

86 Ibid., p. 15.

87 Ibid., p. 166.

88 Ibid., pp. 88, 204.

89 Ibid., p. 111.

90 Jose, 'Food production', p. 75.

91 Kerkvliet, 'Withdrawal and resistance', p. 303.

92 Jose, 'Food production', pp. 75, 90.

93 Kerkvliet, 'Withdrawal and resistance', p. 311.

94 Ibid., p. 308.

95 Ibid., p. 313.

96 Ibid., p. 311.

97 Sato, 'Oppression and romanticism', p. 177.

98 Kurasawa, 'Transportation and rice', p. 34.

99 Reid, 'Indonesia', p. 20; Sato, 'Oppression and romanticism', p. 168.

100 Kennett, *G.I.*, p. 187.

101 Jessup, Changi Diary, NLA, MS 3924, p. 52.

102 Frank, *Downfall*, p. 160.

103 Jessup, Changi Diary, NLA, MS 3924, p. 35.

104 Ibid., p. 51.

105 Ibid., p. 54.

106 Ibid., p. 67.

107 Ibid., pp. 86, 91.

108 Teruko Blair, interviewed March 2006.

109 Shin'ichi, *Manchuria*, pp. 204–5.

110 Johnston, *Japanese Food Management*, p. 145.

111 Japanese Pamphlet No. 19, AWM 54 423/5/22 Air Dept. Wellington N.Z. Japanese Pamphlets.

112 Ibid.

113 Ibid.

114 Shin'ichi, *Manchuria*, p. 205.

115 Ibid.

12. China Divided

1 White and Jacoby, *Thunder out of China*, p. 72.

2 Ven, *War and Nationalism*, p. 2.

3 Ibid., p. 295.

4 Mitter, *Modern China*, pp. 38–9.

5 Ibid., p. 44.

6 Ibid.

7 Ven, *War and Nationalism*, pp. 15–16.

8 Wang, 'Urban life in China's wars', p. 95.

9 Pusen, 'To feed a country at war', p. 158.

10 White and Jacoby, *Thunder out of China*, pp. 60–61.

11 Ven, *War and Nationalism*, p. 275.

12 Shen, 'Food production', p. 168; MacKinnon, 'Refugee flight', p. 122.

13 Pusen, 'To feed a country at war', p. 159.

14 Ven, *War and Nationalism*, p. 295.

15 Ibid.

16 Ibid., pp. 256–7; Ellis, *The World War II Databook*, p. 229.

17 Shen, 'Food production', p. 176; Ven, *War and Nationalism*, pp. 260–61.

18 Ven, *War and Nationalism*, pp. 260, 268.

19 White and Jacoby, *Thunder out of China*, pp. 74–5.

20 Bayly and Harper, *Forgotten Armies*, pp. 3, 89.

21 US Army Air Forces Statistical Digest, World War II, Table 211 – ATC Operations from Assam, India, to China (over the Hump): Jan 1943 to Aug 1945, http://www.usaaf.net/digest/t211.htm.

22 Ven, *War and Nationalism*, p. 269.

23 Pusen, 'To feed a country at war', p. 159.

24 Shen, 'Food production', p. 182.

25 Eastman, 'Nationalist China during the Sino-Japanese war', pp. 154–5.

26 Ronning, *A Memoir*, p. 146.

27 Wang, 'Urban life in China's wars', p. 104.

28 Eastman, 'Nationalist China during the Sino-Japanese war', pp. 155–6.

29 Ven, *War and Nationalism*, p. 276.

30 White and Jacoby, *Thunder out of China*, p. 71.

31 Pusen, 'To feed a country at war', p. 166.

32 Shen, 'Food production', pp. 187–8.

33 White and Jacoby, *Thunder out of China*, p. 74.

34 Ven, *War and Nationalism*, p. 272.

35 White and Jacoby, *Thunder out of China*, pp. 73–4.

36 Ven, *War and Nationalism*, p. 272.

37 Ibid., p. 278.

38 Eastman, 'Nationalist China during the Sino-Japanese war', pp. 173–4.

39 Eastman, *Seeds of Destruction*, p. 67; Pusen, 'To feed a country at war', p. 167.

40 Ibid., p. 158.

41 Eastman, *Seeds of Destruction*, p. 68.

42 Ven, *War and Nationalism*, p. 284.

43 White and Jacoby, *Thunder out of China*, pp. 166–7.

44 Rummel, *China's Bloody Century*, p. 117.

45 Eastman, *Seeds of Destruction*, p. 69.

46 Xinran, *China Witness*, pp. 339–40.

47 White and Jacoby, *Thunder out of China*, p. 164.

48 Eastman, *Seeds of Destruction*, p. 69.

49 Rummel, *China's Bloody Century*, p. 116.

50 Ibid., p. 113.

51 Ven, *War and Nationalism*, p. 273.

52 Rummel, *China's Bloody Century*, p. 113.

53 Ibid., p. 118.

54 Eastman, 'Nationalist China during the Sino-Japanese war', p. 174; White and Jacoby, *Thunder out of China*, p. 170.

55 Ven, *War and Nationalism*, p. 17.

56 Smith, *The War's Long Shadow*, p. 48.

57 White and Jacoby, *Thunder out of China*, p. 169.

58 Ch'en, 'The communist movement', p. 114; Slyke, 'The Chinese Communist movement', p. 200.

59 Tiedemann, 'Wartime guerrilla economy', p. 18; Slyke, 'The Chinese Communist movement', p. 200.

60 Levich, *The Kwangsi Way*, p. 227; Chen, *Making Revolution*, pp. 219–20.

61 Tiedemann, 'Wartime guerrilla economy', pp. 19–20.

62 Gatu, *Toward Revolution*, pp. 219–20.

63 Pusen, 'To feed a country at war', pp. 158–9.

64 Gatu, *Toward Revolution*, p. 217; Hongmin, 'Traditional responses to modern war', pp. 195–6.

65 Ibid., p. 196.

66 Ibid., pp. 197–8.

67 Xinran, *China Witness*, p. 245.
68 Hongmin, 'Traditional responses to modern war', p. 198.
69 Ibid., pp. 197, 199.
70 Slyke, 'The Chinese Communist movement', p. 222.
71 Gatu, *Toward Revolution*, pp. 218–19.
72 Ven, *War and Nationalism*, p. 283.
73 Eastman, *Seeds of Destruction*, p. 88.
74 Mitter, *Modern China*, p. 48.
75 Xinran, *China Witness*, p. 276.
76 Mitter, *Modern China*, p. 54.
77 Ibid., p. 48; Mitter, *Bitter Revolution*, p. 184.
78 Ven, *War and Nationalism*, p. 296; Gordon, 'The China–Japan war', p. 162.
79 Ven, *War and Nationalism*, p. 296.
80 Ibid., p. 5.
81 Mitter, *Bitter Revolution*, p. 183.
82 Milward, *War, Economy and Society*, p. 289.
83 Magaeva, 'Physiological and psychosomatic prerequisites for survival', p. 131.
84 Ibid., pp. 141–2.
85 Ibid., p. 141.
86 Macintyre, 'Famine and the female mortality advantage', p. 254; Cherepenina, 'Assessing the scale of famine and death', p. 39.
87 Myron Winick, 'Hunger disease: studies by the Jewish physicians in the Warsaw ghetto, their historical importance and their relevance today', 27 October 2005, http://www.columbia.edu/cu/epic/pdf/winick_lecture, pp. 2–3; Fliederbaum, 'Metabolic changes', pp. 69–124; Apfelbaum, 'Pathophysiology of the circulatory system', pp. 125–60.
88 Brown et al., 'Increased risk of affective disorders in males', pp. 601–6.
89 Lumley, 'Reproductive outcomes', pp. 129–35.
90 Barker, 'Fetal origins', pp. 171–4.
91 Stanner et al., 'Does malnutrition in utero determine diabetes?', pp. 1342–9; Joseph and Kramer, 'Review of the evidence', pp. 158–74.
92 Duigan and Gann, *The Rebirth*, p. 2.
93 Hobsbawm, *Age of Extremes*, p. 290.
94 Short et al., '"The front line of freedom"', p. 15.
95 Martin, 'Agriculture and food supply', p. 203.
96 Milward, 'Long-term change in world agriculture', p. 6.
97 Ibid., p. 12.
98 Kershaw, *Fateful Choices*, p. 128.

PART III THE POLITICS OF FOOD

1 Kravchenko, *I Chose Freedom*, p. 417.
2 Mayhew, 'The 1930s nutrition controversy', p. 447.
3 Overy, *Russia's War*, p. 327; Hastings, *Das Reich*, pp. 2–3.
4 Crew, 'General introduction', p. 8.
5 Harris, 'Great Britain', p. 241.
6 Drea, *In the Service of the Emperor*, pp. 66–7.
7 Baer, *One Hundred Years*, p. 201.
8 Reynolds, *Rich Relations*, p. 86.
9 Ibid., p. 62.
10 Richmond, *The Japanese Forces in New Guinea*, p. 42.
11 Cited in ibid., pp. 165–6.
12 Edgerton, *Warriors of the Rising Sun*, p. 235.
13 Imamura, 'Extracts from the tenor of my life', NLA, mfm PMB 569, III, p. 151.

13. Japan – Starving for the Emperor

1 Cook and Cook, *Japan at War*, pp. 278–80.
2 Kershaw, *Fateful Choices*, p. 331.
3 Morris, *Traveller from Tokyo*, p. 121.
4 Research Report No. 122, 'Antagonism between officers and men in the Japanese armed forces', AWM 55 12/94, p. 6.
5 Drea, *In the Service of the Emperor*, p. 72.
6 Harries and Harries, *Soldiers of the Sun*, p. 351.
7 Soviak, *A Diary of Darkness*, p. 285.
8 Imamura, 'Extracts from the tenor of my life', NLA, mfm PMB 569, III, p. 151.
9 Cwiertka, 'Popularizing a military diet in wartime Japan and postwar Japan', IIAS Newsletter, 38, http://www.iias.nl/iias/show/id=51553, p. 10.
10 Cwiertka, *Modern Japanese Cuisine*, p. 77.
11 Ibid., pp. 78–9; Cwiertka, 'Popularizing a military diet in wartime Japan and postwar Japan', IIAS Newsletter, 38, http://www.iias.nl/iias/show/id=51553, pp. 8–10.
12 Ibid., p. 11.
13 Cwiertka, *Modern Japanese Cuisine*, p. 81.
14 Ibid., p. 84.
15 Ibid.; Cwiertka, 'Popularizing a military diet in wartime Japan and postwar Japan', IIAS Newsletter, 38, http://www.iias.nl/iias/show/id=51553, p. 13.
16 Ibid., p. 16.
17 Ibid., p. 19.

18 Cwiertka, *Modern Japanese Cuisine*, pp. 117, 119.

19 Pauer, 'Neighbourhood associations', p. 222.

20 Tomita, *Dear Miye*, p. 56.

21 Pauer, 'Neighbourhood associations', p. 222; Cwiertka, *Modern Japanese Cuisine*, p. 130.

22 Tomita, *Dear Miye*, p. 97.

23 Ibid., p. 113.

24 Pauer, 'Neighbourhood associations', p. 237.

25 Morris, *Traveller from Tokyo*, p. 123.

26 Author in conversation with Katarzyna Cwiertka.

27 Morris, *Traveller from Tokyo*, pp. 121–2.

28 Johnston, *Japanese Food Management*, p. 150.

29 Ibid., p. 151.

30 Senoh, *A Boy Called H*, p. 170.

31 Havens, *Valley of Darkness*, p. 77; Pauer, 'Neighbourhood associations', p. 240.

32 Ibid., p. 231.

33 Havens, *Valley of Darkness*, p. 86; Martin, 'Agriculture and food supply', p. 197.

34 Cwiertka, *Modern Japanese Cuisine*, p. 82.

35 Martin, 'Agriculture and food supply', p. 193.

36 Milward, *War, Economy and Society*, p. 288.

37 Katarzyna Cwiertka, 'Feeding the troops in the Pacific and the Korean War', talk given to the East Asian Studies seminar, Cambridge, 10 November 2008.

38 Richmond, *The Japanese Forces in New Guinea*, p. 168.

39 Ibid.

40 Ibid., p. 17; Reynolds, *Rich Relations*, p. 63.

41 Harries and Harries, *Soldiers of the Sun*, p. 286.

42 Drea, *In the Service of the Emperor*, p. 65; Calvocoressi and Wint, *Total War*, pp. 270–73.

43 Richmond, *The Japanese Forces in New Guinea*, pp. 165–6.

44 Ibid., p. 166.

45 Calvocoressi and Wint, *Total War*, p. 727.

46 Richmond, *The Japanese Forces in New Guinea*, p. 166.

47 Tamayama and Nunneley, *Tales by Japanese Soldiers*, pp. 37–8.

48 Ibid., pp. 29–30.

49 Ibid., p. 60.

50 Ibid., p. 108.

51 Soviak, *A Diary of Darkness*, p. 14.

52 Onn, *Malaya Upside Down*, p. 47.

53 Cook and Cook, *Japan at War*, p. 100.

54 Tamayama and Nunneley, *Tales by Japanese Soldiers*, pp. 101–2.

55 Drea, *In the Service of the Emperor*, p. 35.

56 'Ration supply and ration scale of Japanese land forces in SWPA', 6 Feb 1944, AWM 55 12/47 (69), p. 1.

57 Richmond, *The Japanese Forces in New Guinea*, p. 145.

58 Keegan, *The Second World War*, p. 104.

59 (1.1 million tons) between December 1941 and April 1943. Johnston, *Japanese Food Management*, pp. 140–41.

60 Ibid., p. 152.

61 Ibid., p. 192.

62 Pauer, 'Neighbourhood associations', pp. 226–7.

63 Senoh, *A Boy Called H*, p. 290.

64 Japanese Pamphlet no. 9, AWM 54 423/5/22 Air Dept. Wellington N.Z. Japanese Pamphlets, p. 7.

65 Johnston, *Japanese Food Management*, p. 162.

66 Morris-Suzuki, *Showa*, p. 161.

67 Cook and Cook, *Japan at War*, pp. 177–8.

68 Ibid., pp. 179–80.

69 Ibid., p. 180.

70 Morris-Suzuki, *Showa*, pp. 161–2.

71 Havens, *Valley of Darkness*, p. 94.

72 Pauer, 'Neighbourhood associations', p. 227.

73 Soviak, *A Diary of Darkness*, p. 115.

74 Ibid., p. 170.

75 Ibid., p. 143.

76 Japanese Pamphlet no. 9, AWM 54 423/5/22 Air Dept. Wellington N.Z. Japanese Pamphlets.

77 Soviak, *A Diary of Darkness*, p. 170.

78 'Ration supply and ration scale of Japanese land forces in SWPA', 6 Feb 1944, AWM 55 12/47 (69), p. 2.

79 Japanese Pamphlet no. 27, 30 December 1943, Air Dept. Wellington N.Z., AWM 54 423/5/22.

80 'Ration supply and ration scale of Japanese land forces in SWPA', 6 Feb 1944, AWM 55 12/47 (69), p. 5.

81 Richmond, *The Japanese Forces in New Guinea*, p. 167.

82 'Ration supply and ration scale of Japanese land forces in SWPA', 6 Feb 1944, AWM 55 12/47 (69), p. 8.

83 Japanese Pamphlet no. 27, 30 December 1943, Air Dept. Wellington N.Z., AWM 54 423/5/22.

84 Imamura, 'Extracts from the tenor of my life', NLA, mfm PMB 569, III, pp. 153–4.

85 'Ration supply and ration scale of Japanese land forces in SWPA', 6 Feb 1944, AWM 55 12/47 (69), p. 5.

86 Japanese Pamphlet no. 27, 30 December 1943, Air Dept. Wellington N.Z., AWM 54 423/5/22.

87 'Ration supply and ration scale of Japanese land forces in SWPA', 6 Feb 1944, AWM 55 12/47 (69), p. 34.

88 Richmond, *The Japanese Forces in New Guinea*, pp. 151–2.

89 Harries and Harries, *Soldiers of the Sun*, p. 340.

90 Ibid., p. 341.

91 Imamura, 'Extracts from the tenor of my life', NLA, mfm PMB 569, III, pp. 141–2.

92 Harries and Harries, *Soldiers of the Sun*, p. 341.

93 Imamura, 'Extracts from the tenor of my life', NLA, mfm PMB 569, III, pp. 145–6.

94 Harries and Harries, *Soldiers of the Sun*, p. 342. The Japanese routinely underestimated the numbers of Japanese soldiers killed in combat. Harries and Harries suggest that the Japanese lost 25,000 men on Guadalcanal, 10,000 of whom succumbed to disease and starvation. Most probably 40,000 Japanese soldiers were sent to Guadalcanal and somewhere close to one half of those 25,000 who died starved to death, or about 12,500.

95 Imamura, 'Extracts from the tenor of my life', NLA, mfm PMB 569, III, p. 151.

96 Beaumont, 'Australia's war: Asia and the Pacific', p. 38.

97 Ibid.

98 Richmond, *The Japanese Forces in New Guinea*, p. 204.

99 Ibid., p. 171.

100 Harries and Harries, *Soldiers of the Sun*, p. 343.

101 Dornan, *The Silent Men*, p. 146.

102 Harries and Harries, *Soldiers of the Sun*, p. 343.

103 Bullard, '"The great enemy"', pp. 215–16.

104 Ibid., p. 212.

105 Drea, *In the Service of the Emperor*, p. 70.

106 Bullard, '"The great enemy"', p. 215.

107 Richmond, *The Japanese Forces in New Guinea*, p. 150.

108 Ibid., p. 178.

109 Thune, 'The making of history', p. 241.

110 Tanaka cited by Richmond, *The Japanese Forces in New Guinea*, pp. 149, 179.

111 Richmond, *The Japanese Forces in New Guinea*, pp. 166–7.

112 Nelson, *'Taim Bilong Pait'*, pp. 253–4.

113 Ibid., p. 256; Denoon, *The Cambridge History of the Pacific Islanders*, p. 316.

114 Japanese Pamphlet no. 27, 30 December 1943, Air Dept. Wellington N.Z., AWM 54 423/5/22.

115 Research Report No. 122, 'Antagonism between officers and men in the Japanese armed forces', AWM 55 12/94, p. 4.

116 Ibid.

117 Richmond, *The Japanese Forces in New Guinea*, pp. 185–6.

118 Ibid., p. 181.
119 Ibid., p. 214.
120 Tanaka, *Hidden Horrors*, p. 115.
121 Ibid. p. 116.
122 Keegan, *The Second World War*, p. 303.
123 Laurence and Tiddy, *From Bully Beef*, p. 43.
124 Falgout, 'From passive pawns', pp. 287–8.
125 McQuarrie, *Strategic Atolls*, pp. 135, 139; McQuarrie, *Conflict in Kiribati*, pp. 89–91.
126 McQuarrie, *Strategic Atolls*, p. 131.
127 Cook and Cook, *Japan at War*, p. 114.
128 Ibid., p. 116.
129 Ibid., p. 117.
130 Ibid., p. 119.
131 Gibney, *Senso*, pp. 156–7.
132 Ooka, *Fires on the Plain*, p. 179.
133 Harries and Harries, *Soldiers of the Sun*, p. 346.
134 Thompson, *The Lifeblood of War*, pp. 80–81; Richmond, *The Japanese Forces in New Guinea*, p. 17.
135 Allen, *Burma*, pp. 158–67.
136 Harries and Harries, *Soldiers of the Sun*, p. 347; Thompson, *The Lifeblood of War*, p. 92.
137 Tamayama and Nunneley, *Tales by Japanese Soldiers*, p. 158.
138 Ibid., p. 170.
139 Ibid., p. 175.
140 Thompson, *The Lifeblood of War*, p. 93.
141 Moharir, *History of the Army Service Corps*, p. 46.
142 Tamayama and Nunneley, *Tales by Japanese Soldiers*, p. 176.
143 Thompson, *The Lifeblood of War*, p. 95.
144 Ibid., p. 87.
145 Tamayama and Nunneley, *Tales by Japanese Soldiers*, p. 177.
146 Allen, *Burma*, p. 292.
147 Tamayama and Nunneley, *Tales by Japanese Soldiers*, pp. 174–8.
148 Ibid., p. 202.
149 Ibid., p. 229.
150 Cook and Cook, *Japan at War*, p. 104.
151 Hastings, *Nemesis*, p. 358.
152 Moharir, *History of the Army Service Corps*, p. 49.
153 Fujiwara, *Uejini shita eireitachi*, pp. 135–8.
154 Tanaka, *Hidden Horrors*, pp. 133–4.
155 Soviak, *Diary of Darkness*, p. 28.
156 Ibid., p. 282.

157 Ibid., p. 156.
158 Ibid., p. 145.
159 Ibid., p. 156.
160 Ibid., p. 207.
161 Ibid., p. 213.
162 Cwiertka, *Modern Japanese Cuisine*, p. 132.
163 Ibid.
164 Senoh, *A Boy Called H*, p. 302.
165 Matsumoto Nakako, interviewed May 2006.
166 Soviak, *A Diary of Darkness*, p. 261.
167 Pauer, 'Neighbourhood associations', p. 230.
168 Soviak, *A Diary of Darkness*, p. 171.
169 Ibid., pp. 174, 180.
170 Martin, 'Agriculture and food supply', p. 197.
171 Soviak, *A Diary of Darkness*, p. 236.
172 Dower, *Embracing Defeat*, pp. 90, 95.
173 Frank, *Downfall*, p. 81.
174 Soviak, *A Diary of Darkness*, p. 215.
175 Havens, *Valley of Darkness*, p. 103.
176 Soviak, *A Diary of Darkness*, p. 256.
177 Senoh, *A Boy Called H*, p. 402.
178 Cook and Cook, *Japan at War*, p. 192.
179 Ibid., p. 190.
180 Ibid., p. 191.
181 Ibid.
182 Soviak, *A Diary of Darkness*, pp. 294, 320.
183 Ibid., p. 326.
184 Havens, *Valley of Darkness*, p. 129.
185 Soviak, *A Diary of Darkness*, p. 329.
186 Frank, *Downfall*, p. 77.
187 Ibid., pp. 149, 156–7.
188 Parillo, *The Japanese Merchant Marine*, p. 204.
189 Martin, 'Japans Kriegswirtschaft', p. 271.
190 Gibney, *Senso*, p. 181.
191 Ibid.
192 Frank, *Downfall*, p. 81.
193 Pauer, 'Neighbourhood associations', p. 227.
194 Johnston, *Japanese Food Management*, p. 150.
195 Parillo, *The Japanese Merchant Marine*, pp. 219–20; Frank, *Downfall*, pp. 80–81, 96.
196 Havens, *Valley of Darkness*, pp. 129–30.
197 Johnston, *Japanese Food Management*, p. 202; Dower, *Embracing Defeat*, p. 91.

198 Frank, *Downfall*, p. 354.
199 Dower, *Embracing Defeat*, p. 92; Honda, 'Differential structure', p. 281.
200 Frank, *Downfall*, p. 343.
201 Soviak, *A Diary of Darkness*, p. 215.
202 Ibid., p. 247.
203 Newman, *Truman*, p. 13.
204 Frank, *Downfall*, pp. 26–7.
205 Newman, *Truman*, pp. 71–3.
206 Ibid., p. 43.
207 Frank, *Downfall*, p. 345.
208 Ibid., p. 351; Dower, *Embracing Defeat*, pp. 95–6.
209 Frank, *Downfall*, p. 352.
210 Newman, *Truman*, p. 37.
211 Ibid., p. 43.
212 Frank, *Downfall*, pp. 188–9.
213 Senoh, *A Boy Called H*, p. 395.
214 Newman, *Truman*, pp. 186–7.
215 Ibid., pp. 3, 186; Frank, *Downfall*, pp. 123, 163.
216 Frank, *Downfall*, p. 71.
217 Higa, *The Girl with the White Flag*, p. 71.
218 Frank, *Downfall*, p. 72.
219 Newman, *Truman*, pp. 25–6.
220 Ibid., p. 17.
221 Ibid., p. 19.
222 Ibid., p. 105; Frank, *Downfall*, pp. 271–2.
223 Frank, *Downfall*, p. 287.
224 Gibney, *Senso*, pp. 254–5.

14. The Soviet Union – Fighting on Empty

1 Kravchenko, *I Chose Freedom*, p. 413.
2 The figure of 30 million has to be calculated in a frustratingly roundabout way. There are no accurate figures for death tolls. Instead it is based on a projection forward from the 1939 population census figures to 1941 and a projection backwards from the 1959 census to 1946, to estimate pre- and post-war population figures. Then, allowing for what would have been a normal 2.5 per cent annual increase in population, the demographers calculate that 28–30 million people were missing in 1946. Linz, 'World War II and Soviet economic growth', p. 18; Wheatcroft and Davies, 'Population', pp. 77–80; Barber and Harrison, *The Soviet Home Front*, pp. ix, 40–42; Ellman and Maksudov, 'Soviet deaths', pp. 671–8.
3 Nine million of the estimated 28–30 million dead are accounted for by the military. The causes of death for the 19–21 million Soviet civilians were many. In

the German-occupied areas of the Soviet Union at least 1 million Soviet Jews were murdered, other Soviets died in German prisons and concentration camps or as a result of mass shootings of civilians, yet more died while fighting the Germans as partisans or working as forced labour in German industry. Then there were those who starved to death as a result of the Hunger Plan. In the unoccupied areas of the Soviet Union the figure encompasses those who died in Soviet gulags and forced labour camps and those killed by enemy bombing (estimated at 500,000). Wheatcroft and Davies, 'Population', p. 79; Overy, *Russia's War*, p. 89.

4 Wheatcroft and Davies, 'Population', p. 79.
5 Bacon, *The Gulag at War*, p. 139.
6 Kravchenko, *I Chose Freedom*, p. 413.
7 Moskoff, *The Bread of Affliction*, p. 37.
8 Miller, 'Impact and aftermath of World War II', p. 284.
9 Merridale, *Ivan's War*, p. 88.
10 Moskoff, *The Bread of Affliction*, pp. 113–15.
11 Harvard Project on the Soviet Social System, Schedule A, Vol. 9, Case 118, pp. 34–5.
12 Ibid., p. 38.
13 Merridale, *Ivan's War*, p. 3.
14 Moskoff, *The Bread of Affliction*, p. 113.
15 Ibid., p. 127; War Office, *Record of Ration Scales*, p. 12.
16 Dunn, *The Soviet Economy*, pp. 56–7.
17 Merridale, *Ivan's War*, p. 120.
18 Harvard Project on the Soviet Social System, Schedule A, Vol. 27, Case 528, p. 11.
19 Merridale, *Ivan's War*, pp. 147–8.
20 Ibid., p. 120.
21 Dunn, *The Soviet Economy*, p. 201.
22 Ibid., p. 197.
23 Harvard Project on the Soviet Social System, Schedule A, Vol. 9, Case 118, pp. 37–8.
24 Moskoff, *The Bread of Affliction*, p. 127.
25 Braithwaite, *Moscow 1941*, p. 324.
26 Moskoff, *The Bread of Affliction*, pp. 123–4.
27 Bellamy, *Absolute War*, p. 525.
28 Ibid.
29 Beevor, *Stalingrad*, p. 155.
30 Moskoff, *The Bread of Affliction*, p. 125.
31 Beevor, *Stalingrad*, p. 280.
32 Steinhoff et al., *Voices*, p. 129.
33 Overy, *Why the Allies Won*, p. 82.

34 Beevor, *Stalingrad*, p. 335.
35 Harvard Project on the Soviet Social System, Schedule A, Vol. 30, Case 641, p. 17.
36 Ibid.
37 Ibid.
38 Merridale, *Ivan's War*, p. 205.
39 Moskoff, *The Bread of Affliction*, p. 131.
40 Simmons and Perlina, *Writing the Siege of Leningrad*, p. 198.
41 Ibid.
42 Fitzpatrick, *Everyday Stalinism*, p. 40.
43 Helmut Geidel, interviewed January 2007.
44 Merridale, *Ivan's War*, p. 98.
45 Bartov, *Hitler's Army*, pp. 7, 26.
46 Steinhoff et al., *Voices*, p. 214.
47 Merridale, *Ivan's War*, p. 5.
48 Harvard Project on the Soviet Social System, Schedule A, Vol. 30, Case 641, p. 35.
49 Trentmann, 'Coping with shortage', p. 24.
50 Harvard Project on the Soviet Social System, Schedule A, Vol. 33, Case 454, pp. 24–5.
51 Fitzpatrick, *Everyday Stalinism*, p. 41.
52 Braithwaite, *Moscow 1941*, p. 27.
53 Overy, *Why the Allies Won*, p. 181.
54 Erickson, 'Soviet women at war', p. 54; Overy, *Russia's War*, p. 170.
55 Two million shells were produced against a target of 6 million. Dunn, *The Soviet Economy*, pp. 33, 36.
56 'Production of shoes dropped from 211 million pairs in 1940 to only 63 million pairs in 1945.' Dunn, *The Soviet Economy*, p. 31.
57 Barber and Harrison, *The Soviet Home Front*, pp. 78–9, 132–4.
58 Kravchenko, *I Chose Freedom*, p. 388.
59 Sakharov, *Memoirs*, pp. 47–8.
60 Rush, Memoir, NLA MS 8316, pp. 177–8.
61 Ibid., pp. 178–9.
62 Braithwaite, *Moscow 1941*, p. 339.
63 Kravchenko, *I Chose Freedom*, p. 388.
64 Barber and Harrison, *The Soviet Home Front*, pp. 204–5.
65 Harrison, *Accounting for War*, p. 170.
66 Barber and Harrison, *The Soviet Home Front*, p. 144.
67 Moskoff, *The Bread of Affliction*, p. 2.
68 Ibid., p. 138.
69 Harvard Project on the Soviet Social System, Schedule A, Vol. 15, Case 305, p. 75.

70 Harrison, 'The Second World War', p. 266.

71 Barber and Harrison, *The Soviet Home Front*, p. 81.

72 Moskoff, *The Bread of Affliction*, p. 149.

73 Ibid.

74 Erickson, 'Soviet women at war', p. 53.

75 Keyssar and Pozner, *Remembering War*, p. 92.

76 Bidlack, 'Survival strategies in Leningrad', p. 93.

77 Barber and Harrison, *The Soviet Home Front*, p. 173.

78 Sakharov, *Memoirs*, pp. 52–3.

79 Ibid., p. 53.

80 Ibid.

81 Moskoff, *The Bread of Affliction*, p. 142.

82 Tuyll, *Feeding the Bear*, p. 138.

83 Harrison, 'The Second World War', pp. 262–3.

84 Overy, *Russia's War*, p. 226.

85 Moskoff, *The Bread of Affliction*, pp. 227–8.

86 Tolley, *Caviar and Commissars*, p. 115.

87 Ibid.

88 Tuyll, *Feeding the Bear*, p. 65.

89 The maximum number of German divisions fighting in Italy never reached thirty. Ron Klages and John Mulholland, 'Number of German divisions by front in World War II', *Axis History Factbook*, http://www.axishistory.com/index.php?id=7288.

90 Barber and Harrison, *The Soviet Home Front*, pp. 159–60.

91 Overy, *Russia's War*, p. 329.

92 Barber and Harrison, *The Soviet Home Front*, pp. 159–60, 186, 204–5.

93 Bacon, *The Gulag at War*, p. 137.

94 Barber and Harrison, *The Soviet Home Front*, pp. 164–5.

95 Harvard Project on the Soviet Social System, Schedule A, Vol. 27, Case 524, pp. 13–15.

96 Kravchenko, *I Chose Freedom*, p. 413.

97 Ibid., p. 389.

98 Ibid., p. 401.

99 Ibid., p. 413.

100 Ibid., p. 414.

101 Ibid., p. 394.

102 Ibid., p. 397. Barber and Harrison, *The Soviet Home Front*, p. 111.

103 Fenby, *Alliance*, p. 21.

104 Fitzpatrick, *Everyday Stalinism*, pp. 54–6.

105 Kravchenko, *I Chose Freedom*, p. 412.

106 Barber and Harrison, *The Soviet Home Front*, pp. 83–4.

107 Erickson, 'Soviet women at war', p. 57.

108 Moskoff, *The Bread of Affliction*, p. 145.

109 Ibid., p. 222.

110 Sakharov, *Memoirs*, p. 53.

111 Bidlack, 'Survival strategies in Leningrad', p. 96.

112 Keyssar and Pozner, *Remembering War*, p. 94.

113 Davies et al., *The Economic Transformation*, p. 263.

114 Goldberg, 'Intake and energy requirements', p. 2095.

115 Bidlack, 'Survival strategies in Leningrad', pp. 92, 95; Macintyre, 'Famine and the female mortality advantage', p. 250.

116 Moskoff, *The Bread of Affliction*, p. 37.

117 Overy, *Why the Allies Won*, p. 183.

118 Merridale, *Ivan's War*, pp. 138–9; Overy, *Russia's War*, pp. 188–92.

119 Overy, *Russia's War*, p. 191.

120 Ibid., pp. 171, 212.

121 Sajer, *The Forgotten Soldier*, p. 302.

122 Overy, *Russia's War*, pp. 193–4.

123 Ibid., p. 210.

124 Harrison, 'The Second World War', p. 244.

125 Overy, *Why the Allies Won*, p. 183.

126 Moskoff, *The Bread of Affliction*, p. 224.

127 Wettlin, *Russian Road*, p. 97.

128 Moskoff, *The Bread of Affliction.*, pp. 108–9.

129 Rush, Memoir, NLA MS 8316, p. 217.

130 Ibid., p. 218.

131 Moskoff, *The Bread of Affliction*, p. 224.

132 Wettlin, *Russian Road*, p. 87.

133 Merridale, *Ivan's War*, p. 182; Ensminger et al., *Foods and Nutrition Encyclopedia*, II, p. 2332.

134 Adamovich and Granin, *A Book of the Blockade*, pp. 53–4.

135 Barber and Harrison, *The Soviet Home Front*, pp. 83–4.

136 2 September 1944, Alexander Papers, NLA, MS2389.

137 Nove, 'Soviet peasantry in World War II', p. 85.

138 Fitzpatrick, *Everyday Stalinism*, p. 57; 16 August 1944, Alexander Papers, NLA, MS2389.

139 Barber and Harrison, *The Soviet Home Front*, p. 111.

140 Wettlin, *Russian Road*, p. 85.

141 Moskoff, *The Bread of Affliction*, p. 163.

142 Rush, Memoir, NLA MS 8316, p. 207.

143 Ibid.

144 Ibid., p. 210.

145 Ibid., p. 215.

146 Ibid., p. 216.

147 Bengelsdorf, *Die Landwirtschaft der Vereinigten Staaten*, p. 319.
148 Tuyll, *Feeding the Bear*, p. 117; Dunn, *The Soviet Economy*, pp. 86–7.
149 Volin, *A Century*, p. 293.
150 Erickson, *The Road to Berlin*, p. 84.
151 Tuyll, *Feeding the Bear*, p. 117.
152 Tolley, *Caviar and Commissars*, p. 80.
153 Dunn, *The Soviet Economy*, p. 86.
154 Rush, Memoir, NLA MS 8316, pp. 217–18.
155 Tuyll, *Feeding the Bear*, p. 83.
156 Bengelsdorf, *Die Landwirtschaft der Vereinigten Staaten*, p. 318.
157 Tuyll, *Feeding the Bear*, p. 117.
158 Harvard Project on the Soviet Social System, Schedule A, Vol. 30, Case 639, pp. 53–4.
159 Moskoff, *The Bread of Affliction*, p. 126.
160 Ibid., p. 130.
161 Ibid., p. 131.
162 Ibid., p. 130.
163 Ibid., pp. 126–8.
164 Figes, *The Whisperers*, p. 441.
165 Harvard Project on the Soviet Social System, Schedule A, Vol. 15, Case 305, pp. 71–2.
166 Ibid., p. 43.
167 Barber and Harrison, *The Soviet Home Front*, pp. 78–9.
168 Rush, Memoir, NLA MS 8316, p. 207.
169 Moskoff, *The Bread of Affliction*, pp. 230–32.
170 2 September 1944, 22 October 1944, Alexander Papers, NLA, MS2389.
171 Barber and Harrison, *The Soviet Home Front*, pp. 87–8.
172 Tolley, *Caviar and Commissars*, p. 149.
173 Wheatcroft and Davies, 'Population', p. 78.
174 Merridale, *Ivan's War*, p. 165.
175 Keyssar and Pozner, *Remembering War*, p. 62.
176 Figes, *The Whisperers*, p. 416.
177 Kravchenko, *I Chose Freedom*, p. 389.
178 Sakharov, *Memoirs*, p. 41.
179 Kravchenko, *I Chose Freedom*, p. 361.
180 Overy, *Why the Allies Won*, pp. 189–90; Barber and Harrison, *The Soviet Home Front*, p. 68.

15. Germany and Britain – Two Approaches to Entitlement

1 Curtis-Bennett, *The Food of the People*, p. 250.
2 Beevor, *Berlin*, p. 39.
3 Spiekermann, 'Brown bread for victory', p. 161.
4 Ibid.
5 Mackay, *Half the Battle*, p. 202.
6 Dewey, *War and Progress*, pp. 130, 150.
7 Laybourn, *Britain on the Breadline*, p. 61.
8 Dewey, *War and Progress*, p. 258.
9 Laybourn, *Britain on the Breadline*, p. 43.
10 Webster, 'Healthy or hungry', p. 117.
11 Ibid., pp. 118, 120.
12 Laybourn, *Britain on the Breadline*, p. 63.
13 Dewey, *War and Progress*, p. 150.
14 Mayhew, 'The 1930s nutrition controversy', p. 455.
15 Ibid., pp. 122–3.
16 Bosworth, 'Eating for the nation', p. 227.
17 Jonsson, 'Changes in food consumption', pp. 25, 40–41.
18 Laybourn, *Britain on the Breadline*, pp. 62–3.
19 Burnett, *Plenty and Want*, p. 281.
20 Orr, *As I Recall*, p. 115.
21 Mayhew, 'The 1930s nutrition controversy', pp. 457–8.
22 Webster, 'Healthy or hungry', p. 117.
23 Ibid., pp. 116–17.
24 Staples, *The Birth of Development*, pp. 72–4.
25 Crew, 'General introduction', p. 8.
26 Huegel, *Kriegsernährungswirtschaft Deutschlands*, p. 261; Berghoff, 'Methoden der Verbrauchslenkung', pp. 283, 287–8.
27 Huegel, *Kriegsernährungswirtschaft Deutschlands*, p. 285.
28 Corni, *Hitler and the Peasants*, p. 170.
29 Proctor, *The Nazi War on Cancer*, pp. 125–6.
30 Spiekermann, 'Vollkorn für die Führer', p. 94.
31 Ibid., p. 95.
32 Spiekermann, 'Brown bread for victory', pp. 150–51.
33 Ibid., p. 153.
34 Ibid., p. 151.
35 Huegel, *Kriegsernährungswirtschaft Deutschlands*, p. 287.
36 Reagin, '*Marktordnung* and autarkic housekeeping', p. 171.
37 Collins, *The Alien Years*, p. 45.
38 Ibid.

39 Gruchmann, 'Korruption', p. 576.

40 Collins, *The Alien Years*, pp. 45–6.

41 Ibid., p. 46.

42 Gordon, 'Fascism, the neo-right and gastronomy', pp. 84–5.

43 Corni, *Hitler and the Peasants*, pp. 50–3.

44 Hachtman, 'Lebenshaltungskosten', p. 50.

45 Hinze, '"Die ungewöhnlich geduldigen Deutschen"', p. 47.

46 Tooze, *The Wages of Destruction*, pp. 192–3.

47 Hachtman, 'Lebenshaltungskosten', p. 52; Baten and Wagner, 'Autarchy, market disintegration and health', p. 19.

48 Huegel, *Kriegsernährungswirtschaft Deutschlands*, p. 285.

49 Collins, *The Alien Years*, p. 26.

50 Geyer, 'Soziale Sicherheit', p. 392; Mason, *Social Policy in the Third Reich*, p. 132.

51 Tooze, *The Wages of Destruction*, p. 709.

52 Baten and Wagner, 'Autarchy, market disintegration and health', p. 22. There are historians who argue that the workers' diet improved under the National Socialists. Farquharson states that between 1934 and 1937 Germans increased their consumption of white flour, sugar and butter by almost one-quarter, and that meat consumption went up by 11 per cent. Farquharson, 'The agrarian policy', p. 244.

53 Reagin, '*Marktordnung* and autarkic housekeeping', p. 166; Baten and Wagner, 'Autarchy, market disintegration and health', p. 2.

54 Proctor, *The Nazi War on Cancer*, p. 125.

55 Haffner, *Defying Hitler*, p. 17.

56 Ibid.

57 Baten and Wagner, 'Autarchy, market disintegration and health', pp. 3–8, 22–4.

58 Gumpert, *Heil Hunger!*, p. 76.

59 On the lack of statistical information in Germany see Von der Decken, 'Die Ernährung in England und Deutschland', pp. 198–9.

60 Heim, *Kalorien, Kautschuk, Karrieren*, p. 107; Corni and Gies, *Brot, Butter, Kanonen*, p. 556.

61 Müller, 'Die Mobilisierung der deutschen Wirtschaft', p. 465.

62 Lüdtke, 'Hunger, Essens-"Genuß" und Politik', p. 124.

63 Kaplan, 'Jewish daily life', p. 397.

64 Lucia and Peter Seidel in conversation with the author.

65 Kaplan, 'Jewish daily life', p. 397.

66 Ibid., pp. 397–8.

67 Ibid., p. 404.

68 Corni and Gies, *Brot, Butter, Kanonen*, p. 565.

69 Gratzer, *Terrors of the Table*, p. 156.

70 Burleigh, *Death and Deliverance*, p. 242.
71 Ibid., p. 231.
72 Ibid., pp. 241–2.
73 Proctor, *The Nazi War on Cancer*, p. 171.
74 Addison, *Churchill*, pp. 338–9; Mackay, *Half the Battle*, p. 53.
75 Hammond, *Food and Agriculture*, pp. 19–20.
76 Oddy, *From Plain Fare*, p. 148.
77 Gardiner, *The 1940s House*, p. 125.
78 Woolton, *Memoirs*, p. 218.
79 Leff, 'The politics of sacrifice', p. 1301.
80 Waller, *London 1945*, p. 88.
81 Woolton, *Memoirs*, p. 218.
82 Garfield, *We Are at War*, pp. 80, 298–9.
83 Hammond, *Food and Agriculture*, pp. 232–3.
84 Oddy, *From Plain Fare*, pp. 142–3.
85 Woolton, *Memoirs*, p. 218.
86 Roodhouse, 'Popular morality', p. 247.
87 Burnett, *Plenty and Want*, p. 293.
88 Bird, *The First Food Empire*, p. 175.
89 Driver, *The British at Table*, p. 33.
90 Sheridan, *Wartime Women*, pp. 148–9.
91 Waller, *London 1945*, p. 198.
92 Garfield, *Private Battles*, p. 290.
93 Zweiniger-Bargielowska, *Austerity in Britain*, p. 74.
94 Don Joseph, comments to http://www.woodlands-junior.kent.sch.uk/Home word/war/rationing.htm.
95 Hardyment, *Slice of Life*, p. 8.
96 Burnett, *Plenty and Want*, p. 293.
97 Doreen Laven, notes on wartime memories.
98 Burnett, *Plenty and Want*, p. 295.
99 Woolton, *Memoirs*, p. 212.
100 Mackay, *Half the Battle*, p. 201.
101 Burnett, *Plenty and Want*, p. 292.
102 Mackay, *Half the Battle*, p. 202.
103 Müller, 'Die Mobilisierung der deutschen Wirtschaft', p. 469; Corni and Gies, *Brot, Butter, Kanonen*, p. 556.
104 Dörr, "*Wer die Zeit nicht miterlebt hat . . .*", II, p. 11.
105 Corni and Gies, *Brot, Butter, Kanonen*, p. 559.
106 Stephenson, *Hitler's Home Front*, p. 202.
107 Rüther, *Köln*, p. 66.
108 Müller, 'Die Mobilisierung der deutschen Wirtschaft', p. 465.
109 Fritz, *Frontsoldaten*, p. 26.

110 Müller, 'Die Mobilisierung der deutschen Wirtschaft', pp. 472–3.

111 Werner, *"Bleib übrig!"*, p. 47.

112 Ibid., p. 56.

113 Ibid., pp. 127–8.

114 Ibid., p. 48.

115 Ibid., p. 128.

116 Müller, 'Die Mobilisierung der deutschen Wirtschaft', p. 468.

117 Werner, *"Bleib übrig!"*, pp. 126–7.

118 Herbert, *Hitler's Foreign Workers*, p. 158.

119 Geyer, 'Soziale Sicherheit', p. 406.

120 Kraut and Bramsel, 'Der Calorienbedarf der Berufe'.

121 Michaelis, 'Über die Wirkung'; Droese, 'Experimentalle Untersuchung'; Droese, 'Die Wirkung von Traubenzucker'; Neumann, 'Nutritional physiology', p. 56.

122 Proctor, *The Nazi War on Cancer*, p. 156.

123 Tooze, *The Wages of Destruction*, p. 517.

124 Ibid., p. 540.

125 Gratzer, *Terrors of the Table*, p. 156.

126 Tooze, *The Wages of Destruction*, p. 540.

127 Herbert, *Hitler's Foreign Workers*, p. 172.

128 Ibid., p. 387.

129 Lammers, 'Levels of collaboration', p. 53.

130 Herbert, *Hitler's Foreign Workers*, p. 183.

131 Scharf, *"Man machte mit uns, was man wollte"*, pp. 118–19.

132 Herbert, *Hitler's Foreign Workers*, p. 85.

133 Levi, *If This is a Man*, p. 80.

134 Obenaus, 'Hunger und Überleben', p. 374.

135 Tooze, *The Wages of Destruction*, pp. 622–3; Evans, *The Third Reich at War*, pp. 664–5.

136 Kopke, 'Der "Ernährungsinspekteur der Waffen-SS"', p. 213.

137 Ibid., p. 215.

138 Ibid., p. 216; Schmidt, *Karl Brandt*, p. 262.

139 The papers of R. P. Evans, Department of Documents, IWM, p. 33.

140 Ibid.

141 Ibid., pp. 38–9.

142 Tooze, *The Wages of Destruction*, p. 194.

143 Roodhouse, 'Popular morality', p. 248.

144 Stephenson, *Hitler's Home Front*, pp. 212–15.

145 Ibid., p. 209.

146 Roodhouse, 'Popular morality', p. 256.

147 Hodgson, *Few Eggs*, p. 119.

148 Dörr, *"Wer die Zeit nicht miterlebt hat . . ."*, II, p. 19.

149 Roodhouse, 'Popular morality', p. 252.

150 Ibid., p. 259.

151 Mackay, *Half the Battle*, p. 200.

152 Ibid., pp. 254–5.

153 Vassiltchikov, *The Berlin Diaries*, p. 42.

154 Evans, *The Third Reich at War*, p. 510; Proctor, *The Nazi War on Cancer*, p. 140; Gordon, 'Fascism, the neo-right and gastronomy', p. 88.

155 Picker, *Hitlers Tischgespräche*, p. 53.

156 Proctor, *The Nazi War on Cancer*, pp. 134–7.

157 Gruchmann, 'Korruption', p. 578.

158 Ibid., pp. 573–4.

159 Ibid., p. 574.

160 Ibid., pp. 585–8.

161 Müller, 'Albert Speer und die Rüstungspolitik', p. 495.

162 Picker, *Hitlers Tischgespräche*, p. 380.

163 Werner, *"Bleib übrig!"*, p. 204.

164 Dörr, *"Wer die Zeit nicht miterlebt hat . . .",* II, p. 23.

165 Werner, *"Bleib übrig!"*, p. 201.

166 Erker, *Ernährungskrise und Nachkriegsgesellschaft*, p. 24.

167 Werner, *"Bleib übrig!"*, pp. 202–3.

168 Beck, *Under the Bombs*, p. 11.

169 Stephenson, *Hitler's Home Front*, p. 184.

170 Corni and Gies, *Brot, Butter, Kanonen*, p. 572.

171 Ibid., p. 567.

172 Beck, *Under the Bombs*, p. 45.

173 Corni and Gies, *Brot, Butter, Kanonen*, pp. 566–7.

174 Bannister, *I Lived Under Hitler*, pp. 104–5.

175 Ibid., pp. 141–2.

176 Ibid., p. 157.

177 Müller, 'Albert Speer und die Rüstungspolitik', p. 491.

178 Rüther, *Köln*, p. 372; Werner, *"Bleib übrig!"*, p. 216.

179 Stephenson, *Hitler's Home Front*, pp. 188, 191.

180 Corni and Gies, *Brot, Butter, Kanonen*, p. 563.

181 Bannister, *I Lived Under Hitler*, p. 220.

182 Beck, *Under the Bombs*, p. 100.

183 Kitchen, *Nazi Germany at War*, p. 82.

184 Huegel, *Kriegsernährungswirtschaft Deutschlands*, p. 311.

185 Dörr, *"Wer die Zeit nicht miterlebt hat . . .",* II, p. 17.

186 Ibid., II, p. 27.

187 Ibid., II, p. 29.

16. The British Empire – War as Welfare

1 Woolton, *Memoirs*, pp. 192–3.
2 Hicks, *"Who Called the Cook a Bastard?"*, p. 83.
3 Oddy, *From Plain Fare*, p. 136.
4 Ibid., pp. 136–7.
5 Mackay, *Half the Battle*, p. 61.
6 Ibid., p. 74.
7 Ashwell, *McCance and Widdowson*, p. 23.
8 Ibid.
9 Ibid., pp. 24–5.
10 Oddy, *From Plain Fare*, p. 137.
11 Wilt, *Food for War*, p. 219.
12 Hammond, *Food and Agriculture*, p. 155; Britnell and Voake, *Canadian Agriculture*, p. 367.
13 Driver, *The British at Table*, p. 12.
14 Burnett, *Plenty and Want*, p. 282.
15 Ibid., p. 281.
16 Buss, 'The British diet', p. 124.
17 Spiekermann, 'Brown bread for victory', p. 163.
18 Oddy, *From Plain Fare*, pp. 138–9.
19 Ibid., p. 140; Burnett, *Plenty and Want*, p. 291.
20 Hammond, *Food and Agriculture*, p. 230.
21 Ashwell, *McCance and Widdowson*, p. 25.
22 Oddy, *From Plain Fare*, p. 162.
23 Burnett, *Plenty and Want*, p. 291.
24 Gardiner, *The 1940s House*, p. 140.
25 The papers of A. W. Winter, Department of Documents, IWM, III, p. 12.
26 Hammond, *Food and Agriculture*, pp. 155–6.
27 Longmate, *How We Lived Then*, p. 145.
28 Gardiner, *The 1940s House*, pp. 141–2.
29 Garfield, *Private Battles*, p. 87.
30 Brassley and Potter, 'A view from the top', pp. 226–7.
31 Oddy, *From Plain Fare*, p. 153.
32 Hardyment, *Slice of Life*, p. 17.
33 Gardiner, *The 1940s House*, p. 136.
34 Patten, *Victory Cookbook*, n.p.
35 Gardiner, *The 1940s House*, p. 138.
36 Waller, *London 1945*, p. 51.
37 Garfield, *Private Battles*, p. 338.
38 Britnell and Voake, *Canadian Agriculture*, p. 367.

39 Driver, *The British at Table*, p. 26.

40 Zweineger-Bargielowska, 'Rationing', p. 179.

41 Gardiner, *The 1940s House*, p. 133.

42 Hammond, *Food and Agriculture*, p. 183.

43 Oddy, *From Plain Fare*, p. 154.

44 Hammond, *Food and Agriculture*, p. 183.

45 Mant, *All Muck*, p. 39. Prisoners of war engaged in manual work were allocated the daily 3,300 calorie army home service ration. War Office, *Record of Ration Scales*, p. 12.

46 Waugh, *Brideshead Revisited*, Preface, p. 42.

47 Zweiniger-Bargielowska, *Austerity in Britain*, p. 71.

48 Mackay, *Half the Battle*, p. 204.

49 Ibid., p. 203. For a discussion of the limits of the levelling-up thesis see Summer-field, 'The "levelling of class"' and Fielding, 'The Good War'.

50 Oddy, *From Plain Fare*, p. 164.

51 Essemyr, 'Food policies in Sweden', p. 171.

52 Darian-Smith, *On the Home Front*, p. 39.

53 Santich, *What the Doctors Ordered*, p. 120.

54 Ibid.; Darian-Smith, *On the Home Front*, p. 48.

55 Britnell and Voake, *Canadian Agriculture*, pp. 150–51.

56 Magnússon, *The Hidden Class*, p. 132; Jonsson, 'Changes in food consumption', p. 41.

57 Webster, 'Healthy or hungry', p. 121.

58 Hammond, *Food and Agriculture*, p. 143.

59 Woolton, *Memoirs*, pp. 34–5.

60 Hammond, *Food and Agriculture*, pp. 144–5.

61 Burnett, *Plenty and Want*, p. 292.

62 Mackay, *Half the Battle*, p. 240.

63 Hammond, *Food and Agriculture*, p. 149; Mackay, *Half the Battle*, p. 242.

64 Maggie Hay in conversation with the author.

65 Burnett, 'The rise and decline of school meals', p. 55.

66 Ibid., p. 65.

67 Oddy, *From Plain Fare*, pp. 165, 209.

68 Jeffreys, 'British politics and social policy', p. 129.

69 Hardyment, *Slice of Life*, p. 3.

70 Burnett, 'The rise and decline of school meals', pp. 65–6.

71 Taylor, *English History*, p. 567.

72 Burnett and Oddy, 'Introduction', pp. 5–6.

73 Harris, 'Great Britain', p. 242.

74 The papers of R. P. Evans, Department of Documents, IWM, p. 21.

75 The papers of R. B. Buckle, Department of Documents, IWM, p. 16.

76 Garfield, *Private Battles*, p. 61.

77 Bruce, *War on the Ground*, p. 27.
78 War Office, *Record of Ration Scales*, p. 3.
79 Reynolds, *Rich Relations*, p. 137.
80 Ibid., p. 69.
81 Crang, 'The British soldier', p. 62.
82 Garfield, *Private Battles*, p. 61.
83 Crew, *The Royal Army Service Corps*, p. 186; Bird, *The First Food Empire*, p. 176.
84 The papers of Fus. H. Simons, 'Army Cookery Notebook, 1944', Department of Documents, IWM, Misc 180 Item 2726.
85 Crang, 'The British soldier', p. 131.
86 Hicks, *"Who Called the Cook a Bastard?"*, pp. 31–3.
87 Ibid., pp. 44–5.
88 Ibid., pp. 38–9.
89 Ibid., p. 73.
90 Beaumont, 'Australia's war: Europe and the Middle East', pp. 17–18; Jackson, *The British Empire*, p. 2.
91 The papers of G. R. Page, Department of Documents, IWM, p. 30.
92 Crimp, *The Diary of a Desert Rat*, pp. 20–21.
93 Bierman and Smith, *Alamein*, p. 151.
94 Crimp, *The Diary of a Desert Rat*, pp. 38–9.
95 Bierman and Smith, *Alamein*, pp. 151–2.
96 Levenstein, *Paradox of Plenty*, p. 93.
97 Jackson, *Botswana*, p. 76.
98 The papers of G. R. Page, Department of Documents, IWM, p. 30.
99 Lloyd, *Food and Inflation*, pp. 273–7; Bayly, 'Spunyarns', p. 33.
100 Jackson, *The British Empire*, p. 105.
101 Collier, 'The logistics of the North African campaign', pp. 202–3.
102 The papers of G. R. Page, Department of Documents, IWM, p. 47.
103 Ibid.
104 Walker, *The Clinical Problems of War*, p. 321; Bullard, '"The great enemy"', pp. 219–20.
105 Brune, *Those Ragged Bloody Heroes*, p. 45.
106 Walker, 'The writers' war', pp. 149–50.
107 Brune, *Those Ragged Bloody Heroes*, p. 101; Dornan, *The Silent Men*, p. 146.
108 Richmond, *The Japanese Forces in New Guinea*, p. 369.
109 Brune, *Those Ragged Bloody Heroes*, p. 93.
110 Ibid., p. 89.
111 Walker, *The Clinical Problems of War*, p. 321.
112 Beaumont, 'Australia's war: Asia and the Pacific', p. 40.
113 Ibid.; Drea, *In the Service of the Emperor*, p. 70.
114 Walker, *The Island Campaigns*, p. 229.

115 Ibid., p. 227.

116 *The Australian Army at War*, p. 70.

117 'Appendix. Sources of Vitamin C etc.', Box 23, Folder 203, Sir Cedric Stanton Hicks Papers, NLA, MS 5623.

118 Ibid.

119 Walker, *The Island Campaigns*, p. 272.

120 Ibid., p. 270.

121 Ibid., p. 227.

122 Health and stamina of the troops. Appendix A. Explanatory Note on Blue Peas and Wheat. JAS. H. Cannan, Quartermaster General, 30 January 1943, AWM 54 351/6/2.

123 Laurence and Tiddy, *From Bully Beef*, p. 35.

124 Ibid., pp. 45–6.

125 Ibid., pp. 35–6.

126 Walker, *The Island Campaigns*, pp. 227–8.

127 Ibid., p. 270.

128 'Historical summary of the activities of Sir C. Stanton Hicks from the outbreak of war – showing the influence of applied science on army feeding', Box 23, Folder 203, Sir Cedric Stanton Hicks Papers, NLA, MS 5623.

129 Johnston, *The Australian Army*, p. 58.

130 Laurence and Tiddy, *From Bully Beef*, p. 40.

131 Ibid., p. 41.

132 Walker, *The Island Campaigns*, p. 269.

133 Ibid., p. 228.

134 Ibid., p. 227.

135 Ibid., p. 273.

136 Ibid., p. 270.

137 Australian Defence Force: Good food to stay fighting fit. http://www.dsto.defence.gov.au/research/5170/.

138 Walker, *The Clinical Problems of War*, p. 321.

139 Jackson, *Botswana*, p. 63.

140 Ibid.

141 Moharir, *History of the Army Service Corps*, p. 42; War Office, *Record of Ration Scales*, p. 58.

142 Barkawi, *Globalization and War*, p. 85.

143 MacNalty and Mellor, *Medical Services in War*, p. 745.

144 Kamtekar, 'A different war dance', pp. 190–91.

145 Bayly and Harper, *Forgotten Armies*, pp. 368, 425.

146 Moharir, *History of the Army Service Corps*, p. 45.

147 MacNalty and Mellor, *Medical Services in War*, p. 81.

148 Moharir, *History of the Army Service Corps*, p. 44.

149 Ibid., pp. 42–4; War Office, *Record of Ration Scales*, p. 62.

150 Crew, *The Royal Army Service Corps*, p. 186.
151 Australian Defence Force: Good food to stay fighting fit. http://www.dsto.
defence.gov.au/research/5170/.
152 Pollan, *In Defence of Food*, p. 8.

17. The United States – Out of Depression and into Abundance

1 Terkel, *'The Good War'*, p. 112.
2 Lamont, 'Oral histories of World War II labour corps', p. 403.
3 26 April–12 May 1945, the papers of E. Barrington, Department of Documents, IWM, 88/58/1 (P).
4 Ibid.
5 Ibid.
6 Bernstein, *A Caring Society*, p. 46.
7 Poppendieck, *Breadlines Knee-Deep in Wheat*, pp. 19–20.
8 Levenstein, *Paradox of Plenty*, pp. 58–9.
9 Levine, *School Lunch Politics*, p. 56.
10 Wynn, 'The "good war"', p. 469.
11 Jeffries, *Wartime America*, pp. 63–4.
12 Gluck, *Rosie the Riveter Revisited*, p. 189.
13 Terkel, *'The Good War'*, p. 112.
14 Ibid., pp. 316–17.
15 Levenstein, *Paradox of Plenty*, p. 87.
16 Jacobs, '"How about some meat?"', pp. 931–2.
17 Cohen, *A Consumer's Republic*, p. 70.
18 Campbell, *Women at War*, p. 183.
19 Levenstein, *Paradox of Plenty*, p. 85.
20 Campbell, *Women at War*, p. 181.
21 Levenstein, *Paradox of Plenty*, p. 88.
22 Terkel, *'The Good War'*, p. 316.
23 Reynolds, *Rich Relations*, p. 50.
24 Bentley, *Eating for Victory*, p. 62.
25 Overy, *Why the Allies Won*, p. 192.
26 Ibid., p. 198.
27 Ibid., p. 192.
28 Ibid., p. 191.
29 Ibid., p. 192.
30 Bentley, *Eating for Victory*, pp. 63–4.
31 Ibid., p. 22.
32 Levenstein, *Paradox of Plenty*, p. 65.
33 Ibid., p. 66.
34 Levine, *School Lunch Politics*, p. 64.

35 Ibid., pp. 64–5.
36 Campbell, *Women at War*, pp. 183–4.
37 Leff, 'The politics of sacrifice', p. 1310.
38 Levenstein, *Paradox of Plenty*, p. 76.
39 Goodhart and Pett, 'The wartime nutrition programs', pp. 163–4.
40 Levenstein, *Paradox of Plenty*, p. 77.
41 French, *Waging War*, p. 135.
42 Ibid.
43 Levenstein, *Paradox of Plenty*, pp. 77–8.
44 Kersten, *Labor's Home Front*, p. 177.
45 Ibid., p. 175.
46 Ibid., pp. 179–80.
47 Prendergast, *For God, Country and Coca-Cola*, p. 196.
48 Proctor, *The Nazi War on Cancer*, p. 156.
49 Terkel, *'The Good War'*, p. 110.
50 Bentley, *Eating for Victory*, pp. 9–10.
51 Brandt, *Harlem at War*, p. 217.
52 Ibid., p. 73.
53 Ibid., p. 218.
54 Ibid., p. 93.
55 Kryder, *Divided Arsenal*, pp. 2–3.
56 Brandt, *Harlem at War*, p. 138.
57 Cohen, *A Consumer's Republic*, pp. 85–7.
58 Capeci, *The Harlem Riot*, pp. 64–5.
59 Brandt, *Harlem at War*, pp. 158–9.
60 Levine, *School Lunch Politics*, pp. 55–6.
61 Levenstein, *Paradox of Plenty*, pp. 54, 62; Poppendieck, *Breadlines Knee-Deep in Wheat*, p. 241.
62 Bengelsdorf, *Die Landwirtschaft der Vereinigten Staaten*, pp. 123–4.
63 Poppendieck, *Breadlines Knee-Deep in Wheat*, p. 242.
64 Bengelsdorf, *Die Landwirtschaft der Vereinigten Staaten*, pp. 207–8.
65 Wilcox, *The Farmer*, p. 318.
66 Levine, *School Lunch Politics*, p. 51.
67 Ibid., p. 53.
68 Ibid., p. 58.
69 Ibid., pp. 68–9.
70 Ibid., p. 60.
71 Terkel, *'The Good War'*, p. 112.
72 Cohen, *A Consumer's Republic*, p. 71.
73 Terkel, *'The Good War'*, p. 487.
74 McDermott, *Women Recall the War Years*, pp. 206–7.
75 Duis, 'No time for privacy', p. 39.

76 Cohen, *A Consumer's Republic*, p. 73.

77 Bentley, *Eating for Victory*, p. 61.

78 Goodwin, *No Ordinary Time*, p. 384.

79 Garfield, *Private Battles*, p. 312.

80 Levenstein, *Paradox of Plenty*, p. 82.

81 Bentley, *Eating for Victory*, pp. 103, 109.

82 Wilcox, *The Farmer*, p. 200.

83 Levenstein, *Paradox of Plenty*, p. 82.

84 Bentley, *Eating for Victory*, p. 61.

85 Ibid., p. 10.

86 Ibid., p. 93.

87 Ibid., p. 35.

88 Campbell, *Women at War*, p. 181.

89 Matusow, *Farm Policies*, p. 49.

90 Levenstein, *Paradox of Plenty*, pp. 81–2; Bentley, *Eating for Victory*, pp. 36–7.

91 Fenby, *Alliance*, p. 21.

92 Goodwin, *No Ordinary Time*, p. 384.

93 Duis, 'No time for privacy', pp. 33–4.

94 Gluck, *Rosie the Riveter Revisited*, p. 189.

95 Westbrook, 'Fighting for the American family', p. 203.

96 Cited by Westbrook, 'Fighting for the American family', p. 204.

97 Aquila, *Home Front Soldier*, p. 63.

98 Cohen, *A Consumer's Republic*, p. 55.

99 Ibid., p. 116.

100 Ibid., p. 127.

101 Bentley, *Eating for Victory*, p. 94; Crawford et al., *Wartime Agriculture in Australia*, p. 147.

102 Milward, *War, Economy and Society*, p. 288; Tooze, *The Wages of Destruction*, p. 361.

103 Levenstein, *Paradox of Plenty*, pp. 94–5.

104 The papers of R. B. Buckle, Department of Documents, IWM, pp. 52–5.

105 Kennett, *G.I.*, p. 99.

106 Reynolds, *Rich Relations*, p. 73.

107 Ross and Romanus, *The Quartermaster Corps*, p. 485.

108 Reynolds, *Rich Relations*, p. 80.

109 Ibid., p. 81.

110 Collier, 'Logistics', pp. 5–6.

111 Reynolds, *Rich Relations*, p. 81.

112 *Adapting Livestock Products to War Needs*, p. 14.

113 Levenstein, *Paradox of Plenty*, p. 90.

114 Wilson, 'Who fought and why?', p. 302.

115 Levenstein, *Paradox of Plenty*, p. 90.

116 Ross and Romanus, *The Quartermaster Corps*, p. 136.

117 Stauffer, *The Quartermaster Corps*, p. 67.

118 Levenstein, *Paradox of Plenty*, p. 91.

119 Cited by Potts and Potts, *Yanks*, pp. 289–90.

120 US War Department, *Handbook*, pp. 298–9, 537.

121 Merridale, *Ivan's War*, p. 120.

122 William H. Bauer, Interview, 7 October 1994, Rutgers Oral History Archives, New Brunswick History Department, http://oralhistory.rutgers.edu/Interviews.

123 Reynolds, *Rich Relations*, p. 77.

124 Levine, *School Lunch Politics*, p. 69; Levenstein, *Paradox of Plenty*, p. 93.

125 Bentley, *Eating for Victory*, pp. 82–3.

126 Prendergast, *For God, Country and Coca-Cola*, p. 196.

127 Ibid., p. 197.

128 Ibid., pp. 512–13.

129 Mintz, *Tasting Food*, p. 27.

130 Prendergast, *For God, Country and Coca-Cola*, p. 203.

131 Mintz, *Tasting Food*, p. 27.

132 Prendergast, *For God, Country and Coca-Cola*, p. 206.

133 Mintz, *Tasting Food*, p. 28.

134 Prendergast, *For God, Country and Coca-Cola*, p. 194.

135 Ross and Romanus, *The Quartermaster Corps*, p. 485.

136 Risch, *The Quartermaster Corps*, p. 55.

137 Ibid., p. 196.

138 Ross and Romanus, *The Quartermaster Corps*, p. 131.

139 Risch, *The Quartermaster Corps*, p. 182.

140 Ross and Romanus, *The Quartermaster Corps*, p. 131.

141 Ibid.

142 Risch, *The Quartermaster Corps*, p. 187.

143 US War Department, *Handbook*, p. 299.

144 Richmond, *The Japanese Forces in New Guinea*, pp. 28–9, 35–6.

145 Ellis, *Sharp End of War*, p. 280.

146 Kennett, *G.I.*, p. 100.

147 Ellis, *The Sharp End of War*, p. 288.

148 Ross and Romanus, *The Quartermaster Corps*, p. 132.

149 Ibid., pp. 485–6.

150 Ibid., p. 129.

151 Ibid., p. 133.

152 Ibid., p. 490.

153 Katarzyna Cwiertka, 'Feeding the troops in the Pacific and the Korean War', talk given to the East Asian Studies seminar, Cambridge, 10 November 2008.

154 Beaumont, 'Australia's war: Europe and the Middle East', pp. 9, 47.

155 Potts and Potts, *Yanks*, pp. 14–15.

156 Mellor, *The Role of Science and Industry*, pp. 609–10.

157 Stauffer, *The Quartermaster Corps*, p. 48.

158 Freeman, 'Australian universities at war', p. 123.

159 *Forty Facts about Australia's Wartime Agriculture*.

160 Mellor, *The Role of Science and Industry*, p. 573; Butlin and Schedvin, *War Economy*, pp. 196–7.

161 Mellor, *The Role of Science and Industry*, p. 582.

162 Ibid.

163 Ibid., p. 586.

164 Ibid., p. 587.

165 Ibid., p. 596.

166 Ibid., pp. 589–90.

167 *Forty Facts about Australia's Wartime Agriculture*, n.p.

168 Cramp, 'Food – the first munition of war', p. 76.

169 Cited by Potts and Potts, *Yanks*, p. 247.

170 Mellor, *The Role of Science and Industry*, p. 592.

171 Ibid., p. 598.

172 Ibid., pp. 596–7; Stauffer, *The Quartermaster Corps*, pp. 103–8.

173 Potts and Potts, *Yanks*, p. 247; *Forty Facts about Australia's Wartime Agriculture*, n.p.

174 Mellor, *The Role of Science and Industry*, pp. 599–600; Crawford et al., *Wartime Agriculture in Australia*, p. 153.

175 Cited by Potts and Potts, *Yanks*, p. 88.

176 Cramp, 'Food – the first munition of war', p. 74. Australians ate 17 lbs of pork while Americans ate 63 lbs.

177 Potts and Potts, *Yanks*, p. 15.

178 Laurence and Tiddy, *From Bully Beef*, p. 43.

179 Potts and Potts, *Yanks*, p. 288.

180 Cited in ibid., p. 87.

181 Ibid., p. 245.

182 Ibid., p. 156; Bosworth, 'Eating for the nation', p. 228.

183 Bosworth, 'Eating for the nation', pp. 231–2.

184 Potts and Potts, *Yanks*, p. 243.

185 Ibid., p. 258.

186 Houldsworth, *The Morning Side of the Hill*, p. 137.

187 Ibid., p. 170.

188 Ibid.

189 Ibid., p. 177.

190 Ibid., p. 175.

191 Potts and Potts, *Yanks*, p. 264.

192 'Food requirements for the Allied fighting forces', Dept. of Defence, ANA,

Series A816/1 File no: 42/301/397; 'Food requirements of the Allied fighting forces and ration supply – United States Forces', ANA, Series A5954/69 File no: 291/6.

193 Potts and Potts, *Yanks*, p. 287.

194 Reynolds, *Rich Relations*, p. 148.

195 War Office, *Record of Ration Scales*, pp. 3–4, 11.

196 Reynolds, *Rich Relations*, pp. 148–9.

197 Stauffer, *The Quartermaster Corps*, p. 113.

198 Ibid., pp. 110–11.

199 Ibid., p. 110.

200 Sledge, *With the Old Breed*, p. 32.

201 Ibid.

202 Stauffer, *The Quartermaster Corps*, pp. 49–53, 96–7.

203 Ibid., p. 191.

204 Ibid., pp. 182–9.

205 Ibid., p. 192. Other causes of wastage were 'losses at sea, pilferage, enemy action, operational movements, extra issues, and . . . errors in distribution'. Ross and Romanus, *The Quartermaster Corps*, p. 136.

206 Stauffer, *The Quartermaster Corps*, pp. 193, 196.

207 Ibid., pp. 194–5.

208 Ibid., p. 199.

209 Italics added. Hastings, *Nemesis*, pp. 56–7.

210 Cited by Reynolds, *Rich Relations*, pp. 67–8.

211 Cook and Cook, *Japan at War*, p. 280.

212 Harries and Harries, *Soldiers of the Sun*, p. 314.

213 McQuarrie, *Strategic Atolls*, p. 28.

214 Ibid., pp. 26–30.

215 Lindstrom and White, 'War stories', p. 4.

216 McQuarrie, *Strategic Atolls*, p. xiv.

217 Denoon, *The Cambridge History*, p. 312.

218 Kahn and Sexton, 'The fresh and the canned', p. 11.

219 McQuarrie, *Strategic Atolls*, p. 31.

220 Ibid., pp. 40–41.

221 Ibid., pp. 32–3.

222 Ibid., p. 35.

223 White et al., *The Big Death*, p. 211.

224 Lindstrom and White, 'War stories', p. 10.

225 Kahn and Sexton, 'The fresh and the canned', p. 6.

226 Denoon, *The Cambridge History of the Pacific Islanders*, p. 315.

227 McQuarrie, *Strategic Atolls*, p. 145.

228 Ibid., p. 153.

229 Bindon, 'Breadfruit', p. 50.

230 Franco, 'Samoan representations', p. 375.
231 Ibid., p. 379.
232 Ibid., p. 386.
233 Ibid., p. 385.
234 Bindon, 'Taro or rice', p. 64.
235 Neubarth, *Dental Conditions*, p. 1.
236 Bindon, 'Taro or rice', p. 76.
237 Ibid., pp. 66–7.
238 Malcolm, *Diet and Nutrition*, n.p.
239 McQuarrie, *Conflict in Kiribati*, p. 149.
240 Nero, 'Time of famine', pp. 119, 122.
241 Ibid., p. 120.
242 Ibid., p. 129.
243 Ibid., pp. 129–30.
244 Ibid., pp. 132–3.
245 Counts, 'Shadows of war', p. 203.
246 Nero, 'Time of famine', p. 141.
247 Ibid., p. 132.
248 Stanner, *The South Seas*, p. 326.
249 Weeks, 'The United States occupation', p. 415.
250 Nero, 'Time of famine', p. 142.
251 Lindstrom and White, 'War stories', pp. 26–7; Franco, 'Samoan representations', pp. 373–4.
252 Stanner, *The South Seas*, p. 328.
253 Kahn and Sexton, 'The fresh and the canned', pp. 12–13.
254 Weeks, 'The United States occupation', p. 425.
255 Prendergast, *For God, Country and Coca-Cola*, pp. 208–9.
256 Kahn and Sexton, 'The fresh and the canned', p. 6.
257 Coyne, *The Effect of Urbanisation*, p. 18.
258 Blum, *V Was for Victory*, p. 67.
259 Reynolds, *Rich Relations*, p. 88.
260 Ibid.
261 Helmut Geidel, interviewed January 2007.
262 Gibney, *Senso*, p. 145.
263 Ibid., p. 146.
264 Sledge, *With the Old Breed*, pp. 31–2.
265 Stauffer, *The Quartermaster Corps*, pp. 13–14; Bird, *American POWs of World War II*, pp. 4–5.
266 Frank, *Downfall*, p. 160.
267 Reynolds, *Rich Relations*, p. 69.
268 Harrison, 'The Second World War', p. 240.
269 Harris, 'Great Britain', pp. 244–45.

270 Overy, *Why the Allies Won*, p. 321.
271 Frank, *Downfall*, p. 345.

PART IV THE AFTERMATH

18. A Hungry World

1 Harvard Project on the Soviet Social System, Schedule A, Vol. 30, Case 639, p. 8.
2 Bentley, *Eating for Victory*, p. 143.
3 Dower, *Embracing Defeat*, p. 93.
4 Bengelsdorf, *Die Landwirtschaft der Vereinigten Staaten*, pp. 273–4; Erker, *Ernährungskrise und Nachkriegsgesellschaft*, p. 49.
5 Trittel, 'Hungerkrise und kollektiver Protest', pp. 382–3.
6 Black, *A Cause for Our Times*, pp. 23–4, 28.
7 Tooze, *The Wages of Destruction*, p. 673.
8 Cited by Black, *A Cause for Our Times*, p. 3.
9 Dower, *Embracing Defeat*, pp. 45–7; Frank, *Downfall*, p. 334.
10 Duigan and Gann, *The Rebirth of the West*, pp. 23–4.
11 Teruko Blair, interviewed March 2006.
12 Kennedy, 'Herbert Hoover', p. 101.
13 Bengelsdorf, *Die Landwirtschaft der Vereinigten Staaten*, p. 270; Kratoska, 'Malayan food shortages', p. 109; Kurasawa, 'Transportation and rice distribution', p. 58.
14 Bentley, *Eating for Victory*, p. 144.
15 Gold, *Wartime Economic Planning*, p. 458.
16 Bentley, *Eating for Victory*, p. 144.
17 Gold, *Wartime Economic Planning*, p. 458.
18 Eastman, *Seeds of Destruction*, pp. 72–3.
19 Medvedev, *Soviet Agriculture*, p. 135.
20 Smith, *The War's Long Shadow*, p. 171.
21 Harvard Project on the Soviet Social System, Schedule A, Vol. 30, Case 639, p. 8.
22 Ibid., pp. 56–7.
23 Zubkova, *Russia after the War*, p. 38.
24 Harvard Project on the Soviet Social System, Schedule B, Vol. 13, Case 645, pp. 3, 18–19; ibid., Schedule A, Vol. 30, Case 641, pp. 42–3; ibid., Schedule A, Vol. 29, Case 623, p. 34.
25 Medvedev, *Soviet Agriculture*, pp. 137–8.
26 Volin, *A Century*, pp. 302–3.
27 Zubkova, *Russia after the War*, pp. 40–41.
28 Ibid., pp. 48–9.

29 Medvedev, *Soviet Agriculture*, pp. 132–4.

30 Harvard Project on the Soviet Social System, Schedule A, Vol. 5, Case 62, pp. 14–15.

31 Zubkova, *Russia after the War*, pp. 41–2, 47.

32 Farquharson, *The Western Allies*, p. 243.

33 Hollingsworth, 'Rationing', p. 261.

34 Kroen, 'Negotiations', pp. 263–4.

35 Oddy, *From Plain Fare*, p. 166; Zweiniger-Bargielowska, 'Rationing', p. 179.

36 Doreen Laven, notes on wartime memories.

37 Driver, *The British at Table*, p. 40.

38 Calvin Trillin, 'Dissed fish. The strange attraction of snoek', *New Yorker*, 6 September 2004, p. 86.

39 Driver, *The British at Table*, p. 41.

40 Zweiniger-Bargielowska, 'Rationing', p. 181.

41 Panter-Downes, *One Fine Day*, p. 15.

42 Zweiniger-Bargielowska, *Austerity in Britain*, pp. 3–4.

43 Duigan and Gann, *The Rebirth of the West*, p. 109.

44 Ibid., pp. 109–10.

45 Hans-Ulrich Wehler, interviewed February 2004.

46 Dower, *Embracing Defeat*, p. 110.

47 Prendergast, *For God, Country and Coca-Cola*, p. 211.

48 Wagenleitner, *Coca-Colonization*, p. 277.

49 Pells, 'American culture abroad', p. 77.

50 Terkel, *'The Good War'*, pp. 206–7.

51 Cited by Bentley, *Eating for Victory*, p. 170.

19. A World of Plenty

1 Matusow, *Farm Policies*, p. 3.

2 Bentley, *Eating for Victory*, p. 143.

3 Gold, *Wartime Economic Planning*, p. 457.

4 Kennedy, 'Herbert Hoover', p. 98.

5 Matusow, *Farm Policies*, p. 18.

6 Perkins, *Geopolitics*, p. 127; Wilcox, *The Farmer*, p. 279.

7 Gold, *Wartime Economic Planning*, pp. 444–5.

8 Ibid., pp. 435–6.

9 Matusow, *Farm Policies*, p. 8.

10 Bentley, *Eating for Victory*, pp. 146, 157.

11 Ibid., p. 144.

12 Gold, *Wartime Economic Planning*, p. 450.

13 Miller, *Call of Duty*, p. 120.

14 Matusow, *Farm Policies*, pp. 19, 23–5.

15 Gold, *Wartime Economic Planning*, p. 467.
16 Ibid., pp. 470–71.
17 Kennedy, 'Herbert Hoover', pp. 98–9.
18 Ibid., p. 101.
19 Gold, *Wartime Economic Planning*, p. 469.
20 Moore, 'The western Allies', p. 106.
21 Hammond, *Food and Agriculture*, p. 187.
22 Britnell and Voake, *Canadian Agriculture*, pp. 166–9, 269–272.
23 Gold, *Wartime Economic Planning*, p. 474.
24 Ibid., pp. 480–81.
25 Matusow, *Farm Policies*, p. 168.
26 Ibid., p. 150; Gold, *Wartime Economic Planning*, pp. 474, 476–7.
27 Ibid., p. 463.
28 Staples, *The Birth of Development*, p. 76.
29 Vernon, *Hunger*, p. 158; Boon, 'Agreement and disagreement', p. 171.
30 Ibid., p. 172.
31 Vernon, *Hunger*, p. 153.
32 Boon, 'Agreement and disagreement', p. 173; Trentmann, 'Coping with shortage', p. 32.
33 Extracts from the Report of the Hot Springs Conference, http://www.world fooddayusa.org/?id-16367; Evang, 'The Hot Springs Conference', p. 168.
34 Matusow, *Farm Policies*, p. 85.
35 Vernon, *Hunger*, p. 153.
36 Staples, *The Birth of Development*, p. 82.
37 Vernon, *Hunger*, p. 156.
38 Orr, *As I Recall*, pp. 176–7, 193.
39 Matusow, *Farm Policies*, pp. 89–90.
40 Cohen, *A Consumer's Republic*, p. 114.
41 Gold, *Wartime Economic Planning*, pp. 463, 465.
42 Erker, *Ernährungskrise und Nachkriegsgesellschaft*, pp. 49–50.
43 Trittel, 'Hungerkrise und kollektiver Protest', p. 378.
44 Ibid., p. 379.
45 Ibid, p. 389.
46 Gardner, *Architects of Illusion*, p. 259.
47 Henderson, 'German economic miracle', *The Concise Encyclopedia of Economics*, http://www.econlib.org.
48 Trittel, 'Hungerkrise und kollektiver Protest', p. 391.
49 Wexler, 'The Marshall Plan', p. 151.
50 Hogan, *The Marshall Plan*, p. 415.
51 Tracy, *Government and Agriculture*, pp. 218, 223.
52 Kroen, 'Negotiations', pp. 252, 255–6.
53 Cohen, *A Consumer's Republic*, p. 127.

54 Kroen, 'Negotiations', p. 265.

55 Bell and Bell, *Implicated*, p. 94.

56 Ibid., p. 105; Brash, *The Hegemony of International Business*, pp. 8–9.

57 Lowe, *Menzies*, pp. 136–7.

58 Trentmann, 'Coping with shortage', p. 35.

59 Hobsbawm, *The Age of Extremes*, p. 260; Tracy, *Government and Agriculture*, pp. 230, 238.

60 Smith, *The War's Long Shadow*, p. 176.

61 Medvedev, *Soviet Agriculture*, p. 131; Nove, 'Soviet peasantry in World War II', pp. 87–8.

62 Becker, *Hungry Ghosts*, p. 57.

63 Mitter, *Modern China*, pp. 57–8.

64 Mitter, *Bitter Revolution*, pp. 196–8; Becker, *Hungry Ghosts*, p. 57.

65 Rasmussen, 'Plant hormones in war and peace', p. 291.

66 Martin, *The Development of Modern Agriculture*, p. 102; Pollan, *In Defence of Food*, p. 101.

67 Martin, *The Development of Modern Agriculture*, p. 197.

68 Matusow, *Farm Policies*, p. 111.

69 Short et al., '"The front line of freedom"', p. 15.

70 Brown, *Who Will Feed China?*, p. 106.

71 Martin, *The Development of Modern Agriculture*, p. 128.

72 Blythe, *Akenfield*, p. 260.

73 Ibid., p. 262.

74 Ibid., p. 264.

75 Mira Kamdar, 'The threat of global food shortages – Part II', Yaleglobal online, http://yaleglobal.yale.edu/content/threat-global-food-shortages-%E2%80%93-part-ii, n.p.

76 Farrer, *To Feed a Nation*, p. 129.

77 Ibid., p. 130.

78 Ibid., p. 170.

79 Ibid., pp. 129, 169, 177.

80 Milward, *The Fascist Economy in Norway*, p. 243.

81 Hobsbawm, *The Age of Extremes*, p. 263; Hardyment, *Slice of Life*, pp. 79–80.

82 Hobsbawm, *The Age of Extremes*, p. 269; Driver, *The British at Table*, p. 66.

83 Cohen, *A Consumer's Republic*, p. 404.

84 Kuisel, *Seducing the French*, p. 105.

85 Duigan and Gann, *The Rebirth of the West*, p. 533.

86 Buss, 'The British diet', p. 127; Oddy, *From Plain Fare*, pp. 208–10.

87 Barkawi, *Globalization and War*, p. 92.

88 Bruce, *War on the Ground*, p. 301.

89 Richard Eickelmann, interviewed February 2004.

90 Morehouse, *Fighting in the Jim Crow Army*, p. 200.

91 Potts and Potts, *Yanks*, p. 246.

92 Jaffrey, *Climbing the Mango Trees*, pp. 183–4.

93 Knight, *Food Administration in India*, p. 97.

94 Lloyd, *Food and Inflation*, p. 58.

95 Dower, *Embracing Defeat*, pp. 90, 529.

96 Ibid., p. 169.

97 Ibid., pp. 169–70.

98 Cwiertka, 'Culinary culture', p. 423; Oki Chiyo, interviewed by Catherine Oki, October 2006.

99 Cwiertka, 'Militarization of nutrition', p. 15; Cwiertka, *Modern Japanese Cuisine*, p. 131; Ohnuki-Tierney, *Rice as Self*, p. 39.

100 Pollan, *In Defence of Food*, pp. 8–10, 28–9, 35–6, 107–21.

101 Mitter, *Modern China*, pp. 57–8.

102 Naylor and Falcon, 'Our daily bread', p. 13.

103 Scrimshaw, 'World nutritional problems', p. 353; Food and Agriculture Organization, 'Assessment of the world food security and nutrition situation', Committee on World Food Security, Thirty-fourth Session, Rome, 14–17 October 2008. Agenda Item II http//ftp.fao.org/docrep/fao/meeting/014/k3175e.pdf, p. 1.

104 'Quarter of US grain crop feeds cars not people', *Guardian*, 23 January 2010.

105 Mira Kamdar, 'The threat of global food shortages – Part II', Yaleglobal online, http://yaleglobal.yale.edu/content/threat-global-food-shortages-%E2%80%93-part-ii, n.p.; Stern, 'Climate change, internationalism and India in the 21st century', the Jawaharlal Nehru Memorial Lecture, Chatham House, 15 July 2009, http://www.chathamhouse.org.uk/files/14384-15070.

Bibliography

MANUSCRIPT SOURCES

National Library of Australia, Canberra (NLA)

J. A. Alexander Papers 1892–1983, MS2389
Sir Cedric Stanton Hicks Papers, MS5623
Hitoshi Imamura, 'Extracts from the tenor of my life', mfm PMB 569
H. E. Jessup, Changi Diary, MS3924
Irene Rush, Memoir, MS8316
Harry Simon, Memoirs, MS7514

Imperial War Museum, London (IWM)

E. Barrington Papers, Department of Documents, 88/58/1 (P)
Miss E. Blaikley Papers, Department of Documents, 86/46/1
R. B. Buckle Papers, Department of Documents
R. P. Evans Papers, Department of Documents
G. R. Page Papers, Department of Documents
Fus. H(arold Walter) Simons Papers, 'Army Cookery Notebook, 1944', Department of Documents, Misc180 Item 2726
A. W. Winter Papers, Department of Documents

OFFICIAL PAPERS

Australian National Archives (ANA)

Records:
Series A816/1
Series A5954/69

Australian War Memorial (AWM)

Allied Translator and Interpreter Section Reports, 1942–46, AWM 54 & 55

NEWSPAPERS

Guardian
New Yorker

INTERNET SITES

Australian Defence Force: Good food to stay fighting fit. http://www.dsto.defence.gov.au/research/5170/

William H. Bauer, Interview, 7 October 1994, Rutgers Oral History Archives, New Brunswick History Department, http://oralhistory.rutgers.edu/Interviews

Katarzyna Cwiertka, 'Popularizing a military diet in wartime Japan and postwar Japan', *IIAS Newsletter*, 38, http://www.iias.nl/iias/show/id=51553

Extracts from the Report of the Hot Springs Conference, http://www.worldfooddayusa.org/?id-16367

Food and Agriculture Organization, 'Assessment of the world food security and nutrition situation', Committee on World Food Security, Thirty-fourth Session, Rome, 14–17 October 2008. Agenda Item II, http//ftp.fao.org/docrep/fao/meeting/014/k3175e.pdf

Harvard Project on the Soviet Social System Online, http://hcl.harvard.edu/collections/hpsss/index.html

David R. Henderson, 'German economic miracle', *The Concise Encyclopedia of Economics*, http://www.econlib.org

Don Joseph, comments to http://www.woodlands-junior.kent.sch.uk/Homeword/war/rationing.htm

Mira Kamdar, 'The threat of global food shortages – Part II', Yaleglobal online, http://yaleglobal.yale.edu/content/threat-global-food-shortages-%E2%80%93-part-ii

Ron Klages and John Mulholland, 'Number of German divisions by front in World War II, *Axis History Factbook*, http://www.axishistory.com/index.php?id=7288

'Eduard Schulte', US Holocaust Memorial Museum, http://www.ushmm.org/wlc/article.php?lang=en&ModulId=10005682

Seabrook Farms, New Jersey, http://www.usgennet.org/usa/nj/state/seabrook_farms_nj.htm

Nicholas Stern, 'Climate change, internationalism and India in the 21st century', the Jawaharlal Nehru Memorial Lecture, Chatham House, 15 July 2009, http://www.chathamhouse.org.uk/files/14384-15070

'The things we forgot to remember', BBC Radio 4, 7 January 2008, http://www.opennet/thingsweforgot/bengalfamine_programme.html

C. Peter Timmer, 'The threat of global food shortages – Part I', Yaleglobal online, http://yaleglobal.yale.edu/content/threat-global-food-shortages-%E2%80%93-part-i

US Army Air Forces Statistical Digest, World War II, Table 211 – ATC Operations from Assam, India, to China (over the Hump): Jan 1943 to Aug 1945, http://www.usaaf.net/digest/t211.htm

Myron Winick, 'Hunger disease: studies by the Jewish physicians in the Warsaw ghetto, their historical importance and their relevance today', 27 October 2005, http://www.columbia.edu/cu/epic/pdf/winick_lecture

BOOKS AND ARTICLES

Adamovich, Ales and Daniil Granin, *A Book of the Blockade* (trans. Hilda Perham, Raduga Publishers, Moscow, 1983).

Adams, R. L., *Farm Problems in Meeting Food Needs* (University of California Press, Berkeley, 1942).

Adapting Livestock Products to War Needs, by members of the staffs of the divisions of dairy industry, animal husbandry, and poultry husbandry, College of Agriculture, University of California (University of California Press, Berkeley, 1943).

Addison, Paul, *Churchill on the Home Front 1900–1955* (Jonathan Cape, London, 1992).

—— and Angus Calder (eds), *Time to Kill. The Soldier's Experience of War in the West 1939–1945* (Pimlico, London, 1997).

Ahmad, Abu Talib, 'The Malay community and memory of the Japanese occupation', in P. Lim Pui Huen and Diana Wong (eds), *War and Memory in Malaysia and Singapore* (Institute of Southeast Asia Studies, Singapore, 2000).

Ajayi, J. F. A. and Michael Crowder (eds), *History of West Africa*, 2 vols (Longman, London, 1974).

Akashi, Yoji, 'Japanese policy towards the Malayan Chinese, 1941–45', *Journal of Southeast Asian Studies* 1 (2) (1970): 61–89.

Allen, Louis, *Burma. The Longest War 1941–45* (J. M. Dent & Sons, London, 1986).

Anderson, David and David Throup, 'Africans and agricultural production in colonial Kenya: the myth of the war as a watershed', *Journal of African History* 26 (1985): 327–45.

Anh, Nguyên Thê, 'Japanese food policies and the 1945 great famine in Indochina', in Paul H. Kratoska (ed.), *Food Supplies and the Japanese Occupation in South-East Asia* (Macmillan, London, 1998), pp. 208–26.

Apfelbaum, Emil, 'Pathophysiology of the circulatory system in hunger disease', in Myron Winick (ed.), *Hunger Disease. Studies by the Jewish Physicians in the Warsaw Ghetto* (trans. Martha Osnos, John Wiley & Sons, New York, 1979), pp. 125–60.

Aquila, Richard, *Home Front Soldier. The Story of a GI and his Italian American Family During World War II* (State University of New York Press, Albany, 1999).

Arnason, Ragnar, *The Icelandic Fisheries. Evolution and Management of a Fishing Industry* (Fishing News Books, Oxford, 1995).

Ashwell, Margaret (ed.), *McCance and Widdowson. A Scientific Partnership of 60 Years 1933 to 1993* (British Nutrition Foundation, London, 1993).

The Australian Army at War. An Official Record of Service in Two Hemispheres 1939–1944 (Australian Army Staff, Merriam Press, Bennington, VT, 2008).

Backe, Herbert, *Um die Nahrungsfreiheit Europas. Weltwirtschaft oder Großraum* (Wilhelm Goldmann Verlag, Leipzig, 1942).

Bacon, Edwin, *The Gulag at War. Stalin's Forced Labour System in the Light of the Archives* (Macmillan, London, 1994).

Baer, George W., *One Hundred Years of Sea Power: The US Navy 1890–1990* (Stanford University Press, Stanford, CA, 1996).

Baker, J. V. T., *The New Zealand People at War. War Economy* (Historical Publications, Department of Internal Affairs, Wellington, 1965).

Bankier, David (ed.), *Probing the Depths of German Antisemitism. German Society and the Persecution of the Jews, 1933–1941* (Berghahn Books, Oxford, 2000).

Bannister, Sybil, *I Lived Under Hitler. An Englishwoman's Story* (Rockliff, London, 1957).

Barber, John and Andrei Dzeniskevich (eds), *Life and Death in Besieged Leningrad, 1941–44* (Palgrave Macmillan, London, 2005).

Barber, John and Mark Harrison, *The Soviet Home Front, 1941–1945: A Social and Economic History of the USSR in World War II* (Longman, London, 1991).

Barkawi, Tarak, *Globalization and War* (Rowman & Littlefield, Oxford, 2006).

Barker, D. J. P., 'Fetal origins of coronary heart disease', *British Medical Journal* 311 (July 1995): 171–4.

Barnhart, Michael A., *Japan Prepares for Total War. The Search for Economic Security, 1919–1941* (Cornell University Press, London, 1987).

Barral, Pierre, 'Agriculture and food supply in France during the Second World War', in Bernd Martin and Alan S. Milward (eds), *Agriculture and Food Supply in the Second World War. Landwirtschaft und Versorgung im Zweiten Weltkrieg* (Scripta Mercaturae Verlag, Ostfildern, 1985), pp. 89–102.

Barrett, David P. and Larry N. Shyu (eds), *China in the Anti-Japanese War, 1937–1945. Politics, Culture and Society* (Peter Lang, Oxford, 2001).

Bartov, Omer, *The Eastern Front, 1941–45. German Troops and the Barbarisation of Warfare* (Macmillan, London, 1985).

——, *Hitler's Army. Soldiers, Nazis and War in the Third Reich* (Oxford University Press, Oxford, 1991).

——, *Germany's War and the Holocaust. Disputed Histories* (Cornell University Press, London, 2003).

Baten, Jörg and Andrea Wagner, 'Autarchy, market disintegration and health: the mortality and nutritional crisis in Nazi Germany, 1933–37', *Economics and Human Biology* 1 (1) (2002): 1–28.

Bayly, Christopher and Tim Harper, *Forgotten Armies. The Fall of British Asia 1941–1945* (Allen Lane, London, 2004).

Beasley, W. G., *Japanese Imperialism 1894–1945* (Clarendon Press, Oxford, 1987).

Beaumont, Joan (ed.), *Australia's War, 1939–1945* (Allen & Unwin, St Leonards, NSW, 1996).

——, 'Australia's war: Asia and the Pacific', in Joan Beaumont (ed.), *Australia's War, 1939–1945* (Allen & Unwin, St Leonards, NSW, 1996).

——, 'Australia's war: Europe and the Middle East', in Joan Beaumont (ed.), *Australia's War, 1939–1945* (Allen & Unwin, St Leonards, NSW, 1996).

——, 'Starving for democracy: Britain's blockade of and relief for occupied Europe, 1939–1945', *War and Society* 8 (2) (1990): 57–82.

Beck, Earl R., *Under the Bombs. The German Home Front 1942–1945* (University Press of Kentucky, Lexington, KY, 1986).

Becker, Jasper, *Hungry Ghosts. China's Secret Famine* (John Murray, London, 1996).

Beer, Edith Hahn, *The Nazi Officer's Wife. How One Jewish Woman Survived the Holocaust* (Little Brown & Company, London, 2000).

Beevor, Antony, *Berlin. The Downfall 1945* (Penguin, London, 2004).

——, *Stalingrad* (first pub. 1998, Penguin, London, 2007).

Behrens, C. B. A., *Merchant Shipping and the Demands of War* (HMSO and Kraus Reprint, London, 1978).

Belcham, John, *Industrialization and the Working Class: The English Experience, 1750–1900* (Scolar Press, Aldershot, 1990).

Bell, Philip and Roger Bell, *Implicated. The United States in Australia* (Oxford University Press, Oxford, 1993).

Bellamy, Chris, *Absolute War. Soviet Russia in the Second World War: A Modern History* (Macmillan, London, 2007).

Bengelsdorf, Joachim, *Die Landwirtschaft der Vereinigten Staaten von Amerika im Zweiten Weltkrieg* (Scripta Mercaturae Verlag, St Katharinen, 1997).

Bennett, George, 'British settlers north of the Zambezi, 1920 to 1960', in L. H. Gann and Peter Duigan (eds), *Colonialism in Africa 1870–1960. Vol. 2. The History and Politics of Colonialism 1914–1960* (Cambridge University Press, Cambridge, 1970), pp. 58–91.

Bentley, Amy, *Eating for Victory. Food Rationing and the Politics of Domesticity* (University of Illinois Press, Chicago, 1998).

Berghoff, Hartmut, 'Methoden der Verbrauchslenkung im Nationalsozialismus. Konsumpolitische Normensetzung zwischen totalitärem Anspruch und widerspenstiger Praxis', in Dieter Gosewinkel (ed.), *Wirtschaftskontrollen und Recht in der nationalsozialistischen Diktatur* (Klostermann, Frankfurt am Main, 2005), pp. 281–316.

Berkhoff, Karel C., *Harvest of Despair. Life and Death in Ukraine under Nazi Rule* (Belknap Press of Harvard University Press, Cambridge, MA, 2004).

Bernstein, Irving, *A Caring Society. The New Deal, the Worker, and the Great Depression* (Houghton Mifflin Company, Boston, 1985).

Betts, Raymond F., *Uncertain Dimensions: Western Overseas Empires in the Twentieth Century* (Oxford University Press, Oxford, 1985).

Bidlack, Richard, 'Survival strategies in Leningrad during the first year of the Soviet–German war', in Robert W. Thurston and Bernd Bonwetsch (eds), *The People's War. Responses to World War II in the Soviet Union* (University of Illinois Press, Chicago, 2000), pp. 84–107.

Bierman, John, and Colin Smith, *Alamein. War without Hate* (Viking, London, 2002).

Bindon, James R., 'Breadfruit, banana, beef and beer: modernization of the Samoan diet', *Ecology of Food and Nutrition* 12 (1982): 49–60.

——, 'Taro or rice, plantation or market: dietary choice in American Samoa', *Food and Foodways* 3 (1989): 59–78.

Bird, John, *American POWs of World War II. Forgotten Men Tell their Stories* (Praeger, London, 1992).

Bird, Peter, *The First Food Empire. A History of J. Lyons & Co.* (Phillimore, Chichester, 2000).

Bix, Herbert P., *Hirohito and the Making of Modern Japan* (Duckworth, London, 2001).

Black, Maggie, *A Cause for Our Times. Oxfam the First Fifty Years* (Oxfam, Oxford, 1992).

Blum, John Morton, *V Was for Victory. Politics and American Culture During World War II* (Harcourt Brace Jovanovich, New York, 1976).

Blythe, Ronald, *Akenfield. Portrait of an English Village* (Allen Lane, London, 1969).

Bohn, Robert (ed.), *Die Deutsche Herrschaft in den 'germanischen' Ländern 1940–1945* (Franz Steiner Verlag, Stuttgart, 1997).

Boog, Horst, Joachim Hoffmann, Ernst Kluk, Rolf-Dieter Müller, Gerd Ueberschör, *Der Angriff auf die Sowjet Union* (Deutsche Verlags-Anstalt, Stuttgart, 1983).

Boog, Horst, Werner Rahn, Reinhard Stumpf and Bernd Wegner, *Germany and the Second World War. Volume 6. The Global War. Widening of the Conflict into a World War and the Shift of the Initiative 1941–43* (Clarendon Press, Oxford, 2001).

Boon, Timothy, 'Agreement and disagreement in the making of World of Plenty', in David F. Smith (ed.), *Nutrition in Britain. Science, Scientists and Politics in the Twentieth Century* (Routledge, London, 1997), pp. 166–89.

Bordiugov, Gennadi, 'The popular mood in the unoccupied Soviet Union: continuity and change during the war', in Robert W. Thurston and Bernd Bonwetsch (eds), *The People's War. Responses to World War II in the Soviet Union* (University of Illinois Press, Chicago, 2000), pp. 54–70.

Bose, Sugata, 'Starvation amidst plenty: the making of famine in Bengal, Honan and Tonkin, 1942–45', *Modern Asian Studies* 24 (4) (1990): 699–727.

Bosma, Koos, 'Verbindungen zwischen Ost- und Westkolonisation', in Mechtild Rössler, Sabine Schleiermacher and Cordula Tollmien (eds), *Der "Generalplan Ost". Hauptlinien der nationalsozialistischen Planungs- und Vernichtungspolitik* (Akademie Verlag, Berlin, 1993), pp. 198–214.

Bosworth, Michal, 'Eating for the nation: food and nutrition on the home front', in Jenny Gregory (ed.), *On the Home Front. Western Australia and World War II* (University of Western Australia, Nedlands, 1996).

Boyce, Robert and Esmonde M. Robertson (eds), *Paths to War. New Essays on the Origins of the Second World War* (Macmillan, London, 1989).

Braithwaite, Rodric, *Moscow 1941. A City and its People at War* (Profile Books, London, 2007).

Bramwell, Anna, *Blood and Soil. Richard Walther Darré and Hitler's 'Green Party'* (Kensal Press, Abbotsbrook, Buckinghamshire,1985).

Brandt, Karl, in collaboration with Otto Schiller and Franz Ahlgrimm, *Management of Agriculture and Food in the German-Occupied and Other Areas of Fortress Europe. A Study in Military Government* (Stanford University Press, Stanford, CA, 1953).

Brandt, Nat, *Harlem at War. The Black Experience in WWII* (Syracuse University Press, Syracuse, 1996).

Brash, D. T., *The Hegemony of International Business 1945–1970*. Vol. 5. *American Investment in Australian Industry* (Routledge, London, 1966).

Brassley, Paul, 'British farming between the wars', in Paul Brassley, Jeremy Burchardt and Lynee Thompson (eds), *The English Countryside between the Wars. Regeneration or Decline?* (Boydell Press, Woodbridge, 2006), pp. 187–99.

—— 'Wartime productivity and innovation, 1939–45', in Brian Short, Charles Watkins and John Martin (eds), *The Front Line of Freedom. British Farming in the Second World War* (British Agricultural History Society, Exeter, 2006), pp. 36–54.

——, Jeremy Burchardt and Lynee Thompson (eds), *The English Countryside between the Wars. Regeneration or Decline?* (Boydell Press, Woodbridge, 2006).

—— and Angela Potter, 'A view from the top: social elites and food consumption in Britain, 1930s–1940s', in Frank Trentmann and Flemming Just (eds), *Food and Conflict in Europe in the Age of the Two World Wars* (Palgrave Macmillan, Basingstoke, 2006), pp. 223–42.

Brewer, John and Frank Trentmann (eds), *Consuming Cultures, Global Perspectives. Historical Trajectories, Transnational Exchanges* (Berg, Oxford, 2006).

Britnell, G. E. and V. C. Voake, *Canadian Agriculture in War and Peace 1935–50* (Stanford University Press, Stanford, CA, 1962).

Brown, Alan S., Ezra S. Susser, P. Lin Shang, Richard Neugebauer and Jack M. Gorman, 'Increased risk of affective disorders in males after second trimester prenatal exposure to the Dutch Hunger Winter of 1944–45', *British Journal of Psychiatry* 166 (1995): 601–6.

Brown, Lester, *Who Will Feed China? Wake-up Call for a Small Planet* (Earthscan, London, 1995).

Bruce, Colin John, *War on the Ground* (Constable, London, 1995).

Brune, Peter, *Those Ragged Bloody Heroes: From the Kokoda Trail to Gona Beach 1942* (Allen & Unwin, London, 2005).

Brzeska, Maria, *Through a Woman's Eyes. Life in Poland under the German Occupation* (Max Love Publishing, London, 1945).

Bullard, Steven, '"The great enemy of humanity". Malaria and the Japanese medical corps in Papua, 1942–43', *Journal of Pacific History* 39 (2) (2004): 203–20.

Burchardt, Lothar, 'The impact of the war economy on the civilian population of Germany during the First and Second World Wars', in Wilhelm Deist (ed.), *The German Military in the Age of Total War* (Berg, Leamington Spa, 1985), pp. 40–70.

Burleigh, Michael, *The Third Reich. A New History* (Macmillan, London, 2000).

——, *Death and Deliverance. 'Euthanasia' in Germany c.1900–1945* (Pan Books, London, 2002).

Burnett, John, *Plenty and Want. A Social History of Diet in England from 1815 to the Present Day* (first pub. 1966, 3rd edn, Routledge, London, 1985).

——, 'The rise and decline of school meals in Britain, 1860–1990', in John Burnett and Derek J. Oddy (eds), *The Origins and Development of Food Policies in Europe* (Leicester University Press, London, 1994), pp. 55–69.

—— and Derek J. Oddy, 'Introduction', in John Burnett and Derek J. Oddy (eds), *The Origins and Development of Food Policies in Europe* (Leicester University Press, London, 1994), pp. 1–6.

—— and —— (eds), *The Origins and Development of Food Policies in Europe* (Leicester University Press, London, 1994).

Buss, D. H., 'The British diet since the end of food rationing', in Catherine Geissler and Derek J. Oddy (eds), *Food, Diet and Economic Change Past and Present* (Leicester University Press, London, 1993), pp. 121–32.

Butlin, S. J. and C. B. Schedvin, *War Economy 1942–1945* (Australian War Memorial, Canberra, 1977).

Calder, Angus, *The People's War. Britain 1939–1945* (first pub. 1969, Pimlico, London, 1992).

Calvocoressi, Peter and Guy Wint, *Total War. Causes and Courses of the Second World War* (Allen Lane, London, 1972).

Campbell, D'Ann, *Women at War with America. Private Lives in a Patriotic Era* (Harvard University Press, London, 1984).

Capeci, Dominic, *The Harlem Riot of 1943* (Temple University Press, Philadelphia, 1977).

Carpenter, Stephanie A., *On the Farm Front. The Women's Land Army in World War II* (Northern Illinois University Press, DeKalb, IL, 2003).

Carruthers, Bob, *Servants of Evil. New First-hand Accounts of the Second World War from Survivors of Hitler's Armed Forces* (André Deutsch, London, 2001).

Chamberlin, William Charles, *Economic Development of Iceland through World War II* (Columbia University Press, New York, 1947).

Chandos, Viscount (Oliver Lyttelton), *The Memoirs of Viscount Chandos* (Bodley Head, London, 1962).

Ch'en, Jerome, 'The communist movement, 1927–1937', in Lloyd E. Eastman, Jerome Ch'en, Suzanne Pepper and Lyman P. van Slyke, *The Nationalist Era in China, 1927–1949* (Cambridge University Press, Cambridge, 1991), pp. 53–114.

Chen, Yung-fa, *Making Revolution. The Communist Movement in Eastern and Central China, 1937–1945* (University of California Press, Berkeley, 1986).

Cherepenina, Nadezhda, 'Assessing the scale of famine and death in the besieged city', in John Barber and Andrei Dzeniskevich (eds), *Life and Death in Besieged Leningrad, 1941–44* (Palgrave Macmillan, London, 2005), pp. 28–70.

Cherrington, John, *On the Smell of an Oily Rag. My 50 Years in Farming* (Farming Press, Ipswich, 1993).

Chopra, R. N., *Evolution of Food Policy in India* (Macmillan, London, 1981).

Citizen of Kharkiw, A, 'Lest we forget. Hunger in Kharkiv in the winter 1941–1942', *Ukrainian Quarterly* 4 (1) (Winter 1948): 72–9.

Cohen, Lizabeth, *A Consumer's Republic. The Politics of Mass Consumption in Postwar America* (Alfred A. Knopf, New York, 2003).

Collins, Sarah Mabel, *The Alien Years: being the Autobiography of an English-woman in Germany and Austria: 1938–1946* (Hodder & Stoughton, London, 1949).

Cook, Haruko Taya and Theodore F. Cook (eds), *Japan at War. An Oral History* (Phoenix Press, London, 2000).

Cooper, Artemis, *Cairo in the War 1939–1945* (Penguin, London, 1995).

Corner, Paul, 'Fascist agrarian policy and the Italian economy in the inter-war years', in John A. Davis (ed.), *Gramsci and Italy's Passive Revolution* (Croom Helm, London, 1979), pp. 239–74.

Corni, Gustavo, *Hitler and the Peasants. Agrarian Policy of the Third Reich, 1930–1939* (Berg, Oxford, 1990).

—— and Horst Gies, *Brot, Butter, Kanonen. Die Ernährungswirtschaft in Deutschland unter der Diktatur Hitlers* (Akademie Verlag, Berlin, 1997).

Costello, John and Terry Hughes, *The Battle of the Atlantic. The Epic Story of Britain's Wartime Fight for Survival* (Fontana, London, 1980).

Counts, David, 'Shadows of war: changing remembrance through twenty years in New Britain', in Geoffrey M. White and Lamont Lindstrom (eds), *The Pacific*

Theater. Island Representations of World War II (University of Hawaii Press, Honolulu, 1989), pp. 187–203.

Coyne, Terry, *The Effect of Urbanisation and Western Diet on the Health of Pacific Island Populations* (South Pacific Commission, Noumea, New Caledonia, 1984).

Cramp, K. R., 'Food – the first munition of war', *Royal Australian Historical Society Journal and Proceedings* 31 (2) (1945): 65–91.

Crang, J. A., 'The British soldier on the home front: army morale reports, 1940–45', in Paul Addison and Angus Calder (eds), *Time to Kill. The Soldier's Experience of War in the West 1939–1945* (Pimlico, London, 1997), pp. 60–74.

Crawford, J. G., C. M. Donald, C. P. Dowsett, D. B. Williams and A. A. Ross, *Wartime Agriculture in Australia and New Zealand 1939–50* (Stanford University Press, Stanford, 1954).

Crew, David, 'General introduction', in David F. Crew, *Nazism and German Society, 1933–1945* (Routledge, London, 1994), pp. 1–40.

Crew, Graeme, *The Royal Army Service Corps* (Leo Cooper Ltd., London, 1970).

Crimp, R. L., *The Diary of a Desert Rat* (Leo Cooper, London, 1971).

Crowder, Michael, 'The 1939–45 war and West Africa', in J. F. A. Ajayi and Michael Crowder (eds), *History of West Africa*, Vol. 2 (Longman, London, 1974), pp. 596–621.

Curtis-Bennett, Noel, *The Food of the People being the History of Industrial Feeding* (Faber & Faber, London, 1949).

Cwiertka, Katarzyna Joanna, 'Culinary culture and the making of a national cuisine', in Jennifer Robertson (ed.), *A Companion to the Anthropology of Japan* (Blackwell, Oxford, 2005), pp. 415–28.

——, 'Militarization of nutrition in wartime Japan', *IIAS Newsletter* (September 2005): 15.

——, *Modern Japanese Cuisine. Food, Politics and National Identity* (Reaktion, London, 2006).

Dallin, Alexander, *German Rule in Russia 1941–1945. A Study of Occupation Policies* (first pub. 1957, 2nd edn, Macmillan Press, London, 1981).

Danbom, David B., *Born in the Country. A History of Rural America* (Johns Hopkins University Press, London, 1995).

Darian-Smith, Kate, *On the Home Front. Melbourne in Wartime 1939–1945* (Oxford University Press, Oxford, 1990).

Davidson, R. and M. A. Eastwood, *Human Nutrition and Dietetics* (Churchill Livingstone, London, 1986).

Davies, David, *The Case of Labourers in Husbandry Stated and Considered with an appendix containing a collection of accounts shewing the earnings and expenses of labouring families in different parts of the Kingdom* (first published 1795, Augustus M. Kelley Publishers, Fairfield, New Jersey, 1977).

Davies, Norman, *Europe at War 1939–1945. No Simple Victory* (Macmillan, London, 2006).

Davies, Robert William, Mark Harrison, S. G. Wheatcroft, *The Economic Transformation of the Soviet Union 1913–1945* (Cambridge University Press, Cambridge, 1994).

Davis, Belinda J., *Home Fires Burning. Food, Politics, and Everyday Life in World War I Berlin* (University of North Carolina Press, London, 2000).

Davis, Lance Edwin and Stanley L. Engerman, *Naval Blockades in Peace and War: An Economic History since 1750* (Cambridge University Press, New York, 2006).

Deist, Wilhelm (ed.), *The German Military in the Age of Total War* (Berg, Leamington Spa, 1985).

Denoon, Donald (ed.), *The Cambridge History of the Pacific Islanders* (Cambridge University Press, Cambridge, 1997).

Dewey, Peter, *War and Progress. Britain 1914–45* (Longman, London, 1997).

——, 'The supply of tractors in wartime', in Brian Short, Charles Watkins and John Martin (eds), *The Front Line of Freedom. British Farming in the Second World War* (British Agricultural History Society, Exeter, 2006), pp. 89–100.

Dlugoborski, Waclaw, 'Die Landwirtschaft in der Sowjetunion 1941–1944. Ein Vergleich der Situation in den besetzten und den unbesetzten Gebieten', in Bernd Martin and Alan S. Milward (eds), *Agriculture and Food Supply in the Second World War. Landwirtschaft und Versorgung im Zweiten Weltkrieg* (Scripta Mercaturae Verlag, Ostfildern, 1985), pp. 143–60.

Dore, Ronald, *Shinohata. A Portrait of a Japanese Village* (Allen Lane, London, 1978).

—— and Tsutomu Ouchi, 'Rural origins of Japanese fascism', in James William Morley (ed.), *Dilemmas of Growth in Prewar Japan* (Princeton University Press, Princeton, NJ, 1971), pp. 181–210.

Dornan, Peter, *The Silent Men. Syria to Kokoda and on to Gona* (Allen & Unwin, London, 1999).

Dörr, Margarete, *"Wer die Zeit nicht miterlebt hat ..." Frauenerfahrungen im Zweiten Weltkrieg und in den Jahren danach*, 3 vols (Campus Verlag, Frankfurt, 1998).

Doughty, Martin, *Merchant Shipping and War: A Study in Defence Planning in Twentieth-Century Britain* (Royal Historical Society, London, 1982).

Dower, John W., *Embracing Defeat. Japan in the Aftermath of World War II* (Penguin, London, 2000).

Drea, Edward J., *In the Service of the Emperor. Essays on the Imperial Japanese Army* (University of Nebraska Press, Lincoln, 1998).

Driver, Christopher, *The British at Table 1940–1980* (Chatto and Windus, London, 1983).

Droese, Werner, 'Die Wirkung von Traubenzucker und Traubenzucker B1 – Kombinationen auf die Leistungsfähigkeit bei Hitzarbeit' *Arbeitsphysiologie*, 12 (2) (1942): 124–33.

——, 'Experimentalle Untersuchung über die Vitamin B1 – Versorgung der großstädtischen Bevölkerung in den Jahren 1941/42 und 43', *Arbeitsphysiologie*, 13 (1) (1944): 63–77.

Duigan, Peter and L. H. Gann, *The Rebirth of the West. The Americanization of the Democratic World, 1945–1958* (Blackwell, Oxford, 1992).

Duis, Perry R., 'No time for privacy: World War II and Chicago's families', in Lewis A. Erenberg and Susan E. Hirsch (eds), *The War in American Culture. Society and Consciousness During World War II* (University of Chicago Press, London, 1996).

Dung, Bui Minh, 'Japan's role in the Vietnamese starvation of 1944–45', *Modern Asian Studies* 29 (3) (1995): 573–618.

Dunn, Walter S., Jr., *The Soviet Economy and the Red Army, 1930–1945* (Praeger, Westport, CT, 1995).

Duus, Peter, 'Economic dimensions of Meiji imperialism: the case of Korea, 1895–1910', in Ramon H. Myers and Mark R. Peattie, *The Japanese Colonial Empire, 1895–1945* (Princeton University Press, Princeton, NJ, 1984), pp. 128–71.

——, *The Abacus and the Sword. The Japanese Penetration of Korea, 1895–1910* (University of California Press, Berkeley, 1995).

——, 'Introduction. Japan's wartime empire: problems and issues', in Peter Duus, Ramon H. Myers and Mark R. Peattie (eds), *The Japanese Wartime Empire, 1931–1945* (Princeton University Press, Princeton, NJ, 1996), pp. xi–xlvii.

——, Ramon H. Myers and Mark R. Peattie (eds), *The Japanese Wartime Empire, 1931–1945* (Princeton University Press, Princeton, NJ, 1996).

Dyson, Tim and Cormac Ó Gráda (eds), *Famine Demography. Perspectives from the Past and Present* (Oxford University Press, Oxford, 2002).

Eastman, Lloyd E., *Seeds of Destruction. Nationalist China in War and Revolution 1937–1949* (Stanford University Press, Stanford, CA, 1984).

——, 'Nationalist China during the Sino-Japanese war, 1937–1945', in Lloyd E. Eastman, Jerome Ch'en, Suzanne Pepper and Lyman P. van Slyke, *The Nationalist Era in China, 1927–1949* (Cambridge University Press, Cambridge, 1991), pp. 115–76.

——, Jerome Ch'en, Suzanne Pepper and Lyman P. van Slyke, *The Nationalist Era in China, 1927–1949* (Cambridge University Press, Cambridge, 1991).

Eckart, Wolfgang Uwe (ed.), *Man, Medicine and the State. The Human Body as an Object of Government* (Franz Steiner Verlag, Stuttgart, 2006).

Eckert, Carter J., 'Total war, industrialization, and social change in late colonial Korea', in Peter Duus, Ramon H. Myers and Mark R. Peattie (eds), *The Japanese Wartime Empire, 1931–1945* (Princeton University Press, Princeton, NJ, 1996), pp. 3–39.

Eden, Sir Frederic Morton, *The State of the Poor. A History of the Labouring Classes in England, with parochial reports* (abridged and edited by A. G. L. Rogers, first pub. 1797, George Routledge & Sons, London, 1928).

Edgerton, Robert B., *Warriors of the Rising Sun. A History of the Japanese Military* (W. W. Norton & Co., London, 1977).

Eichholtz, Dietrich and Almuth Püschel (eds), *Verfolgung, Alltag, Widerstand. Brandenburg in der NS-Zeit. Studien und Dokumente* (Verlag Volk & Welt, Berlin, 1993).

Ellis, John, *World War II: The Sharp End of War* (Windrow & Green, London, 1990).

——, *The World War II Databook. The Essential Facts and Figures for All the Combatants* (Aurum Press, London, 1993).

Ellman, Michael and S. Maksudov, 'Soviet deaths in the Great Patriotic War', *Europe–Asia Studies* 46 (4) (1994), pp. 671–80.

Ensminger Audrey H., M. E. Ensminger, James E. Konland and John R. Robson, *Foods and Nutrition Enclyopedia*, 2 vols (2nd edn, CRC Press, London, 1994).

Erenberg, Lewis A. and Susan E. Hirsch (eds), *The War in American Culture. Society and Consciousness During World War II* (University of Chicago Press, London, 1996).

Erickson, John, *The Road to Berlin. Stalin's War with Germany*, Vol. 2 (Weidenfeld & Nicolson, London, 1983).

——, 'Soviet women at war', in John Garrard and Carol Garrard (eds), *World War Two and the Soviet People. Selected Papers from the Fourth World Congress for Soviet and East European Studies, Harrogate 1990* (St Martin's Press, New York, 1993), pp. 50–76.

Erker, Paul, *Ernährungskrise und Nachkriegsgesellschaft. Bauern und Arbeiterschaft in Bayern 1943–1953* (Klett-Cotta, Stuttgart, 1990).

Essemyr, Mats, 'Food policies in Sweden during the World Wars', in John Burnett and Derek J. Oddy (eds), *The Origins and Development of Food Policies in Europe* (Leicester University Press, London, 1994), pp. 161–77.

Etlin, Richard A. (ed.), *Art, Culture, and Media under the Third Reich* (University of Chicago Press, Chicago, 2002).

Evang, K., 'The Hot Springs Conference', *Proceedings of the Nutrition Society* 2 (1944): 163–76.

Evans, Richard, *The Third Reich in Power 1933–1939* (Allen Lane, London, 2005).

—— *The Third Reich at War 1939–1945* (Allen Lane, London, 2008).

Falgout, Suzanne, 'From passive pawns to political strategists: wartime lessons for the people of Pohnpei', in Geoffrey M. White and Lamont Lindstrom (eds), *The Pacific Theater. Island Representations of World War II* (University of Hawaii Press, Honolulu, 1989), pp. 279–97.

Farquharson, John E., *The Plough and the Swastika. The NSDAP and Agriculture in Germany 1928–45* (Sage Publications, London, 1976).

——, *The Western Allies and the Politics of Food. Agrarian Management in Postwar Germany* (Berg Publishers, Leamington Spa, 1985).

——, 'The agrarian policy of National Socialist Germany', in Robert G. Moeller (ed.), *Peasants and Lords in Modern Germany. Recent Studies in Agricultural History* (Allen & Unwin, London, 1986), pp. 233–59.

Farrer, Keith Thomas Henry, *To Feed a Nation* (CSIRO, Canberra, 2005).

Fenby, Jonathan, *Alliance. The Inside Story of How Roosevelt, Stalin and Churchill Won One War and Began Another* (Simon & Schuster, London, 2006).

Fieldhouse, David, 'War and the origins of the Gold Coast Cocoa Marketing Board, 1939–40', in Michael Twaddle (ed.), *Imperialism, the State and the Third World* (British Academic Press, London, 1992), pp. 153–82.

Fielding, Steven, 'The Good War: 1939–1945', in Nick Tiratsoo (ed.), *From Blitz to Blair: A New History of Britain since 1939* (Weidenfeld & Nicolson, London, 1997), pp. 25–52.

Figes, Orlando, *The Whisperers. Private Lives in Stalin's Russia* (Allen Lane, London, 2007).

Fischer, Fritz, *World Power or Decline. The Controversy over Germany's Aims in the First World War* (W. W. Norton & Co., New York, 1974).

Fitzpatrick, Sheila, *Everyday Stalinism. Ordinary Life in Extraordinary Times: Soviet Russia in the 1930s* (Oxford University Press, Oxford, 1999).

Fliederbaum, 'Metabolic changes in hunger disease', in Myron Winick (ed.), *Hunger Disease. Studies by the Jewish Physicians in the Warsaw Ghetto* (trans. Martha Osnos, John Wiley & Sons, New York, 1979), pp. 69–124.

Flynn, George Q., *The Mess in Washington. Manpower Mobilization in World War II* (Greenwood Press, London, 1979).

Foot, William, 'The impact of the military on the agricultural landscape of England and Wales in the Second World War', in Brian Short, Charles Watkins and John Martin (eds), *The Front Line of Freedom. British Farming in the Second World War* (British Agricultural History Society, Exeter, 2006), pp. 132–42.

Forstmeier, Friedrich and Hans-Erich Volkmann (eds), *Kriegswirtschaft und Rüstung 1939– 1945* (Droste Verlag, Düsseldorf, 1977).

Forty Facts about Australia's Wartime Agriculture (Issued under the direction and by the authority of the Australian Minister for Information The Hon. A. A. Calwell, M. H. R., Alfred Henry Pettifer, Acting Government Printer, 1944).

Fox, Richard Wightman and T. J. Jackson Lears (eds), *The Power of Culture. Critical Essays in American History* (University of Chicago Press, Chicago, 1993).

Franco, Robert W., 'Samoan representations of World War II and military work: the emergence of international movement networks', in Geoffrey M. White and Lamont Lindstrom (eds), *The Pacific Theater. Island Representations of World War II* (University of Hawaii Press, Honolulu, 1989), pp. 373–94.

Frank, Richard B., *Downfall. The End of the Imperial Japanese Empire* (Random House, New York, 1999).

Freeman, Michelle, 'Australian universities at war: the mobilization of universities in the battle for the Pacific', in Roy M. Macleod, *Science and the Pacific War. Science and Survival in the Pacific, 1939–1945* (Kluwer Academic Publishers, London, 2000), pp. 119–38.

Frei, Norbert, Sybille Steinbacher and Bernd C. Wagner (eds), *Ausbeutung, Vernichtung, Öffentlichkeit. Neue Studien zur nationalsozialistischen Lagerpolitik* (K. G. Saur, Munich, 2000).

French, Chauncey Del, *Waging War on the Home Front. An Illustrated Memoir of World War II* (ed. Lois Mack and Ted van Arsdol, Oregon State University Press, Corvallis, OR, 2004).

Fritz, Stephen G., *Frontsoldaten. The German Soldier in World War II* (University Press of Kentucky, Lexington, KY, 1995).

Fujiwara, Akira, *Uejini shita eireitachi* (Aoki Shoten, Tokyo, 2001).

Fulbrook, Mary, 'Hitler's willing robbers: the deadly sin of greed, and guilt by extension', *neue politische literatur* 2 (2005): 203–10.

Furuta, Motoo, 'A survey of village conditions during the 1945 famine in Vietnam', in Paul H. Kratoska (ed.), *Food Supplies and the Japanese Occupation in South-East Asia* (Macmillan, London, 1998), pp. 227–37.

Futselaar, Ralf, 'The mystery of the dying Dutch: can micronutrient deficiencies explain the difference between Danish and Dutch wartime mortality?', in Frank Trentmann and Flemming Just (eds), *Food and Conflict in Europe in the Age of the Two World Wars* (Palgrave Macmillan, Basingstoke, 2006), pp. 193–222.

Fuykschot, Cornelia, *Hunger in Holland. Life During the Nazi Occupation* (Prometheus Books, New York, 1995).

Gailus, Manfred and Heinrich Volkmann (eds), *Der Kampf um das tägliche Brot. Nahrungsmangel, versorgungspolitik und Protest 1770–1990* (Westdeutscher Verlag, Opladen, 1994).

Gann, L. H., 'Reflections on the Japanese and German Empires of World War II', in Peter Duus, Ramon H. Myers and Mark R. Peattie (eds), *The Japanese Wartime Empire, 1931–1945* (Princeton University Press, Princeton, NJ, 1996), pp. 335–62.

—— and Peter Duigan (eds), *Colonialism in Africa 1870–1960. Vol. 2. The History and Politics of Colonialism 1914–1960* (Cambridge University Press, Cambridge, 1970).

—— and ——, 'Introduction', in L. H. Gann and Peter Duigan (eds), *Colonialism in Africa 1870–1960. Vol. 2. The History and Politics of Colonialism 1914–1960* (Cambridge University Press, Cambridge, 1970), pp. 1–30.

Gardiner, Juliet, *The 1940s House* (4 Books, London, 2002).

Gardner, Lloyd C., *Architects of Illusion. Men and Ideas in American Foreign Policy 1941–1949* (Quadrangle Books, Chicago, 1970).

Garfield, Simon, *Private Battles. How the War Almost Defeated Us* (Ebury Press, London, 2006).

——, *We Are at War. The Diaries of Five Ordinary People in Extraordinary Times* (Ebury Press, London, 2006).

Garrard, John and Carol Garrard (eds), *World War Two and the Soviet People. Selected Papers from the Fourth World Congress for Soviet and East European Studies, Harrogate 1990* (St Martin's Press, New York, 1993).

Gatu, Dagfinn, *Toward Revolution. War, Social Change and the Chinese Communist Party in North China 1937–45* (Skrifter utgivna as Föreningen för Orientliska Studier 16, Stockholm, 1983).

Geissler, Catherine and Derek J. Oddy (eds), *Food, Diet and Economic Change Past and Present* (Leicester University Press, London, 1993).

Gerlach, Christian, *Krieg, Ernährung, Völkermord. Forschungen zur deutschen Vernichtungspolitik im Zweiten Weltkrieg* (Hamburger Edition, Hamburg, 1998).

——, *Kalkulierte Morde. Die deutsche Wirtschafts- und Vernichtungspolitik in Weissrussland 1941 bis 1944* (Hamburger Edition, Hamburg, 1999).

——, 'Militärische "Versorgungszwänge", Besatzungspolitik und Massenverbrechen: Die Rolle des Generalquartiermeisters des Heeres und seiner Dienststellen im Krieg gegen die Sowjetunion', in Norbert Frei, Sybille Steinbacher and Bernd C. Wagner (eds), *Ausbeutung, Vernichtung, Öffentlichkeit. Neue Studien zur nationalsozialistischen Lagerpolitik* (K. G. Saur, Munich, 2000), pp. 175–209.

Geyer, Martin H., 'Soziale Sicherheit und wirtschaftlicher Fortschritt. Überlegungen zum Verhältnis von Arbeitsideologie und Sozialpolitik im "Dritten Reich"', *Geschichte und Gesellschaft* 15 (1989): 382–406.

Gibney, Frank (ed.), *Senso. The Japanese Remember the Pacific War. Letters to the Editor of Asahi Shimbun* (M. E. Sharpe, London, 1995).

Gildea, Robert, *Marianne in Chains. In Search of the German Occupation 1940–1945* (Macmillan, London, 2002).

——, Olivier Wieviorka and Anette Warring (eds), *Surviving Hitler and Mussolini. Daily Life in Occupied Europe* (Berg, Oxford, 2006).

Gillingham, John, 'How Belgium survived: the food supply problems of an occupied nation', in Bernd Martin and Alan S. Milward (eds), *Agriculture and Food Supply in the Second World War. Landwirtschaft und Versorgung im Zweiten Weltkrieg* (Scripta Mercaturae Verlag, Ostfildern, 1985), pp. 69–88.

Gluck, Sherna Berger, *Rosie the Riveter Revisited: Women, the War and Social Change* (Twayne Publishers, Boston, 1987).

Gold, Bella, *Wartime Economic Planning in Agriculture. A Study in the Allocation of Resources* (Columbia University Press, New York, 1949).

Goldberg, G. R., 'Intake and energy requirements', *Encyclopedia of Food Sciences and Nutrition*, Vol. 4 (2nd edn, Academic Press, London, 2003), pp. 2091–8.

Goodhart, Robert S. and L. B. Pett, 'The wartime nutrition programs for workers in the United States and Canada', *Milbank Memorial Fund Quarterly* 23 (2) (April 1945): 161–79.

Goodwin, Doris Kearns, *No Ordinary Time. Franklin and Eleanor Roosevelt: The Home Front in World War II* (Simon & Schuster, London, 1994).

Gordon, Bertram M., 'Fascism, the neo-right and gastronomy. A case in the theory of the social engineering of taste', *Oxford Symposium on Food and Cookery. 1987. Taste Proceedings* (Oxford, 1988).

Gordon, David M., 'The China–Japan war, 1931–1945', *Journal of Military History* 70 (1) (2006): 137–82.

Gosewinkel, Dieter (ed.), *Wirtschaftskontrollen und Recht in der nationalsozialistischen Diktatur* (Klostermann, Frankfurt am Main, 2005).

Graham, Malcolm, *Oxfordshire at War* (Alan Sutton Publishing, Stroud, 1994).

Gratzer, Walter, *Terrors of the Table. The Curious History of Nutrition* (Oxford University Press, Oxford, 2005).

Greenough, Paul R., *Prosperity and Misery in Modern Bengal. The Famine of 1943–1944* (Oxford University Press, Oxford, 1982).

Gregory, Jenny (ed.), *On the Home Front. Western Australia and World War II* (University of Western Australia, Nedlands, 1996).

Grönung, Gert, 'Die "Allgemeine Anordnung Nr. 20/VI/42" – Über die Gestaltung der Landwirtschaft in den eingegliederten Ostgebieten', in Mechtild Rössler, Sabine Schleiermacher and Cordula Tollmien (eds), *Der "Generalplan Ost". Hauptlinien der nationalsozialistischen Planungs- und Vernichtungspolitik* (Akademie Verlag, Berlin, 1993), pp. 131–5.

Grover, Roy Lee, *Incidents in the Life of a B-25 Pilot* (Author House, Bloomington, IN, 2006).

Gruchmann, Lothar, 'Korruption im Dritten Reich. Zur Lebensmittelversorgung der NS-Führerschaft', *Vierteljahreshefte für Zeitgeschichte* 4 (1994): 571–93.

Gumpert, Dr Martin, *Heil Hunger! Health under Hitler* (first published 1940, George Allen & Unwin, London, 1965).

Hachtman, Rüdiger, 'Lebenshaltungskosten und Reallöhne während des "Dritten Reichs"', *Vierteljahrschrift für Sozial- und Wirtschaftsgeschichte* 75 (1988): 32–73.

Haffner, Sebastian, *Anmerkumgen zu Hitler* (first pub. 1978, Fischer Taschenbuch Verlag, Frankfurt am Main, 1997).

——, *Defying Hitler. A Memoir* (first pub. 2002, trans. Oliver Pretzel, Phoenix, London, 2003).

Hall, Anne, *Land Girl. Her Story of Six Years in the Women's Land Army, 1940–46* (Ex Libris Press, Bradford-on-Avon, 1993).

Hammond, R. J., *Food and Agriculture in Britain 1939–45. Aspects of Wartime Control* (Stanford University Press, Stanford, CA, 1954).

Hane, Mikiso, *Peasants, Rebels and Outcastes. The Underside of Modern Japan* (Pantheon Books, New York, 1982).

Hardyment, Christina, *Slice of Life. The British Way of Eating since 1945* (Penguin Books/BBC Books, London, 1995).

Harman, Tony, *Seventy Summers. The Story of a Farm* (BBC Publications, London, 1986).

Harper, T. N., *The End of Empire and the Making of Malaya* (Cambridge University Press, Cambridge, 1998).

Harries, Meirion and Susie Harries, *Soldiers of the Sun. The Rise and Fall of the Imperial Japanese Army 1868–1945* (Heinemann, London, 1991).

Harris, José, 'Great Britain: The People's War?', in David Reynolds, Warren F. Kimball and A. O. Chubarian (eds), *Allies at War. The Soviet, American and British Experience, 1939–1945* (Macmillan, London, 1994), pp. 233–60.

Harrison, Charles H., *Growing a Global Village. Making History at Seabrook Farms* (Holmes & Meier, New York, 2003).

Harrison, Mark, 'The Second World War', in R. W. Davies, Mark Harrison and S. G. Wheatcroft (eds), *The Economic Transformation of the Soviet Union, 1913–1945* (Cambridge University Press, Cambridge, 1994), pp. 238–67.

——, *Accounting for War. Soviet Production, Employment, and the Defence Burden 1940–1945* (Cambridge University Press, Cambridge, 1996).

Harvey, Elizabeth, *Women and the Nazi East. Agents and Witnesses of Germanization* (Yale University Press, London, 2003).

Hastings, Max, *Nemesis. The Battle for Japan, 1944–45* (Harper Perennial, London, 2008).

——, *Das Reich. The March of the 2nd Panzer Division through France, June 1944* (first pub. 1981, Pan Books, London, 2009).

Hatano, Sumio and Sadao Asada, 'The Japanese decision to move south', in Robert Boyce and Esmonde M. Robertson (eds), *Paths to War. New Essays on the Origins of the Second World War* (Macmillan, London, 1989), pp. 383–407.

Havens, Thomas R. H., *Valley of Darkness. The Japanese People and World War Two* (W. W. Norton & Company, New York, 1978).

Heim, Susanne, *Kalorien, Kautschuk, Karrieren. Pflanzenzüchtung und landwirtschaftliche Forschung in Kaiser-Wilhelm-Instituten 1933–1945* (Wallstein, Göttingen, 2003).

Heinemann, Isabel, 'Wissenschaft und Homogenisierungsplanungen für Osteuropa: Konrad Meyer, der "Generalplan Ost" und die Deutsche Forschungsgemeinschaft', in Isabel Heinemann and Patrick Wagner (eds), *Wissenschaft, Planung, Vertreibung: Neuordnungskonzepte und Umsiedlungspolitik im 20. Jahrhundert* (Franz Steiner Verlag, Stuttgart, 2006), pp. 45–72.

—— and Patrick Wagner (eds), *Wissenschaft, Planung, Vertreibung: Neuordnungskonzepte und Umsiedlungspolitik im 20. Jahrhundert* (Franz Steiner Verlag, Stuttgart, 2006).

Helstosky, Carol, *Garlic and Oil. Food and Politics in Italy* (Berg, Oxford, 2004).

Herbert, Ulrich, *Hitler's Foreign Workers. Enforced Foreign Labor in Germany under the Third Reich* (Cambridge University Press, Cambridge, 1997).

Hernández-Sandoica, Elena and Enrique Moradiellos, 'Spain and the Second World War, 1939–1945', in Neville Wylie (ed.), *European Neutrals and Non-Belligerents During the Second World War* (Cambridge University Press, Cambridge, 2002), pp. 241–68.

Hicks, Brigadier Sir C. Stanton, *"Who Called the Cook a Bastard?"* (Keyline Publishing, Sydney, 1972).

Higa, Tomiko, *The Girl with the White Flag. An Inspiring Story of Love and Courage in War Time* (Kodansha International, London, 1991).

Hinze, Sibylle, '"Die ungewöhnlich geduldigen Deutschen". Arbeiterleben 1934–36 im Spiegel ausgewählter Gestapodokumente (Regierungsbezirk Potsdam)', in Dietrich Eichholtz and Almuth Püschel (eds), *Verfolgung, Alltag, Widerstand. Brandenburg in der NS-Zeit. Studien und Dokumente* (Verlag Volk & Welt, Berlin, 1993), pp. 32–62.

Hionidou, Violetta, '"Send us either food or coffins": the 1941–2 famine on the Aegean island of Syros', in Tim Dyson and Cormac Ó Gráda (eds), *Famine Demography. Perspectives from the Past and Present* (Oxford University Press, Oxford, 2002), pp. 181–203.

Hobsbawm, Eric, *The Age of Extremes. The Short Twentieth Century 1914–1991* (Michael Joseph, London, 1994).

Hodgson, Vere, *Few Eggs and No Oranges. A Diary Showing How Unimportant People in London and Birmingham Lived through the War Years 1940–45* (Dennis Dobson, London, 1976).

Hogan, Michael J., *The Marshall Plan. America, Britain and the Reconstruction of Western Europe, 1947–1952* (Cambridge University Press, Cambridge, 1987).

Holland, Roy Fraser, 'Mobilization, rejuvenation and liquidation: colonialism and global war', in Lloyd E. Lee, *World War II. Crucible of the Contemporary World: Commentary and Readings* (M. E. Sharpe, London, 1991), pp. 159–90.

Hollingsworth, Dorothy, 'Rationing and economic constraints on food consumption in Britain since the Second World War', in Derek J. Oddy and Derek S. Miller (eds), *Diet and Health in Modern Britain* (Croom Helm, London, 1985).

Honda, Gail, 'Differential structure, differential health: industrialization in Japan, 1868–1940', in Richard H. Steckel and Roderick Floud (eds), *Health and Welfare during Industrialization* (University of Chicago Press, Chicago, 1997), pp. 251–84.

Hongmin, Chen, 'Traditional responses to modern war: the Nationalist post-stage system and the Communist Great Production Movement', in David P. Barrett and Larry N. Shyu (eds), *China in the Anti-Japanese War, 1937–1945. Politics, Culture and Society* (Peter Lang, Oxford, 2001), pp. 189–203.

Houldsworth, Marion, *The Morning Side of the Hill. A Townsville Childhood 1939–45* (Department of History and Politics, James Cook University, 1995).

Howard, N. P., 'The social and political consequences of the Allied food blockade of Germany, 1918–19', *German History* 11 (2) (1993): 161–88.

Huegel, Arnulf, *Kriegsernährungswirtschaft Deutschlands während des Ersten und Zweiten Weltkrieges im Vergleich* (Hartung-Gorre Verlag, Konstanz, 2003).

Huen, P. Lim Pui and Diana Wong (eds), *War and Memory in Malaysia and Singapore* (Institute of Southeast Asia Studies, Singapore, 2000).

Humburg, Martin, *Das Gesicht des Krieges. Feldpostbriefe von Wehrmachtssoldaten aus der Sowjetunion 1941–1944* (Westdeutscher Verlag, Wiesbaden, 1998).

Hurd, Anthony, *A Farmer in Whitehall. Britain's Farming Revolution 1939–1950 and Future Prospects* (Country Life Ltd., London, 1951).

Hurt, Douglas R., *American Agriculture. A Brief History* (Iowa State University Press, Ames, IA, 1994).

——, *Problems of Plenty. The American Farmer in the Twentieth Century* (Ivan R. Dee, Chicago, 2002).

Illife, John, *A Modern History of Tanganyika* (Cambridge University Press, Cambridge, 1979).

Ingham, Barbara and Colin Simmons (eds), *Development Studies and Colonial Policy* (Frank Cass, London, 1987).

Iriye, Akira, *The Origins of the Second World War in Asia and the Pacific* (Longman, London, 1987).

Ishige, Naomichi, 'Japan', in Kenneth Kiple and Kriemhild Coneè Ornelas (eds), *The Cambridge World History of Food*, 2 vols (Cambridge University Press, Cambridge, 2000), vol. 2, pp. 1175–83.

Jackson, Ashley, *Botswana 1939–1945. An African Country at War* (Clarendon Press, Oxford, 1999).

——, 'Supplying war: the High Commission Territories' military-logistical contribution in the Second World War', *Journal of Military History* 66 (3) (2002): 719–60.

——, *The British Empire and the Second World War* (Hambledon Continuum, London, 2006).

Jacobs, Meg, '"How about some meat?": The Office of Price Administration, consumption politics, and state building from the bottom up, 1941–1946', *Journal of American History* 84 (December 1997): 911–41.

Jaffrey, Madhur, *Climbing the Mango Trees. A Memoir of a Childhood in India* (Ebury Press, London, 2006.)

James, W. Philip T., 'Food and nutrition policy in this century', in Nancy Milio and Elisabet Helsing, *European Food and Nutrition Policies in Action* (WHO Regional Office, Europe, 1998), pp. 17–22.

Jeffreys, Kevin, 'British politics and social policy during the Second World War', *Historical Journal* 30 (1987), pp. 123–44.

Jeffries, John W., *Wartime America. The World War II Home Front* (Ivan R. Dee, Chicago, 1996).

Jenkins, Roy, *Churchill* (Pan Books, London, 2001).

Johnson, David, 'Settler farmers and coerced African labour in Southern Rhodesia, 1936–1946', *Journal of African History* 33 (1992): 111–28.

Johnston, B. F., with Mosaburo Hosoda and Yoshio Kusumi, *Japanese Food Management in World War II* (Stanford University Press, Stanford, CA, 1953).

Johnston, Mark, *The Australian Army in World War II* (Osprey, Oxford, 2007).

Jonsson, Guðmundur, 'Changes in food consumption in Iceland, 1770–1940', *Scandinavian Economic History Review* 46 (1) (1998): 24–41.

Jose, Ricardo Trota, 'Food production and food distribution programmes in the Philippines during the Japanese occupation', in Paul H. Kratoska (ed.), *Food Supplies and the Japanese Occupation in South-East Asia* (Macmillan, London, 1998), pp. 67–100.

Joseph, K. S. and M. S. Kramer, 'Review of the evidence on fetal and early childhood antecedents of adult chronic disease', *Epidemiologic Reviews* 18 (1996): 158–74.

Joseph, Shirley, *If Their Mothers Only Knew. An Unofficial Account of Life in the Women's Land Army* (Faber & Faber, London, 1956).

Kahn, Miriam and Lorraine Sexton, 'The fresh and the canned: food choices in the Pacific', *Food and Foodways* 3 (1998): 1–18.

Kamtekar, Indivar, 'A different war dance: state and class in India 1939–1945', *Past and Present* 176 (2002): 187–221.

Kaplan, Marion, 'Jewish daily life in wartime Germany', in David Bankier (ed.), *Probing the Depths of German Antisemitism. German Society and the Persecution of the Jews, 1933–1941* (Berghahn Books, Oxford, 2000), pp. 395–414.

Kay, Alex J., *Exploitation, Resettlement, Mass Murder. Political and Economic Planning for German Occupation Policy in the Soviet Union, 1940–1941* (Berghahn Books, Oxford, 2006).

Keay, John, *India. A History* (HarperCollins, London, 2001).

Keegan, John, *The Second World War* (Hutchinson, London, 1989).

Kennedy, Susan Estabrook, 'Herbert Hoover and the two great food crusades of the 1940s', in Lee Nash (ed.), *Understanding Herbert Hoover* (Stanford University Press, Stanford, CA, 1978), pp. 87–106.

Kennett, Lee, *G.I. The American Soldier in World War Two* (Charles Scribner's Son, New York, 1987).

Kerkvliet, Benedict, J. Tria, 'Withdrawal and resistance: the political significance of food, agriculture and how people lived during the Japanese occupation in the Philippines', in Bernd Martin and Alan S. Milward (eds), *Agriculture and Food Supply in the Second World War. Landwirtschaft und Versorgung im Zweiten Weltkrieg* (Scripta Mercaturae Verlag, Ostfildern, 1985), pp. 297–315.

Kershaw, Ian, *Hitler. 1889–1936: Hubris* (Allen Lane, London, 1998).

——, *Fateful Choices. Ten Decisions that Changed the World, 1940–1941* (Allen Lane, London, 2007).

Kerslake, R. T., *Time and the Hour. Nigeria, East Africa and the Second World War* (Radcliffe Press, London, 1997).

Kersten, Andrew E., *Labor's Home Front. The American Federation of Labor during World War II* (New York University Press, London, 2006).

Keyssar, Helene and Vladimir Pozner, *Remembering War. A US–Soviet Dialogue* (Oxford University Press, Oxford, 1990).

Kheng, Cheah Boon, 'Memory as history and moral judgement. Oral and written accounts of the Japanese occupation of Malaya', in P. Lim Pui Huen and Diana

Wong (eds), *War and Memory in Malaysia and Singapore* (Institute of Southeast Asia Studies, Singapore, 2000), pp. 23–44.

Killingray, David, 'African civilians in the era of the Second World War *c.*1935–1950', in John Laband (ed.), *Daily Lives of Civilians in Wartime Africa. From Slavery Days to Rwandan Genocide* (Greenwood Press, London, 2007), pp. 139–68.

—— and Richard Rathbone (eds), *Africa and the Second World War* (Macmillan, London, 1986).

Kingston, Paul, R. G. Tiedemann and Nicholas Westcott, *Managed Economies in World War II* (School of Oriental and African Studies, University of London, 1991).

Kitchen, Martin, *Nazi Germany at War* (Longman, London, 1995).

Klukowski, Zygmunt, *Diary from the Years of Occupation 1939–44* (trans. George Klukowski; ed. Andrew Klukowski and Helen Klukowski May, University of Illinois Press, Urbana, 1993).

Knight, Sir Henry, *Food Administration in India 1939–47* (Stanford University Press, Stanford, CA, 1954).

Kopke, Christoph, 'Der "Ernährungsinspekteur der Waffen-SS". Zur Rolle des Mediziners Ernst Günther Schenck im Nationalsozialismus', in Christoph Kopke (ed.), *Medizin und Verbrechen. Festschrift zum 60. Geburtstag von Walther Wuttke* (Klemm & Oelschläger, Ulm, 2001), pp. 208–20.

—— (ed.), *Medizin und Verbrechen. Festschrift zum 60. Geburtstag von Walther Wuttke* (Klemm & Oelschläger, Ulm, 2001).

Kratoska, Paul H. (ed.), *Food Supplies and the Japanese Occupation in South-East Asia* (Macmillan, London, 1998).

——, 'The impact of the Second World War on commercial rice production in mainland South-East Asia', in Paul H. Kratoska (ed.), *Food Supplies and the Japanese Occupation in South-East Asia* (Macmillan, London, 1998), pp. 9–31.

——, 'Introduction', in Paul H. Kratoska (ed.), *Food Supplies and the Japanese Occupation in South-East Asia* (Macmillan, London, 1998), pp. 1–8.

——, *The Japanese Occupation of Malaya. A Social and Economic History* (Hurst & Company, London, 1998).

——, 'Malayan food shortages and the Kedah rice industry during the Japanese Occupation', in Paul H. Kratoska (ed.), *Food Supplies and the Japanese Occupation in South-East Asia* (Macmillan, London, 1998), pp. 101–34.

Kraut, Heinrich and Herbert Bramsel, 'Der Calorienbedarf der Berufe ermittelt aus den Erhebungen von Wirtschaftsrechnungen im Deutschen Reich vom Jahre 1927/28', *Arbeitsphysiologie* 12 (3) (1942): 197–221.

Kravchenko, Victor, *I Chose Freedom. The Personal and Political Life of a Soviet Official* (Robert Hale, London, 1947).

Kroen, Sheryl, 'Negotiations with the American way: the consumer and the social contract in post-war Europe', in John Brewer and Frank Trentmann (eds),

Consuming Cultures, Global Perspectives. Historical Trajectories, Transnational Exchanges (Berg, Oxford, 2006), pp. 251–78.

Kroener, Bernhard R., Rolf-Dieter Müller and Hans Umbriet, *Das Deutsche Reich und Der Zweite Weltkrieg*, 10 vols (Deutsche Verlags-Anstalt, Stuttgart, 1988–99).

Kroes, R., R.W. Rydell and D. F. J. Bosscher (eds), *Cultural Transmission and Receptions. American Mass Culture in Europe* (V. U. University Press, Amsterdam, 1993).

Kryder, Daniel, *Divided Arsenal: Race and the American State During World War II* (Cambridge University Press, Cambridge, 2000).

Kuisel, Richard F., *Seducing the French. The Dilemma of Americanization* (University of California Press, Berkeley, 1993).

Kuramoto, Kazuko, *Manchurian Legacy. Memoirs of a Japanese Colonist* (Michigan State University Press, East Lansing, 1999).

Kurasawa, Aiko, 'Transportation and rice distribution in South-East Asia during the Second World War', in Paul H. Kratoska (ed.), *Food Supplies and the Japanese Occupation in South-East Asia* (Macmillan, London, 1998), pp. 32–66.

Kutz, Martin, 'Kriegserfahrung und Kriegsvorbereitung. Die agrarwirtschaftliche Vorbereitung des Zweiten Weltkrieges in Deutschland vor dem Hintergrund der Weltkrieg I – Erfahrung', *Zeitschrift für Agrargeschichte und Agrarsoziologie* 32 (1984): 59–82, 135–63.

Laband, John (ed.), *Daily Lives of Civilians in Wartime Africa. From Slavery Days to Rwandan Genocide* (Greenwood Press, London, 2007).

Lamer, Mirko, *The World Fertilizer Economy* (Stanford University Press, Stanford, CA, 1957).

Lammers, Cornelis J., 'Levels of collaboration. A comparative study of German occupation regimes during the Second World War', in Robert Bohn (ed.), *Die Deutsche Herrschaft in den "germanischen" Ländern 1940–1945* (Franz Steiner Verlag, Stuttgart, 1997), pp. 47–69.

Lamont, Lindstrom, 'Oral histories of World War II labor corps from Tanna, Vanuatu', in Geoffrey M. White and Lamont Lindstrom (eds), *The Pacific Theater. Island Representations of World War II* (University of Hawaii Press, Honolulu, 1989), pp. 395–417.

Laqueur, Walter and Richard Breitman, *Breaking the Silence. The Secret Mission of Eduard Schulte, Who Brought the World News of the Final Solution* (Bodley Head, London, 1986).

Lawrence, Felicity, *Eat Your Heart Out: Why the Food Business is Bad for the Planet and Your Health* (Penguin, London, 2008).

Laybourn, Keith, *Britain on the Breadline. A Social and Political History of Britain between the Wars* (Alan Sutton, Gloucester, 1990).

Lee, Dwight E. (ed.), *The Outbreak of the First World War. Causes and Responsibilities* (D. C. Heath & Company, Lexington, MA, 1975).

Lee, Lloyd E., *World War II. Crucible of the Contemporary World: Commentary and Readings* (M. E. Sharpe, London, 1991).

Leff, Mark H., 'The politics of sacrifice on the American home front in World War II', *Journal of American History* 77 (3–4) (March 1991): 1296–1318.

Lehmann, Joachim, 'Agrarpolitik und Landwirtschaft in Deutschland 1939 bis 1945', in Bernd Martin and Alan S. Milward (eds), *Agriculture and Food Supply in the Second World War. Landwirtschaft und Versorgung im Zweiten Weltkrieg* (Scripta Mercaturae Verlag, Ostfildern, 1985), pp. 29–49.

——, 'Herbert Backe – Technocrat und Agrarideologe', in Ronald Smelser, Enrico Syring and Rainer Zitelman (eds), *Die Braune Elite II: 21 weitere biographische Skizzen* (Wissenschaftliche Buchgesellschaft, Darmstadt, 1993), pp. 1–12.

Levenstein, Harvey, *Paradox of Plenty. A Social History of Eating in Modern America* (Oxford University Press, Oxford, 1993).

Levi, Primo, *If This Is a Man* and *The Truce* (first published 1958 and 1963, Abacus, London, 1987).

Levich, Eugene William, *The Kwangsi Way in Kuomintang China 1931–39* (M. E. Sharpe, London, 1993).

Levine, Susan, *School Lunch Politics. The Surprising History of America's Favorite Welfare Program* (Princeton University Press, Princeton, 2008).

Lewis, Michael, *Rioters and Citizens Mass. Protest in Imperial Japan* (University of California Press, Berkeley, 1990).

Lindstrom, Lamont and Geoffrey M. White, 'War stories', in Geoffrey M. White and Lamont Lindstrom (eds), *The Pacific Theater. Island Representations of World War II* (University of Hawaii Press, Honolulu, 1989), pp. 3–40.

Linz, Susan J. (ed.), *The Impact of World War II on the Soviet Union* (Rowman & Allanheld, Totowa, NJ, 1985).

——, 'World War II and Soviet economic growth, 1940–1953', in Susan J. Linz (ed.), *The Impact of World War II on the Soviet Union* (Rowman & Allanheld, Totowa, NJ, 1985), pp. 11–38.

Litoff, Judy Barrett and David C. Smith (eds), *Since You Went Away. World War II Letters from American Women on the Home Front* (Oxford University Press, Oxford, 1991).

Lloyd, E. M. H., *Food and Inflation in the Middle East 1940–1945* (Stanford University Press, Stanford, CA, 1956).

Longmate, N., *How We Lived Then. A History of Everyday Life during the Second World War* (Hutchinson, London, 1971).

Lonsdale, John, 'The Depression and the Second World War in the transformation of Kenya', in David Killingray and Richard Rathbone (eds), *Africa and the Second World War* (Macmillan, London, 1986), pp. 97–142.

Lovin, Clifford R., 'Blut und Boden: the ideological basis of the Nazi agricultural program', *Journal of the History of Ideas* 28 (1967): 279–88.

——, 'Agricultural reorganization in the Third Reich: the Reich Food Corporation (Reichsnährstand), 1933–1936', *Agricultural History* 43 (1969): 447–61.

Lowe, David, *Menzies and the 'Great World Struggle'. Australia's Cold War, 1948–1954* (University of New South Wales Press, Sydney, 1999).

Lucas, James, *The War on the Eastern Front 1941–1945. The German Soldier in Russia* (Jane's Publishing Company, London, 1979).

Luczak, Czeslaw, 'Landwirtschaft und Ernährung in Polen während der deutschen Besatzungszeit 1939–1945', in Bernd Martin and Alan S. Milward (eds), *Agriculture and Food Supply in the Second World War. Landwirtschaft und Versorgung im Zweiten Weltkrieg* (Scripta Mercaturae Verlag, Ostfildern, 1985), pp. 117–27.

Lüdtke, Alf, 'Hunger, Essens-"Genuß" und Politik bei Fabrikarbeitern und Arbeiterfrauen. Beispiele aus dem rheinisch-westfälischen Industriegebiet, 1910–1940', *Sozialwissenschaftliche Informationen* 14 (2) (1985): 118–25.

Lumley, L. H., 'Reproductive outcomes in women prenatally exposed to undernutrition: a review of findings from the Dutch famine birth cohort', *Proceedings of the Nutrition Society* 57 (1998): 129–35.

McCoy, Alfred W. (ed.), *Southeast Asia under Japanese Occupation* (Yale University Press, New Haven, 1980).

McDermott, George L., *Women Recall the War Years: Memories of World War II* (Professional Press, Chapel Hill, NC, 1998).

Macintyre, Kate, 'Famine and the female mortality advantage', in Tim Dyson and Cormac Ó Gráda (eds), *Famine Demography. Perspectives from the Past and Present* (Oxford University Press, Oxford, 2002), pp. 240–59.

Mackay, Robert, *Half the Battle. Civilian Morale in Britain During the Second World War* (Manchester University Press, Manchester, 2002).

MacKinnon, Stephen, 'Refugee flight at the outset of the Anti-Japanese War', in Diana Lary and Stephen MacKinnon (eds), *Scars of War: The Impact of Warfare on Modern China* (UBC Press, Vancouver, 2001), pp. 118–35.

MacNalty, Arthur Salusbury and W. Franklin Mellor, *Medical Services in War. The Principal Medical Lessons of the Second World War. Based on the Official Medical Histories of the United Kingdom, Canada, Australia, New Zealand and India* (HMSO, London, 1968).

McQuarrie, Peter, *Strategic Atolls. Tuvalu and the Second World War* (Macmillan Brown Centre for Pacific Studies, University of Canterbury and Institute of Pacific Studies, University of South Pacific, Christchurch, New Zealand, 1993).

——, *Conflict in Kiribati. A History of the Second World War* (Macmillan Brown Centre for Pacific Studies, University of Canterbury and Institute of Pacific Studies, University of South Pacific, Christchurch, New Zealand, 2000).

Madajczyk, Czeslaw, 'Vom "Generalplan Ost" zum "Generalsiedlungsplan"', in Mechtild Rössler, Sabine Schleiermacher and Cordula Tollmien (eds), *Der "Generalplan Ost". Hauptlinien der nationalsozialistischen Planungs- und Vernichtungspolitik* (Akademie Verlag, Berlin, 1993), pp. 12–17.

Magaeva, Svetlana, 'Physiological and psychosomatic prerequisites for survival and recovery', in John Barber and Andrei Dzeniskevich (eds), *Life and Death in Besieged Leningrad, 1941–44* (Palgrave Macmillan, London, 2005), pp. 123–59.

Magee, H. E., 'Some effects of inanition and their treatment', *Proceedings of the Nutritional Society*, 3 (1945): 53–7.

Magnússon, Finnur, *The Hidden Class. Culture and Class in a Maritime Setting – Iceland 1880–1942* (Aarhus University Press, Denmark, 1990).

Mai, Uwe, *"Rasse und Raum". Agrarpolitik, Sozial- und Raumplanung im NS-Staat* (Ferdinand Schöningh, Paderborn, 2002).

Malcolm, Sheila, *Diet and Nutrition in American Samoa. A Survey* (South Pacific Commission, Noumea, New Caledonia, August 1954).

Mant, Joan, *All Muck, No Medals. Land Girls by Land Girls* (Book Guild, Lewes, 1994).

Martin, Bernd, 'Japans Kriegswirtschaft 1941–1945', in Friedrich Forstmeier and Hans-Erich Volkmann (eds), *Kriegswirtschaft und Rüstung 1939–1945* (Droste Verlag, Düsseldorf, 1977), pp. 256–86.

——, 'Agriculture and food supply in Japan during the Second World War', in Bernd Martin and Alan S. Milward (eds), *Agriculture and Food Supply in the Second World War. Landwirtschaft und Versorgung im Zweiten Weltkrieg* (Scripta Mercaturae Verlag, Ostfildern, 1985).

——, *Japan and Germany in the Modern World* (Berghahn Books, Oxford, 1995).

—— and Alan S. Milward (eds), *Agriculture and Food Supply in the Second World War. Landwirtschaft und Versorgung im Zweiten Weltkrieg* (Scripta Mercaturae Verlag, Ostfildern, 1985).

Martin, John, *The Development of Modern Agriculture. British Farming since 1931* (Macmillan, London, 2000).

——, 'The structural transformation of British agriculture: the resurgence of progressive high-input arable farming', in Brian Short, Charles Watkins and John Martin (eds), *The Front Line of Freedom. British Farming in the Second World War* (British Agricultural Society, Exeter, 2006), History pp. 16–35.

Mason, Timothy W., *Social Policy in the Third Reich. The Working Class and the 'National Community'* (Berg, Oxford, 1993).

Matusow, Allen J., *Farm Policies and Politics in the Truman Years* (Harvard University Press, Cambridge, MA, 1967).

Mayhew, Madeleine, 'The 1930s nutrition controversy', *Journal of Contemporary History* 23 (3) (1988): 445–64.

Mazower, Mark, *Inside Hitler's Greece. The Experience of Occupation, 1941–44* (Yale University Press, London, 1993).

——, *Hitler's Empire. Nazi Rule in Occupied Europe* (Allen Lane, London, 2008).

Medvedev, Zhores, *Soviet Agriculture* (W. W. Norton & Company, London, 1987).

Mellor, D. P., *The Role of Science and Industry. Australia in the War of 1939–1945*, Series 4, Vol. 5 (Australian War Memorial, Canberra, 1958).

Meredith, David, 'State controlled marketing and economic "development": the case of West African produce during the Second World War', *Economic History Review* 39 (1) (1986): 77–91.

Merridale, Catherine, *Ivan's War. The Red Army 1939–1945* (Faber & Faber, London, 2005).

Michaelis, Hans Ferdinand, 'Über die Wirkung einer warmen Mahlzeit auf die Leistungsfähigkeit von Frauen bei Nachtarbeit', *Arbeitsphysiologie* 12 (2) (1942): 134–41.

Milio, Nancy and Elisabet Helsing, *European Food and Nutrition Policies in Action* (WHO Regional Office, Europe, 1998).

Miller, Grace Porter, *Call of Duty. A Montana Girl in World War II* (Louisiana State University Press, Baton Rouge, 1999).

Miller, James R., 'Conclusion: impact and aftermath of World War II', in Susan J. Linz (ed.), *The Impact of World War II on the Soviet Union* (Rowman & Allanheld, Totowa, NJ, 1985), pp. 283–91.

Milward, Alan S., *The Fascist Economy in Norway* (Clarendon Press, Oxford, 1972).

——, 'The Second World War and long-term change in world agriculture', in Bernd Martin and Alan S. Milward (eds), *Agriculture and Food Supply in the Second World War. Landwirtschaft und Versorgung im Zweiten Weltkrieg* (Scripta Mercaturae Verlag, Ostfildern, 1985), pp. 5–15.

——, *War, Economy and Society 1939–1945* (Penguin, London, 1987).

Mintz, Sidney, *Tasting Food, Tasting Freedom. Excursions into Eating, Culture and the Past* (Beacon Press, Boston, 1996).

Mitter, Rana, *A Bitter Revolution. China's Struggle with the Modern World* (Oxford University Press, Oxford, 2004).

——, *Modern China. A Very Short Introduction* (Oxford University Press, Oxford, 2008).

Moeller, Robert G. (eds.), *Peasants and Lords in Modern Germany. Recent Studies in Agricultural History* (Allen & Unwin, London, 1986).

Moharir, V. J., *History of the Army Service Corps (1939–1946)* (Sterling Publishers, New Delhi, 1979).

Moore, Bob, 'The western Allies and food relief to the occupied Netherlands, 1944–1945', *War and Society* 10 (2) (October 1992): 91–118.

Moore, Martin, *Fourth Shore. Italy's Mass Colonization of Libya* (George Routledge & Sons, London, 1940).

Morehouse, Maggi M., *Fighting in the Jim Crow Army. Black Men and Women Remember World War II* (Rowman & Littlefield, New York, Oxford, 2000).

Morley, James William (ed.), *Dilemmas of Growth in Prewar Japan* (Princeton University Press, Princeton, NJ, 1971).

Morris, John, *Traveller from Tokyo* (Cresset Press, London, 1943).

Morris-Suzuki, Tessa, *Showa. An Inside History of Hirohito's Japan* (Athlone Press, London, 1984).

Moskoff, William, *The Bread of Affliction. The Food Supply in the USSR During World War II* (Cambridge University Press, Cambridge, 1990).

Müller, Rolf-Dieter, 'Die Mobilisierung der deutschen Wirtschaft für Hitlers Kriegführung', in Bernhard R. Kroener, Rolf-Dieter Müller and Hans Umbriet, *Das Deutsche Reich und der Zweite Weltkrieg*. Vol. 5/1. *Organisation und Mobilisierung des deutschen Machtbereichs. Kriegsverwaltung, Wirtschaft und Personelle Resourcen 1939–1941* (Deutsche Verlags-Anstalt, Stuttgart, 1988), pp. 349–692.

——, 'Albert Speer und die Rüstungspolitik im totalen Krieg', in Bernhard R. Kroener, Rolf-Dieter Müller and Hans Umbriet, *Das Deutsche Reich und der Zweite Weltkrieg*. Vol. 5/2. *Organisation und Mobilisierung des deutschen Machtbereichs. Kriegsverwaltung, Wirtschaft und Personelle Resourcen 1942–1944/45* (Deutsche Verlags-Anstalt, Stuttgart, 1999), pp. 275–776.

Murray, Keith A., *Agriculture* (first pub. 1955, HMSO and Kraus Reprint, London, 1975).

Myers, Ramon H. and Mark R. Peattie, *The Japanese Colonial Empire, 1895–1945* (Princeton University Press, Princeton, NJ, 1984).

—— and Yamada Saburo, 'Agricultural development in the Empire,' in Ramon H. Myers and Mark R. Peattie, *The Japanese Colonial Empire, 1895–1945* (Princeton University Press, Princeton, NJ, 1984) pp. 420–54.

Nash, Lee (ed.), *Understanding Herbert Hoover* (Stanford University Press, Stanford, CA, 1978).

Naylor, Rosamund L. and Walter P. Falcon, 'Our daily bread: without public intervention the food crisis will only get worse', *Boston Review* (October 2008): 13–18.

Nelson, Hank, '*Taim Bilong Pait*: The impact of the Second World War on Papua New Guinea', in Alfred W. McCoy (ed.), *Southeast Asia Under Japanese Occupation* (Yale University Press, New Haven, 1980), pp. 246–66.

Nero, Karen L., 'Time of famine, time of transformation: hell in the Pacific, Palau', in Geoffrey M. White and Lamont Lindstrom (eds), *The Pacific Theater. Island Representations of World War II* (University of Hawaii Press, Honolulu, 1989), pp. 117–47.

Neubarth, Raymond G., *Dental Conditions in School Children of American Samoa* (South Pacific Commission, Noumea, New Caledonia, 1954).

Neumann, Alexander, 'Nutritional physiology in the Third Reich 1933–45', in Wolfgang Uwe Eckart (ed.), *Man, Medicine and the State. The Human Body as an Object of Government* (Franz Steiner Verlag, Stuttgart, 2006), pp. 49–60.

Newman, Lucile F. (ed.), *Hunger in History. Food Shortage, Poverty, and Deprivation* (Basil Blackwell, Oxford, 1990).

Newman, Robert P., *Truman and the Hiroshima Cult* (Michigan State University Press, East Lansing, 1995).

Nissen, Mogens R., 'Danish food production in the German war economy', in Frank Trentmann and Flemming Just (eds), *Food and Conflict in Europe in the Age of the Two World Wars* (Palgrave Macmillan, Basingstoke, 2006), pp. 172–92.

Nove, Alec, 'Soviet peasantry in World War II', in Susan J. Linz (ed.), *The Impact of World War II on the Soviet Union* (Rowman and Allanheld, Totowa, NJ, 1985), pp. 77–90.

Nützenadel, Alexander, 'Dictating food: autarchy, food provision, and consumer politics in fascist Italy, 1922–1943', in Frank Trentmann and Flemming Just (eds), *Food and Conflict in Europe in the Age of the Two World Wars* (Palgrave Macmillan, Basingstoke, 2006), pp. 88–108.

Obenaus, Herbert, 'Hunger und Überleben in den nationalsozialistischen Konzentrationslagern (1938–1945)', in Manfred Gailus and Heinrich Volkmann (eds), *Der Kampf um das tägliche Brot. Nahrungsmangel, versorgungspolitik und Protest 1770–1990* (Westdeutscher Verlag, Opladen, 1994), pp. 361–76.

Oddy, Derek J., *From Plain Fare to Fusion Food. British Diet from the 1890s to the 1990s* (Boydell Press, Woodbridge, 2003).

—— and Derek S. Miller (eds), *Diet and Health in Modern Britain* (Croom Helm, London, 1985).

Offer, Avner, *The First World War. An Agrarian Interpretation* (Clarendon Press, Oxford, 1989).

Ohnuki-Tierney, Emiko, *Rice as Self. Japanese Identities Through Time* (Princeton University Press, Princeton, NJ, 1993).

Onn, Chin Kee, *Malaya Upside Down* (Federal Publications, Singapore, 1976).

Ooka, Shohei, *Fires on the Plain* (trans. Ivan Morris, Charles E. Tuttle Company, Tokyo, 1957).

Orr, Lord John Boyd, *As I Recall* (MacGibbon & Kee, London, 1966).

Ousby, Ian, *Occupation. The Ordeal of France 1940–1944* (John Murray, London, 1997).

Overy, Richard, *Why the Allies Won* (Pimlico, London, 1995).

——, *Russia's War* (Penguin, London, 1998).

Panter-Downes, Mollie, *One Fine Day* (first pub. 1947, Virago, London, 1985).

Parillo, Mark P., *The Japanese Merchant Marine in World War II* (Naval Institute Press, Annapolis, MD, 1993).

Partner, Simon, 'Daily life of civilians in wartime Japan, 1937–1945', in Stewart Lone (ed.), *Daily Lives of Civilians in Wartime Asia* (Greenwood Publishing Group, Westport, CT, 2007), pp. 127–54.

Patten, Marguerite, *Victory Cookbook. Nostalgic Food and Facts from 1940–1954* (Chancellor Press, London, 2004).

Patterson, James T., *Grand Expectations. The United States 1945–1974* (Oxford University Press, Oxford, 1996).

Pauer, Erich, 'Neighbourhood associations and food distribution in Japanese cities in World War II', in Bernd Martin and Alan S. Milward (eds), *Agriculture and*

Food Supply in the Second World War. Landwirtschaft und Versorgung im Zweiten Weltkrieg (Scripta Mercaturae Verlag, Ostfildern, 1985), pp. 219–41.

Pearce, Robert, 'The colonial economy: Nigeria and the Second World War', in Barbara Ingham and Colin Simmons (eds), *Development Studies and Colonial Policy* (Frank Cass, London, 1987), pp. 263–92.

Peattie, Mark R., 'Japanese attitudes towards colonialism, 1895–1945', in Ramon H. Myers and Mark R. Peattie, *The Japanese Colonial Empire, 1895–1945* (Princeton University Press, Princeton, NJ, 1984), pp. 80–127.

——, '*Nanshin*: the "Southward Advance", 1931–1941, as a prelude to the Japanese occupation of Southeast Asia', in Peter Duus, Ramon H. Myers and Mark R. Peattie (eds), *The Japanese Wartime Empire, 1931–1945* (Princeton University Press, Princeton, NJ, 1996), pp. 189–242.

Pells, Richard, 'American culture abroad: the European experience since 1945', in R. Kroes, R.W. Rydell and D. F. J. Bosscher (eds), *Cultural Transmission and Receptions. American Mass Culture in Europe* (V. U. University Press, Amsterdam, 1993), pp. 67–83.

Perkins, John H., *Geopolitics and the Green Revolution. Wheat, Genes and the Cold War* (Oxford University Press, Oxford, 1997).

Picker, Henry, *Hitlers Tischgespräche im Führerhauptquartier. Vollständig überarbeitete und erweiterte Neuausgabe mit bisher unbekannten Selbstzeugnissen Adolf Hitlers, Abbildungen, Augenzeugenberichten und Erläuterungen des Autors: Hitler, wie er wirklich war* (Seewald Verlag, Stuttgart, 1976).

Pitkin, Donald S., *The House that Giacomo Built. History of an Italian Family, 1898–1978* (Cambridge University Press, Cambridge, 1985).

Polenberg, Richard, *War and Society. The United States 1941–1945* (J. B. Lippincott Company, Philadelphia, New York, Toronto, 1972).

Pollan, Michael, *In Defence of Food. The Myth of Nutrition and the Pleasures of Eating* (Allen Lane, London, 2008).

Pollard, Sidney, *The Development of the British Economy 1914–1990* (first pub. 1962, 4th edn, Edward Arnold, London, 1992).

Poppendieck, Janet, *Breadlines Knee-Deep in Wheat. Food Assistance in the Great Depression* (Rutgers University Press, New Brunswick, NJ, 1986).

Potts, E. Daniel and Annette Potts, *Yanks Down Under 1941–45* (Oxford University Press, Melbourne, 1985).

Prendergast, Mark, *For God, Country and Coca-Cola. The Definitive History of the World's Most Popular Soft Drink* (Orion Business Books, London, 2000).

Proctor, Robert N., *The Nazi War on Cancer* (Princeton University Press, Princeton, NJ, 1999).

Production of Food Crops in Mauritius during the War, The (J. Eliel Felix, Acting Government Printer, Port Louis, Mauritius, 1947).

Pusen, Jin, 'To feed a country at war: China's supply and consumption of grain during the war of resistance', in David P. Barrett and Larry N. Shyu (eds), *China in the Anti-Japanese War, 1937–1945. Politics, Culture and Society* (Peter Lang, Oxford, 2001), 157–69.

Rahn, Werner, 'The war at sea in the Atlantic and in the Arctic Ocean', in Horst Boog, Werner Rahn, Reinhard Stumpf and Bernd Wegner, *Germany and the Second World War. Vol. 6. The Global War. Widening of the Conflict into a World War and the Shift of the Initiative 1941–43* (Clarendon Press, Oxford, 2001), pp. 301–441.

Rama, M. V. and P. Narasimham, 'The root crop and its uses', *Encyclopedia of Food Sciences and Nutrition*, 2nd edn, vol. 7 (Academic Press, London, 2003).

Rankine, Kerry, *Soya: The Ubiquitous Bean. A Look at the Environmental and Social Aspects of Soya Production* (Food Facts No. 5, Sustainable Agriculture, Food and Environment Alliance, London, 1999).

Rasmussen, Nicolas, 'Plant hormones in war and peace: science, industry, and government in the development of herbicides in 1940s America', *Isis* 92 (2) (2001): 291–316.

Reagin, Nancy R., '*Marktordnung* and autarkic housekeeping: housewives and private consumption under the Four-Year Plan, 1936–1939', *German History* 19 (2) (2001): 162–84.

——, *Sweeping the German Nation. Domesticity and National Identity in Germany, 1870–1945* (Cambridge University Press, Cambridge, 2007).

Reid, Anthony, 'Indonesia: from briefcase to Samurai sword', in Alfred W. McCoy (ed.), *Southeast Asia under Japanese Occupation* (Yale University Press, New Haven, CT, 1980), pp. 16–32.

Reynolds, David, *Rich Relations: The American Occupation of Britain 1942–1945* (Phoenix Press, London, 2000).

——, Warren F. Kimball and A. O. Chubarian (eds), *Allies at War. The Soviet, American and British Experience, 1939–1945* (Macmillan, London, 1994).

Risch, Erna, *The Quartermaster Corps: Organization, Supply, and Services. United States Army in World War II. The Technical Services* (Office of the Chief of Military History, Department of the Army, Washington, DC, 1953).

Robertson, Jennifer (ed.), *A Companion to the Anthropology of Japan* (Blackwell Publishing, Oxford, 2005).

Roland, Charles G., *Courage under Siege. Starvation, Disease and Death in the Warsaw Ghetto* (Oxford University Press, Oxford, 1992).

Roll, Eric, *The Combined Food Board. A Study in Wartime International Planning* (Stanford University Press, Stanford, CA, 1956).

Ronning, Chester, *A Memoir of China in Revolution. From the Boxer Rebellion to the People's Republic* (Pantheon Books, New York, 1974).

Roodhouse, Mark, 'Popular morality and the black market in Britain, 1939–1955', in Frank Trentmann and Flemming Just (eds), *Food and Conflict in Europe in the Age of the Two World Wars* (Palgrave Macmillan, Basingstoke, 2006), pp. 243–65.

Rosenberger, Leif Roderick, 'The strategic importance of the world food supply', *Parameters* (Spring 1997): 84–105.

Ross, William F. and Charles F. Romanus, *The Quartermaster Corps: Operations in the War against Germany* (Office of the Chief of Military History, Department of the Army, Washington, DC, 1965).

Rössler, Mechtild, 'Konrad Meyer und der "Generalplan Ost" in der Beurteilung der Nürnberger Prozesse', in Mechtild Rössler, Sabine Schleiermacher and Cordula Tollmien (eds), *Der "Generalplan Ost". Hauptlinien der nationalsozialistischen Planungs- und Vernichtungspolitik* (Akademie Verlag, Berlin, 1993), pp. 356–67.

—— and Sabine Schleiermacher, 'Der "Generalplan Ost" und die "Modernität" der Großraumordnung. Eine Einführung', in Mechtild Rössler, Sabine Schleiermacher and Cordula Tollmien (eds), *Der "Generalplan Ost". Hauptlinien der nationalsozialistischen Planungs- und Vernichtungspolitik* (Akademie Verlag, Berlin, 1993), pp. 7–11.

—— Sabine Schleiermacher and Cordula Tollmien (eds), *Der "Generalplan Ost". Hauptlinien der nationalsozialistischen Planungs- und Vernichtungspolitik* (Akademie Verlag, Berlin, 1993).

Roth, Karl Heinz, '"Generalplan Ost" – "Gesamtplan Ost". Forschungsstand, Quellenprobleme, neue Ergebnisse', in Mechtild Rössler, Sabine Schleiermacher and Cordula Tollmien (eds), *Der "Generalplan Ost". Hauptlinien der nationalsozialistischen Planungs- und Vernichtungspolitik* (Akademie Verlag, Berlin, 1993), pp. 25–95.

Rothermund, Dietmar, *An Economic History of India: From Pre-colonial Times to 1991* (Routledge, London, 1993).

Rummel, R. J., *China's Bloody Century. Genocide and Mass Murder Since 1900* (first pub. 1991, Transaction Publishers, London, 2007).

Russell, Sir Herbert, *Sea Shepherds. Wardens of our Food Flocks* (John Murray, London, 1941).

Rüther, Martin, *Köln im Zweiten Weltkrieg. Alltag und Erfahrungen zwischen 1939 und 1945. Darstellung – Bilder – Quellen* (Emons Verlag, Cologne, 2005).

Sajer, Guy, *The Forgotten Soldier. The True Story of a Young German Soldier on the Russian Front* (first pub. 1967, Phoenix, London, 2000).

Sakharov, Andrei, *Memoirs* (trans. Richard Lourie, Hutchinson, London, 1990).

Santich, Barbara, *What the Doctors Ordered. 150 Years of Dietary Advice in Australia* (Hyland House, Melbourne, 1995).

Sarkar, Sumit, *Modern India 1885–1947* (Macmillan, London, 1989).

Sato, Shigeru, 'Oppression and romanticism: the food supply of Java during the Japanese occupation', in Paul H. Kratoska (ed.), *Food Supplies and the Japanese Occupation in South-East Asia* (Macmillan, London, 1998), pp. 167–86.

Schain, Martin (ed.), *The Marshall Plan: Fifty Years After* (Palgrave, Basingstoke, 2001).

Scharf, Eginhard, *"Man machte mit uns, was man wollte". Ausländische Zwangs-arbeiter in Ludwigshafen am Rhein 1939–1945* (Verlag Regionalkultur, Heidelberg, 2004).

Schleiermacher, Sabine, 'Begleitende Forschung zum "Generalplan Ost"', in Mechtild Rössler, Sabine Schleiermacher and Cordula Tollmien (eds), *Der "Generalplan Ost". Hauptlinien der nationalsozialistischen Planungs- und Vernichtungspolitik* (Akademie Verlag, Berlin, 1993), pp. 339–45.

Schmidt, Ulf, *Karl Brandt. The Nazi Doctor: Medicine and Power in the Third Reich* (Hambledon Continuum, London, 2007).

Schulte, Theo J., *The German Army and Nazi Policies in Occupied Russia* (Berg, Oxford, 1989).

Scott, James, 'An approach to the problems of food supply in Southeast Asia during World War Two', in Bernd Martin and Alan S. Milward (eds), *Agriculture and Food Supply in the Second World War. Landwirtschaft und Versorgung im Zweiten Weltkrieg* (Scripta Mercaturae Verlag, Ostfildern, 1985), pp. 269–96.

Scrimshaw, Nevin, 'World nutritional problems', in Lucile F. Newman (ed.), *Hunger in History. Food Shortage, Poverty, and Deprivation* (Basil Blackwell, Oxford, 1990), pp. 353–73.

Sen, Amartya, *Poverty and Famines. An Essay on Entitlement and Deprivation* (Clarendon Press, Oxford, 1981).

Senoh, Kappa, *A Boy Called H. A Childhood in Wartime Japan* (Kodansha International, Tokyo, 1997).

Service, Robert, *A History of Twentieth-Century Russia* (Allen Lane, London, 1997).

Shen, Tsung-han, 'Food production and distribution for civilian and military needs in wartime China, 1937–1945', in Paul Sih (ed.), *Nationalist China During the Sino-Japanese War, 1937–1945* (Exposition Press, New York, 1977), pp. 167–93.

Sheridan, Dorothy (ed.), *Wartime Women. An Anthology of Women's Wartime Writing for Mass-Observation 1937–45* (Heinemann, London, 1990).

Shin'ichi, Yamamuro, *Manchuria under Japanese Dominion* (University of Pennsylvania Press, Philadelphia, 2006).

Short, Brian, 'The dispossession of farmers in England and Wales during and after the Second World War', in Brian Short, Charles Watkins and John Martin (eds), *The Front Line of Freedom. British Farming in the Second World War* (British Agricultural History Society, Exeter, 2006), pp. 158–78.

——, Charles Watkins and John Martin (eds), *The Front Line of Freedom. British Farming in the Second World War* (British Agricultural History Society, Exeter, 2006).

——, Charles Watkins and John Martin, '"The front line of freedom": state-led agricultural revolution in Britain, 1939–1945', in Brian Short, Charles Watkins and John Martin (eds), *The Front Line of Freedom. British Farming in the Second World War* (British Agricultural History Society, Exeter, 2006), pp. 1–15.

Simmons, Cynthia and Nina Perlina, *Writing the Siege of Leningrad: Women's Diaries, Memories and Documentary Prose* (University of Pittsburgh Press, Pittsburgh, PA, 2002).

Sledge, E. B., *With the Old Breed at Peleliu and Okinawa* (Oxford University Press, Oxford, 1981).

Slyke, Lyman P. van, 'The Chinese Communist movement during the Sino-Japanese War, 1937–1945', in Lloyd E. Eastman, Jerome Ch'en, Suzanne Pepper and Lyman P. van Slyke (eds), *The Nationalist Era in China, 1927–1949* (Cambridge University Press, Cambridge, 1991), pp. 177–290.

Smelser, Ronald, Enrico Syring and Rainer Zitelman (eds), *Die Braune Elite II: 21 weitere biographische Skizzen* (Wissenschaftliche Buchgesellschaft, Darmstadt, 1993).

Smith, Bradley F., *The War's Long Shadow. The Second World War and its Aftermath – China, Russia, Britain, America* (André Deutsch, London, 1986).

Smith, David F., (ed.), *Nutrition in Britain. Science, Scientists and Politics in the Twentieth Century* (Routledge, London, 1997).

—— 'Nutrition science and the two world wars', in David F. Smith (ed.), *Nutrition in Britain. Science, Scientists and Politics in the Twentieth Century* (Routledge, London, 1997), pp. 142–65.

Smith, Harold L. (ed.), *War and Social Change. British Society in the Second World War* (Manchester University Press, Manchester, 1986).

Smith, Kerry, *A Time of Crisis: Japan, the Great Depression and Rural Revitalization* (Harvard University Press, Cambridge, MA, 2001).

Smith, Kevin, *Conflict over Convoys. Anglo-American Logistics Diplomacy in the Second World War* (Cambridge University Press, Cambridge, 1996).

Soviak, Eugene (ed.), *A Diary of Darkness. The Wartime Diary of Kiyosawa Kiyoshi* (Princeton University Press, Princeton, NJ, 1999).

Spencer, Ian, 'Settler dominance, agricultural production and the Second World War in Kenya', *Journal of African History* 21 (4) (1980): 497–514.

Spiekermann, Uwe, 'Vollkorn für die Führer. Zur Geschichte der Vollkornbrotpolitik im "Dritten Reich"', *Zeitschrift für Sozialgeschichte des 20 & 21 Jahrhunderts* 16 (1) (2001): 91–128.

——, 'Brown bread for victory: German and British wholemeal politics in the inter-war period', in Frank Trentmann and Flemming Just (eds), *Food and Conflict in Europe in the Age of the Two World Wars* (Palgrave Macmillan, Basingstoke, 2006), pp. 143–71.

Standish, Meacham, *A Life Apart. The English Working Class 1890–1914* (Thames & Hudson, London, 1977).

Stanner, S. A. K., Andrès C. Bulmer, O. E. Lantseva, V. Borodina, V. V. Poteen and J. S. Yudkin, 'Does malnutrition in utero determine diabetes and coronary heart disease in adulthood? Results from the Leningrad siege survey', *British Medical Journal* 315 (1997): 1342–9.

Stanner, W. E. H., *The South Seas in Transition. A Study of Post-War Rehabilitation and Reconstruction in Three British Pacific Dependencies* (Australasian Publishing Company, Sydney, Wellington, London, 1953).

Staples, Amy L. S., *The Birth of Development. How the World Bank, Food and Agriculture Organization, and World Health Organization Changed the World, 1945–1965* (Kent State University Press, Kent, OH, 2006).

Stauffer, Alvin, *The Quartermaster Corps: Operations in the War Against Japan. United States Army in World War II. The Technical Services.* (Office of the Chief of Military History, Department of the Army, Washington, DC, 1956).

Steckel, Richard H. and Roderick Floud (eds), *Health and Welfare during Industrialization* (University of Chicago Press, Chicago, 1997).

Steinhoff, Johannes, Peter Pechel and Dennis Showalter, *Voices from the Third Reich. An Oral History* (Grafton Books, London, 1991).

Stephens, Ian, *Monsoon Morning* (Ernest Benn, London, 1966).

Stephenson, Jill, 'Nazism, modern war and rural society in Württemberg, 1939–45', *Journal of Contemporary History* 32 (3) (1997): 339–56.

——, *Hitler's Home Front. Württemberg under the Nazis* (Hambledon Continuum, London, 2006).

Stevenson, Richard, *Bengal Tiger and British Lion: An Account of the Bengal Famine of 1943* (XLibris Corporation, 2005).

Summerfield, Penny, 'The "levelling of class"', in Harold L. Smith (ed.), *War and Social Change. British Society in the Second World War* (Manchester University Press, Manchester, 1986), pp. 179–207.

Swinton, Viscount, *I Remember* (Hutchinson & Co., London, n.d.).

Talib, Naimah S., 'Memory and its historical context. The Japanese occupation in Sarawak and its impact on a Kuching Malay community', in P. Lim Pui Huen and Diana Wong (eds), *War and Memory in Malaysia and Singapore* (Institute of Southeast Asia Studies, Singapore, 2000).

Tamayama, Kazuo and John Nunneley, *Tales by Japanese Soldiers of the Burma Campaign 1942–1945* (Cassell & Co., London, 1992).

Tanaka, Yuki, *Hidden Horrors. Japanese War Crimes in World War II* (Westview Press, Oxford, 1996).

Tauger, Mark B., 'Entitlement, shortage, and the Bengal famine of 1943: another look', *Journal of Peasant Studies* 31 (1) (2003): 45–72.

——, 'Stalin, Soviet agriculture, and collectivisation', in Frank Trentmann and Flemming Just (eds), *Food and Conflict in Europe in the Age of the Two World Wars* (Palgrave Macmillan, Basingstoke, 2006), pp. 109–42.

Taylor, A. J. P., *English History 1914–1945* (first pub. 1965, Oxford University Press, Oxford, 1992).

Tennant, Roger, *A History of Korea* (Kegan Paul International, London, 1996).

Terkel, Studs, *'The Good War'. An American Oral History of World War II* (Phoenix Press, London, 1984).

Teuteberg, Hans J., *Der Wandel der Nahrungsgewohnheiten unter dem Einfluß der Industrialisierung* (Vandenhoeck & Ruprecht, Göttingen, 1972).

Thompson, Major-General Julian, *The Lifeblood of War. Logistics in Armed Conflict* (Brassey's, London, 1991).

Thune, Carl E., 'The making of history: the representation of World War II on Normanby Island', in Geoffrey M. White and Lamont Lindstrom (eds), *The Pacific Theater. Island Representations of World War II* (University of Hawaii Press, Honolulu, 1989), pp. 231–56.

Thurston, Robert W. and Bernd Bonwetsch (eds), *The People's War. Responses to World War II in the Soviet Union* (University of Illinois Press, Chicago, 2000).

Tiedemann, R. G., 'Wartime guerrilla economy and the Chinese road to development', in Paul Kingston, R. G. Tiedemann and Nicholas Westcott, *Managed Economies in World War II* (School of Oriental and African Studies, University of London, 1991), pp. 16–34.

Tinley, J. M., *Wartime Transportation and Distribution of Foods* (University of California Press, Berkeley, 1942).

Tiratsoo, Nick (ed.), *From Blitz to Blair: A New History of Britain since 1939* (Weidenfeld & Nicolson, London, 1997).

Tolley, Kemp, *Caviar and Commissars. The Experiences of a U.S. Naval Officer in Stalin's Russia* (Naval Institute Press, Annapolis, MD, 1983).

Tomasson, Richard F., *Iceland. The First New Society* (University of Minnesota Press, Minneapolis, 1980).

Tomita, Mary Kimoto, *Dear Miye. Letters Home from Japan 1939–1946* (Stanford University Press, Stanford, CA, 1995).

Tomlinson, B. R., 'The historical roots of Indian poverty: issues in the economic and social history of modern South Asia: 1880–1960', *Modern Asian Studies* 22 (1) (1988): 123–40.

Tooze, Adam, *The Wages of Destruction. The Making and Breaking of the Nazi Economy* (Allen Lane, London, 2006).

Tracy, Michael, *Government and Agriculture in Western Europe 1880–1988* (3rd edn, Harvester Wheatsheaf, London, 1989).

Trentmann, Frank, 'Coping with shortage: the problem of food security and global visions of coordination, *c.*1890s–1950', in Frank Trentmann and Flemming Just (eds), *Food and Conflict in Europe in the Age of the Two World Wars* (Palgrave Macmillan, Basingstoke, 2006), pp. 13–48.

—— and Flemming Just (eds), *Food and Conflict in Europe in the Age of the Two World Wars* (Palgrave Macmillan, Basingstoke, 2006).

Trittel, Günter J., 'Hungerkrise und kollektiver Protest in Westdeutschland (1945–1949)', in Manfred Gailus and Heinrich Volkmann (eds), *Der Kampf um das tägliche Brot. Nahrungsmangel, Versorgungspolitik und Protest 1770–1990* (Westdeutscher Verlag, Opladen, 1994), pp. 377–91.

Tunzelmann, Alex von, *Indian Summer. The Secret History of the End of Empire* (Simon & Schuster, London, 2007).

Turner, Ben, *About Myself 1863–1930* (Humphrey Toulmin, London, 1930).

Tuyll, Hubert P. van, *Feeding the Bear. American Aid to the Soviet Union, 1941–1945* (Greenwood Press, London, 1989).

Twaddle, Michael (ed.), *Imperialism, the State and the Third World* (British Academic Press, London, 1992).

Tyrer, Nicola, *They Fought in the Fields. The Women's Land Army: The Story of a Forgotten Victory* (Sinclair-Stevenson, London, 1996).

US War Department, *Handbook on German Military Forces* (first pub. 1945, LSU Press, 1995).

Van Creveld, Martin, *Supplying War. Logistics from Wallenstein to Patton* (Cambridge University Press, Cambridge, 1977).

Vassilieva, Tatiana, *A Hostage to War* (first pub. in Leningrad in 1990, Collins, London, 1999).

Vassiltchikov, Marie, *The Berlin Diaries 1940–1945 of Marie 'Missie' Vassiltchikov* (Chatto & Windus, London, 1986).

Vat, Dan van der, *The Atlantic Campaign. The Great Struggle at Sea 1939–1945* (Hodder & Stoughton, London, 1988).

Vaughan, Megan and Henrietta L. Moore, *Cutting down Trees. Gender, Nutrition, and Agricultural Change in the Northern Province of Zambia 1890–1990* (James Currey, London, 1994).

Ven, Hans J. van de, *War and Nationalism in China 1925–1945* (Routledge Curzon, London, 2003).

Vernon, James, *Hunger. A Modern History* (Belknap Press of Harvard University Press, London, 2007).

Vickery, Kenneth P., 'The Second World War and the revival of forced labour in the Rhodesias', *International Journal of African History Studies* 22 (3) (1989): 423–37.

Vincent, C. Paul, *The Politics of Hunger. The Allied Blockade of Germany, 1915–1919* (Ohio University Press, London, 1985).

Vinen, Richard, *A History in Fragments. Europe in the Twentieth Century* (Abacus, London, 2002).

Voglis, Polymeris, 'Surviving hunger: life in the cities and the countryside during the occupation', in Robert Gildea, Olivier Wieviorka and Anette Warring (eds), *Surviving Hitler and Mussolini. Daily Life in Occupied Europe* (Berg, Oxford, 2006), pp. 16–41.

Voigt, Johannes H., *India in the Second World War* (Arnold–Heinemann, London, 1987).

Volin, Lazar, *A Century of Russian Agriculture. From Alexander II to Khrushchev* (Harvard University Press, Cambridge, MA, 1970).

Von der Decken, Hans, 'Die Ernährung in England und Deutschland', *Vierteljahrshefte zur Wirtschaftsforschung* 12 (1937): 177–99.

Wagenleitner, Reinhold, *Coca-Colonization and the Cold War. The Cultural Mission of the United States in Austria after the Second World War* (University of North Carolina Press, London, 1994).

Walker, Allan S., *The Clinical Problems of War* (Australian War Memorial, Canberra, 1952).

—— *The Island Campaigns* (Australian War Memorial, Canberra, 1957).

Walker, David, 'The writers' war', in Joan Beaumont (ed.), *Australia's War, 1939–1945* (Allen & Unwin, St Leonards, New South Wales, 1996), pp. 136–61.

Waller, Maureen, *London 1945. Life in the Debris of War* (John Murray, London, 2004).

Wang, Di, 'Urban life in China's wars, 1937–1949: the view from the teahouse', in Stewart Lone (ed.), *Daily Lives of Civilians in Wartime Asia: From the Taiping Rebellion to the Vietnam War* (Greenwood Publishing Group, Westport, CT, 2007), pp. 95–113.

War Office, *Record of Ration Scales Operative during the Period September 1939–October 1946* (War Office, June 1947).

Wasser, Bruno, 'Die "Germanisierung" im Distrikt Lublin als Generalprobe und erste Realisierungsphase des "Generalplans Ost"', in Mechtild Rössler, Sabine Schleiermacher and Cordula Tollmien (eds), *Der "Generalplan Ost". Hauptlinien der nationalsozialistischen Planungs- und Vernichtungspolitik* (Akademie Verlag, Berlin, 1993), pp. 271–93.

Watters, Mary, *Illinois in the Second World War. Vol. 2. The Production Front* (State of Illinois, Springfield, 1952).

Waugh, Evelyn, *Brideshead Revisted. The Sacred and Profane Memories of Captain Charles Ryder* (first pub. 1945, Penguin, London, 1981).

Webster, Charles, 'Healthy or hungry thirties?', *History Workshop Journal* 13 (1982): 110–29.

Weeks, Charles J., 'The United States occupation of Tonga, 1942–1945: the social and economic impact', *Pacific Historical Review* 56 (1987): 399–426.

Wehler, Hans-Ulrich, *Deutsche Gesellschaftsgeschichte. Vol. 4. Vom Beginn des ersten Weltkriegs bis zur Gründung der beiden deutschen Staaten 1914–1949* (C. H. Beck, Munich, 2003).

Werner, Wolfgang Franz, *"Bleib übrig!" Deutsche Arbeiter in der nationalsozialistischen Kriegswirtschaft* (Schwann, Düsseldorf, 1983).

Westbrook, Robert B., 'Fighting for the American family. Private interests and political obligations in World War II', in Richard Wightman Fox and T. J. Jackson Lears (eds), *The Power of Culture. Critical Essays in American History* (University of Chicago Press, Chicago, 1993), pp. 195–222.

Westcott, Nicholas, 'The slippery slope: economic control in Africa during the Second World War', in Paul Kingston, R. G. Tiedemann and Nicholas Westcott, *Managed Economies in World War II* (School of Oriental and African Studies, University of London, 1991), pp. 1–8.

Wettlin, Margaret, *Russian Road. Three Years of War in Russia as lived through by an American Woman* (Hutchinson & Co., London, 1945).

Wexler, Imanuel, 'The Marshall Plan in economic perspective: goals and accomplishments', in Martin Schain (ed.), *The Marshall Plan: Fifty Years After* (Palgrave, Basingstoke, 2001), pp. 147–52.

Wheatcroft, S. G. and R. W. Davies, 'Population', in R. W. Davies, Mark Harrison and S. G. Wheatcroft (eds), *The Economic Transformation of the Soviet Union, 1913–1945* (Cambridge University Press, Cambridge, 1994), pp. 58–80.

White, Geoffrey M. and Lamont Lindstrom (eds), *The Pacific Theater. Island Representations of World War II* (University of Hawaii Press, Honolulu, 1989).

——, David W. Gegeo, David Akin and Karen Watson-Gegeo (eds), *The Big Death. Solomon Islanders Remember World War II* (Solomon Islands College of Higher Education and the University of the South Pacific, Suva, 1988).

White, Theodore H. and Annalee Jacoby, *Thunder out of China* (Victor Gollancz, London, 1947).

Wickizer, V. D., *Coffee, Tea and Cocoa. An Economic and Political Analysis* (Stanford University Press, Stanford, CA, 1951).

Wilcox, Walter W., *The Farmer in the Second World War* (first pub. 1947, DaCapo Press, New York, 1973).

Wildt, Michael, *Generation des Unbedingten. Das Führungskorps des Reichssicherheitshauptamtes* (Hamburger Edition, Hamburg, 2002).

Wilmington, Martin, *The Middle East Supply Centre* (University of London Press, London, 1972).

Wilson, Sandra, *The Manchurian Crisis and Japanese Society, 1931–33* (Routledge, London, 2002).

Wilson, Theodore A., 'Who fought and why? The assignment of American soldiers to combat', in Paul Addison and Angus Calder (eds), *Time to Kill. The Soldier's Experience of War in the West 1939–1945* (Pimlico, London, 1997), 284–303.

Wilt, Alan F., *Food for War. Agriculture and Rearmament in Britain before the Second World War* (Oxford University Press, Oxford, 2001).

Winick, Myron (ed.), *Hunger Disease. Studies by the Jewish Physicians in the Warsaw Ghetto* (trans. Martha Osnos, John Wiley & Sons, New York, 1979).

Wolschke-Bulmahn, Joachim, 'Gewalt als Grundlage nationalsozialistischer Stadt- und Landwirtschaftsplanung in den "eingegliederten Ostgebieten"', in Mechtild Rössler, Sabine Schleiermacher and Cordula Tollmien (eds), *Der "Generalplan Ost". Hauptlinien der nationalsozialistischen Planungs- und Vernichtungspolitik* (Akademie Verlag, Berlin, 1993), pp. 328–38.

—— and Gert Gröning, 'The National Socialist Garden and Landscape Ideal: Bodenständigkeit (Rootedness in the Soil)', in Richard A. Etlin (ed.), *Art, Culture, and Media Under the Third Reich* (University of Chicago Press, Chicago, 2002), pp. 73–97.

Woolton, The Rt. Hon. the Earl of, *The Memoirs of The Rt. Hon. the Earl of Woolton* (Cassell, London, 1959).

Wright, Donald R., *The World and a Very Small Place in Africa. A History of Globalization in Niumi, The Gambia* (2nd edn, M. E. Sharpe, London, 2004).

Wylie, Neville (ed.), *European Neutrals and Non-Belligerents During the Second World War* (Cambridge University Press, Cambridge, 2002).

Wynn, Neil A., 'The "good war": the Second World War and post-war American society', *Journal of Contemporary History* 31 (3) (1996): 463–82.

Xinran, *China Witness. Voices from a Silent Generation* (Chatto & Windus, London, 2008).

Young, Louise, 'Imagined empire: the cultural construction of Manchukuo', in Peter Duus, Ramon H. Myers and Mark R. Peattie (eds), *The Japanese Wartime Empire, 1931–1945* (Princeton University Press, Princeton, NJ, 1996), pp. 71–96.

——, *Japan's Total Empire. Manchuria and the Culture of Imperialism* (University of California Press, Berkeley, 1998).

Zee, Henri A. van der, *The Hunger Winter. Occupied Holland 1944–5* (Jill Norman & Hobhouse, London, 1982).

Zilliacus, K., 'Economic and social causes of the war', in Dwight E. Lee (ed.), *The Outbreak of the First World War. Causes and Responsibilities* (D. C. Heath and Co., Lexington, MA, 1975), pp. 27–36.

Zubkova, Elena, *Russia after the War. Hopes, Illusions, and Disappointments, 1945–1957* (M. E. Sharpe, London, 1998).

Zweiniger-Bargielowska, Ina, 'Rationing, austerity and the Conservative Party recovery after 1945', *The Historical Journal* 37 (1) (1994): 173–97.

——, *Austerity in Britain. Rationing, Controls and Consumption, 1939–1955* (Oxford University Press, Oxford, 2000).

UNPUBLISHED STUDIES

Amrith, Sunil Siddharth, 'The United Nations and public health in Asia, c. 1940–1960', PhD thesis, University of Cambridge, 2004.

Bayly, Roy E., 'Spunyarns. Some impressions of my years at sea' (by the Bayly family for the Bayly family), July 1993.

Collier, Paul, 'The logistics of the North African campaign 1940–1943', DPhil thesis, University of Oxford, 2001.

Laurence, Caroline and Joanne Tiddy, *From Bully Beef to Ice Cream. The Diet of the Australian Armed Forces in World War I and World War II* (Food History Project, Department of Nutrition and Dietetics, Repatriation General Hospital, Daw Park, South Australia, 1989).

Richmond, Keith, *The Japanese Forces in New Guinea during World War II: A Primer in Logistics* (privately printed by the author, 2003).

Index